Case Studies in Contemporary Criticism

WILLIAM SHAKESPEARE

Hamlet

Case Studies in Contemporary Criticism

SERIES EDITOR: Ross C Murfin

Case Studies in Contemporary Criticism

SERIES EDITOR: Ross C Murfin, *Southern Methodist University*

WILLIAM SHAKESPEARE
Hamlet

Complete, Authoritative Text with
Biographical and Historical Contexts,
Critical History, and Essays from
Five Contemporary Critical Perspectives

EDITED BY

Susanne L. Wofford
University of Wisconsin–Madison

Bedford/St. Martin's
BOSTON ◆ NEW YORK

For Bedford/St. Martin's
President and Publisher: Charles H. Christensen
Associate Publisher/General Manager: Joan E. Feinberg
Managing Editor: Elizabeth M. Schaaf
Developmental Editor: Stephen A. Scipione
Production Editor: Lori Chong
Copyeditor: Cynthia Benn
Text Design: Sandra Rigney, The Book Department
Cover Design: Richard Emery Design, Inc.

Library of Congress Catalog Card Number: 92–50033

Manufactured in the United States of America.

4   3   2   1   0   9
n   m   l   k   j   i

For information, write: Bedford/St. Martin's, 75 Arlington Street, Boston,
MA 02116 (617–399–4000)

ISBN: 0–312–05544–7 (paperback)
ISBN: 0–312–08986–4 (hardcover)

Published and distributed outside North America by:

MACMILLAN PRESS LTD.
Houndmills, Basingstoke, Hampshire RG21 2XS and London
Companies and representatives throughout the world.

ISBN: 0–333–59492–4

Acknowledgments

    Hamlet, Prince of Denmark. From *The Riverside Shakespeare.* G. Blakemore Evans,
Editor. Copyright © 1974 by Houghton Mifflin Company. Used by permission.

    *Acknowledgments and copyrights are continued at the back of the book on page 418,
which constitutes an extension of the copyright page.*

About the Series

Volumes in the Case Studies in Contemporary Criticism series provide college students with an entrée into the current critical and theoretical ferment in literary studies. Each volume reprints the complete text of a classic literary work and presents critical essays that approach the work from different theoretical perspectives, together with the editors' introductions to both the literary work and the critics' theoretical perspectives.

The volume editor of each Case Study has selected and prepared an authoritative text of the classic work, written an introduction to the work's biographical and historical contexts, and surveyed the critical responses to the work since its initial publication. Thus situated biographically, historically, and critically, the work is examined in five critical essays, each representing a theoretical perspective of importance to contemporary literary studies. These essays, prepared especially for undergraduates, show theory in praxis; whether written by established scholars or exceptional young critics, they demonstrate how current theoretical approaches can generate compelling readings of great literature.

As series editor, I have prepared introductions, with bibliographies, to the theoretical perspectives represented in the five critical essays. Each introduction presents the principal concepts of a particular theory in their historical context and discusses the major figures and key works that have influenced their formulation. It is my hope that these introductions will reveal to students that effective criticism is informed by a set of coherent assumptions, and will encourage them to recognize and examine their own assumptions about literature. After each introduction, a selective bibliography presents a partially annotated list of important works from the literature of the particular theoretical perspective, including the most recent and readily available editions and translations of the works cited in the introduction. Finally, I have compiled a glossary of key terms that recur in these volumes and in the discourse of contemporary theory and criticism. We hope that the Case Studies in Contemporary Criticism series will reaffirm the richness of its literary works, even as it introduces invigorating new ways to mine their apparently inexhaustible wealth.

Ross C Murfin
Series Editor
Southern Methodist University

About This Volume

Part One presents in full *The Riverside Shakespeare's* version of *Hamlet*, along with its excellent notes and textual commentary. The editors at Bedford Books and I chose G. Blakemore Evans's text because it has become, for scholars and students alike, one of the most admired and most widely used modern editions of the play.

Part Two includes five exemplary critical essays, prepared especially for students, that examine *Hamlet* from different contemporary theoretical perspectives: feminist, psychoanalytic, deconstructionist, Marxist, and new historicist. Selecting these from the many contemporary approaches was difficult. The range of work on *Hamlet* is exceptionally wide, so inevitably certain approaches, methods, or perspectives have not been included here — most notably, perhaps, performance criticism. Choosing psychoanalysis as one field to include in a volume on contemporary approaches to *Hamlet* was not really a choice, for *Hamlet* has long been a crucial text in the development of psychoanalytic literary criticism. The play has also received considerable attention from feminist critics and from deconstructionists. It has received less attention from new historicist critics, and, although several critics who work within one or another of the several Marxist traditions have written about the play, Marxist criticism also has not focused on *Hamlet*. Both these perspectives are important to include, however, for they bring to the play the political and historical analyses that inform much contemporary interpretation.

As is characteristic of the best of modern criticism, these essays tend to resist being placed in only one theoretical category, and several of them overlap in critical methods. Thus Janet Adelman's fine psychoanalytic essay, which draws on the work of D. W. Winnicott and Melanie Klein and the object relations school of psychoanalysis, could also have been included under the category of feminist criticism. Elaine Showalter's study of representations of Ophelia could have been listed under cultural criticism (not one of the five critical approaches included formally in this volume). Marjorie Garber's essay also provides an example of cultural criticism, to which she adds deconstructive strategies of interpretation and the methods of Lacanian psychoanalysis.

I selected Janet Adelman's essay because I thought it represented the best of contemporary psychoanalytic approaches to the play. Elaine Showalter's feminist essay on Ophelia, which helpfully outlines three different feminist approaches before undertaking to demonstrate one, reveals the cultural influence of Shakespeare in shaping views of identity and femininity, describing especially the cultural linking of femininity and madness. Karin S. Coddon's exemplary new historicist essay also takes madness as its topic but focuses on its contemporary context, historicizing the subject by emphasizing the difficulty of distinguishing madness from treason in either the case of Robert Devereux, second Earl of Essex, or in *Hamlet*. Marjorie Garber's deconstructive account of the way memory works in the text of the play and of our culture argues that the play is based on an uncanny causality. Just as Hamlet is haunted by the ghost of his father, so too, Garber suggests, are we haunted by the ghosts of Shakespeare.

Michael D. Bristol's essay, written especially for this volume, draws on the theories about the role of Carnival in English Renaissance society first articulated in his book *Carnival and Theater*. It exemplifies through a Bakhtinian analysis how *Hamlet* becomes a site of struggle between proletarian interpretations of value and those represented as characteristic of the nobles and great princes of the play. Bristol's work is Marxist in its focus on class divisions, in its use of the concept of class consciousness, in its focus on the text as a locus of cultural contestation — even of class struggle — and in its concern to render audible the silenced voices of Elizabethan society.

Acknowledgments

I owe thanks first to the five authors whose work is represented here. They all helped me to prepare their essays for this volume. I'd like to thank especially Janet Adelman, Michael D. Bristol, and Marjorie Garber for their bibliographical and editing advice and for their help in surveying the state of their fields. I owe special thanks to my husband, Jacques Lezra, for his assistance in revising three of the introductions to the theoretical approaches represented here, and to my colleague at Wisconsin, Richard Knowles, who read my essays with care, corrected them where they were wrong, rewrote what I had said about the Quarto and Folio texts to make my descriptions more precise, and gave me invaluable bibliographical help. Heather James, my colleague at Yale (where this book was begun), cheerfully listened to many frustrated discussions about the difficulty of making the initial selection of essays and shared with me her knowledge of the field. Mihoko Suzuki and Michael Cadden similarly lent me their ears at several key moments and gave much needed encouragement. I owe thanks to David Engelstad, my research assistant at Wisconsin, for patiently working through all the bibliographies and for helping to prepare and proofread the manuscript for press. I also wish to thank Roger Ladd, Susannah Brietz, and especially Thomas Fulton for their help in proofreading the manuscript. I warmly thank Steve Scipione at Bedford Books for his encouragement, support, and patience and for his thoughtful responses to my choices of critical essays for the volume. At Bedford Books I would also like to thank Lori Chong for her assiduous work as the book's production editor and Cynthia Benn for her painstaking copyediting. Finally, I thank Ross Murfin for the invitation to work on the project, for his faith in me when it counted, and for his encouragement throughout the many delays that my move to Wisconsin created.

Susanne L. Wofford
University of Wisconsin–Madison

Contents

xi

Case Studies in Contemporary Criticism

WILLIAM SHAKESPEARE

Hamlet

PART ONE

Hamlet:
The Complete Text

Introduction:
Biographical and
Historical Contexts

Perhaps one of the most surprising things about Shakespeare is how little we know of his life, especially about his early years as an actor and playwright, and about his decision to go to London. We do know more about the life of Shakespeare than about that of any other contemporary dramatist (except for Ben Jonson), but much of the information we have provides the details of his family background, his business affairs and financial successes. The central questions about his activities as a dramatist and actor remain to tantalize and frustrate us. Shakespeare was born in 1564 and died on April 23, 1616 (since Cervantes also died in 1616 this date is often used as a marker of the end of the European Renaissance). He was born, raised, and married in Stratford-on-Avon, a provincial town northwest of London, but by the beginning of the 1590s he had been in London for several years. One of the more frustrating gaps in the historical evidence is our lack of information about Shakespeare's last years in Stratford and his early years in London. By 1592, when Shakespeare would have been twenty-eight years old, he was prominent enough in the London theater world to be attacked in print by an envious rival playwright, Robert Greene, and so we have our first record of Shakespeare as a man of the theater.[1]

---

[1] About forty documents mention Shakespeare, while others mention his family. For a good sense of how thorough is the accounting of the basic facts of Shakespeare's life, see Schoenbaum and Bentley. See also Kay for a good, readable biography that covers

From this first reference on, he is consistently described as a successful actor and playwright. In 1608, for instance, eight years before his death, he is still listed as being one of the "men players." In 1594 Shakespeare became one of the founding members of a company of actors called the Chamberlain's Men (the name refers to the noble patron of the company). This company changed its name to the King's Men when James I came to the throne in 1603 but otherwise remained remarkably stable and profitable throughout Shakespeare's lifetime. When the company built the Globe Theatre in 1599, Shakespeare held a one-tenth interest in it, so he was also a successful businessman. Shakespeare seems to have been unique among Elizabethan dramatists for playing this threefold role in the theater as actor, playwright, and theater owner/business partner in the theatrical company. We know that Shakespeare made good money out of the theater, that he was a practical man of the theater above all else, and that he himself never oversaw the publication of his plays, though some were published in his lifetime. Indeed, as a writer and actor, Shakespeare probably was not very interested in publishing his plays because he wanted people to have to come to the theater to see them (to pay admission to the theater company rather than to buy the book from a bookseller).

Shakespeare's parents were among the important figures in Stratford. They were of sufficient wealth and social standing to be respected members of the community, but they were not noble. His mother, Mary Arden, was the daughter of a substantial landowner, while his father, John Shakespeare, was a glover and a trader in farm commodities. John Shakespeare held a number of local offices: member of the governing body of Stratford, a constable of the borough, one of the two town chamberlains, and an alderman. In 1568, he became high bailiff, the town's highest political office. In 1596 John Shakespeare was granted a coat of arms, a business arrangement probably made by his son William, who was already very successful in London by this time. In later years documents occasionally refer to William Shakespeare as a "gentleman." Shakespeare and his family seem to have had significant social ambitions and to have desired to "gentle" their condition, as it would have been put in Elizabethan English (in other words, to become gentlemen), but they never attained noble rank.

Shakespeare's life and works. The relative lack of information about Shakespeare's life — relative to what we would know about a modern writer of such prominence — has in part led to the controversy about whether the man from Stratford was truly the author of Shakespeare's works.

William Shakespeare and Anne Hathaway were issued a marriage license on November 27, 1582, when he was eighteen. She was eight years his senior. Their first child was born in May 1583. It may have been that their marriage was necessary. Two years later Anne gave birth to twins, one of whom, Shakespeare's only son, was named Hamnet. Several of Shakespeare's children, including Hamnet, died in their childhood or youth. Those who like to find biographical connections between Shakespeare's life and his plays thus point to Shakespeare's experience as a father and emphasize in particular that Hamnet died in 1596. Sometime in the half-decade after Hamnet's death, Shakespeare began meditating on the plot of the play *Hamlet*.

As the son of prominent citizens, Shakespeare probably attended the local grammar school, where he would have learned Latin, studied logic and rhetoric, and read a goodly amount of Latin literature. Shakespeare thus would have received a decent but undistinguished education that did not continue to the university. Although to readers today Shakespeare's many allusions to classical figures seem evidence of impressive learning, in his own day Shakespeare would not have been identified as a particularly learned writer. Indeed, Ben Jonson, who prided himself on his knowledge, mocked Shakespeare, saying that Shakespeare had "little Latin and less Greek." Jonson was a great humanist linguist and writer who drew on both Greek and Latin plentifully for his own plays and poetry, and from his perspective he was right. Shakespeare was not an expert on classical literature. His greatness lay elsewhere — in his ability to combine a good understanding of European and classical literature with the native English popular and learned theatrical traditions to produce a dramatic poetry still unequaled in power and range in English today.

By various kinds of evidence including publication dates of the plays (we have records from the Stationers' Register, a book located in the guildhall of the Company of Stationers, the organization for all printers and publishers in England), records of performances, descriptions in diaries or journals of members of the audience, and allusions made in the plays to events of the day, we are able to make a rough chronology of Shakespeare's thirty-seven plays. This evidence places *Hamlet* somewhere around 1600–01, near the midpoint of Shakespeare's career as playwright and actor, at the end of the reign of Queen Elizabeth I and near the beginning of Shakespeare's great tragic period. One of the unsolved and unsolvable questions abut the trajectory of Shakespeare's career is why he seems to have devoted his writing to tragedies after 1600. There are probably as many proposed answers to this question as there are scholars. It requires a complicated gesture of the historical imagination to try to imagine how the future would have looked to an Elizabethan subject as his queen was approaching her death, yet anxiety or fear about the end of a monarch's reign hardly seems sufficient to explain the shift in Shakespeare's literary interests from primarily history and comedy to tragedy. Moreover, once James I was securely on the throne, such anxiety would seem misplaced, though perhaps it was replaced with other concerns — dislike of James's politics, for instance, or an alienation from the image of the nation projected by the court. Such speculations seem unfruitful, yet there is a temporal congruence between the historical shift from Elizabeth to James and Shakespeare's artistic turn toward tragedy. Another theory would look for biographical explanations, perhaps in the fact of his son's death four years or so before Shakespeare probably began work on *Hamlet*. But Shakespeare wrote many comedies after Hamnet's death. Moreover, many playwrights wrote tragedies in this period — Shakespeare was certainly not alone in responding to the taste for tragedy, and there is no particular reason to interpret his turn toward tragedy in the early seventeenth century as having been caused by some private experience. Like any person living in this period, he lost many members of his family to sickness, but that fact does not seem sufficient to explain the broad shift in English aesthetic taste that ushered in the era of Jacobean tragedy. In any case, *Hamlet* was one of Shakespeare's last Elizabethan plays and remains the play that most insistently led Shakespeare, and with him his audiences and readers, into tragedy.[2]

SHAKESPEARE'S THEATER

Hamlet was performed in the Globe Theatre, which Shakespeare's company built from the timbers of their previous theater, known simply as the Theatre. The Theatre, the first building in England constructed for the sole purpose of performing plays, had been built in 1576. In the next twenty years, London saw an extraordinary growth in theatergoing and theater building. The reviser of Stowe's *Annales* captures the excitement and sense of historical moment felt by those observing this major cultural development:

[2]For one theory about why *Hamlet* initiates Shakespeare's tragic period (though he did write some tragedies before it, and some comedies after it), see the essay by Janet Adelman included in this volume.

In the yeere one thousand sixe hundred twenty nine, there was builded a new faire Play-house, neere the white Fryers. And this is the seaventeenth Stage, or Common Play-house which hath beene new made within the space of three-score yeeres within London and the suburbs. . . . Before the space of three-score yeares . . . I neither knew, heard, nor read, of any such Theaters, set Stages or Play-houses, as have beene purposely built within mans memory. (Qtd. in Chambers 2: 373)

The extent of the cultural change should not be underestimated. In the twenty-five or so years between the construction of the Theatre and the production of *Hamlet,* theatergoing had become an extremely popular entertainment. Estimates suggest that the London population of the period was somewhere from 150,000 to 200,000, while in 1595 about 15,000 people attended weekly performances. In 1620, when six play-houses were open, probably more like 25,000 people visited the the-aters weekly. Using these estimates, Andrew Gurr, an historian of the Elizabethan stage, comments that "perhaps about 15 or 20 percent of the people living within reach of Shoreditch and Southwark [the sub-urbs where the theaters were located] were regular playgoers" (*The Shakespearean Stage* 213).

The Globe Theatre opened in 1599, and from then on Shake-speare's company principally performed there. We know the design and general characteristics of the Globe partly by comparison to other Eliz-abethan playhouses. Several representations of the theaters of the day, including one important drawing (the De Witt drawing of the Swan Theatre from about 1596), provide a glimpse of their structure, as does the one remaining contract for the building of a theater (the contract for the building of the Fortune, built about six months after the Globe and apparently modeled on it). There is now some archaeological evi-dence about the shape of the Globe amphitheater from recent excava-tions of the foundations of the second Globe Theatre (built on the site of the original Globe after the latter was destroyed by fire). The excava-tions have exposed the polygonal shape of the Globe, which may have had as many as twenty sides, and also tell us that the "yard" of the Globe was about eighty feet in diameter, but they do not tell us much about the shape of the stage or about any of the other construction in timber above the ground (including the galleries). (On the excavations, see Gurr, *The Shakespearean Stage* 142–45.) Of course, we also guess about stage design from the stage directions included in the plays. Drawing on all this information, we are able to describe a composite Elizabethan theater and to be fairly certain that the Globe Theatre shared most, if not all, of these attributes.

The basic Elizabethan theater was modeled originally on two types of building: the courtyards of inns, where plays were often performed on improvised stages before any theaters were built, and bearbaiting arenas. Both of these were "in the round," with spectators sitting and standing nearly all the way around the performers. The public buildings based on these structures, such as the Globe, were usually round or po-lygonal buildings made of wood and several stories high. Performance was also in the round, with only the area directly behind the stage inac-cessible to the audience. The image Shakespeare gives us for the shape and performance space in the public theaters is "The Wooden O" (from the prologue to *Henry V*). The poorer people, whom Shakespeare calls "the groundlings," stood in what was called "the yard," the flat ground near and around the stage. Like most of the stage itself, the yard was open to the sky. There the poorer spectators watched the play, milled about, sometimes heckled or cheered the actors on, and bought the food being peddled. The Elizabethans organized their theaters in a way opposite to ours, so that those closest to the stage were the poorest and paid the least. It cost one penny to enter the yard, two to enter the galleries (what we would call the balconies) that surrounded the yard, and three to sit in comfort in the higher galleries. There were also lord's rooms costing about sixpence, which were partitioned off from the gal-leries in the section near the stage, comparable to the boxes in a modern theater (see Gurr, *The Shakespearean Stage* 122).

For the groundlings, this entertainment was reasonably cheap. To gauge the value of the one-penny entrance charge, it seems useful to know that the average London artisan's weekly wage was about seventy-two pence (six shillings), that tobacco was threepence for a small pipe-ful, and that the nuts that spectators commonly munched during the performances cost up to sixpence (see Gurr, *The Shakespearean Stage* 214–15). Only bearbaiting was as cheap an entertainment, and indeed bearbaiting was a pastime frequently compared to theatergoing by its critics, notably the mayor and city elders of London and Puritan writers or pamphleteers. These public theaters were very large by our standards for theaters. The yard probably held as many as 800 spectators, and the galleries as many as 1,500. A contemporary visitor estimated that one public theater was able to hold up to 3,000 spectators, but most mod-ern estimates point to 2,500 as the maximum. This is still a very large gathering of people, however, a fact that perhaps explains why the the-

aters seem often to have served as meeting places at times of social upheaval, resistance, or even revolt.

In public theaters like the Globe, actors performed during the day
and out of doors, without the effects of artificial lighting to which we
are accustomed. The many night scenes in Shakespeare's plays (such as
the opening scene of *Hamlet*) would have been performed in broad
daylight, with poetic language and the viewer's imagination creating
whatever effects of darkness needed to be conveyed. The stage itself was
a platform about forty feet wide extending at least as far out into the
yard as it was wide (an apron stage). The Shakespearean actor walked
way out into his audience when he moved to the edge of the stage,
rather as runway models do today in a fashion show, except that the
stage was also very wide, and there were people above him in the galleries. The thrust of the stage allowed the actor to talk with an immediacy
and an intimacy surprising in such a large group of people and hard to
create on most modern stages. By walking out to nearly the middle of
the yard, he could speak introspectively and be heard by the 2,000 or so
people sitting and standing around him.

Although it is a matter of the constitution of the acting companies
and not of theater design, we should also emphasize that no women
performed on the Shakespearean stage. Throughout the sixteenth and
seventeenth centuries until the closing of the theaters in 1642, women
were excluded from the profession of acting, and all female parts were
played by adolescent boys whose voices had not yet deepened and
whose beards had not yet grown. For this reason, the stage in this period is today sometimes called transvestite, and some of Shakespeare's
works, especially several of the comedies that involve cross-dressing, call
attention to this circumstance. The effects of femininity that were
needed were created by costume and cosmetics, by the skill of the boy
actor, and by the imagination of the audience. The use of boy actors to
play female parts was a matter of convention, and perhaps it struck the
audience as odd only in those occasions where the plays specifically
called attention to it. Nonetheless, the role of Gertrude may have been
substantially affected by the fact that the actor playing the part was so
young. We have some sense of how unsuccessful the illusion of femininity may sometimes have been from the lines spoken by Cleopatra near
the moment of her death. She expresses her fear that she would be
mocked and led in triumph were she to capitulate to Octavius Caesar,
and complains that they would make plays of her life, plays that would
in no way do her justice:

> The quick comedians
> Extemporally will stage us, and present
> Our Alexandrian revels: Antony
> Shall be brought drunken forth, and I shall see
> Some squeaking Cleopatra boy my greatness
> I' th' posture of a whore.
> (*Antony and Cleopatra* 5.2.216–21)

Here the boy actor to play Cleopatra is imagined as squeaking out his lines, his boyish efforts to capture this paragon of femininity fail, producing only a travesty or parody in her mind. Presumably some boy actors were better than others — including, perhaps, the actor playing the role of Cleopatra, who in this tour-de-force of theatrical trompe l'oeil convinces the audience that she, the fictional Cleopatra, is more real than is he, the actor playing the role.

At the rear of the stage was the "tiring" (or in modern English, "attiring") house. This was the actors' dressing room, and from it there were at least two doors onto the stage. At the first gallery level above the tiring house was a balcony that was a part of the stage (important for such moments as the balcony scenes in *Romeo and Juliet*). Near the front of the stage in some playhouses (and almost certainly the Globe) was a large trapdoor big enough for two men to crawl through. It led to the "hell," a space below the stage useful for scenes such as Hamlet's farewell to the ghost of his father. In act 1, scene 5 of *Hamlet*, while Hamlet is making Marcellus and Horatio swear secrecy about the visitations of the ghost, the stage direction tells us, "Ghost cries under the stage." Hamlet, with a grotesque humor, calls the ghost "old mole" and refers to "this fellow in the cellarage" (1.5.162,151). This same space may well have been used in *Hamlet* for the grave-digger's scene, at the end of which Hamlet and Laertes literally jump into the grave. References like the stage direction about the ghost allow us to be sure that the Globe Theatre included this understage area and trapdoor. Above a good part of the stage was a roof or covering (to make the play a drier affair on rainy days) called "the heavens." When Jaques in *As You Like It* says, "All the world's a stage," his comment reflects an intentional analogy built into the playhouse's construction. The theater thus was understood to represent a world with the heavens above it and hell below: it was the "wooden O," the theatrical "Globe" that mirrored the globe of the world.

Structurally the Globe Theatre evoked the theatrical metaphor and actualized a concern that recurred in a number of Shakespeare's plays: the extent to which the human being can be defined as an actor. The comparison of the stage, with its hell below and the heavens above, to the world was a version of the more general and widely used comparison of the human self and the actor. This form of the theatrical metaphor was used with great emphasis by Pico della Mirandola, Erasmus, and other prominent humanist writers long before Shakespeare adapted it for his dramatic purposes. An English example from one of Shakespeare's contemporaries suggests how conventional and widely used it was. Sir Walter Raleigh's poem "On the Life of Man" works out each detail of the comparison with a grim humor:

> What is our life? a play of passion,
> Our mirth the musicke of division,
> Our mothers wombes the tyring houses be,
> When we are drest for this short Comedy,
> Heaven the Judicious sharpe spector° is,
> That sits and markes still who doth act amisse.
> Our graves that hide us from the searching Sun,
> Are like drawne curtaynes when the play is done.
> Thus march we playing to our latest rest,
> Onely we dye in earnest, that's no Jest.

The comparison of human being to actor seemed to celebrate human flexibility and the power to shape the self for good or evil, but as the Renaissance progressed, writers came to recognize that the freedom to play any role, to take on any shape or quality of being — to be the consummate actor — also had its darker side, emphasized particularly by Puritan critics of the theater. They saw that to take seriously the idea of human being as actor is to accept that there may be no single, intrinsic or essential self (see Agnew 125–35). This sense of multiplicity is expressed in Hamlet's own radical use of the theatrical metaphor. As his father's ghost disappears, Hamlet responds to the ghost's command "remember me" with these words:

> Remember thee!
> Ay, thou poor ghost, whiles memory holds a seat
> In this distracted globe.
>
> (1.5.95–97)

spector: Spectator, but also specter.

He refers here simultaneously to his own head (the globe wherein his memory is lodged) and to the Globe Theatre. By comparing the workings of his mind to a play being played out on stage, he acknowledges both the theatricality of the self, even the inner self, and his own feelings of fragmentation. He implies that he finds within not simply the mourner he had insisted on a few scenes earlier but a multiple self, perhaps even a fragmented self, the different parts of which are vying to be chief actor. "That within which passes show," Hamlet's phrase to describe the sincerity and power of his grief for his father a little earlier in the play, thus turns out to be a kind of theater after all.

A similar acknowledgment through the theatrical metaphor of human multiplicity occurs, though more playfully, in a sonnet (1595) by Edmund Spenser:

> Of this worlds Theatre in which we stay,
> My love lyke the Spectator ydly sits
> Beholding me that all the pageants play,
> Disguysing diversly my troubled wits.
> Sometimes I joy when glad occasion fits,
> And mask in myrth lyke to a Comedy:
> Soone after when my joy to sorrow flits,
> I waile and make my woes a Tragedy.
> Yet she beholding me with constant eye,
> Delights not in my merth nor rues my smart:
> But when I laugh she mocks, and when I cry
> She laughes, and hardens evermore her hart.
>   What then can move her? if nor merth nor mone,
>   She is no woman, but a sencelesse stone.
>   (Sonnet 54 from Spenser's *Amoretti*)

Here the alternative to the mobile, shifting persona of the lover is the beloved's resistance: a senseless stone. But what may be comic in a love poem intended to express the multiplicity of human eroticism and emotion becomes much darker when taken as a metaphor for human life. To celebrate the analogy between human self and actor, as poets, writers, and the critics of the theater found, is to recognize the possibility for manipulation and falsehood and even to court the very emptiness or absence in being that might deny any divine origin to human life. We can see this darker reading of human theatrical capacities in Shakespeare's bleakest use of the idea that all the world's a stage, Macbeth's near-final soliloquy about the emptiness in life:

Life's but a walking shadow, a poor player,
That struts and frets his hour upon the stage,
And then is heard no more. It is a tale
Told by an idiot, full of sound and fury,
Signifying nothing.
                                    (*Macbeth* 5.5.24–28)

His use of a similar idea in *King Lear* — "When we are born, we cry that we are come / To this great stage of fools" (4.6.183–84) — is less pessimistic in its estimate of the value in human life, since at least in Lear's invocation of it the first person "we" brings a vision of a bleak, comradely spirit to the stage of fools. The theatrical metaphor, suggesting as it did the power of self-consciousness to create a division within the mind — a division, for Hamlet, between emotion and memory — suggested the flexibility and complexity of the human self. It also showed, however, that histrionic power can expose an inner emptiness, upon which other uses and forms of power — political, sexual, linguistic — can be founded, since it allowed the individual to play any role necessary to gain power. Such histrionic power could also become politically subversive just as it was morally disturbing in suggesting that there may not be any absolutes in human nature to govern behavior. The power of theatricality in royal hands was thus often dedicated to containing precisely this "flexibility" of the self within determined ideologies and social forms.

In a society much more stratified and hierarchical than our own, the theatrical metaphor then also had a socially disturbing quality, because it suggested that rank itself might have no more intrinsic validity than any other role. Indeed, in the theater, commoners with no claim to aristocratic lineage frequently paraded about as kings or noblemen. Equally threatening, as we have seen, boys dressed as women played all the female roles. Among the many qualities of the stage that disturbed Puritan critics, this uncomfortable instability of gender was perhaps one of the most serious. Not only was gender treated as a role, but cross-dressing and transvestism provided a source of entertainment that greatly disturbed critics of the theater. Attacks on the theater stressed the danger to actor and audience of such promiscuity.

Stephen Gosson stands as a case in point. He became one of the leaders of the attack on the players when he published his *School of Abuse* in 1579, a work that may have been commissioned by the London authorities (see Agnew 125–28). Gosson comments on the dangers of disrupting the hierarchies of gender and social station:

[T]o declare ourselves by wordes or by gestures to be otherwise than we are, is [an] acte executed where it should not, therefore a lye. The profe is evident, the consequent is necessarie, that in Stage Playes for a boy to put on the attyre, the gesture, the passions of a woman; for a meane person to take upon him the title of a Prince with counterfeit porte and traine, is by outwarde signes to shewe themselves other wise then they are, and so within the compasse of a lye. . . . (Qtd. in Agnew 128)

The two theatrical lies on which Gosson focuses here are telling ones for the Shakespearean stage. For, when applied to kings, the theatrical metaphor posed the question of authority in a radical form. Is the king merely someone acting as king, someone with no special authority to be king other than that given him by his power as actor? Political uses of the theatrical metaphor are especially important for *Hamlet,* since Claudius is implicitly compared to the "Player King" (the actor playing the king in the play-within-the-play). Claudius's claim to his position of authority is made to seem not only tenuous but criminal by this association. The actor playing Claudius was of course literally an actor, playing the king in borrowed robes that he would not have been allowed to wear when not performing on the stage. Elizabethan law carefully regulated clothing, conferring on certain classes the right to wear certain kinds of cloth (see Whigham 157–69). Although these regulations were clearly broken as often as they were kept, especially by the wealthy merchant class and by the gentry, nonetheless the theater seemed morally and even politically suspect to many contemporaries of Shakespeare in part because of its apparent license to transgress class and gender boundaries.

The sixteenth-century Puritan critics repeated objections to the theater made in earlier periods. They echoed Tertullian's third-century complaints about the licentiousness of Roman plays and Plato's condemnation of all fiction as false representation. The Puritans objected to imaginative literature because it aroused desire and to acting because it was a form of hypocrisy or lying. They objected most strenuously to theater: not only did plays represent and endorse licentious conduct, they argued, but the playhouse served as a marketplace for prostitutes and a meeting place for the "masterless men" so prominent in Elizabethan documents about the theater (see Chambers, vol. 4, app. 3–4). The accusations of promiscuity and lustful behavior thus referred at once to the perceived function of the playhouse, to the disturbing fact of people taking on selves different from their own, and to the stories represented in the plays.

THE TEXT

In spite of the efforts of theater companies to keep sole control of their plays, publishers of the day had a variety of ways of getting hold of them and usually published these editions in quarto form. Quartos of plays were cheaply printed paperbacks for popular consumption, about the size of a modern hardback novel and selling for six pennies. The term *quarto*, which means "four," refers to the fact that the printer printed eight pages on one large sheet of paper which he then folded twice to make *four* leaves (with one printed page on each side of a leaf); several such sheets loosely sewn together made up a book. Eighteen of Shakespeare's plays appeared in quarto editions; since he did not supervise their publication, some of the plays appear in mangled form and sometimes in widely differing versions of the same play. Six years after Shakespeare's death, in 1623, two senior members of his company, John Heminges and Henry Condell, in order to honor his memory, published a (nearly) complete works in the large, expensive folio format used for important books such as Bibles and histories. The name *folio*, which means "leaf," refers to the fact that the printer set four pages of type on each sheet and then folded it only once, making two *leaves* of four large, usually double-column pages, one on each side of a leaf somewhat larger than a city telephone directory. The so-called First Folio is a priceless volume because it preserves not only the eighteen plays previously printed in quarto editions but also eighteen others that had not previously been published and so might not otherwise have survived. For half the plays, this Folio version is the only surviving version and so must form the basis of all modern editions of those plays. For the other half, the plays that had appeared in both quarto and Folio versions, sometimes one of the quarto editions provides the most purely Shakespearean text (least corrupted by errors, omissions, and alterations) and sometimes the Folio. Modern editions of these plays are based on the best text and they import from others any lines that seem to be authentically Shakespeare's.

The most important point to be learned from this historical problem is that for some plays, and *Hamlet* is among them, there is no single authorized text. Indeed, the *Hamlet* we read today is not identical to any one of the three existing Renaissance printings of the play. It may well have been that such a single, stable text did not exist in the Globe Theatre either. Like any drama company, Shakespeare's company probably added and cut scenes from plays when they went on the road or performed at court. So when a modern director decides to cut a speech or even moves it to a different part of the play, he or she may be treating the text of the play more in the way that Shakespeare and his company would have done than is a critic who challenges such practices. A play text is not like a modern lyric poem or a novel, for which there is a secure text, and the complications of printing history only exaggerate this point for the text of a Renaissance play like *Hamlet*. As we shall see, in *Hamlet*, the relation of the differing contemporary versions of the play is particularly vexed.

The quarto texts represent printings that were unsupervised by the author, and many of them present a text that seems quite mangled or otherwise distorted. There are also examples of "good" quartos — and this is the case for *Hamlet* — in which the text printed may well be closer to Shakespeare's original. In trying to understand where the "bad" versions of the plays may have come from, scholars have speculated that sometimes an actor in need of money would piece together a play from memory for a publisher, with disastrous results if the actor had only a minor part in the play, as seems to have been the case with the First Quarto of *Hamlet*. It may even have been the case that members of the audience attempted to reconstruct plays by memory, presumably with even worse results. And of course, sometimes a theatrical company would agree to sell a play to a publisher either because it was in need of money or because the play no longer seemed to draw audiences.

In challenging this theory of "memorial reconstruction," scholars have recently argued that the differing printed versions may in fact reflect differing theatrical conditions or even different versions by Shakespeare. According to this line of argument, the so-called bad quartos may well have been versions used for acting when a shorter and less complicated text might have been desirable, as when the show went on the road. While this theory does not explain the extent to which these texts are garbled, it does help us to see that the various versions of Shakespeare's plays may include clues about how the plays were sometimes revised, and may represent texts whose differences should be respected. In the case of *Hamlet*, for instance, the character of Gertrude changes dramatically from the First (and "bad") Quarto to the Folio. In the First Quarto, Gertrude takes Hamlet's side quite clearly from the closet scene (3.4) on, swearing to assist him in his revenge, and is thus made much more sympathetic, while lingering questions about her guilt disappear (see Clayton 105–06 and 201–02). The First Quarto also includes an entirely new scene between Gertrude and Horatio that replaces act 4, scene 6 in the later editions. In this new scene Gertrude learns from Horatio the news imparted to Horatio by Hamlet's letter in the act 4, scene 6 printed as the main text in this volume. She thus learns of Hamlet's escape and his impending return, news told to her because she is understood in the text to be Hamlet's ally. This simplification of Gertrude's character, in which a number of the mysteries about her in the Folio text are cleared up, may represent a shorter acting version of Shakespeare's fuller play (see Melchiori's article in Clayton 195–210). It also represents, however, a very different interpretation of Gertrude's character that precludes the hovering doubt and even disgust at his mother that is so characteristic of the Hamlet we know. Feminist critics have recently begun to question therefore even the principles that have caused editors to reject the Gertrude of the First Quarto and to select always the more ambiguous figure of the later printed versions (these critics have pointed out that the later versions are more misogynistic). While no one suggests that we should cease to be concerned about which version may represent the best, most authentic text, such questions help to indicate how complicated the project of editing Shakespeare can be and how deeply implicated any edition is in the shaping of cultural values.

The text of *Hamlet* provides an editor with an especially complicated problem. The version of the play first printed appeared in 1603, and is called the First or "Bad" Quarto (abbreviated as Q1 by scholarly agreement). Although printed first, however, it doesn't necessarily represent the earliest version of the play since it clearly is a memorial reconstruction of a performance, not a version printed from an early, pre-performance rough draft. This version seems to be particularly corrupt. Since act 1, scene 1 is present nearly in its entirety, scholars have speculated that this quarto may have relied on a recitation of the play by one of the actors in that scene, probably by the actor who played Marcellus. Only two copies of this First Quarto exist, and before 1823, when the first of these was discovered, the First Quarto was entirely unknown. In 1604, the Second Quarto (known as Q2) was printed. On its title page it claims to be an enlargement and a correction of the First Quarto. The title page reads in part: "*The Tragical History of Hamlet, Prince of Denmark,* by William Shakespeare, Newly Imprinted and Enlarged to almost as much againe as it was, according to the true and perfect Coppie."[3] This version, which shows signs of being based on Shakespeare's own manuscript, is the fullest and, in the opinion of most

---

[3]See the introduction to the Arden edition of *Hamlet,* 36–53, for a detailed account of the relation between the First and Second Quartos.

editors, best version of the play. It is about twice as long as the First
Quarto. The third version of the play appears in the First Folio (1623;
known as F1), where the text seems to have been based on a theater
transcript of the play. The Folio thus may well be one step further from
Shakespeare's original than is the Second Quarto, incorporating cuts
and additions possibly made or authorized by Shakespeare but just as
possibly made by someone else sometime before 1623. The Folio includes about ninety lines not in the Second Quarto, while the Second
Quarto includes about two hundred lines not in the Folio. The Folio
also includes many more stage directions, as would be expected in a text
deriving from a theatrical playbook. Modern editions usually represent
a conflation of the Second Quarto and the First Folio. The text of *Hamlet* that we read today thus does not match anything that was printed in
the Renaissance, and what we read today may be longer than any version an audience in sixteenth- or seventeenth-century London might
have encountered. (For an outline of one theory about the relations
between the three versions, see Edwards 31.)

The version of the "To be, or not to be" soliloquy in the First
Quarto can show the difficulties with the Quarto text:

> To be or not to be, ay there's the point;
> To die, to sleep, is that all? Ay, all.
> No, to sleep, to dream; ay marry, there it goes.
> For in that dream of death, when we awake
> And borne before an everlasting judge,
> From whence no passenger ever returned,
> The undiscovered country, at whose sight
> The happy smile, and the accursed damned. . . .

Comparing this to the Riverside Shakespeare Edition version, reprinted
in this volume, can make the First Quarto indeed seem "bad":

> To be, or not to be, that is the question:
> Whether 'tis nobler in the mind to suffer
> The slings and arrows of outrageous fortune,
> Or to take arms against a sea of troubles,
> And by opposing, end them. To die, to sleep —
> No more, and by a sleep to say we end
> The heart-ache and the thousand natural shocks
> That flesh is heir to; 'tis a consummation
> Devoutly to be wish'd. To die, to sleep —
> To sleep, perchance to dream — ay, there's the rub. . . .
>   (3.1.55–64)

Here the comparison seems merely comic, and yet the First Quarto, although garbled at points because of mistakes of memory, may provide the best link we have to how the play may have been acted at the Globe. This actor's version is shorter, places the "To be, or not to be" soliloquy and the nunnery scene much earlier, and speeds up the action after the death of Polonius (see Edwards 24–26), something modern directors of the play also often try to accomplish. The textual notes that follow the play in this volume will allow any curious reader to discover the differences between the three versions, and to read sections from the First Quarto in their entirety.

SOURCE AND GENRE

Praise for artistic originality would not have been the first words to come to the lips of a critic of great art in the Renaissance. Whereas in the modern period originality is one of the most valued traits a work can have, in the Renaissance intellectuals, poets, and writers admired the capacity to imitate and reproduce (with a difference, of course) the devices, concepts, plots, and even vision of an already existing work of art, especially if it was created by a Greek or Roman artist. It often surprises students of Shakespeare to discover that he took many of his plots from collections of stories and from historical narratives, and sometimes even from other plays. All of these were the case with *Hamlet,* for its story is very old. It appears first in Saxo Grammaticus's *Historia Danica* (or *Danish History*), written in the second half of the twelfth century. There were a number of Renaissance retellings of this tale, which appeared in English translation several times in the sixteenth century, and before Shakespeare wrote his *Hamlet,* there existed another play by that name which possibly was written by Thomas Kyd. This play of the 1580s, which is referred to as the "Ur-Hamlet," was almost certainly Shakespeare's immediate source. We can only guess what this play was like, but it seems certain that it contained a ghost (there is no ghost in Saxo's version) who tells Hamlet of the murder and urges revenge. We assume that it was a revenge tragedy, like *The Spanish Tragedy* (ca. 1587), another play by Kyd, which means that it may have been more of a melodrama than a tragedy and very gory, ending with the stage covered with bodies. Whether or not this description of the Ur-Hamlet is correct, Shakespeare's *Hamlet* clearly incorporates, responds to, and critiques the genre of the revenge tragedy (see Bowers, *Elizabethan Revenge Tragedy*). Indeed, we might argue that Hamlet's difficulty is in part his dislike, or distrust, of the role of revenger thrust upon him by his father. The fate of Laertes, who tries in acts 4 and 5 to become a revenger of the old school, tellingly suggests why Hamlet may be right in his delay, for Laertes fulfills not his own plan, but Claudius's. There seems to be no exit from the trap set by revenge in this play: Laertes, the simple revenger who does just the sort of thing Hamlet's father seems to urge on his son, is manipulated into becoming the agent of the king's corrupt schemes, whereas Hamlet, whose relation to revenge is far more complex, becomes his victim. It seems that Hamlet may be right to delay in taking his revenge, since taking any action at all seems to depend directly on his willingness to commit murder. Hamlet's first act, once he has assumed the role of "Hamlet the Dane" and has started on the path of revenge, is to send his treacherous former school friends to their deaths (see Ferguson 299). In these ways, as well as others, Shakespeare's play gives us a commentary on the genre from which it arose.

SHAKESPEARE'S AUDIENCE

Plays, as we have noted, were attended by a very broad spectrum of social classes and indeed seem to have provided the unlikely setting for a meeting of social groups that otherwise might have kept their distance from one another.[4] Similarly, the combination in Shakespeare's plays of popular and more serious, highbrow elements, including especially the incorporation of popular comic traditions, suggests that the plays aimed to please a rather diverse audience (see Weimann, esp. 185–92 and 208–46). The evidence we have suggests that this diverse audience must have responded rather diversely to the plays. For our interpretations today this means that we not only lack a single stable text for the plays, we also should not imagine that in earlier periods they evoked a more unified response than they might today.

Although there were no women on the stage, there were certainly women in the audience, from the higher as well as the lower social

---

[4]Ann Jennalie Cook, a recent historian of the stage, has challenged this consensus and argued that the audiences in the public theaters were largely constituted of the privileged classes. See her *The Privileged Playgoers of Shakespeare's London.* Her data and argument have been seriously questioned, however, by Gurr, *Playgoing in Shakespeare's London.* Although Shakespeare's audiences may not have represented the ideal unity of all parts of English society as was claimed by stage historians a generation or two ago, they were not simply made up of the wealthy.

groups. Some of the early attacks on playgoing mention plays as places where young people might have illicit and "vnchaste" meetings, and Puritan critics of the theaters frequently complain about the presence of women in the audience. City elders and critics of the theater associated theatergoing with prostitution. Thus William Prynne, an archenemy of the theater who attacked the theater viciously in his *Histriomastix, The Players Scourge* (1633) writes that "our Theatres if they are not Bawdy-houses [houses of prostitution] (as they easily may be, since many play-ers, if reports be true, are common panders [pimps, go-betweens]), yet they are cousins-german, at least neighbors to them." This concern about prostitutes working the theaters and about impropriety goes back to some of the early complaints about playgoing. In 1574, for instance, two years before the first theater was built, the London city authorities, describing a scene at a play performed in an inn yard, objected to

> the inordynate hauntyinge of great multitudes of people, speciallye youthe, to playes, enterludes and shewes, namelye oc-casyon of ffrayes and quarrelles, eavell [evil] practizes of in-continencye in greate Innes, havinge chambers and secrete places adioyninge to their open stagies and gallyries, inveglynge and al-leuringe of maides, speciallye orphanes and Good Cityzens Chil-dren vnder Age, to previe [privy] and vnmeete Contractes, the publishinge of vnchaste vncomelye and vnshamefaste speeches and doynges, withdrawinge of the Queenes Maiesties Subiects from dyvyne service on Sonndaies and hollydayes . . . vnthriftye waste of the moneye of the poore and fond persons, sondrye robberies by pickinge and Cuttinge of purses, vtteringe of popular busye and sedycious matters, and manie other Corruptions of youthe and other enormyties, besydes that allso soundrye slaughters and may-hemings of the Quenes Subiectes have happened by ruines of Skaffoldes, fframes, and Stagies, and by engynes, weapons, and powder vsed in plaies. (Qtd. in Chambers, 4: 273–74)

Although this document is early, similar complaints continued to be leveled against the theaters for the next forty years. The authorities were distressed not only by what went on in the plays — "the publishing of vnchaste vncomely and vnshamefaste speeches and doynges" seems to be the only reference to the contents of the plays — but also by the various kinds of unseemly behavior in the audience. The stress on youth, on unregulated sexuality, and on the possibility that large public gatherings would breed sedition all point to a distrust of theater as pro-viding a space largely outside official control. This document represents one side of a polemic, of course, but there is evidence to suggest that the playgoers themselves, and aristocrats who were not involved in the attacks on the theater, may have seen the theaters as at least potentially subversive. In 1592, a group of Southwark feltmakers (mostly apprentices) confronted the guards of the Marshalsea debtors' prison in a rowdy and violent demonstration by means of which they attempted to rescue one of their fellows from the prison. The documents about the case stress that the "principal actors" in the riot had "assembled by occasion of a play," perhaps using the theater as a meeting point (qtd. in Patterson 35). In several earlier cases, revolts were associated with the theater, and the authorities seem to have taken the threat represented by the stage quite seriously.

One occasion at about the time when *Hamlet* was being performed suggests the way in which theatrical representation and playgoing could suddenly come to seem subversive. On the day before the abortive uprising of Essex against Queen Elizabeth in 1601, Shakespeare's company, The Lord Chamberlain's Men, was paid forty shillings to revive their by then out-of-date play about the deposition and murder of King Richard II. The idea seems to have been that this representation of a revolt against royal power would encourage the populace to rise up with Essex against Elizabeth. Although many modern readers have felt that the play could hardly be seen as sufficiently subversive to send the audience out into the streets, the principals in this story were not so sure. We believe that the play was performed only once, on the eve of the rebellion, at the Globe Theatre, but in Queen Elizabeth's account, the event has multiplied: "this tragedy was played forty times in open streets and houses," she claimed (qtd. in Greenblatt 3). Queen Elizabeth was said to have seen a personal attack in the play's treatment of the deposition of Richard II: "I am Richard II. Know ye not that?" she supposedly said (Greenblatt 4).

This kind of overt association of the theaters with rebellion is perhaps less important than the prevailing sense among London authorities that what went on in the theaters was beyond their control. This was literally the case, for the theaters, along with the hospitals, gaming places, houses of prostitution, and the sites of public executions were located outside the boundaries of the city of London, in suburban areas called "the Liberties" (see Mullaney 26–55). These "licentious liberties," as Puritan critics called them, were beyond the control of the London city government; they were "licensed" — by custom allowed to encourage behavior that elsewhere was deemed illegal and immoral — and thus provided a space in which the laws of the city of London had no power. The location of hospitals in the Liberties was partly a matter of health — to protect the citizens from infection and contagion — but the analogy to the playhouses was not overlooked by critics of the theater. We have already seen how Prynne argues that the location of the playhouses near the houses of prostitution reveals the true, licentious character of the drama. Puritan critics similarly were quick to pick up the language of contagion from the descriptions of nearby hospitals, and to insist that audiences would catch diseases as bad, or worse, by attendance at plays (Mullaney 34–35, Agnew 123–24). Indeed, in times of plague, the theaters were closed, for the authorities feared the spreading of disease in public gathering places. But it is moral not physical disease that particularly concerned those attacking the theater, whether they were Puritan or not. The treatment of the stage as a place of contamination matches the concern about pollution prominent in Elizabethan and Jacobean attacks on the actor. Anthony Munday's *Second and Third Blast of Retrait from Plaies and Theaters* (1580) makes this double point explicitly because it connects the power of theater to contaminate its audiences with the guilt of the actors themselves. He observes that all other evils "pollute the doers onlie, not the beholders, or the hearers. . . . Onlie the filthines of plaies, and spectacles is such, as maketh both the actors & beholders giltie alike" (qtd. in Agnew 123). Similarly, William Rankins in his *Mirrour of Monsters* (1587) argues that plays present "spectacles of human deceit, incontinence and general depravity" that can contaminate their audiences with these same vices. Rankins's "monsters" are "the manifold vices, and spotted enormities, that can be caused by infectious sight of Playes" (qtd. in Mullaney 34).

The Lord Mayor of London and his aldermen, who wrote frequently to the Privy Council urging that plays be more strictly controlled or even outlawed, attribute to drama the power to impress the evils that are represented onto the minds of the audience so as to ensure repetition of them. The principal danger of the stage, according to the Lord Mayor, was that the playhouses were the haunt of the poor and of "masterless men" and rebellious apprentices, people who had no stable place within the social hierarchy, but he also mentions the dangerous influence of the plays. On November 3, 1594, for instance, the Lord Mayor complains to Lord Burghley:

> the sayed playes . . . ar of that sort . . . conteining nothing ells but vnchaste fables, lascivious divises, shifts of cozenage, and matters of lyke sort, which ar so framed & represented by them, that such as resort to see & hear the same, beeing of the base & refuse sort of people or such yong gentlemen as haue small regard of credit

or conscience, draue the same into example of imitation and not
of avoyding the sayed lewd offences. (Qtd. in Chambers 4: 317)

This concluding formula appears over and over again in letters from the
city government in the course of the 1590s. These documents reveal a
striking concern with the powers of representational art, and with the
danger that plays "impress" or infect their audiences with evil ideas or
behavior. Many of these same complaints are still made today by critics
of the theater, of modern art, and, of course, of movies and television.

What does it matter for a reading of *Hamlet* today that the "Liberties" of London and the plays performed there were considered licentious and threatening to social order? Tragedy itself is a dramatic genre
or mode that often represents the disruption or failure of traditional
forms of government, particularly, in this period, the disruption and
fragmentation of royal authority, the kind of "uncrowning" that Michael Bristol writes about in his essay included in this volume. In *Hamlet* the moral corruption that the play focuses on cannot be distinguished from a political corruption undermining all value in the Danish
state. Although *Hamlet* may seem more of a philosophical than a political play, one of the difficulties that Hamlet encounters is precisely that
he has trouble separating his moral outrage from his political ambitions.
As Franco Moretti puts it,

> Elizabethan and Jacobean tragedy was in fact one of the decisive
> influences in the creation of a "public" that for the first time in his-
> tory assumed the right to bring a king to justice. . . . Tragedy dis-
> entitled the absolute monarch to all ethical and rational legitima-
> tion. Having deconsecrated the king, it thus made it possible to
> decapitate him. (7–8)

Not all critics by any means would agree that tragedy had this disruptive
power, but it nonetheless seems significant for *Hamlet* that the play was
performed in a location specifically associated with transgression and
with a tendency to ignore or to undermine authority (see also
Dollimore on the association of tragedy with the deconsecration of
royal authority). To whatever extent the representation of a fraudulent
player-king in *Hamlet* might serve to make its audiences question the
essential authority of monarchs, the volatile and shifting position of the
actor and the moral ambiguity of the Liberties would have rendered
the experience of seeing the play all the more unsettling.

Susanne L. Wofford

WORKS CITED

Agnew, Jean-Christophe. *Worlds Apart: The Market and the Theater in Anglo-American Thought, 1550–1750.* Cambridge, Eng.: Cambridge UP, 1986.

Allen, Michael, and Kenneth Muir, eds. *Shakespeare's Plays in Quarto.* Berkeley: U of California P, 1981.

Barnet, Sylvan. "Shakespeare: Prefatory Remarks." *Hamlet.* Signet Classic Shakespeare. New York: NAL-Penguin, 1963.

Bentley, G. E. *Shakespeare: A Biographical Handbook.* New Haven: Yale UP, 1962.

Bowers, Fredson Thayer. *Elizabethan Revenge Tragedy, 1587–1642.* Princeton: Princeton UP, 1940.

Butler, Martin. *Theatre and Crisis 1632–1642.* Cambridge, Eng.: Cambridge UP, 1984.

Chambers, E. K. *The Elizabethan Stage.* Oxford, Eng.: Clarendon, 1923. 4 vols.

Clayton, Thomas, ed. *The "Hamlet" First Published Q1, 1603: Origins, Forms, Intertextualities.* Newark: U of Delaware P, 1992.

Cook, Ann Jennalie. *The Privileged Playgoers of Shakespeare's London, 1576–1642.* Princeton: Princeton UP, 1981.

Dollimore, Jonathan. *Radical Tragedy: Religion, Ideology, and Power in the Drama of Shakespeare and His Contemporaries.* Chicago: U of Chicago P, 1984.

Edwards, Philip, ed. *Hamlet, Prince of Denmark.* New Cambridge Shakespeare. Cambridge, Eng.: Cambridge UP, 1985.

Felperin, Howard. *Shakespearean Representation: Mimesis and Modernity in Elizabethan Tragedy.* Princeton: Princeton UP, 1977.

Ferguson, Margaret. "*Hamlet:* Letters and Spirits." *Shakespeare and the Question of Theory.* Ed. Patricia Parker and Geoffrey Hartman. New York: Methuen, 1987. 292–309.

Greenblatt, Stephen, ed. *The Power of Forms in the English Renaissance.* Norman: Pilgrim, 1982.

———. Introduction. Greenblatt 3–6.

Gurr, Andrew. *Playgoing in Shakespeare's London.* Cambridge, Eng.: Cambridge, UP, 1987.

———. *The Shakespearean Stage, 1574–1642.* 3rd ed. Cambridge, Eng.: Cambridge UP, 1992.

Jenkins, Harold, ed. *Hamlet.* Arden Shakespeare. London: Methuen, 1982.

Kay, Dennis. *Shakespeare: His Life, Work, and Era.* New York: Morrow, 1992.

Montrose, Louis Adrian. "The Purpose of Playing: Reflections on a Shakespearean Anthropology." *Helios* 7.2 (1979–80): 51–74.

Moretti, Franco. "'A Huge Eclipse': Tragic Form and the Deconsecration of Sovereignty." Greenblatt 7–40.

Mullaney, Steven. *The Place of the Stage: License, Play, and Power in Renaissance England.* Chicago: U of Chicago P, 1988.

Patterson, Annabel. *Shakespeare and the Popular Voice.* Cambridge: Basil Blackwell, 1989.

Schoenbaum, Samuel. *William Shakespeare: A Compact Documentary Life.* Oxford, Eng.: Clarendon, 1977.

Weimann, Robert. *Shakespeare and the Popular Tradition in the Theater: Studies in the Social Dimension of Dramatic Form and Function.* Ed. Robert Schwartz. Baltimore: Johns Hopkins UP, 1978.

Whigham, Frank. *Ambition and Privilege: The Social Tropes of Elizabethan Courtesy Theory.* Berkeley: U of California P, 1984.

The Tragedy of Hamlet, Prince of Denmark

[DRAMATIS PERSONAE

CLAUDIUS, *King of Denmark*
HAMLET, *son to the late King*
  Hamlet, and nephew to the
  present King
POLONIUS, *Lord Chamberlain*
HORATIO, *friend to Hamlet*
LAERTES, *son to Polonius*
VOLTEMAND ⎤
CORNELIUS ⎟
ROSENCRANTZ ⎟ *courtiers*
GUILDENSTERN ⎟
OSRIC ⎟
GENTLEMAN ⎦
MARCELLUS ⎤ *officers*
BARNARDO ⎦
FRANCISCO, *a soldier*

REYNALDO, *servant to Polonius*
FORTINBRAS, *Prince of Norway*
NORWEGIAN CAPTAIN
DOCTOR OF DIVINITY
PLAYERS
Two CLOWNS, *grave-diggers*
ENGLISH AMBASSADORS

GERTRUDE, *Queen of Denmark,*
  and mother to Hamlet
OPHELIA, *daughter to Polonius*

GHOST *of Hamlet's Father*

LORDS, LADIES, OFFICERS,
  SOLDIERS, SAILORS, MESSENGERS,
  and ATTENDANTS

SCENE: *Denmark*]

27

ACT 1, Scene 1°

Enter BARNARDO *and* FRANCISCO, *two sentinels,* [*meeting*].

BARNARDO: Who's there?
FRANCISCO: Nay, answer me.° Stand and unfold yourself.°
BARNARDO: Long live the King!°
FRANCISCO: Barnardo.
BARNARDO: He.   5
FRANCISCO: You come most carefully upon your hour.
BARNARDO: 'Tis now strook twelf.° Get thee to bed, Francisco.
FRANCISCO: For this relief much thanks. 'Tis bitter cold,
    And I am sick at heart.°
BARNARDO: Have you had quiet guard?
FRANCISCO: Not a mouse stirring.   10
BARNARDO: Well, good night.
    If you do meet Horatio and Marcellus,
    The rivals° of my watch, bid them make haste.

Enter HORATIO *and* MARCELLUS.

FRANCISCO: I think I hear them. Stand ho! Who is there?
HORATIO: Friends to this ground.
MARCELLUS: And liegemen to the Dane.°   15
FRANCISCO: Give° you good night.
MARCELLUS: O, farewell, honest [soldier].
    Who hath reliev'd you?
FRANCISCO: Barnardo hath my place.
    Give you good night.   *Exit Francisco.*
MARCELLUS: Holla, Barnardo!
BARNARDO: Say —
    What, is Horatio there?
HORATIO: A piece of him.

Words and passages enclosed in square brackets in the text above are either emendations of the copy-text or additions to it. The Textual Notes immediately following the play cite the earliest authority [e.g., Rowe, Pope, Theobald] for every such change or insertion and supply the reading of the copy-text wherever it is emended in this edition.

1.1. Location: Elsinore. A guard-platform of the castle.   **2. answer me:** I.e. *you* answer *me*. Francisco is on watch; Barnardo has come to relieve him.   **unfold yourself:** Make known who you are.   **3. Long . . . King:** Perhaps a password, perhaps simply an utterance to allow the voice to be recognized.   **7. strook twelf:** Struck twelve.   **9. sick at heart:** In low spirits.   **13. rivals:** Partners.   **15. liegemen . . . Dane:** Loyal subjects to the King of Denmark.   **16. Give:** God give.

BARNARDO: Welcome, Horatio, welcome, good Marcellus.   20
HORATIO: What, has this thing appear'd again to-night?
BARNARDO: I have seen nothing.
MARCELLUS: Horatio says 'tis but our fantasy,°
    And will not let belief take hold of him
    Touching this dreaded sight twice seen of us;   25
    Therefore I have entreated him along,
    With us to watch the minutes of this night,
    That if again this apparition come,
    He may approve° our eyes and speak to it.
HORATIO: Tush, tush, 'twill not appear.
BARNARDO: Sit down a while,   30
    And let us once again assail your ears,
    That are so fortified against our story,
    What we have two nights seen.
HORATIO: Well, sit we down,
    And let us hear Barnardo speak of this.
BARNARDO: Last night of all,   35
    When yond same star that's westward from the pole°
    Had made his° course t' illume that part of heaven
    Where now it burns, Marcellus and myself,
    The bell then beating one —

Enter GHOST.

MARCELLUS: Peace, break thee off! Look where it comes again!   40
BARNARDO: In the same figure like° the King that's dead.
MARCELLUS: Thou art a scholar,° speak to it, Horatio.
BARNARDO: Looks 'a° not like the King? Mark it, Horatio.
HORATIO: Most like; it [harrows] me with fear and wonder.
BARNARDO: It would be spoke to.°
MARCELLUS: Speak to it, Horatio.   45
HORATIO: What art thou that usurp'st° this time of night,
    Together with that fair and warlike form
    In which the majesty of buried Denmark°
    Did sometimes° march? By heaven I charge thee speak!

---

23. fantasy: Imagination.   **29. approve:** Corroborate.   **36. pole:** Pole star.   **37. his:**
Its (the commonest form of the neuter possessive singular in Shakespeare's day).   **41.**
like: In the likeness of.   **42. a scholar:** I.e. one who knows how best to address it.
43. 'a: He.   **45. It . . . to:** A ghost had to be spoken to before it could speak.   **46.**
usurp'st: The ghost, a supernatural being, has invaded the realm of nature.   **48. majesty**
. . . Denmark: Late King of Denmark.

MARCELLUS: It is offended.
BARNARDO: See, it stalks away!   50
HORATIO: Stay! Speak, speak, I charge thee speak!   *Exit Ghost.*
MARCELLUS: 'Tis gone, and will not answer.
BARNARDO: How now, Horatio? you tremble and look pale.
    Is not this something more than fantasy?
    What think you on't?   55
HORATIO: Before my God, I might not this believe
    Without the sensible° and true avouch°
    Of mine own eyes.
MARCELLUS: Is it not like the King?
HORATIO: As thou art to thyself.
    Such was the very armor he had on   60
    When he the ambitious Norway° combated.
    So frown'd he once when in an angry parle°
    He smote the sledded° [Polacks°] on the ice.
    'Tis strange.
MARCELLUS: Thus twice before, and jump° at this dead hour,   65
    With martial stalk hath he gone by our watch.
HORATIO: In what particular thought to work I know not,
    But in the gross and scope of mine opinion,°
    This bodes some strange eruption° to our state.
MARCELLUS: Good now, sit down, and tell me, he that knows,   70
    Why this same strict and most observant watch
    So nightly toils° the subject° of the land,
    And [why] such daily [cast] of brazen cannon,
    And foreign mart° for implements of war,
    Why such impress° of shipwrights, whose sore task   75
    Does not divide the Sunday from the week,
    What might be toward,° that this sweaty haste
    Doth make the night joint-laborer with the day:
    Who is't that can inform me?

---

49. sometimes: Formerly.   **57. sensible:** Relating to the senses.   **avouch:** Guarantee.
61. Norway: King of Norway.   **62. parle:** Parley.   **63. sledded:** Using sleds or
sledges.   **Polacks:** Poles.   **65. jump:** Precisely.   **67–68. In . . . opinion:** While I
have no precise theory about it, my general feeling is that. *Gross* = wholeness, totality; *scope*
= range.   **69. eruption:** Upheaval.   **72. toils:** Causes to work.   **subject:** Subjects.
74. foreign mart: Dealing with foreign markets.   **75. impress:** Forced service.   **77.
toward:** In preparation.

HORATIO: That can I,
At least the whisper goes so: our last king,   80
Whose image even but now appear'd to us,
Was, as you know, by Fortinbras of Norway,
Thereto prick'd on by a most emulate° pride,
Dar'd to the combat; in which our valiant Hamlet
(For so this side of our known world esteem'd him)   85
Did slay this Fortinbras, who, by a seal'd compact
Well ratified by law and heraldy,°
Did forfeit (with his life) all [those] his lands
Which he stood seiz'd of,° to the conqueror;
Against the which a moi'ty° competent°   90
Was gaged° by our king, which had° [return'd]
To the inheritance° of Fortinbras,
Had he been vanquisher; as by the same comart°
And carriage° of the article [design'd°],
His fell to Hamlet. Now, sir, young Fortinbras,   95
Of unimproved° mettle hot and full,
Hath in the skirts° of Norway here and there
Shark'd up° a list of lawless resolutes
For food and diet to some enterprise
That hath a stomach° in't, which is no other,   100
As it doth well appear unto our state,
But to recover of us, by strong hand
And terms compulsatory, those foresaid lands
So by his father lost; and this, I take it,
Is the main motive of our preparations,   105
The source of this our watch, and the chief head°
Of this post-haste and romage° in the land.
BARNARDO: I think it be no other but e'en so.
Well may it sort° that this portentous° figure
Comes armed through our watch so like the King   110

---

83. emulate: Emulous, proceeding from rivalry.   **87. law and heraldy:** Heraldic law
(governing combat). *Heraldy* is a variant of *heraldry*.   **89. seiz'd of:** Possessed of.   **90.
moi'ty:** Portion.   **competent:** Adequate, i.e. equivalent.   **91. gaged:** Pledged.   **had:**
Would have.   **92. inheritance:** Possession.   **93. comart:** Bargain.   **94. carriage:**
Tenor.   **design'd:** Drawn up.   **96. unimproved:** Untried (?) or not directed to any
useful end (?).   **97. skirts:** Outlying territories.   **98. Shark'd up:** Gathered up hastily
and indiscriminately.   **100. stomach:** Relish of danger (?) or demand for courage (?).
106. head: Source.   **107. romage:** Rummage, bustling activity.   **109. sort:** Fit.
portentous: Ominous.

That was and is the question of these wars.
HORATIO: A mote it is to trouble the mind's eye.
In the most high and palmy state of Rome,
A little ere the mightiest Julius fell,
The graves stood [tenantless] and the sheeted dead   115
Did squeak and gibber in the Roman streets.°
As stars with trains of fire, and dews of blood,
Disasters° in the sun; and the moist star°
Upon whose influence Neptune's empire stands°
Was sick almost to doomsday° with eclipse.°   120
And even the like precurse° of [fear'd] events,
As harbingers° preceding still° the fates
And prologue to the omen° coming on,
Have heaven and earth together demonstrated
Unto our climatures° and countrymen.   125

Enter GHOST.

But soft, behold! lo where it comes again!
                                    It spreads his° arms.
I'll cross it° though it blast° me. Stay, illusion!
If thou hast any sound or use of voice,
Speak to me.
If there be any good thing to be done   130
That may to thee do ease, and grace to me,
Speak to me.
If thou art privy to thy country's fate,
Which happily° foreknowing may avoid,
O speak!   135
Or if thou hast uphoarded in thy life
Extorted treasure in the womb of earth,
For which, they say, your° spirits oft walk in death,

---

116. One or more lines may have been lost between this line and the next. **118. Disasters:** Ominous signs. **moist star:** Moon. **119. Neptune's empire stands:** The seas are dependent. **120. sick . . . doomsday:** I.e. almost totally darkened. When the Day of Judgment is imminent, says Matthew 24:29, "the moon shall not give her light." **eclipse:** There were a solar and two total lunar eclipses visible in England in 1598; they caused gloomy speculation. **121. precurse:** Foreshadowing. **122. harbingers:** Advance messengers. **still:** Always. **123. omen:** I.e. the events portended. **125. climatures:** Regions. **126. s.d. his:** Its. **127. cross it:** Cross its path, confront it directly. **blast:** Wither (by supernatural means). **134. happily:** Haply, perhaps. **138. your:** Colloquial and impersonal; cf. 1.5.167, 4.3.20–21, 22. Most editors adopt *you* from F1.

Speak of it, stay and speak! *(The cock crows.)* Stop it, Mar-
   cellus.
MARCELLUS: Shall I strike it with my partisan?°   140
HORATIO: Do, if it will not stand.
BARNARDO: 'Tis here!
HORATIO: 'Tis here!
MARCELLUS: 'Tis gone!   [*Exit Ghost.*]
   We do it wrong, being so majestical,
   To offer it the show of violence,
   For it is as the air, invulnerable,   145
   And our vain blows malicious mockery.°
BARNARDO: It was about to speak when the cock crew.
HORATIO: And then it started like a guilty thing
   Upon a fearful summons. I have heard
   The cock, that is the trumpet° to the morn,   150
   Doth with his lofty and shrill-sounding throat
   Awake the god of day, and at his warning,
   Whether in sea or fire, in earth or air,
   Th' extravagant° and erring° spirit hies°
   To his confine; and of the truth herein   155
   This present object° made probation.°
MARCELLUS: It faded on the crowing of the cock.
   Some say that ever 'gainst° that season comes
   Wherein our Saviour's birth is celebrated,
   This bird of dawning singeth all night long,   160
   And then they say no spirit dare stir abroad,
   The nights are wholesome, then no planets strike,°
   No fairy takes,° nor witch hath power to charm,
   So hallowed, and so gracious,° is that time.
HORATIO: So have I heard and do in part believe it.   165
   But look, the morn in russet° mantle clad
   Walks o'er the dew of yon high eastward hill.
   Break we our watch up, and by my advice
   Let us impart what we have seen to-night

---

140. partisan: Long-handled spear.   **146. malicious mockery:** Mockery of malice, i.e.
empty pretenses of harming it.   **150. trumpet:** Trumpeter.   **154. extravagant:** Wandering outside its proper bounds.   **erring:** Wandering abroad.   **hies:** Hastens.   **156.**
object: Sight.   **probation:** Proof.   **158. 'gainst:** Just before.   **162. strike:** Exert malevolent influence.   **163. takes:** Bewitches, charms.   **164. gracious:** Blessed.   **166.**
russet: Coarse greyish-brown cloth.

Unto young Hamlet, for, upon my life,   170
This spirit, dumb to us, will speak to him.
Do you consent we shall acquaint him with it,
As needful in our loves, fitting our duty?
MARCELLUS: Let's do't, I pray, and I this morning know
Where we shall find him most convenient.   *Exeunt.*   175

[Scene 2]°

Flourish.° Enter CLAUDIUS, KING OF DENMARK, GERTRUDE THE
QUEEN; COUNCIL: *as* POLONIUS; *and his son* LAERTES, HAMLET,
cum aliis° [*including* VOLTEMAND *and* CORNELIUS].

KING: Though yet of Hamlet our dear brother's death
The memory be green, and that it us befitted°
To bear our hearts in grief, and our whole kingdom
To be contracted in° one brow of woe,°
Yet so far hath discretion fought with nature   5
That we with wisest sorrow think on him
Together with remembrance of ourselves.
Therefore our sometime sister, now our queen,
Th' imperial jointress° to this warlike state,
Have we, as 'twere with a defeated° joy,   10
With an auspicious, and a dropping° eye,
With mirth in funeral, and with dirge in marriage,
In equal scale weighing delight and dole,
Taken to wife; nor have we herein barr'd
Your better wisdoms, which have freely° gone   15
With this affair along. For all, our thanks.
Now follows that you know° young Fortinbras,
Holding a weak supposal° of our worth,
Or thinking by our late dear brother's death
Our state to be disjoint and out of frame,   20
Co-leagued° with this dream of his advantage,
He hath not fail'd to pester us with message°

1.2. Location: The castle.   o.s.d. Flourish: Trumpet fanfare.   cum aliis: With others.
2. befitted: Would befit.   4. contracted in: (1) Reduced to; (2) knit or wrinkled in.
brow of woe: Mournful brow.   9. jointress: Joint holder.   10. defeated: Impaired.
11. auspicious . . . dropping: Cheerful . . . weeping.   15. freely: Fully, without reser-
vation.   17. know: Be informed, learn.   18. supposal: Conjecture, estimate.   21.
Co-leagued: Joined.   22. pester . . . message: Trouble me with persistent messages
(the original sense of *pester* is "overcrowd").

Importing° the surrender of those lands
Lost by his father, with all bands° of law,
To our most valiant brother. So much for him.   25
Now for ourself, and for this time of meeting,
Thus much the business is: we have here writ
To Norway, uncle of young Fortinbras —
Who, impotent and bedred,° scarcely hears
Of this his nephew's purpose — to suppress   30
His further gait° herein, in that the levies,
The lists, and full proportions are all made
Out of his subject;° and we here dispatch
You, good Cornelius, and you, Voltemand,
For bearers of this greeting to old Norway,   35
Giving to you no further personal power
To business with the King, more than the scope
Of these delated° articles allow.   [*Giving a paper.*]
Farewell, and let your haste commend your duty.
CORNELIUS, VOLTEMAND: In that, and all things, will we show
    our duty.   40
KING: We doubt it nothing;° heartily farewell.
            [*Exeunt Voltemand and Cornelius.*]
And now, Laertes, what's the news with you?
You told us of some suit, what is't, Laertes?
You cannot speak of reason to the Dane
And lose° your voice. What wouldst thou beg, Laertes,   45
That shall not be my offer, not thy asking?
The head is not more native° to the heart,
The hand more instrumental° to the mouth,
Than is the throne of Denmark to thy father.
What wouldst thou have, Laertes?
LAERTES: My dread lord,   50
Your leave and favor° to return to France,
From whence though willingly I came to Denmark
To show my duty in your coronation,
Yet now I must confess, that duty done,
My thoughts and wishes bend again toward France,   55

---

23. Importing: Having as import.   **24. bands:** bonds, binding terms.   **29. impotent
and bedred:** Feeble and bedridden.   **31. gait:** Proceeding.   **31–33. in . . . subject:**
Since the troops are all drawn from his subjects.   **38. delated:** Extended, detailed (a
variant of *dilated*).   **41. nothing:** Not at all.   **45. lose:** Waste.   **47. native:** Closely
related.   **48. instrumental:** Serviceable.   **51. leave and favor:** Gracious permission.

And bow them to your gracious leave and pardon.°
KING: Have you your father's leave? What says Polonius?
POLONIUS: H'ath,° my lord, wrung from me my slow leave
By laborsome petition, and at last
Upon his will I seal'd my hard° consent.   60
I do beseech you give him leave to go.
KING: Take thy fair hour, Laertes, time be thine,
And thy best graces spend it at thy will!
But now, my cousin° Hamlet, and my son —
HAMLET: [Aside.] A little more than kin, and less than kind.°   65
KING: How is it that the clouds still hang on you?
HAMLET: Not so, my lord, I am too much in the sun.°
QUEEN: Good Hamlet, cast thy nighted color off,
And let thine eye look like a friend on Denmark.
Do not for ever with thy vailed° lids   70
Seek for thy noble father in the dust.
Thou know'st 'tis common,° all that lives must die,
Passing through nature to eternity.
HAMLET: Ay, madam, it is common.
QUEEN: If it be,
Why seems it so particular° with thee?   75
HAMLET: Seems, madam? nay, it is, I know not "seems."
'Tis not alone my inky cloak, [good] mother,
Nor customary suits of solemn black,
Nor windy suspiration of forc'd breath,
No, nor the fruitful° river in the eye,   80
Nor the dejected havior of the visage,
Together with all forms, moods, [shapes] of grief,
That can [denote] me truly. These indeed seem,
For they are actions that a man might play,
But I have that within which passes show,   85
These but the trappings and the suits of woe.
KING: 'Tis sweet and commendable in your nature, Hamlet,
To give these mourning duties to your father.
But you must know your father lost a father,

---

56. pardon: Permission to depart.   **58. H'ath:** He hath.   **60. hard:** Reluctant.   **64. cousin:** Kinsman (used in familiar address to any collateral relative more distant than a brother or sister; here to a nephew).   **65. A little . . . kind:** Closer than a nephew, since you are my mother's husband; yet more distant than a son, too (and not well disposed to you).   **67. sun:** With obvious quibble on *son*.   **70. vailed:** Downcast.   **72. common:** General, universal.   **75. particular:** Individual, personal.   **80. fruitful:** Copious.

That father lost, lost his, and the survivor bound   90
In filial obligation for some term
To do obsequious° sorrow. But to persever
In obstinate condolement° is a course
Of impious stubbornness, 'tis unmanly grief,
It shows a will most incorrect° to heaven,   95
A heart unfortified, or mind impatient,
An understanding simple and unschool'd:
For what we know must be, and is as common
As any the most vulgar thing to sense,°
Why should we in our peevish opposition   100
Take it to heart? Fie, 'tis a fault to° heaven,
A fault against the dead, a fault to nature,
To reason most absurd,° whose common theme
Is death of fathers, and who still hath cried,
From the first corse till he that died to-day,   105
"This must be so." We pray you throw to earth
This unprevailing° woe, and think of us
As of a father, for let the world take note
You are the most immediate to our throne,
And with no less nobility of love   110
Than that which dearest° father bears his son
Do I impart° toward you. For your intent
In going back to school in Wittenberg,
It is most retrograde to our desire,
And we beseech you bend you to remain   115
Here in the cheer and comfort of our eye,
Our chiefest courtier, cousin, and our son.
QUEEN: Let not thy mother lose her prayers, Hamlet,
    I pray thee stay with us, go not to Wittenberg.
HAMLET: I shall in all my best obey you, madam.   120
KING: Why, 'tis a loving and a fair reply.
    Be as ourself in Denmark. Madam, come.
    This gentle and unforc'd accord of Hamlet
    Sits smiling to my heart, in grace whereof,
    No jocund health that Denmark drinks to-day,   125

---

92. obsequious: Proper to obsequies.   **93. condolement:** Grief.   **95. incorrect:** Unsubmissive.   **99. any . . . sense:** What is perceived to be commonest.   **101. to:** Against.   **103. absurd:** Contrary.   **107. unprevailing:** Unavailing.   **111. dearest:** Most loving.   **112. impart:** I.e. impart love.

But the great cannon to the clouds shall tell,
And the King's rouse° the heaven shall bruit° again,
Respeaking earthly thunder. Come away.
                              Flourish. Exeunt all but Hamlet.
HAMLET: O that this too too sallied° flesh would melt,
Thaw, and resolve itself into a dew!   130
Or that the Everlasting had not fix'd
His canon° 'gainst [self-]slaughter! O God, God,
How [weary], stale, flat, and unprofitable
Seem to me all the uses° of this world!
Fie on't, ah fie! 'tis an unweeded garden   135
That grows to seed, things rank and gross in nature
Possess it merely.° That it should come [to this]!
But two months dead, nay, not so much, not two.
So excellent a king, that was to° this
Hyperion° to a satyr, so loving to my mother   140
That he might not beteem° the winds of heaven
Visit her face too roughly. Heaven and earth,
Must I remember? Why, she should hang on him
As if increase of appetite had grown
By what it fed on, and yet, within a month —   145
Let me not think on't! Frailty, thy name is woman! —
A little month, or ere° those shoes were old
With which she followed my poor father's body,
Like Niobe,° all tears — why, she, [even she] —
O God, a beast that wants discourse of reason°   150
Would have mourn'd longer — married with my uncle,
My father's brother, but no more like my father
Than I to Hercules. Within a month,
Ere yet the salt of most unrighteous° tears
Had left the flushing° in her galled° eyes,   155
She married — O most wicked speed: to post

---

127. **rouse:** Bumper, drink.   **bruit:** Loudly declare.   129. **sallied:** Sullied. See the
Textual Notes. Many editors prefer the F1 reading, *solid*.   132. **canon:** Law.   134.
uses: Customs.   137. **merely:** Utterly.   139. **to:** In comparison with.   140. **Hyperion:** The sun-god.   141. **beteem:** Allow.   147. **or ere:** Before.   149. **Niobe:** She
wept endlessly for her children, whom Apollo and Artemis had killed.   150. **wants . . .
reason:** Lacks the power of reason (which distinguishes men from beasts).   154. **un-
righteous:** I.e. hypocritical.   155. **flushing:** Redness.   **galled:** Inflamed.

With such dexterity to incestious° sheets,
It is not, nor it cannot come to good,
But break my heart, for I must hold my tongue.

Enter HORATIO, MARCELLUS, *and* BARNARDO.

HORATIO: Hail to your lordship!
HAMLET: I am glad to see you well.   160
   Horatio — or I do forget myself.
HORATIO: The same, my lord, and your poor servant ever.
HAMLET: Sir, my good friend — I'll change° that name with
   you.
   And what make you from° Wittenberg, Horatio?
   Marcellus.   165
MARCELLUS: My good lord.
HAMLET: I am very glad to see you. [*To Barnardo.*] Good even,
   sir. —
   But what, in faith, make you from Wittenberg?
HORATIO: A truant disposition,° good my lord.
HAMLET: I would not hear your enemy say so,   170
   Nor shall you do my ear that violence
   To make it truster of your own report
   Against yourself. I know you are no truant.
   But what is your affair in Elsinore?
   We'll teach you to drink [deep] ere you depart.   175
HORATIO: My lord, I came to see your father's funeral.
HAMLET: I prithee do not mock me, fellow student,°
   I think it was to [see] my mother's wedding.
HORATIO: Indeed, my lord, it followed hard upon.
HAMLET: Thrift, thrift, Horatio, the funeral bak'd-meats   180
   Did coldly° furnish forth the marriage tables.
   Would I had met my dearest° foe in heaven
   Or° ever I had seen that day, Horatio!
   My father — methinks I see my father.
HORATIO: Where, my lord?

---

157. **incestious:** Incestuous. The marriage of a man to his brother's widow was so regarded until long after Shakespeare's day.   163. **change:** Exchange.   164. **what . . .
from:** What are you doing away from.   169. **truant disposition:** Inclination to play
truant.   177. **student:** Student.   181. **coldly:** When cold.   182. **dearest:** Most intensely hated.   183. **Or:** Ere, before.

HAMLET: In my mind's eye, Horatio.   185
HORATIO: I saw him once, 'a was a goodly king.
HAMLET: 'A was a man, take him for all in all,
    I shall not look upon his like again.
HORATIO: My lord, I think I saw him yesternight.
HAMLET: Saw, who?   190
HORATIO: My lord, the King your father.
HAMLET: The King my father?
HORATIO: Season° your admiration° for a while
    With an attent ear, till I may deliver,°
    Upon the witness of these gentlemen,
    This marvel to you.
HAMLET: For God's love let me hear!   195
HORATIO: Two nights together had these gentlemen,
    Marcellus and Barnardo, on their watch,
    In the dead waste° and middle of the night,
    Been thus encount'red: a figure like your father,
    Armed at point exactly,° cap-a-pe,°   200
    Appears before them, and with solemn march
    Goes slow and stately by them; thrice he walk'd
    By their oppress'd and fear-surprised° eyes
    Within his truncheon's° length, whilst they, distill'd
    Almost to jelly with the act° of fear,   205
    Stand dumb and speak not to him. This to me
    In dreadful° secrecy impart they did,
    And I with them the third night kept the watch,
    Where, as they had delivered, both in time,
    Form of the thing, each word made true and good,   210
    The apparition comes. I knew your father,
    These hands are not more like.°
HAMLET: But where was this?
MARCELLUS: My lord, upon the platform where we watch.
HAMLET: Did you not speak to it?
HORATIO: My lord, I did,
    But answer made it none. Yet once methought   215

---

192. **Season:** Temper.   **admiration:** Wonder.   **193. deliver:** Report.   **198. waste:**
Empty expanse.   **200. at point exactly:** In every particular.   **cap-a-pe:** From head to
foot.   **203. fear-surprised:** Overwhelmed by fear.   **204. truncheon:** Short staff carried as a symbol of military command.   **205. act:** Action, operation.   **207. dreadful:**
Held in awe, i.e. solemnly sworn.   **212. are . . . like:** I.e. do not resemble each other
more closely than the apparition resembled him.

It lifted up it° head and did address
Itself to motion° like as it would speak;
But even then the morning cock crew loud,
And at the sound it shrunk in haste away
And vanish'd from our sight.
HAMLET: 'Tis very strange.   220
HORATIO: As I do live, my honor'd lord, 'tis true,
And we did think it writ down in our duty
To let you know of it.
HAMLET: Indeed, [indeed,] sirs. But this troubles me.
Hold you the watch to-night?
[MARCELLUS, BARNARDO]:   We do, my lord.   225
HAMLET: Arm'd, say you?
[MARCELLUS, BARNARDO]: Arm'd, my lord.
HAMLET: From top to toe?
[MARCELLUS, BARNARDO]: My lord, from head to foot.
HAMLET: Then saw you not his face.
HORATIO: O yes, my lord, he wore his beaver° up.   230
HAMLET: What, look'd he frowningly?
HORATIO: A countenance more
In sorrow than in anger.
HAMLET: Pale, or red?
HORATIO: Nay, very pale.
HAMLET: And fix'd his eyes upon you?
HORATIO: Most constantly.
HAMLET: I would I had been there.
HORATIO: It would have much amaz'd you.   235
HAMLET: Very like, [very like]. Stay'd it long?
HORATIO: While one with moderate haste might tell a
    hundreth.°
BOTH [MARCELLUS, BARNARDO]: Longer, longer.
HORATIO: Not when I saw't.
HAMLET: His beard was grisl'd,° no?
HORATIO: It was, as I have seen it in his life,   240
A sable silver'd.
HAMLET: I will watch to-night,
Perchance 'twill walk again.

---

216. it: Its.   **216–17. address . . . motion:** Begin to make a gesture.   **230. beaver:**
Visor.   **237. tell a hundreth:** Count a hundred.   **239. grisl'd:** Grizzled, mixed with
grey.

HORATIO: I warr'nt it will.
HAMLET: If it assume my noble father's person,
    I'll speak to it though hell itself should gape
    And bid me hold my peace. I pray you all,   245
    If you have hitherto conceal'd this sight,
    Let it be tenable° in your silence still,
    And whatsomever else shall hap to-night,
    Give it an understanding but no tongue.
    I will requite your loves. So fare you well.   250
    Upon the platform 'twixt aleven° and twelf
    I'll visit you.
ALL: Our duty to your honor.
HAMLET: Your loves, as mine to you; farewell.
                                    Exeunt [*all but Hamlet*].
    My father's spirit — in arms! All is not well,
    I doubt° some foul play. Would the night were come!   255
    Till then sit still, my soul. [Foul] deeds will rise,
    Though all the earth o'erwhelm them, to men's eyes. *Exit.*

[**Scene 3**]°

Enter LAERTES *and* OPHELIA, *his sister.*

LAERTES: My necessaries are inbark'd.° Farewell.
    And, sister, as the winds give benefit
    And convey [is] assistant,° do not sleep,
    But let me hear from you.
OPHELIA: Do you doubt that?
LAERTES: For Hamlet, and the trifling of his favor,   5
    Hold it a fashion° and a toy in blood,°
    A violet in the youth of primy° nature,
    Forward,° not permanent, sweet, not lasting,
    The perfume and suppliance° of a minute —
    No more.
OPHELIA: No more but so?
LAERTES: Think it no more: 10

---

247. **tenable:** Held close.   251. **aleven:** Eleven.   255. **doubt:** Suspect.   **1.3. Location:** Polonius's quarters in the castle.   1. **inbark'd:** Embarked, abroad.   3. **convey is
assistant:** Means of transport is available.   6. **a fashion:** I.e. standard behavior for a
young man.   **toy in blood:** Idle fancy of youthful passion.   7. **primy:** Springlike.   8.
Forward: Early of growth.   9. **suppliance:** Pastime.

For nature crescent° does not grow alone
In thews° and [bulk], but as this temple waxes,
The inward service of the mind and soul
Grows wide withal.° Perhaps he loves you now,
And now no soil° nor cautel° doth besmirch   15
The virtue of his will,° but you must fear,
His greatness weigh'd,° his will is not his own,
[For he himself is subject to his birth:]
He may not, as unvalued° persons do,
Carve for himself,° for on his choice depends   20
The safety and health of this whole state,
And therefore must his choice be circumscrib'd
Unto the voice° and yielding° of that body°
Whereof he is the head. Then if he says he loves you,
It fits your wisdom so far to believe it   25
As he in his particular act and place°
May give his saying deed, which is no further
Than the main° voice of Denmark goes withal.°
Then weigh what loss your honor may sustain
If with too credent° ear you list his songs,   30
Or lose your heart, or your chaste treasure open
To his unmast'red importunity.
Fear it, Ophelia, fear it, my dear sister,
And keep you in the rear of your affection,
Out of the shot° and danger of desire.   35
The chariest maid is prodigal enough
If she unmask her beauty to the moon.
Virtue itself scapes not calumnious strokes.
The canker° galls the infants of the spring
Too oft before their buttons° be disclos'd,°   40
And in the morn and liquid dew of youth
Contagious blastments° are most imminent.

---

11. **crescent:** growing, increasing.   12. **thews:** Muscles, sinews.   **12–14. as . . . withal:** As the body develops, the powers of mind and spirit grow along with it.   **15. soil:** Stain.   **cautel:** Deceit.   **16. will:** Desire.   **17. His greatness weigh'd:** Considering his princely status.   **19. unvalued:** Of low rank.   **20. Carve for himself:** Indulge his own wishes.   **23. voice:** Vote, approval.   **yielding:** Consent.   **that body:** I.e. the state.   **26. in . . . place:** I.e. acting as he must act in the position he occupies.   **28. main:** General.   **goes withal:** Accord with.   **30. credent:** Credulous.   **35. shot:** Range.   **39. canker:** Canker-worm.   **40. buttons:** Buds.   **disclos'd:** Opened.   **42. blastments:** Withering blights.

Be wary then, best safety lies in fear:
Youth to° itself rebels, though none else near.
OPHELIA: I shall the effect of this good lesson keep   45
As watchman to my heart. But, good my brother,
Do not, as some ungracious° pastors do,
Show me the steep and thorny way to heaven,
Whiles, [like] a puff'd° and reckless libertine,
Himself the primrose path of dalliance treads,   50
And reaks° not his own rede.°
LAERTES: O, fear me not.°

Enter POLONIUS.

I stay too long — but here my father comes.
A double blessing is a double grace,
Occasion° smiles upon° a second leave.
POLONIUS: Yet here, Laertes? Aboard, aboard, for shame!   55
The wind sits in the shoulder of your sail,
And you are stay'd for. There — [*laying his hand on
Laertes' head*] my blessing with thee!
And these few precepts in thy memory
Look thou character.° Give thy thoughts no tongue,
Nor any unproportion'd° thought his act.   60
Be thou familiar,° but by no means vulgar:°
Those friends thou hast, and their adoption tried,°
Grapple them unto thy soul with hoops of steel,
But do not dull thy palm with entertainment
Of each new-hatch'd, unfledg'd courage.° Beware   65
Of entrance to a quarrel, but being in,
Bear't that° th' opposed may beware of thee.
Give every man thy ear, but few thy voice,
Take° each man's censure,° but reserve thy judgment.
Costly thy habit as thy purse can buy,   70
But not express'd in fancy, rich, not gaudy,
For the apparel oft proclaims the man,

---

44. to: Of.   **47. ungracious:** Graceless.   **49. puff'd:** Bloated.   **51. reaks:** Recks,
heeds.   **rede:** Advice.   **fear me not:** Don't worry about me.   **54. Occasion:** Opportunity (here personified, as often).   **smiles upon:** I.e. graciously bestows.   **59. character:** Inscribe.   **60. unproportion'd:** Unfitting.   **61. familiar:** Affable, sociable.   **vulgar:** Friendly with everybody.   **62. their adoption tried:** Their association with you
tested and proved.   **65. courage:** Spirited, young blood.   **67. Bear't that:** Manage it
in such a way that.   **69. Take:** Listen to.   **censure:** Opinion.

And they in France of the best rank and station
[Are] of a most select and generous° chief° in that.
Neither a borrower nor a lender [be],   75
For [loan] oft loses both itself and friend,
And borrowing dulleth [th'] edge of husbandry.°
This above all: to thine own self be true,
And it must follow, as the night the day,
Thou canst not then be false to any man.   80
Farewell, my blessing season° this in thee!
LAERTES: Most humbly do I take my leave, my lord.
POLONIUS: The time invests° you, go, your servants tend.°
LAERTES: Farewell, Ophelia, and remember well
    What I have said to you.
OPHELIA: 'Tis in my memory lock'd,   85
    And you yourself shall keep the key of it.
LAERTES: Farewell.   *Exit Laertes.*
POLONIUS: What is't, Ophelia, he hath said to you?
OPHELIA: So please you, something touching the Lord Hamlet.
POLONIUS: Marry,° well bethought.   90
    'Tis told me, he hath very oft of late
    Given private time to you, and you yourself
    Have of your audience been most free and bounteous.
    If it be so — as so 'tis put on° me,
    And that in way of caution — I must tell you,   95
    You do not understand yourself so clearly
    As it behooves my daughter and your honor.
    What is between you? Give me up the truth.
OPHELIA: He hath, my lord, of late made many tenders°
    Of his affection to me.   100
POLONIUS: Affection, puh! You speak like a green girl,
    Unsifted° in such perilous circumstance.
    Do you believe his tenders, as you call them?
OPHELIA: I do not know, my lord, what I should think.
POLONIUS: Marry, I will teach you: think yourself a baby   105
    That you have ta'en these tenders° for true pay,

---

74. generous: Noble.   chief: Eminence (?). But the line is probably corrupt. Perhaps *of a* is intrusive, in which case *chief* = chiefly.   77. husbandry: Thrift.   81. season: Preserve (?) or ripen, make fruitful (?).   83. invests: Besieges.   tend: Wait.   90. Marry: Indeed (originally the name of the Virgin Mary used as an oath).   94. put on: Told to.   99. tenders: Offers.   102. Unsifted: Untried.   106. tenders: With play on the sense "money offered in payment" (as in *legal tender*).

Which are not sterling. Tender° yourself more dearly,
Or (not to crack the wind of the poor phrase,
[Wringing°] it thus) you'll tender me a fool.°
OPHELIA: My lord, he hath importun'd me with love   110
In honorable fashion.
POLONIUS: Ay, fashion° you may call it. Go to, go to.
OPHELIA: And hath given countenance° to his speech, my lord,
With almost all the holy vows of heaven.
POLONIUS: Ay, springes° to catch woodcocks.° I do know,   115
When the blood burns, how prodigal the soul
Lends the tongue vows. These blazes, daughter,
Giving more light than heat, extinct in both
Even in their promise, as it is a-making,
You must not take for fire. From this time   120
Be something scanter of your maiden presence,
Set your entreatments at a higher rate
Than a command to parle.° For Lord Hamlet,
Believe so much in him,° that he is young,
And with a larger teder° may he walk   125
Than may be given you. In few, Ophelia,
Do not believe his vows, for they are brokers,°
Not of that dye which their investments show,°
But mere° [implorators] of unholy suits,
Breathing like sanctified and pious bonds,°   130
The better to [beguile]. This is for all:
I would not, in plain terms, from this time forth
Have you so slander° any moment° leisure
As to give words or talk with the Lord Hamlet.
Look to't, I charge you. Come your ways.°   135
OPHELIA: I shall obey, my lord.   *Exeunt.*

---

107. **Tender:** Hold, value.   109. **Wringing:** Straining, forcing to the limit.   **tender
. . . fool:** (1) Show me that you are a fool; (2) make me look like a fool; (3) present me
with a (bastard) grandchild.   112. **fashion:** See note on line 6.   113. **countenance:**
Authority.   115. **springes:** Snares.   **woodcocks:** Proverbially gullible birds.   **122–
23. Set . . . parle:** Place a higher value on your favors; do not grant interviews simply
because he asks for them. Polonius uses a military figure: *entreatments* = negotiations for
surrender; *parle* = parley, discuss terms.   124. **so . . . him:** No more than this with
respect to him.   125. **larger teder:** Longer tether.   127. **brokers:** Procurers.   **128.
Not . . . show:** Not of the color that their garments (*investments*) exhibit, i.e. not what
they seem.   129. **mere:** Out-and-out.   130. **bonds:** (Lover's) vows or assurances.
Many editors follow Theobald in reading *bawds*.   133. **slander:** Disgrace.   **moment:**
Momentary.   135. **Come your ways:** Come along.

[Scene 4]°

Enter HAMLET, HORATIO, *and* MARCELLUS.

HAMLET: The air bites shrowdly,° it is very cold.
HORATIO: It is [a] nipping and an eager° air.
HAMLET: What hour now?
HORATIO: I think it lacks of twelf.
MARCELLUS: No, it is strook.
HORATIO: Indeed? I heard it not. It then draws near the season   5
  Wherein the spirit held his wont to walk.
    A flourish of trumpets, and two pieces° goes off [*within*].
  What does this mean, my lord?
HAMLET: The King doth wake to-night and takes his rouse,°
  Keeps wassail,° and the swagg'ring up-spring° reels;
  And as he drains his draughts of Rhenish° down,   10
  The kettle-drum and trumpet thus bray out
  The triumph of his pledge.°
HORATIO: Is it a custom?
HAMLET: Ay, marry, is't,
  But to my mind, though I am native here
  And to the manner° born, it is a custom   15
  More honor'd in the breach than the observance.°
  This heavy-headed revel east and west
  Makes us traduc'd and tax'd of° other nations.
  They clip° us drunkards, and with swinish phrase
  Soil our addition,° and indeed it takes   20
  From our achievements, though perform'd at height,°
  The pith and marrow of our attribute.°
  So, oft it chances in particular° men,
  That for some vicious mole of nature° in them,
  As in their birth, wherein they are not guilty   25
  (Since nature cannot choose his° origin),

1.4. **Location:** The guard-platform of the castle.   1. **shrowdly:** Shrewdly, wickedly.
2. **eager:** Sharp.   6. **s.d. pieces:** Cannon.   8. **doth . . . rouse:** I.e. holds revels far into
the night.   9. **wassail:** Carousal.   **up-spring:** Wild dance.   10. **Rhenish:** Rhine wine.
12. **triumph . . . pledge:** Accomplishment of his toast (by draining his cup at a single
draught).   15. **manner:** Custom (of carousing).   16. **More . . . observance:** Which it
is more honorable to break than to observe.   18. **tax'd of:** Censured by.   19. **clip:**
Clepe, call.   20. **addition:** Titles of honor.   21. **at height:** Most excellently.   22.
attribute: Reputation.   23. **particular:** Individual.   24. **vicious . . . nature:** Small
natural blemish.   26. **his:** Its.

By their o'ergrowth of some complexion°
Oft breaking down the pales° and forts of reason,
Or by some habit, that too much o'er-leavens°
The form of plausive° manners — that these men,   30
Carrying, I say, the stamp of one defect,
Being nature's livery, or fortune's star,°
His virtues else, be they as pure as grace,
As infinite as man may undergo,°
Shall in the general censure° take corruption   35
From that particular fault: the dram° of [ev'l°]
Doth all the noble substance of a doubt°
To his own scandal.°

Enter GHOST.

HORATIO: Look, my lord, it comes!
HAMLET: Angels and ministers of grace defend us!
Be thou a spirit of health,° or goblin damn'd,   40
Bring with thee airs from heaven, or blasts from hell,
Be thy intents wicked, or charitable,
Thou com'st in such a questionable° shape
That I will speak to thee. I'll call thee Hamlet,
King, father, royal Dane. O, answer me!   45
Let me not burst in ignorance, but tell
Why thy canoniz'd° bones, hearsed in death,
Have burst their cerements;° why the sepulchre,
Wherein we saw thee quietly [inurn'd,]
Hath op'd his ponderous and marble jaws   50
To cast thee up again. What may this mean,
That thou, dead corse, again in complete steel°
Revisits° thus the glimpses of the moon,

---

27. By . . . complexion: By the excess of some one of the humors (which were thought
to govern the disposition).   28. pales: Fences.   29. o'er-leavens: Makes itself felt
throughout (as leaven works in the whole mass of dough).   30. plausive: Pleasing.
32. Being . . . star: I.e. whether they were born with it, or got it by misfortune. *Star*
means "blemish."   34. undergo: Carry the weight of, sustain.   35. general censure:
Popular opinion.   36. dram: Minute amount.   ev'l: Evil, with a pun on *eale*, "yeast"
(cf. *o'er-leavens* in line 29).   37. of a doubt: A famous crux, for which many emendations have been suggested, the most widely accepted being Steevens's *often dout* (i.e. ex-
tinguish).   38. To . . . scandal: I.e. so that it all shares in the disgrace.   40. of health:
Wholesome, good.   43. questionable: Inviting talk.   47. canoniz'd: Buried with
the prescribed rites.   48. cerements: Grave-clothes.   52. complete steel: Full armor.
53. Revisits: The -*s* ending in the second person singular is common.

Making night hideous, and we fools of nature°
So horridly to shake our disposition°   55
With thoughts beyond the reaches of our souls?
Say why is this? wherefore? what should we do?
                              [*Ghost*] *beckons* [*Hamlet*].
HORATIO: It beckons you to go away with it,
    As if it some impartment° did desire
    To you alone.
MARCELLUS: Look with what courteous action   60
    It waves you to a more removed ground,
    But do not go with it.
HORATIO: No, by no means.
HAMLET: It will not speak, then I will follow it.
HORATIO: Do not, my lord.
HAMLET: Why, what should be the fear?
    I do not set my life at a pin's fee,°   65
    And for my soul, what can it do to that,
    Being a thing immortal as itself?
    It waves me forth again, I'll follow it.
HORATIO: What if it tempt you toward the flood, my lord,
    Or to the dreadful summit of the cliff   70
    That beetles o'er his base into the sea,
    And there assume some other horrible form
    Which might deprive your sovereignty of reason,°
    And draw you into madness? Think of it.
    The very place puts toys of desperation,°   75
    Without more motive, into every brain
    That looks so many fadoms° to the sea
    And hears it roar beneath.
HAMLET: It waves me still. —
    Go on, I'll follow thee.
MARCELLUS: You shall not go, my lord.
HAMLET: Hold off your hands.   80
HORATIO: Be rul'd, you shall not go.
HAMLET: My fate cries out,

---

54. fools of nature: The children (or the dupes) of a purely natural order, baffled by
the supernatural.   **55. disposition:** Nature.   **59. impartment:** Communication.
65. fee: Worth.   **73. deprive . . . reason:** Unseat reason from the rule of your mind.
75. toys of desperation: Fancies of desperate action, i.e. inclinations to jump off.   **77.
fadoms:** Fathoms.

And makes each petty artere° in this body
As hardy as the Nemean lion's° nerve.°
Still am I call'd. Unhand me, gentlemen.
By heaven, I'll make a ghost of him that lets° me!   85
I say away! — Go on, I'll follow thee.
                              Exeunt Ghost and Hamlet.
HORATIO: He waxes desperate with [imagination].
MARCELLUS: Let's follow. 'Tis not fit thus to obey him.
HORATIO: Have after. To what issue will this come?
MARCELLUS: Something is rotten in the state of Denmark.   90
HORATIO: Heaven will direct it.°
MARCELLUS: Nay, let's follow him. *Exeunt.*

[Scene 5]°

Enter GHOST *and* HAMLET.

HAMLET: Whither wilt thou lead me? Speak, I'll go no further.
GHOST: Mark me.
HAMLET: I will.
GHOST: My hour is almost come
     When I to sulph'rous and tormenting flames
     Must render up myself.
HAMLET: Alas, poor ghost!
GHOST: Pity me not, but lend thy serious hearing   5
     To what I shall unfold.
HAMLET: Speak, I am bound to hear.
GHOST: So art thou to revenge, when thou shalt hear.
HAMLET: What?
GHOST: I am thy father's spirit,
     Doom'd for a certain term to walk the night,   10
     And for the day confin'd to fast° in fires,
     Till the foul crimes° done in my days of nature
     Are burnt and purg'd away. But that I am forbid
     To tell the secrets of my prison-house,
     I could a tale unfold whose lightest word   15
     Would harrow up thy soul, freeze thy young blood,

---

82. artere: Variant spelling of *artery;* here, ligament, sinew.   **83. Nemean lion:** Slain by
Hercules as one of his twelve labors.   **nerve:** Sinew.   **85. lets:** Hinders.   **91. it:** I.e.
the issue.   **1.5. Location:** On the battlements of the castle.   **11. fast:** Do penance.
12. crimes: Sins.

Make thy two eyes like stars start from their spheres,°
Thy knotted and combined locks to part,
And each particular hair to stand an end,°
Like quills upon the fearful porpentine.°   20
But this eternal blazon° must not be
To ears of flesh and blood. List, list, O, list!
If thou didst ever thy dear father love —
HAMLET: O God!
GHOST: Revenge his foul and most unnatural murther.   25
HAMLET: Murther!
GHOST: Murther most foul, as in the best it is,
But this most foul, strange, and unnatural.
HAMLET: Haste me to know't, that I with wings as swift
As meditation,° or the thoughts of love,   30
May sweep to my revenge.
GHOST: I find thee apt,
And duller shouldst thou be than the fat weed
That roots itself in ease on Lethe° wharf,°
Wouldst thou not stir in this. Now, Hamlet, hear:
'Tis given out that, sleeping in my orchard,°   35
A serpent stung me, so the whole ear of Denmark
Is by a forged process° of my death
Rankly abus'd;° but know, thou noble youth,
The serpent that did sting thy father's life
Now wears his crown.
HAMLET: O my prophetic soul!   40
My uncle?
GHOST: Ay, that incestuous, that adulterate° beast,
With witchcraft of his wits, with traitorous gifts —
O wicked wit and gifts that have the power
So to seduce! — won to his shameful lust   45
The will of my most seeming virtuous queen.
O Hamlet, what [a] falling-off was there
From me, whose love was of that dignity
That it went hand in hand even with the vow

17. **spheres:** Eye-sockets; with allusion to the revolving spheres in which, according to the Ptolemaic astronomy, the stars were fixed. **19. an end:** On end. **20. fearful porpentine:** Frightened porcupine. **21. eternal blazon:** Revelation of eternal things. **30. meditation:** Thought. **33. Lethe:** River of Hades, the water of which made the drinker forget the past. **wharf:** Bank. **35. orchard:** Garden. **37. forged process:** False account. **38. abus'd:** Deceived. **42. adulterate:** Adulterous.

I made to her in marriage, and to decline 50
Upon a wretch whose natural gifts were poor
To those of mine!
But virtue, as it never will be moved,
Though lewdness court it in a shape of heaven,°
So [lust], though to a radiant angel link'd, 55
Will [sate] itself in a celestial bed
And prey on garbage.
But soft, methinks I scent the morning air,
Brief let me be. Sleeping within my orchard,
My custom always of the afternoon, 60
Upon my secure° hour thy uncle stole,
With juice of cursed hebona° in a vial,
And in the porches of my ears did pour
The leprous distillment, whose effect
Holds such an enmity with blood of man 65
That swift as quicksilver it courses through
The natural gates and alleys of the body,
And with a sudden vigor it doth [posset°]
And curd, like eager° droppings into milk,
The thin and wholesome blood. So did it mine, 70
And a most instant tetter° bark'd° about,
Most lazar-like,° with vile and loathsome crust
All my smooth body.
Thus was I, sleeping, by a brother's hand
Of life, of crown, of queen, at once° dispatch'd,° 75
Cut off even in the blossoms of my sin,
Unhous'led,° disappointed,° unanel'd,°
No reck'ning made, but sent to my account
With all my imperfections on my head.
O, horrible, O, horrible, most horrible! 80
If thou hast nature° in thee, bear it not,
Let not the royal bed of Denmark be

---

54. shape of heaven: Angelic form. 61. secure: Carefree. 62. hebona: Ebony
(which Shakespeare, following a literary tradition, and perhaps also associating the word
with *henbane,* thought the name of a poison). 68. posset: Curdle. 69. eager: Sour.
71. tetter: Scabby eruption. bark'd: Formed a hard covering, like bark on a tree. 72.
lazar-like: Leper-like. 75. at once: All at the same time. dispatch'd: Deprived.
77. Unhous'led: Without the Eucharist. disappointed: Without (spiritual) preparation. unanel'd: Unanointed, without extreme unction. 81. nature: Natural feeling.

A couch for luxury° and damned incest.
But howsomever thou pursues this act,
Taint not thy mind, nor let thy soul contrive   85
Against thy mother aught. Leave her to heaven,
And to those thorns that in her bosom lodge
To prick and sting her. Fare thee well at once!
The glow-worm shows the matin° to be near,
And gins° to pale his uneffectual fire.   90
Adieu, adieu, adieu! remember me.   [*Exit.*]
HAMLET: O all you host of heaven! O earth! What else?
And shall I couple hell? O fie, hold, hold, my heart,
And you, my sinows,° grow not instant old,
But bear me [stiffly] up. Remember thee!   95
Ay, thou poor ghost, whiles memory holds a seat
In this distracted globe.° Remember thee!
Yea, from the table° of my memory
I'll wipe away all trivial fond° records,
All saws° of books, all forms,° all pressures° past   100
That youth and observation copied there,
And thy commandement all alone shall live
Within the book and volume of my brain,
Unmix'd with baser matter. Yes, by heaven!
O most pernicious woman!   105
O villain, villain, smiling, damned villain!
My tables — meet it is I set it down
That one may smile, and smile, and be a villain!
At least I am sure it may be so in Denmark.   [*He writes.*]
So, uncle, there you are. Now to my word:°   110
It is "Adieu, adieu! remember me."
I have sworn't.
HORATIO: [*Within.*] My lord, my lord!
MARCELLUS: [*Within.*]   Lord Hamlet!

Enter HORATIO *and* MARCELLUS.

HORATIO: Heavens secure him!

---

83. luxury: Lust.   **89. matin:** Morning.   **90. gins:** Begins.   **94. sinows:** Sinews.
97. globe: Head.   **98. table:** Writing tablet.   **99. fond:** Foolish.   **100. saws:** Wise
sayings.   **forms:** Shapes, images.   **pressures:** Impressions.   **110. word:** I.e. word of
command from the Ghost.

HAMLET: So be it!
MARCELLUS: Illo, ho, ho, my lord!   115
HAMLET: Hillo, ho, ho, boy! Come, [bird,] come.°
MARCELLUS: How is't, my noble lord?
HORATIO: What news, my lord?
HAMLET: O, wonderful!
HORATIO: Good my lord, tell it.
HAMLET: No, you will reveal it.
HORATIO: Not I, my lord, by heaven.
MARCELLUS: Nor I, my lord.   120
HAMLET: How say you then, would heart of man once think
       it? —
    But you'll be secret?
BOTH [HORATIO, MARCELLUS]:   Ay, by heaven, [my lord].
HAMLET: There's never a villain dwelling in all Denmark
    But he's an arrant knave.
HORATIO: There needs no ghost, my lord, come from the grave   125
    To tell us this.
HAMLET: Why, right, you are in the right,
    And so, without more circumstance° at all,
    I hold it fit that we shake hands and part,
    You, as your business and desire shall point you,
    For every man hath business and desire,   130
    Such as it is, and for my own poor part,
    I will go pray.
HORATIO: These are but wild and whirling words, my lord.
HAMLET: I am sorry they offend you, heartily,
    Yes, faith, heartily.
HORATIO: There's no offense, my lord.   135
HAMLET: Yes, by Saint Patrick, but there is, Horatio,
    And much offense too. Touching this vision here,
    It is an honest° ghost, that let me tell you.
    For your desire to know what is between us,
    O'ermaster't as you may. And now, good friends,   140
    As you are friends, scholars, and soldiers,
    Give me one poor request.

---

116. Hillo ... come: Hamlet answers Marcellus's halloo with a falconer's cry. **127.**
circumstance: Ceremony.   **138. honest:** True, genuine.

HORATIO: What is't,° my lord, we will.
HAMLET: Never make known what you have seen to-night.
BOTH [HORATIO, MARCELLUS]: My lord, we will not.
HAMLET: Nay, but swear't.
HORATIO: In faith,   145
    My lord, not I.
MARCELLUS: Nor I, my lord, in faith.
HAMLET: Upon my sword.°
MARCELLUS: We have sworn, my lord, already.
HAMLET: Indeed, upon my sword, indeed.
                               Ghost cries under the stage.
GHOST: Swear.
HAMLET: Ha, ha, boy, say'st thou so? Art thou there, true-
    penny?°   150
    Come on, you hear this fellow in the cellarage,
    Consent to swear.
HORATIO: Propose the oath, my lord.
HAMLET: Never to speak of this that you have seen,
    Swear by my sword.
GHOST: [*Beneath.*] Swear.   155
HAMLET: *Hic et ubique?* ° Then we'll shift our ground.
    Come hither, gentlemen,
    And lay your hands again upon my sword.
    Swear by my sword
    Never to speak of this that you have heard.   160
GHOST: [*Beneath.*] Swear by his sword.
HAMLET: Well said, old mole, canst work i' th' earth so fast?
    A worthy pioner!° Once more remove, good friends.
HORATIO: O day and night, but this is wondrous strange!
HAMLET: And therefore as a stranger give it welcome.°   165
    There are more things in heaven and earth, Horatio,
    Than are dreamt of in your° philosophy.°
    But come —
    Here, as before, never, so help you mercy,

---

143. **What is't:** Whatever it is.   147. **Upon my sword:** I.e. on the cross formed by the hilt.   150. **truepenny:** Trusty fellow.   156. *Hic et ubique:* Here and everywhere.   163. **pioner:** Digger, miner (variant of *pioneer*).   165. **as . . . welcome:** Give it the welcome due in courtesy to strangers.   167. **your:** See note on 1.1.138.   **philosophy:** I.e. natural philosophy, science.

How strange or odd some'er I bear myself —   170
As I perchance hereafter shall think meet
· To put an antic disposition on° —
That you, at such times seeing me, never shall,
With arms encumb'red° thus, or this headshake,
Or by pronouncing of some doubtful phrase,   175
As "Well, well, we know," or "We could, and if° we
    would,"
Or "If we list° to speak," or "There be, and if they might,"
Or such ambiguous giving out, to note°
That you know aught of me — this do swear,
So grace and mercy at your most need help you.   180
GHOST: [*Beneath.*] Swear.   [*They swear.*]
HAMLET: Rest, rest, perturbed spirit! So, gentlemen,
With all my love I do commend me to you,
And what so poor a man as Hamlet is
May do t' express his love and friending to you,   185
God willing, shall not lack. Let us go in together,
And still° your fingers on your lips, I pray.
The time is out of joint — O cursed spite,
That ever I was born to set it right!
Nay, come, let's go together.°   *Exeunt.*   190

[ACT 2, Scene 1]°

Enter old POLONIUS *with his man* [REYNALDO].

POLONIUS: Give him this money and these notes, Reynaldo.
REYNALDO: I will, my lord.
POLONIUS: You shall do marvell's° wisely, good Reynaldo,
Before you visit him, to make inquire
Of his behavior.
REYNALDO: My lord, I did intend it.   5
POLONIUS: Marry, well said, very well said. Look you, sir,

---

172. put . . . on: Behave in some fantastic manner, act like a madman.   **174.**
encumb'red: Folded.   **176. and if:** If.   **177. list:** Cared, had a mind.   **178. note:**
Indicate.   **187. still:** Always.   **190. Nay . . . together:** They are holding back to let
him go first.   **2.1. Location:** Polonius's quarters in the castle.   **3. marvell's:** Marvel-
lous(ly).

Inquire me first what Danskers° are in Paris,
And how, and who, what means, and where they keep,°
What company, at what expense; and finding
By this encompassment° and drift of question°   10
That they do know my son, come you more nearer
Than your particular demands° will touch it.
Take you as 'twere some distant knowledge of him,
As thus, "I know his father and his friends,
And in part him." Do you mark this, Reynaldo?   15
REYNALDO: Ay, very well, my lord.
POLONIUS: "And in part him — but," you may say, "not well.
But if't be he I mean, he's very wild,
Addicted so and so," and there put on him
What forgeries° you please: marry, none so rank   20
As may dishonor him, take heed of that,
But, sir, such wanton,° wild, and usual slips
As are companions noted and most known
To youth and liberty.
REYNALDO: As gaming, my lord.
POLONIUS: Ay, or drinking, fencing, swearing, quarrelling,   25
Drabbing° — you may go so far.
REYNALDO: My lord, that would dishonor him.
POLONIUS: Faith,° as you may season° it in the charge:
You must not put another scandal on him,
That he is open to incontinency° —   30
That's not my meaning. But breathe his faults so quaintly°
That they may seem the taints of liberty,
The flash and outbreak of a fiery mind,
A savageness in unreclaimed° blood,
Of general assault.°
REYNALDO: But, my good lord —   35
POLONIUS: Wherefore should you do this?
REYNALDO: Ay, my lord,
I would know that.

---

7. Danskers: Danes, **8. keep:** Lodge **10. encompassment:** Circuitousness. **drift
of question:** Directing of the conversation. **12. particular demands:** Direct questions. **20. forgeries:** Invented charges. **22. wanton:** Sportive. **26. Drabbing:**
Whoring. **28. Faith:** Most editors read *Faith, no,* following F1; this makes easier sense.
season: Qualify, temper. **30. open to incontinency:** Habitually profligate. **31.
quaintly:** Artfully. **34. unreclaimed:** Untamed. **35. Of general assault:** I.e. to
which young men are generally subject.

POLONIUS: Marry, sir, here's my drift,
And I believe it is a fetch of wit:°
You laying these slight sallies° on my son,
As 'twere a thing soil'd [wi' th'] working,°   40
Mark you,
Your party in converse, him you would sound,
Having° ever seen in the prenominate crimes°
The youth you breathe of guilty, be assur'd
He closes° with you in this consequence:°   45
"Good sir," or so, or "friend," or "gentleman,"
According to the phrase or the addition°
Of man and country.
REYNALDO: Very good, my lord.
POLONIUS: And then, sir, does 'a this — 'a does — what was I
      about to say?
By the mass, I was about to say something.   50
Where did I leave?
REYNALDO: At "closes in the consequence."
POLONIUS: At "closes in the consequence," ay, marry.
He closes thus: "I know the gentleman.
I saw him yesterday, or th' other day,
Or then, or then, with such or such, and as you say,   55
There was 'a gaming, there o'ertook in 's rouse,°
There falling out at tennis"; or, perchance,
"I saw him enter such a house of sale,"
Videlicet, a brothel, or so forth. See you now,
Your bait of falsehood take this carp of truth,   60
And thus do we of wisdom and of reach,°
With windlasses° and with assays of bias,°
By indirections find directions° out;
So by my former lecture and advice
Shall you my son. You have me,° have you not?   65
REYNALDO: My lord, I have.

---

38. fetch of wit: Ingenious device.   **39. sallies:** Sullies, blemishes.   **40. soil'd . . .
working:** I.e. shopworn.   **43. Having:** If he has.   **prenominate crimes:** Aforemen-
tioned faults.   **45. closes:** Falls in.   **in this consequence:** As follows.   **47. addition:**
Style of address.   **56. o'ertook in 's rouse:** Overcome by drink.   **61. reach:** Capacity,
understanding.   **62. windlasses:** Roundabout methods.   **assays of bias:** Indirect attempts (a figure from the game of bowls, in which the player must make allowance for the
curving course his bowl will take toward its mark).   **63. directions:** The way things are
going.   **65. have me:** Understand me.

POLONIUS: God buy ye,° fare ye well.
REYNALDO: Good my lord.
POLONIUS: Observe his inclination in° yourself.
REYNALDO: I shall, my lord.
POLONIUS: And let him ply° his music.
REYNALDO: Well, my lord.   70
POLONIUS: Farewell.   *Exit Reynaldo.*

Enter OPHELIA.

                        How now, Ophelia, what's the matter?
OPHELIA: O my lord, my lord, I have been so affrighted!
POLONIUS: With what, i' th' name of God?
OPHELIA: My lord, as I was sewing in my closet,°
    Lord Hamlet, with his doublet all unbrac'd,°   75
    No hat upon his head, his stockins fouled,°
    Ungart'red, and down-gyved° to his ankle,
    Pale as his shirt, his knees knocking each other,
    And with a look so piteous in purport
    As if he had been loosed out of hell   80
    To speak of horrors — he comes before me.
POLONIUS: Mad for thy love?
OPHELIA: My lord, I do not know,
    But truly I do fear it.
POLONIUS: What said he?
OPHELIA: He took me by the wrist, and held me hard,
    Then goes he to the length of all his arm,   85
    And with his other hand thus o'er his brow,
    He falls to such perusal of my face
    As 'a would draw it. Long stay'd he so.
    At last, a little shaking of mine arm,
    And thrice his head thus waving up and down,   90
    He rais'd a sigh so piteous and profound
    As it did seem to shatter all his bulk°
    And end his being. That done, he lets me go,
    And with his head over his shoulder turn'd,

---

66. God buy ye: Good-bye (a contraction of *God be with you*). **68. in:** By. Polonius asks him to observe Laertes directly, as well as making inquiries. **70. let him ply:** See that he goes on with. **74. closet:** Private room. **75. unbrac'd:** Unlaced. **76. stockins fouled:** Stockings dirty. **77. down-gyved:** Hanging down like fetters on a prisoner's legs. **92. bulk:** Body.

He seem'd to find his way without his eyes,   95
For out a' doors he went without their helps,
And to the last bended their light on me.
POLONIUS: Come, go with me. I will go seek the King.
This is the very ecstasy° of love,
Whose violent property° fordoes° itself,   100
And leads the will to desperate undertakings
As oft as any passions under heaven
That does afflict our natures. I am sorry —
What, have you given him any hard words of late?
OPHELIA: No, my good lord, but as you did command   105
I did repel his letters, and denied
His access to me.
POLONIUS: That hath made him mad.
I am sorry that with better heed and judgment
I had not coted° him. I fear'd he did but trifle
And meant to wrack thee, but beshrow° my jealousy!°   110
By heaven, it is as proper to our age°
To cast beyond ourselves° in our opinions,
As it is common for the younger sort
To lack discretion. Come, go we to the King.
This must be known, which, being kept close,° might move   115
More grief to hide, than hate to utter love.°
Come.   *Exeunt.*

[Scene 2]°

Flourish. Enter KING *and* QUEEN, ROSENCRANTZ *and* GUILDEN-
STERN [*cum aliis*].

KING: Welcome, dear Rosencrantz and Guildenstern!
Moreover that we much did long to see you,°
The need we have to use you did provoke
Our hasty sending. Something have you heard
Of Hamlet's transformation; so call it,   5

---

99. ecstasy: Madness.   **100. property:** Quality.   **fordoes:** Destroys.   **109. coted:**
Observed.   **110. beshrow:** Beshrew, plague take.   **jealousy:** Suspicious mind.   **111.**
proper . . . age: Characteristic of men of my age.   **112. cast beyond ourselves:** Over-
shoot, go too far (by way of caution).   **115. close:** Secret.   **115–16. move . . . love:**
Cause more grievous consequences by its concealment than we shall incur displeasure by
making it known.   **2.2. Location:** The castle.   **2. Moreover . . . you:** Besides the fact
that we wanted to see you for your own sakes.

Sith° nor th' exterior nor the inward man
Resembles that it was. What it should be,
More than his father's death, that thus hath put him
So much from th' understanding of himself,
I cannot dream of. I entreat you both   10
That, being of ° so young days brought up with him,
And sith so neighbored to his youth and havior,
That you voutsafe your rest° here in our court
Some little time, so by your companies
To draw him on to pleasures, and to gather   15
So much as from occasion you may glean,
Whether aught to us unknown afflicts him thus,
That, open'd, lies within our remedy.
QUEEN: Good gentlemen, he hath much talk'd of you,
And sure I am two men there is not living   20
To whom he more adheres.° If it will please you
To show us so much gentry° and good will
As to expend your time with us a while
For the supply and profit° of our hope,
Your visitation shall receive such thanks   25
As fits a king's remembrance.
ROSENCRANTZ: Both your Majesties
Might, by the sovereign power you have of us,
Put your dread pleasures more into command
Than to entreaty.
GUILDENSTERN: But we both obey,
And here give up ourselves, in the full bent,°   30
To lay our service freely at your feet,
To be commanded.
KING: Thanks, Rosencrantz and gentle Guildenstern.
QUEEN: Thanks, Guildenstern and gentle Rosencrantz.
And I beseech you instantly to visit   35
My too much changed son. Go some of you
And bring these gentlemen where Hamlet is.
GUILDENSTERN: Heavens make our presence and our practices
Pleasant and helpful to him!
QUEEN: Ay, amen!

---

6. **Sith:** Since.   11. **of:** From.   13. **voutsafe your rest:** Vouchsafe to remain.   21.
more adheres: Is more attached.   22. **gentry:** Courtesy.   24. **supply and profit:** Support and advancement.   30. **in . . . bent:** To our utmost.

*Exeunt Rosencrantz and Guildenstern [with some Atten-
dants].*

Enter POLONIUS.

POLONIUS: Th' embassadors° from Norway, my good lord,   40
  Are joyfully return'd.
KING: Thou still° hast been the father of good news.
POLONIUS: Have I, my lord? I assure my good liege°
  I hold my duty as I hold my soul,
  Both to my God and to my gracious king;   45
  And I do think, or else this brain of mine
  Hunts not the trail of policy° so sure
  As it hath us'd to do, that I have found
  The very cause of Hamlet's lunacy.
KING: O, speak of that, that do I long to hear.   50
POLONIUS: Give first admittance to th' embassadors;
  My news shall be the fruit° to that great feast.
KING: Thyself do grace to them, and bring them in.
                                 [Exit Polonius.]
  He tells me, my dear Gertrude, he hath found
  The head° and source of all your son's distemper.°   55
QUEEN: I doubt° it is no other but the main,°
  His father's death and our [o'erhasty] marriage.

*Enter [*POLONIUS *with* VOLTEMAND *and* CORNELIUS, *the*] Embassadors.*

KING: Well, we shall sift him. — Welcome, my good friends!
  Say, Voltemand, what from our brother Norway?
VOLTEMAND: Most fair return of greetings and desires.   60
  Upon our first,° he sent out to suppress
  His nephew's levies, which to him appear'd
  To be a preparation 'gainst the Polack;
  But better look'd into, he truly found
  It was against your Highness. Whereat griev'd,°   65
  That so his sickness, age, and impotence

---

40. **embassadors:** Ambassadors.   42. **still:** Always.   43. **liege:** Sovereign.   47. **pol-icy:** Statecraft.   52. **fruit:** Dessert.   55. **head:** Synonymous with *source*.   **distemper:** (Mental) illness.   56. **doubt:** Suspect.   **main:** Main cause.   61. **Upon our first:** At our first representation.   65. **griev'd:** Aggrieved, offended.

Was falsely borne in hand,° sends out arrests
On Fortinbras, which he, in brief, obeys,
Receives rebuke from Norway, and in fine,°
Makes vow before his uncle never more   70
To give th' assay° of arms against your Majesty.
Whereon old Norway, overcome with joy,
Gives him threescore thousand crowns in annual fee,
And his commission to employ those soldiers,
So levied, as before, against the Polack,   75
With an entreaty, herein further shown,   [*Giving a paper.*]
That it might please you to give quiet pass
Through your dominions for this enterprise,
On such regards of safety and allowance°
As therein are set down.
KING: It likes° us well,   80
And at our more consider'd° time we'll read,
Answer, and think upon this business.
Mean time, we thank you for your well-took labor.
Go to your rest, at night we'll feast together.
Most welcome home!
          Exeunt Embassadors [and Attendants].
POLONIUS: This business is well ended.   85
My liege, and madam, to expostulate°
What majesty should be, what duty is,
Why day is day, night night, and time is time,
Were nothing but to waste night, day, and time;
Therefore, [since] brevity is the soul of wit,°   90
And tediousness the limbs and outward flourishes,
I will be brief. Your noble son is mad:
Mad call I it, for to define true madness,
What is't but to be nothing else but mad?
But let that go.
QUEEN: More matter with less art.°   95
POLONIUS: Madam, I swear I use no art at all.
That he's mad, 'tis true, 'tis true 'tis pity,
And pity 'tis 'tis true — a foolish figure,°

---

67. **borne in hand:** Taken advantage of.   69. **in fine:** In the end.   71. **assay:** Trial.
79. **On . . . allowance:** With such safeguards and provisos.   80. **likes:** Pleases.   81.
consider'd: Suitable for consideration.   86. **expostulate:** Expound.   90. **wit:** Understanding, wisdom.   95. **art:** I.e. rhetorical art.   98. **figure:** Figure of speech.

But farewell it, for I will use no art.
Mad let us grant him then, and now remains   100
That we find out the cause of this effect,
Or rather say, the cause of this defect,
For this effect defective comes by cause:°
Thus it remains, and the remainder thus.
Perpend.°   105
I have a daughter — have while she is mine —
Who in her duty and obedience, mark,
Hath given me this. Now gather, and surmise.
                        [*Reads the salutation of the letter.*]
"To the celestial and my soul's idol, the most beautified°
Ophelia" —   110
That's an ill phrase, a vile phrase, "beautified" is a vile
phrase. But you shall hear. Thus:
"In her excellent white bosom, these, etc."
QUEEN: Came this from Hamlet to her?
POLONIUS: Good madam, stay awhile. I will be faithful.   115
                          [*Reads the*] *letter.*
      "Doubt thou the stars are fire,
        Doubt that the sun doth move,
        Doubt° truth to be a liar,
        But never doubt I love.
O dear Ophelia, I am ill at these numbers.° I have not art to   120
reckon° my groans, but that I love thee best, O most best,
believe it. Adieu.
                Thine evermore, most dear lady,
                whilst this machine° is to him, Hamlet."
This in obedience hath my daughter shown me,   125
And more [above°], hath his solicitings,
As they fell out by time, by means, and place,
All given to mine ear.
KING: But how hath she
Receiv'd his love?
POLONIUS: What do you think of me?

---

103. For . . . cause: For this effect (which shows as a defect in Hamlet's reason) is not merely accidental, and has a cause we may trace.   **105. Perpend:** Consider.   **109. beautified:** Beautiful (not an uncommon usage).   **118. Doubt:** Suspect.   **120. ill . . . numbers:** Bad at versifying.   **121. reckon:** Count (with a quibble on *numbers*).   **124. machine:** Body.   **126. more above:** Furthermore.

KING: As of a man faithful and honorable.   130
POLONIUS: I would fain° prove so. But what might you think,
    When I had seen this hot love on the wing —
    As I perceiv'd it (I must tell you that)
    Before my daughter told me — what might you,
    Or my dear Majesty your queen here, think,   135
    If I had play'd the desk or table-book,°
    Or given my heart a [winking,°] mute and dumb,
    Or look'd upon this love with idle sight,°
    What might you think? No, I went round° to work,
    And my young mistress thus I did bespeak:°   140
    "Lord Hamlet is a prince out of thy star;°
    This must not be"; and then I prescripts gave her,
    That she should lock herself from [his] resort,
    Admit no messengers, receive no tokens.
    Which done, she took the fruits of ° my advice;   145
    And he repell'd,° a short tale to make,
    Fell into a sadness, then into a fast,
    Thence to a watch,° thence into a weakness,
    Thence to [a] lightness,° and by this declension,
    Into the madness wherein now he raves,   150
    And all we mourn for.
KING: Do you think ['tis] this?
QUEEN: It may be, very like.
POLONIUS: Hath there been such a time — I would fain know
    that —
    That I have positively said, "'Tis so,"
    When it prov'd otherwise?
KING: Not that I know.   155
POLONIUS: [Points to his head and shoulder.] Take this from this,
    if this be otherwise.
    If circumstances lead me, I will find
    Where truth is hid, though it were hid indeed
    Within the centre.°
KING: How may we try it further?

---

131. fain: Willingly, gladly.   136. play'd . . . table-book: I.e. noted the matter secretly.   137. winking: Closing of the eyes.   138. idle sight: Noncomprehending
eyes.   139. round: Straightforwardly.   140. bespeak: Address.   141. star: I.e.
sphere, lot in life.   145. took . . . of: Profited by, i.e. carried out.   146. repell'd: Repulsed.   148. watch: Sleeplessness.   149. lightness: Lightheadedness.   159. centre:
I.e. of the earth (which in the Ptolemaic system is also the center of the universe).

POLONIUS: You know sometimes he walks four hours together   160
  Here in the lobby.
QUEEN: So he does indeed.
POLONIUS: At such a time I'll loose my daughter to him.
  Be you and I behind an arras° then,
  Mark the encounter: if he love her not,
  And be not from his reason fall'n thereon,°   165
  Let me be no assistant for a state,
  But keep a farm and carters.
KING: We will try it.

Enter HAMLET [*reading on a book*].

QUEEN: But look where sadly the poor wretch comes reading.
POLONIUS: Away, I do beseech you, both away.
  I'll board° him presently.°   *Exeunt King and Queen.*
                    O, give me leave,   170
  How does my good Lord Hamlet?
HAMLET: Well, God-a-mercy.°
POLONIUS: Do you know me, my lord?
HAMLET: Excellent well, you are a fishmonger.°
POLONIUS: Not I, my lord.   175
HAMLET: Then I would you were so honest a man.
POLONIUS: Honest, my lord?
HAMLET: Ay, sir, to be honest, as this world goes, is to be one
  man pick'd out of ten thousand.
POLONIUS: That's very true, my lord.   180
HAMLET: For if the sun breed maggots in a dead dog, being a
  good kissing carrion° — Have you a daughter?
POLONIUS: I have, my lord.
HAMLET: Let her not walk i' th' sun. Conception° is a blessing,
  but as your daughter may conceive, friend, look to't.   185
POLONIUS: [*Aside.*] How say you by that? still harping on my
  daughter. Yet he knew me not at first, 'a said I was a fishmonger. 'A is far gone. And truly in my youth I suff'red
  much extremity for love — very near this. I'll speak to him
  again. — What do you read, my lord?   190

163. arras: Hanging tapestry.   165. thereon: Because of that.   170. board: Accost.
presently: At once.   172. God-a-mercy: Thank you.   174. fishmonger: Usually explained as slang for "bawd," but no evidence has been produced for such a usage in
Shakespeare's day.   182. good kissing carrion: Flesh good enough for the sun to kiss.
184. Conception: Understanding (with following play on the sense "conceiving a child").

HAMLET: Words, words, words.
POLONIUS: What is the matter,° my lord?
HAMLET: Between who?
POLONIUS: I mean, the matter that you read, my lord.
HAMLET: Slanders, sir; for the satirical rogue says here that old   195
    men have grey beards, that their faces are wrinkled, their
    eyes purging thick amber and plum-tree gum, and that they
    have a plentiful lack of wit, together with most weak hams;
    all which, sir, though I most powerfully and potently be-
    lieve, yet I hold it not honesty° to have it thus set down, for   200
    yourself, sir, shall grow old as I am, if like a crab you could
    go backward.
POLONIUS: [*Aside.*] Though this be madness, yet there is
    method° in't. — Will you walk out of the air,° my lord?
HAMLET: Into my grave.   205
POLONIUS: Indeed that's out of the air. [*Aside.*] How pregnant°
    sometimes his replies are! a happiness that often madness
    hits on, which reason and [sanity] could not so prosper-
    ously be deliver'd of. I will leave him, [and suddenly° con-
    trive the means of meeting between him] and my daughter.   210
    — My lord, I will take my leave of you.
HAMLET: You cannot take from me any thing that I will not
    more willingly part withal — except my life, except my life,
    except my life.
POLONIUS: Fare you well, my lord.   215
HAMLET: These tedious old fools!

Enter GUILDENSTERN *and* ROSENCRANTZ.

POLONIUS: You go to seek the Lord Hamlet, there he is.
ROSENCRANTZ: [*To Polonius.*] God save you, sir!
                                     [*Exit Polonius.*]
GUILDENSTERN: My honor'd lord!
ROSENCRANTZ: My most dear lord!   220
HAMLET: My [excellent] good friends! How dost thou,
    Guildenstern? Ah, Rosencrantz! Good lads, how do you
    both?

---

192. **matter:** Subject; but Hamlet replies as if he had understood Polonius to mean
"cause for a quarrel."   200. **honesty:** A fitting thing.   204. **method:** Orderly arrangement, sequence of ideas.   **out . . . air:** Outdoor air was thought to be bad for invalids.
206. **pregnant:** Apt.   209. **suddenly:** At once.

ROSENCRANTZ: As the indifferent° children of the earth.

GUILDENSTERN: Happy, in that we are not [over-]happy, on   225
Fortune's [cap] we are not the very button.

HAMLET: Nor the soles of her shoe?

ROSENCRANTZ: Neither, my lord.

HAMLET: Then you live about her waist, or in the middle of her
favors?   230

GUILDENSTERN: Faith, her privates° we.

HAMLET: In the secret parts of Fortune? O, most true, she is a
strumpet.° What news?

ROSENCRANTZ: None, my lord, but the world's grown honest.

HAMLET: Then is doomsday near. But your news is not true.   235
[Let me question more in particular. What have you, my
good friends, deserv'd at the hands of Fortune, that she
sends you to prison hither?

GUILDENSTERN: Prison, my lord?

HAMLET: Denmark's a prison.   240

ROSENCRANTZ: Then is the world one.

HAMLET: A goodly one, in which there are many confines,
wards,° and dungeons, Denmark being one o' th' worst.

ROSENCRANTZ: We think not so, my lord.

HAMLET: Why then 'tis none to you; for there is nothing either   245
good or bad, but thinking makes it so. To me it is a prison.

ROSENCRANTZ: Why then your ambition makes it one. 'Tis too
narrow for your mind.

HAMLET: O God, I could be bounded in a nutshell, and count
myself a king of infinite space — were it not that I have bad   250
dreams.

GUILDENSTERN: Which dreams indeed are ambition, for the very
substance of the ambitious is merely the shadow of a
dream.

HAMLET: A dream itself is but a shadow.   255

ROSENCRANTZ: Truly, and I hold ambition of so airy and light a
quality that it is but a shadow's shadow.

HAMLET: Then are our beggars bodies,° and our monarchs and

---

224. indifferent: Average.   231. privates: (1) Intimate friends; (2) genitalia.   233.
strumpet: A common epithet for Fortune, because she grants favors to all men.   243.
wards: Cells.   258. bodies: I.e. not shadows (since they lack ambition).

outstretch'd° heroes the beggars' shadows. Shall we to th'
court? for, by my fay,° I cannot reason.   260
BOTH [ROSENCRANTZ, GUILDENSTERN]: We'll wait upon you.°
HAMLET: No such matter. I will not sort° you with the rest of
my servants; for to speak to you like an honest man, I am
most dreadfully° attended.] But in the beaten way of
friendship, what make you at Elsinore?   265
ROSENCRANTZ: To visit you, my lord, no other occasion.
HAMLET: Beggar that I am, I am [even] poor in thanks — but I
thank you, and sure, dear friends, my thanks are too dear a
halfpenny.° Were you not sent for? is it your own inclining?
is it a free visitation? Come, come, deal justly° with me.   270
Come, come — nay, speak.
GUILDENSTERN: What should we say, my lord?
HAMLET: Any thing but° to th' purpose. You were sent for, and
there is a kind of confession in your looks, which your
modesties° have not craft enough to color. I know the   275
good King and Queen have sent for you.
ROSENCRANTZ: To what end, my lord?
HAMLET: That you must teach me. But let me conjure you, by
the rights of our fellowship, by the consonancy of our
youth,° by the obligation of our ever-preserv'd love, and by   280
what more dear a better proposer can charge° you withal,
be even° and direct with me, whether you were sent for or
no!
ROSENCRANTZ: [Aside to Guildenstern.] What say you?
HAMLET: [Aside.] Nay then I have an eye of° you! — If you   285
love me, hold not off.
GUILDENSTERN: My lord, we were sent for.
HAMLET: I will tell you why, so shall my anticipation prevent
your discovery,° and your secrecy to the King and Queen

---

259. outstretch'd: I.e. with their ambition extended to the utmost (and hence producing
stretched-out or elongated shadows).   **260. fay:** Faith.   **261. wait upon you:** Attend
you thither.   **262. sort:** Associate.   **264. dreadfully:** Execrably.   **269. too . . . halfpenny:** Too expensive priced at a halfpenny, i.e. not worth much.   **270. justly:** Hon-
estly.   **273. but:** Ordinarily punctuated with a comma preceding, to give the sense "provided that it is"; but Q2 has no comma, and Hamlet may intend, or include, the sense
"except."   **275. modesties:** Sense of shame.   **279–80. consonancy . . . youth:** Similarity of our ages.   **281. charge:** Urge, adjure.   **282. even:** Frank, honest (cf. modern
"level with me").   **285. of:** On.   **288–89. prevent your discovery:** Forestall your disclosure (of what the King and Queen have said to you in confidence).

moult no feather.° I have of late — but wherefore I know   290
not — lost all my mirth, forgone all custom of exercises;°
and indeed it goes so heavily with my disposition, that this
goodly frame, the earth, seems to me a sterile promontory;
this most excellent canopy, the air, look you, this brave°
o'erhanging firmament, this majestical roof fretted° with   295
golden fire, why, it appeareth nothing to me but a foul and
pestilent congregation of vapors. What [a] piece of work° is
a man, how noble in reason, how infinite in faculties, in
form and moving, how express° and admirable in action,
how like an angel in apprehension, how like a god!° the   300
beauty of the world; the paragon of animals; and yet to me
what is this quintessence° of dust? Man delights not me —
nor women neither, though by your smiling you seem to
say so.

ROSENCRANTZ: My lord, there was no such stuff in my thoughts.   305

HAMLET: Why did ye laugh then, when I said, "Man delights
not me"?

ROSENCRANTZ: To think, my lord, if you delight not in man,
what lenten entertainment° the players shall receive from
you. We coted° them on the way, and hither are they com-   310
ing to offer you service.

HAMLET: He that plays the king shall be welcome — his Majesty shall have tribute on° me, the adventerous° knight shall
use his foil and target,° the lover shall not sigh gratis,° the
humorous° man shall end his part in peace, [the clown shall   315
make those laugh whose lungs are [tickle] a' th' sere,°] and
the lady shall say her mind freely, or the [blank] verse shall
halt° for't. What players are they?

290. **moult no feather:** Not be impaired in the least.   291. **custom of exercises:** My
usual athletic activities.   294. **brave:** Splendid.   295. **fretted:** Ornamented as with
fretwork.   297. **piece of work:** Masterpiece.   298–300. **how infinite . . . god:** See
the Textual Notes for the different punctuation in F1.   299. **express:** Exact.   302.
quintessence: Finest and purest extract.   309. **lenten entertainment:** Meager reception.   310. **coted:** Outstripped.   313. **on:** Of, from.   **adventerous:** Adventurous,
i.e. wandering in search of adventure.   314. **foil and target:** Light fencing sword and
small shield.   **gratis:** Without reward.   315. **humorous:** Dominated by some eccentric
trait (like the melancholy Jaques in *As You Like It*).   316. **tickle . . . sere:** I.e. easily
made to laugh (literally, describing a gun that goes off easily; *sere* = a catch in the gunlock;
tickle = easily affected, highly sensitive to stimulus).   318. **halt:** Limp, come off lamely
(the verse will not scan if she omits indecent words).

ROSENCRANTZ: Even those you were wont to take such delight
in, the tragedians of the city. 320
HAMLET: How chances it they travel? Their residence, both in
reputation and profit, was better both ways.
ROSENCRANTZ: I think their inhibition° comes by the means of
the late innovation.°
HAMLET: Do they hold the same estimation they did when I 325
was in the city? Are they so follow'd?
ROSENCRANTZ: No indeed are they not.
[HAMLET: How comes it? do they grow rusty?°
ROSENCRANTZ: Nay, their endeavor keeps in the wonted pace;
but there is, sir, an aery° of children, little eyases,° that cry 330
out on the top of question,° and are most tyrannically°
clapp'd for't. These are now the fashion, and so [berattle°]
the common stages° — so they call them — that many
wearing rapiers are afraid of goose-quills° and dare scarce
come thither. 335
HAMLET: What, are they children? Who maintains 'em? How
are they escoted?° Will they pursue the quality° no longer
than they can sing?° Will they not say afterwards, if they
should grow themselves to common players (as it is [most
like], if their means are [no] better), their writers do them 340
wrong, to make them exclaim against their own succession?°

323. inhibition: Hindrance (to playing in the city). The word could be used of an official
prohibition. See next note. 324. innovation: Shakespeare elsewhere uses this word of
a political uprising or revolt, and lines 323–24 are often explained as meaning that the
company had been forbidden to play in the city as the result of some disturbance. It is
commonly conjectured that the allusion is to the Essex rebellion of 1601, but it is known
that Shakespeare's company, though to some extent involved on account of the special
performance of *Richard II* they were commissioned to give on the eve of the rising, were
not in fact punished by inhibition. A second interpretation explains *innovation* as referring
to the new theatrical vogue described in lines 330 ff., and conjectures that *inhibition* may
allude to a Privy Council order of 1600 restricting the number of London playhouses to
two and the number of performances to two a week. 328–52. How . . . too: This
passage refers topically to the "War of the Theaters" between the child actors and their
poet Jonson on the one side, and on the other the adults, with Dekker, Marston, and
possibly Shakespeare as spokesmen, in 1600–01. 330. aery: Nest. eyases: Unfledged
hawks. 330–31. cry . . . question: Cry shrilly above others in controversy. 331. tyran
nically: Outrageously. 332. berattle: Cry down, satirize. 333. common stages: Public
theaters (the children played at the Blackfriars, a private theater). 334. goose-quills: Pens
(of satirical playwrights). 337. escoted: Supported. quality: Profession (of acting).
337–38. no . . . sing: I.e. only until their voices change. 341–42. succession: Future.

ROSENCRANTZ: Faith, there has been much to do° on both sides,
and the nation holds it no sin to tarre° them to controversy.
There was for a while no money bid for argument,° unless   345
the poet and the player went to cuffs in the question.°
HAMLET: Is't possible?
GUILDENSTERN: O, there has been much throwing about of
brains.
HAMLET: Do the boys carry it away?°   350
ROSENCRANTZ: Ay, that they do, my lord — Hercules and his
load too.°]
HAMLET: It is not very strange, for my uncle is King of Denmark, and those that would make mouths° at him while
my father liv'd, give twenty, forty, fifty, a hundred ducats   355
a-piece for his picture in little. 'Sblood,° there is something
in this more than natural, if philosophy could find it out.
                              A flourish [for the Players].
GUILDENSTERN: There are the players.
HAMLET: Gentlemen, you are welcome to Elsinore. Your
hands, come then: th' appurtenance of welcome is fashion   360
and ceremony. Let me comply° with you in this garb,° [lest
my] extent° to the players, which, I tell you, must show
fairly outwards, should more appear like entertainment
than yours.° You are welcome; but my uncle-father and
aunt-mother are deceiv'd.   365
GUILDENSTERN: In what, my dear lord?
HAMLET: I am but mad north-north-west. When the wind is
southerly I know a hawk from a hand-saw.°

Enter POLONIUS.

POLONIUS: Well be with you, gentlemen!
HAMLET: [*Aside to them.*] Hark you, Guildenstern, and you   370

---

343. to do: Ado.   344. tarre: Incite.   345. argument: Plot of a play.   346. in the
question: I.e. as part of the script.   350. carry it away: Win.   351–52. Hercules . . .
too: Hercules in the course of one of his twelve labors supported the world for Atlas; the
children do better, for they carry away the world and Hercules as well. There is an allusion
to the Globe playhouse, which reportedly had for its sign the figure of Hercules upholding
the world.   354. mouths: Derisive faces.   356. 'Sblood: By God's (Christ's) blood.
361. comply: Observe the formalities.   garb: Fashion, manner.   362. my extent: I.e.
the degree of courtesy I show.   363–64. more . . . yours: Seem to be a warmer reception than I have given you.   368. hawk, hand-saw: Both cutting-tools; but also both
birds, if *hand-saw* quibbles on *hernshaw,* "heron," a bird preyed upon by the hawk.

too — at each ear a hearer — that great baby you see there
is not yet out of his swaddling-clouts.°
ROSENCRANTZ: Happily° he is the second time come to them,
for they say an old man is twice° a child.
HAMLET: I will prophesy, he comes to tell me of the players,   375
mark it. [*Aloud.*] You say right, sir, a' Monday morning,
'twas then indeed.
POLONIUS: My lord, I have news to tell you.
HAMLET: My lord, I have news to tell you. When Roscius° was
an actor in Rome —   380
POLONIUS: The actors are come hither, my lord.
HAMLET: Buzz, buzz!°
POLONIUS: Upon my honor —
HAMLET: "Then came each actor on his ass" —
POLONIUS: The best actors in the world, either for tragedy,   385
comedy, history, pastoral, pastoral-comical, historical-
pastoral, [tragical-historical, tragical-comical-historical-
pastoral,] scene individable,° or poem unlimited;° Seneca°
cannot be too heavy, nor Plautus° too light, for the law of
writ and the liberty:° these are the only° men.   390
HAMLET: O Jephthah, judge of Israel,° what a treasure hadst
thou!
POLONIUS: What a treasure had he, my lord?
HAMLET: Why —
"One fair daughter, and no more,   395
The which he loved passing well."
POLONIUS: [*Aside.*] Still on my daughter.
HAMLET: Am I not i' th' right, old Jephthah?
POLONIUS: If you call me Jephthah, my lord, I have a daughter
that I love passing well.   400

---

372. swaddling-clouts: Swaddling clothes.   **373. Happily:** Haply, perhaps.   **374.**
twice: I.e. for the second time.   **379. Roscius:** The most famous of Roman actors (died
62 B.C.). News about him would be stale news indeed.   **382. Buzz:** Exclamation of
impatience at someone who tells news already known.   **388. scene individable:** Play
observing the unity of place.   **poem unlimited:** Play ignoring rules such as the three
unities.   **Seneca:** Roman writer of tragedies.   **389. Plautus:** Roman writer of comedies.   **389–90. for . . . liberty:** For strict observance of the rules, or for freedom from
them (with possible allusion to the location of playhouses, which were not built in properties under city jurisdiction, but in the "liberties" — land once monastic and now outside
the jurisdiction of the city authorities).   **390. only:** Very best (a frequent use).   **391.**
Jephthah . . . Israel: Title of a ballad, from which Hamlet goes on to quote. For the story
of Jephthah and his daughter, see Judges 11.

HAMLET: Nay, that follows not.
POLONIUS: What follows then, my lord?
HAMLET: Why —
          "As by lot, God wot,"
and then, you know,   405
          "It came to pass, as most like it was" —
the first row° of the pious chanson° will show you more, for
look where my abridgment° comes.

Enter the PLAYERS, [*four or five*].

You are welcome, masters, welcome all. I am glad to see
thee well. Welcome, good friends. O, old friend! why, thy   410
face is valanc'd° since I saw thee last; com'st thou to beard°
me in Denmark? What, my young lady and mistress! by'
lady,° your ladyship is nearer to heaven than when I saw
you last, by the altitude of a chopine.° Pray God your voice,
like a piece of uncurrent gold, be not crack'd within the   415
ring.° Masters, you are all welcome. We'll e'en to't like
[French] falc'ners — fly at any thing we see; we'll have a
speech straight.° Come give us a taste of your quality,°
come, a passionate speech.
[FIRST] PLAYER: What speech, my good lord?   420
HAMLET: I heard thee speak me a speech once, but it was never
acted, or if it was, not above once; for the play, I remember,
pleas'd not the million, 'twas caviary to the general,° but it
was — as I receiv'd it, and others, whose judgments in such
matters cried in the top of° mine — an excellent play, well   425
digested in the scenes, set down with as much modesty as
cunning. I remember one said there were no sallets° in the
lines to make the matter savory,° nor no matter in the
phrase that might indict the author of affection,° but call'd

---

407. row: Stanza.   **chanson:** Song, ballad.   **408. abridgment:** (1) Interruption; (2)
pastime.   **411. valanc'd:** Fringed, i.e. bearded.   **beard:** Confront boldly (with obvious
pun).   **412–13. by' lady:** By Our Lady.   **414. chopine:** Thick-soled shoe.   **415–16.
crack'd . . . ring:** I.e. broken to the point where you can no longer play female roles. A
coin with a crack extending far enough in from the edge to cross the circle surrounding
the stamp of the sovereign's head was unacceptable in exchange (*uncurrent*).   **418.
straight:** Straightway.   **quality:** Professional skill.   **423. caviary . . . general:** Caviar
to the common people, i.e. too choice for the multitude.   **425. cried . . . of:** Were
louder than, i.e. carried more authority than.   **427. sallets:** Salads, i.e. spicy jokes.   **428.
savory:** Zesty.   **429. affection:** Affectation.

it an honest method, as wholesome as sweet, and by very   430
much more handsome than fine.° One speech in't I chiefly
lov'd, 'twas Aeneas' [tale] to Dido, and thereabout of it
especially when he speaks of Priam's slaughter.° If it live in
your memory, begin at this line — let me see, let me see:
"The rugged Pyrrhus,° like th' Hyrcanian beast° — "   435
'Tis not so, it begins with Pyrrhus:
"The rugged Pyrrhus, he whose sable arms,°
Black as his purpose, did the night resemble
When he lay couched in th' ominous horse,
Hath now this dread and black complexion smear'd   440
With heraldy° more dismal:° head to foot
Now is he total gules,° horridly trick'd°
With blood of fathers, mothers, daughters, sons,
Bak'd° and impasted° with the parching streets,°
That lend a tyrannous and a damned light   445
To their lord's murther. Roasted in wrath and fire,
And thus o'er-sized° with coagulate gore,
With eyes like carbuncles,° the hellish Pyrrhus
Old grandsire Priam seeks."
So proceed you.   450
POLONIUS: 'Fore God, my lord, well spoken, with good accent
and good discretion.
[FIRST] PLAYER: "Anon he finds him
Striking too short at Greeks. His antique sword,
Rebellious to his arm, lies where it falls,   455
Repugnant° to command. Unequal match'd,
Pyrrhus at Priam drives, in rage strikes wide,
But with the whiff and wind of his fell° sword
Th' unnerved° father falls. [Then senseless° Ilium,°]
Seeming to feel this blow, with flaming top   460
Stoops to his base, and with a hideous crash

---

431. fine: Showily dressed (in language).   433. Priam's slaughter: The slaying of
Priam (at the fall of Troy).   435. Pyrrhus: Another name for Neoptolemus, Achilles'
son.   Hyrcanian beast: Hyrcania in the Caucasus was notorious for its tigers.   437.
sable arms: The Greeks within the Trojan horse had blackened their skin so as to be
inconspicuous when they emerged at night.   441. heraldy: Heraldry.   dismal: Ill-
boding.   442. gules: Red (heraldic term).   trick'd: Adorned.   444. Bak'd: Caked.
impasted: Crusted.   with . . . streets: I.e. by the heat from the burning streets.   447.
o'er-sized: Covered over as with a coat of sizing.   448. carbuncles: Jewels believed to
shine in the dark.   456. Repugnant: Resistant, hostile.   458. fell: Cruel.   459. un-
nerved: Drained of strength.   senseless: Insensible.   Ilium: The citadel of Troy.

Takes prisoner Pyrrhus' ear; for lo his sword,
Which was declining on the milky head
Of reverent° Priam, seem'd i' th' air to stick.
So as a painted tyrant Pyrrhus stood   465
[And,] like a neutral to his will and matter,°
Did nothing.
But as we often see, against° some storm,
A silence in the heavens, the rack° stand still,
The bold winds speechless, and the orb below   470
As hush as death, anon the dreadful thunder
Doth rend the region;° so after Pyrrhus' pause,
A roused vengeance sets him new a-work,
And never did the Cyclops'°· hammers fall
On Mars's armor forg'd for proof eterne°   475
With less remorse° than Pyrrhus' bleeding sword
Now falls on Priam.
Out, out, thou strumpet Fortune! All you gods,
In general synod take away her power!
Break all the spokes and [fellies°] from her wheel,   480
And bowl the round nave° down the hill of heaven
As low as to the fiends!"
POLONIUS: This is too long.
HAMLET: It shall to the barber's with your beard. Prithee say
    on, he's for a jig° or a tale of bawdry, or he sleeps. Say on,   485
    come to Hecuba.
[FIRST] PLAYER: "But who, ah woe, had seen the mobled°
    queen" —
HAMLET: "The mobled queen"?
POLONIUS: That's good, ["[mobled] queen" is good].
[FIRST] PLAYER: "Run barefoot up and down, threat'ning the
    flames   490
    With bisson rheum,° a clout° upon that head
    Where late the diadem stood, and for a robe,
    About her lank and all o'er-teemed° loins,

---

464. reverent: Reverend, aged.   **466. like . . . matter:** I.e. poised midway between intention and performance.   **468. against:** Just before.   **469. rack:** Cloud-mass. **472. region:** I.e. air.   **474. Cyclops:** Giants who worked in Vulcan's smithy, where armor was made for the gods.   **475. proof eterne:** Eternal endurance.   **476. remorse:** Pity.   **480. fellies:** Rims.   **481. nave:** Hub.   **485. jig:** Song-and-dance entertainment performed after the main play.   **487. mobled:** Muffled.   **491. bisson rheum:** Blinding tears.   **clout:** Cloth.   **493. o'er-teemed:** Worn out by childbearing.

A blanket, in the alarm of fear caught up —
Who this had seen, with tongue in venom steep'd,   495
'Gainst Fortune's state° would treason have pronounc'd.
But if the gods themselves did see her then,
When she saw Pyrrhus make malicious sport
In mincing with his sword her [husband's] limbs,
The instant burst of clamor that she made,   500
Unless things mortal move them not at all,
Would have made milch° the burning eyes of heaven,
And passion° in the gods."
POLONIUS: Look whe'er he has not° turn'd his color and has
tears in 's eyes. Prithee no more.   505
HAMLET: 'Tis well, I'll have thee speak out the rest of this soon.
Good my lord, will you see the players well bestow'd?° Do
you hear, let them be well us'd,° for they are the abstract
and brief chronicles of the time. After your death you were
better have a bad epitaph than their ill report while you live.   510
POLONIUS: My lord, I will use them according to their desert.
HAMLET: God's bodkin,° man, much better: use every man
after his desert, and who shall scape whipping? Use them
after your own honor and dignity — the less they deserve,
the more merit is in your bounty. Take them in.   515
POLONIUS: Come, sirs.   [*Exit.*]
HAMLET: Follow him, friends, we'll hear a play to-morrow. [*Ex-
eunt all the Players but the First.*] Dost thou hear me, old
friend? Can you play "The Murther of Gonzago"?
[FIRST] PLAYER: Ay, my lord.   520
HAMLET: We'll ha't to-morrow night. You could for need°
study a speech of some dozen lines, or sixteen lines, which
I would set down and insert in't, could you not?
[FIRST] PLAYER: Ay, my lord.
HAMLET: Very well. Follow that lord, and look you mock him   525
not. [*Exit First Player.*] My good friends, I'll leave you [till]
night. You are welcome to Elsinore.
ROSENCRANTZ: Good my lord!
HAMLET: Ay so, God buy to you.

---

496. state: Rule, government.   **502. milch:** Moist (literally, milky).   **503. passion:**
Grief.   **504. Look . . . not:** I.e. note how he has.   **507. bestow'd:** Lodged.   **508.**
us'd: Treated.   **512. God's bodkin:** By God's (Christ's) little body.   **521. for need:**
If necessary.

Exeunt [Rosencrantz and Guildenstern].
Now I am alone.
O, what a rogue and peasant slave am I!   530
Is it not monstrous that this player here,
But in a fiction, in a dream of passion,
Could force his soul so to his own conceit°
That from her working all the visage wann'd,
Tears in his eyes, distraction in his aspect,   535
A broken voice, an' his whole function° suiting
With forms° to his conceit? And all for nothing,
For Hecuba!
What's Hecuba to him, or he to [Hecuba],
That he should weep for her? What would he do   540
Had he the motive and [the cue] for passion
That I have? He would drown the stage with tears,
And cleave the general ear with horrid speech,
Make mad the guilty, and appall the free,°
Confound the ignorant, and amaze° indeed   545
The very faculties of eyes and ears. Yet I,
A dull and muddy-mettled° rascal, peak°
Like John-a-dreams,° unpregnant of ° my cause,
And can say nothing; no, not for a king,
Upon whose property and most dear life   550
A damn'd defeat° was made. Am I a coward?
Who calls me villain, breaks my pate across,
Plucks off my beard and blows it in my face,
Tweaks me by the nose, gives me the lie i' th' throat
As deep as to the lungs?° Who does me this?   555
Hah, 'swounds,° I should° take it; for it cannot be
But I am pigeon-liver'd, and lack gall°
To make oppression bitter, or ere this
I should 'a' fatted all the region kites°
With this slave's offal.° Bloody, bawdy villain!   560

---

533. conceit: Imaginative conception.   **536. his whole function:** The operation of his whole body.   **537. forms:** Actions, expressions.   **544. free:** Innocent.   **545. amaze:** Confound.   **547. muddy-mettled:** Dull-spirited.   **peak:** Mope.   **548. John-a-dreams:** A sleepy fellow.   **unpregnant of:** Unquickened by.   **551. defeat:** destruction.   **554–55. gives . . . lungs:** Calls me a liar in the extremest degree.   **556. 'swounds:** By God's (Christ's) wounds.   **should:** Would certainly.   **557. am . . . gall:** I.e. am constitutionally incapable of resentment. That doves were mild because they had no gall was a popular belief.   **559. region kites:** Kites of the air.   **560. offal:** Entrails.

Remorseless, treacherous, lecherous, kindless° villain!
Why, what an ass am I! This is most brave,
That I, the son of a dear [father] murthered,
Prompted to my revenge by heaven and hell,
Must like a whore unpack my heart with words,   565
And fall a-cursing like a very drab,
A stallion.° Fie upon't, foh!
About,° my brains! Hum — I have heard
That guilty creatures sitting at a play
Have by the very cunning of the scene   570
Been strook so to the soul, that presently°
They have proclaim'd their malefactions:
For murther, though it have no tongue, will speak
With most miraculous organ. I'll have these players
Play something like the murther of my father   575
Before mine uncle. I'll observe his looks,
I'll tent° him to the quick. If 'a do blench,°
I know my course. The spirit that I have seen
May be a [dev'l], and the [dev'l] hath power
T' assume a pleasing shape, yea, and perhaps,   580
Out of my weakness and my melancholy,
As he is very potent with such spirits,°
Abuses° me to damn me. I'll have grounds
More relative° than this — the play's the thing
Wherein I'll catch the conscience of the King.   *Exit.* 585

[ACT 3, Scene 1]°

Enter KING, QUEEN, POLONIUS, OPHELIA, ROSENCRANTZ, GUIL-
DENSTERN, LORDS.

KING: An'° can you by no drift of conference°
Get from him why he puts on this confusion,
Grating so harshly all his days of quiet
With turbulent and dangerous lunacy?

---

561. kindless: Unnatural.   **567. stallion:** Male whore. Most editors adopt the F1 reading *scullion,* "kitchen menial."   **568. About:** To work.   **571. presently:** At once, then
and there.   **577. tent:** Probe.   **blench:** Flinch.   **582. spirits:** States of temperament.
583. Abuses: Deludes.   **584. relative:** Closely related (to fact), i.e. conclusive.   **3.1.
Location:** The castle. See the Textual Notes for the Q1 version of parts of this scene.   **1.
An':** And.   **drift of conference:** Leading on of conversation.

ROSENCRANTZ: He does confess he feels himself distracted,   5
  But from what cause 'a will by no means speak.
GUILDENSTERN: Nor do we find him forward° to be sounded,°
  But with a crafty madness° keeps aloof
  When we would bring him on to some confession
  Of his true state.
QUEEN: Did he receive you well?   10
ROSENCRANTZ: Most like a gentleman.
GUILDENSTERN: But with much forcing of his disposition.°
ROSENCRANTZ: Niggard of question,° but of our demands°
  Most free in his reply.
QUEEN: Did you assay° him
  To any pastime?   15
ROSENCRANTZ: Madam, it so fell out that certain players
  We o'erraught° on the way; of these we told him,
  And there did seem in him a kind of joy
  To hear of it. They are here about the court,
  And as I think, they have already order   20
  This night to play before him.
POLONIUS: 'Tis most true,
  And he beseech'd me to entreat your Majesties
  To hear and see the matter.
KING: With all my heart, and it doth much content me
  To hear him so inclin'd.   25
  Good gentlemen, give him a further edge,°
  And drive his purpose into° these delights.
ROSENCRANTZ: We shall, my lord.
                    Exeunt Rosencrantz and Guildenstern.
KING: Sweet Gertrude, leave us two,
  For we have closely° sent for Hamlet hither,
  That he, as 'twere by accident, may here   30
  Affront° Ophelia. Her father and myself,
  We'll so bestow ourselves that, seeing unseen,
  We may of their encounter frankly° judge,
  And gather by him, as he is behav'd,
  If't be th' affliction of his love or no   35

---

7. **forward:** Readily willing.   **sounded:** Plumbed, probed.   **8. crafty madness:** I.e.
mad craftiness, the shrewdness that mad people sometimes exhibit.   **12. disposition:**
Inclination.   **13. question:** Conversation.   **demands:** Questions.   **14. assay:** Attempt to win.   **17. o'erraught:** Passed (literally, overreached).   **26. edge:** Stimulus.
27. into: On to.   **29. closely:** Privately.   **31. Affront:** Meet.   **33. frankly:** Freely.

That thus he suffers for.
QUEEN: I shall obey you.
And for your part, Ophelia, I do wish
That your good beauties be the happy cause
Of Hamlet's wildness. So shall I hope your virtues
Will bring him to his wonted way again,   40
To both your honors.
OPHELIA: Madam, I wish it may.
                                        [Exit Queen.]
POLONIUS: Ophelia, walk you here. — Gracious, so please you,
We will bestow ourselves. [To Ophelia.] Read on this book,
That show of such an exercise° may color
Your [loneliness].° We are oft to blame in this —   45
'Tis too much prov'd° — that with devotion's visage
And pious action° we do sugar o'er
The devil himself.
KING: [Aside.] O, 'tis too true!
How smart a lash that speech doth give my conscience!
The harlot's cheek, beautied with plast'ring art,   50
Is not more ugly to the thing that helps it°
Than is my deed to my most painted word.
O heavy burthen!
POLONIUS: I hear him coming. Withdraw, my lord.
                                        [Exeunt King and Polonius.]

Enter HAMLET.

HAMLET: To be, or not to be, that is the question:°   55
Whether 'tis nobler in the mind to suffer°
The slings and arrows of outrageous fortune,
Or to take arms against a sea of troubles,
And by opposing, end them. To die, to sleep —
No more, and by a sleep to say we end   60
The heart-ache and the thousand natural shocks
That flesh is heir to; 'tis a consummation°
Devoutly to be wish'd. To die, to sleep —

---

44. exercise: I.e. religious exercise (as the next sentence makes clear).   **44–45. color Your loneliness:** Make your solitude seem natural.   **46. too much prov'd:** Too often proved true.   **47. action:** Demeanor.   **51. to . . . it:** In comparison with the paint that makes it look beautiful.   **55–89.** See the Textual Notes for the version of this soliloquy in Q1.   **56. suffer:** Submit to, endure patiently.   **62. consummation:** Completion, end.

To sleep, perchance to dream — ay, there's the rub,°
For in that sleep of death what dreams may come,   65
When we have shuffled off ° this mortal coil,°
Must give us pause; there's the respect°
That makes calamity of so long life:°
For who would bear the whips and scorns of time,°
Th' oppressor's wrong, the proud man's contumely,   70
The pangs of despis'd love, the law's delay,
The insolence of office, and the spurns
That patient merit of th' unworthy takes,
When he himself might his quietus make°
With a bare bodkin;° who would fardels° bear,   75
To grunt and sweat under a weary life,
But that the dread of something after death,
The undiscover'd° country, from whose bourn°
No traveller returns, puzzles° the will,
And makes us rather bear those ills we have,   80
Than fly to others that we know not of?
Thus conscience° does make cowards [of us all],
And thus the native hue° of resolution
Is sicklied o'er with the pale cast° of thought,°
And enterprises of great pitch° and moment   85
With this regard their currents turn awry,
And lose the name of action. — Soft you now,
The fair Ophelia. Nymph, in thy orisons°
Be all my sins rememb'red.
OPHELIA: Good my lord,
How does your honor for this many a day?   90
HAMLET: I humbly thank you, well, [well, well].
OPHELIA: My lord, I have remembrances of yours
That I have longed long to redeliver.
I pray you now receive them.

---

64. rub: Obstacle (a term from the game of bowls).   **66. shuffled off:** Freed ourselves
from.   **this mortal coil:** The turmoil of this mortal life.   **67. respect:** Consideration.   **68. of . . . life:** So long-lived.   **69. time:** The world.   **74. his quietus make:**
Write paid to his account.   **75. bare bodkin:** Mere dagger.   **fardels:** Burdens.   **78.
undiscover'd:** Not disclosed to knowledge; about which men have no information.
bourn: Boundary, i.e. region.   **79. puzzles:** Paralyzes.   **83. native hue:** Reflection
(but with some of the modern sense, too).   **83. native hue:** Natural (ruddy) complexion.   **84. pale cast:** Pallor.   **thought:** I.e. melancholy thought, brooding.   **85. pitch:**
Loftiness (a term from falconry, signifying the highest point of a hawk's flight).   **88.
orisons:** Prayers.

HAMLET: No, not I,
I never gave you aught.   95
OPHELIA: My honor'd lord, you know right well you did,
And with them words of so sweet breath compos'd
As made these things more rich. Their perfume lost,
Take these again, for to the noble mind
Rich gifts wax poor when givers prove unkind.   100
There, my lord.
HAMLET: Ha, ha! are you honest?°
OPHELIA: My lord?
HAMLET: Are you fair?
OPHELIA: What means your lordship?   105
HAMLET: That if you be honest and fair, [your honesty] should
admit no discourse to your beauty.
OPHELIA: Could beauty, my lord, have better commerce than
with honesty?
HAMLET: Ay, truly, for the power of beauty will sooner trans-   110
form honesty from what it is to a bawd than the force of
honesty can translate beauty into his likeness. This was
sometime° a paradox,° but now the time gives it proof. I
did love you once.
OPHELIA: Indeed, my lord, you made me believe so.   115
HAMLET: You should not have believ'd me, for virtue cannot so
[inoculate] our old stock but we shall relish of it.° I lov'd
you not.
OPHELIA: I was the more deceiv'd.
HAMLET: Get thee [to] a nunn'ry, why wouldst thou be a   120
breeder of sinners? I am myself indifferent honest,° but yet
I could accuse me of such things that it were better my
mother had not borne me: I am very proud, revengeful,
ambitious, with more offenses at my beck than I have
thoughts to put them in, imagination to give them shape,   125
or time to act them in. What should such fellows as I do
crawling between earth and heaven? We are arrant knaves,
believe none of us. Go thy ways to a nunn'ry. Where's your
father?

102. honest: Chaste.   113. sometime: Formerly.   paradox: Tenet contrary to accepted belief.   116–17. virtue . . . it: Virtue, engrafted on our old stock (of vicious-
ness), cannot so change the nature of the plant that no trace of the original will remain.
121. indifferent honest: Tolerably virtuous.

OPHELIA: At home, my lord.   130
HAMLET: Let the doors be shut upon him, that he may play the
  fool no where but in 's own house. Farewell.
OPHELIA: O, help him, you sweet heavens!
HAMLET: If thou dost marry, I'll give thee this plague for thy
  dowry: be thou as chaste as ice, as pure as snow, thou shalt   135
  not escape calumny. Get thee to a nunn'ry, farewell. Or if
  thou wilt needs marry, marry a fool, for wise men know
  well enough what monsters° you° make of them. To a
  nunn'ry, go, and quickly too. Farewell.
OPHELIA: Heavenly powers, restore him!   140
HAMLET: I have heard of your paintings, well enough. God
  hath given you one face, and you make yourselves another.
  You jig and amble, and you [lisp,] you nickname God's
  creatures° and make your wantonness [your] ignorance.°
  Go to, I'll no more on't, it hath made me mad. I say we will   145
  have no moe° marriage. Those that are married already (all
  but one) shall live, the rest shall keep as they are. To a
  nunn'ry, go.   *Exit.*
OPHELIA: O, what a noble mind is here o'erthrown!
  The courtier's, soldier's, scholar's, eye, tongue, sword,   150
  Th' expectation° and rose° of the fair° state,
  The glass° of fashion and the mould of form,°
  Th' observ'd of all observers,° quite, quite down!
  And I, of ladies most deject and wretched,
  That suck'd the honey of his [music] vows,   155
  Now see [that] noble and most sovereign reason
  Like sweet bells jangled out of time, and harsh;
  That unmatch'd form and stature of blown° youth
  Blasted° with ecstasy.° O, woe is me
  T' have seen what I have seen, see what I see!   160
                              [*Ophelia withdraws.*]

Enter KING *and* POLONIUS.

---

138. monsters: Alluding to the notion that the husbands of unfaithful wives grew horns.
you: You women.   **143–44. You . . . creatures:** I.e. you walk and talk affectedly.   **144.
make . . . ignorance:** Excuse your affectation as ignorance.   **146. moe:** More.   **151.
expectation:** Hope.   **rose:** Ornament.   **fair:** Probably proleptic: "(the kingdom) made
fair by his presence."   **152. glass:** Mirror.   **mould of form:** Pattern of (courtly) behavior.   **153. observ'd . . . observers:** Shakespeare uses *observe* to mean not only "behold,
mark attentively" but also "pay honor to."   **158. blown:** In full bloom.   **159.
Blasted:** Withered.   **ecstasy:** Madness.

KING: Love? his affections° do not that way tend,
Nor what he spake, though it lack'd form a little,
Was not like madness. There's something in his soul
O'er which his melancholy sits on brood,
And I do doubt° the hatch and the disclose°   165
Will be some danger; which for to prevent,
I have in quick determination
Thus set it down: he shall with speed to England
For the demand of our neglected° tribute.
Haply the seas, and countries different,   170
With variable objects, shall expel
This something-settled matter in his heart,
Whereon his brains still beating puts him thus
From fashion of himself. What think you on't?
POLONIUS: It shall do well; but yet do I believe   175
The origin and commencement of his grief
Sprung from neglected° love. [*Ophelia comes forward.*]
    How now, Ophelia?
You need not tell us what Lord Hamlet said,
We heard it all. My lord, do as you please,
But if you hold it fit, after the play   180
Let his queen-mother all alone entreat him
To show his grief.° Let her be round° with him,
And I'll be plac'd (so please you) in the ear
Of all their conference. If she find him° not,
To England send him, or confine him where   185
Your wisdom best shall think.
KING: It shall be so.
Madness in great ones must not [unwatch'd] go. *Exeunt.*

[Scene 2]°

Enter HAMLET *and three of the* PLAYERS.

HAMLET: Speak the speech, I pray you, as I pronounc'd it to
    you, trippingly on the tongue, but if you mouth° it, as many

---

161. **affections:** Inclinations, feelings.   165. **doubt:** Fear.   **disclose:** Synonymous
with *hatch;* see also 5.1.273.   177. **neglected:** Unrequited.   182. **his grief:** What is
troubling him.   **round:** Blunt, outspoken.   184. **find him:** Learn the truth about
him.   3.2. **Location:** The castle.   2. **mouth:** Pronounce with exaggerated distinctness
or declamatory effect.

of our players do, I had as live° the town-crier spoke my
lines. Nor do not saw the air too much with your hand,
thus, but use all gently, for in the very torrent, tempest,   5
and, as I may say, whirlwind of your passion, you must ac-
quire and beget a temperance that may give it smoothness.
O, it offends me to the soul to hear a robustious periwig-
pated fellow tear a passion to totters,° to very rags, to
spleet° the ears of the groundlings,° who for the most part   10
are capable of ° nothing but inexplicable dumb shows and
noise. I would have such a fellow whipt for o'erdoing
Termagant,° it out-Herods Herod, pray you avoid it.
[FIRST] PLAYER: I warrant your honor.
HAMLET: Be not too tame neither, but let your own discretion   15
be your tutor. Suit the action to the word, the word to the
action, with this special observance, that you o'erstep not
the modesty° of nature: for any thing so o'erdone is from°
the purpose of playing, whose end, both at the first and
now, was and is, to hold as 'twere the mirror up to nature: 20
to show virtue her feature, scorn° her own image, and the
very age and body of the time his form and pressure.° Now
this overdone, or come tardy° off, though it makes the
unskillful laugh, cannot but make the judicious grieve; the
censure° of which one° must in your allowance° o'er-   25
weigh a whole theatre of others. O, there be players that
I have seen play — and heard others [praise], and that
highly — not to speak it profanely,° that, neither having th'
accent of Christians nor the gait of Christian, pagan, nor
man, have so strutted and bellow'd that I have thought   30
some of Nature's journeymen had made men, and not
made them well, they imitated humanity so abominably.°

---

3. **live:** Lief, willingly.   9. **totters:** Tatters.   10. **spleet:** Split.   **groundlings:** Those
who paid the lowest admission price and stood on the ground in the "yard" or pit of the
theater.   11. **capable of:** Able to take in.   13. **Termagant:** A supposed god of the
Saracens, whose role in medieval drama, like that of Herod (line 13), was noisy and violent.   18. **modesty:** Moderation.   **from:** Contrary to.   21. **scorn:** I.e. that which is
worthy of scorn.   22. **pressure:** Impression (as of a seal), exact image.   23. **tardy:** Inad-
equately.   25. **censure:** Judgment.   **which one:** (Even) one of whom.   **allowance:**
Estimation.   28. **profanely:** Irreverently.   31–32. **some . . . abominably:** I.e. they
were so unlike men that it seemed Nature had not made them herself but had delegated
the task to mediocre assistants.

[FIRST] PLAYER: I hope we have reform'd that indifferently°
with us, [sir].
HAMLET: O, reform it altogether. And let those that play your   35
clowns speak no more than is set down for them, for there
be of them° that will themselves laugh to set on some quantity of barren spectators to laugh too, though in the mean
time some necessary question of the play be then to be
consider'd. That's villainous, and shows a most pitiful am-   40
bition in the fool° that uses it.° Go make you ready.

                                                    [*Exeunt Players.*]

Enter POLONIUS, GUILDENSTERN, *and* ROSENCRANTZ.

How now, my lord? Will the King hear this piece of work?°
POLONIUS: And the Queen too, and that presently.°
HAMLET: Bid the players make haste.   [*Exit Polonius.*]
Will you two help to hasten them?   45
ROSENCRANTZ: Ay, my lord.   *Exeunt they two.*
HAMLET: What ho, Horatio!

Enter HORATIO.

HORATIO: Here, sweet lord, at your service.
HAMLET: Horatio, thou art e'en as just a man°
As e'er my conversation cop'd withal.°   50
HORATIO: O my dear lord —
HAMLET: Nay, do not think I flatter,
For what advancement may I hope from thee
That no revenue hast but thy good spirits
To feed and clothe thee? Why should the poor be flatter'd?
No, let the candied° tongue lick absurd° pomp,   55
And crook the pregnant° hinges of the knee
Where thrift° may follow fawning. Dost thou hear?
Since my dear soul was mistress of her choice
And could of men distinguish her election,

---

33. **indifferently:** Pretty well.   37. **of them:** Some of them.   41. **fool:** (1) Stupid
person; (2) actor playing a fool's role.   **uses it:** See the Textual Notes for an interesting
passage following these words in Q1.   42. **piece of work:** Masterpiece (said jocu-
larly).   43. **presently:** At once.   49. **thou . . . man:** I.e. you come as close to being
what a man should be (*just* = exact, precise).   50. **my . . . withal:** My association with
people has brought me into contact with.   55. **candied:** Sugared, i.e. flattering.   **absurd:** Tasteless (Latin sense).   56. **pregnant:** Moving readily.   57. **thrift:** Thriving,
profit.

Sh' hath seal'd thee for herself, for thou hast been   60
As one in suff'ring all that suffers nothing,
A man that Fortune's buffets and rewards
Hast ta'en with equal thanks; and blest are those
Whose blood° and judgment are so well co-meddled,°
That they are not a pipe for Fortune's finger   65
To sound what stop she please. Give me that man
That is not passion's slave, and I will wear him
In my heart's core, ay, in my heart of heart,°
As I do thee. Something too much of this.
There is a play to-night before the King,   70
One scene of it comes near the circumstance
Which I have told thee of my father's death.
I prithee, when thou seest that act afoot,
Even with the very comment of thy soul°
Observe my uncle. If his occulted° guilt   75
Do not itself unkennel° in one speech,
It is a damned ghost° that we have seen,
And my imaginations are as foul
As Vulcan's stithy.° Give him heedful note,
For I mine eyes will rivet to his face,   80
And after we will both our judgments join
In censure of his seeming.°
HORATIO: Well, my lord.
If 'a steal aught the whilst this play is playing,
And scape [detecting], I will pay the theft.

[*Sound a flourish. Danish march.*] *Enter Trumpets and Kettle-drums,* KING, QUEEN, POLONIUS, OPHELIA, [ROSENCRANTZ, GUILDENSTERN, *and other* LORDS *attendant, with his* GUARD *carrying torches*].

HAMLET: They are coming to the play. I must be idle;°   85
     Get you a place.
KING: How fares° our cousin Hamlet?

---

64. blood: Passions.   **co-meddled:** Mixed, blended.   **68. my heart of heart:** The heart of my heart.   **74. very . . . soul:** Your most intense critical observation.   **75. occulted:** Hidden.   **76. unkennel:** Bring into the open.   **77. damned ghost:** Evil spirit, devil.   **79. stithy:** Forge.   **82. censure . . . seeming:** Reaching a verdict on his behavior.   **85. be idle:** Act foolish, pretend to be crazy.   **87. fares:** Hamlet takes up this word in another sense.

HAMLET: Excellent, i' faith, of the chameleon's dish:° I eat the
air, promise-cramm'd — you cannot feed capons so.

KING: I have nothing with° this answer, Hamlet, these words   90
are not mine.

HAMLET: No, nor mine° now. [*To Polonius.*] My lord, you
play'd once i' th' university, you say?

POLONIUS: That did I, my lord, and was accounted a good
actor.   95

HAMLET: What did you enact?

POLONIUS: I did enact Julius Caesar. I was kill'd i' th' Capitol;
Brutus kill'd me.

HAMLET: It was a brute part° of him to kill so capital a calf
there. Be the players ready?   100

ROSENCRANTZ: Ay, my lord, they stay upon your patience.

QUEEN: Come hither, my dear Hamlet, sit by me.

HAMLET: No, good mother, here's metal more attractive.

                    [*Lying down at Ophelia's feet.*]

POLONIUS: [*To the King.*] O ho, do you mark that?

HAMLET: Lady, shall I lie in your lap?   105

OPHELIA: No, my lord.

[HAMLET: I mean, my head upon your lap?

OPHELIA: Ay, my lord.]

HAMLET: Do you think I meant country matters?°

OPHELIA: I think nothing, my lord.   110

HAMLET: That's a fair thought to lie between maids' legs.

OPHELIA: What is, my lord?

HAMLET: Nothing.

OPHELIA: You are merry, my lord.

HAMLET: Who, I?   115

OPHELIA: Ay, my lord.

HAMLET: O God, your only° jig-maker.° What should a man do
but be merry, for look you how cheerfully my mother
looks, and my father died within 's° two hours.

OPHELIA: Nay, 'tis twice two months, my lord.   120

---

88. chameleon's dish: Chameleons were thought to feed on air. Hamlet says that he
subsists on an equally nourishing diet, the promise of succession. There is probably a pun
on *air/heir.*   **90. have nothing with:** Do not understand.   **92. mine:** I.e. an answer to
my question.   **99. part:** Action.   **109. country matters:** Indecency.   **117. only:**
Very best.   **jig-maker:** One who composed or played in the farcical song-and-dance en-
tertainments that followed plays.   **119. 's:** This.

HAMLET: So long? Nay then let the dev'l wear black, for I'll
have a suit of sables.° O heavens, die two months ago, and
not forgotten yet? Then there's hope a great man's memory may outlive his life half a year, but, by'r lady, 'a must
build churches then, or else shall 'a suffer not thinking on,°   125
with the hobby-horse, whose epitaph is, "For O, for O, the
hobby-horse is forgot."°

The trumpets sounds. Dumb show follows.

*Enter a King and a Queen [very lovingly], the Queen embracing
him and he her. [She kneels and makes show of protestation unto
him.] He takes her up and declines his head upon her neck. He lies
him down upon a bank of flowers. She, seeing him asleep, leaves
him. Anon come in another man, takes off his crown, kisses it,
pours poison in the sleeper's ears, and leaves him. The Queen returns, finds the King dead, makes passionate action. The pois'ner
with some three or four [mutes] come in again, seem to condole
with her. The dead body is carried away. The pois'ner woos the
Queen with gifts; she seems harsh [and unwilling] awhile, but in
the end accepts love.   [Exeunt.]*

OPHELIA: What means this, my lord?
HAMLET: Marry, this' [miching] mallecho,° it means mischief.
OPHELIA: Belike this show imports the argument° of the play.   130

Enter PROLOGUE.

HAMLET: We shall know by this fellow. The players cannot keep
[counsel°], they'll tell all.
OPHELIA: Will 'a tell us what this show meant?
HAMLET: Ay, or any show that you will show him. Be not you°
asham'd to show, he'll not shame to tell you what it means.   135
OPHELIA: You are naught,° you are naught. I'll mark the play.

121–22. let . . . sables: I.e. to the devil with my garments; after so long a time I am
ready for the old man's garb of sables (fine fur).   **125. not thinking on:** Not being
thought of, i.e. being forgotten.   **126–27. For . . . forgot:** Line from a popular ballad
lamenting puritanical suppression of such country sports as the May-games, in which
the hobby-horse, a character costumed to resemble a horse, traditionally appeared.
129. this' miching mallecho: This is sneaking mischief.   **130. argument:** Subject,
plot.   **132. counsel:** Secrets.   **134. Be not you:** If you are not.   **136. naught:**
Wicked.

PROLOGUE: For us, and for our tragedy,
    Here stooping to your clemency,
    We beg your hearing patiently.   [*Exit.*]
HAMLET: Is this a prologue, or the posy of a ring?°   140
OPHELIA: 'Tis brief, my lord.
HAMLET: As woman's love.

Enter [*two Players,*] KING *and* QUEEN.

[PLAYER] KING: Full thirty times hath Phoebus' cart° gone
    round
    Neptune's salt wash and Tellus'° orbed ground,
    And thirty dozen moons with borrowed sheen   145
    About the world have times twelve thirties been,
    Since love our hearts and Hymen° did our hands
    Unite comutual in most sacred bands.°
[PLAYER] QUEEN: So many journeys may the sun and moon
    Make us again count o'er ere love be done!   150
    But woe is me, you are so sick of late,
    So far from cheer and from [your] former state,
    That I distrust you. Yet though I distrust,°
    Discomfort you, my lord, it nothing must,
    [For] women's fear and love hold quantity,°   155
    In neither aught, or in extremity.
    Now what my [love] is, proof° hath made you know,
    And as my love is siz'd, my fear is so.
    Where love is great, the littlest doubts are fear;
    Where little fears grow great, great love grows there.   160
[PLAYER] KING: Faith, I must leave thee, love, and shortly too;
    My operant° powers their functions leave to do,°
    And thou shalt live in this fair world behind,
    Honor'd, belov'd, and haply one as kind
    For husband shalt thou —
[PLAYER] QUEEN: O, confound the rest!°   165
    Such love must needs be treason in my breast.

---

140. posy . . . ring: Verse motto inscribed in a ring (necessarily short).   **143–61.** See the Textual Notes for the corresponding lines in Q1.   **143. Phoebus' cart:** The sun-god's chariot.   **144. Tellus:** Goddess of the earth.   **147. Hymen:** God of marriage. **148. bands:** Bonds.   **153. distrust:** Fear for.   **155. hold quantity:** Are related in direct proportion.   **157. proof:** Experience.   **162. operant:** Active, vital.   **leave to do:** Cease to perform.   **165. confound the rest:** May destruction befall what you are about to speak of — a second marriage on my part.

In second husband let me be accurs'd!
None wed the second but who kill'd the first.
HAMLET: [*Aside.*] That's wormwood!
[PLAYER QUEEN]: The instances° that second marriage move°   170
Are base respects of thrift,° but none of love.
A second time I kill my husband dead,
When second husband kisses me in bed.
[PLAYER] KING: I do believe you think what now you speak,
But what we do determine, oft we break.   175
Purpose is but the slave to memory,
Of violent birth, but poor validity,°
Which now, the fruit unripe, sticks on the tree,
But fall unshaken when they mellow be.
Most necessary 'tis that we forget   180
To pay ourselves what to ourselves is debt.°
What to ourselves in passion° we propose,
The passion ending, doth the purpose lose.
The violence of either grief or joy
Their own enactures with themselves destroy.°   185
Where joy most revels, grief doth most lament;
Grief [joys], joy grieves, on slender accident.°
This world is not for aye, nor 'tis not strange
That even our loves should with our fortunes change:
For 'tis a question left us yet to prove,   190
Whether love lead fortune, or else fortune love.
The great man down, you mark his favorite flies,
The poor advanc'd makes friends of enemies.
And hitherto doth love on fortune tend,
For who not needs shall never lack a friend,   195
And who in want a hollow friend doth try,
Directly seasons° him his enemy.
But orderly to end where I begun,
Our wills and fates do so contrary run
That our devices° still° are overthrown,   200

---

170. instances: Motives.   **move:** Give rise to.   **171. respects of thrift:** Considerations
of advantage.   **177. validity:** Strength, power to last.   **180–81. Most . . . debt:** I.e.
such resolutions are debts we owe to ourselves, and it would be foolish to pay such debts.
182. passion: Violent emotion.   **184–85. The violence . . . destroy:** I.e. both violent
grief and violent joy fail of their intended acts because they destroy themselves by their
very violence.   **187. slender accident:** Slight occasion.   **197. seasons:** Ripens, con-
verts into.   **200. devices:** Devisings, intentions.   **still:** Always.

Our thoughts are ours, their ends none of our own:
So think thou wilt no second husband wed,
But die thy thoughts when thy first lord is dead.
[PLAYER] QUEEN: Nor earth to me give food, nor heaven light,
   Sport and repose lock from me day and night,   205
To desperation turn my trust and hope,
[An] anchor's cheer° in prison be my scope!°
Each opposite that blanks° the face of joy
Meet what I would have well and it destroy!
Both here and hence pursue me lasting strife,   210
If once I be a widow, ever I be a wife!
HAMLET: If she should break it now!
[PLAYER] KING: 'Tis deeply sworn. Sweet, leave me here a while,
   My spirits grow dull, and fain I would beguile
The tedious day with sleep.   [*Sleeps.*]
[PLAYER] QUEEN: Sleep rock thy brain,   215
And never come mischance between us twain!   *Exit.*
HAMLET: Madam, how like you this play?
QUEEN: The lady doth protest too much, methinks.
HAMLET: O but she'll keep her word.
KING: Have you heard the argument? is there no offense° in't?   220
HAMLET: No, no, they do but jest,° poison in jest — no offense
   i' th' world.
KING: What do you call the play?
HAMLET: "The Mouse-trap." Marry, how? tropically:° this play
   is the image° of a murther done in Vienna; Gonzago is the   225
duke's name, his wife, Baptista. You shall see anon. 'Tis a
knavish piece of work, but what of that? Your Majesty, and
we that have free souls,° it touches us not. Let the gall'd
jade° winch,° our withers° are unwrung.°

Enter LUCIANUS.

This is one Lucianus, nephew to the king.   230

---

207. **anchor's cheer:** Hermit's fare.   **my scope:** The extent of my comforts.   **208.
blanks:** Blanches, makes pale (a symptom of grief).   **220. offense:** Offensive matter
(but Hamlet quibbles on the sense "crime").   **221. jest:** I.e. pretend.   **224. tropically:** Figuratively (with play on *trapically* — which is the reading of Q1 — and probably
with allusion to the children's saying *marry trap,* meaning "now you're caught").   **225.
image:** Representation.   **228. free souls:** Clear consciences.   **228–29. gall'd jade:**
Chafed horse.   **229. winch:** Wince.   **withers:** Ridge between a horse's shoulders.
unwrung: Not rubbed sore.

OPHELIA: You are as good as a chorus,° my lord.

HAMLET: I could interpret between you and your love, if I
could see the puppets dallying.°

OPHELIA: You are keen,° my lord, you are keen.

HAMLET: It would cost you a groaning to take off mine edge.   235

OPHELIA: Still better, and worse.°

HAMLET: So° you mistake° your husbands. Begin, murtherer,
leave thy damnable faces° and begin. Come, the croaking
raven doth bellow for revenge.°

LUCIANUS: Thoughts black, hands apt, drugs fit, and time
agreeing,   240
[Confederate] season,° else no creature seeing,
Thou mixture rank, of midnight weeds collected,
With Hecat's ban° thrice blasted, thrice [infected],
Thy natural magic and dire property
On wholesome life usurps immediately.   245
                    [*Pours the poison in his ears.*]

HAMLET: 'A poisons him i' th' garden for his estate. His name's
Gonzago, the story is extant, and written in very choice
Italian. You shall see anon how the murtherer gets the love
of Gonzago's wife.

OPHELIA: The King arises.   250

[HAMLET: What, frighted with false fire?°]

QUEEN: How fares my lord?

POLONIUS: Give o'er the play.

KING: Give me some light. Away!

POLONIUS: Lights, lights, lights!   255
                    Exeunt all but Hamlet and Horatio.

HAMLET: "Why, let the strooken° deer go weep,
          The hart ungalled° play,
     For some must watch° while some must sleep,
          Thus runs the world away."

---

231. chorus: I.e. one who explains the forthcoming action.   **232–33. I . . . dallying:** I
could speak the dialogue between you and your lover like a puppet-master (with an indecent jest).   **234. keen:** Bitter, sharp.   **236. better, and worse:** I.e. more pointed and
less decent.   **237. So:** I.e. "for better, for worse," in the words of the marriage service.
mistake: I.e. mis-take, take wrongfully. Their vows, Hamlet suggests, prove false.   **238.
faces:** Facial expressions.   **238–39. the croaking . . . revenge:** Misquoted from an old
play, *The True Tragedy of Richard III.*   **241. Confederate season:** The time being my
ally.   **243. Hecat's ban:** The curse of Hecate, goddess of witchcraft.   **251. false fire:**
I.e. a blank cartridge.   **256. strooken:** Struck, i.e. wounded.   **257. ungalled:** Un-
wounded.   **258. watch:** Stay awake.

Would not this, sir, and a forest of feathers° — if the rest of   260
my fortunes turn Turk° with me — with [two] Provincial
roses° on my raz'd° shoes, get me a fellowship° in a cry° of
players?
HORATIO: Half a share.
HAMLET: A whole one, I.   265
    "For thou dost know, O Damon dear,
      This realm dismantled° was
    Of Jove himself, and now reigns here
    A very, very" — pajock.°
HORATIO: You might have rhym'd.   270
HAMLET: O good Horatio, I'll take the ghost's word for a thou-
sand pound. Didst perceive?
HORATIO: Very well, my lord.
HAMLET: Upon the talk of the pois'ning?
HORATIO: I did very well note him.   275
HAMLET: Ah, ha! Come, some music! Come, the recorders!
    For if the King like not the comedy,
    Why then belike he likes it not, perdy.°
  Come, some music!

Enter ROSENCRANTZ *and* GUILDENSTERN.

GUILDENSTERN: Good my lord, voutsafe me a word with you.   280
HAMLET: Sir, a whole history.
GUILDENSTERN: The King, sir —
HAMLET: Ay, sir, what of him?
GUILDENSTERN: Is in his retirement marvellous distemp'red.
HAMLET: With drink, sir?   285
GUILDENSTERN: No, my lord, with choler.°
HAMLET: Your wisdom should show itself more richer to signify
  this to the doctor, for for me to put him to his purgation°
  would perhaps plunge him into more choler.

---

260. feathers: The plumes worn by tragic actors.   **261. turn Turk:** I.e. go to the bad.
261–62. Provincial roses: Rosettes designed to look like a variety of French rose.   **262.
raz'd:** With decorative slashing.   **fellowship:** Partnership.   **cry:** Company.   **267.
dismantled:** Divested, deprived.   **269. pajock:** Peacock (substituting for the rhyme-
word *ass*). The natural history of the time attributed many vicious qualities to the peacock.
278. perdy: Assuredly (French *pardieu,* "by God").   **286. choler:** Anger (but Hamlet
willfully takes up the word in the sense "biliousness").   **288. put . . . purgation:** I.e.
prescribe for what's wrong with him.

GUILDENSTERN: Good my lord, put your discourse into some   290
frame,° and [start] not so wildly from my affair.
HAMLET: I am tame, sir. Pronounce.
GUILDENSTERN: The Queen, your mother, in most great afflic-
tion of spirit, hath sent me to you.
HAMLET: You are welcome.   295
GUILDENSTERN: Nay, good my lord, this courtesy is not of the
right breed. If it shall please you to make me a wholesome°
answer, I will do your mother's commandement; if not, your
pardon° and my return shall be the end of [my] business.
HAMLET: Sir, I cannot.   300
ROSENCRANTZ: What, my lord?
HAMLET: Make you a wholesome answer — my wit's diseas'd.
But, sir, such answer as I can make, you shall command, or
rather, as you say, my mother. Therefore no more, but to
the matter: my mother, you say —   305
ROSENCRANTZ: Then thus she says: your behavior hath strook
her into amazement and admiration.°
HAMLET: O wonderful son, that can so stonish° a mother! But
is there no sequel at the heels of this mother's admiration?
Impart.   310
ROSENCRANTZ: She desires to speak with you in her closet° ere
you go to bed.
HAMLET: We shall obey, were she ten times our mother. Have
you any further trade with us?
ROSENCRANTZ: My lord, you once did love me.   315
HAMLET: And do still, by these pickers and stealers.°
ROSENCRANTZ: Good my lord, what is your cause of distemper?
You do surely bar the door upon your own liberty if you
deny your griefs to your friend.
HAMLET: Sir, I lack advancement.   320
ROSENCRANTZ: How can that be, when you have the voice of
the King himself for your succession in Denmark?
HAMLET: Ay, sir, but "While the grass grows" — the proverb°
is something musty.°

---

291. frame: Logical structure.   **297. wholesome:** Sensible, rational.   **299. pardon:**
Permission for departure.   **307. amazement and admiration:** Bewilderment and wonder.   **308. stonish:** Astound.   **311. closet:** Private room.   **316. pickers and stealers:**
Hands; which, as the Catechism says, we must keep "from picking and stealing."   **323:
proverb:** I.e. "While the grass grows, the steed starves."   **something musty:** Somewhat
stale.

Enter the PLAYERS *with recorders.*

O, the recorders! Let me see one. — To withdraw with   325
you — why do you go about to recover the wind° of me, as
if you would drive me into a toil?°
GUILDENSTERN: O my lord, if my duty be too bold, my love is
too unmannerly.
HAMLET: I do not well understand that. Will you play upon this   330
pipe?
GUILDENSTERN: My lord, I cannot.
HAMLET: I pray you.
GUILDENSTERN: Believe me, I cannot.
HAMLET: I do beseech you.   335
GUILDENSTERN: I know no touch of it, my lord.
HAMLET: It is as easy as lying. Govern these ventages° with your
fingers and [thumbs], give it breath with your mouth, and
it will discourse most eloquent music. Look you, these are
the stops.   340
GUILDENSTERN: But these cannot I command to any utt'rance
of harmony. I have not the skill.
HAMLET: Why, look you now, how unworthy a thing you make
of me! You would play upon me, you would seem to know
my stops, you would pluck out the heart of my mystery,   345
you would sound me from my lowest note to [the top of]
my compass; and there is much music, excellent voice, in
this little organ,° yet cannot you make it speak. 'Sblood, do
you think I am easier to be play'd on than a pipe? Call me
what instrument you will, though you fret° me, [yet] you   350
cannot play upon me.

Enter POLONIUS.

God bless you, sir.
POLONIUS: My lord, the Queen would speak with you, and
presently.°
HAMLET: Do you see yonder cloud that's almost in shape of a   355
camel?
POLONIUS: By th' mass and 'tis, like a camel indeed.
HAMLET: Methinks it is like a weasel.

---

326. recover the wind: Get to windward.   **327. toil:** Snare.   **337. ventages:** Stops.
348. organ: Instrument.   **350. fret:** (1) Finger (an instrument); (2) vex.   **354. presently:** At once.

POLONIUS: It is back'd like a weasel.
HAMLET: Or like a whale.   360
POLONIUS: Very like a whale.
HAMLET: Then I will come to my mother by and by. [*Aside.*]
   They fool me to the top of my bent.° — I will come by and
   by.°
[POLONIUS:] I will say so.   [*Exit.*]   365
HAMLET: "By and by" is easily said. Leave me, friends.
                              [*Exeunt all but Hamlet.*]
   'Tis now the very witching° time of night,
   When churchyards yawn and hell itself [breathes] out
   Contagion to this world. Now could I drink hot blood,
   And do such [bitter business as the] day   370
   Would quake to look on. Soft, now to my mother.
   O heart, lose not thy nature!° let not ever
   The soul of Nero° enter this firm bosom,
   Let me be cruel, not unnatural;
   I will speak [daggers] to her, but use none.   375
   My tongue and soul in this be hypocrites —
   How in my words somever she be shent,°
   To give them seals° never my soul consent!   *Exit.*

[Scene 3]°

Enter KING, ROSENCRANTZ, *and* GUILDENSTERN.

KING: I like him° not, nor stands it safe with us
   To let his madness range. Therefore prepare you.
   I your commission will forthwith dispatch,°
   And he to England shall along with you.
   The terms° of our estate° may not endure   5
   Hazard so near 's as doth hourly grow
   Out of his brows.°

363. They . . . bent: They make me play the fool to the limit of my ability.   363–
64. by and by: At once.   367. witching: I.e. when the powers of evil are at large.
372. nature: Natural affection, filial feeling.   373. Nero: Murderer of his mother.
377. shent: Rebuked.   378. give them seals: Confirm them by deeds.   3.3. Location: The castle.   1. him: I.e. his state of mind, his behavior.   3. dispatch: Have
drawn up.   5. terms: Conditions, nature.   our estate: My position (as king).   7. his
brows: The madness visible in his face (?).

GUILDENSTERN: We will ourselves provide.
Most holy and religious fear° it is
To keep those many many bodies safe
That live and feed upon your Majesty.   10
ROSENCRANTZ: The single and peculiar° life is bound
With all the strength and armor of the mind
To keep itself from noyance,° but much more
That spirit upon whose weal depends and rests
The lives of many. The cess° of majesty   15
Dies not alone, but like a gulf ° doth draw
What's near it with it. Or it is a massy wheel
Fix'd on the summit of the highest mount,
To whose [huge] spokes ten thousand lesser things
Are mortis'd° and adjoin'd, which when it falls,   20
Each small annexment, petty consequence,
Attends° the boist'rous [ruin°]. Never alone
Did the King sigh, but [with] a general groan.
KING: Arm° you, I pray you, to this speedy viage,°
For we will fetters put about this fear,°   25
Which now goes too free-footed.
ROSENCRANTZ: We will haste us.
        Exeunt Gentlemen [Rosencrantz and Guildenstern].

Enter POLONIUS.

POLONIUS: My lord, he's going to his mother's closet.
Behind the arras I'll convey myself
To hear the process.° I'll warrant she'll tax him home,°
And as you said, and wisely was it said,   30
'Tis meet that some more audience than a mother,
Since nature makes them partial, should o'erhear
The speech, of vantage.° Fare you well, my liege,
I'll call upon you ere you go to bed,
And tell you what I know.
KING: Thanks, dear my lord.   35
                                Exit [Polonius].

---

8. fear: Concern.   **11. single and peculiar:** Individual and private.   **13. noyance:** Injury.   **15. cess:** Cessation, death.   **16. gulf:** Whirlpool.   **20. mortis'd:** Fixed.   **22.
Attends:** Accompanies.   **ruin:** Fall.   **24. Arm:** Prepare.   **viage:** Voyage.   **25. fear:**
Object of fear.   **29. process:** Course of the talk.   **tax him home:** Take him severely to
task.   **33. of vantage:** From an advantageous position (?) or in addition (?).

O, my offense is rank, it smells to heaven,°
It hath the primal eldest curse° upon't,
A brother's murther. Pray can I not,
Though inclination be as sharp as will.°
My stronger guilt defeats my strong intent,   40
And, like a man to double business bound,°
I stand in pause where I shall first begin,
And both neglect.° What if this cursed hand
Were thicker than itself with brother's blood,
Is there not rain enough in the sweet heavens   45
To wash it white as snow? Whereto serves mercy
But to confront the visage of offense?°
And what's in prayer but this twofold force,
To be forestalled ere we come to fall,
Or [pardon'd] being down? then I'll look up.   50
My fault is past, but, O, what form of prayer
Can serve my turn? "Forgive me my foul murther"?
That cannot be, since I am still possess'd
Of those effects for which I did the murther:
My crown, mine own ambition, and my queen.   55
May one be pardon'd and retain th' offense?°
In the corrupted currents° of this world
Offense's gilded° hand may [shove] by justice,
And oft 'tis seen the wicked prize° itself
Buys out the law, but 'tis not so above: 60
There is no shuffling,° there the action lies°
In his true nature, and we ourselves compell'd,
Even to the teeth and forehead° of our faults,
To give in evidence. What then? What rests?°
Try what repentance can. What can it not?   65
Yet what can it, when one can not repent?
O wretched state! O bosom black as death!

36–72. See the Textual Notes for the corresponding lines in Q1.   **37. primal eldest curse:** I.e. God's curse on Cain, who also slew his brother.   **39. Though . . . will:** Though my desire is as strong as my resolve to do so.   **41. bound:** Committed.   **43. neglect:** Omit.   **46–47. Whereto . . . offense:** I.e. what function has mercy except when there has been sin.   **56. th' offense:** I.e. the "effects" or fruits of the offense.   **57. currents:** Courses.   **58. gilded:** I.e. bribing.   **59. wicked prize:** Rewards of vice.   **61. shuffling:** Evasion.   **the action lies:** The charge comes for legal consideration.   **63. Even . . . forehead:** I.e. fully recognizing their features, extenuating nothing.   **64. rests:** Remains.

O limed° soul, that struggling to be free
Art more engag'd!° Help, angels! Make assay,
Bow, stubborn knees, and heart, with strings of steel,   70
Be soft as sinews of the new-born babe!
All may be well.   [*He kneels.*]

Enter HAMLET.

HAMLET: Now might I do it [pat], now 'a is a-praying;
  And now I'll do't — and so 'a goes to heaven,
  And so am I [reveng'd]. That would be scann'd:°   75
  A villain kills my father, and for that
  I, his sole son, do this same villain send
  To heaven.
  Why, this is [hire and salary], not revenge.
  'A took my father grossly,° full of bread,   80
  With all his crimes° broad blown,° as flush° as May,
  And how his audit° stands who knows save heaven?
  But in our circumstance and course of thought°
  'Tis heavy with him. And am I then revenged,
  To take him in the purging of his soul,   85
  When he is fit and season'd for his passage?
  No!
  Up,° sword, and know thou a more horrid hent:°
  When he is drunk asleep, or in his rage,
  Or in th' incestious pleasure of his bed,   90
  At game a-swearing, or about some act
  That has no relish° of salvation in't —
  Then trip him, that his heels may kick at heaven,
  And that his soul may be as damn'd and black
  As hell, whereto it goes. My mother stays,   95
  This physic° but prolongs thy sickly days.   *Exit.*
KING: [*Rising.*] My words fly up, my thoughts remain below:
  Words without thoughts never to heaven go.   *Exit.*

---

68. limed: Caught (as in birdlime, a sticky substance used for catching birds).   **69. engag'd:** Entangled.   **75. would be scann'd:** Must be carefully considered.   **80. grossly:** In a gross state; not spiritually prepared.   **81. crimes:** Sins.   **broad blown:** In full bloom.   **flush:** Lusty, vigorous.   **82. audit:** Account.   **83. in . . . thought:** I.e. to the best of our knowledge and belief.   **88. Up:** Into the sheath.   **know . . . hent:** Be grasped at a more dreadful time.   **92. relish:** Trace.   **96. physic:** (Attempted) remedy, i.e. prayer.

[Scene 4]°

Enter [QUEEN] GERTRUDE *and* POLONIUS.

POLONIUS: 'A will come straight. Look you lay home to him.°
    Tell him his pranks have been too broad° to bear with,
    And that your Grace hath screen'd and stood between
    Much heat and him. I'll silence me even here;
    Pray you be round° [with him].   5
QUEEN: I'll [warr'nt] you, fear me not.° Withdraw,
    I hear him coming.   [*Polonius hides behind the arras.*]

Enter HAMLET.

HAMLET: Now, mother, what's the matter?
QUEEN: Hamlet, thou hast thy father much offended.
HAMLET: Mother, you have my father much offended.   10
QUEEN: Come, come, you answer with an idle° tongue.
HAMLET: Go, go, you question with a wicked tongue.
QUEEN: Why, how now, Hamlet?
HAMLET: What's the matter now?
QUEEN: Have you forgot me?
HAMLET: No, by the rood,° not so:
    You are the Queen, your husband's brother's wife,   15
    And would it were not so, you are my mother.
QUEEN: Nay, then I'll set those to you that can speak.
HAMLET: Come, come, and sit you down, you shall not
        boudge;°
    You go not till I set you up a glass
    Where you may see the [inmost] part of you.   20
QUEEN: What wilt thou do? Thou wilt not murther me?
    Help ho!
POLONIUS: [*Behind.*] What ho, help!
HAMLET: [*Drawing.*] How now? A rat? Dead, for a ducat,°
        dead!   [*Kills Polonius through the arras.*]
POLONIUS: [*Behind.*] O, I am slain.
QUEEN: O me, what hast thou done?   25
HAMLET: Nay, I know not, is it the King?

3.4. Location: The Queen's closet in the castle.   **1. lay . . . him:** Reprove him severely.
2. broad: Unrestrained.   **5. round:** Plain-spoken.   **6. fear me not:** Have no fears
about my handling of the situation.   **11. idle:** Foolish.   **14. rood:** Cross.   **18.**
boudge: Budge.   **24. for a ducat:** I'll wager a ducat.

QUEEN: O, what a rash and bloody deed is this!
HAMLET: A bloody deed! almost as bad, good mother,
  As kill a king, and marry with his brother.
QUEEN: As kill a king!
HAMLET: Ay, lady, it was my word.   30
  [*Parts the arras and discovers Polonius.*]
  Thou wretched, rash, intruding fool, farewell!
  I took thee for thy better. Take thy fortune;
  Thou find'st to be too busy° is some danger. —
  Leave wringing of your hands. Peace, sit you down,
  And let me wring your heart, for so I shall   35
  If it be made of penetrable stuff,
  If damned custom° have not brass'd° it so
  That it be proof ° and bulwark against sense.°
QUEEN: What have I done, that thou dar'st wag thy tongue
  In noise so rude against me?
HAMLET: Such an act   40
  That blurs the grace and blush of modesty,
  Calls virtue hypocrite, takes off the rose
  From the fair forehead of an innocent love
  And sets a blister° there, makes marriage vows
  As false as dicers' oaths, O, such a deed   45
  As from the body of contraction° plucks
  The very soul, and sweet religion° makes
  A rhapsody° of words. Heaven's face does glow°
  O'er this solidity and compound mass°
  With heated visage, as against the doom;°   50
  Is thought-sick at the act.
QUEEN: Ay me, what act,
  That roars so loud and thunders in the index?°
HAMLET: Look here upon this picture, and on this,
  The counterfeit presentment° of two brothers.
  See what a grace was seated on this brow: 55

---

33. busy: Officious, meddlesome.   **37. damned custom:** I.e. the habit of ill-doing.
brass'd: Hardened, literally, plated with brass.   **38. proof:** Armor.   **sense:** Feeling.
44. blister: Brand of shame.   **46. contraction:** The making of contracts, i.e. the assuming of solemn obligation.   **47. religion:** I.e. sacred vows.   **48. rhapsody:** Miscellaneous
collection, jumble.   **glow:** I.e. with anger.   **49. this . . . mass:** I.e. the earth. *Compound* = compounded of the four elements.   **50. as . . . doom:** As if for Judgment Day.
52. index: I.e. table of contents. The index was formerly placed at the beginning of a
book.   **54. counterfeit presentment:** Painted likenesses.

Hyperion's° curls, the front° of Jove himself,
An eye like Mars, to threaten and command,
A station° like the herald Mercury
New lighted on a [heaven-]kissing hill,
A combination and a form indeed,   60
Where every god did seem to set his seal
To give the world assurance of a man.
This was your husband. Look you now what follows:
Here is your husband, like a mildewed ear,°
Blasting his wholesome brother. Have you eyes?   65
Could you on this fair mountain leave to feed,
And batten° on this moor? ha, have you eyes?
You cannot call it love, for at your age
The heyday° in the blood is tame, it's humble,
And waits upon the judgment, and what judgment   70
Would step from this to this? Sense° sure you have,
Else could you not have motion, but sure that sense
Is apoplex'd,° for madness would not err,
Nor sense to ecstasy was ne'er so thrall'd
But it reserv'd some quantity of choice   75
To serve in such a difference.° What devil was't
That thus hath cozen'd° you at hoodman-blind?°
Eyes without feeling, feeling without sight,
Ears without hands or eyes, smelling sans° all,
Or but a sickly part of one true sense   80
Could not so mope.° O shame, where is thy blush?
Rebellious hell,
If thou canst mutine° in a matron's bones,
To flaming youth let virtue be as wax
And melt in her own fire. Proclaim no shame   85
When the compulsive ardure gives the charge,
Since frost itself as actively doth burn,
And reason [panders] will.°

---

56. **Hyperion's:** The sun-god's.   **front:** Forehead.   **58. station:** Bearing.   **64. ear:** I.e.
of grain.   **67. batten:** Gorge.   **69. heyday:** Excitement.   **71. Sense:** Sense perception, the five senses.   **73. apoplex'd:** Paralyzed.   **73–76. madness . . . difference:** I.e.
madness itself could not go so far astray, nor were the senses ever so enslaved by lunacy
that they did not retain the power to make so obvious a distinction.   **77. cozen'd:**
Cheated.   **hoodman-blind:** Blindman's bluff.   **79. sans:** Without.   **81. mope:** Be
dazed.   **83. mutine:** Rebel.   **85–88. Proclaim . . . will:** Do not call it sin when the
hot blood of youth is responsible for lechery, since here we see people of calmer age on
fire for it; and reason acts as procurer for desire, instead of restraining it. *Ardure* = ardor.

QUEEN: O Hamlet, speak no more!
Thou turn'st my [eyes into my very] soul,
And there I see such black and [grained°] spots   90
And will [not] leave their tinct.°
HAMLET: Nay, but to live
In the rank sweat of an enseamed° bed,
Stew'd in corruption, honeying and making love
Over the nasty sty!
QUEEN: O, speak to me no more!
These words like daggers enter in my ears.   95
No more, sweet Hamlet!
HAMLET: A murtherer and a villain!
A slave that is not twentith° part the [tithe]
Of your precedent° lord, a Vice° of kings,
A cutpurse of the empire and the rule,
That from a shelf the precious diadem stole,   100
And put it in his pocket —
QUEEN: No more!

Enter GHOST [*in his night-gown°*].

HAMLET: A king of shreds and patches° —
Save me, and hover o'er me with your wings,
You heavenly guards! What would your gracious figure?
QUEEN: Alas, he's mad!   105
HAMLET: Do you not come your tardy son to chide,
That, laps'd in time and passion,° lets go by
Th' important° acting of your dread command?
O, say!
GHOST: Do not forget! This visitation   110
Is but to whet thy almost blunted purpose.
But look, amazement° on thy mother sits,
O, step between her and her fighting soul.
Conceit° in weakest bodies strongest works,
Speak to her, Hamlet.

90. grained: Fast-dyed, indelible   **91. leave their tinct:** Lose their color.   **92. en-**
seamed: Greasy.   **97. twentith:** Twentieth.   **98. precedent:** Former.   **Vice:** Buffoon
(like the Vice of the morality plays).   **101. s.d. night-gown:** Dressing gown.   **102.**
of . . . patches: Clownish (alluding to the motley worn by jesters) (?) or patched-up,
beggarly (?).   **107. laps'd . . . passion:** "having suffered time to slip and passion to
cool" (Johnson).   **108. important:** Urgent.   **112. amazement:** Utter bewilderment.
114. Conceit: Imagination.

HAMLET: How is it with you, lady?   115
QUEEN: Alas, how is't with you,
    That you do bend your eye on vacancy,
    And with th' incorporal air do hold discourse?
    Forth at your eyes your spirits wildly peep,
    And as the sleeping soldiers in th' alarm,°   120
    Your bedded hair, like life in excrements,°
    Start up and stand an end.° O gentle son,
    Upon the heat and flame of thy distemper
    Sprinkle cool patience.° Whereon do you look?
HAMLET: On him, on him! look you how pale he glares!   125
    His form and cause° conjoin'd, preaching to stones,
    Would make them capable.° — Do not look upon me,
    Lest with this piteous action you convert°
    My stern effects,° then what I have to do
    Will want true color° — tears perchance for blood.   130
QUEEN: To whom do you speak this?
HAMLET: Do you see nothing there?
QUEEN: Nothing at all, yet all that is I see.
HAMLET: Nor did you nothing hear?
QUEEN: No, nothing but ourselves.
HAMLET: Why, look you there, look how it steals away!
    My father, in his habit° as he lived!   135
    Look where he goes, even now, out at the portal!
                                   Exit Ghost.
QUEEN: This is the very coinage of your brain,°
    This bodiless creation ecstasy°
    Is very cunning in.
HAMLET: [Ecstasy?]
    My pulse as yours doth temperately keep time,   140
    And makes as healthful music. It is not madness
    That I have utt'red. Bring me to the test,
    And [I] the matter will reword, which madness
    Would gambol° from. Mother, for love of grace,

120. **in th' alarm:** When the call to arms is sounded.   121. **excrements:** Outgrowths;
here, hair (also used of nails).   122. **an end:** On end.   124. **patience:** Self-control.
126. **His . . . cause:** His appearance and what he has to say.   127. **capable:** Sensitive,
receptive.   128. **convert:** Alter.   129. **effects:** (Purposed) actions.   130. **want true
color:** Lack its proper appearance.   135. **habit:** Dress.   137–217. See the Textual
Notes for the conclusion of the scene in Q1.   138. **ecstasy:** Madness.   144. **gambol:**
Start, jerk away.

Lay not that flattering unction° to your soul,   145
That not your trespass but my madness speaks;
It will but skin and film the ulcerous place,
Whiles rank corruption, mining all within,
Infects unseen. Confess yourself to heaven,
Repent what's past, avoid what is to come,   150
And do not spread the compost° on the weeds
To make them ranker. Forgive me this my virtue,
For in the fatness of these pursy° times
Virtue itself of vice must pardon beg,
Yea, curb and woo° for leave to do him good.   155
QUEEN: O Hamlet, thou hast cleft my heart in twain.
HAMLET: O, throw away the worser part of it,
And [live] the purer with the other half.
Good night, but go not to my uncle's bed —
Assume a virtue, if you have it not.   160
That monster custom, who all sense doth eat,°
Of habits devil,° is angel yet in this,
That to the use of actions fair and good
He likewise gives a frock or livery
That aptly is put on.° Refrain [to-]night,   165
And that shall lend a kind of easiness
To the next abstinence, the next more easy;
For use° almost can change the stamp of nature,
And either [. . . . °] the devil or throw him out
With wondrous potency. Once more good night,   170
And when you are desirous to be blest,°
I'll blessing beg of you. For this same lord,

                           [*Pointing to Polonius.*]
I do repent; but heaven hath pleas'd it so
To punish me with this, and this with me,
That I must be their scourge and minister.°   175

---

145. flattering unction: Soothing ointment.   **151. compost:** Manure.   **153. pursy:**
Puffy, out of condition.   **155. curb and woo:** Bow and entreat.   **161. all . . . eat:**
Wears away all natural feeling.   **162. Of habits devil:** I.e. though it acts like a devil in
establishing bad habits. Most editors read (in lines 161–62) *eat / Of habits evil*, following
Theobald.   **164–65. frock . . . on:** I.e. a "habit" or customary garment, readily put on
without need of any decision.   **168. use:** Habit.   **169.** A word seems to be wanting after
either; for conjectures see the Textual Notes.   **171. desirous . . . blest:** I.e. repentant.
175. scourge and minister: The agent of heavenly justice against human crime. *Scourge*
suggests a permissive cruelty (Tamburlaine was the "scourge of God"), but "woe to him
by whom the offense cometh"; the scourge must suffer for the evil it performs.

I will bestow° him, and will answer° well
The death I gave him. So again good night.
I must be cruel only to be kind.
This bad begins and worse remains behind.°
One word more, good lady.
QUEEN: What shall I do?   180
HAMLET: Not this, by no means, that I bid you do:
Let the bloat king tempt you again to bed,
Pinch wanton on your cheek, call you his mouse,
And let him, for a pair of reechy° kisses,
Or paddling in your neck with his damn'd fingers,   185
Make you to ravel all this matter out,
That I essentially am not in madness,
But mad in craft. 'Twere good you let him know,
For who that's but a queen, fair, sober, wise,
Would from a paddock,° from a bat, a gib,°   190
Such dear concernings° hide? Who would do so?
No, in despite of sense and secrecy,
Unpeg the basket° on the house's top,
Let the birds fly, and like the famous ape,°
To try conclusions° in the basket creep,   195
And break your own neck down.°
QUEEN: Be thou assur'd, if words be made of breath,
And breath of life, I have no life to breathe
What thou hast said to me.
HAMLET: I must to England, you know that?
QUEEN: Alack,   200
I had forgot. 'Tis so concluded on.
HAMLET: There's letters seal'd, and my two schoolfellows,
Whom I will trust as I will adders fang'd,
They bear the mandate, they must sweep my way
And marshal me to knavery.° Let it work,   205
For 'tis the sport to have the enginer°
Hoist with° his own petar,° an't shall go hard

---

176. bestow: Dispose of.   **answer:** Answer for.   **179. behind:** To come.   **184. reechy:**
Filthy.   **190. paddock:** Toad.   **gib:** Tom-cat.   **191. dear concernings:** Matters of intense concern.   **193. Unpeg the basket:** Open the door of the cage.   **194. famous
ape:** The actual story has been lost.   **195. conclusions:** Experiments (to see whether he
too can fly if he enters the cage and then leaps out).   **196. down:** By the fall.   **205.
knavery:** Some knavish scheme against me.   **206. enginer:** Deviser of military "en-
gines" or contrivances.   **207. Hoist with:** Blown up by.   **petar:** Petard, bomb.

But I will delve one yard below their mines,
And blow them at the moon. O, 'tis most sweet
When in one line two crafts° directly meet.   210
This man shall set me packing;°
I'll lug the guts into the neighbor room.
Mother, good night indeed. This counsellor
Is now most still, most secret, and most grave,
Who was in life a foolish prating knave.   215
Come, sir, to draw toward an end° with you.
Good night, mother.
           Exeunt [severally, Hamlet tugging in Polonius].

[ACT 4, Scene 1]°

Enter KING *and* QUEEN *with* ROSENCRANTZ *and* GUILDENSTERN.

KING: There's matter in these sighs, these profound heaves —
You must translate, 'tis fit we understand them.
Where is your son?
QUEEN: Bestow this place on us a little while.
           [*Exeunt Rosencrantz and Guildenstern.*]
Ah, mine own lord, what have I seen to-night!   5
KING: What, Gertrude? How does Hamlet?
QUEEN: Mad as the sea and wind when both contend
Which is the mightier. In his lawless fit,
Behind the arras hearing something stir,
Whips out his rapier, cries, "A rat, a rat!"   10
And in this brainish apprehension° kills
The unseen good old man.
KING: O heavy deed!
It had been so with us had we been there.
His liberty is full of threats to all,
To you yourself, to us, to every one.   15
Alas, how shall this bloody deed be answer'd?°
It will be laid to us, whose providence°
Should have kept short,° restrain'd, and out of haunt°

---

210. **crafts:** Plots. 211. **packing:** (1) Taking on a load; (2) leaving in a hurry. **216. draw . . . end:** Finish my conversation. **4.1. Location:** The castle. **11. brainish apprehension:** Crazy notion. **16. answer'd:** I.e. satisfactorily accounted for to the public. **17. providence:** Foresight. **18. short:** On a short leash. **out of haunt:** Away from other people.

This mad young man; but so much was our love,
We would not understand what was most fit,   20
But like the owner of a foul disease,
To keep it from divulging,° let it feed
Even on the pith of life. Where is he gone?
QUEEN: To draw apart the body he hath kill'd,
O'er whom his very madness, like some ore°   25
Among a mineral° of metals base,
Shows itself pure: 'a weeps for what is done.
KING: O Gertrude, come away!
The sun no sooner shall the mountains touch,
But we will ship him hence, and this vile deed   30
We must with all our majesty and skill
Both countenance and excuse. Ho, Guildenstern!

Enter ROSENCRANTZ *and* GUILDENSTERN.

Friends both, go join you with some further aid:
Hamlet in madness hath Polonius slain,
And from his mother's closet hath he dragg'd him.   35
Go seek him out, speak fair, and bring the body
Into the chapel. I pray you haste in this.
                    [*Exeunt Rosencrantz and Guildenstern.*]
Come, Gertrude, we'll call up our wisest friends
And let them know both what we mean to do
And what's untimely done, [. . . . °]   40
Whose whisper o'er the world's diameter,
As level° as the cannon to his blank,°
Transports his pois'ned shot, may miss our name,
And hit the woundless° air. O, come away!
My soul is full of discord and dismay.   *Exeunt.*   45

[**Scene 2**]°

Enter HAMLET.

HAMLET: Safely stow'd.
[GENTLEMEN: *(Within.)* Hamlet! Lord Hamlet!]

---

22. divulging: Being revealed.   **25. ore:** Vein of gold.   **26. mineral:** Mine.   **40.**
Some words are wanting at the end of the line. Capell's conjecture, *so, haply, slander,*
probably indicates the intended sense of the passage.   **42. As level:** With aim as good.
blank: Target.   **44. woundless:** Incapable of being hurt.   **4.2. Location:** The castle.

[HAMLET]: But soft, what noise? Who calls on Hamlet? O, here they come.

Enter ROSENCRANTZ *and* [GUILDENSTERN].

ROSENCRANTZ: What have you done, my lord, with the dead body? 5

HAMLET: [Compounded] it with dust, whereto 'tis kin.

ROSENCRANTZ: Tell us where 'tis, that we may take it thence, And bear it to the chapel.

HAMLET: Do not believe it.

ROSENCRANTZ: Believe what? 10

HAMLET: That I can keep your counsel and not mine own. Besides, to be demanded of° a spunge,° what replication° should be made by the son of a king?

ROSENCRANTZ: Take you me for a spunge, my lord?

HAMLET: Ay, sir, that soaks up the King's countenance,° his re- 15 wards, his authorities. But such officers do the King best service in the end: he keeps them, like [an ape] an apple, in the corner of his jaw, first mouth'd, to be last swallow'd. When he needs what you have glean'd, it is but squeezing you, and, spunge, you shall be dry again. 20

ROSENCRANTZ: I understand you not, my lord.

HAMLET: I am glad of it, a knavish speech sleeps° in a foolish ear.

ROSENCRANTZ: My lord, you must tell us where the body is, and go with us to the King. 25

HAMLET: The body is with the King, but the King is not with the body.° The King is a thing —

GUILDENSTERN: A thing, my lord?

HAMLET: Of nothing,° bring me to him. [Hide fox, and all after.]°   *Exeunt.* 30

---

12. demanded of: Questioned by.   **spunge:** Sponge.   **replication:** Reply.   **15. countenance:** Favor.   **22. sleeps:** Is meaningless.   **26–27. The body . . . the body:** Possibly alluding to the legal fiction that the king's dignity is separate from his mortal body.   **29. Of nothing:** Of no account. Cf. "Man is like a thing of nought, his time passeth away like a shadow" (Psalm 144:4 in the Prayer Book version). "Hamlet at once insults the King and hints that his days are numbered" (Dover Wilson).   **29–30. Hide . . . after:** Probably a cry in some game resembling hide-and-seek.

[Scene 3]°

Enter KING *and two or three.*

KING: I have sent to seek him, and to find the body.
How dangerous is it that this man goes loose!
Yet must not we put the strong law on him.
He's lov'd of the distracted° multitude,
Who like not in their judgment, but their eyes,   5
And where 'tis so, th' offender's scourge° is weigh'd,
But never the offense. To bear° all smooth and even,
This sudden sending him away must seem
Deliberate pause.° Diseases desperate grown
By desperate appliance are reliev'd,   10
Or not at all.

Enter ROSENCRANTZ.

　　　　　　　　How now, what hath befall'n?
ROSENCRANTZ: Where the dead body is bestow'd, my lord,
We cannot get from him.
KING:　　　　　　　　　But where is he?
ROSENCRANTZ: Without, my lord, guarded, to know your plea-
sure.
KING: Bring him before us.
ROSENCRANTZ:　　　　　　Ho, bring in the lord.   15

They [HAMLET *and* GUILDENSTERN] *enter.*

KING: Now, Hamlet, where's Polonius?
HAMLET: At supper.
KING: At supper? where?
HAMLET: Not where he eats, but where 'a is eaten; a certain
convocation of politic° worms are e'en° at him. Your worm   20
is your only emperor for diet:° we fat all creatures else to fat
us, and we fat ourselves for maggots; your fat king and your
lean beggar is but variable service,° two dishes, but to one
table — that's the end.
KING: Alas, alas!   25

4.3. Location: The castle.　**4. distracted:** Unstable.　**6. scourge:** I.e. punishment.
7. bear: Manage.　**8–9. must . . . pause:** I.e. must be represented as a maturely considered decision.　**20. politic:** Crafty, prying; "such worms as might breed in a politician's
corpse" (Dowden).　**e'en:** Even now.　**21. for diet:** With respect to what it eats.
23. variable service: Different courses of a meal.

HAMLET: A man may fish with the worm that hath eat of a king, and eat of the fish that hath fed of that worm.
KING: What dost thou mean by this?
HAMLET: Nothing but to show you how a king may go a progress° through the guts of a beggar.   30
KING: Where is Polonius?
HAMLET: In heaven, send thither to see; if your messenger find him not there, seek him i' th' other place yourself. But if indeed you find him not within this month, you shall nose him as you go up the stairs into the lobby.   35
KING: [*To Attendants.*] Go seek him there.
HAMLET: 'A will stay till you come.   [*Exeunt Attendants.*]
KING: Hamlet, this deed, for thine especial safety —
  Which we do tender,° as we dearly° grieve
  For that which thou hast done — must send thee hence   40
  [With fiery quickness]; therefore prepare thyself,
  The bark is ready, and the wind at help,°
  Th'° associates tend,° and every thing is bent°
  For England.
HAMLET: For England.
KING: Ay, Hamlet.
HAMLET: Good.
KING: So is it, if thou knew'st our purposes.   45
HAMLET: I see a cherub that sees them.° But come, for England! Farewell, dear mother.
KING: Thy loving father, Hamlet.
HAMLET: My mother: father and mother is man and wife, man and wife is one flesh — so, my mother. Come, for England!   50
                         Exit.
KING: Follow him at foot,° tempt him with speed aboard.
  Delay it not, I'll have him hence to-night.
  Away, for every thing is seal'd and done
  That else leans on° th' affair. Pray you make haste.
          [*Exeunt Rosencrantz and Guildenstern.*]
  And, England,° if my love thou hold'st at aught —   55
  As my great power thereof may give thee sense,

---

30. progress: Royal journey of state.   **39. tender:** Regard with tenderness, hold dear. **dearly:** With intense feeling.   **42. at help:** Favorable.   **43. Th':** Thy.   **tend:** Await. **bent:** Made ready.   **46. I . . . them:** I.e. heaven sees them.   **51. at foot:** At his heels, close behind.   **54. leans on:** Relates to.   **55. England:** King of England.

Since yet thy cicatrice° looks raw and red
After the Danish sword, and thy free awe
Pays° homage to us — thou mayst not coldly set°
Our sovereign process,° which imports at full,   60
By letters congruing to° that effect,
The present° death of Hamlet. Do it, England,
For like the hectic° in my blood he rages,
And thou must cure me. Till I know 'tis done,
How e'er my haps,° my joys [were] ne'er [begun].   *Exit.*   65

[Scene 4]°

Enter FORTINBRAS *with his army over the stage.*

FORTINBRAS: Go, captain, from me greet the Danish king.
    Tell him that by his license Fortinbras
    Craves the conveyance° of a promis'd march
    Over his kingdom. You know the rendezvous.
    If that his Majesty would aught with us,   5
    We shall express our duty in his eye,°
    And let him know so.
CAPTAIN: I will do't, my lord.
FORTINBRAS: Go softly° on.   [*Exeunt all but the Captain.*]

Enter HAMLET, ROSENCRANTZ, [GUILDENSTERN,] *etc.*

HAMLET: Good sir, whose powers° are these?
CAPTAIN: They are of Norway, sir.   10
HAMLET: How purpos'd, sir, I pray you?
CAPTAIN: Against some part of Poland.
HAMLET: Who commands them, sir?
CAPTAIN: The nephew to old Norway, Fortinbras.
HAMLET: Goes it against the main° of Poland, sir,
    Or for some frontier?   15
CAPTAIN: Truly to speak, and with no addition,
    We go to gain a little patch of ground
    That hath in it no profit but the name.

---

57. cicatrice: Scar.   **58–59. thy . . . Pays:** Your fear makes you pay voluntarily.   **59. coldly set:** Undervalue, disregard.   **60. process:** Command.   **61. congruing to:** In accord with.   **62. present:** Immediate.   **63. hectic:** Continuous fever.   **65. haps:** Fortunes.   **4.4. Location:** The Danish coast, near the castle.   **3. conveyance of:** Escort for.   **6. eye:** Presence.   **8. softly:** Slowly.   **9. powers:** Forces.   **15. main:** Main territory.

To pay° five ducats, five, I would not farm° it;   20
Nor will it yield to Norway or the Pole
A ranker° rate, should it be sold in fee.°
HAMLET: Why then the Polack never will defend it.
CAPTAIN: Yes, it is already garrison'd.
HAMLET: Two thousand souls and twenty thousand ducats   25
Will not debate° the question of this straw.
This is th' imposthume° of much wealth and peace,
That inward breaks, and shows no cause without
Why the man dies. I humbly thank you, sir.
CAPTAIN: God buy you, sir.   [Exit.]
ROSENCRANTZ: Will't please you go, my lord?   30
HAMLET: I'll be with you straight — go a little before.
                              [Exeunt all but Hamlet.]
How all occasions do inform against° me,
And spur my dull revenge! What is a man,
If his chief good and market° of his time
Be but to sleep and feed? a beast, no more.   35
Sure He that made us with such large discourse,°
Looking before and after, gave us not
That capability and godlike reason
To fust° in us unus'd. Now whether it be
Bestial oblivion,° or some craven scruple   40
Of thinking too precisely on th' event° —
A thought which quarter'd hath but one part wisdom
And ever three parts coward — I do not know
Why yet I live to say, "This thing's to do,"
Sith I have cause, and will, and strength, and means   45
To do't. Examples gross° as earth exhort me:
Witness this army of such mass and charge,°
Led by a delicate and tender prince,
Whose spirit with divine ambition puff'd
Makes mouths at° the invisible° event,   50
Exposing what is mortal and unsure
To all that fortune, death, and danger dare,

20. To pay: I.e. for an annual rent of.   farm: Lease.   22. ranker: Higher.   in fee: Outright.   26. Will not debate: I.e. will scarcely be enough to fight out.   27. imposthume:
Abscess.   32. inform against: Denounce, accuse.   34. market: Purchase, profit.
36. discourse: Reasoning power.   39. fust: Grow moldy.   40. oblivion: Forgetful-
ness.   41. event: Outcome.   46. gross: Large, obvious.   47. mass and charge: Size
and expense.   50. Makes mouths at: Treats scornfully.   invisible: I.e. unforeseeable.

Even for an egg-shell. Rightly to be great
Is not to° stir without great argument,°
But greatly° to find quarrel in a straw   55
When honor's at the stake. How stand I then,
That have a father kill'd, a mother stain'd,
Excitements of ° my reason and my blood,
And let all sleep, while to my shame I see
The imminent death of twenty thousand men,   60
That for a fantasy° and trick° of fame
Go to their graves like beds, fight for a plot
Whereon the numbers cannot try the cause,°
Which is not tomb enough and continent°
To hide the slain? O, from this time forth,   65
My thoughts be bloody, or be nothing worth!   *Exit.*

[Scene 5]°

Enter HORATIO, [QUEEN] GERTRUDE, *and a* GENTLEMAN.

QUEEN: I will not speak with her.°
GENTLEMAN: She is importunate, indeed distract.
    Her mood will needs be pitied.
QUEEN: What would she have?
GENTLEMAN: She speaks much of her father, says she hears
    There's tricks i' th' world, and hems, and beats her heart,   5
    Spurns enviously at straws,° speaks things in doubt°
    That carry but half sense. Her speech° is nothing,
    Yet the unshaped use° of it doth move
    The hearers to collection;° they yawn at° it,
    And botch° the words up fit to their own thoughts,   10
    Which° as her winks and nods and gestures yield them,
    Indeed would make one think there might be thought,°
    Though nothing sure, yet much unhappily.

---

54. Is not to: I.e. is *not* not to.   **argument:** Cause.   **55. greatly:** Nobly.   **58. Excitements of:** Urgings by.   **61. fantasy:** Caprice.   **trick:** Trifle.   **63. Whereon . . . cause:** Which isn't large enough to let the opposing armies engage upon it.   **64. continent:** Container.   **4.5. Location:** The castle.   **1–20.** See the Textual Notes for the lines that replace these in Q1.   **6. Spurns . . . straws:** Spitefully takes offense at trifles. **in doubt:** Obscurely.   **7. Her speech:** What she says.   **8. unshaped use:** Distracted manner.   **9. collection:** Attempts to gather the meaning.   **yawn at:** Gape eagerly (as if to swallow). Most editors adopt the F1 reading *aim at*.   **10. botch:** Patch.   **11. Which:** I.e. the words.   **12. thought:** Inferred, conjectured.

HORATIO: 'Twere good she were spoken with, for she may
  strew
Dangerous conjectures in ill-breeding° minds.   15
[QUEEN:] Let her come in.   [*Exit Gentleman.*]
[*Aside.*] To my sick soul, as sin's true nature is,
Each toy° seems prologue to some great amiss,°
So full of artless jealousy° is guilt,
It spills° itself in fearing to be spilt.   ·20

Enter OPHELIA [*distracted, with her hair down, playing on a
lute*].

OPHELIA: Where is the beauteous majesty of Denmark?
QUEEN: How now, Ophelia?
OPHELIA: "How should I your true-love know   *She sings.*
      From another one?°
      By his cockle hat° and staff,°   25
      And his sandal shoon."°
QUEEN: Alas, sweet lady, what imports this song?
OPHELIA: Say you? Nay, pray you mark.
      "He is dead and gone, lady,   *Song.*
      He is dead and gone,   30
      At his head a grass-green turf,
      At his heels a stone."
  O ho!
QUEEN: Nay, but, Ophelia —
OPHELIA: Pray you mark.   35
  [*Sings.*] "White his shroud as the mountain snow" —

Enter KING.

QUEEN: Alas, look here, my lord.
OPHELIA: "Larded° all with sweet flowers,   *Song.*
      Which bewept to the ground did not° go

---

15. ill-breeding: Conceiving ill thoughts, prone to think the worst.   **18. toy:** Trifle.
amiss: Calamity.   **19. artless jealousy:** Uncontrolled suspicion.   **20. spills:** Destroys.
23–24. These lines resemble a passage in an earlier ballad beginning "As you came from
the holy land / Of Walsingham." Probably all the song fragments sung by Ophelia were
familiar to the Globe audience, but only one other line (184) is from a ballad still extant.
25. cockle hat: Hat bearing a cockle shell, the badge of a pilgrim to the shrine of St.
James of Compostela in Spain.   **staff:** Another mark of a pilgrim.   **26. shoon:** Shoes
(already an archaic form in Shakespeare's day).   **38. Larded:** Adorned.   **39. not:** Contrary to the expected sense, and unmetrical; explained as Ophelia's alteration of the line to
accord with the facts of Polonius's burial (see line 83).

    With true-love showers."   40
KING: How do you, pretty lady?
OPHELIA: Well, God dild° you! They say the owl° was a baker's
    daughter. Lord, we know what we are, but know not what
    we may be. God be at your table!
KING: Conceit° upon her father.   45
OPHELIA: Pray let's have no words of this, but when they ask
    you what it means, say you this:
        "To-morrow is Saint Valentine's day,   *Song.*
        All in the morning betime,
        And I a maid at your window,   50
        To be your Valentine.

        "Then up he rose and donn'd his clo'es,
        And dupp'd° the chamber-door,
        Let in the maid, that out a maid
        Never departed more."   55
KING: Pretty Ophelia!
OPHELIA: Indeed without an oath I'll make an end on't.
    [*Sings.*] "By Gis,° and by Saint Charity,
        Alack, and fie for shame!
        Young men will do't if they come to't,   60
        By Cock,° they are to blame.

        "Quoth she, 'Before you tumbled me,
        You promis'd me to wed.'"
    (He answers.)
        "'So would I 'a' done, by yonder sun,   65
        And° thou hadst not come to my bed.'"
KING: How long hath she been thus?
OPHELIA: I hope all will be well. We must be patient, but I can-
    not choose but weep to think they would lay him i' th' cold
    ground. My brother shall know of it, and so I thank you for   70
    your good counsel. Come, my coach! Good night, ladies,
    good night. Sweet ladies, good night, good night.   [*Exit.*]
KING: Follow her close, give her good watch, I pray you.
                                        [*Exit Horatio.*]

---

42. dild: Yield, reward.   **owl:** Alluding to the legend of a baker's daughter whom Jesus
turned into an owl because she did not respond generously to his request for bread.   **45.**
Conceit: Fanciful brooding.   **53. dupp'd:** Opened.   **58. Gis:** Contraction of *Jesus*.
61. Cock: Corruption of *God*.   **66. And:** If.

O, this is the poison of deep grief, it springs
All from her father's death — and now behold!   75
O Gertrude, Gertrude,
When sorrows come, they come not single spies,°
But in battalions: first, her father slain;
Next, your son gone, and he most violent author
Of his own just remove; the people muddied,°   80
Thick and unwholesome in [their] thoughts and whispers
For good Polonius' death; and we have done but greenly°
In hugger-mugger° to inter him; poor Ophelia
Divided from herself and her fair judgment,
Without the which we are pictures, or mere beasts;   85
Last, and as much containing as all these,
Her brother is in secret come from France,
Feeds on this wonder, keeps himself in clouds,°
And wants° not buzzers° to infect his ear
With pestilent speeches of his father's death,   90
Wherein necessity, of matter beggar'd,°
Will nothing stick our person to arraign°
In ear and ear. O my dear Gertrude, this,
Like to a murd'ring-piece,° in many places
Gives me superfluous death.   *A noise within.*
[QUEEN: Alack, what noise is this?]   95
KING: Attend!
Where is my Swissers?° Let them guard the door.

Enter a MESSENGER.

What is the matter?
MESSENGER: Save yourself, my lord!
The ocean, overpeering of his list,°
Eats not the flats with more impiteous haste   100
Than young Laertes, in a riotous head,°
O'erbears your officers. The rabble call him lord,

---

77. **spies:** I.e. soldiers sent ahead of the main force to reconnoiter, scouts.   80. **mud-died:** Confused.   82. **greenly:** Unwisely.   83. **In hugger-mugger:** Secretly and hast-ily.   88. **in clouds:** I.e. in cloudy surmise and suspicion (rather than the light of fact).   89. **wants:** Lacks.   **buzzers:** Whispering informers.   91. **of matter beggar'd:** Desti-tute of facts.   92. **nothing . . . arraign:** Scruple not at all to charge me with the crime.   94. **murd'ring-piece:** Cannon firing a scattering charge.   97. **Swissers:** Swiss guards.   99. **overpeering . . . list:** Rising higher than its shores.   101. **in . . . head:** With a re-bellious force.

And as° the world were now but to begin,
Antiquity forgot, custom not known,
The ratifiers and props of every word,°   105
[They] cry, "Choose we, Laertes shall be king!"
Caps, hands, and tongues applaud it to the clouds,
"Laertes shall be king, Laertes king!"   *A noise within.*
QUEEN: How cheerfully on the false trail they cry!
O, this is counter,° you false Danish dogs!   110

Enter LAERTES *with others.*

KING: The doors are broke.
LAERTES: Where is this king? Sirs, stand you all without.
ALL: No, let's come in.
LAERTES: I pray you give me leave.
ALL: We will, we will.
LAERTES: I thank you, keep the door. [*Exeunt Laertes' follow-*
    ers.] O thou vile king,   115
    Give me my father!
QUEEN: Calmly, good Laertes.
LAERTES: That drop of blood that's calm proclaims me bastard,
    Cries cuckold to my father, brands the harlot
    Even here between the chaste unsmirched brow
    Of my true mother.
KING: What is the cause, Laertes,   120
    That thy rebellion looks so giant-like?
    Let him go, Gertrude, do not fear° our person:
    There's such divinity doth hedge a king
    That treason can but peep to what it would,°
    Acts little of his will. Tell me, Laertes,   125
    Why thou art thus incens'd. Let him go, Gertrude.
    Speak, man.
LAERTES: Where is my father?
KING: Dead.
QUEEN: But not by him.
KING: Let him demand his fill.
LAERTES: How came he dead? I'll not be juggled with.   130
    To hell, allegiance! vows, to the blackest devil!

___

103. as: As if.   **105. word:** Pledge, promise.   **110. counter:** On the wrong scent (literally, following the scent backward).   **122. fear:** Fear for.   **124. would:** I.e. would
like to do.

Conscience and grace, to the profoundest pit!
I dare damnation. To this point I stand,
That both the worlds I give to negligence,°
Let come what comes, only I'll be reveng'd   135
Most throughly° for my father.
KING: Who shall stay you?
LAERTES: My will, not all the world's:°
And for my means, I'll husband them so well,
They shall go far with little.
KING: Good Laertes,
If you desire to know the certainty   140
Of your dear father, is't writ in your revenge
That, swoopstake,° you will draw both friend and foe,
Winner and loser?
LAERTES: None but his enemies.
KING: Will you know them then?
LAERTES: To his good friends thus wide I'll ope my arms,   145
And like the kind life-rend'ring pelican,°
Repast them with my blood.
KING: Why, now you speak
Like a good child° and a true gentleman.
That I am guiltless of your father's death,
And am most sensibly° in grief for it,   150
It shall as level° to your judgment 'pear
As day does to your eye.
                 A noise within: "Let her come in!"
LAERTES: How now, what noise is that?

Enter OPHELIA.

O heat, dry up my brains! tears seven times salt
Burn out the sense and virtue° of mine eye!   155
By heaven, thy madness shall be paid with weight
[Till] our scale turn the beam. O rose of May!
Dear maid, kind sister, sweet Ophelia!
O heavens, is't possible a young maid's wits

---

134. both . . . negligence: I.e. I don't care what the consequences are in this world or in the next. **136. throughly:** Thoroughly. **137. world's:** I.c. world's will. **142. swoopstake:** Sweeping up everything without discrimination (modern *sweepstake*). **146. pelican:** The female pelican was believed to draw blood from her own breast to nourish her young. **148. good child:** Faithful son. **150. sensibly:** Feelingly. **151. level:** Plain. **155. virtue:** Faculty.

Should be as mortal as [an old] man's life?   160
[Nature is fine in° love, and where 'tis fine,
It sends some precious instance° of itself
After the thing it loves.]
OPHELIA: "They bore him barefac'd on the bier,   *Song.*
   [Hey non nonny, nonny, hey nonny,]   165
   And in his grave rain'd many a tear" —
Fare you well, my dove!
LAERTES: Hadst thou they wits and didst persuade° revenge,
It could not move thus.
OPHELIA: You must sing, "A-down, a-down," and you call him   170
a-down-a.° O how the wheel° becomes it! It is the false
steward, that stole his master's daughter.
LAERTES: This nothing's more than matter.°
OPHELIA: There's rosemary, that's for remembrance; pray you,
love, remember. And there is pansies, that's for thoughts.   175
LAERTES: A document in madness,° thoughts and remembrance
fitted.
OPHELIA: [*To Claudius.*] There's fennel for you, and colum-
bines.° [*To Gertrude.*] There's rue° for you, and here's
some for me; we may call it herb of grace a' Sundays. You   180
may wear your rue with a difference.° There's a daisy. I
would give you some violets,° but they wither'd all when
my father died. They say 'a made a good end —
[*Sings.*] "For bonny sweet Robin is all my joy."
LAERTES: Thought° and afflictions, passion, hell itself,   185
She turns to favor° and to prettiness.
OPHELIA: "And will 'a not come again?   *Song.*
      And will 'a not come again?
      No, no, he is dead,

---

161. fine in: Refined or spiritualized by.   **162. instance:** Proof, token. So delicate is
Ophelia's love for her father that her sanity has pursued him into the grave.   **168. persuade:** Argue logically for.   **170–71. and . . . a-down-a:** "If he indeed agrees
that Polonius is 'a-down,' i.e. fallen low" (Dover Wilson).   **171. wheel:** Refrain (?) or
spinning-wheel, at which women sang ballads (?).   **173. matter:** Lucid speech.   **176.
A document in madness:** A lesson contained in mad talk.   **178, 179. fennel, colum-
bines:** Symbols respectively of flattery and ingratitude.   **179. rue:** Symbolic of sorrow
and repentance.   **181. with a difference:** I.e. to represent a different cause of sorrow.
Difference is a term from heraldry, meaning a variation in a coat of arms made to distinguish different members of a family.   **181, 182. daisy, violets:** Symbolic respectively of
dissembling and faithfulness. It is not clear who are the recipients of these.   **185.
Thought:** Melancholy.   **186. favor:** Grace, charm.

Go to thy death-bed,   190
He never will come again.

"His beard was as white as snow,
[All] flaxen° was his pole,°
He is gone, he is gone,
And we cast away moan,   195
God 'a' mercy on his soul!"
And of all Christians' souls, [I pray God]. God buy you.
                                                    [*Exit.*]
LAERTES: Do you [see] this, O God?
KING: Laertes, I must commune with your grief,
Or you deny me right. Go but apart,   200
Make choice of whom your wisest friends you will,
And they shall hear and judge 'twixt you and me.
If by direct or by collateral° hand
They find us touch'd,° we will our kingdom give,
Our crown, our life, and all that we call ours,   205
To you in satisfaction; but if not,
By you content to lend your patience to us,
And we shall jointly labor with your soul
To give it due content.
LAERTES: Let this be so.
His means of death, his obscure funeral —   210
No trophy,° sword, nor hatchment° o'er his bones,
No noble rite nor formal ostentation° —
Cry to be heard, as 'twere from heaven to earth,
That° I must call't in question.
KING: So you shall,
And where th' offense is, let the great axe fall.   215
I pray you go with me.   *Exeunt.*

---

193. flaxen: White.   pole: Poll, head.   203. collateral: I.e., indirect.   204. touch'd:
Guilty.   211. trophy: Memorial.   hatchment: Heraldic memorial tablet.   212. formal ostentation: Fitting and customary ceremony.   214. That: So that.

[Scene 6]°

Enter HORATIO *and others.*

HORATIO: What are they that would speak with me?
GENTLEMAN: Sea-faring men, sir. They say they have letters for you.
HORATIO: Let them come in.   [*Exit Gentleman.*]
    I do not know from what part of the world   5
    I should be greeted, if not from Lord Hamlet.

Enter SAILORS.

[FIRST] SAILOR: God bless you, sir.
HORATIO: Let him bless thee too.
[FIRST] SAILOR: 'A shall, sir, and['t] please him. There's a letter
for you, sir — it came from th' embassador that was bound   10
for England — if your name be Horatio, as I am let to
know it is.
HORATIO: [*Reads.*] "Horatio, when thou shalt have overlook'd
this, give these fellows some means to the King, they have
letters for him. Ere we were two days old at sea, a pirate of   15
very warlike appointment gave us chase. Finding ourselves
too slow of sail, we put on a compell'd valor, and in the
grapple I boarded them. On the instant they got clear of
our ship, so I alone became their prisoner. They have dealt
with me like thieves of mercy,° but they knew what they   20
did: I am to do a [good] turn for them. Let the King have
the letters I have sent, and repair thou to me with as much
speed as thou wouldest fly death. I have words to speak in
thine ear will make thee dumb, yet are they much too light
for the [bore°] of the matter. These good fellows will bring   25
thee where I am. Rosencrantz and Guildenstern hold their
course for England, of them I have much to tell thee. Farewell.

                [He] that thou knowest thine,
                        Hamlet."   30

4.6. Location: The castle. See the Textual Notes for a scene unique to Q1.   **20. thieves of mercy:** Merciful thieves.   **25. bore:** Caliber, size (gunnery term).

Come, I will [give] you way for these your letters,
And do't the speedier that you may direct me
To him from whom you brought them.   *Exeunt.*

[Scene 7]°

Enter KING *and* LAERTES.

KING: Now must your conscience my acquittance seal,°
  And you must put me in your heart for friend,
  Sith you have heard, and with a knowing ear,
  That he which hath your noble father slain
  Pursued my life.
LAERTES: It well appears. But tell me   5
  Why you [proceeded] not against these feats°
  So criminal and so capital in nature,
  As by your safety,° greatness, wisdom, all things else
  You mainly° were stirr'd up.
KING: O, for two special reasons,
  Which may to you perhaps seem much unsinow'd,°   10
  But yet to me th' are strong. The Queen his mother
  Lives almost by his looks, and for myself —
  My virtue or my plague, be it either which° —
  She is so [conjunctive°] to my life and soul,
  That, as the star moves not but in his sphere,°   15
  I could not but by her. The other motive,
  Why to a public count° I might not go,
  Is the great love the general gender° bear him,
  Who, dipping all his faults in their affection,
  Work like the spring that turneth wood to stone,   20
  Convert his gyves° to graces, so that my arrows,
  Too slightly timber'd for so [loud a wind],
  Would have reverted to my bow again,

4.7. **Location:** The castle.   **1. my acquittance seal:** Ratify my acquittal, i.e. acknowledge my innocence in Polonius's death.   **6. feats:** Acts.   **8. safety:** I.e. regard for your own safety.   **9. mainly:** Powerfully.   **10. unsinow'd:** Unsinewed, i.e. weak.   **13. either which:** One or the other.   **14. conjunctive:** Closely joined.   **15. in his sphere:** By the movement of the sphere in which it is fixed (as the Ptolemaic astronomy taught).   **17. count:** Reckoning.   **18. the general gender:** Everybody.   **21. gyves:** Fetters.

But not where I have aim'd them.
LAERTES: And so have I a noble father lost,   25
A sister driven into desp'rate terms,°
Whose worth, if praises may go back again,°
Stood challenger on mount° of all the age
For her perfections — but my revenge will come.
KING: Break not your sleeps for that.° You must not think   30
That we are made of stuff so flat° and dull
That we can let our beard be shook° with° danger
And think it pastime. You shortly shall hear more.
I lov'd your father, and we love ourself,
And that, I hope, will teach you to imagine —   35

Enter a MESSENGER *with letters.*

[How now? What news?
MESSENGER: Letters, my lord, from Hamlet:]
These to your Majesty, this to the Queen.
KING: From Hamlet? Who brought them?
MESSENGER: Sailors, my lord, they say, I saw them not.
They were given me by Claudio. He receiv'd them   40
Of him that brought them.
KING: Laertes, you shall hear them.
— Leave us.   [*Exit Messenger.*]
[*Reads.*] "High and mighty, You shall know I am set
naked° on your kingdom. To-morrow shall I beg leave to
see your kingly eyes, when I shall, first asking you pardon   45
thereunto,° recount the occasion of my sudden [and more
strange] return.

[Hamlet.]"
What should this mean? Are all the rest come back?
Or is it some abuse,° and no such thing?   50
LAERTES: Know you the hand?
KING: 'Tis Hamlet's character.° "Naked"!
And in a postscript here he says "alone."
Can you devise me?°

---

26. terms: Condition.   **27. go back again:** I.e. refer to what she was before she went
mad.   **28. on mount:** Preeminent.   **30. for that:** I.e. for fear of losing your revenge.
31. flat: Spiritless.   **32. let . . . shook:** To ruffle or tweak a man's beard was an act of
insolent defiance that he could not disregard without loss of honor. Cf. 2.2.553.   **with:**
By.   **44. naked:** Destitute.   **45–46. pardon thereunto:** Permission to do so.   **50.
abuse:** Deceit.   **51. character:** Handwriting.   **53. devise me:** Explain it to me.

LAERTES: I am lost in it, my lord. But let him come,
   It warms the very sickness in my heart   55
   That I [shall] live and tell him to his teeth,
   "Thus didst thou."
KING: If it be so, Laertes —
   As how should it be so? how otherwise?° —
   Will you be rul'd by me?
LAERTES: Ay, my lord,
   So° you will o'errule me to a peace.   60
KING: To thine own peace. If he be now returned
   As [checking] at° his voyage, and that he means
   No more to undertake it, I will work him
   To an exploit, now ripe in my device,
   Under the which he shall not choose but fall;   65
   And for his death no wind of blame shall breathe,
   But even his mother shall uncharge the practice,°
   And call it accident.
LAERTES: My lord, I will be rul'd,
   The rather if you could devise it so
   That I might be the organ.°
KING: It falls right.   70
   You have been talk'd of since your travel much,
   And that in Hamlet's hearing, for a quality°
   Wherein they say you shine. Your sum of parts°
   Did not together pluck such envy from him
   As did that one, and that, in my regard,   75
   Of the unworthiest° siege.°
LAERTES: What part is that, my lord?
KING: A very riband in the cap of youth,
   Yet needful too, for youth no less becomes
   The light and careless livery that it wears
   Than settled age his sables and his weeds,°   80
   Importing health and graveness.° Two months since
   Here was a gentleman of Normandy:

---

58. As . . . otherwise: How can he have come back? Yet he obviously has.   60. So:
Provided that.   62. checking at: Turning from (like a falcon diverted from its quarry by
other prey).   67. uncharge the practice: Adjudge the plot no plot, i.e. fail to see the
plot.   70. organ: Instrument, agent.   72. quality: Skill.   73. Your . . . parts: All
your (other) accomplishments put together.   76. unworthiest: I.e. least important
(with no implication of unsuitableness).   siege: Status, position.   80. weeds: (Characteristic) garb.   81. Importing . . . graveness: Signifying prosperity and dignity.

I have seen myself, and serv'd against, the French,
And they can well on horseback,° but this gallant
Had witchcraft in't, he grew unto his seat,   85
And to such wondrous doing brought his horse,
As had he been incorps'd° and demi-natur'd°
With the brave beast. So far he topp'd [my] thought,
That I in forgery° of shapes and tricks
Come short of what he did.
LAERTES: A Norman was't?   90
KING: A Norman.
LAERTES: Upon my life, Lamord.
KING: The very same.
LAERTES: I know him well. He is the brooch° indeed
And gem of all the nation.
KING: He made confession of you,°   95
And gave you such a masterly report
For art and exercise in your defense,
And for your rapier most especial,
That he cried out 'twould be a sight indeed
If one could match you. The scrimers° of their nation   100
He swore had neither motion, guard, nor eye,
If you oppos'd them. Sir, this report of his
Did Hamlet so envenom with his envy
That he could nothing do but wish and beg
Your sudden° coming o'er to play with you.   105
Now, out of this —
LAERTES: What out of this, my lord?
KING: Laertes, was your father dear to you?
Or are you like the painting of a sorrow,
A face without a heart?
LAERTES: Why ask you this?
KING: Not that I think you did not love your father,   110
But that I know love is begun by time,°
And that I see, in passages of proof,°
Time qualifies° the spark and fire of it.

84. can . . . horseback: Are excellent riders.   87. incorps'd: Made one body.   demi-
natur'd: I.e. become half of a composite animal.   89. forgery: Mere imagining.   93.
brooch: Ornament (worn in the hat).   95. made . . . you: Acknowledged your excellence.   100. scrimers: Fencers.   105. sudden: Speedy.   111. time: I.e. a particular
set of circumstances.   112. in . . . proof: I.e. by the test of experience, by actual examples.   113. qualifies: Moderates.

There lives within the very flame of love
A kind of week° or snuff that will abate it,   115
And nothing is at a like goodness still,°
For goodness, growing to a plurisy,°
Dies in his own too much.° That we would do,
We should do when we would; for this "would" changes,
And hath abatements and delays as many   120
As there are tongues, are hands, are accidents,
And then this "should" is like a spendthrift's sigh,°
That hurts by easing.° But to the quick of th' ulcer:
Hamlet comes back. What would you undertake
To show yourself indeed your father's son   125
More than in words?
LAERTES: To cut his throat i' th' church.
KING: No place indeed should murther sanctuarize,°
Revenge should have no bounds. But, good Laertes,
Will you do this,° keep close within your chamber.
Hamlet return'd shall know you are come home.   130
We'll put on those° shall praise your excellence,
And set a double varnish° on the fame
The Frenchman gave you, bring you in fine° together,
And wager o'er your heads. He, being remiss,°
Most generous,° and free from all contriving,°   135
Will not peruse° the foils, so that with ease,
Or with a little shuffling,° you may choose
A sword unbated,° and in a [pass] of practice°
Requite him for your father.
LAERTES: I will do't,
And for [that] purpose I'll anoint my sword.   140
I bought an unction° of a mountebank,°

---

115. week: Wick.   **116. nothing . . . still:** Nothing remains forever at the same pitch of perfection.   **117. plurisy:** Plethora (a variant spelling of *pleurisy*, which was erroneously related to *plus*, stem *plur-*, "more, overmuch."   **118. too much:** Excess.   **122. spendthrift's sigh:** A sigh was supposed to draw blood from the heart.   **123. hurts by easing:** Injures us at the same time that it gives us relief.   **127. sanctuarize:** Offer asylum to.   **129. Will . . . this:** If you want to undertake this.   **131. put on those:** Incite those who.   **132. double varnish:** Second coat of varnish.   **133. in fine:** Finally.   **134. remiss:** Careless, overtrustful.   **135. generous:** Noble-minded.   **free . . . contriving:** Innocent of sharp practices.   **136. peruse:** Examine.   **137. shuffling:** Cunning exchange.   **138. unbated:** Not blunted.   **pass of practice:** Tricky thrust.   **141. unction:** Ointment.   **mountebank:** Traveling quack-doctor.

So mortal° that, but dip a knife in it,
Where it draws blood, no cataplasm° so rare,
Collected from all simples° that have virtue°
Under the moon, can save the thing from death   145
That is but scratch'd withal. I'll touch my point
With this contagion, that if I gall° him slightly,
It may be death.

KING: Let's further think of this,
Weigh what convenience both of time and means
May fit us to our shape.° If this should fail,   150
And that our drift° look through° our bad performance,
'Twere better not assay'd; therefore this project
Should have a back or second,° that might hold
If this did blast in proof.° Soft, let me see.
We'll make a solemn wager on your cunnings —   155
I ha't!
When in your motion you are hot and dry —
As° make your bouts more violent to that end —
And that he calls for drink, I'll have preferr'd° him
A chalice for the nonce,° whereon but sipping,   160
If he by chance escape your venom'd stuck,°
Our purpose may hold there. But stay, what noise?

Enter QUEEN.

QUEEN: One woe doth tread upon another's heel,
So fast they follow. Your sister's drown'd, Laertes.
LAERTES: Drown'd! O, where?   165
QUEEN: There is a willow grows askaunt° the brook,
That shows his hoary° leaves in the glassy stream,
Therewith° fantastic garlands did she make
Of crow-flowers, nettles, daisies, and long purples°
That liberal° shepherds give a grosser name,   170

---

142. **mortal:** Deadly.   143. **cataplasm:** Poultice.   144. **simples:** Medicinal herbs.
virtue: Curative power.   147. **gall:** Graze.   150. **fit . . . shape:** I.e., suit our purposes
best.   151. **drift:** Purpose.   **look through:** Become visible, be detected.   153. **back
or second:** I.e. a second plot in reserve for emergency.   154. **blast in proof:** Blow up
while being tried (an image from gunnery).   158. **As:** I.e. and you should.   159.
preferr'd: Offered to. Most editors adopt the F1 reading *prepar'd*.   160. **nonce:** Occasion.   161. **stuck:** Thrust (from *stoccado*, a fencing term).   166. **askaunt:** Sideways
over.   167. **hoary:** Grey-white.   168. **Therewith:** I.e. with willow branches.   169.
long purples: Wild orchids.   170. **liberal:** Free-spoken.

But our cull-cold° maids do dead men's fingers call them.
There on the pendant boughs her crownet° weeds
Clamb'ring to hang, an envious sliver° broke,
When down her weedy trophies and herself
Fell in the weeping brook. Her clothes spread wide,   175
And mermaid-like awhile they bore her up,
Which time she chaunted snatches of old lauds,°
As one incapable° of her own distress,
Or like a creature native and indued°
Unto that element. But long it could not be   180
Till that her garments, heavy with their drink,
Pull'd the poor wretch from her melodious lay
To muddy death.
LAERTES: Alas, then she is drown'd?
QUEEN: Drown'd, drown'd.
LAERTES: Too much of water hast thou, poor Ophelia,   185
And therefore I forbid my tears; but yet
It° is our trick,° Nature her custom holds,
Let shame say what it will; when these° are gone,
The woman will be out.° Adieu, my lord,
I have a speech a' fire that fain would blaze,   190
But that this folly drowns it.   *Exit.*
KING: Let's follow, Gertrude.
How much I had to do to calm his rage!
Now fear I this will give it start again,
Therefore let's follow.   *Exeunt.*

ACT 5, Scene 1]°

Enter two CLOWNS° [*with spades and mattocks*].

FIRST CLOWN: Is she to be buried in Christian burial when she
willfully seeks her own salvation?
SECOND CLOWN: I tell thee she is, therefore make her grave
straight.° The crowner° hath sate on her, and finds it Christian burial.   5

171. cull-cold: Chaste. 172. crownet: Made into coronets. 173. envious sliver:
Malicious branch. 177. lauds: Hymns. 178. incapable: Insensible. 179. indued:
Habituated. 187. It: I.e. weeping. trick: Natural way. 188. these: These tears.
189. The woman . . . out: My womanish traits will be gone for good. 5.1. Location: A churchyard. o.s.d. Clowns: Rustics. 4. straight: Immediately. crowner:
coroner.

FIRST CLOWN: How can that be, unless she drown'd herself in
    her own defense?
SECOND CLOWN: Why, 'tis found so.
FIRST CLOWN: It must be [*se offendendo°*], it cannot be else. For
    here lies the point: if I drown myself wittingly, it argues an   10
    act, and an act hath three branches — it is to act, to do, to
    perform; [argal°], she drown'd herself wittingly.
SECOND CLOWN: Nay, but hear you, goodman delver —
FIRST CLOWN: Give me leave. Here° lies the water; good. Here
    stands the man; good. If the man go to this water and   15
    drown himself, it is, will he, nill he,° he goes, mark you
    that. But if the water come to him and drown him, he
    drowns not himself; argal, he that is not guilty of his own
    death shortens not his own life.
SECOND CLOWN: But is this law?   20
FIRST CLOWN: Ay, marry, is't — crowner's quest° law.
SECOND CLOWN: Will you ha' the truth an't? If this had not
    been a gentlewoman, she should have been buried out a'
    Christian burial.
FIRST CLOWN: Why, there thou say'st, and the more pity that   25
    great folk should have count'nance in this world to drown
    or hang themselves, more than their even-Christen.°
    Come, my spade. There is no ancient gentlemen but
    gard'ners, ditchers, and grave-makers; they hold up Adam's
    profession.   30
SECOND CLOWN: Was he a gentleman?
FIRST CLOWN: 'A was the first that ever bore arms.
[SECOND CLOWN: Why, he had none.°
FIRST CLOWN: What, art a heathen? How dost thou understand
    the Scripture? The Scripture says Adam digg'd; could he   35
    dig without arms?] I'll put another question to thee. If
    thou answerest me not to the purpose, confess thyself —
SECOND CLOWN: Go to.
FIRST CLOWN: What is he that builds stronger than either the
    mason, the shipwright, or the carpenter?   40

---

9. *se offendendo*: Blunder for *se defendendo*, "in self-defense."   **12. argal:** Blunder for
ergo, "therefore."   **14–19. Here . . . life:** Alluding to a very famous suicide case, that of
Sir James Hales, a judge who drowned himself in 1554; it was long cited in the courts.
The clown gives a garbled account of the defense summing-up and the verdict.   **16. nill
he:** Will he not.   **21. quest:** Inquest.   **27. even-Christen:** Fellow-Christians.   **33.
none:** I.e. no coat of arms.

SECOND CLOWN: The gallows-maker, for that outlives a thou-
sand tenants.
FIRST CLOWN: I like thy wit well, in good faith. The gallows
does well; but how does it well? It does well to those that
do ill. Now thou dost ill to say the gallows is built stronger   45
than the church; argal, the gallows may do well to thee.
To't again, come.
SECOND CLOWN: Who builds stronger than a mason, a ship-
wright, or a carpenter?
FIRST CLOWN: Ay, tell me that, and unyoke.°   50
SECOND CLOWN: Marry, now I can tell.
FIRST CLOWN: To't.
SECOND CLOWN: Mass,° I cannot tell.

Enter HAMLET *and* HORATIO [*afar off*].

FIRST CLOWN: Cudgel thy brains no more about it, for your dull
ass will not mend his pace with beating, and when you are   55
ask'd this question next, say "a grave-maker": the houses
he makes lasts till doomsday. Go get thee in, and fetch me
a sup of liquor.   [*Exit Second Clown. First Clown digs.*]
"In youth when I did love, did love,   *Song.*
    Methought it was very sweet,   60
    To contract — O — the time for — a — my behove,°
    O, methought there — a — was nothing — a — meet."
HAMLET: Has this fellow no feeling of his business? 'a sings in
grave-making.
HORATIO: Custom° hath made it in him a property of easiness.°   65
HAMLET: 'Tis e'en so, the hand of little employment hath the
daintier sense.°
FIRST CLOWN: "But age with his stealing steps   *Song.*
    Hath clawed me in his clutch,
    And hath shipped me into the land,   70
    As if I had never been such."
[*Throws up a shovelful of earth with a skull in it.*]

---

50. unyoke: I.e. cease to labor, call it a day.   **53. Mass:** By the mass.   **61. contract . . . behove:** Shorten, i.e. spend agreeably . . . advantage. The song, punctuated by
the grunts of the clown as he digs, is a garbled version of a poem by Thomas Lord Vaux,
entitled "The Aged Lover Renounceth Love."   **65. Custom:** Habit.   **a property of
easiness:** I.e. a thing he can do with complete ease of mind.   **67. daintier sense:** More
delicate sensitivity.

HAMLET: That skull had a tongue in it, and could sing once.
How the knave jowls° it to the ground, as if 'twere Cain's
jaw-bone, that did the first murder! This might be the pate
of a politician,° which this ass now o'erreaches,° one that   75
would circumvent God,° might it not?
HORATIO: It might, my lord.
HAMLET: Or of a courtier, which could say, "Good morrow,
sweet lord! How dost thou, sweet lord?" This might be my
Lord Such-a-one, that prais'd my Lord Such-a-one's horse   80
when 'a [meant] to beg it, might it not?
HORATIO: Ay, my lord.
HAMLET: Why, e'en so, and now my Lady Worm's, chopless,°
and knock'd about the [mazzard°] with a sexton's spade.
Here's fine revolution,° and° we had the trick° to see't. Did   85
these bones cost° no more the breeding, but to play at
loggats° with them? Mine ache to think on't.
FIRST CLOWN: "A pickaxe and a spade, a spade,   *Song.*
          For and a shrouding sheet:
          O, a pit of clay for to be made   90
          For such a guest is meet."
                                   [*Throws up another skull.*]
HAMLET: There's another. Why may not that be the skull of a
lawyer? Where be his quiddities° now, his quillities,° his
cases, his tenures,° and his tricks? Why does he suffer this
mad knave now to knock him about the sconce° with a   95
dirty shovel, and will not tell him of his action of battery?
Hum! This fellow might be in 's time a great buyer of land,
with his statutes,° his recognizances, his fines,° his double
vouchers,° his recoveries. [Is this the fine° of his fines, and
the recovery of his recoveries,] to have his fine pate full of   100
fine dirt? Will [his] vouchers vouch him no more of his pur-

---

73. **jowls:** Dashes.   75. **politician:** Schemer, intriguer.   **o'erreaches:** Gets the better
of (with play on the literal sense).   76. **circumvent God:** Bypass God's law.   **83.
chopless:** Lacking the lower jaw.   84. **mazzard:** Head.   85. **revolution:** Change.
and: If.   **trick:** Knack, ability.   **85–86. Did . . . cost:** Were . . . worth.   87. **loggats:** A
game in which blocks of wood were thrown at a stake.   93. **quiddities:** Subtleties, quibbles.   **quillities:** Fine distinctions.   94. **tenures:** Titles to real estate.   95. **sconce:**
Head.   98. **statutes, recognizances:** Bonds securing debts by attaching land and property.   98, 99. **fines, recoveries:** Procedures for converting an entailed estate to freehold.
98–99. **double vouchers:** Documents guaranteeing title to real estate, signed by two
persons.   99. **fine:** End.

chases, and [double ones too], than the length and breadth
of a pair of indentures?° The very conveyances° of his lands
will scarcely lie in this box,° and must th' inheritor° himself
have no more, ha?   105
HORATIO: Not a jot more, my lord.
HAMLET: Is not parchment made of sheep-skins?
HORATIO: Ay, my lord, and of calves'-skins too.
HAMLET: They are sheep and calves which seek out assurance in
that. I will speak to this fellow. Whose grave's this, sirrah?°   110
FIRST CLOWN: Mine, sir.
   [*Sings.*] "[O], a pit of clay for to be made
   [For such a guest is meet]."
HAMLET: I think it be thine indeed, for thou liest in't.
FIRST CLOWN: You lie out on't, sir, and therefore 'tis not yours;   115
for my part, I do not lie in't, yet it is mine.
HAMLET: Thou dost lie in't, to be in't and say it is thine. 'Tis for
the dead, not for the quick; therefore thou liest.
FIRST CLOWN: 'Tis a quick lie, sir, 'twill away again from me to
you.   120
HAMLET: What man dost thou dig it for?
FIRST CLOWN: For no man, sir.
HAMLET: What woman then?
FIRST CLOWN: For none neither.
HAMLET: Who is to be buried in't?   125
FIRST CLOWN: One that was a woman, sir, but, rest her soul,
she's dead.
HAMLET: How absolute° the knave is! we must speak by the
card,° or equivocation° will undo us. By the Lord, Horatio,
this three years I have took note of it: the age is grown so   130
pick'd° that the toe of the peasant comes so near the heel of
the courtier, he galls his kibe.° How long hast thou been
grave-maker?
FIRST CLOWN: Of [all] the days i' th' year, I came to't that day
that our last king Hamlet overcame Fortinbras.   135

---

103. **pair of indentures:** Legal document cut into two parts which fitted together on a
serrated edge. Perhaps Hamlet thus refers to the two rows of teeth in the skull, or to the
bone sutures. **conveyances:** Documents relating to transfer of property. **104. this
box:** I.e. the skull itself. **inheritor:** Owner. **110. sirrah:** Term of address to inferiors.
128. absolute: Positive. **128–29. by the card:** By the compass, i.e. punctiliously. **129.
equivocation:** Ambiguity. **131. pick'd:** Refined. **132. galls his kibe:** Rubs the
courtier's chilblain.

HAMLET: How long is that since?

FIRST CLOWN: Cannot you tell that? Every fool can tell that. It was that very day that young Hamlet was born — he that is mad, and sent into England.

HAMLET: Ay, marry, why was he sent into England?   140

FIRST CLOWN: Why, because 'a was mad. 'A shall recover his wits there, or if 'a do not, 'tis no great matter there.

HAMLET: Why?

FIRST CLOWN: 'Twill not be seen in him there, there the men are as mad as he.   145

HAMLET: How came he mad?

FIRST CLOWN: Very strangely, they say.

HAMLET: How strangely?

FIRST CLOWN: Faith, e'en with losing his wits.

HAMLET: Upon what ground?   150

FIRST CLOWN: Why, here in Denmark. I have been sexton here, man and boy, thirty years.

HAMLET: How long will a man lie i' th' earth ere he rot?

FIRST CLOWN: Faith, if 'a be not rotten before 'a die — as we have many pocky° corses, that will scarce hold the laying in°   155
— 'a will last you some eight year or nine year. A tanner will last you nine year.

HAMLET: Why he more than another?

FIRST CLOWN: Why, sir, his hide is so tann'd with his trade that 'a will keep out water a great while, and your water is a sore   160
decayer of your whoreson dead body. Here's a skull now hath lien you i' th' earth three and twenty years.

HAMLET: Whose was it?

FIRST CLOWN: A whoreson mad fellow's it was. Whose do you think it was?   165

HAMLET: Nay, I know not.

FIRST CLOWN: A pestilence on him for a mad rogue! 'a pour'd a flagon of Rhenish on my head once. This same skull, sir, was, sir, Yorick's skull, the King's jester.

HAMLET: This?   [*Takes the skull.*]   170

FIRST CLOWN: E'en that.

HAMLET: Alas, poor Yorick! I knew him, Horatio, a fellow of infinite jest, of most excellent fancy. He hath bore me on

---

155. pocky: Rotten with venereal disease.   **hold . . . in:** Last out the burial.

his back a thousand times, and now how abhorr'd in my
imagination it is! my gorge rises at it. Here hung those lips   175
that I have kiss'd I know not how oft. Where be your gibes
now, your gambols, your songs, your flashes of merriment,
that were wont to set the table on a roar? Not one now to
mock your own grinning — quite chop-fall'n.° Now get
you to my lady's [chamber], and tell her, let her paint an   180
inch thick, to this favor° she must come; make her laugh at
that. Prithee, Horatio, tell me one thing.
HORATIO: What's that, my lord?
HAMLET: Dost thou think Alexander look'd a' this fashion i' th'
earth?   185
HORATIO: E'en so.
HAMLET: And smelt so? pah!   [*Puts down the skull.*]
HORATIO: E'en so, my lord.
HAMLET: To what base uses we may return, Horatio! Why may
not imagination trace the noble dust of Alexander, till 'a   190
find it stopping a bunghole?
HORATIO: 'Twere to consider too curiously,° to consider so.
HAMLET: No, faith, not a jot, but to follow him thither with
modesty° enough and likelihood to lead it: Alexander died,
Alexander was buried, Alexander returneth to dust, the   195
dust is earth, of earth we make loam,° and why of that loam
whereto he was converted might they not stop a beer-
barrel?
Imperious° Caesar, dead and turn'd to clay,
Might stop a hole to keep the wind away.   200
O that that earth which kept the world in awe
Should patch a wall t' expel the [winter's] flaw!°
But soft, but soft awhile, here comes the King,

Enter KING, QUEEN, LAERTES, *and* [*a* DOCTOR OF DIVINITY, *following*] *the corse,* [*with* LORDS *attendant*].

The Queen, the courtiers. Who is this they follow?
And with such maimed rites?° This doth betoken   205
The corse they follow did with desp'rate hand

---

179. chop-fall'n: (1) Lacking the lower jaw; (2) downcast.   181. favor: Appearance.
192. curiously: Closely, minutely.   194. modesty: Moderation.   196. loam: A mixture of moistened clay with sand, straw, etc.   199. Imperious: Imperial.   202. flaw:
Gust.   205. maimed rites: Lack of customary ceremony.

Foredo° it° own life. 'Twas of some estate.°
Couch we° a while and mark.   [*Retiring with Horatio.*]
LAERTES: What ceremony else?
HAMLET: That is Laertes, a very noble youth. Mark.   210
LAERTES: What ceremony else?
DOCTOR: Her obsequies have been as far enlarg'd
     As we have warranty. Her death was doubtful,°
     And but that great command o'ersways the order,°
     She should° in ground unsanctified been lodg'd   215
     Till the last trumpet; for° charitable prayers,
     [Shards,] flints, and pebbles should be thrown on her.
     Yet here she is allow'd her virgin crants,°
     Her maiden strewments,° and the bringing home
     Of bell and burial.°   220
LAERTES: Must there no more be done?
DOCTOR: No more be done:
     We should profane the service of the dead
     To sing a requiem° and such rest to her
     As to peace-parted souls.
LAERTES: Lay her i' th' earth,
     And from her fair and unpolluted flesh   225
     May violets spring! I tell thee, churlish priest,
     A minist'ring angel shall my sister be
     When though liest howling.
HAMLET: What, the fair Ophelia!
QUEEN: [*Scattering flowers.*] Sweets° to the sweet, farewell!
     I hop'd thou shouldst have been my Hamlet's wife.   230
     I thought thy bride-bed to have deck'd, sweet maid,
     And not have strew'd thy grave.
LAERTES: O, treble woe
     Fall ten times [treble] on that cursed head
     Whose wicked deed thy most ingenious° sense
     Depriv'd thee of ! Hold off the earth a while,   235
     Till I have caught her once more in mine arms.
                                      [*Leaps in the grave.*]

---

207. **Foredo:** Fordo, destroy.   **it:** Its.   **estate:** rank.   **208. Couch we:** Let us conceal ourselves.   **213. doubtful:** I.e. the subject of an "open verdict."   **214. order:** Customary procedure.   **215. should:** Would certainly.   **216. for:** Instead of.   **218. crants:** Garland.   **219. maiden strewments:** Flowers scattered on the grave of an unmarried girl.   **219–20. bringing . . . burial:** I.e. burial in consecrated ground, with the bell tolling.   **223. requiem:** Dirge.   **229. Sweets:** Flowers.   **234. ingenious:** Intelligent.

Now pile your dust upon the quick and dead,
Till of this flat a mountain you have made
T' o'ertop old Pelion, or the skyish head
Of blue Olympus.°
HAMLET: [*Coming forward.*] What is he whose grief   240
Bears such an emphasis, whose phrase° of sorrow
Conjures° the wand'ring stars° and makes them stand
Like wonder-wounded hearers? This is I,
Hamlet the Dane!°   [*Hamlet leaps in after Laertes.*]
LAERTES: The devil take thy soul!   [*Grappling with him.*]
HAMLET: Thou pray'st not well.   245
I prithee take thy fingers from my throat.
For though I am not splenitive° [and] rash,
Yet have I in me something dangerous,
Which let thy wisdom fear. Hold off thy hand!
KING: Pluck them asunder.
QUEEN: Hamlet, Hamlet!
ALL: Gentlemen!   250
HORATIO: Good my lord, be quiet.
[*The Attendants part them, and they come out of the grave.*]
HAMLET: Why, I will fight with him upon this theme
Until my eyelids will no longer wag.
QUEEN: O my son, what theme?
HAMLET: I lov'd Ophelia. Forty thousand brothers   255
Could not with all their quantity of love
Make up my sum. What wilt thou do for her?
KING: O, he is mad, Laertes.
QUEEN: For love of God, forbear him.
HAMLET: 'Swounds, show me what thou't° do.   260
Woo't° weep, woo't fight, woo't fast, woo't tear thyself?
Woo't drink up eisel,° eat a crocadile?°
I'll do't. Dost [thou] come here to whine?
To outface me with leaping in her grave?
Be buried quick with her, and so will I.   265
And if thou prate of mountains,° let them throw

239, 240. Pelion, Olympus: Mountains in northeastern Greece.   **241. emphasis,
phrase:** Rhetorical terms, here used in disparaging reference to Laertes' inflated language.
242. Conjures: Puts a spell upon.   **wand'ring stars:** Planets.   **244. the Dane:** This
title normally signifies the King.   **247. splenitive:** Impetuous.   **260. thou't:** Thou
wilt.   **261. Woo't:** Wilt thou.   **262. eisel:** Vinegar.   **crocadile:** Crocodile.   **266.
if . . . mountains:** Referring to lines 237–40.

Millions of acres on us, till our ground,
Singeing his pate against the burning zone,°
Make Ossa° like a wart! Nay, and thou'lt mouth,°
I'll rant as well as thou.
QUEEN: This is mere° madness,   270
And [thus] a while the fit will work on him;
Anon, as patient° as the female dove,
When that her golden couplets° are disclosed,°
His silence will sit drooping.
HAMLET: Hear you, sir,
What is the reason that you use me thus?   275
I lov'd you ever. But it is no matter.
Let Hercules himself do what he may,
The cat will mew, and dog will have his day.° Exit Hamlet.
KING: I pray thee, good Horatio, wait upon him.
                                        [Exit] Horatio.
[To Laertes.]° Strengthen your patience in° our last night's
    speech,   280
We'll put the matter to the present push.° —
Good Gertrude, set some watch over your son.
This grave shall have a living° monument.
An hour of quiet [shortly] shall we see,
Till then in patience our proceeding be.   Exeunt.   285

[Scene 2]°

Enter HAMLET and HORATIO.

HAMLET: So much for this, sir, now shall you see the other° —
You do remember all the circumstance?
HORATIO: Remember it, my lord!
HAMLET: Sir, in my heart there was a kind of fighting
That would not let me sleep. [Methought] I lay   5

---

268. burning zone: Sphere of the sun.   269. Ossa: Another mountain in Greece, near
Pelion and Olympus.   mouth: Talk bombast (synonymous with rant in the next line).
270. mere: Utter.   272. patient: Calm.   273. golden couplets: Pair of baby birds,
covered with yellow down.   disclosed: Hatched.   277–78. Let . . . day: I.e. nobody
can prevent another from making the scenes he feels he has a right to.   280–85. See the
Textual Notes for the lines that replace these in Q1.   280. in: I.e. by recalling.   281.
present push: Immediate test.   283. living: Enduring (?) or in the form of a lifelike
effigy (?).   5.2. Location: The castle.   1. see the other: I.e. hear the other news I have
to tell you (hinted at in the letter to Horatio, 4.6.23–24).

Worse than the mutines° in the [bilboes°]. Rashly° —
And prais'd be rashness for it — let us know°
Our indiscretion sometime serves us well
When our deep plots do pall,° and that should learn° us
There's a divinity that shapes our ends,°   10
Rough-hew them° how we will —
HORATIO: That is most certain.
HAMLET: Up from my cabin,
My sea-gown scarf'd about me, in the dark
Grop'd I to find out them, had my desire,
Finger'd° their packet, and in fine withdrew   15
To mine own room again, making so bold,
My fears forgetting manners, to [unseal]
Their grand commission; where I found, Horatio —
Ah, royal knavery! — an exact command,
Larded° with many several sorts of reasons,   20
Importing° Denmark's health and England's too,
With, ho, such bugs and goblins in my life,°
That, on the supervise,° no leisure bated,°
No, not to stay° the grinding of the axe,
My head should be strook off.
HORATIO: Is't possible?   25
HAMLET: Here's the commission, read it at more leisure.
But wilt thou hear now how I did proceed?
HORATIO: I beseech you.
HAMLET: Being thus benetted round with [villainies],
Or° I could make a prologue to my brains,   30
They had begun the play. I sat me down,
Devis'd a new commission, wrote it fair.°
I once did hold it, as our statists° do,
A baseness° to write fair, and labor'd much

---

6. mutines: Mutineers (but the term *mutiny* was in Shakespeare's day used of almost any act of rebellion against authority).   **bilboes:** Fetters attached to a heavy iron bar.   **Rashly:** On impulse.   **7. know:** Recognize, acknowledge.   **9. pall:** Lose force, come to nothing.   **learn:** Teach.   **10. shapes our ends:** Gives final shape to our designs.   **11. Rough-hew them:** Block them out in initial form.   **15. Finger'd:** Filched, "pinched."   **20. Larded:** Garnished.   **21. Importing:** Relating to.   **22. bugs . . . life:** Terrifying things in prospect if I were permitted to remain alive. *Bugs* = bugaboos.   **23. supervise:** Perusal.   **bated:** Deducted (from the stipulated speediness).   **24. stay:** Wait for.   **30. Or:** Before.   **32. fair:** I.e. in a beautiful hand (such as a professional scribe would use).   **33. statists:** Statesmen, public officials.   **34. A baseness:** I.e. a skill befitting men of low rank.

How to forget that learning, but, sir, now   35
It did me yeman's° service. Wilt thou know
Th' effect° of what I wrote?
HORATIO: Ay, good my lord.
HAMLET: An earnest conjuration from the King,
  As England was his faithful tributary,
  As love between them like the palm might flourish,   40
  As peace should still her wheaten garland wear
  And stand a comma° 'tween their amities,
  And many such-like [as's] of great charge,°
  That on the view and knowing of these contents,
  Without debatement further, more or less,   45
  He should those bearers put to sudden death,
  Not shriving time° allow'd.
HORATIO: How was this seal'd?
HAMLET: Why, even in that was heaven ordinant.°
  I had my father's signet in my purse,
  Which was the model° of that Danish seal;   50
  Folded the writ up in the form of th' other,
  [Subscrib'd°] it, gave't th' impression, plac'd it safely,
  The changeling° never known.° Now the next day
  Was our sea-fight, and what to this was sequent
  Thou knowest already.   55
HORATIO: So Guildenstern and Rosencrantz go to't.°
HAMLET: [Why, man, they did make love to this employment,]
  They are not near my conscience. Their defeat°
  Does by their own insinuation° grow.
  'Tis dangerous when the baser° nature comes   60
  Between the pass° and fell° incensed points
  Of mighty opposites.
HORATIO: Why, what a king is this!
HAMLET: Does it not, think thee, stand me now upon° —

---

36. yeman's: Yeoman's, i.e. solid, substantial.   37. effect: Purport, gist.   42. comma:
Connective, link.   43. as's . . . charge: (1) Weighty clauses beginning with *as;* (2) asses
with heavy loads.   47. shriving time: Time for confession and absolution.   48. ordinant: In charge, guiding.   50. model: Small copy.   52. Subscrib'd: Signed.   53.
changeling: I.e. Hamlet's letter, substituted secretly for the genuine letter, as fairies substituted their children for human children.   never known: Never recognized as a substitution (unlike the fairies' changelings).   56. go to't: I.e. are going to their death.   58.
defeat: Ruin, overthrow.   59. insinuation: Winding their way into the affair.   60.
baser: Inferior.   61. pass: Thrust.   fell: Fierce.   63. stand . . . upon: I.e. rest upon
me as a duty.

He that hath kill'd my king and whor'd my mother,
Popp'd in between th' election° and my hopes,   65
Thrown out his angle° for my proper° life,
And with such coz'nage° — is't not perfect conscience
[To quit him° with this arm? And is't not to be damn'd,
To let this canker° of our nature come
In° further evil?   70
HORATIO: It must be shortly known to him from England
    What is the issue of the business there.
HAMLET: It will be short; the interim's mine,
    And a man's life's no more° than to say "one."°
    But I am very sorry, good Horatio,   75
    That to Laertes I forgot myself,
    For by the image° of my cause I see
    The portraiture of his. I'll [court] his favors.
    But sure the bravery° of his grief did put me
    Into a tow'ring passion.
HORATIO: Peace, who comes here?]   80

Enter [young OSRIC,] *a courtier.*

OSRIC: Your lordship is right welcome back to Denmark.
HAMLET: I [humbly] thank you, sir. — Dost know this water-
    fly?°
HORATIO: No, my good lord.
HAMLET: Thy state is the more gracious,° for 'tis a vice to know
    him. He hath much land, and fertile; let a beast be lord of   85
    beasts, and his crib shall stand at the King's mess.° 'Tis a
    chough,° but, as I say, spacious in the possession of dirt.
OSRIC: Sweet lord, if your lordship were at leisure, I should im-
    part a thing to you from his Majesty.
HAMLET: I will receive it, sir, with all diligence of spirit. [Put]   90
    your bonnet° to his right use, 'tis for the head.

---

65. election: I.e. as King of Denmark.   **66. angle:** Hook and line.   **proper:** Very.
67. coz'nage: Trickery.   **68. quit him:** Pay him back.   **69. canker:** Cancerous sore.
69–70. come In: Grow into.   **74. a man's . . . more:** I.e. to kill a man takes no more
time.   **say "one":** Perhaps this is equivalent to "deliver one sword thrust"; see line 262
below, where Hamlet says "One" as he makes the first hit.   **77. image:** Likeness.   **79.
bravery:** Ostentatious expression.   **82. water-fly:** I.e. tiny, vainly agitated creature.
84. gracious: Virtuous.   **85–86. let . . . mess:** I.e. if a beast owned as many cattle as
Osric, he could feast with the King.   **87. chough:** Jackdaw, a bird that could be taught
to speak.   **91. bonnet:** Hat.

OSRIC: I thank your lordship, it is very hot.
HAMLET: No, believe me, 'tis very cold, the wind is northerly.
OSRIC: It is indifferent° cold, my lord, indeed.
HAMLET: But yet methinks it is very [sultry] and hot [for] my   95
    complexion.°
OSRIC: Exceedingly, my lord, it is very sultry — as 'twere — I
    cannot tell how. My lord, his Majesty bade me signify to
    you that 'a has laid a great wager on your head. Sir, this is
    the matter —   100
HAMLET: I beseech you remember.
                 [*Hamlet moves him to put on his hat.*]
OSRIC: Nay, good my lord, for my ease,° in good faith. Sir, here
    is newly come to court Laertes, believe me, an absolute°
    [gentleman], full of most excellent differences,° of very soft°
    society, and great showing;° indeed, to speak sellingly° of   105
    him, he is the card or calendar° of gentry;° for you shall find
    in him the continent of what part° a gentleman would see.
HAMLET: Sir, his definement suffers no ·perdition° in you,
    though I know to divide him inventorially would dozy° th'
    arithmetic of memory, and yet but yaw° neither° in respect   110
    of° his quick sail; but in the verity of extolment,° I take him
    to be a soul of great article,° and his infusion° of such
    dearth° and rareness as, to make true diction° of him, his
    semblable° is his mirror, and who else would trace him,° his
    umbrage,° nothing more.   115
OSRIC: Your lordship speaks most infallibly of him.
HAMLET: The concernancy,° sir? Why do we wrap the gentle-
    man in our more rawer breath?°

---

94. indifferent: Somewhat. **96. complexion:** Temperament. **102. for my ease:** I.e.
I am really more comfortable with my hat off (a polite insistence on maintaining ceremony). **103. absolute:** Complete, possessing every quality a gentleman should have.
104. differences: Distinguishing characteristics, personal qualities. **soft:** Agreeable.
105. great showing: Splendid appearance. **sellingly:** I.e. like a seller to a prospective
buyer; in a fashion to do full justice. Most editors follow Q3 in reading *feelingly* = with
exactitude, as he deserves. **106. card or calendar:** Chart or register, i.e. compendious
guide. **gentry:** Gentlemanly behavior. **107. the continent . . . part:** One who contains every quality. **108. perdition:** Loss. **109. dozy:** Make dizzy. **110. yaw:**
Keep deviating erratically from its course (said of a ship). **neither:** For all that. **110–
11. in respect of:** Compared with. **111. in . . . extolment:** To praise him truly.
112. article: Scope (?) or importance (?). **infusion:** Essence, quality. **113. dearth:**
Scarceness. **make true diction:** Speak truly. **113–14. his semblable:** His only likeness or equal. **114. who . . . him:** Anyone else who tries to follow him. **115. um-
brage:** Shadow. **117. concernancy:** Relevance. **118. more rawer breath:** I.e. words
too crude to describe him properly.

OSRIC: Sir?

HORATIO: Is't not possible to understand in another tongue?°   120
You will to't, sir, really.°

HAMLET: What imports the nomination° of this gentleman?

OSRIC: Of Laertes?

HORATIO: His purse is empty already: all 's golden words are
spent.   125

HAMLET: Of him, sir.

OSRIC: I know you are not ignorant —

HAMLET: I would you did, sir, yet, in faith, if you did, it would
not much approve° me. Well, sir?

OSRIC: You are not ignorant of what excellence Laertes is —   130

HAMLET: I dare not confess that, lest I should compare with
him in excellence,° but° to know a man well were to know
himself.°

OSRIC: I mean, sir, for [his] weapon, but in the imputation laid
on him by them,° in his meed° he's unfellow'd.   135

HAMLET: What's his weapon?

OSRIC: Rapier and dagger.

HAMLET: That's two of his weapons — but well.

OSRIC: The King, sir, hath wager'd with him six Barbary horses,
against the which he has impawn'd,° as I take it, six French   140
rapiers and poniards, with their assigns,° as girdle,
[hangers°], and so. Three of the carriages,° in faith, are very
dear to fancy,° very responsive to° the hilts, most delicate
carriages, and of very liberal conceit.°

HAMLET: What call you the carriages?   145

HORATIO: I knew you must be edified by the margent° ere you
had done.

OSRIC: The [carriages], sir, are the hangers.

HAMLET: The phrase would be more germane to the matter if
we could carry a cannon by our sides; I would it [might be]   150

---

120. in another tongue: I.e. when someone else is the speaker.   121. You . . . really:
I.e. you can do it if you try.   122. nomination: Naming, mention.   129. approve:
Commend.   131–32. compare . . . excellence: I.e. seem to claim the same degree of
excellence for myself.   132. but: The sense seems to require *for*.   133. himself: I.e.
oneself.   134–35. in . . . them: I.e. in popular estimation.   135. meed: Merit.   140.
impawn'd: Staked.   141. assigns: Appurtenances.   142. hangers: Straps on which
the swords hang from the girdle.   carriages: Properly, gun-carriages; here used affectedly in place of *hangers*.   143. fancy: Taste.   143. very responsive to: Matching well.
144. liberal conceit: Elegant design.   146. must . . . margent: Would require enlight-
enment from a marginal note.

hangers till then. But on: six Barb'ry horses against six
French swords, their assigns, and three liberal-conceited
carriages; that's the French bet against the Danish. Why is
this all [impawn'd, as] you call it?

OSRIC: The King, sir, hath laid,° sir, that in a dozen passes be-   155
tween yourself and him, he shall not exceed you three hits;°
he hath laid on twelve for nine;° and it would come to immediate trial, if your lordship would vouchsafe the answer.°

HAMLET: How if I answer no?

OSRIC: I mean, my lord, the opposition of your person in trial.   160

HAMLET: Sir, I will walk here in the hall. If it please his Majesty,
it is the breathing time of day with me.° Let the foils be
brought, the gentleman willing, and the King hold his purpose, I will win for him and I can; if not, I will gain nothing
but my shame and the odd hits.   165

OSRIC: Shall I deliver you so?

HAMLET: To this effect, sir — after what flourish° your nature
will.

OSRIC: I commend my duty° to your lordship.

HAMLET: Yours. [*Exit Osric.*] ['A] does well to commend it   170
himself, there are no tongues else for 's turn.

HORATIO: This lapwing° runs away with the shell on his head.

HAMLET: 'A did [comply], sir, with his dug° before 'a suck'd it.
Thus has he, and many more of the same breed that I know
the drossy° age dotes on, only got the tune of the time,°   175
and out of an habit of encounter,° a kind of [yesty°] collection,° which carries them through and through the most

---

155. laid: Wagered.   **156. he . . . hits:** Laertes must win by at least eight to four (if
none of the "passes" or bouts are draws), since at seven to five he would be only two up.
157. he . . . nine: Not satisfactorily explained despite much discussion. One suggestion is
that Laertes has raised the odds against himself by wagering that out of twelve bouts he
will win nine.   **158. answer:** Encounter (as Hamlet's following quibble forces Osric to
explain in his next speech).   **162. breathing . . . me:** My usual hour for exercise.
167. after what flourish: With whatever embellishment of language.   **169. commend
my duty:** Offer my dutiful respects (but Hamlet picks up the phrase in the sense "praise
my manner of bowing").   **172. lapwing:** A foolish bird which upon hatching was supposed to run with part of the eggshell still over its head. (Osric has put his hat on at last.)
173. comply . . . dug: Bow politely to his mother's nipple.   **175. drossy:** I.e. worth-
less.   **tune . . . time:** I.e. fashionable ways of talk.   **176. habit of encounter:** Mode of
social intercourse.   **yesty:** Yeasty, frothy.   **176–77. collection:** I.e. anthology of fine
phrases.

[profound] and [winnow'd°] opinions,° and do but blow
them to their trial,° the bubbles are out.°

Enter a LORD.

LORD: My lord, his Majesty commended him to you by young   180
Osric, who brings back to him that you attend him in the
hall. He sends to know if your pleasure hold to play with
Laertes, or that you will take longer time.
HAMLET: I am constant to my purposes, they follow the King's
pleasure. If his fitness speaks, mine is ready;° now or when-   185
soever, provided I be so able as now.
LORD: The King and Queen and all are coming down.
HAMLET: In happy time.
LORD: The Queen desires you to use some gentle enter-
tainment° to Laertes before you fall to play.   190
HAMLET: She well instructs me.   [*Exit Lord.*]
HORATIO: You will lose, my lord.
HAMLET: I do not think so; since he went into France I have
been in continual practice. I shall win at the odds. Thou
wouldst not think how ill all's here about my heart — but   195
it is no matter.
HORATIO: Nay, good my lord —
HAMLET: It is but foolery, but it is such a kind of [gain-]giving,°
as would perhaps trouble a woman.
HORATIO: If your mind dislike any thing, obey it. I will forestall 200
their repair hither, and say you are not fit.
HAMLET: Not a whit, we defy augury. There is special providence in the fall of a sparrow.° If it be [now], 'tis not to
come; if it be not to come, it will be now; if it be not now,
yet it [will] come — the readiness is all. Since no man, of   205
aught° he leaves, knows what is't to leave betimes,° let be.

A table prepar'd, [*and flagons of wine on it. Enter*] *Trumpets,*

---

178. **winnow'd:** Sifted, choice. **opinions:** Judgments. **178–79. blow . . . trial:**
Test them by blowing on them, i.e. make even the least demanding trial of them. **179.**
out: Blown away (?) or at an end, done for (?). **185. If . . . ready:** I.e. If this is a good
moment for him, it is for me also. **189–90. gentle entertainment:** Courteous greeting.
198. gain-giving: Misgiving. **202–03. special . . . sparrow:** See Matthew 10:29.
205–06. of aught: I.e. whatever. **knows . . . betimes:** Knows what is the best time to
leave it.

Drums, and Officers with cushions, foils, daggers; KING, QUEEN,
LAERTES, [OSRIC,] *and all the State.°*

KING: Come, Hamlet, come, and take this hand from me.
          [*The King puts Laertes' hand into Hamlet's.*]
HAMLET: Give me your pardon, sir. I have done you wrong,
  But pardon't as you are a gentleman.
  This presence° knows,   210
  And you must needs have heard, how I am punish'd°
  With a sore distraction. What I have done
  That might your nature, honor, and exception°
  Roughly awake, I here proclaim was madness.
  Was't Hamlet wrong'd Laertes? Never Hamlet!   215
  If Hamlet from himself be ta'en away,
  And when he's not himself does wrong Laertes,
  Then Hamlet does it not, Hamlet denies it.
  Who does it then? His madness. If't be so,
  Hamlet is of the faction that is wronged,   220
  His madness is poor Hamlet's enemy.
  [Sir, in this audience,]
  Let my disclaiming from a purpos'd evil°
  Free° me so far in your most generous thoughts,
  That I have shot my arrow o'er the house   225
  And hurt my brother.
LAERTES: I am satisfied in nature,°
  Whose motive in this case should stir me most
  To my revenge, but in my terms of honor°
  I stand aloof, and will no reconcilement
  Till by some elder masters of known honor   230
  I have a voice and president of peace
  To [keep] my name ungor'd.° But [till] that time
  I do receive your offer'd love like love,
  And will not wrong it.
HAMLET: I embrace it freely,
  And will this brothers'° wager frankly° play.   235

---

206. s.d. State: Nobles.   **210. presence:** Assembled court.   **211. punish'd:** Afflicted.
213. exception: Objection.   **223. my . . . evil:** My declaration that I intended no harm.
224. Free: Absolve.   **226. in nature:** So far as my personal feelings are concerned.
228. in . . . honor: I.e. as a man governed by an established code of honor.   **231–32.
have . . . ungor'd:** Can secure an opinion backed by precedent that I can make peace with
you without injury to my reputation.   **235. brothers':** I.e. amicable, as if between
brothers.   **frankly:** Freely, without constraint.

Give us the foils. [Come on.]
LAERTES: Come, one for me.
HAMLET: I'll be your foil,° Laertes; in mine ignorance
   Your skill shall like a star i' th' darkest night
   Stick fiery off ° indeed.
LAERTES: You mock me, sir.
HAMLET: No, by this hand.   240
KING: Give them the foils, young Osric. Cousin Hamlet,
   You know the wager?
HAMLET: Very well, my lord.
   Your Grace has laid the odds° a' th' weaker side.
KING: I do not fear it, I have seen you both;
   But since he is [better'd°], we have therefore odds.°   245
LAERTES: This is too heavy; let me see another.
HAMLET: This likes° me well. These foils have all a length?°
                              [*Prepare to play.*]
OSRIC: Ay, my good lord.
KING: Set me the stoups° of wine upon that table.
   If Hamlet give the first or second hit,   250
   Or quit in answer of the third exchange,°
   Let all the battlements their ord'nance fire.
   The King shall drink to Hamlet's better breath,
   And in the cup an [union°] shall he throw,
   Richer than that which four successive kings   255
   In Denmark's crown have worn. Give me the cups,
   And let the kettle° to the trumpet speak,
   The trumpet to the cannoneer without,
   The cannons to the heavens, the heaven to earth,
   "Now the King drinks to Hamlet." Come begin;   260
                              Trumpets the while.
   And you, the judges, bear a wary eye.
HAMLET: Come on, sir.
LAERTES: Come, my lord.
            [*They play and Hamlet scores a hit.*]

237, foil: Thin sheet of metal placed behind a jewel to set it off.   239. Stick . . . off:
Blaze out in contrast.   243. laid the odds: I.e. wagered a higher stake (horses to rapiers).   245. is better'd: Has perfected his skill.   odds: I.e. the arrangement that Laertes
must take more bouts than Hamlet to win.   247. likes: Pleases.   a length: The same
length.   249. stoups: Tankards.   251. quit . . . exchange: Pays back wins by Laertes
in the first and second bouts by taking the third.   254. union: An especially fine pearl.
257. kettle: Kettle-drum.

HAMLET: One.
LAERTES: No.
HAMLET: Judgment.
OSRIC: A hit, a very palpable hit.
LAERTES: Well, again.
KING: Stay, give me drink. Hamlet, this pearl is thine,
   Here's to thy health! Give him the cup.   265
    Drum, trumpets [*sound*] *flourish. A piece goes off* [*within*].
HAMLET: I'll play this bout first, set it by a while.
   Come. [*They play again.*] Another hit; what say you?
LAERTES: [A touch, a touch,] I do confess't.
KING: Our son shall win.
QUEEN: He's fat,° and scant of breath.
   Here, Hamlet, take my napkin, rub thy brows.   270
   The Queen carouses° to thy fortune, Hamlet.
HAMLET: Good madam!
KING: Gertrude, do not drink.
QUEEN: I will, my lord, I pray you pardon me.
KING: [*Aside.*] It is the pois'ned cup, it is too late.
HAMLET: I dare not drink yet, madam; by and by.   275
QUEEN: Come, let me wipe thy face.
LAERTES: My lord, I'll hit him now.
KING: I do not think't.
LAERTES: [*Aside.*] And yet it is almost against my conscience.
HAMLET: Come, for the third, Laertes, you do but dally.
   I pray you pass with your best violence;   280
   I am sure you make a wanton of me.°
LAERTES: Say you so? Come on.   [*They play.*]
OSRIC: Nothing, neither way.
LAERTES: Have at you now!
   [*Laertes wounds Hamlet; then, in scuffling, they change
   rapiers.*]
KING: Part them, they are incens'd.
HAMLET: Nay, come again.
    [*Hamlet wounds Laertes. The Queen falls.*]
OSRIC: Look to the Queen there ho!   285
HORATIO: They bleed on both sides. How is it, my lord?
OSRIC: How is't, Laertes?

---

269. fat: Sweaty.   **271. carouses:** Drinks a toast.   **281. make . . . me:** I.e. are holding
back in order to let me win, as one does with a spoiled child (*wanton*).

LAERTES: Why, as a woodcock to mine own springe,° Osric:
    I am justly kill'd with mine own treachery.
HAMLET: How does the Queen?
KING: She sounds° to see them bleed.   290
QUEEN: No, no, the drink, the drink — O my dear Hamlet —
    The drink, the drink! I am pois'ned.   [*Dies.*]
HAMLET: O villainy! Ho, let the door be lock'd!
    Treachery! Seek it out.
LAERTES: It is here, Hamlet. [Hamlet,] thou art slain.   295
    No med'cine in the world can do thee good;
    In thee there is not half an hour's life.
    The treacherous instrument is in [thy] hand,
    Unbated° and envenom'd. The foul practice°
    Hath turn'd itself on me. Lo here I lie,   300
    Never to rise again. Thy mother's pois'ned.
    I can no more — the King, the King's to blame.
HAMLET: The point envenom'd too!
    Then, venom, to thy work.   [*Hurts° the King.*]
ALL. Treason! treason!   305
KING: O, yet defend me, friends, I am but hurt.
HAMLET: Here, thou incestious, [murd'rous], damned Dane,
    Drink [off] this potion! Is [thy union] here?
    Follow my mother!   [*King dies.*]
LAERTES: He is justly served,
    It is a poison temper'd° by himself.   310
    Exchange forgiveness with me, noble Hamlet.
    Mine and my father's death come not upon thee,
    Nor thine on me!   [*Dies.*]
HAMLET: Heaven make thee free° of it! I follow thee.
    I am dead, Horatio. Wretched queen, adieu!   315
    You that look pale, and tremble at this chance,
    That are but mutes or audience° to this act,
    Had I but time — as this fell° sergeant,° Death,
    Is strict in his arrest — O, I could tell you —
    But let it be. Horatio, I am dead,   320
    Thou livest. Report me and my cause aright

---

288. springe: Snare.   **290. sounds:** Swoons.   **299. Unbated:** Not blunted.   **foul practice:** Vile plot.   **304. s.d. Hurts:** Wounds.   **310. temper'd:** Mixed.   **314. make thee free:** Absolve you.   **317. mutes or audience:** Silent spectators.   **318. fell:** Cruel. **sergeant:** Sheriff's officer.

To the unsatisfied.
HORATIO: Never believe it;
I am more an antique Roman° than a Dane.
Here's yet some liquor left.
HAMLET: As th' art a man,
Give me the cup. Let go! By heaven, I'll ha't!   325
O God, Horatio, what a wounded name,
Things standing thus unknown, shall I leave behind me!
If thou didst ever hold me in thy heart,
Absent thee from felicity a while,
And in this harsh world draw thy breath in pain   330
To tell my story. *A march afar off* [*and a shot within*].
What warlike noise is this?
                [*Osric goes to the door and returns.*]
OSRIC: Young Fortinbras, with conquest come from Poland,
To th' embassadors of England gives
This warlike volley.
HAMLET: O, I die, Horatio,
The potent poison quite o'er-crows° my spirit.°   335
I cannot live to hear the news from England,
But I do prophesy th' election lights
On Fortinbras, he has my dying voice.°
So tell him, with th' occurrents° more and less
Which have solicited° — the rest is silence.   [*Dies.*]   340
HORATIO: Now cracks a noble heart. Good night, sweet prince,
And flights of angels sing thee to thy rest! [*March within.*]
Why does the drum come hither?

Enter FORTINBRAS *with the* [ENGLISH] EMBASSADORS, [*with
Drum, Colors, and Attendants*].

FORTINBRAS: Where is this sight?
HORATIO: What is it you would see?
If aught of woe or wonder, cease your search.   345
FORTINBRAS: This quarry cries on havoc.° O proud death,
What feast is toward° in thine eternal cell,

---

323. antique Roman: I.e. one who will commit suicide on such an occasion.   335.
o'er-crows: Triumphs over (a term derived from cockfighting).   spirit: Vital energy.
338. voice: Vote.   339. occurrents: Occurrences.   340. solicited: Instigated.   346.
This . . . havoc: This heap of corpses proclaims a massacre.   347. toward: In preparation.

That thou so many princes at a shot
So bloodily hast strook?
FIRST EMBASSADOR: The sight is dismal,
And our affairs from England come too late.   350
The ears are senseless that should give us hearing,
To tell him his° commandment is fulfill'd,
That Rosencrantz and Guildenstern are dead.
Where should we have our thanks?
HORATIO: Not from his mouth,
Had it th' ability of life to thank you.   355
He never gave commandement for their death.
But since so jump° upon this bloody question,°
You from the Polack wars, and you from England,
Are here arrived, give order that these bodies
High on a stage° be placed to the view,   360
And let me speak to [th'] yet unknowing world
How these things came about. So shall you hear
Of carnal, bloody, and unnatural acts,
Of accidental judgments,° casual° slaughters,
Of deaths put on° by cunning and [forc'd] cause,   365
And in this upshot, purposes mistook
Fall'n on th' inventors' heads: all this can I
Truly deliver.
FORTINBRAS: Let us haste to hear it,
And call the noblest to the audience.
For me, with sorrow I embrace my fortune.   370
I have some rights, of memory° in this kingdom,
Which now to claim my vantage° doth invite me.
HORATIO: Of that I shall have also cause to speak,
And from his mouth whose voice will draw [on] more.°
But let this same be presently° perform'd   375
Even while men's minds are wild,° lest more mischance
On plots and errors happen.
FORTINBRAS: Let four captains

---

352. his: I.e. the King's.   357. jump: Precisely, pat.   question: Matter.   360. stage:
Platform.   364. judgments: Retributions.   casual: Happening by chance.   365. put
on: Instigated.   371. of memory: Unforgotten.   372. my vantage: I.e. my oppor-
tune presence at a moment when the throne is empty.   374. his . . . more: The mouth
of one (Hamlet) whose vote will induce others to support your claim.   375. presently:
At once.   376. wild: Distraught.

Bear Hamlet like a soldier to the stage,
For he was likely, had he been put on,°
To have prov'd most royal; and for his passage,°   380
The soldiers' music and the rite of war
Speak loudly for him.
Take up the bodies. Such a sight as this
Becomes the field, but here shows much amiss.°
Go bid the soldiers shoot.   385
    Exeunt [marching; after the which a peal of ordinance
    are shot off].

---

379. **put on:** Put to the test (by becoming king).   380. **passage:** Death.   384. **Becomes . . . amiss:** Befits the battlefield, but appears very much out of place here.

NOTE ON THE TEXT

Hamlet offers a textual situation too complicated to permit here more than a sketch of the principal problems involved.

There are three early and significant editions of *Hamlet:* First Quarto (Q1), 1603; Second Quarto (Q2), 1604/5; First Folio (F1), 1623. Three more quartos, stemming from Q2, appeared before the Restoration: Q3 (1611); Q4 (undated); Q5 (1637). The first of several Players' Quartos (Betterton's acting version) was printed in 1676.

Q1, which is approximately half the length of Q2, is one of the so-called "bad" quartos, i.e. a memorially reconstructed version, made probably for some provincial touring company, perhaps by the actor who doubled in the roles of Marcellus and Lucianus. Thus, although in one sense a substantive test, Q1 is without any real textual authority, but its stage directions and very occasionally its readings are valuable in supplementing, corroborating, or correcting Q2 and F1. It also contains one scene (see Textual Notes, 4.6) not found in Q2–4 or F1.

Since the pioneer work of J. D. Wilson in 1934, the position of Q2 as basic copy-text for a critical edition has never been seriously questioned. Wilson was able to show with near certainty that Q2 was printed from some form of Shakespeare's autograph, probably the "foul papers." One qualification of this view, however, is now generally admitted: act 1, as Greg had earlier suggested, seems to have been printed not directly from the manuscript but from a copy of Q1 corrected and enlarged by collation with the manuscript. This qualification has important bearings on the relative authority of the Q2 text in act 1 where its readings agree with Q1 against those of F1. Another influential theory advanced by Wilson — that Q2 was badly printed because the work was set up by a young and inexperienced compositor — must now be abandoned. Fredson Bowers and J. R. Brown have proved that two compositors set Q2 and that the printing errors and supposed omissions, etc. are pretty evenly distributed between them. Such a view means that many words and passages found only in F1 were probably not accidentally omitted by Wilson's hypothetical inexperienced compositor of Q2 but were in fact not present in Shakespeare's manuscript when it served as copy for Q2. This conclusion raises one of several questions about the provenience of the F1 text.

The exact status of the F1 text has become increasingly uncertain in recent years. Two principal theories, each with important implications, are advanced: (a) F1 is based on a playhouse manuscript, a transcript at one or two removes from Shakespeare's "foul papers" as used for Q2, the printer occasionally consulting Q2 on difficult passages; (b) F1 is based on a copy of Q2 which had been brought into some measure of conformity (by verbal substitutions, deletion of some 230 lines, and addition of some 83 lines) with a playhouse manuscript of the kind described under (a). Theory (a) obviously allows the F1 text an independent authority apart from Q2 and strengthens the authority of all readings in which F1 and Q2 agree; theory (b), while still allowing a degree of independence to F1, limits the cumulative authority of all readings common to F1 and Q2. Whichever view is taken, F1 contains a number of readings which seem to reflect early stage usage, as is shown by the fairly frequent agreement, against Q2, between F1 and Q1. Whether such readings (as well as some of the additions in F1) represent possible Shakespearean revision (the major additions presumably do) or actors' or bookholder's changes must in the present state of our knowledge remain uncertain. Harold Jenkins, who in part supports theory (a), has recently gone so far as to suggest that F1 has many of the characteristics of a reported text, a view which, of course, further undermines its already ambiguous authority. The treatment of F1 in the present text has been influenced by Jenkins's position.

Since the textual situation in *Hamlet* is so intricate, the Textual Notes offer as complete a picture of the interrelations between Q2, F1, and Q1 as considerations of space allow. All significant variants, as well as additions and omissions, are listed, together with a record of Q1's concurrence or disagreement with Q2 and F1 in these and some other readings. (*Q1*) immediately after the square bracket or following other sigla indicates that Q1 here agrees with Q2 or with the other editions listed. The absence of citation of Q1 in any entry indicates that the reading of the lemma occurs in a passage which in Q1 is either omitted or so differently worded that it offers no recognizable equivalent. To help the reader in appreciating the debased nature of the Q1 text, especially where it differs most markedly from Q2–4 and F1, some longer passages (including the Q1 version of "To be, or not to be," 3.1.55–89) are given in the Textual Notes (see 1.3.135–36, 2.2.526–28, 3.1 opening, 3.2.41, 143–61, 3.3.36–72, 3.4.137, 4.5 opening and line 95, 4.6, 4.7.140, 5.1.278–85, 5.2.155–58).

Der bestrafte Brudermord, oder Prinz Hamlet aus Dännemark (Fratricide Punished), referred to occasionally in the Textual Notes, is a German adaptation of *Hamlet* played by visiting English comedians in the early years of the seventeenth century. It shows several interesting points of contact with Q1, but it is ultimately derived from Shakespeare's text as it appears in Q2, probably through performance.

For further information, see: J. D. Wilson, *The Manuscript of Shakespeare's "Hamlet,"* 2 vols. (Cambridge, 1934), and ed., New Cambridge *Hamlet* (Cambridge, 1934; rev. ed., 1948); G. I. Duthie, *The "Bad" Quarto of "Hamlet," A Critical Study* (Cambridge, 1941); Alice Walker, *Textual Problems of the First Folio* (Cambridge, 1953); W. W. Greg, *The Shakespeare First Folio* (Oxford, 1955); J. R. Brown, "The Compositors of *Hamlet* Q2 and *The Merchant of Venice*," SB [*Shakespeare Bulletin*], VII (1955), 17–40; Fredson Bowers, "The Printing of *Hamlet*, Q2," *SB*, VII (1955), 41–50; Harold Jenkins, "The Relation between the Second Quarto and the Folio Text of *Hamlet*," *SB*, VII (1955), 69–83; J. M. Nosworthy, *Shakespeare's Occasional Plays* (London, 1965).

THE TEXTUAL NOTES

Title: The . . . Denmark] *F1;* The Tragicall Historie of Hamlet, Prince of Denmarke. By William Shakespeare. Newly imprinted and enlarged to almost as much againe as it was, according to the true and perfect Coppie. *Q2 (title-page);* The Tragicall Historie of Hamlet Prince of Denmarke By William Shake-speare. As it hath beene diuerse times acted by his Highnesse seruants in the Cittie of London: as also in the two Vniuersities of Cambridge and Oxford, and else-where *Q1 (title-page)*

Dramatis personae: *subs. as first given in Q (1676)*

Act-scene division: *none in Q1–4; F1 marks 1.1–3, act 2, 2.2; other act-scene divisions*

from Q (1676), Rowe, and later editors (see first note to each scene); present act-scene division as a whole first established by Capell

―――――――― 1.1 ――――――――

1.1] I.i *F1*

Location: *Alexander (after Rowe)*

o.s.d. meeting] *ed.; Q1 s.d. reads:* Enter two Centinels. (*with s.pp. distinguishing Barnardo and Francisco only as* 1. *and* 2.)

4 **Barnardo.**] Barnardo? *F1*

7 **twelf**] twelue *Q3–4, F1*

14 **ho! Who is**] who's *F1;* who is *Q1*

16 **soldier**] *F1 (Q1);* souldiers *Q2–4*

17 **hath my**] *(Q1);* ha's my *F1*

21 **s.p. Horatio**] Mar. *F1 (Q1)*
33 **have two nights**] *(Q1)*; two **Nights haue** *F1*
40 **off**] *Q3–4 (Q1)*; of *Q2, F1*
41 **figure**] figure, *F1*
43 **'a**] it *F1 (Q1)*
44 **harrows**] *F1*; horrowes *Q2–4*; horrors *Q1*
45 **Speak to**] Question *F1 (Q1)*
51 **s.d. Exit Ghost.**] *placed as in F1; after* offended, *l. 50, Q2–4*
55 **you on't**] *F1 (Q1)*; you-ont *Q2*; you of it *Q3–4*
61 **he**] *(Q1)*; *om. F1*
61 **the**] *(Q1)*; th' *F1*
63 **smote**] *Q3–4*; smot *Q2, F1 (Q1)*
63 **sledded**] *F1*; sleaded *Q2–4 (Q1)*
63 **Polacks**] *Malone*; pollax *Q2–4, F1 (Q1)*
65 **jump**] *(Q1)*; iust *F1*
68 **mine**] my *F1 (Q1)*
73 **why**] *F1 (Q1)*; with *Q2–4*
73 **cast**] *F1*; cost *Q2–4 (Q1)*
79 **I,**] *F1 (Q1)*; I. *Q2–4*
87 **heraldy**] Heraldrie *F1, Q3–4 (Q1)*
88 **those**] *F1 (Q1)*; these *Q2–4*
89 **of**] *(Q1)*; on *F1*
91 **return'd**] *F1*; returne *Q2–4*
93 **comart**] Cou'nant *F1*
94 **design'd**] *F2*; desseigne *Q2–4, F1*
98 **lawless**] *(Q1)*; Landlesse *F1*
101 **As**] And *F1*
103 **compulsatory**] Compulsatiue *F1*
108–25 **I . . . countrymen.**] *om. F1 (Q1)*
108 **e'en so**] *Collier*; enso *Q2*; euen so *Q3–4*
112 **mote**] *Q4*; moth *Q2–3*
115 **tenantless**] *Q3–4*; tennatlesse *Q2*
116 **streets.**] *Theobald (subs.)*; streets *Q2–4*
121 **fear'd**] *Collier conj.*; feare *Q2*; fearce *Q3*; fierce *Q4*
125 **s.d. Ghost**] Ghost againe *F1*
126 **again!**] *F1 (subs.)*; againe *Q2–4*; againe, *Q1*
126 **s.d. It . . . arms.**] *om. F1 (Q1)*
138 **your**] you *F1 (Q1)*
139 **s.d. The cock crows.**] *placed as in Cambridge; after l. 138, Q2–4; om. F1 (Q1)*
140 **it**] at ir *F1*
142 **s.d. Exit Ghost.**] *F1 (Q1)*
150 **morn**] day *F1*; morning *Q1*
151 **shrill-sounding**] *hyphen, F1*; shrill crowing *Q1*
158 **say**] *(Q1)*; sayes *F1*
160 **This**] The *F1 (Q1)*
161 **dare stir**] can walke *F1*; dare walke *Q1*
163 **takes**] *(Q1)*; talkes *F1*
164 **that**] *(Q1)*; the *F1*
167 **eastward hill.**] *Q3–4 (subs.)*; Eastward hill *Q2*; Easterne Hill, *F1*; mountaine top, *Q1*
168 **advice**] *F1*; aduise *Q2–4 (Q1)*
175 **convenient**] conueniently *F1 (Q1)*

_____ 1.2 _____

1.2] I.ii *F1*
Location: *Capell (subs., after Rowe)*
o.s.d. **Flourish . . . aliis**] Enter Claudius King of Denmarke, Gertrude the Queene, Hamlet, Polonius, Laertes, and his Sister Ophelia, Lords Attendant. *F1*; Enter King, Queene, Hamlet, Leartes, Corambis, and the two Ambassadors, with Attendants. *Q1* (Leartes *for* Laertes *and* Corambis *for* Polonius *throughout; cf.* Corambus *in Der bestrafte Brudermord*)
o.s.d. **Gertrude**] *(throughout)*; Gertrad *Q2–4 (or* Gertrard *throughout, except* Gertrud *at 2.2.54 in Q3–4)*; Gertred *Q1 (or* Gerterd *throughout)*
o.s.d. **including . . . Cornelius**] *from Q1 (see above); F1 brings in the Ambassadors at l. 25.*
8 **sometime**] sometimes *F1*
9 **to**] of *F1*
11 **an . . . a**] one . . . one *F1*
16 **all,**] *Pope*; all *Q2–4, F1*
17 **follows**] follows, *F1*
21 **Co-leagued**] *Capell*; Coleagued *Q2*; Colegued *Q3*; Collegued *Q4*; Col-leagued *F1*
21 **this**] the *F1*
22 **pester**] *F1, Q3–4*; pestur *Q2*
24 **bands**] Bonds *F1*
29 **bedred**] *cf.* Love's Labor's Lost, *1.1.138, and* Lucrece, *l. 975)*; bedrid *F1*; bed-rid *Q1*
34 **Cornelius**] Cornelia *Q1*
34 **Voltemand**] *F1*; Valtemand *Q2–4*; Voltemar *Q1 (throughout)*
35 **bearers**] *(Q1)*; bearing *F1*
38 **delated**] dilated *F1*; related *Q1*
38 **s.d. Giving a paper.**] *Collier MS (subs., after Capell)*
40 **s.p. Cornelius, Voltemand**] Volt. *F1*
41 **s.d. Exeunt . . . Cornelius.**] *F1 (Exit . . .)*
50 **My dread**] Dread my *F1*; My gratious *Q1*
55 **toward**] towards *F1*; for *Q1*
58 **H'ath**] *ed.*; Hath *Q2*; He hath *Q3–4, F1(Q1)*
58–60 **wrung . . . consent.**] *om. F1*; wrung from me a forced graunt, *Q1*
58 **wrung**] *Q3–4 (Q1)*; wroung *Q2*
65 **s.d. Aside.**] *Theobald*
67 **so**] *F1*; so much *Q2–4*
67 **in the**] i' th' *F1*
67 **sun**] *F1*; sonne *Q2–4*
68 **nighted**] nightly *F1*
72 **common,**] *F1*; common *Q2–4*
77 **good mother**] *F1*; coold mother *Q2*; could smother *Q3–4*
82 **shapes**] *Q3–4*; chapes *Q2*; shewes *F1*
83 **denote**] *F1*; deuote *Q2–3*; deuoute *Q4*
85 **passes**] passeth *F1*
96 **or**] a *F1*
97 **unschool'd:**] *F1*; vnschoold *Q2*; vnschoold, *Q3–4*

105 **corse**] *Capell;* course *Q2–4;* Coarse *F1*
112 **toward**] towards *F1*
112 **you.**] *F1;* you *Q2–4*
114 **retrograde**] *F1;* retrogard *Q2–3;* retro-grad *Q4*
119 **pray thee**] prythee *F1*
126 **tell,**] *F1;* tell. *Q2–4;* tell *Q1*
127 **rouse**] *Malone;* rowse *Q2–4* (*Q1*); Rouce *F1*
127 **heaven**] Heauens *F1*
128 **s.d. Flourish**] *om. F1* (*Q1*)
128 **s.d. Exeunt . . . Hamlet.**] (*Q1*); Exeunt Manet Hamlet. *F1*
129 **sallied**] *cf.* sallies *at 2.1.39 and* vnsallied *in* Love's Labor's Lost, *5.2.352;* solid *F1;* grieu'd and sallied *Q1*
132 **self-slaughter**] *F1;* seale slaughter *Q2–4*
132 **God, God,**] God, O God! *F1*
133 **weary**] *F1;* wary *Q2–4*
134 **Seem**] Seemes *F1*
135 **ah fie**] Oh fie, fie *F1*
137 **merely. That**] *F1;* meerely that *Q2–4*
137 **to this**] *F1;* thus *Q2–4*
140 **satyr**] *F4;* satire *Q2–3;* Satyre *F1, Q4*
141 **beteem**] beteene *F1*
143 **Why,**] *Pope;* why *Q2–4, F1*
143 **should**] would *F1* (*Q1*)
147 **month, or**] *F1;* month or *Q2;* month. Or *Q3–4*
149 **even she**] *F1*
150 **God**] (*Q1*); Heauen *F1*
151 **my**] mine *F1* (*Q1*)
155 **in**] (*Q1*); of *F1*
156 **married — O**] *ed.;* married, ô *Q2;* married Oh! *Q3–4;* married. O *F1;* married, well *Q1*
156 **speed:**] *ed.;* speed; *Q2–4;* speed, *F1* (*Q1*)
157 **incestious**] Incestuous *F1* (*Q1*)
158 **good,**] good. *F1;* good: *Q1*
159 **s.d. Barnardo**] *Wilson;* Bernardo *Q2–4;* Barnard *F1; Q1 s.d. om. Barnardo*
167 **s.d. To Barnardo.**] *Cambridge*
170 **hear**] haue *F1*
171 **my**] mine *F1*
174 **Elsinore**] *Malone;* Elsonoure *Q2–4;* Elsenour *F1;* Elsenoure *Q1*
175 **to drink deep**] *F1* (*Q1*); for to drinke *Q2–4*
177 **prithee**] pray thee *F1;* O I pre thee *Q1*
177 **studient**] (*Q1*); Student *F1, Q3–4*
178 **see**] *F1* (*Q1*)
183 **Or . . . had**] Ere I had euer *F1;* Ere euer I had *Q1*
185 **Where**] (*Q1*); Oh where *F1*
186 **'a**] he *F1* (*Q1*) (*the usual F1 form*)
187 **'A**] He *F1* (*Q1*)
191 **lord,**] *F1* (*Q1*); Lord *Q2–4*
195 **God's**] (*Q1*); Heauens *F1*
198 **waste**] *F2;* wast *Q2–3, F1;* vast *Q4* (*Q1*)
200 **Armed at point**] Arm'd at all points *F1;* Armed to poynt *Q1*
200 **point exactly, cap-a-pe**] *F1* (points);

poynt, exactly Capapea *Q2* (*Q1*); poynt, exactly Cap apea *Q3–4*
203 **fear-surprised**] *hyphen, F1;* feare oppressed *Q1*
204 **distill'd**] bestil'd *F1;* distilled *Q1*
209 **Where, as**] *Q5;* Whereas *Q2–4, F1;* Where as *Q1*
213 **watch**] watcht *F1;* watched *Q1*
224 **indeed**] *F1* (*Q1*)
225, 227, 228 **s.pp.** Marcellus, Barnardo] Mar., Bar. *Capell (after F1* Both.); All. *Q2–4* (*Q1*)
231 **What, look'd**] *F1;* What look't *Q2–4;* How look't *Q1* (*with a comma after* he)
236 **very like**] *F1* (*Q1*)
237 **hundreth**] hundred *F1* (*Q1*)
238 **s.p.** Marcellus, Barnardo] Mar., Bar. *Capell; F1 s.p.* All.; *Q1 s.p.* Mar.
239 **grisl'd**] *Warburton;* grissl'd *Q2–3;* grisseld *Q4;* grisly *F1;* grisleld Q1
241 **I will**] (*Q1*); Ile *F1*
241 **to-night**] *F1, Q3–4* (*Q1*); to nigh *Q2*
242 **warr'nt**] *Kittredge (after Wilson);* warn't *Q2–4;* warrant you *F1;* warrant *Q1*
247 **tenable**] treble *F1;* tenible *Q1*
248 **whatsomever**] *Wilson;* what someuer *Q2;* what what soeuer *Q3;* whatsoeuer *F1, Q4* (*Q1*)
250 **fare**] *F1, Q3–4* (*Q1*); farre *Q2*
250 **you**] (*Q1*); ye *F1*
251 **aleven**] *ed.;* a leauen *Q2–3;* eleuen *F1, Q4* (*Q1*)
251 **twelf**] twelue *Q3–4, F1* (*Q1*)
253 **Your loves**] Your loue *F1;* O your loues, your loues *Q1*
253 **s.d. all but Hamlet**] *Cambridge (after Capell); s.d. after l. 252, Q2–4, F1* (*Q1*); *placed as in Capell*
256 **Foul**] *F1, Q3–4* (*Q1*); fonde *Q2*

──────────── 1.3 ────────────

1.3] I.iii *F1*
Location: *ed.* (*after Pope*)
o.s.d. Ophelia] Ofelia *Q1* (*throughout*)
o.s.d. his sister] *om. F1* (*Q1*)
1 **inbark'd**] (*Q1*); imbark't *F1, Q4*
3 **convey**] *ed.;* conuay, *Q2–4;* Conuoy *F1*
3 **is**] *F1;* in *Q2–4*
5 **favor**] fauours *F1*
8 **Forward**] Froward *F1*
9 **perfume and**] *om. F1* (*Q1*)
9 **minute —**] *F2* (*subs.*); minute *Q2–4;* minute? *F1*
10 **so?**] *Rowe;* so. *Q2–4, F1*
12 **bulk**] *F1;* bulkes *Q2–4*
12 **this**] his *F1*
16 **will**] feare *F1*
18 **For . . . birth:**] *F1*
21 **safety**] sanctity *F1*
21 **this whole**] the weole *F1;* the whole *F2*
26 **particular . . . place**] peculiar Sect and force *F1*
34 **you in**] within *F1*

36, 38, 39] Q2–4 mark these lines with gnomic quotes
37 moon.] Q1; Moone Q2–4; Moone: F1
40 their] the F1
46 watchman] watchmen F1
49 Whiles] Whilst F1
49 like] F1 (Q1)
51 reaks] recks Q1
51 s.d. Enter Polonius.] placed as in F1; after rede. l. 51, Q2–4; Enter Corambis. Q1 (after l. 54)
57 stay'd] F1 (Q1); stayed Q2–4
57 for. There —] Theobald; for, there Q2–4 (Q1); for there: F1
57 s.d. laying . . . head] Theobald
57 thee] (Q1); you F1
59 Look] See F1
62 Those] (Q1); The F1
63 unto thy soul] to thy Soule F1; to thee Q1
65 new-hatch'd] hyphen, Pope; vnhatch't F1; new Q1
65 courage] (Q1); Comrade F1
68 thy ear] thine eare F1
74 Are] F1, Q4 (Q1); Or Q2; Ar Q3
74 generous] F1; generous, Q2–4; generall Q1
74 chief] (Q1); cheff F1
75 be] F1; boy Q2–4
76 loan] (lone); loue Q2–4
77 dulleth th' edge] Q3–4 (reading the); dulleth edge Q2; duls the edge F1
83 invests] inuites F1
97–98 honor. What] F1; honor, / What Q2–4
98 you?] Q5; you Q2–4; you, F1
105 I will] Ile F1
106 these] his F1
109 Wringing] Theobald; Wrong Q2–4; Roaming F1; tendring Q1
114 almost. . . vows] all the vowes F1; Q1 reads the line: And withall, such earnest vowes.
115 springes] F1, Q3–4 (Q1); springs Q2
117 Lends] (Q1); Giues F1
120 fire. From] Q3–4 (subs.); fire, from Q2; fire. For F1
120 time] time Daughter F1
121 something] somewhat F1
123 parle] parley F1
125 teder] Q3–4; tider Q2; tether F1
128 that dye] the eye F1
129 implorators] F1, Q3–4; imploratotors Q2
131 beguile] F1, Q3–4; beguide Q2
135–36 Come . . . lord.] Q1 ends the scene with the following lines: Cor. Ofelia, receiue none of his letters, / "For louers lines are snares to intrap the heart; / "Refuse his tokens, both of them are keyes / To vnlocke Chastitie vnto Desire; / Come in Ofelia, such men often proue, / "Great in their wordes, but little in their loue. (the final couplet seems to be a recollection of Twelfth Night, 2.4.117–18)

———————— 1.4 ————————

1.4] I.iv Capell
Location: Alexander (after Rowe)
1 shrowdly] shrewdly F1; shrewd Q1
1 it . . . cold.] is it very cold? F1
2 a] F1; An Q1
3 twelf] twelue F1, Q3–4 (Q1)
5 It then] then it F1
6 s.d. off] Q3–4; of Q2; s.d. om. F1; Q1 gives Sound Trumpets. after l. 3
6 s.d. within] Rowe
9 wassail] (Q1); wassels F1
14 But] And F1
17–38 This . . . scandal.] om. F1 (Q1)
17 heavy-headed] hyphen, Q3–4
17 revel] Q3–4; reueale Q2
18 traduc'd] Q3 (tradu'cd) –4; tradust Q2
18 tax'd] Pope; taxed Q2–4
23 So,] Theobald; So Q2–4
36 ev'l] ed. (after Keightley); eale Q2; ease Q3–4
42 intents] euents F1
45 Dane. O] F1 (Dane: Oh, oh); Dane, ô Q2–4
48 cerements] cerments F1; ceremonies Q1
49 inurn'd] F1 (enurn'd); interr'd Q2–4 (Q1)
56 the] (Q1); thee; F1
57 s.d. Ghost beckons Hamlet.] F1; Beckins Q2–4
61 waves] (Q1); wafts F1
63 I will] will I F1 (Q1)
70 summit] Rowe; somnet Q2–4; Sonnet F1
70 cliff] F1; cleefe Q2–4
71 beetles] F1; bettles Q2; bettels Q3–4; beckles Q1
72 assume] (Q1); assumes F1
75–78 The . . . beneath.] om. F1 (Q1)
78 waves] wafts F1
80 hands] hand F1
82 artere] Wilson; arture Q2; artyre Q3; attire Q4; artcry Q5; Artire F1, Artiue Q1
83 Nemean] Q3–4; Nemeon Q2 (Q1); Nemian F1
86 s.d. Exeunt] F1; Exit Q2–4
87 imagination] F1, Q3–4 (Q1); imagion Q2

———————— 1.5 ————————

1.5] I.v Capell
Location: Alexander
1 Whither] Q1; Whether Q2–4; Where F1
3 sulph'rous] Kittredge (after Q3–4 sulphrous); sulphrus Q2; sulphurous F1
18 knotted] (Q1); knotty F1
20 fearful] fretfull F1 (Q1)

22 **List . . . list!**] list *Hamlet*, oh list, *F1;* Hamlet, *Q1*
24 **God**] (*Q1*); Heauen *F1*
29 **Haste . . . that** I] Hast, hast me to know it / That *F1;* Haste me to knowe it that *Q1*
33 **roots**] (*Q1*); rots *F1*
35 **'Tis**] (*Q1*); It's *F1*
35 **my**] (*Q1*); mine *F1*
38 **know,**] *F4;* knowe *Q2–4, F1* (*Q1*)
41 **My uncle?**] mine Vncle *F1;* my vncle! my vncle! *Q1*
43 **with traitorous gifts — **] *Pope (subs., after Rowe);* with trayterous gifts, *Q2–4;* hath Traitorous guifts. *F1;* with gifts, *Q1*
45 **to his**] (*Q1*); to to this *F1*
47 **a**] *F1*
47 **falling-off**] *hyphen, Capell*
55 **lust**] *F1* (*Q1*); but *Q2–4*
55 **angel**] *F1;* Angle *Q2–4* (*Q1*)
56 **sate**] *F1;* sort *Q2–4;* fate *Q1*
58 **morning**] Mornings *F1* (*Q1*)
59 **my**] (*Q1*); mine *F1*
60 **of**] in *F1* (*Q1*)
62 **hebona**] (*Q1*); Hebenon *F1*
62 **vial**] (*Q1*); Violl *F1*
63 **my**] (*Q1*); mine *F1*
64 **leprous**] (*Q1*); leaperous *F1*
67 **alleys**] *Hanmer;* allies *Q2–4, F1*
68 **posset**] *F1;* possesse *Q2–4*
69 **eager**] (*Q1*); Aygre *F1*
71 **bark'd**] bak'd *F1;* barked *Q1*
75 **of queen**] (*Q1*); and Queene *F1*
77 **Unhous'led**] *ed. (after Theobald);* Vnhuzled *Q2;* Vnnuzled *Q3–4;* Vnhouzzled *F1*
77 **unanel'd**] *Pope;* vnanueld *Q2;* vn-anueld *Q3–4;* vnnaneld *F1*
79 **With all**] *F1, Q3–4* (*Q1*); Withall *Q2*
84 **howsomever**] howsoeuer *F1* (*Q1*)
84 **pursues**] pursuest *F1*
91 **adieu, adieu!**] adue, *Hamlet: F1; Q1 reads the line:* Hamlet adue, adue, adue: remember me.
91 **s.d. Exit.**] *F1*
93 **hold,**] *om. F1* (*Q1*)
94 **sinows**] sinnewes *F1*
95 **stiffly**] *F1;* swiftly *Q2–4*
96 **whiles**] while *F1*
102 **commandement**] Commandment *F1*
104 **Yes**] yes, yes *F1* (*Q1*)
107 **My tables — **] *Pope;* My tables, *Q2–4;* My Tables, my Tables; *F1;* (My tables) *Q1*
109 **I am**] (*Q1*); I'm *F1*
109 **s.d. He writes.**] *Rowe (subs.)*
113 **s.p. Horatio**] Hor. & Mar. *F1*
113 **s.d.d. Within.**] *F1 gives the first, Capell the second*
113 **s.d. Enter . . . Marcellus.**] *placed by ed.; after l. 112, Q2–4; after* lord! *l. 113, F1; opposite l. 113, Q1*
113 **Heavens**] (*Q1*); Heauen *F1*

114 **s.p. Hamlet**] Mar. *F1*
115 **s.p. Marcellus**] Hor. *F1* (*Q1*)
116 **boy! Come, bird,**] *F1 (subs.);* boy come, and *Q2–4;* so, come boy, *Q1*
119 **you will**] you'l *F1* (*Q1*)
121 **it?**] *F1* (*Q1*); it, *Q2–4*
122 **secret?**] *F1;* secret, *Q2–4* (*Q1*)
122 **s.p. Horatio, Marcellus**] Hor., Mar. *Capell*
122 **my lord**] *F1* (*Q1*)
123 **never**] (*Q1*); nere *F1*
126 **in the**] (*Q1*); i' th' *F1*
129 **desire**] desires *F1* (*Q1*)
130 **hath**] (*Q1*); ha's *F1*
131 **my**] (*Q1*); mine *F1*
132 **I will**] Looke you, Ile *F1;* ile *Q1*
133 **whirling**] *Theobald;* whurling *Q2–4;* hurling *F1;* wherling *Q1*
134 **I am**] (*Q1*); I'm *F1*
136 **Horatio**] (*Q1*); my Lord *F1*
137 **too.**] *Q5 (subs.);* to, *Q2–4;* too, *F1* (*Q1*)
140 **O'ermaster't**] *F1, Q3–4;* Oremastret *Q2;* Or'emaister it *Q1*
145 **s.p. Horatio, Marcellus**] Hor., Mar. *Capell*
150 **Ha**] (*Q1*); Ah *F1*
151 **on, you hear**] one you here *F1;* you here, *Q1*
151 **cellarage**] *Johnson;* Sellerige *Q2* (*Q1*); selleredge *F1*
155, 161, 181 **s.dd. Beneath.**] *Capell*
156 **ubique?**] *F1;* vbique, *Q2–4* (*Q1*)
156 **our**] (*Q1*); for *F1*
159 **Swear . . . sword,**] *follows l. 160, F1* (*Q1*)
161 **by his sword**] *om. F1* (*Q1*)
162 **i' th'**] *F1;* it'h *Q2–4;* in the *Q1*
162 **earth**] (*Q1*); ground *F1*
167 **your**] (*Q1*); our *F1*
170–78 **How . . . note**] *F1 (subs.);* (How . . . note) *Q2–4*
170 **some'er**] *Wilson;* so mere *Q2–4;* so ere *F1;* soere *Q1*
173 **times**] (*Q1*); time *F1*
174 **this**] (*Q1*); thus, *F1*
176 **Well, well,**] (*Q1*); well, *F1*
177 **they**] (*Q1*); there *F1*
179 **do swear,**] not to doe: *F1*
180 **you.**] you: / Sweare. *F1* (*Q1*)
181 **s.d. They swear.**] *Globe (after l. 182); placed as in Kittredge*
183 **With all**] *F1, Q3–4;* Withall *Q2;* In all *Q1*
187 **pray.**] *Rowe;* pray, *Q2–4, F1* (*Q1*)

──────────── **2.1** ────────────

2.1] II.i *Q (1676);* Actus Secundus. *F1*
Location: *ed. (after Rowe)*
o.s.d. with . . . Reynaldo] *from Q2–4, F1 s.d.:* with his man or two *Q2–4;* and Reynoldo *F1; Q1 s.d. reads:* Enter Corambis, and Montano.
1 **this**] his *F1;* this same *Q1*

1 **Reynaldo**] Reynoldo *F1 (throughout);*
  Montano *Q1 (throughout)*
3 **marvell's**] *Dyce;* meruiles *Q2;* marue-
  lous *Q3–4;* maruels *F1*
4 **to make inquire**] you make inquiry *F1;*
  To inquire *Q1*
6 **Marry**] *F1, Q4;* Mary *Q2–3*
14 **As**] *(Q1);* And *F1*
18 **if 't**] *F1;* y'ft *Q2–4*
28 **Faith,**] Faith no, *F1;* I faith not a whit,
  no not a whit, *Q1*
34 **unreclaimed**] *Q4;* vnreclamed *Q2–3;*
  vnreclaim'd *F1*
38 **wit**] warrant *F1*
39 **sallies**] *see 1.2.129;* sullies *Q3–4;* sulleyes
  F1
40 **wi' th'**] *ed.,* with *Q2–4;* i' th' *F1*
43 **seen**] seene. *F1*
43 **prenominate**] *F1, Q4;* prenominat
  Q2–3
47 **or**] and *F1*
47 **addition**] *F1, Q3–4;* addistion *Q2*
49 **'a . . . 'a**] he . . . He *F1*
49 **this — . . . does —**] *Capell (after
  Rowe);* this, . . . doos, *Q2;* this . . . doos:
  Q3–4; this? . . . does: *F1*
50 **By the mass**] *om. F1 (Q1)*
51 **consequence.**] consequence: / At
  friend, or so, and Gentleman. *F1*
53 **closes thus:**] closes with you thus. *F1;*
  closeth with him thus, *Q1*
54 **th' other**] tother *F1 (Q1)*
55 **or such**] and such *F1*
56 **'a**] he *F1*
56 **gaming, there o'ertook**] *F1;* gaming
  there, or tooke *Q2–4*
58 **sale**] saile *F1;* lightnes *Q1*
59 **forth.**] *F1;* forth, *Q2–4*
60 **take**] takes *F1*
60 **carp**] Cape *F1*
64 **advice**] *F1;* aduise *Q2–4*
66 **ye . . . ye**] you . . . you *F1*
71 s.d. **Exit Reynaldo.**] *placed as in Dyce
  (after Singer); after l. 70, Q2–4;* Exit. *F1
  (Q1) (after l. 70)*
71 s.d. **Enter Ophelia.**] *placed as in
  Singer; after l. 70, Q2–4, F1 (Q1)*
72 **O . . . I**] Alas, my Lord, I *F1*
73 **i' th'**] in the *F1*
73 **God**] Heauen *F1*
74 **closet**] Chamber *F1*
76 **stockins**] stockings *F1*
77 **down-gyved**] *hyphen, F2*
88 **'a**] he *F1*
92 **As**] That *F1*
94 **shoulder**] *(Q1);* shoulders *F1*
96 **a' doors**] *Q3* (a doores); adoores *Q2;* of
  doores *Q4 (Q1);* adores *F1*
96 **helps**] helpe *F1 (Q1)*
98 **Come**] *om. F1 (Q1)*
102 **passions**] passion *F1*
103 **sorry —**] *Capell;* sorry, *Q2–4, F1*
108 **heed**] speed *F1*
109 **coted**] quoted *F1*

109 **fear'd**] feare *F1*
111 **By heaven**] It seemes *F1;* By heau'n *Q1*
117 **Come.**] *om. F1 (Q1)*

_____ **2.2** _____

2.2] II.ii *F1*
Location: *Capell (after Rowe)*
o.s.d. **Flourish.**] *om. F1 (Q1)*
o.s.d. **Rosencrantz**] *Malone;* Rosencraus
  *Q2–4 (so generally throughout, except
  Rosencrans at 2.2.34);* Rosincrane *F1
  (also Rosencrance and Rosincran elsewhere);* Rossencraft *Q1*
o.s.d. **Guildenstern**] Guyldensterne *Q2–4
  (also Guyldersterne elsewhere), F1;* Gilderstone *Q1*
o.s.d **cum aliis**] *F1*
5 **so**] so I *F1*
6 **Sith nor**] Since not *F1*
10 **dream**] deeme *F1*
12 **sith**] since *F1*
12 **neighbored**] *Q3–4;* nabored *Q2;*
  Neighbour'd *F1*
12 **havior**] humour *F1*
13 **voutsafe**] vouchsafe *F1, Q4*
16 **occasion**] Occasions *F1*
17 **Whether . . . thus,**] *om. F1 (Q1)*
20 **is**] are *F1*
29 **But**] *om. F1 (Q1)*
31 **service**] Seruices *F1*
36 **you**] ye *F1*
37 **these**] the *F1*
39 **Ay**] *Capell;* I *Q2–4; om. F1 (Q1)*
39 s.d. **with some Attendants**] *Capell; F1
  s.d. is* Exit. *(after* him! *l. 39)*
43 **I assure**] *(Q1);* Assure you, *F1*
45 **and**] *(Q1);* one *F1*
48 **it hath**] I haue *F1;* it had *Q1*
50 **do I**] I do *F1*
52 **fruit**] Newes *F1*
53 s.d. **Exit Polonius.**] *Rowe*
54 **dear Gertrude**] *Q5;* deere Gertrard *Q2;*
  decree: Gertrud *Q3–4;* sweet Queene,
  that *F1*
57 **o'erhasty**] *F1;* hastie *Q2–4*
57 s.d. **Polonius . . . the**] *F1 (subs., reading* Voltumand)
58 **my**] *om. F1 (Q1)*
63, 75 **Polack**] *(Q1);* Poleak *F1*
73 **threescore**] three *F1 (Q1)*
76 **shown**] *F1* (shewne) *(Q1);* shone *Q2–4*
76 s.d. **Giving a paper.**] *Malone (after
  Capell)*
78 **this**] his *F1;* that *Q1*
85 s.d. **Exeunt Embassadors**] *(Q1 subs.);*
  Exit. Ambass. *F1*
85 s.d. **and Attendants**] *Alexander*
85 **well**] very well *F1*
90 **since**] *F1*
97 **he's**] he is *F1*
98 **'tis 'tis**] it is *F1*
104 **thus.**] *F1;* thus *Q2–4*
106 **while**] *(Q1);* whil'st *F1*

108 **s.d. Reads . . . letter.**] *ed.;* The Letter. *F1*
111 **vile . . . vile**] vilde . . . vilde *F1*
112 **hear. Thus:**] *Jennens (subs.);* heare: thus *Q2–4 (Polonius's comments are given as part of the letter in Q2–4);* heare these *F1*
113 **etc.**] *om. F1 (Q1)*
115 **s.d. Reads the**] *Rowe*
125 **This**] *F1; Pol.* This *Q2–4 (repeated s.p.)*
125 **shown**] shew'd *F1*
126 **above**] *F1;* about *Q2–4*
126 **solicitings**] soliciting *F1*
137 **winking,**] *F1;* working *Q2–4*
142 **prescripts**] Precepts *F1*
143 **his**] *F1, Q3–4;* her *Q2*
145 **advice**] *F1;* aduise *Q2–4*
146 **repell'd**] repulsed *F1*
148 **watch**] *F1, Q3–4;* wath *Q2*
149 **a**] *F1*
150 **wherein**] whereon *F1*
151 **mourn**] waile *F1*
151 **'tis**] *F1 (Q1)*
152 **be,**] *Capell;* be *Q2–4, F1*
152 **like**] likely *F1*
153 **I would**] I'de *F1;* I would very *Q1*
156 **s.d. Points . . . shoulder.**] *Theobald*
161 **does**] ha's *F1*
167 **But**] And *F1*
167 **s.d. reading on a book**] *F1; in Q1 the King describes the entrance of Hamlet* poring vppon a booke; *Q1 (like Der* bestrafte Brudermord) *inserts at this point its version of 3.1.43–174*
169 **you,**] *F1;* you *Q2–4*
170 **s.d. Exeunt**] *Rowe;* Exit *Q2–4, F1; s.d. placed as in F1; after l. 169, Q2–4*
174 **Excellent**] Excellent, excellent *F1;* Yea very *Q1*
174 **you are**] y'are *F1 (Q1)*
177 **lord?**] *F1;* Lord, *Q2–4*
178–79 **Ay . . . thousand.**] *as prose, F1; as verse, Q2–4 (Q1)*
179 **ten**] *(Q1);* two *F1*
184–85 **Let . . . to't.**] *as prose, F1; as verse, Q2–4*
185 **but**] but not *F1*
186 **s.d. Aside.**] *Capell*
187 **'a**] he *F1 (Q1)*
188 **'A**] he *F1*
188 **gone**] gone, farre gone *F1*
194 **that**] *om. F1 (Q1)*
194 **read**] *(Q1);* meane *F1*
195 **rogue**] slaue *F1;* Satyre *Q1*
197 **and**] or *F1*
198 **lack**] locke *F1*
199 **most**] *om. F1;* pittifull *Q1*
201 **yourself**] *(Q1);* you your selfe *F1*
201 **shall grow**] should be *F1;* shalbe *Q1*
203 **s.d. Aside.**] *Johnson*
206 **that's . . . the**] *(Q1);* that is out o' th' *F1*
206 **s.d. Aside.**] *Capell*
208 **sanity**] *F1;* sanctity *Q2–4*
209–10 **and . . . him**] *F1*

211 **lord . . . take**] *(Q1);* Honourable Lord, I will most humbly / Take *F1*
212 **cannot . . . thing**] cannot Sir . . . thing *F1;* can take nothing from me sir *Q1*
212 **not**] *om. F1 (Q1)*
213–14 **withal — . . . life.**] withall, except my life, my life. *F1*
216 **s.d. Enter . . . Rosencrantz.**] *placed as in Capell; after l. 214, Q2–4; after l. 217, F1; after l. 211, Q1*
217 **the**] my *F1*
218 **s.d. To Polonius.**] *Malone*
218 **s.d. Exit Polonius.**] *Q1* (exit.)
219 **My**] Mine *F1*
221 **excellent**] *F1, Q4;* extent *Q2;* exelent *Q3*
222 **Ah**] *Q5;* A *Q2–4;* Oh *F1*
222 **you**] ye *F1*
225 **over-happy,**] *F1* (ouer-happy:); euer happy *Q2–4*
226 **cap**] *F1;* lap *Q2–4*
227 **shoe?**] *F1;* shooe. *Q2–4*
230 **favors**] fauour *F1*
233 **What**] What's the *F1*
234 **but**] but that *F1*
236–64 **s.d. Let . . . attended.**] *F1*
261 **s.p. Rosencrantz, Guildenstern**] Ros., Guil. *Capell*
265 **Elsinore**] *Malone;* Elsonoure *Q2–4;* Elsonower *F1;* Elsanoure *Q1*
267 **even**] *F1;* euer *Q2–4*
270 **come**] *om. F1 (Q1)*
273 **Any thing**] Why any thing. *F1*
274 **of**] *(Q1); om. F1*
281 **can**] could *F1*
284 **s.d. Aside to Guildenstern.**] *Globe (after Theobald)*
285 **s.d. Aside.**] *Steevens*
289 **and**] of *F1*
291 **exercises**] exercise *F1*
292 **heavily**] heauenly *F1*
295 **firmament**] *om. F1 (Q1)*
296 **appeareth . . . but**] appeares no other thing to me then *F1*
297 **a**] *F1*
298–300 **how infinite . . . god:**] how infinite in faculty? in forme and mouing how expresse and admirable? in Action, how like an Angel? in apprehension, how like a God? *F1 (c) (the uncorrected state has no pointing after* God)
303 **nor**] no, nor *F1 (Q1)*
303 **women**] Woman *F1, Q3–4 (Q1)*
306 **ye**] you *F1 (Q1)*
306 **then**] *(Q1); om. F1*
310 **coted**] coated *F1;* boorded *Q1*
313 **on**] of *F1 (Q1)*
315–16 **the . . . sere,**] *F1 (Q1, in part)*
316 **tickle**] *Staunton conj.;* tickled *F1 (Q1)*
317 **blank**] *F1, Q3–4 (Q1);* black *Q2*
319 **such**] *om. F1 (Q1)*
321 **travel**] *Q1;* trauaile *Q2–4, F1*
327 **are they**] they are *F1*
328–52 **Ham. How . . . too.**] *F1*

330 eyases] *Theobald;* Yases *F1*
332 berattle] *F3* (be-rattle); be-ratled *F1;* be ratle *F2*
339–40 most like] *Pope;* like most *F1*
340 no] *Rowe;* not *F1* (*the* t *is uncertain*), *F2*
353 very] *om. F1* (*Q1*)
354 mouths at him] mowes at him *F1;* mops and moes / At my vncle *Q1*
355 fifty] *om. F1* (*Q1*)
355 a] (*Q1*); an *F1*
356 'Sblood] *om. F1* (*Q1*)
357 s.d. for the Players] *F1; Q1 s.d. reads:* The Trumpets sound,
360 hands, come then:] *F1* (*which om.* then); hands come then. *Q2;* hands, Come then *Q3–4*
361 this] the *F1*
361–62 lest my] *F1;* let me *Q2;* let my *Q3–4*
363 outwards] outward *F1*
368 hand-saw] *Q3–4;* hand saw *Q2;* Hand-saw *F1*
370 s.d. Aside to them.] *Neilson*
372 swaddling-clouts] (*Q1*); swathing clouts *F1*
373 he is] he's *F1*
376 s.d. Aloud.] *Neilson*
376 a'] (*Q1*); for a *F1*
377 then] so *F1* (*Q1*)
379 was] (*Q1*); *om. F1*
383 my] mine *F1*
384 "Then ... ass"] *quotes, Johnson conj.*
384 came] can *F1*
386–87 pastoral-comical, historical-pastoral] hyphens, *Q3–4;* Pastoricall-Comicall-Historicall-Pastorall *F1;* Pastorall, Historicall, Historicall, Comicall *Q1*
387–88 tragical- . . . -pastoral,] *F1;* Comicall historicall, Pastorall, Tragedy historicall: *Q1*
388 Seneca] *F1, Q3–4* (*Q1*); Sceneca *Q2*
391, 398, 399 Jephthah] *Hanmer;* Ieptha *Q2–4;* Iephta *F1;* Iepha *Q1* (*om. l. 398*)
395–96 One . . . well.] *as verse,* F1 (*Q1*); *as prose, Q2–4; quotes, Pope*
397 s.d. Aside.] *Capell*
404–06 "As . . . was"] *as partly quoted verse, Malone* (*after Pope*); *as prose, Q2–4,* F1; *as irregular verse, Q1, reading:* Why by lot, or God wot, or as it came to passe, / And so it was,
407 pious chanson] Pons Chanson *F1* (*in italics*); godly Ballet *Q1*
408 abridgment comes] (*Q1*); Abridgements come *F1*
408 s.d. four or five] *F1* (*before* Players)
409 You] *F1* (*reading* Y'); *Ham.* You *Q2–4* (*repeated s.p.*); *s.p. and* You are *om. Q1*
410 old] my olde *F1* (*Q1*)
410 why] *om. F1* (*Q1*)
411 valanc'd] *Q3–4;* valanct *Q2;* valiant *F1;* vallanced *Q1*
412—13 by' lady] *ed.;* by lady *Q2–3;* my Ladie *Q4;* Byrlady *F1;* burlady *Q1*

413 to] *om. F1* (*Q1*)
416 e'en to't] *F1;* ento't *Q2–4;* euen too't *Q1*
417 French] *F1* (*Q1*); friendly *Q2–4*
417 falc'ners] *Q3–4* (Faukners); Fankners *Q2;* Faulconers *F1* (*Q1*)
420, 453, 487, 489, s.pp. First Player]1. Play. *F1;* Player. *or* Play. *Q2–4;* Players *Q1* (*later* Play.)
420 good] (*Q1*); *om. F1*
424 judgments] (*Q1*); iudgement *F1*
427 were] was *F1* (*Q1*)
429 affection] affectation *F1*
430–31 as wholesome . . . fine.] *om. F1* (*Q1, in part*)
431 speech] (*Q1*); cheefe Speech *F1*
432 tale] *F1* (*Q1*); talke *Q2–4*
432 thereabout] *F1;* there about *Q2–4;* . then *Q1* (*om.* of it)
433 when] (*Q1*); where *F1*
435 "The . . . beast"] *as verse, Q1, Capell; as prose, Q2–Q4, F1*
435 Hyrcanian] *F1;* ircanian *Q2–4;* arganian *Q1*
436 'Tis] It is *F1;* No t'is *Q1*
439 th'] the *F1*
441 heraldy] Heraldry *F1* (*Q1*)
441 dismal:] *F1;* dismall *Q2–4;* dismall, *Q1*
442 total gules] to take Geulles *F1;* totall guise *Q1*
445 and a] and *F1*
446 lord's murther] (*apostrophe, Steevens*); vilde Murthers *F1*
447 o'ersized] *F1;* ore-cised *Q2–4*
450 So proceed you.] *om. F1;* So goe on. *Q1*
454 antique] *Pope;* anticke *Q2–4,* F1 (*Q1*)
456 match'd] match *F1*
459 Then senseless Ilium,] *F1*
460 this] his *F1*
466 And] *F1*
473 a-work] *F1;* a worke *Q2–4*
475 Mars's armor] *Capell;* Marses Armor *Q2–4;* Mars his Armours *F1*
480 fellies] *F4;* follies *Q2;* folles *Q3;* fellowes *Q4;* Fallies *F1*
484 to the] (*Q1*); to'th *F1*
487 ah woe] *Q5;* a woe *Q2–4;* O who *F1* (*Q1*)
487, 488 mobled] (*Q1, l.* 487; *om. l.* 488); inobled *F1*
489 mobled . . . good] *F2;* Inobled . . . good *F1; Q1 reads the line:* Mobled Queene is good, faith very good.
490 flames] flame *F1*
491 bisson rheum] *F1; Bison* rehume *Q2; Bison* rhume *Q3–4*
491 clout upon] clout about *F1;* kercher on *Q1*
494 alarm] Alarum *F1* (*Q1*)
499 husband's] *F1, Q3–4* (*Q1*); husband *Q2*
504 whe'er] *Theobald* (*subs.*); where *Q2–4,* F1; if *Q1*

505 **Prithee**] Pray you *F1;* no more good
heart *Q1*
506 **of this**] *om. F1 (Q1)*
508 **you**] ye *F1*
508 **abstract**] Abstracts *F1 (Q1)*
510 **live**] *(Q1);* liued *F1*
512 **bodkin**] bodykins *F1*
512 **much**] *om. F1;* farre *Q1*
513 **shall**] should *F1 (Q1)*
516 **s.d. Exit.**] *F1 (Q1); Q2–4 give exit for
Polonius and Players after l. 525*
517–18 **s.d. Exeunt . . . First.**] *Dyce*
520, 524 **s.pp. First Player**] 1. Play. *Capell;*
Play. *Q2–4, F1;* players *Q1*
521 **ha't**] *F1;* hate *Q2;* hau't *Q3–4*
521 **need**] a need *F1 (Q1)*
522 **lines**] *om. F1 (Q1)*
523 **you**] ye *F1*
526 **s.d. Exit First Player.**] *Dyce*
526–28 **My . . . lord!**] Gentlemen, for your
kindnes I thanke you, / And for a time
I would desire you leaue me. / *Gil.* Our
loue and duetie is at your commaund.
Q1
526 **till**] *F1, Q3–4;* tell *Q2*
527 **Elsinore**] *Malone;* Elsonoure *Q2–4;*
Elsonower *F1*
529 **Ay so,**] *F1* (I so,), *Q3–4;* I so *Q2*
529 **to**] *om. F1 (Q1)*
529 **you.**] *pointing after F1* ('ye:); you,
Q2–4
529 **s.d. Rosencrantz and Guildenstern**]
*Capell; s.d. placed as in Globe; after l.
528, Q2–4, F1 (Q1)*
533 **own**] whole *F1*
534 **the**] his *F1*
534 **wann'd**] *Steevens (after Warburton);*
wand *Q2–4;* warm'd *F1*
535 **in his**] in's *F1*
536 **an'**] *ed.;* an *Q2;* and *F1, Q3–4*
539 **Hecuba**] *F1 (Q1);* her *Q2–4*
541 **the cue**] *F1;* that *Q2–4; Q1 reads l. 541
as:* and if he had my losse?
544 **appall**] *Rowe;* appale *Q2;* appeale *Q3–4;*
apale *F1*
546 **faculties**] faculty *F1*
547 **muddy-mettled**] *hyphen, F1*
556 **'swounds**] Why *F1;* Sure *Q1*
557 **pigeon-liver'd**] *hyphen, F1*
559 **'a'**] *ed.;* a *Q2 (Q1);* haue *F1, Q3–4*
560 **offal. Bloody,**] *Q5 (subs.);* offall,
bloody, *Q2–4;* Offall, bloudy: a *F1;*
offell, this *Q1 (substituting* damned
villaine *for* bawdy villain)
561 **villain!**] villaine! / Oh Vengeance! *F1*
562 **Why,**] Who? *F1*
562 **This**] I sure, this *F1*
563 **a dear father**] *Q3–4;* a deere *Q2;* the
Deere *F1;* my deare father *Q1*
567 **stallion**] Scullion *F1;* scalion *Q1*
568 **About,**] *Theobald;* About *Q2–4, F1
(Q1)*
568 **brains**] *Q2* (*c*), *Q3–4;* braues *Q2* (*u*);
Braine *F1 (Q1)*

568 **Hum**] *om. F1 (Q1)*
577 **If 'a do**] If he but *F1;* And if he doe not
Q1
579 **a dev'l . . . dev'l**] *ed.;* a deale . . . deale
Q2; a diuell . . . diuell *Q3–4;* the Diuell
. . . Diuel *F1;* the Diuell, *Q1*

_____ 3.1 _____

3.1] III.i *Q* (1676)
Location: *Capell (subs., after Rowe)*
*Cf. the following version of this scene in Q1 (see
note at l. 43 s.d. below): Enter the King,
Queene, and Lordes. / King* Lordes, can
you by no meanes finde / The cause of
our sonne Hamlets lunacie? / You
being so neere in loue, euen from his
youth, / Me thinkes should gaine more
than a stranger should. / *Gil.* My lord,
we haue done all the best we could, /
To wring from him the cause of all his
griefe, / But still he puts vs off, and by
no meanes / Would make an answere to
that we exposde. / *Ross.* Yet was he
something more inclin'd to mirth / Before we left him, and I take it, / He hath
giuen order for a play to night, / At
which he craues your highnesse company. / *King* With all our heart, it likes
vs very well: / Gentlemen, seeke still to
increase his mirth, / Spare for no cost,
our coffers shall be open, / And we
vnto your selues will still be thankefull.
/ *Both* In all wee can, be sure you shall
commaund. / *Queene* Thankes gentlemen, and what the Queene of
Denmarke / May pleasure you, be sure
you shall not want. / *Gil.* Weele once
againe vnto the noble Prince. / *King*
Thankes to you both: Gertred you'l see
this play. / *Queene* My lord I will, and it
ioyes me at the soule / He is inclin'd to
any kinde of mirth. / *Cor.* Madame, I
pray be ruled by me: / And my good
Soueraigne, giue me leaue to speake, /
We cannot yet finde out the very
ground / Of his distemperance, therefore / I holde it meete, if so it please
you, / Else they shall not meete, and
thus it is. / *King* What i'st *Corambis?* /
Cor. Mary my good lord this, soone
when the sports are done, / Madam,
send you in haste to speake with him, /
And I myselfe will stand behind the
Arras, / There question you the cause
of all his griefe, / And then in loue and
nature vnto you, hee'le tell you all: /
My Lord, how thinke you on't? / *King*
It likes vs well, Gerterd, what say you?/
Queene With all my heart, soone will I
send for him. / *Cor.* My selfe will be
that happy messenger, / Who hopes his
griefe will be reueal'd to her. *exeunt
omnes*

1 **An'**] *ed.*; An *Q2*; And *F1, Q3–4*
1 **conference**] circumstance *F1;* meanes
   Q1
6 **'a**] he *F1*
17 **o'erraught**] ore-wrought *F1*
19 **here**] *om. F1 (Q1)*
27 **into**] on / To *F1*
28 **s.d. Exeunt . . . Guildenstern.**] Exeunt. *F1*
28 **two**] too *F1*
30 **here**] there *F1*
31–32 **myself, We'll**] my selfe (lawful espials) / Will *F1*
41 **s.d. Exit Queen.**] *Theobald*
42 **please you**] please ye *F1*
43 **s.d. To Ophelia.**] *Johnson;* the *Q1 version of ll. 43–174 appears in 2.2 following l. 167*
45 **loneliness**] *F1;* lowlines *Q2–4*
47 **sugar**] surge *F1*
48 **s.d. Aside.**] *Capell (after Pope, at l. 49)*
48 **too**] *om. F1 (Q1)*
54 **Withdraw**] let's withdraw *F1*
54 **s.d. Exeunt**] *F1*
54 **s.d. King and Polonius**] *Capell*
54 **s.d. Enter Hamlet.**] *placed as in F1; after l. 53, Q2–4*
55–89 **To . . . rememb'red.**] *This soliloquy appears in the following form in Q1:* To be, or not to be, I there's the point, / To Die, to sleepe, is that all? I all: / No, to sleepe, to dreame, I mary there it goes, / For in that dreame of death, when wee awake, / And borne before an euerlasting Iudge, / From whence no passenger euer retur'nd, / The vndiscouered country, at whose sight / The happy smile, and the accursed damn'd. / But for this, the ioyfull hope of this, / Whol'd beare the scornes and flattery of the world, / Scorned by the right rich, the rich curssed of the poore? / The widow being oppressed, the orphan wrong'd, / The taste of hunger, or a tirants raigne, / And thousand more calamities besides, / To grunt and sweate vnder this weary life, / When that he may his full *Quietus* make, / With a bare bodkin, who would this indure, / But for a hope of something after death? / Which pusles the braine, and doth confound the sence, / Which makes vs rather beare those euilles we haue, / Than flie to others that we know not of. / I that, O this conscience makes cowardes of vs all, / Lady in thy orizons, be all my sinnes remembred. *(Q1 places this soliloquy, and the interview between Hamlet and Ophelia which follows, in 2.2 after the equivalent of ll. 169–70; Der bestrafte Brudermord, though it omits the soliloquy, also places the Hamlet-Ophelia interview essentially as in Q1.)*

59 **them.**] *F1, Q3–4 (subs.);* them, *Q2*
59 **die,**] *F1 (Q1);* die *Q2–4*
59 **sleep — **] *Pope;* sleepe *Q2–4, F1;* sleepe, *Q1*
63 **wish'd.**] *F1;* wisht *Q2–4*
63 **die,**] *Globe (after Pope);* die *Q2–4, F1*
70 **proud**] poore *F1*
71 **despis'd**] dispriz'd *F1*
74 **quietus**] *F1, Q4 (Q1);* quietas *Q2–3*
75 **fardels**] these Fardles *F1*
78 **bourn**] *Capell (after Pope);* borne *Q2–4, F1*
82 **of us all**] *F1 (Q1)*
84 **sicklied**] *F1;* sickled *Q2–4*
85 **pitch**] pith *F1*
86 **awry**] away *F1*
91 **well, well**] *F1*
94 **No, not I**] No, no *F1*
96 **you know**] I know *F1*
98 **these**] the *F1*
98 **rich. Their**] *Q3–4 (subs.);* rich, their *Q2;* rich, then *F1*
98 **lost,**] left: *F1*
106 **your honesty**] *F1;* you *Q2–4;* Your beauty *Q1*
108–09 **Could . . . honesty?**] *as prose, F1; as verse, Q2–4 (Q1)*
109 **with**] *(Q1);* your *F1*
117 **inoculate**] *F1;* euocutat *Q2;* euacuat *Q3;* euacuate *Q4*
120 **to**] *F1 (Q1)*
127 **earth and heaven**] Heauen and Earth *F1 (Q1)*
127 **knaves**] Knaues all *F1 (Q1)*
131–132 **Let . . . Farewell!**] *as prose, F1; as verse, Q2–4 (Q1)*
132 **where**] *(Q1);* way *F1*
136 **nunn'ry,**] Nunnery. Go, *F1 (Q1)*
140 **Heavenly powers**] O heavenly Powers *F1;* Pray God *Q1*
141 **paintings**] pratlings too *F1;* paintings too *Q1*
142 **hath . . . face**] *(Q1);* has . . . pace *F1*
142 **yourselves**] *Q4 (Q1);* your selfes *Q2–3;* your selfe *F1*
143 **jig and**] gidge, you *F1;* fig, and you *Q1*
143 **lisp, you**] *from F1* lispe, and; list you *Q2–4*
144 **your**] *F1 (Q1)*
146 **moe marriage**] more Marriages *F1 (Q1)*
151 **expectation**] expectansie *F1*
154 **And**] Haue *F1*
155 **music**] *F1, Q4;* musickt *Q2–3*
156 **that**] *F1;* what *Q2–4*
157 **time**] tune *F1*
158 **stature**] Feature *F1*
160 **s.d. Ophelia withdraws.**] *ed (after Wilson);* Exit. *Q2–4 (Q1)*
161 **Love?**] *F1 (Q1);* Loue, *Q2;* Loue: *Q3–4*
166 **for**] *om. F1 (Q1)*
172 **something-settled**] *hyphen, Warburton*
176 **his**] this *F1*
177 **s.d. Ophelia comes forward.**] *Wilson*

182 grief] Greefes *F1*
187 unwatch'd] *F1;* vnmatcht *Q2–4*

––––––––––––––– 3.2 –––––––––––––––

3.2] III.ii *Capell*
Location: *Alexander (after Capell)*
o.s.d. three . . . Players] two or three of the
  Players *F1;* the Players *Q1*
1 pronounc'd] *F1, Q3–4;* pronoun'd *Q2*
3 our] your *F1 (Q1)*
3 spoke] had spoke *F1*
4 with] *(Q1); om. F1*
5 torrent,] *F1;* torrent *Q2–4*
6 whirlwind of your] the Whirle-winde
  of *F1*
8 hear] *(Q1);* see *F1*
8–9 periwig-pated] *F1 (subs.);* perwig-
  pated *Q2–4;* periwig *Q1*
9 totters] *(Q1);* tatters *F1*
10 spleet] split *F1 (Q1)*
12 would] *(Q1);* could *F1*
13 out-Herods] *hyphen, F1;* out, Herodes
  Q1
14, 33 s.pp. First Player] 1. Play. *Capell;*
  Player. *or* Play. *Q2–4, F1;* players
  Q1
17 o'erstep] ore-stop *F1*
18 o'erdone] ouer-done *F1*
21 feature] owne Feature *F1*
23 makes] make *F1*
25 which] the which *F1*
27 praise] *F1;* praysd *Q2–4*
29–30 nor man] or Norman *F1;* Nor
  Turke *Q1*
32 abominably] *Q3–4;* abhominably *Q2,
  F1;* abhominable *Q1*
34 sir] *F1*
41 uses it.] *following these words Q1 reads:*
  And then you haue some agen, that
  keepes one sute / Of ieasts, as a man is
  knowne by one sute of / Apparell, and
  Gentlemen quotes his ieasts downe / In
  their tables, before they come to the
  play, as thus: / Cannot you stay till I
  eate my porrige? and, you owe me / A
  quarters wages: and, my coate wants a
  cullison: / And, your beere is sowre:
  and, blabbering with his lips, / And
  thus keeping in his cinkapase of ieasts, /
  When, God knows, the warme Clowne
  cannot make a iest / Vnlesse by chance,
  as the blinde man catcheth a hare: /
  Maisters tell him of it.
41 s.d. Exeunt Players.] *F1* (Exit) *(Q1)*
41 s.d. Enter . . . Rosencrantz.] *placed as
  in F1; after l. 43, Q2–4*
44 s.d. Exit Polonius.] *F1*
46 Rosencrantz: Ay] Both. We will *F1*
46 s.d. they two] *om. F1; Q1 om. the entrance of Rosencrantz, Guildenstern,
  and Polonius at l. 43*
47 ho] *F4;* howe *Q2–4;* hoa *F1*
55 lick] like *F1*
57 fawning] faining *F1*
58 her] my *F1*

60 Sh' hath] *Wilson;* S'hath *Q2;* S hath *Q3;*
  Shath *Q4;* Hath *F1*
63 Hast] Hath *F1*
64 co-meddled] co-mingled *F1*
73 afoot] *F1 (Q1);* a foote *Q2–4*
74 thy] my *F1*
75 my] mine *F1*
79 stithy] Stythe *F1*
79 heedful] needfull *F1*
82 In] To *F1*
83 'a] he *F1*
84 detecting] *F1;* detected *Q2–4*
84 s.d. Sound . . . march.] *F1 (at end of
  s.d.)*
84 s.d. Rosencrantz . . . torches] *F1; Q1
  s.d. reads:* Enter King, Queene,
  Corambis, and other Lords.
88–93 Excellent . . . say?] *as prose, F1; as
  verse, Q2–4*
89 promise-cramm'd] *hyphen, F1, Q3–4;*
  Promiscram'd *Q2;* capon cramm'd *Q1*
92 mine now.] *Johnson;* mine now *Q2–4;*
  mine, Now *F1*
92 s.d. To Polonius.] *Rowe*
94 did I] I did *F1 (Q1)*
96 What] *(Q1);* And what *F1*
97–100 I . . . ready?] *as prose, F1 (Q1, in
  part); as verse, Q2–4*
102 s.p. Queen.] *F1 (Q1);* Ger. *Q2–4*
102 dear] good *F1*
103 metal] *Q5;* mettle *Q2–4, F1 (Q1)*
103 s.d. Lying . . . feet.] *Rowe*
104 s.d. To the King.] *Capell*
107–08 Hamlet: I . . . lord.] *F1 (Q1, in
  part)*
109 country] contrary *Q1*
121 dev'l] *ed.;* deule *Q2;* diuell *Q3–4;* Diuel
  F1
124 by'r] *F1;* ber *Q2–4*
124–25 'a . . . 'a] he . . . he *F1 (Q1)*
127 s.d. The trumpets sounds.] Hoboyes
  play. *F1*
127 s.d. Dumb show follows.] The dumbe
  shew enters. *F1; Q1 s.d. reads:* Enter in a
  Dumbe Shew, the King and the
  Queene, he sits downe in an Arbor, she
  leaues him: Then enters Lucianus with
  poyson in a Viall, and powres it in his
  eares, and goes away: Then the Queene
  commeth and findes him dead: and
  goes away with the other.
127 s.d. a Queen] Queene *F1*
127 s.d. very lovingly] *F1*
127 s.d. and he her] *om. F1*
127 s.d. She . . . him.] *F1*
127 s.d. he lies] Layes *F1*
127 s.d. come] comes *F1, Q3–4*
127 s.d. another man] a Fellow *F1*
127 s.d. pours] and powres *F1*
127 s.d. sleeper's . . . him] Kings eares, and
  Exits *F1*
127 s.d. makes] and makes *F1*
127 s.d. pois'ner . . . pois'ner] poysoner . . .
  poisoner *F1, Q3–4*
127 s.d. three or four] two or three *F1*

127 **s.d. mutes**] *F1*
127 **s.d. come**] comes *F1, Q3–4*
127 **s.d. seem to condole**] seeming to lament *F1*
127 **s.d. harsh**] loath *F1*
127 **s.d. and unwilling**] *F1*
127 **s.d. love**] his loue *F1*
127 **s.d. Exeunt.**] *F1*
129 **this'**] *ed.*, this *Q2;* tis *Q3;* it is *Q4;* this is *F1 (Q1)*
129 **miching**] *F1 (Q1);* munching *Q2–4* (miching *is a Middle English variant of* munching)
129 **mallecho**] *Malone;* Mallico *Q2–4 (Q1);* Malicho *F1*
129 **it**] that *F1 (Q1)*
130 **s.d. Enter Prologue.**] *placed as in Theobald; after* fellow. *l. 131, Q2–4; after l. 138, F1; after l. 129, Q1*
131–32 **We ... all.**] *as prose, F1; as verse, Q2–4; Q1 reduces to:* you shall heare anone, this fellow will tell you all.
131 **this fellow**] *(Q1);* these Fellowes *F1*
132 **counsel**] *F1 (Q1)*
133 **'a**] they *F1;* he *Q1*
134 **you will**] you'l *F1 (Q1)*
139 **s.d. Exit.**] *Globe*
140 **posy**] Poesie *F1 (Q1)*
142 **s.d. two Players.**] *Globe; Q1 s.d. reads:* Enter the Duke and Dutchesse.
143 **etc. s.pp. Player King**] *Steevens;* King. *Q2–4, F1;* Duke *Q1*
143–61] *Cf. the following version of these lines in Q1:* Duke Full fortie yeares are past, their date is gone, / Since happy time ioyn'd both our hearts as one: / And now the blood that fill'd my youthfull veines, / Runnes weakely in their pipes, and all the straines / Of musicke, which whilome pleasde mine eare, / Is now a burthen that Age cannot beare: / And therefore sweete Nature must pay his due, / To heauen must I, and leaue the earth with you. / Dutchesse O say not so, lest that you kill my heart, / When death takes you, let life from me depart.
144 **orbed**] *F1;* orb'd the *Q2–4*
149 **etc. s.pp. Player Queen**] P. Queen *Steevens;* Quee. *Q2–4;* Bap. *F1 (except* Qu. *at l. 215);* Dutchesse *Q1*
152 **your**] *F1, Q3–4;* our *Q2*
154 *In Q2–4 this line is followed by what appears to be a first draft of l. 155:* For women feare too much, euen as they loue, (*note the absence of a rhyming line, and see note on l. 156 below*)
155 **For**] *F1;* And *Q2–4*
155 **hold**] holds *F1*
156 **In neither aught**] *an apparent first draft of these words precedes them in Q2–4:* Eyther none, (*cf. l. 154 above*)
156 **aught**] *Malone;* ought *Q2–4, F1*
157 **love**] *F1;* Lord *Q2–4*
158 **siz'd**] *F1;* ciz'd *Q2;* ciz'st *Q3–4*

159–60 **Where ... there.**] *om. F1 (Q1)*
162 **their**] my *F1*
169 **s.d. Aside.**] *Capell*
169 **That's wormwood!**] Wormwood, Wormwood. *F1;* O wormewood, wormewood! *Q1*
170 **s.p. Player Queen**] P. Queen *Steevens (after Rowe); om. Q2–4;* Bapt. *F1*
178 **the fruit**] like Fruite *F1*
184 **either**] other *F1*
185 **cnactures**] ennactors *F1*
187 **joys**] *F1;* ioy *Q2–4*
187 **grieves**] *F1;* griefes *Q2–4*
192 **favorite**] fauourites *F1*
200 **devices**] *F1, Q3–4;* deuises *Q2;* demises *Q1*
204 **me give**] giue me *F1*
206–07 **To ... scope!**] *om. F1 (Q1)*
207 **An**] *Theobald;* And *Q2 4*
211 **once ... wife**] once a Widdow, euer I be Wife *F1 (Q1)*
215 **s.d. Sleeps.**] *F1 (after l. 215); placed as in Rowe*
216 **s.d. Exit.**] *F1;* Exeunt. *Q2–4;* exit Lady *Q1*
218 **doth protest**] protests *F1 (Q1)*
224 **Marry**] *F1;* mary *Q2–4 (Q1)*
224 **how? tropically:**] *F1;* how tropically, *Q2–4;* how trapically: *Q1*
225 **Vienna**] guyana *Q1*
225 **Gonzago**] Albertus *Q1*
227 **of that**] o'that *F1;* A that *Q1*
229 **unwrung**] *Q3–4;* vnwrong *Q2;* vnrung *F1*
229 **s.d. Enter Lucianus.**] *placed as in F1; after l. 230, Q2–4*
231 **as good as a**] *(Q1);* a good *F1*
232–33 **I ... dallying.**] *as prose, F1 (Q1); as verse, Q2–4*
235 **mine**] *my F1*
237 **mistake**] must take *Q1*
237 **your**] *(Q1); om. F1*
238 **leave**] Pox, leaue *F1;* a poxe, leaue *Q1*
241 **Confederate**] *F1 (Q1);* Considerat *Q2–3;* Considerate *Q4*
243 **ban**] bane *Q1*
243 **infected**] *F1, Q3–4 (Q1);* inuected *Q2*
245 **usurps**] *(Q1);* vsurpe *F1*
245 **s.d. Pours ... ears.**] *F1*
246 **'A**] He *F1 (Q1)*
246 **for his**] *(Q1);* for's *F1*
246 **name's**] *F1;* names *Q2–4*
247 **written in very**] writ in *F1*
251 **Hamlet: What ... fire?**] *F1 (Q1, reading* fires)
255 **s.p. Polonius**] All. *F1;* Cor. *Q1 (thus supporting Q2)*
256 **Why,**] *Theobald;* Why *Q2–4, F1;* Then *Q1*
256 **strooken**] strucken *F1;* stricken *Q1*
259 **Thus**] *(Q1);* So *F1*
261 **two**] *F1*
263 **players?**] Players sir. *F1*
269 **very —**] *Warburton;* very *Q2–4, F1*
276 **Ah**] Oh *F1*

280 **voutsafe**] vouchsafe *F1*
286 **with**] rather with *F1*
288 **the**] his *F1*
289 **more**] farre more *F1*
291 **start**] *F1;* stare *Q2–4*
299 **my**] *F1*
301 s.p. **Rosencrantz**] Guild. *F1*
303 **answer**] answers *F1*
304 **as**] *om. F1 (Q1, which om. ll. 282–310, 318–30* (You do . . . that.)
308 **stonish**] astonish *F1*
310 **impart.**] *om. F1 (Q1)*
316 **And**] So I *F1*
318 **surely**] freely *F1*
318 **upon**] of *F1*
323 **sir**] *om. F1 (Q1)*
324 s.d. **the . . . recorders**] one with a Recorder *F1; s.d. placed as in F1; after l. 322, Q2–4*
325 **recorders**] Recorder *F1*
325 **one. —**] *Capell (after Rowe);* one, *Q2–4; om. F1 (Q1)*
337 **It is**] 'Tis *F1*
338 **fingers**] finger *F1*
338 **thumbs**] *Wilson;* the vmber *Q2;* the thumb *Q3–4;* thumbe *F1*
339 **eloquent**] excellent *F1;* delicate *Q1*
346 **the top of**] *F1*
348 **it speak. 'Sblood**] it. Why *F1;* Zownds *Q1*
349 **think**] *(Q1);* thinke, that *F1*
350 **fret**] can fret *F1 (Q1)*
350 **yet**] *Q1;* not *Q2–4; om. F1*
351 s.d. **Enter Polonius.**] *placed as in Capell; after l. 352, Q2–4, F1 (Q1)*
355 **yonder**] *(Q1);* that *F1*
355 **of**] *(Q1);* like *F1*
357 **mass**] Misse *F1*
357 **'tis,**] it's *F1;* T'is *Q1*
362 s.p. **Hamlet**] *from catchword in Q2; om. in text proper*
362–64 **Then . . . by.**] *as prose, Pope; as verse Q2–4, F1 (Q1)*
362 **I will**] will I *F1;* i'le *Q1*
362 s.d. **Aside.**] *Staunton*
365 **Polonius: I will say so.**] *F1; Q2–4 read* I will, say so. *and continue the line to* Hamlet. *The Q2 arrangement (see also l. 366 below) is perhaps what Shakespeare originally intended; l. 365 as printed in Q2 and spoken by Hamlet means:* "Yes, I will come. Say so." *and should be taken as addressed to Polonius, who has lingered after the others have gone out in obedience to Hamlet's* Leave me, friends. *(immediately preceding l. 365 in Q2). Q1, significantly perhaps, gives Corambis (i.e. Polonius) no exit line, suggesting that the F1 arrangement may be a later sophistication.*
365 s.d. **Exit.**] *F1;* exit Coram. *Q1 (after l. 362)*
366 **Leave me, friends.**] *placed as in F1; after* by and by. *l. 364, Q2–4*

366 s.d. **Exeunt . . . Hamlet.**] *Capell (subs.)*
368 **breathes**] *F1;* breakes *Q2–4*
370 **bitter . . . the**] *F1;* business as the bitter *Q2–4*
375 **daggers**] *F1 (Q1);* dagger *Q2–4*
378 s.d. **Exit.**] *(Q1); om. F1*

───────────── 3.3 ─────────────

3.3] III. iii *Capell*
Location: *Alexander (after Capell)*
6 **near 's**] dangerous *F1*
7 **brows**] Lunacies *F1*
14 **weal**] spirit *F1*
15 **many. The**] *Q5;* many, the *Q2–4, F1*
15 **cess**] *cease F1*
17 **Or**] *om. F1 (Q1, see ll. 36–72 below)*
18 **summit**] *Rowe;* somnet *Q2–4, F1 (see 1.4.70)*
19 **huge**] *F1, Q4;* hough *Q2;* hugh *Q3*
22 **ruin**] *F1;* raine *Q2–4*
23 **with**] *F1*
24 **viage**] Voyage *F1*
25 **about**] vpon *F1*
26 s.p. **Rosencrantz**] Both. *F1*
26 s.d. **Gentlemen**] *Warburton;* Gent. *Q2–4, F1*
26 s.d. **Rosencrantz and Guildenstern**] *Hanmer*
33 **speech,**] *Theobald;* speech *Q2–4, F1*
35 s.d. **Exit Polonius.**] *Capell;* Exit. *Q2–4 (after know. l. 35)*
36–72] *Q1, om. everything before, begins the scene with Claudius's soliloquy, which reads as follows: King* O that this wet that falles vpon my face / Would wash the crime cleere from my conscience! / When I looke vp to heauen, I see my trespasse, / The earth doth still crie out vpon my fact, / Pay me the murder of a brother and a king, / And the adulterous fault I haue committed: / O these are sinnes that are vnpardonable: / Why say thy sinnes were blacker then is ieat, / Yet may contrition make them as white as snowe: / I but still to persuer in a sinne, / It is an act gainst the vniuersall power, / Most wretched man, stoope, bend thee to thy prayer, / Aske grace of heauen to keepe thee from despaire. / *hee kneeles. enters* Hamlet
39 **will.**] *F1 (subs.);* will, *Q2–4*
43 **neglect,**] *F1, Q3–4 (subs.);* neglect, *Q2*
50 **pardon'd**] *F1;* pardon *Q2–4*
58 **shove**] *F1;* showe *Q2–4*
66 **can not**] *Capell;* cannot *Q2–4, F1*
69 **engag'd**] *F1;* ingaged *Q2–4*
69 **angels! Make**] *Theobald (subs.);* Angels make *Q2;* Angles make *Q3–4;* Angels, make *F1*
72 s.d. **He kneels.**] *Q1*
73 **it pat**] *F1;* it, but *Q2–4*
73 **'a**] he *F1*
73 **a-praying**] praying *F1*

74 'a] he *F1*
75 reveng'd] *F1;* reuendge *Q2–3;* reuenged *Q4 (Q1)*
77 sole] foule *F1*
79 Why] Oh *F1*
79 hire and salary] *F1;* base and silly *Q2–4;* a benefit *Q1*
80 'A] He *F1 (Q1)*
81 With all] *F1;* Withall *Q2–4*
81 flush] fresh *F1*
89 drunk asleep] *F1;* drunke, a sleepe *Q2–4;* drinking drunke *Q1*
90 incestious] incestuous *F1 (Q1)*
91 game a-swearing] *ed. (after Cambridge);* game a swearing *Q2;* game, a swearing *Q3–4;* gaming, swearing *F1;* game swaring *Q1*
97 s.d. Rising.] *Capell*

——————— 3.4 ———————

3.4] III.iv *Capell*
Location: *Steevens*
1 'A] He *F1*
4 I'll ... here] I'le shrowde my selfe behinde the Arras. *exit Cor. Q1*
4 even] e'ene *F1*
5 with him] *F1*
5 him] him. / *Ham. within.* Mother, mother, mother. *F1; Q1 reads: Ham.* Mother, mother, O are you here?
6 warr'nt] *Wilson (subs.);* wait *Q2–4;* warrant *F1*
7 s.d. Polonius ... arras.] *Rowe, supported by the Q1 reading quoted at l. 4 above*
7 s.d. Enter Hamlet.] *placed as in F1; after round l. 5, Q2–4*
12 wicked] idle *F1*
16 And would it] But would you *F1*
20 inmost] *F1;* most *Q2–4*
22 Help ho] *Q3–4 (Q1);* Helpe how *Q2;* Helpe, helpe, hoa *F1*
23 s.d. Behind.] *Rowe (subs.)*
23 What ho, help] *Q3–4 (subs.);* What how helpe *Q2;* What hoa, helpe, helpe, helpe *F1;* Helpe for the Queene *Q1*
24 s.d. Drawing.] *Malone (after* rat?*);* placed as in Globe
24 s.d. Kills Polonius] *F1 (after* slain. *l. 25); placed as in Warburton*
24 s.d. through the arras] *Capell*
25 s.d. Behind.] *Capell*
30 it was] 'twas *F1*
30 s.d. Parts ... Polonius.] *Capell (subs., after l. 25); placed as in Dyce*
32 better] Betters *F1*
37 brass'd] braz'd *F1*
38 be] is *F1*
42 off] *F1;* of *Q2–4*
44 sets] makes *F1*
48 does] doth *F1*
49 O'er] Yea *F1*
50 heated] tristfull *F1*
50 doom;] *ed.;* doome *Q2–4;* doome, *F1*

51 thought-sick] hyphen, *F1, Q3–4*
51 act.] *Q3–4, F1;* act *Q2*
52 That ... index?] continued to Queen, *F1;* assigned to Hamlet, *Q2–4*
55 this] his *F1*
57 and] or *F1*
59 heaven-kissing] *F1;* heaue, a kissing *Q2–4*
65 brother] breath *F1*
71–76 Sense ... difference.] *om. F1 (Q1)*
76 was't] *F1;* wast *Q2–4*
77 hoodman-blind] *F1;* hodman blind *Q2;* hodman-blind *Q3–4;* hob-man blinde *Q1*
78–81 Eyes ... mope.] *om. F1 (Q1)*
88 And] As *F1*
88 panders] *F1;* pardons *Q2–4*
89 turn'st my] turn'st mine *F1*
89 eyes ... very] *F1;* very eyes into my *Q2–4*
90 grained] *F1;* greeued *Q2–4*
91 not leave] *F1;* leaue there *Q2–4*
92 enseamed] *F1;* inseemed *Q2;* incestuous *Q3–4; cf. Q1:* To liue in the incestuous pleasure of his bed?
93 Stew'd] *F1;* Stewed *Q2–4*
97 twentith part] twentieth patt *F1*
97 tithe] *F1;* kyth *Q2–4*
101 s.d. in his nightgown] *Q1*
104 your] you *F1*
117 you do] you *F1;* thus you *Q1*
118 th' incorporal] their corporall *F1*
131 whom] who *F1*
137] *The greatly abridged and variant conclusion of this scene in Q1 begins at the equivalent of this line and is interesting in view of Gertrude's active role in aiding Hamlet against Claudius in the sources and her attitude in the Q1 text of 4.6 (see* Textual Notes*):* Queene *Alas, it is the weakenesse of thy braine, / Which makes thy tongue to blazon thy hearts griefe: / But as I haue a soule, I sweare by heauen, / I neuer knew of this most horride murder: / But Hamlet, this is onely fantasie, / And for my loue forget these idle fits. / Ham.* Idle, no mother, *my pulse doth beate like yours, / It is not madnesse that possesseth Hamlet. / O mother, if euer you did my deare father loue, / Forbeare the adulterous bed to night, / And win your selfe by little as you may, / In time it may be you wil lothe him quite: / And mother, but assist mee in reuenge, / And in his death your infamy shall die. / Queene Hamlet,* I vow by that maiesty, */ That knowes our thoughts, and lookes into our hearts, / I will conceale, consent, / and doe my best, / What strategem soe're thou shalt deuise. [*The last two lines seem to be a recollection of Kyd's* Spanish Tragedy, 4.1.46–47.] *Ham.* It is enough, mother good night: / Come

sir, I'le prouide for you a graue, / Who
was in life a foolish prating knaue. /
Exit Hamlet with the dead body.
139 **Ecstasy?**] *F1*
143 **I**] *F1*
145 **that**] a *F1*
148 **Whiles**] Whil'st *F1*
151 **on**] or *F1*
152 **ranker**] ranke *F1*
153 **these**] this *F1*
158 **live**] *F1;* leaue *Q2–4*
160 **Assume**] *F1, Q3–4;* Assune *Q2*
161-65 **That . . . on.**] *om. F1 (Q1)*
161-62 **eat,** . . . this,] *Q5;* eate . . . this *Q2–4*
1-65 **on. Refrain to-night**] *F1 (om. through*
on.; *see above, ll. 161–65);* on to refraine
night *Q2–4;* Forbeare the adulterous
bed to night *Q1*
167-70 **the next . . . potency.**] *om. F1 (Q1)*
169 **either. . . . the devil**] *a word apparently*
om. Q2; many emendations suggested:
master (*Q3–4*), curb (*Malone*), quell
(*Singer*), shame (*Hudson*), etc.; *C. J.*
Monro (in Cambridge) suggests reading
entertain *in place of* either, *a reading*
strongly argued for by A. S. Cairncross in
SQ, IX (1958)
170 **wondrous**] *Q4;* wonderous *Q2–3*
172 **you. For**] *F1;* you, for *Q2–4*
172 **s.d. Pointing to Polonius.**] *Rowe*
179 **This**] Thus *F1*
180 **One . . . lady.**] *om. F1 (Q1)*
182 **bloat**] *Warburton;* blowt *Q2–4;* blunt
F1
186 **ravel**] *F1;* rouell *Q2–4*
188 **mad**] made *F1*
188 **craft. 'Twere**] *F1;* craft, t'were *Q2–4*
190 **paddock**] *F1;* paddock *Q2–4*
200 **that?**] *F1;* that. *Q2;* that, *Q3–4*
202-10 **There's . . . meet.**] *om. F1 (Q1)*
210 **meet.**] *Q5;* meete, *Q2–4*
215 **foolish**] *F1 (Q1);* most foolish *Q2–4*
217 **s.d. Exeunt . . . Polonius.**] *F1 (Capell*
adding severally); Exit, *Q2–4;* Exit
Hamlet with the dead body. *Q1*

——————————— 4.1 ———————————

4.1] IV.i *Q (1676); Q2–4, F1, Q1 indicate no*
scene or act break here, the Queen re-
maining on stage to meet Claudius (see
3.4.217 s.d.); Q2–4, however, also re-
enter the Queen as for a new scene
Location: *Alexander (after Rowe)*
o.s.d. Enter . . . Guildenstern.] Enter King.
F1; Enter the King and Lordes. *Q1*
(Lordes *being Rosencrantz and*
Guildenstern)
1 **matter**] matters *F1*
1 **heaves —**] *Rowe (subs.);* heaues, *Q2–4;*
heaues *F1*
4 **Bestow . . . while.**] *om. F1 (Q1); note*
that Rosencrantz and Guildenstern are
absent in F1
4 **s.d. Exeunt . . . Guildenstern.**] *Capell*

5 **mine own**] my good *F1*
7 **sea**] (*Q1*); Seas *F1*
8 **mightier.**] *Rowe (subs.);* mightier, *Q2,*
F1; mightier *Q3–4*
9 **something**] *F1;* some thing *Q2–4*
10 **Whips . . . rapier,**] He whips his Rapier
out, and *F1;* but whips me / Out his rapier, and *Q1*
11 **this**] his *F1 (Q1)*
22 **let**] let's *F1*
27 **a'**] He *F1*
30 **vile**] vilde *F1*
32 **s.d. Enter . . . Guildenstern.**] *placed as*
in Dyce; after l. 31, Q2–4; after excuse.
l. 32, F1
35 **mother's closet**] Mother Clossets *F1*
35 **dragg'd**] *F1, Q3–4;* dreg'd *Q2*
37 **s.d. Exeunt . . . Guildenstern.**] *Rowe;*
Exit Gent. *F1;* Exeunt Lordes. *Q1*
39 **And**] To *F1*
40 **done, ...**] *apparently the last part of*
this line is missing in Q2–4 (om. F1, Q1
as part of a cut); Capell suggests reading
so, haply, slander,
41-44 **Whose . . . air.**] *om. F1 (Q1)*

——————————— 4.2 ———————————

4.2] IV.ii *Pope*
Scene om. Q1
Location: *Alexander (after Capell)*
o.s.d. Enter Hamlet.] *F1;* Enter Hamlet
Rosencraus, and others. *Q2–4*
2 **Gentlemen: (Within.) Hamlet! Lord
Hamlet!**] *F1*
3 **s.p. Hamlet**] Ham. *F1*
3 **But soft**] *om. F1*
4 **s.d. Enter . . . Guildenstern.**] *F1; for*
Q2–4, see o.s.d. above
6 **Compounded**] *F1, Q3–4;* Compound
Q2
17-18 **like . . . apple**] *Farmer conj.;* like an
apple *Q2–4;* like an Ape *F1;* as an Ape
doth nuttes *Q1*
28 **thing —**] *F1;* thing. *Q2–4*
29-30 **Hide . . . after.**] *F1*

——————————— 4.3 ———————————

4.3] IV.iii *Pope*
Location: *Alexander (after Capell)*
o.s.d. Enter . . . three.] Enter King. *F1*
6 **weigh'd**] *F1;* wayed *Q2–4*
7 **never**] neerer *F1*
11 **s.d. Enter Rosencrantz.**] *F1 (Rosin-*
crane); Enter Rosencraus and all the
rest. *Q2–4;* Enter Hamlet and the
Lordes, *Q1*
11 **How**] *F1; King.* How *Q2–4 (repeated*
s.p.)
15 **Ho, . . . lord.**] *Q3–4;* How, . . . Lord.
Q2; Hoa, Guildensterne? Bring in my
Lord. *F1*
15 **s.d. Hamlet and Guildenstern**] *F1*
19 **'a**] he *F1 (Q1)*

20 **convocation**] *F1, Q4;* conuacation *Q2–*
    3; company *Q1*
20 **politic**] (*Q1*); *om. F1*
22 **ourselves**] our selfe *F1*
23 **two**] (*Q1*); to *F1*
25–27 **King: Alas . . . worm.**] *om. F1;*
    Looke you, a man may fish with that
    worme / That hath eaten of a King, /
    And a Beggar eate that fish, / Which
    that worme hath caught. *Q1*
28 **s.p. King.**] *F1, Q3–4* (*Q1*); King. King.
    Q2
33 **there**] *F1, Q3–4* (*Q1*); thrre *Q2*
33–34 **if indeed**] indeed, if *F1;* if *Q1*
34 **within**] *om. F1* (*Q1*)
36 **s.d. To Attendants.**] *Capell* (*subs.*)
37 **'A will**] He will *F1;* hee'le *Q1*
37 **you**] (*Q1*); ye *F1*
37 **s.d. Exeunt Attendants.**] *Capell*
38 **deed,**] deed of thine, *F1*
41 **With fiery quickness**] *F1*
43 **is**] at *F1*
46–47 **I . . . mother.**] *as prose, F1; as verse,*
    Q2–4
46 **them**] him *F1*
49–50 **My . . . England!**] *as prose, F1; as*
    verse, Q2–4 (*Q1*)
50 **so**] and so *F1* (*Q1*)
54 **s.d. Exeunt . . . Guildenstern.**] *The-*
    obald
61 **congruing**] coniuring *F1*
65 **were ne'er begun**] *F1;* will nere begin
    Q2–4

_____ 4.4 _____

4.4] IV.iii *Pope*
Location: *ed.* (*after Pelican*)
o.s.d. Enter . . . stage.] Enter Fortenbrasse,
    Drumme and Souldiers. *Q1*
3 **Craves**] (*Q1*); Claimes *F1*
8 **softly**] safely *F1*
8 **s.d. Exeunt . . . Captain.**] *Kittredge*
    (*after Theobald*); Exit. *F1;* Exeunt all.
    Q1
8 **s.d. Guildenstern.**] *Dyce; s.d. om. F1*
    (*Q1*)
9–66 **Hamlet: Good . . . worth!**] *om. F1*
    (*Q1*)
19 **name.**] *Pope;* name *Q2–4;* name, *Q5*
30 **s.d. Exit.**] *Capell*
31 **s.d. Exeunt . . . Hamlet.**] *Rowe* (*subs.*)

_____ 4.5 _____

4.5] IV.v *Pope*
Location: *Alexander* (*after Rowe*)
o.s.d., 1–20] *For this passage in Q2–4, F1, the*
    following lines are substituted in Q1:
    enter King and Queene. / King Hamlet
    is ship't for England, fare him well, / I
    hope to heare good newes from thence
    'ere long, / If euery thing fall out to our
    content, / As I doe make no doubt but
    so it shall. / Queene God grant it may,

heau'ns keep my *Hamlet* safe: / But this
mischance of olde *Corambis* death, /
Hath piersed so the yong *Ofeliaes* heart,
/ That she, poore maide, is quite bereft
her wittes, / *King* Alas deere heart! And
on the other side, / We vnderstand her
brother's come from *France*, / And he
hath halfe the heart of all our Land, /
And hardly hee'le forget his fathers
death, / Vnlesse by some meanes he be
pacified. / *Qu.* O see where the yong
Ofelia is! [*There are some vague echoes*
here of ll. 73–93 below.]
o.s.d a Gentleman.] *om. F1* (*which assigns his*
    speeches to Horatio)
2, 4 **s.pp. Gentlemen**] Hor. *F1*
9 **yawn**] ayme *F1*
12 **might**] would *F1*
15 **ill-breeding**] *hyphen, Rowe*
15 **minds.**] *F1;* mindes, *Q2–4*
16 **s.p. Queen**] *from F1 at l. 14* (*F1 gives*
    ll. 14–20 to Queen); *Q2–4 continue l. 16*
    to Horatio
16 **s.d. Exit Gentleman.**] *Hanmer*
17 **s.d. Aside.**] *Capell*
17–20 **To . . . spilt.**] *marked with gnomic*
    quotes, Q2–4
20 **s.d. distracted . . . lute**] *from F1* (dis-
    tracted) *and Q1, which reads:* playing on
    a Lute, and her haire downe singing.;
    Q2–4 s.d. follows l. 16; placed as in F1
23 **true-love**] *hyphen, Capell*
23 **s.d. She sings.**] *om. F1* (*see l. 20 s.d. for*
    Q1)
26 **sandal**] *F1* (*Q1*); Sendall *Q2–4*
28 **you?**] *F1;* you, *Q2–4*
29 **etc. s.dd. Song.**] *om. F1* (*Q1*) (*through-*
    out scene; in F1 the songs are in italics)
33 **O ho!**] *om. F1* (*Q1*)
36, 58 **s.dd. Sings.**] *Capell*
36 **s.d. Enter King.**] *after l. 32, F1*
38 **all**] *om. F1* (*Q1*)
39 **bewept**] *F1* (*Q1*); beweept *Q2–4*
39 **ground**] graue *F1* (*Q1*)
40 **true-love**] *F1;* true-loue *Q2–4;* true
    louers *Q1*
41 **do you**] do ye *F1;* i'st with you *Q1*
42 **God**] *F1* (*Q1*); good *Q2–4*
46 **Pray**] Pray you *F1* (*Q1*)
48–55 **"To-morrow . . . more."**] *Q1*
    transfers this song so that it follows l. 172
    below. It is thus heard by Laertes, on
    whom its implications might be expected
    to have an especially powerful effect in
    arousing him further against Hamlet;
    Q1 also transfers the song at ll. 187–96,
    making it follow Ophelia's first song at ll.
    23–32.
52 **clo'es**] *ed.;* close *Q2–4;* clothes *F1* (*Q1*)
57 **Indeed**] Indeed la? *F1*
64 **(He answers.)**] *om. F1* (*Q1*)
65 **'a'**] *Kittredge;* a *Q2–4* (*Q1*); ha *F1*
67 **thus**] this *F1*
69 **would**] should *F1*

71–72 **Good . . . night.**] *pointing from
Q2–4, which, however, read* God *and*
god *for* Good *and* good; Goodnight
Ladies: Goodnight sweet Ladies: Goodnight, goodnight. *F1;* God be with you
Ladies, God be with you. *Q1*
72 **s.d. Exit.**] *F1 (Q1)*
73 **s.d. Exit Horatio.**] *Theobald*
75 **and now behold!**] *om. F1 (Q1)*
77 **come,**] comes, *F1*
78 **battalions**] *Q (1676);* battalians *Q2–4;*
Battaliaes *F1*
81 **their**] *F1*
88 **Feeds**] Keepes *F1*
88 **this**] his *F1*
91 **Wherein**] Where in *F1*
92 **person**] persons *F1*
95 **Queen: Alack . . . this?**] *F1;* How now,
what noyse is that? *Q1 (spoken by the
King and preceded by four lines found
only in Q1:* king A pretty wretch! this is
a change indeede: / O Time, how
swiftly runnes our ioyes away? / Content on earth was neuer certaine bred, /
To day we laugh and liue, to morrow
dead.)
96 **Attend!**] *om. F1 (Q1)*
97 **is**] are *F1*
97 **Swissers**] Switzers *F1*
97 **s.d. Enter a Messenger.**] *placed as in
Capell; after* death. *l. 95, Q2–4, F1*
106 **They**] *F1;* The *Q2–4*
110 **s.d. with others**] *om. F1 (Q1); Laertes'
followers do not enter in Q1*
112 **this**] the *F1*
115 **s.d. Exeunt Laertes' followers.**] *Kittredge (after Theobald)*
115 **vile**] vilde *F1 (Q1)*
117 **that's calm**] that calmes *F1*
128 **Where is**] Where's *F1 (Q1)*
132–33 **pit! . . . damnation.**] *F1 (subs.);* pit
. . . damnation, *Q2–4*
137 **world's**] *Pope;* worlds *Q2–4;* world *F1
(Q1)*
141 **father**] Fathers death *F1*
141 **is't**] *Q5;* i'st *Q2–4;* if *F1*
142 **swoopstake**] *from Q1* Swoop-stake-
like; soopstake *Q2;* soope-stake *Q3;*
soop-stake *Q4, F1*
143 **loser?**] *Q5;* looser. *Q2–4, F1;* all? *Q1*
146 **pelican**] Politician *F1*
150 **sensibly**] sensible *F1, Q4;* sencible *Q3*
151 **'pear**] *Johnson;* peare *Q2–4;* pierce *F1*
152 **s.d. "Let . . . in!"**] *as F1; given to
Laertes, Q2–4*
153 **s.d. Enter Ophelia.**] *placed as in Theobald; before Laertes' speech in Q2–4, F1
(see preceding note)*
156 **paid with**] payed by *F1*
157 **Till**] *F1, Q3–4;* Tell *Q2*
157 **turn**] turnes *F1*
160 **an old**] *F1 (Q1);* a poore *Q2–4*
161–63 **Nature . . . loves.**] *F1*
164 **barefac'd**] *F1, Q3–4;* bare-faste *Q2*
165 **Hey . . . nonny,**] *F1*

166 **in**] on *F1*
166 **rain'd**] raines *F1*
170–72 **You . . . daughter.**] *as prose, F1; as
verse, Q2–4 (Q1)*
170–71 **"A-down, a-down," . . . a-down-
a.**] *hyphens, F1 (but reading* downe a-
downe,); a downe, And you a downe a,
Q1; quotes, Wilson (after Capell)
174 **you**] *om. F1 (Q1)*
175 **pansies**] *Johnson;* Pancies *Q2–4;*
Paconcies *F1;* pansey *Q1*
178 **s.d. To Claudius.**] *Wilson*
179 **s.d. To Gertrude.**] *Wilson*
180 **herb of grace**] Herb-Grace *F1;* hearb a
grace *Q1*
180–81 **You may**] Oh you must *F1;* you
must *Q1*
183 **'a**] he *F1*
184 **s.d. Sings.**] *Capell*
185 **afflictions**] *(Q1);* Affliction *F1*
187–88 **'a . . . 'a**] he . . . he *F1 (Q1)*
192 **was**] *om. F1 (Q1)*
193 **All**] *F1 (Q1)*
196 **God 'a' mercy**] *Kittredge;* God a mercy
Q2–4 (Q1); Gramercy *F1*
197 **Christians'**] *ed.;* Christians *Q2–4;*
Christian *F1;* christen *Q1*
197 **I pray God**] *F1 (Q1)*
197 **buy you**] buy ye *F1;* buy yous *Q3–4;* be
with you *Q2*
197 **s.d. Exit.**] *F1 (Q1)*
198 **see**] *F1*
198 **O God**] you Gods *F1;* O God, O God
Q1
199 **commune**] common *F1*
203 **collateral**] *F1;* colaturall *Q2–4*
210 **funeral**] buriall *F1*
211 **trophy**] *Q5;* Trophee *F1;* trophe *Q2;*
trophae *Q3–4*
212 **rite**] *F1;* right *Q2–4*
214 **call't**] call *F1*

————————— **4.6** —————————

4.6] IV.vi *Capell*
Location: *Alexander (after Capell)*
*Scene om. Q1, which at this point contains the
following scene not found in Q2–4 or F1:
Enter Horatio and the Queene. / Hor.
Madame, your sonne is safe arriv'de in
Denmarke, / This letter I euen now
receiv'd of him, / Whereas he writes
how he escap't the danger, / And subtle
treason that the king had plotted, /
Being crossed by the contention of the
windes, / He found the Packet sent to
the king of England, / Wherein he saw
himselfe betray'd to death, / As at his
next conuersion with your grace, / He
will relate the circumstance at full. /
Queene Then I perceiue there's treason
in his lookes / That seem'd to sugar
o're his villanie: / But I will soothe and
please him for a time, / For murderous
mindes are alwayes jealous, / But know
not you Horatio where he is? / Hor.* Yes

Madame, and he hath appoynted me/ To meete him on the east side of the Cittie / To morrow morning. / *Queene* O faile not, good *Horatio,* and withall, commend me / A mothers care to him, bid him a while / Be wary of his presence, lest that he / Faile in that he goes about. / *Hor.* Madam, neuer make doubt of that: / I thinke by this the news be come to court: / He is arriv'de, obserue the king, and you shall / Quickely finde, *Hamlet* being here, / Things fell not to his minde. / *Queene* But what became of *Gilderstone* and *Rossencraft?* / *Hor.* He being set ashore, they went for *England,* / And in the Packet there writ down that doome / To be perform'd on them poynted for him: / And by great chance he had his fathers Seale, / So all was done without discouerie. / *Queene* Thankes be to heauen for blessing of the prince, / *Horatio* once againe I take my leaue, / With thowsand mothers blessings to my sonne. / *Horat.* Madam adue. *(four of Horatio's lines seem to echo passages in 4.6 and 5.2)*

o.s.d and others] with an Attendant *F1*
2 Gentleman: Sea-faring men] *Ser. Saylors F1*
4 s.d. Exit Gentleman.] *Hanmer*
6 greeted,] *F1*; greeted. *Q2–4*
6 s.d. Sailors] Saylor *F1*
7, 9 s.pp. First Sailor] 1. Sail. *Capell*; Say. *Q2–4, F1*
9 'A] Hee *F1*
9 and't] *F1*; and *Q2–4*
10 came] comes *F1*
10 embassador] Ambassadours *F1*
13 s.d. Reads.] *F1* (Reads the Letter.)
16 warlike] Warlicke *F1*
17 and] *om. F1*
21 good] *F1*
23 speed] hast *F1*
24 thine] your *F1*
25 bore] *F1*; bord *Q2–4*
29 He] *F1*; so *Q2–4*
29 thine,] *F1*; thinc *Q2–4*
31 Come] *F1*; *Hor.* Come *Q2–4 (repeated s.p.)*
31 give] *F1*; *om. Q2*; make *Q3–4*

———————— 4.7 ————————

4.7] IV.vii *Capell*
Location: *Alexander (after Capell)*
6 proceeded] *F1*; proceede *Q2–4*
7 criminal] crimefull *F1*
8 greatness] *om. F1* (*Q1, om. everything down to about l. 50*)
10 unsinow'd] v̇nsinnowed *F1*
11 But] And *F1*
11 th' are] *Alexander;* tha'r *Q2–4*; they are *F1*
14 She is] She's *F1*
14 conjunctive] *F1; concliue Q2–4*

22 loud a wind] *F1;* loued Arm'd *Q2;* loued armes *Q3–4*
24 But . . . have aim'd] And . . . had arm'd *F1*
26 desp'rate] *ed.;* desprat *Q2;* desperate *F1, Q3–4*
27 Whose worth] Who was *F1*
29 perfections —] *Pope;* perfections, *Q2–4;* perfections. *F1*
34 lov'd] *F1, Q3–4;* loued *Q2*
35 imagine —] *F1 (subs.);* imagine. *Q2–4*
35 s.d. with letters] *om. F1 (Q1)*
36 How . . . Hamlet:] *F1*
37 These] This *F1*
40 receiv'd] *F1;* recceiued *Q2–4*
41 Of . . . them.] *om. F1 (Q1)*
42 s.d. Exit Messenger.] *F1*
43 s.d. Reads.] *Capell*
45 you] your *F1*
45 pardon thereunto,] *F1 (subs.);* pardon, there-vnto *Q2–4*
46 the occasion] th'Occasions *F1*
46 and more strange] *F1*
48 Hamlet.] *F1*
49 What] *F1; King.* What *Q2–4 (repeated s.p.)*
50 and] Or *F1*
53 devise] aduise *F1*
54 I am] I'm *F1*
56 shall] *F1 (Q1)*
57 didst] diddest *F1*
59 Ay, my lord,] *om. F1 (Q1)*
60 So you will] If so you'l *F1*
62 checking at] *F1;* the King at *Q2–3;* liking not *Q4*
64 device] *F1;* deuise *Q2–4*
68–81 Laertes: My . . . graveness.] *om. F1 (Q1, except l. 68)*
71 travel] *Q4;* trauaile *Q2–3*
77 riband] *Q3–4;* ribaud *Q2*
81 Two months since] Some two Monthes hence *F1*
83 I have] I'ue *F1*
83 against,] *Hanmer;* against *Q2–4, F1*
84 can] ran *F1*
85 unto] into *F1*
88 topp'd] past *F1*
88 my] *F1;* me *Q2–4*
90 was't] *F1;* wast *Q2–4*
92 Lamord] Lamound *F1*
94 the] our *F1*
95 made] mad *F1*
98 especial] especially *F1*
100–02 The . . . them.] *om F1 (Q1)*
100 scrimers] *Q3–4;* Scrimures *Q2*
105 you] him *F1*
106 What out of] Why out of *F1;* And how for *Q1*
114–23 There . . . ulcer:] *om. F1 (Q1)*
121 accidents] *Q4;* accedents *Q2–3*
122 spendthrift's] *Q3–4 (subs.);* spend thirfts *Q2;* spend-thrift *Q5*
125 indeed . . . son] your Fathers sonne indeed *F1*
127 sanctuarize] Sancturize *F1*

129 **chamber.**] *Steevens;* chamber, *Q2 F1;* chamber *Q3–4*
133 **Frenchman**] *F1,* Q4; french man *Q2–3*
134 **o'er**] on *F1*
138 **pass**] *F1;* pace *Q2–4*
139 **Requite**] Requit *F1*
140] *In Q1 and* Der bestrafte Brudermord *the suggestion for poisoning Laertes' sword comes from Claudius. In Q1 the King says:* . . . now this being granted, / When you are hot in midst of all your play, / Among the foyles shall a keene rapier lie, / Steeped in a mixture of deadly poyson, / That if it drawes but the least dramme of blood, / In any part of him, he cannot liue: / This being done will free you from suspition, / And not the deerest friend that Hamlet lov'de / Will euer haue Leartes in suspect.
140 **that**] *F1*
142 **that, but dip**] I but dipt *F1*
149 **Weigh**] *F1, Q4;* Wey *Q2–3*
150 **shape. If . . . fail,**] *Rowe;* shape if . . . fayle, *Q2–4;* shape, if . . . faile; *F1;* And lest that all should miss, *Q1*
154 **did**] should *F1*
155 **cunnings**] commings *F1*
156 **ha't**] *F1;* hate *Q2;* hau't *Q3–4*
158 **that**] the *F1*
159 **preferr'd**] *Q3–4;* prefard *Q2;* prepar'd *F1*
162 **But . . . noise?**] how sweet Queene. *F1;* How now Gertred, why looke you heauily? *Q1*
164 **they**] they'l *F1*
166 **askaunt the**] aslant a *F1;* by a *Q1*
167 **hoary**] hore *F1*
168 **Therewith . . . make**] There with . . . come *F1*
171 **cull-cold**] cold *F1*
172 **crownet**] *Wilson;* cronet *Q2;* Coronet *F1, Q3–4*
174 **her**] the *F1*
177 **snatches . . . lauds**] snatches of old tunes *F1;* olde sundry tunes *Q1*
181 **their**] *(Q1);* her *F1*
182 **lay**] buy *F1*
183 **she is**] *(Q1);* is she *F1*
190 **a'**] of *F1*
191 **drowns**] doubts *F1*

────────── 5.1 ──────────

5.1] V.i *Q (1676)*
Location: *Capell (after Rowe)*
o.s.d. **with mattocks**] *Q (1676)*
1 **s.p. First Clown**] 1. Clo. *Rowe;* Clowne. *Q2–4, F1 (Q1) (throughout)*
1 **when she**] that *F1*
3 **s.p. Second Clown**] 2. Clo. *Rowe;* Other. *Q2–4, F1 (throughout);* 2. *Q1*
3 **therefore**] and therefore *F1*
9 **se offendendo**] *F1;* so offended *Q2–4*
11 **to act**] an Act *F1*

11 **do**] doe and *F1*
12 **perform; argal,**] *F1 (subs.);* performe, or all; *Q2–4;* Ergo *Q1*
13 **goodman**] *F1;* good man *Q2–4*
15 **good.**] *F1 (subs.);* good, *Q2–4*
16 **himself**] himsele *F1*
17 **that. But**] *Q5 (subs.);* that, but *Q2–4;* that? But *F1*
22 **an't**] on't *F1*
23 **a'**] of *F1*
27 **even-Christen**] *hyphen, Furness;* euen Christian *F1*
32 **'A**] He *F1*
33–36 **Second Clown: Why . . . arms?**] *F1 (s.p.* Other)
37 **thyself —**] *F1;* thy selfe. *Q2–4*
41 **that**] *(Q1);* that Frame *F1*
53 **s.d. afar off**] *F1; s.d. after l. 62, Q2–4 (Q1); placed as in F1*
56 **houses**] *(Q1);* Houses that *F1*
57 **lasts**] last *Q4 (Q1)*
57 **in, and**] to Yaughan *F1*
58 **sup**] *Kermode conj. (privately);* soope *Q2–4;* stoupe *F1;* stope *Q1*
58 **s.d. Exit . . . digs.**] *Rowe (subs.)*
59 **s.d. Song.**] Sings. *F1*
62 **a — was nothing — a — meet.**] was nothing meete. *F1;* most meete. *Q1*
63–64 **'a . . . grave-making**] that he sings at Graue-making *F1;* That is thus merry in making of a graue *Q1*
67 **daintier**] *F1, Q3–4;* dintier *Q2*
68, 88 **s.dd. Song.**] sings *F1*
69 **clawed**] caught *F1*
70 **into**] intill *F1*
71 **s.d. Throws . . . it.**] *ed., from Q1 and Capell; Q1 reads:* he throwes vp a shouel.
73 **'twere**] it were *F1*
74 **This**] It *F1*
75 **now o'erreaches**] o're Offices *F1*
76 **would**] could *F1*
79 **sweet**] good *F1*
81 **'a**] he *F1 (Q1)*
81 **meant**] *F1, Q3–4 (Q1);* went *Q2*
83 **Worm's,**] *F1 (subs.);* wormes *Q2–4*
83 **chopless**] *Wilson;* Choples *Q2–4;* Chaplesse *F1*
84 **mazzard**] *F1;* massene *Q2;* mazer *Q3–4*
85 **and**] if *F1*
87 **them**] 'em *F1*
88 **pickaxe**] *(Q1);* Pickhaxe *F1*
91 **s.d. Throws . . . skull.**] *Capell*
92 **may**] might *F1 (Q1)*
92 **of**] of of *F1*
93 **quiddities**] Quiddits *F1;* Quirkes *Q1*
93 **quillities**] *Q3–4;* quillites *Q2;* Quillets *F1*
94 **tenures**] *F1, Q4;* tenurs *Q2–3*
95 **mad**] rude *F1*
99–100 **Is . . . recoveries,**] *F1*
101 **his**] *F1*
102 **double ones too**] *F1;* doubles *Q2–4*
104 **scarcely**] hardly *F1;* scarse *Q1*

108 **calves'-skins**] (*Q1*); Calue-skinnes *F1*, *Q3–4*
109 **which**] that *F1*
110 **sirrah**] Sir *F1*; *Q1 reads the line:* Now my friend, whose graue is this?
112 **s.d. Sings.**] *Capell*
112 **O**] *F1*; or *Q2–4*
113 **For . . . meet.**] *F1*
115 **'tis**] it is *F1*
116 **yet**] and yet *F1*
117 **it is**] 'tis *F1*
130 **this three**] these three *F1*; this seauen *Q1*
130 **I . . . of**] I haue taken note of *F1*; haue I noted *Q1*
131–32 **heel . . . courtier**] (*Q1*); heeles of our Courtier *F1*
132 **been**] been a *F1*
134 **all**] *F1*
135 **overcame**] o'recame *F1*
138 **that very**] the very *F1*
138 **is**] was *F1*; 's *Q1*
141 **'a**] he *F1*
141–42 **'A . . . 'a**] hee . . . he *F1* (*Q1*)
142 **'tis**] (*Q1*); it's *F1*
144 **him there,**] him, *F1*
151–52 **I . . . thirty years.**] *Q1 om. this passage which makes Hamlet thirty years old; see l. 162 below.*
151 **sexton**] sixteene *F1*
154 **Faith**] Ifaith *F1* (*Q1*)
154 **'a . . . 'a**] he . . . he *F1* (*Q1*)
155 **corses**] (*Q1*); Coarses now adaies *F1*
156 **'a**] he *F1* (*Q1*)
160 **'a**] he *F1*; it *Q1*
162 **hath . . . years.**] *Q2–4* (23. yeeres); this Scul, has laine in the earth three & twenty years. *F1*; hath bin here this dozen yeare, *Q1* (*Q1 thus makes Hamlet a very young man; see ll. 151–52 above*)
167 **pestilence**] pestlence *F1*; plague *Q1*
168 **This same skull, sir**] *repeated. F1*
168 **sir, Yorick's**] *Wilson:* sir Yoricks *Q2–4*; Yoricks, *F1*; one Yorickes *Q1*
170 **s.d. Takes the skull.**] *Capell*
172 **Alas**] Let me see. Alas *F1*; I prethee let me see it, alas *Q1*
173 **bore**] borne *F1*; caried *Q1*
174 **now**] (*Q1*); *om. F1*
174–75 **in . . . it**] my Imagination *F1*
178 **Not**] No *F1*
179 **grinning**] leering *F1*
180 **chamber**] *F1* (*Q1*); table *Q2–4*
184 **a'**] o' *F1*
187 **so? pah**) *Q5*; so pah *Q2*; so: pah *Q3–4*; so? Puh *F1*
187 **s.d. Puts . . . skull.**] *Collier*
190 **'a**] he *F1*
194 **it:**] it; as thus. *F1*; as thus of *Q1*
195 **to**] into *F1*
199 **Imperious**] (*Q1*); Imperiall *F1*
202 **winter's**] *F1*; waters *Q2–4*
203 **awhile**] aside *F1*
203 **s.d. Enter . . . attendant.**] *based on*

Q2–4, F1; Q1 s.dd. Enter K. Q. Laertes and the corse. *Q2–4;* Enter King, Queene, Laertes, and a Coffin, with Lords attendant. *F1;* Enter King and Queene, Leartes, and other lordes, with a Priest after the coffin. *Q1* (a Doctor of Divinity *from Wilson;* following *from Q1 after*)
206 **desp'rate**] disperate *F1*
207 **of**] *om. F1* (*Q1*)
208 **s.d. Retiring with Horatio.**] *Capell*
212, 221 **s.pp. Doctor**] *Priest. F1* (*Q1, l. 212*)
213 **warranty**] warrantis *F1*
215 **been**] (*Q1*); haue *F1*
216 **prayers**] praier *F1*
217 **Shards**] *F1*
218 **allow'd**] allowed *F1*
218 **crants**] Rites *F1*
223 **a**] sage *F1*
229 **s.d. Scattering flowers.**] *Johnson*
229 **Sweets . . . sweet,**] (*Q1*); Sweets, . . . sweet *F1*
232 **have**] t'haue *F1*
232 **treble woe**] terrible woer *F1*
233 **treble**] *F1*; double *Q2–4*
235 **Depriv'd**] *F1*; Depriued *Q2–4*
236 **s.d. Leaps . . . grave.**] *F1* (*Q1 subs.*)
240 **s.d. Coming forward.**] *Collier MS* (*subs.*)
240 **grief**] griefes *F1*
242 **Conjures**] (*Q1*); Coniure *F1*
243 **wonder-wounded**] *hyphen, F1*
244 **s.d. Hamlet . . . Laertes.**] *Q1*
245 **s.d. Grappling with him.**] *Rowe*
247 **For**] Sir *F1*
247 **and**] *F1*
248 **in me something**] something in me *F1* (*Q1*)
249 **wisdom**] (*Q1*); wisenesse *F1* (*c*); wisensse *F1* (*u*)
249 **Hold off**] (*Q1*); Away *F1*
250 **All: Gentlemen!**] *om. F1* (*Q1*)
251 **s.p. Horatio**] Gen. *F1*
251 **s.d. The . . . grave.**] *Capell* (*subs.*)
255 **lov'd**] *F1, Q3–4* (*Q1*); loued *Q2*
260 **'Swounds**] Come *F1*
260 **thou't**] *Q5;* th'owt *Q2;* th'out *Q3–4;* thou'lt *F1;* thou wilt *Q1*
261 **woo't fast,**] *om. F1;* wilt fast *Q1*
262 **eisel**] *Theobald;* Esill *Q2–4;* Esile *F1;* vessels *Q1*
262 **crocadile**] (*Q1*); Crocodile *F1* (*c*); Crocadile *F1* (*u*)
263 **thou**] *F1* (*Q1*)
270 **s.p. Queen**] Kin. *F1;* King *Q1*
271 **thus**] *F1;* this *Q2–4*
273 **couplets**] Cuplet *F1*
278, 279 **s.dd. Exit Hamlet., Exit Horatio.**] *as in F1 and Pope; Q2–4 combine these in one s.d.* Exit Hamlet / and Horatio. *opposite ll. 278, 279 (so Q1 after l. 278, om l. 279*)
280 **thee**] you *F1*

281–85 *Q1 substitutes the following lines:*
Queene. Alas, it is his madnes makes him
thus, / And not his heart, *Leartes.* /
King. My lord, t'is so: but wee'le no
longer trifle, / This very day shall *Hamlet* drinke his last, / For presently we
meane to send to him, / Therfore
Leartes be in readynes. / *Lear.* My lord,
till then my soule will not bee quiet. /
King. Come *Gertred,* wee'l haue *Leartes,*
and our sonne, / Made friends and
Louers, as befittes them both, / Euen as
they tender vs, and loue their countrie.
/ *Queene* God grant they may. *exeunt
omnes.*
281 s.d. **To Laertes.**] *Rowe*
281 **your**] you *F1*
284 **shortly**]*F1;* thirtie *Q2* (*u*); thereby *Q2*
(*c*), *Q3–4*
284 **see.**] *Q5;* see *Q2–4;* see *F1*
285 **Till**] *F1;* Tell *Q2–4*

─────────── 5.2 ───────────

5.2] V.ii *Rowe*
Location: *Alexander* (*after Theobald*)
1 **shall you**] let me *F1; Q1 om. ll. 1–74*
3 **lord!**] *Capell;* Lord. *Q2–4;* Lord? *F1*
5 **Methought**] *F1, Q3–4;* my thought *Q2*
6 **bilboes**] *F1, Q3–4;* bilbo *Q2*
7 **prais'd**] praise *F1*
8 **sometime**] sometimes *F1, Q4*
9 **deep**] deare *F1*
9 **pall**] *Q2* (*u*); fall *Q2* (*c*), *Q3–4;* paule *F1*
9 **learn**] teach *F1*
11 **Rough-hew**] hyphen, *F1*
13 **me,**] *Q5;* me *Q2–4, F1*
16–17 **bold, . . . manners,**] *F1* (*subs.*);
bold . . . manners *Q2–4*
17 **unseal**] *F1;* vnfold *Q2–4*
19 **Ah**] *Delius conj.;* A *Q2–4;* Oh *F1*
20 **reasons**] reason *F1*
22 **ho**] *Pope;* hoe *Q2–4;* hoo *F1*
27 **now**] me *F1*
29 **villainies**] *Capell;* villaines *Q2–4, F1*
30 **Or**] Ere *F1*
36 **yeman's**] *F3;* yemans *Q2–3;* Yeomans
F1, Q4
37 **Th'effect**] The effects *F1*
40 **like**] as *F1*
40 **might**] should *F1*
43 **as's**] *Rowe;* as sir *Q2–4;* Assis *F1*
44 **knowing**] know *F1*
46 **those**] the *F1*
47 **allow'd**] *Q4;* alow'd *Q2–3;* allowed *F1*
48 **ordinant**] ordinate *F1*
51 **in the**] in *F1*
52 **Subscrib'd**] *F1, Q3–4;* Subscribe *Q2*
54 **sequent**] sement *F1*
55 **knowest**] know'st *F1*
57 **Why . . . employment,**] *F1*
58 **defeat**] debate *F1*
59 **Does**] Doth *F1*
63 **think**] thinkst *F1*

63 **upon** —] *Boswell;* vppon? *Q2–4;* vpon
F1
67 **coz'nage** —] *Boswell* (*subs.*); cusnage,
Q2; cosnage, *Q3–4;* coozenage, *F1*
68–80 **To . . . here?**] *F1; ll. 75–78 in substance in Q1*
78 **court**] *Rowe;* count *F1*
80 s.d. **young Osric**] *F1; s.d. in Q1 reads:*
Enter a Bragart Gentleman.
81, 88, etc. s.pp. **Osric**] Osr. *F1;* Cour.
Q2–4; Gent. *Q1*
82 **humbly**] *Q3–4, F1;* humble *Q2*
87 **say**] saw *F1*
88 **lordship**] friendship *F1*
90 **sir**] (*Q1*); *om. F1*
90 **with all**] *F1, Q3–4;* withall *Q2*
90 **Put**] *F1*
92 **it is**] 'tis *F1*
95 **But yet**] *om. F1* (*Q1*)
95 **sultry**] *F1, Q3–4* (soultry); sully *Q2*
95 **for**] *F1;* or *Q2–4*
97 **soultry**] *F1, Q3–4* (soultry); soultery
Q2; swoltery *Q1*
98 **My**] but my *F1*
99 **'a**] he *F1*
99 **laid**] *F1;* layed *Q2–4*
100 **matter** —] *Rowe;* matter. *Q2–4, F1*
101 s.d. **Hamlet . . . hat.**] *Johnson*
102 **good my lord**] in good faith *F1*
102 **my**] mine *F1*
102–35 **Sir . . . unfellow'd.**] *om. F1, except
for:* Sir, you are not ignorant of what excellence *Laertes* is at / his weapon.; *om
Q1*
104 **gentleman**] *Q3–4;* gentlemen *Q2*
105 **sellingly**] *Q2* (*u*); fellingly *Q2* (*c*); feelingly *Q3–4*
109 **dozy**] *Kittredge;* dosie *Q2* (*u*); dazzie
Q2 (*c*); dizzie *Q3–4*
110 **yaw**] *Q2* (*u*); raw *Q2* (*c*), *Q3–4*
117 **sir? Why**] *Capell;* sir, why *Q2–4*
121 **to't**] too't *Q2* (*u*); doo't *Q2* (*c*), *Q3–4*
129 **me. Well, sir?**] *Globe* (*after Theobald*);
me, well sir. *Q2–4*
134 **his**] *Q5;* this *Q2–4*
135 **them, . . . meed**] *Steevens;* them . . .
meed, *Q2–4*
139 **King, sir**] sir King *F1;* sweete Prince *Q1*
139 **hath wager'd**] ha's wag'd *F1;* hath layd
a wager *Q1*
140 **against**] *F1, Q3–4* (*Q1*); againgst *Q2*
140 **has impawn'd**] impon'd *F1*
142 **hangers**] *F1;* hanger *Q2–4*
142 **and**] or *F1*
146–47 **Horatio: I . . . done.**] *om. F1* (*Q1*)
148 **carriages**] *F1;* carriage *Q2–4*
149 **germane**] *F1* (Germaine); lerman *Q2;*
German *Q3–4;* cosin german *Q1*
149 **matter**] matter: *F1;* phrase, *Q1*
150 **a**] *om. F1;* the *Q1*
150 **might be**] *F1, Q3–4;* be might *Q2* (*c*);
be *Q2* (*u*)
151 **on:**] *Pope;* on, *Q2–4;* on *F1*

151 Barb'ry] Barbary *Fl*
152 liberal-conceited] *hyphen, Pope*
153 bet] but *Fl*
154 all impawn'd, as] *Wilson (after Malone);* all *Q2–4;* impon'd as *Fl*
155–58 Osric: The . . . answer.] *Q1 gives two statements on the wager; the first in 4.7: King.* Mary Leartes thus: I'le lay a wager, / Shalbe on *Hamlets* side, and you shall giue the oddes, / The which will draw him with a more desire. / To try the maistry, that in twelue venies / You gaine not three of him:; *the second, here: Gent.* Mary sir, that yong Leartes in twelue venies / At Rapier and Dagger do not get three oddes of you, / And on your side the King hath laide, / And desires you to be in readinesse.
155 laid, sir,] laid *Fl (Q1)*
156 yourself] you *Fl*
157 laid on] one *Fl*
157 nine] mine *Fl*
157 it] that *Fl*
161 hall.] *Fl (subs.);* hall, *Q2–4*
162 it is] 'tis *Fl*
163–64 purpose,] *Theobald;* purpose; *Q2–4, Fl*
164 him and] him if *Fl*
164 I will] Ile *Fl*
166 deliver you] redeliuer you ee'n *Fl; Q1 reads the line:* I shall deliuer your most sweet answer.
170 Yours.] *Jennens (after Capell);* Yours *Q2–4;* Yours, yours; *Fl*
170 s.d. Exit Osric.] *Capell;* exit. *Q1*
170 'A] *ed.;* hee *Fl; om. Q2–4*
171 turn] tongue *Fl*
173 'A . . . 'a] He . . . hee *Fl*
173 comply] *Fl; om.* Q2 *(u);* so Q2 *(c), Q3–4*
174 has] had *Fl*
174 many] mine *Fl*
174 breed] Beauy *Fl*
176 out of an] outward *Fl*
176 yesty] *Fl;* histy *Q2;* misty *Q3–4*
178 profound] *Bailey conj. (in Cambridge);* prophane *Q2–4;* fond *Fl; Warburton conj. (in Hanmer),* fann'd
178 winnow'd] *Fl* (winnowed); trennowed *Q2;* trennowned *Q3–4*
179 trial] tryalls *Fl*
179 s.d., 180–91 Enter. . . me.] *om. Fl (Q1, except l. 187)*
181 Osric] *from the regular Fl form;* Ostricke *Q2–4 (subs., throughout, except* Osrick *at l. 331 s.d.)*
191 s.d. Exit Lord.] *Theobald*
192 lose] lose this wager *Fl*
194–95 Thou wouldst] but thou wouldest *Fl*
195 ill all's] all *Fl*
198 gain-giving] *Fl;* gamgiuing *Q2;* gamegiuing *Q3–4*

200 it] *om. Fl (Q1)*
200 forestall] *Fl,* Q3–4; forstal *Q2*
202 There is] there's a *Fl (Q1)*
203 now] *Fl (Q1)*
205 will] *Fl,* Q3–4; well *Q2*
205 all.] *Rowe (subs.);* all *Q2–4, Fl*
205–06 of . . . be.] ha's ought of what he leaues. What is't to leaue betimes? *Fl*
206 s.d. A . . . state.] *from Q2–4 and Fl s.dd.:* A table prepard, Trumpets, Drums, and officers with Cushions, King, Queene, and all the state, Foiles, daggars, and Laertes. *Q2–4;* Enter King, Queene, Laertes and Lords, with other Attendants with Foyles, and Gauntlets, a Table and Flagons of Wine on it. *Fl; Q1 reads:* Enter King, Queene, Leartes, Lordes.
206 s.d. Osric] *Theobald*
207 s.d. The . . . Hamlet's.] *Johnson*
208 I have] I'ue *Fl*
212 a] *om. Fl (Q1)*
212 distraction. What] *Q3–4 (subs.);* distraction, what *Q2;* distraction? What *Fl*
213 nature, honor,] nature honour *Fl*
215 Was't . . . wrong'd] *Fl;* Wast . . . wronged *Q2–4*
220 wronged] wrong'd *Fl*
222 Sir . . . audience,] *Fl*
226 brother *(Q1);* Mother *Fl*
232 keep] *Fl*
232 ungor'd] vngorg'd *Fl*
232 till] *Fl;* all *Q2–4*
234–35 I . . . play.] *as verse, Fl;* as prose, *Q2–4*
234 I] I do *Fl*
235 brothers'] *M. Edel (privately);* brothers *Q2–4, Fl*
236 Come on.] *Fl*
239 off] *Fl;* of *Q2–4*
243 has] hath *Fl (Q1)*
243 laid] *Fl,* Q3–4 *(Q1);* layed *Q2*
245 better'd] *Fl;* better *Q2–4*
247 s.d. Prepare to play.] *Fl*
249 stoups] *Johnson;* stoopes *Q2–4;* Stopes *Fl*
252 ord'nance] Ordinance *Fl*
254 union] *Fl;* Vnice Q2 *(u);* Onixe Q2 *(c), Q3–4*
257 trumpet] Trumpets *Fl*
260 s.d. Trumpets the while.] *om. Fl (Q1)*
262 s.d. They . . . hit.] *from Fl and Q1:* They play. *Fl;* a hit. / Heere they play: *Q1 (although* a hit *is in italics and is separated from Hamlet's concluding words* come on sir:, *it is perhaps part of his speech)*
262 my lord] on sir *Fl*
265 s.d. sound flourish] *ed. (after Fl and placed as in Fl);* and shot. / Florish, *Q2–4 (after l. 263); Fl s.d. reads:* Trumpets sound, and shot goes off.
265 s.d. within] *Capell*

266 it] (*Q1*); *om. F1*
267 Come.] *F1* (*subs.*); Come, *Q2–4*
267 s.d. They play again.] *Q1*
268 A touch, a touch,] *F1* (*Q1*)
268 confess't] *Q* (*1676*); confest *Q2–4*; confesse *F1*; grant *Q1*
270 Here... my](*Q1*); Heere's a *F1*
274, 278 s.dd. Aside.] *Rowe*
278 it... against] 'tis almost 'gainst *F1*
279 do] *om. F1* (*Q1*)
281 sure] affear'd *F1*
282 s.d. They play.] *F1* (Play.)
284 s.d. Laertes... rapiers.] *Rowe* (*incorporating F1* In scuffling they change Rapiers.*)*; They catch one anothers Rapiers, and both are wounded, Leartes falles downe, the Queene falles downe and dies. *Q1; the s.d. in* Der bestrafte Brudermord *is interesting at this point:* Dieser [i.e. Leonhardus-Laertes] lässt das Rappier fallen, und ergreift den vergifteten Degen welcher parat lieget, und stösst dem Prinzen die Quarte in den Arm. Hamlet pariret auf Leonhardo, dass sie beyde die Gewehre fallen lassen. Sie laufen ein jeder nach dem Rappier. Hamlet bekommt den vergifteten Degen, und sticht Leonhardus todt. [i.e. He lets his foil fall and seizes the poisoned sword, which is lying ready, and deals him a thrust in the left arm. Hamlet parries, so that both drop their weapons. They each run to pick up a foil. Hamlet takes the poisoned sword and kills Leonhardus (*lit.* sticks Leonhardus dead).]
285 come] come, *F1*
285 s.d. Hamlet wounds Laertes.] *Rowe* (*as end of s.d. at l. 284*); *placed as in Sisson*
285 s.d. The Queen falls.] *Capell after Q1* (*see l. 284 s.d.*)
285 ho] *Q3–4* (hoe); howe *Q2*; hoa *F1*
286 is it] is't *F1*
288 own] *om. F1* (*Q1*)
292 pois'ned] poyson'd *F1*
292 s.d. Dies.] *Rowe after Q1* (*see l. 284 s.d.*)
293 Ho] *Q3–4* (hoe); how *Q2*; How? *F1*
295 Hamlet,] *F1*
296 med'cine] Medicine *F1*; medecine *Q4*
297 hour's] *Q* (*1676*); houres *Q2–4*; houre of *F1* (*Q1*)
298 thy] *F1* (*Q1*); my *Q2–4*
301 pois'ned] (*Q1*); poyson'd *F1*
304 s.d. Hurts the King.] *F1*
307 Here] *F1, Q3–4*; Heare *Q2*

307 incestious] incestuous *F1*
307 murd'rous] *F1*
308 off] *F1; of Q2–4*
308 thy union] *F1* (*Q1*); the Onixe *Q2–4*
309 s.d. King dies.] *F1* (*Q1* The king dies.)
310 temper'd] temp'red *F1*
313 s.d. Dies.] *F1* (*Q1* Leartes dies.)
319 strict] strick'd *F1*
321 cause aright] *Q3–4;* cause a right *Q2;* causes right *F1*
323 antique] *Q5;* anticke *Q2;* Antike *F1, Q3–4*
325 ha't] *Capell;* hate *Q2–4;* haue't *F1*
326 God] good *F1;* fie *Q1*
327 I leave] liue *F1;* thou leaue *Q1*
331 s.d. and... within] *F1* (shout), *Steevens* (shot)
331 s.d. Osric returns.] *ed., based on* Enter Osrick. *at this point in Q2–4, F1*
340 silence.] silence. O, o, o, o. *F1*
340 s.d. Dies.] *F1* (*Q1* Ham. dies.)
341 cracks] cracke *F1*
342 s.d. March within.] *Capell*
343 s.d. English] *F1* (*Q1* from England)
343 s.d. Embassadors] (*Q1, subs.*); Ambassador *F1*
343 s.d. with... Attendants] *F1; Q1 s.d. reads:* Enter Voltemar and the Ambassadors from England. enter Fortenbrasse with his traine.
344 you] ye *F1*
346 This] His *F1*
346 proud] *F1, Q3–4;* prou'd *Q2;* imperious *Q1*
348 a shot] a shoote *F1;* one draft *Q1*
349 s.p. First Embassador] 1. Emb. *Capell;* Embas. *Q2–4;* Amb. *F1* (*Q1*)
356 commandement] command'ment *F1*
358 Polack] *F3;* Pollack *Q2;* Pollock *Q3–4;* Polake *F1*
361 th'] *F1, Q3–4*
365 forc'd] *F1;* for no *Q2–4*
371 rights,] Rites *F1;* rights *Q1*
372 now to] (*Q1*); are ro *F1*
373 also] alwayes *F1*
374 on] *F1;* no *Q2–4*
376 while] whiles *F1*
377 plots] plots, *F1*
380 prov'd] *F1* (*Q1*); prooued *Q2–4*
380 royal] (*Q1*); royally *F1*
381 rite] *Wilson;* right *Q2–4;* rites *F1*
383 bodies] body *F1* (*Q1*)
385 s.d. Exeunt] Exeunt. / FINIS. *Q2–4;* Exeunt... off. / FINIS. *F1* (*see following note*); FINIS. *Q1*
385 s.d. marching... off] *F1*

PART TWO

Hamlet:
A Case Study in
Contemporary Criticism

A Critical History of
Hamlet

To write a critical history of *Hamlet* is in many ways to write a cultural history of Britain and the United States in the last four centuries.[1] Probably no other work in English literature has had as much written about it as *Hamlet* has. Each generation makes Shakespeare its own, both through its scholarly reinterpretations and in the creative reincarnations that individual plays are given onstage, in paintings, in poetry, and on film. This capacity to require reinterpretation and to be sufficient in its own complexity and subtlety to the changing ideas of different periods is one of the defining features of a classic. But the same capacity makes understanding the critical history of such a work a complicated project, requiring us to make subtle distinctions and to develop an awareness of the wider cultural milieu in each period. As Elaine Showalter's essay in this volume shows, the field of cultural history itself has an important subfield in Shakespeare studies. Showalter argues that Shakespeare was not only admired in nineteenth-century Britain; his

---

[1] This overwhelming task has been made somewhat easier for me by the work of those who have gone before. I have relied particularly on the excellent history of *Hamlet* criticism by Harold Jenkins ("*Hamlet* Then Till Now"), and the sections "The Play and the Critics" and "*Hamlet* and the Actors" in Philip Edwards's introduction to the New Cambridge Edition of the play. Readers are urged to consult their works and that of G. K. Hunter for further reading.

plays (or the interpretations given his plays) shaped the way in which madness and femininity were understood. His plays thus determined in large part the imaginative horizons of the culture in its approach to the insane, especially madwomen. Literature created life, then, in the instance she studies, and a thorough history of Shakespeare's influence would no doubt find similar cases of the cultural power of Shakespearean drama in every period. I am able to include only a brief summary of some of these moments here, along with a slightly more detailed account of twentieth-century responses to *Hamlet*.

Praise and criticism of Shakespeare began in his lifetime, and by the time of his death he was already recognized as the major dramatist of his generation, if not of his era. *Hamlet* too was already enroute to being identified as his most famous play. In 1623, at the time of publication of the First Folio, a number of important writers wrote tributes to Shakespeare that were included in that volume as introductory matter. These eulogies served to institute Shakespeare as a major writer; along with the publication of what was represented as the approved and corrected text of the plays in folio form, they told the unsuspecting reader who opened the book that he (or less likely she — many fewer women were literate in this period) was about to encounter a figure whose works were already classics. Today this same point is made not only by the introduction to the First Folio, but by the powerful Shakespeare establishment — the many editions, the libraries full of criticism of the plays — in which even this volume participates. We have determined for Shakespeare a central, shaping and defining role in our culture: in an important sense, it is felt that a person is less fully civilized, less fully instructed in what Western culture values if she or he has not encountered the writings of Shakespeare. This is hardly the role that Shakespeare's works played in his lifetime (as we have seen in the historical and biographical introduction to this volume), but it is precisely the position imagined for them in the First Folio.

One of the most surprising tributes included in the First Folio is a poem "To the memory of my beloved, the AUTHOR, Mr. WILLIAM SHAKESPEARE: and what he hath left us" (Jonson 165–66), by Ben Jonson, Shakespeare's near contemporary and sometime rival. In other writings, as we shall see, Jonson had criticized Shakespeare for lacking "art," that is, the careful practice and technique of artistic method, which Jonson distinguishes from "genius" and "nature." None of his doubts surface, however, in his eulogy in the First Folio, where he comments that Shakespeare owes his success to the combination of art and genius. Jonson begins his praise by invoking Shakespeare, calling his spirit back from the stage, and imbuing the book itself with the living Shakespearean soul.

> I, therefore will begin. Soul of the Age!
> The applause! delight! and wonder of our Stage!
> My *Shakespeare*, rise. . . .
> Thou art a Monument, without a tomb,
> And art alive still, while thy Book doth live,
> And we have wits to read, and praise to give.

Here the First Folio is imagined literally as a living monument. Jonson goes on in good humanist fashion to compare Shakespeare to the great Greek classical dramatists, as well as to contemporary British ones, and concludes,

> He was not of an age, but for all time!

This sense that Shakespeare somehow transcends the boundaries of any determined historical moment is perhaps the most characteristic quality that critics have identified throughout the differing periods in which Shakespeare has commanded so much cultural attention. Everyone recognizes that there are aspects of the plays that are distinctly Elizabethan or Jacobean, and yet playgoers and readers tend to feel that the plays rise above these differences and reach out a hand to us today. They find in Shakespeare's plays a universality of spirit and concern that traverses not only historical periods but national boundaries. In recent times new historicist critics have begun to argue for a more historically grounded approach to Shakespeare — one that points out the distinctions between what one writer calls "the politics of the unconscious" for sixteenth- and seventeenth-century British subjects and for us (where "us" may be multiple and diverse).[2] Nonetheless, criticism that focuses on understanding Shakespeare's ideological role in our culture or the possibly liberating effect of a postcolonial appropriation of the Shakespearean text still acknowledges that Shakespeare's plays cross boundaries of time and space, if in a somewhat different way from the universality celebrated in more traditional essays.

Jonson next suggests that Shakespearean drama depends on a special connection with "Nature" and the natural:

---

[2]The critic quoted is Louis Montrose, in " 'Shaping Fantasies' " (63): "My concern," he explains, "is to emphasize the historical specificity of psychological processes, the politics of the unconscious . . . to glimpse the cultural contours of an Elizabethan psyche."

Nature herself was proud of his designs,
And joy'd to wear the dressing of his lines!
Which were so richly spun, and woven so fit,
As, since, she will vouchsafe no other wit.

Not only is Shakespeare's drama "natural," according to these lines, but it displaces any other claim to the natural. It is uniquely natural, then, and in the centuries after Jonson, it goes on to become precisely the cultural symbol of Nature. Here "Nature" means not so much the Romantic landscape as the nature of each person, the intrinsic qualities and laws that determine who and what we are, that define the "nature" of human beings. Jonson partly meant that the writing of the plays represents genius working with the inspiration of nature, but his invocation of "Nature" becomes prophetic of much later Shakespearean criticism. Our notions today of what is essential to or "natural" for human beings tend to come as much from Shakespeare's plays as they do from the contemplation of life.

Jonson was quite capable of criticizing Shakespeare, however, though he clearly does so with affection and respect:

> I remember, the Players have often mentioned it as an honour to Shakespeare, that in his writing, (whatsoever he penn'd) he never blotted out line. My answer hath been, would he had blotted a thousand. Which they thought a malevolent speech. I had not told posterity this, but for their ignorance, who choose that circumstance to commend their friend by, wherein he most faulted. (9)

Jonson is talking here of the need for stylistic revision, of the hard work and craft of verse-making. Today we may be more inclined to criticize Shakespeare on questions of value, but Jonson's example can nonetheless prove useful as a model. A canonical writer who has shaped English and American literary traditions, and helped to create our very understandings of ourselves, Shakespeare cannot be above criticism. His plays need to be put in the context of their time, but they also should be measured against the values of our own. Each of the writers represented in this volume participates in some way in this project of reading Shakespeare dialectically and critically, and we hope the book as a whole will help to bring to life the dialogue between points of view that the play generates.

A quick look at *Hamlet* in the late seventeenth and eighteenth centuries can help us to see how views of the play have mirrored and, indeed, charted cultural history. Accounts of Thomas Betterton's performance of the role in the late seventeenth century suggest that Hamlet was treated as "vigorous, bold and heroic" (Jenkins 36), a character who stirred his audience to sympathy by providing an exemplary representation of ordinary human emotion intensified by extraordinary circumstance. (We should note that the Davenant-Betterton *Hamlet* involved substantial cuts and alterations of the script, many of which were consistently followed in stage versions for over one hundred years.)[3] The many problems that will provoke the next century are here felt to be of little consequence. In a critical essay written in 1736 (once thought to be by Thomas Hanmer), modern readers may be surprised to hear Hamlet's delay explained as a necessary device of the poet to extend the action (if he hadn't delayed, the play would have ended too soon), his reflections on his mother's hasty marriage called "natural," and the scene between Hamlet and his mother praised for having been managed so "conformably to reason and nature" (all qtd. in Jenkins 36). But by the middle and end of the century, the heroic Hamlet begins to disappear, and with him the emphasis on plot as the main way to explain Hamlet's character. While Dr. Johnson, in 1765, praised Hamlet for his "variety," a nearly contemporaneous critic, Francis Gentleman, in 1770, appreciates the variety but laments Hamlet's "inconsistency." Responding to another stage performance in this same period (by Thomas Sheridan in 1763) Boswell comments that Hamlet appeared "irresolute" and wanting "strength of mind," but that along with this irresoluteness came a delicacy springing from "fine feelings" (Jenkins 37). Ushering in the "Age of Sensibility" in *Hamlet* criticism, Henry Mackenzie (1780) found the unifying principle in the play to be Hamlet's "extreme sensibility of mind" (qtd. in Jenkins 37). This same weaker but sensitive Hamlet was made famous by Goethe in his 1795 novel entitled *Wilhelm Meisters Lehrjahre* where the principal character (not necessarily expressing Goethe's own opinions, though this distinction was seldom noted) describes Shakespeare's intentions as follows (from Thomas Carlyle's translation, qtd. in Jenkins 37–38):

> Shakespeare meant . . . to represent the effects of a great action laid upon a soul unfit for the performance of it. . . . A lovely, pure,

---

[3]For a thorough survey of the actors' versions of the play, see Edwards 61–69; for Davenant's version see Edwards 62–63.

noble and most moral nature, without the strength of nerve which forms a hero, sinks beneath a burden which it cannot bear, and must not cast away.

In *Hamlet* criticism we can thus trace the remarkable shift that occurred in the intellectual world at large from the focus on plot (understood broadly, as Aristotle does in his account of tragedy in the *Poetics*) as the chief virtue of drama, to the emphasis on a dramatist's power to depict character.

But with Goethe we have already reached the Romantics, and the shift from the focus (even in formal criticism) on *Hamlet* as a play to be performed to an emphasis on the individual's discovery of self and of inner truths through his (and, more rarely, her) meditation on litera- ture, now a more private, lyrical, and perhaps philosophical mode. Hamlet's character also underwent a change, this time at the hands of one of the most important literary critics of the day, Samuel Taylor Coleridge, the Romantic poet. Coleridge emphasizes in Hamlet not "sensitivity" of mind, but intellectual power, and he gives us the Hamlet still found today on many stages and in many classrooms, the Hamlet who thinks too much and cannot bring himself to act. Coleridge argued that there ought normally to be a balance between our "attention to outward objects" and our "meditation on inward thoughts," but that this balance does not exist in Hamlet. In Hamlet, then, he finds "great, enormous intellectual activity, and a consequent aversion to real action, with all its symptoms and accompanying qualities" (1: 34). In Cole- ridge's reading, Hamlet is a philosopher; he is the Hamlet of the "To be, or not to be" soliloquy, whose "endless reasoning and hesitating" provides an "escape from action" (2: 150). "I have a smack of Hamlet myself, if I may say so," Coleridge commented. Here is Coleridge sum- ming up both Hamlet's character and the moral lesson Shakespeare in- tended us to learn from his tragedy: Hamlet's constant delay is

> not from cowardice, for he is drawn as one of the bravest of his time — not from want of forethought or slowness of apprehen- sion . . . but merely from that aversion to action, which prevails among such as have a world in themselves. (Lecture 12, 2: 150)
>
> Shakespeare wished to impress on us the truth, that action is the chief end of existence — that no faculties of intellect, however brilliant, can be considered valuable, or indeed otherwise than as misfortunes, if they withdraw us from, or render us repugnant to action, and lead us to think and think of doing, until the time has

elapsed when we can do anything effectually. In enforcing this moral truth, Shakespeare has shown the fulness and force of his powers: all that is amiable and excellent in nature is combined in Hamlet, with the exception of one quality. He is a man living in meditation, called upon to act by every motive human and divine, but the great object of his life is defeated by continually resolving to do, yet doing nothing but resolve. (Lecture 12, 2: 154–55)

At more or less the same time, in Germany, A. W. Schlegel had argued in his *Lectures on Dramatic Art and Literature* (1808) that Hamlet's tendency to philosophize and meditate made him unable to act. Schlegel's ideas seem to have influenced Coleridge, though the latter claimed to have arrived at his formulations in lectures that preceded Schlegel's. In any case, these two writers, and nearly a century of those after them, gave emphasis, not to Hamlet's sensitivity, but to his intellect. His philosophical or speculative qualities were admired because they inspired readers to ponder with Hamlet the great questions of human existence. Hamlet became at once a figure who generalizes his own tragedy and an individual whose experience and thoughts individual readers shared. Thus William Hazlitt like Coleridge identified with Hamlet: in 1817, he described Hamlet as transferring his own distress to the "general account of humanity. Whatever happens to him we apply to ourselves" for, Hazlitt says, his thoughts and speeches are "as real as our own thoughts. . . . It is we who are Hamlet" (New Variorum *Hamlet* 2: 155; qtd. in Edwards 33).

In the nineteenth century, then, Hamlet took on a Romantic persona, rebellious against the politics of the court, a philosophic individual set aside and against a social world found to be corrupt and corrupting. This emphasis on Hamlet's character also raised a number of questions which not only shaped nineteenth-century responses to Hamlet but have continued to be asked in our own age. Of these, the most famous is the question "Why does Hamlet delay?" The notion that this delay was simply a plot device would have been scorned by Romantic and late-Romantic critics, who sought an answer in the depths of Hamlet's character. For Coleridge, as we have seen, Hamlet delays because he is too busy thinking, and his philosophical meditations prevent him from taking action — his "native hue of resolution / Is sicklied o'er with the pale cast of thought" (this is a quotation from Hamlet's own description of himself in the "To be, or not to be" soliloquy, 3.1.55). Perhaps the greatest character critic, A. C. Bradley, devoted his analysis of Hamlet to answering this question in his book *Shakespearean Tragedy*, which appeared in 1904. It summed up many of the arguments of the previous century and took them a step further, becoming in the process the principal articulation of a view of *Hamlet* that twentieth-century criticism would strongly challenge.

But before discussing Bradley, a brief survey of the questions that nineteenth- and twentieth-century critics have put to the play can help to show how problematic it has become in the modern era. We have already considered the question that seemed foremost to nineteenth-century readers: Why does Hamlet delay? But not far behind in urgency came the debate about Hamlet's madness. Is Hamlet really mad, or is his madness feigned? Other questions that have come to dominate writing about *Hamlet,* especially since J. Dover Wilson's influential formulation of them in his book *What Happens in Hamlet* (1935), include: Why does Claudius watch the "dumb show," and then wait for a second reenactment of his crime before responding in 3.2, the "play-within-the-play"? Did Hamlet know that Ophelia was being spied upon in the nunnery scene (3.1)? If not, what has Ophelia done to provoke such anger and disgust from him? When did she receive the letter from Hamlet that she gives her father? Such questions led some writers to view *Hamlet* as a "problem play" more in line with *Measure for Measure* or *All's Well That Ends Well* than with his tragedies. But a more characteristic, or at least more important, response was articulated in the writings of two very different, but highly influential writers of the turn of the century, A. C. Bradley and Sigmund Freud. Both respond to the many questions the play presents by focusing on the character of Hamlet as itself a kind of brooding mystery that hides the deeper secrets of the play.

A. C. Bradley's chapter on *Hamlet* in *Shakespearean Tragedy* proved enormously influential in part because it summed up and intensified the wisdom of the previous century on the play and in part because much twentieth-century criticism of the play began by defining itself against Bradley and the kind of reading he urges. For Bradley, Hamlet is a character whose psychology must be imagined to be as complete as that of any living man, however silent the text may be about one or another detail. We must "reconstruct" (Bradley 95) Hamlet's sensibility from the play, he argues, beginning by speculating on Hamlet's state of mind just before his father's death. Bradley found Hamlet to be suffering from an excess of melancholy, an abnormal and "morbid" melancholy that colors every aspect of his sensibility and prevents him from acting. For Bradley this melancholy is a sickness, not a mood, producing a diseased mental condition that Hamlet himself does not fully understand. What causes this "cloud of melancholy" to fall on Hamlet? Bradley argues that it was "the moral shock of the sudden ghastly disclosure of his mother's true nature" (101). Watching Gertrude change her affections and turn to someone Hamlet sees as base and unworthy causes Hamlet in Bradley's view to see in her "not only an astounding shallowness of feeling, but an eruption of coarse sensuality. . . . Is it possible to conceive an experience more desolating to a man, such as we have seen Hamlet to be . . . ?" (102). Bradley's sympathy with Hamlet's reaction provides yet another example of the extent to which *Hamlet* causes readers and audiences to identify themselves with the protagonist, and in its passion it also suggests that Bradley has found in the play many of his own deepest concerns and values.

Bradley emphasizes that Hamlet himself does not understand why he delays, and he quotes Hamlet's mystified self-questioning at length. He proposes that in these moments the cloud of melancholy lifts from Hamlet, leaving him baffled at his own passivity and inaction, and he at least raises the question of whether Hamlet is a man "whose conscience secretly condemned the act which his explicit consciousness approved" (109). From this sense of a divided Hamlet — with both a consciousness and a more secret conscience inaccessible to himself — a divided Hamlet in need of analysis, it was not a long step to Freud.

At almost exactly the same time that Bradley was imagining Hamlet as a complete person, capable of medical and psychological analysis beyond the detail of the text, Sigmund Freud was using *Hamlet,* along with Sophocles' play *Oedipus the King,* in his own psychoanalysis, and in consequence was analyzing their protagonists. Freud was a great admirer of Shakespeare, and especially of *Hamlet,* a work he mentions in his published writing more than twenty times. He was conversant with Shakespeare in the original English. In *The Interpretation of Dreams* (1900), a work in which Freud describes his discovery of the unconscious and of the value of dream analysis, he traces his own self-analysis, which, in somewhat changed form, produces several of his key examples of how to interpret dreams. It becomes clear that his reading of *Hamlet* was a central event in this self-analysis, which comes to its conclusion with the discovery of the Oedipus complex, a psychic phenomenon that Freud sees especially clearly upon his father's death. One can see the importance of the play in Freud's thought by the fact that he uses Hamlet as a figure for dreams themselves, the very medium through which he believes he can gain access to the unconscious:

The prince in the play, who had to disguise himself as a madman, was behaving just as dreams do in reality; so we can say of dreams what Hamlet says of himself, concealing the true circumstances under a cloak of wit and unintelligibility: "I am but mad north-by-north-west." (Freud, *Interpretation of Dreams* 480–81)

Marjorie Garber's essay in this volume begins from precisely this place in Freud's thought to read the play as a locus and example of the uncanny, in literature and in literary history.

Freud makes his most famous statement about *Hamlet* in a footnote in the 1900 *Interpretation of Dreams* (which in later editions was incorporated into the text) that follows the description of the Oedipus complex, itself put forward through a lengthy account of Sophocles' play. What differentiates *Oedipus the King* and *Hamlet,* Freud argues, is largely the degree of repression, and he says that civilization has become more repressed than it was:

> In the *Oedipus* the child's wishful fantasy that underlies it is brought out into the open and realized as it would be in a dream. In *Hamlet* it remains repressed; and — just as in the case of a neurosis — we only learn of its existence from its inhibiting consequences. . . .
> Hamlet is able to do anything — except take vengeance on the man who did away with his father and took that father's place with his mother, the man who shows him the repressed wishes of his childhood realized. (298–99)

He makes this point at greater length in an earlier letter to Wilhelm Fliess, dated October 15, 1897:

> Everyone in the audience was once a budding Oedipus in fantasy, and each recoils in horror from the dream fulfillment here transplanted into reality, with the full quantity of repression which separates his infantile state from his present one.
> Fleetingly the thought passed through my head that the same thing might be at the bottom of *Hamlet* as well. I am not thinking of Shakespeare's conscious intentions, but believe, rather, that a real event stimulated the poet to his representation, in that his unconscious understood the unconscious of his hero. . . . How does [Hamlet] explain his irresolution in avenging his father? . . . How better than through the torment roused in him by the obscure memory that he himself had contemplated the same deed against his father out of passion for his mother. . . . And is not his sexual alienation in his conversation with Ophelia typically hysterical? . . . And does he not in the end, in the same marvellous way

as my hysterical patients do, bring down punishment on himself
by suffering the same fate as his father of being poisoned by the
same rival? (*Complete Letters* 272–73)

For both Freud and Bradley, though for somewhat different reasons,
Hamlet becomes the locus of a hidden, unacknowledged emotion that
it is the job of criticism to retrieve and understand, and this emotion is
evoked most specifically not by grief for his father but by his affection
for his mother.

Freud's interest in *Hamlet* goes beyond the specific comments he
proposes about the play. His essay "Mourning and Melancholia," for
instance, reads at times as an extended meditation on the play *Hamlet*.
Although he mentions Hamlet only parenthetically, his words make it
clear that he reads Hamlet as the archetypal melancholic (see 246). (It
is, of course, characteristic of Freud's method to acknowledge a central
topic of the essay in this indirect fashion, as though in his own writing
he were trying to represent the work of repression.) Indeed, one might
wonder reading the following symptoms of melancholy whether
Freud's opinion about his patients was not also influenced by his reading of the play, so closely do the symptoms of the melancholic match
those Shakespeare dramatizes in Hamlet:

> The distinguishing features of melancholia are a profoundly pain-
> ful dejection, cessation of interest in the outside world, loss of the
> capacity to love, inhibition of all activity, and a lowering of the
> self-regarding feelings to a degree that finds utterance in self-
> reproaches and self-revilings, and culminates in a delusional expec-
> tation of punishment. ("Mourning and Melancholia" 244)

Freud goes on to distinguish mourning from melancholia precisely by
the difference that while in mourning what has been lost is fully conscious (and mourned), in melancholia that loss is hidden — unconscious, or, at any rate, not apparent. Mourning and melancholia share
most traits, but melancholia is distinguished by harsh self-criticism absent in normal mourning. Freud argues that this derogatory view of the
self comes about because the melancholic identifies himself with the
loved "object" (person) he has lost, and thus directs toward himself
the anger he feels at the loss of the beloved person. The withdrawal of
this desired "object" leaves free-floating emotional energy that does not
get displaced onto something new in the case of melancholia, but

> served to establish an *identification* of the ego with the aban-
> doned object. Thus the shadow of the object fell upon the ego,

and the latter could henceforth be judged . . . as though it were
an object, the forsaken object. In this way, the object-loss was
transformed into ego-loss. . . . (249)

A quick look at *Hamlet* will show that the "lost object" for Hamlet is
multiplied, not single — his lost father; his mother, lost to Claudius;
Ophelia, who betrays him to her father; his school friends, who spy on
him; all could qualify — so that Hamlet's melancholic stance is given
too many causes.[4] Freud's paradigm helps to see how Hamlet comes to
find his melancholia, like his world, inescapable, and it identifies one
precise way in which Hamlet's experience becomes an intensified but
exemplary case of ordinary emotional life. Freud's analysis of the melancholia of his patients thus seems to draw powerfully from his understanding of Hamlet's drama and emotional struggles.

Perhaps Freud's and Bradley's emphasis on Hamlet's proximity to
madness, an emphasis on disease or unhealthy repression, may return us
to an aspect of sixteenth- and seventeenth-century views of the play, for
it is clear that Hamlet's madness was taken quite seriously by his early
audiences, and that it was a much more violent affair onstage than is
generally represented today (Jenkins 35). Numerous references to his
madness in contemporary plays, diaries, and poems suggest that audiences went to see the play partly to find out how the madness would be
played.

The theory that Freud made public in *The Interpretation of Dreams*
has its own important history in *Hamlet* criticism and production because one of Freud's disciples, Ernest Jones, undertook to extend it in
an analysis of the play that eventually was published under the title of
Hamlet and Oedipus. He wrote an essay titled "The Oedipus Complex
as an Explanation of Hamlet's Mystery" in 1910; "A Psychoanalytic
Study of Hamlet" appeared in 1923; and finally *Hamlet and Oedipus* in
1949. Jones, whose reading of the play was not as subtle or as complicated as Freud's, was an important influence on Laurence Olivier's film
version (1947). Olivier's film incorporates the main elements of the
Freud-Jones theory of the play: the erotic treatment of the relationship
between Hamlet and Gertrude, emphasized by the use of an unusually
large bed in the "closet scene" (which doesn't call for a bed at all) on
which Hamlet and Gertrude roll in a sexually suggestive manner during

----

[4]Thanks to Ross Hamilton, my colleague and friend, who first proposed
this interpretation of the relation between *Hamlet* and Freud's essay in a seminar I sat in
on.

their struggle of wills in 3.4; the attribution of Hamlet's delay to an implicit comparison between himself and Claudius; and the interpretation of his final acts as self-destructive. The choice of Eileen Herlie to play Gertrude helped to bring out the erotic ties between her and her son, since Herlie was twenty-seven when she played the role and Olivier was forty. Peter Donaldson has cogently pointed out that while this casting made the relationship appear more sexualized to the audience of the film, it made it seem less oedipal for Olivier as actor — less likely to draw him into an experience of reenacting his own relations to his parents. Donaldson comments that "the wish to distance himself from the role [by dyeing his hair, by casting a twenty-seven-year-old as Gertrude] may have been partly the result of the Freudian interpretation he intended to give it" (37). Olivier's Hamlet is romantic, sublime, intellectually brilliant, and courageous but ultimately an isolated figure. Unlike Freud's, Olivier's *Hamlet* is, as Donaldson has suggested, "a tragedy not of guilt but of the grandiose self and its unmet need for context and validation" (63). Such an important cultural landmark as the Olivier *Hamlet* permanently alters our intellectual landscape. After Olivier, any director working on the closet scene (3.4), to take just one example, must decide whether or not it should be played as having a sexual quality. It can no longer be played or watched or read without the consciousness of its primacy in one tradition of interpreting the play.

It is Gertrude that T. S. Eliot singles out for analysis in his account of *Hamlet* (1919), an essay that provides the location and example for his famous theory of the "objective correlative." Eliot argues that

the only way of expressing emotion in the form of art is by finding an "objective correlative"; in other words, a set of objects, a situation, a chain of events which shall be the formula of that *particular* emotion; such that when the external facts, which must terminate in sensory experience, are given, the emotion is immediately evoked.

The centrality of *Hamlet* in twentieth-century English and American culture is well indicated by Eliot's use of this text to articulate a major aesthetic principle of this kind. Jacqueline Rose has argued that the logic of Eliot's account of the objective correlative leads him implicitly to reproach Gertrude for not being "good enough aesthetically, that is, *bad* enough psychologically" (Rose, *Hamlet* 35). Eliot urged that criticism move away from what he saw as the overemphasis on psychology of the previous century (summed up in Bradley), but he remained interested in the causes of the emotion of the protagonist, which he finds wanting. He attributes this difficulty in part to the recalcitrance of the material of the play, finding that there is "some stuff that the writer could not drag to light, contemplate or manipulate into art" (123). Eliot's language suggests some similarities between his theory and those of Freud and Bradley, though that which cannot be dragged to light or contemplated or made into art differs in each case. For Eliot, *Hamlet* is an aesthetic failure because it does not provide an adequate objective correlative for Hamlet's emotion. Hamlet's emotional responses seem to Eliot to be in excess of the facts, and this is particularly true of his feelings about Gertrude. Thus, as Rose points out, had Gertrude been more clearly corrupt sexually or evil (implicated in the murder, for instance), Hamlet's emotions would not be in excess of the facts and Eliot would have deemed the play an aesthetic success. If Gertrude is inadequate as an objective correlative for Hamlet's feelings of disgust, then presumably the fault is Shakespeare's, not Gertrude's. But in analyzing Gertrude in this way the critic reproduces at a different level Hamlet's logic; the theory leads the critic to retrace Hamlet's path and to search for evidence of just how sexually disgusting his mother had become. The results of such a search can be seen in J. Dover Wilson's appendices to *What Happens in Hamlet,* where he argues with Eliot, stressing that Hamlet has plenty of good motives and cause for his emotion — nothing lacking to support Hamlet's intense disgust. Dover Wilson finds what he views as proof that Gertrude committed adultery with Claudius even before the murder (see his appendices A, "The Adultery of Gertrude" 292–94, and D, "Mr. T. S. Eliot's Theory of *Hamlet*" 305–08). Dover Wilson thus illustrates Rose's point: because, for him, Gertrude is certainly and profoundly corrupt, Hamlet's responses are understandable and the play a success.

Jacqueline Rose's hypothesis about Eliot illustrates precisely the turn to questions of gender and aesthetic politics that the critical focus on Gertrude, and on feminine sexuality, has evoked among feminist readers of Shakespeare:

> The fact that it is a woman who is seen as cause of the excess and deficiency in the play and again a woman who symbolizes its aesthetic failure begins to look like a repetition. Firstly, of the play itself — Hamlet and his dead father united in the reproach they make of Gertrude for her sexual failing. . . . Secondly, a repetition of a more fundamental drama of psychic experience as described by Freud, the drama of sexual difference in which the woman is seen as the cause of just such a failure in representation, as something deficient, lacking or threatening to the system and identities

which are the precondition not only of integrated aesthetic form but also of so-called normal adult psychic and sexual life. . . . (*Hamlet* 37)

Rose's reading of the play goes on to establish the ways in which Gertrude, and through her, sexualized femininity, becomes — at the symbolic level — the scapegoat of the play, that which interrupts any possible resolutions of the oedipal conflict and that which disrupts the ideal aesthetic unity. Femininity functions always as a disruptive excess and as deficiency (not-male), not only in the play but in the criticism. The essay by Janet Adelman in this volume exemplifies a related feminist critique of the play's evocations of fears about and disgust for the sexualized maternal body, and of the incorporation into later Western aesthetics and culture of precisely this view of the mother. Adelman argues that the source of the tragic action in *Hamlet*, and of the tragedies to come, is the return of the sexualized body of the mother to the stage.[5]

Much of twentieth-century *Hamlet* criticism can be understood as an effort to "disengage the play from its Romantic associations and reach an independent assessment" (Hunter 31) as powerful and coherent as that of Bradley, but different in assumption and focus. The first critics to argue with Bradley were historically minded scholars of the Elizabethan stage who discussed how the play arose out of its Elizabethan sources, argued about its critique of revenge plays, and insisted in various ways on putting the prince back into the play and back into his historical context. Critics began to emphasize the symbolic order of the play as a whole more than the individually imagined character of its protagonist, and to turn away from "character" as the principal category of aesthetic value and interest. This shift involved a new assumption about how to analyze dramatic texts, an assumption or approach articulated powerfully by G. Wilson Knight in *The Wheel of Fire* (1930) and by L. C. Knights in his essay "How Many Children Had Lady Macbeth?" and was important as an example of the widespread twentieth-century challenge to Bradley's views. L. C. Knights argues specifically against the tendency in psychological criticism to abstract an imagined charac-

---

[5]There is an important tradition of psychoanalytic studies of *Hamlet* to which this introduction cannot do justice, but see the critical introduction to psychoanalysis in this volume. These psychoanalytic studies include the reading of *Hamlet* by Jacques Lacan and several crucial essays on the play by critics influenced by object-relations psychoanalysis (which puts an emphasis on the period of the infant's or child's relation to the mother, locating the essential psychic action as pre-oedipal). See the essays listed in the bibliography under "Psychoanalytic Criticism of Shakespeare and *Hamlet*" on page 254.

ter from a play, to supply answers to questions that the text doesn't
answer in order to imagine the character more fully. And G. Wilson
Knight, one of the most important figures in the turn toward a more
modernist understanding of Shakespeare, argues in the introduction to
Wheel of Fire that we must pay more attention to the structure of
themes and images, and in this way work to place Hamlet in relation to
his dramatic environment. In his emphasis on poetic imagery, Wilson
Knight implies that a Shakespearean play could be read as a long poem,
with many of the tools that illumine lyric poetry. His claims about critical interpretation were congruent with the aims of the American New
Critics, whose influence has been profound on the teaching of literature
in this country. Most students reading this volume were themselves
taught in high school, if not in college, by teachers trained either directly or indirectly by the New Critics, so discussion of close reading
and attention to patterns of imagery (among other things) will bring
many readers home to familiar ground.

If one direction taken from the nineteenth century's intense scrutiny
of the plot's apparent inconsistencies and of the play's "problems"
("Why does Hamlet delay?" and all the other questions listed thus far)
was the turn to what we might call psychological analysis in Freud and
Bradley (and an aestheticizing of psychological analysis in Eliot) and the
finding of value in enigma, another was toward a more metaphysical and
epistemological response to the play in which what had been viewed as
puzzling difficulty became mystery. This approach suggests that what is
"wrong" with Hamlet is not a private psychological or intellectual problem, but rather something in the nature of the universe, and especially
of the human position in the universe. By the 1950s, critical interest had
shifted toward the poetic and the metaphysical, toward the mysteriousness of life and toward a focus on mortality. Maynard Mack's essay "The
World of Hamlet" (1952) can serve as a characteristic example of this
more metaphysical approach, though readers are urged to see also
Harry Levin's book *The Question of Hamlet* (1959). Mack writes that
"Hamlet's world is pre-eminently in the interrogative mood. It rever-
berates with questions, anguished, meditative, alarmed" (237). Some
questions even reach beyond their immediate contexts, Mack writes,
and thus "point towards some pervasive inscrutability in Hamlet's world
as a whole" (237). It is also a world of riddles, so Mack comments that
the mysteriousness of Hamlet's world is all part of the design — "an
important part of what the play wishes to say to us" (238). For Mack,
this mysteriousness lends itself quickly to a philosophical exploration of
the nature of existence:

We need not be surprised that critics and playgoers alike have
been tempted to see in [this opening scene] an evocation not simply of Hamlet's world but of their own. Man in his aspect of baf-
flement, moving in darkness on a rampart between two worlds,
unable to reject, or quite accept, the one that, when he faces it,
"to-shakes" his disposition with thoughts beyond the reaches of
his soul. . . . (239)

The interest here is in part epistemological. The mysteriousness of the
universe translates for the human being into the question of how one
can know anything for certain. If we cannot, how then can we act?

This shift toward a more poetic and metaphysical interest also entailed a shift in emphasis. Now the opening scene and much of act 1
come to represent the play's fascination with messages brought from
beyond the grave. Special attention is focused on the graveyard scene
itself, with Hamlet's classic *memento mori* gesture as he picks up the
skull (of Yorick? how can the grave-digger tell one skull from another?)
to meditate on life and death. That scene and the ending of the play
similarly become central to interpretations of the play that emphasize
the boundary of mortality as that which is fundamental to human consciousness. In this reading, the corruption that causes the world to become "fallen," or diseased, is neither a generalized corruption, found in
Hamlet and in the whole state of Denmark, nor a sexual corruption, but
rather mortality itself, the snake in the garden. The grave-digger has
after all been digging graves since the birth of Hamlet, as if Hamlet had
been born only to confront mortality — and thus to symbolize the belatedness or secondariness of human consciousness, located in the world
of sons and not fathers — in some special way.

This emphasis on mortality and death does not always come along
with philosophical or existential speculation, but what is consistent is
the shift of interest away from the scenes that had been central to the
Romantic Hamlet and toward the *memento mori* scenes and toward a
philosophic meditation on death itself. G. Wilson Knight in his essay on
Hamlet in *The Wheel of Fire* (1930) entitled "The Embassy of Death"
articulates an extreme version of the view that mortality itself is the
play's real focus by writing of Hamlet himself as a death bringer. He sees
Hamlet as a diseased consciousness in an otherwise healthy world, who
by his very presence infects the kingdom. Hamlet's philosophical speculations, riddles, and wit become in Wilson Knight's account a cynicism
so intense that it becomes a principle of negation. Hamlet's poison, he
argues, is "the poison of negation, nothingness, threatening to a world
of positive assertion" (41); "one element in Hamlet . . . is the negation

of any passion. His disease — or vision — is primarily one of negation, of death" (41–42). The principle of negation may be divided in
two: "love-cynicism and death-consciousness" (43). Wilson Knight's
focus, then, is finally on the consciousness of death, though he sees this
consciousness as morbid and destructive, as a negation of life rather
than a philosophic study of its boundaries. Soon thereafter, Caroline
Spurgeon in *Shakespeare's Imagery* (1935) found that the predominant
metaphors in the play were those of disease and rottenness, and she argued that this disease was generalized: Denmark, and therefore not
Hamlet in particular, was sick, was rotten.

   In their emphasis on the poetic imagery as a clue to the play's meaning, Wilson Knight and Spurgeon provide two examples of what came
to be a dominant mode of reading literature in the middle of the century, literary formalism. Dover Wilson's *What Happens in Hamlet* is another example: almost a plot summary, this study works through exactly
what is going on behind the words in every speech and in every scene.
A number of other writers discussed in this survey are formalists —
Maynard Mack, for instance — though they often appear in connection
with specific interpretations they have proposed for the play rather than
with their method.

   Wilson Knight's view that Hamlet is somehow at the source of this
disease, connected to it in some fundamental way as he is by the plot to
mortality, may reflect the theories about the play put forward toward
the end of the nineteenth century by Stéphane Mallarmé, which were
echoed by Joyce in *Ulysses* (1922). In his article titled "Hamlet and
Fortinbras" (1896), Mallarmé had emphasized not only Hamlet's soli-
tariness but his violence — he is "a killer who kills without concern, and
even if he does not do the killing — people die. The black presence of
this doubter causes this poison, of which all of the characters die: without his even having to bother to pierce them through the arras" ("Il tue
indifféremment ou, du moins, on meurt. La noire présence du douteur
cause ce poison, que tous les personnages trépassent: sans même que lui
prenne toujours la peine de les percer, dans la tapisserie" (in part my
translation; qtd. in Edwards 35). Mallarmé's insight reappears in Stephen Dedalus's meditations on the play in the Library (Scylla and
Charybdis) chapter in Joyce's *Ulysses,* where Stephen quotes Mallarmé
and expostulates on what he imagines as the play's "sumptuous and
stagnant exaggeration of murder":

       — A deathsman of the soul Robert Greene called him, Stephen
   said. Not for nothing was he a butcher's son wielding the sledded

poleaxe and spitting in his palm. Nine lives are taken off for his
father's one. Our father who art in purgatory. Khaki Hamlets
don't hesitate to shoot. The bloodboltered shambles in act five is
a forecast of the concentration camp sung by Mr Swinburne. (187)

Mallarmé's sinister figure, given authority by Joyce and scholarly
form by Wilson Knight, appears thereafter in a number of influential
twentieth-century interpretations. Mark Van Doren's Hamlet also
"scatters death like a universal plague," for instance, while Fortinbras,
the active soldier, is interpreted as living "on the bright ice beyond
tragedy's frontier" (171). A recent essay by Margaret Ferguson returns
to Hamlet as the death bringer by commenting on the way kingship
itself is associated in the play with the power to kill. A key example for
Ferguson is the moment Hamlet exchanges Claudius's letter to the king
of England with a copy, and so arranges to have Rosencrantz and
Guildenstern killed. Hamlet seals this letter with his father's signet ring,
the sign of royal power; Hamlet's first deed once he reclaims the signet
ring is thus to arrange a murder. We value Hamlet's delay, in Ferguson's
interpretation, precisely for its extension of the time during which
Hamlet can resist this kingly obligation/prerogative. Rather than being
his problem, then, his delay marks his humanity, his capacity to resist
coming to resemble Claudius in his murderous power.

A third focus of twentieth-century *Hamlet* criticism has been the
play's highlighting of its own theatricality — its metatheatrical self-
consciousness (*metatheatrical* means "theater about theater"). It is precisely this aspect of the play that Bertolt Brecht, probably the most important Marxist playwright in this century, and also a literary critic,
singles out for emphasis in *The Messingkauf Dialogues* where he speaks
of the Elizabethan theater as being "full of alienation effects." "Alienation effects" refers to a method of dramaturgy that Brecht had theo-
rized and put into practice in his own plays. It was intended to require
the actor to express the distance he or she felt from his or her role, and
thus functioned to allow the audience to maintain its critical judgment
and not to sink into passive acceptance of conditions or plots that should,
Brecht felt, be resisted. Since this technique itself emphasized self-consciousness and the theatricality of the medium, what Brecht found in
the Elizabethan theater was a sympathy of aesthetic interest and method.

The self-consciousness in the play about itself as drama parallels
Hamlet's self-consciousness, his anguished meditation on epistemology
and conscience. Here the play-within-the-play and Hamlet's speech to
the traveling players are seen as touchstones for interpretation, along

with the omnipresent pun on the words "to act," which reminds us that onstage all action is also an act played out by actors. The play itself places the pun in the foreground. Puns on "act," on "sun/son," on "kin/kind," not to mention the bawdy double meanings of "nothing" and "country matters" in 3.2 or of Ophelia's mad songs can practically alone chart the play's main preoccupations. Modern critics, both modernist and postmodernist, have seized with delight on these self-reflexive plays with language and found in Shakespearean text (especially this Shakespearean text) a shared sensibility that seems to authorize criticism that will make its central points by, through, and about the pun. Whether it is the psychoanalytic use of the pun as the hint of an alternative but suppressed story, or the epistemological emphasis on the ways puns intensify and express Hamlet's questioning of the grounds of meaning ("grounds / More relative" [2.2.583–84] are always being sought), the pun, along with studies of metaphor, gets pride of place (see Levin, for instance).

The twentieth century's affirmation of the philosophical value of such textual and dramatic self-consciousness brings out a self-consciousness in critics about the techniques of literary response to match Hamlet's and *Hamlet*'s own. Many essays on the play have a major metacritical dimension. They become essays about the ways interpretation of the play has shaped culture or society, and about the ways the interpretive techniques and energies themselves may participate precisely in the uncertainties and philosophical mysteries of the play. Both Elaine Showalter's and Marjorie Garber's essays in this volume show significant metacritical tendencies. Both are interested in the cultural influence either of the play or of its images and categories, and both seek to describe how the play came to have that power.

Early and middle twentieth-century responses to *Hamlet* can be distinguished, then, by which parts of the play they give special prominence. Although critical opinion about this play is more diverse than such a strategy allows, we can generalize by pointing to three different traditions (never entirely separate) that emphasize three different aspects of the play represented most potently perhaps in three specific scenes that are treated as dramatic, emotional, or philosophical high points. One of these traditions is the psychological or psychoanalytic, focusing as it does on the closet scene and on Hamlet's disgust toward women, especially when women are encountered as sexual beings. For Bradley and for Freud, the closet scene is perhaps the emotional center of the play, and both their interpretations identify Hamlet's attachment to Gertrude as the origin of the tragic impasse. The metatheatrical approach, with its focus on the play's self-consciousness of itself as a play and on the theatricality of self and life, gives special place to the play-within-the-play, literally the center of the drama, and to Hamlet's conversation with the traveling players where he expounds his theory of acting. According to the metaphysical or epistemological interpretation — by critics who see in *Hamlet* a dramatization of the universal human desire and incapacity to reach absolute or stable meaning — the scenes with the ghost and then later in the graveyard become the emotional high points of a play that is philosophical and meditative at its core, focusing on mortality as the corruption that causes the "rank" garden to fall, and as that "bourne" (boundary) from beyond which no traveler returns. A focus on sexuality, especially the sexuality of women; a focus on theatricality; a focus on mortality, the *memento mori* of the graveyard; and the "interrogative mood" of the play: all are mutually implicated even as they may help to delineate the main threads of concern in twentieth-century *Hamlet* criticism.

Any survey such as this one must of necessity be radically selective. Two other contemporary methods that deserve at least brief mention are what we might call historical criticism — the effort to try to discover what the Elizabethan issues in the play were — and performance criticism. First, historical criticism. Recent books by Roland Frye and Arthur McGee will send readers in useful directions as they search out "The Renaissance Hamlet." These books pick up and extend debates already underway concerning moral and religious questions about revenge in the play, about fate and free will, and about the meaning of Hamlet's several comments about Providence in act 5 (among other things). These scholars argue that one cannot talk intelligently about why Hamlet delays if one does not understand the issues that face Hamlet. Hamlet fears the ghost is a devil, and at least one scholar, Eleanor Prosser, has argued that he is. Readers are encouraged to look at Nigel Alexander's *Poison, Play, and Duel: A Study of "Hamlet"* and Fredson Thayer Bowers's *Hamlet as Scourge and Minister* as well as works by Arthur McGee and Roland Frye to discover how profoundly the text is shaped by its complex reevaluation of revenge as plot and as moral (or immoral) deed.

A major field through the centuries in Shakespeare study, performance criticism has become especially lively and reinvigorated in the last decade. For a classic example of attention to the theatrical, readers are encouraged to consult Harley Granville-Barker's *Prefaces to Shakespeare*.

In the "Reading List" appended to his edition of the play, Philip Edwards lists a large number of earlier works devoted to the history of *Hamlet* on the stage. In addition to those works, readers may wish to consult John Mills and J. C. Trewin; several essays in *The Hamlet First Published* discuss the use of the First Quarto as the basis of modern productions of the play. Performance criticism treats the play not as material for interpretation, but as a work of art that has its own separate, powerful, and primary existence on the stage.

The essays included in this volume participate in very diverse critical traditions and illustrate quite divergent modes of contemporary criticism. Nonetheless, it is instructive to note some of the ways in which they share the critical interests or tendencies of the century as a whole. Like Freud, Jones, Eliot, and Bradley, both Janet Adelman and Elaine Showalter address the problem of the feminine, and particularly the sexualized female body, whether maternal (Adelman's focus) or virginal (Showalter's focus). For Adelman, Hamlet's confrontation with maternal sexual desire and the maternal body remains central. Showalter focuses on the scenes that had been painted and imitated in the nineteenth century, especially Ophelia's mad scenes and suicide. Adelman, Showalter, and Garber are all engaged, like Jacqueline Rose (whose work was discussed earlier in connection with T. S. Eliot), in providing a feminist critique of the traditional treatment of female sexuality in the play, which led critics to reduplicate in their essays precisely the misogyny that Hamlet expresses when responding to his mother's marriage. Karin S. Coddon, like Showalter, is concerned with the representation and construction of madness, though not with a focus on Ophelia.

The emphasis in metaphysical or epistemological criticism on the mysteriousness and uncertainty of the world of *Hamlet* is present also in Marjorie Garber's essay in her discussion of the uncanny as both the central experience of Hamlet, of the audience watching the play, and of the play's cultural presence and history. Similarly, Michael D. Bristol's essay, though it addresses the question in social and political ways, shares the metaphysical emphasis on the graveyard scene. In his account of the juxtaposition of the scene's *memento mori* images with the gravedigger's more radical humor, he suggests that this metaphysical view of the play's mysteries is challenged by the humor from below that will not acknowledge or give place to the play's high-minded speculation on mortality.

In character with the general trend of literary interpretation, a more political emphasis has become dominant in *Hamlet* and Shakespeare studies of the last two decades and especially since the 1980s. The essays included here all participate in and exemplify these newer methods of approaching the play. While these newer modes of criticism draw from and continue many of the traditions of the past, they have in common a complex aesthetic and political project (with divergent directions, of course): to relate the dramatic work to its political role in its own time or to its current political effects, or both — to read history politically, and politics historically, and to place the literary text in both these readings.[6] One of the characteristic moves of many of these critics is to challenge the assertions of closure made in the plays, and to argue that *Hamlet* (like other plays) should be seen, in Terence Hawkes's words, as "a site, or arena of conflicting and often contradictory potential interpretations, no single one or group of which can claim 'intrinsic' primacy or 'inherent' authority, and all of which are always ideological in nature and subject to extrinsic political and economic determinants" (330). These words form part of the conclusion of Hawkes's essay "Telmah," whose title is Hamlet spelled backward.

The methods have been diverse — from cultural criticism's study of the role of Shakespeare in the A-Level (high school graduation) examination system in Britain to psychoanalytic feminism's close study of the implications of metaphor — but the changes in the critical landscape of Shakespeare studies have been dramatic. One vehicle of this change has been the publication of a number of collections of essays on the plays that take a particular approach or argue for the value of a specific political understanding. A brief list of some of the most prominent of these collections will give a sense of how extensive the territory claimed by these contemporary critics has become (the works are listed in chronological order):

The Woman's Part: Feminist Criticism of Shakespeare. Ed. Carolyn Ruth Swift Lenz, Gayle Greene, and Carol Thomas Neely. Urbana: University of Illinois Press, 1980.

Representing Shakespeare: New Psychoanalytic Essays. Ed. Murray M. Schwartz and Coppélia Kahn. Baltimore and London; Johns Hopkins University Press, 1980.

Women's Studies 9 (1–2) (1981–82): *Feminist Criticism of Shakespeare.*

---

[6]For a useful introduction to these works, see especially Walter Cohen's essay "Political Criticism of Shakespeare" and Don E. Wayne's "Power, Politics and the Shakespearean Text," both in *Shakespeare Reproduced,* ed. Howard and O'Connor. Cohen's essay also includes an extensive, useful bibliography of works of this kind published in the 1980s.

The Forms of Power and the Power of Forms in the Renaissance. Ed. Stephen Greenblatt. Norman: University of Oklahoma Press, 1982.

alternative shakespeares. Ed. John Drakakis. London: Methuen, 1985.

Political Shakespeare: New Essays in Cultural Materialism. Ed. Jonathan Dollimore and Alan Sinfield. Ithaca: Cornell University Press; and Manchester University Press in England, 1985.

Shakespeare and the Question of Theory. Ed. Patricia Parker and Geoffrey Hartman. New York: Methuen, 1985.

Rewriting the Renaissance: The Discourses of Sexual Difference in Early Modern Europe. Ed. Margaret Ferguson, Maureen Quilligan, and Nancy Vickers. Chicago: University of Chicago Press, 1986.

Cannibals, Witches, and Divorce: Estranging the Renaissance. Ed. Marjorie Garber. English Institute Essays. Baltimore: Johns Hopkins University Press, 1986.

Shakespeare Reproduced: The Text in History and Ideology. Ed. Jean Howard and Marion O'Connor. New York: Methuen, 1987.

Staging the Renaissance: Essays on Elizabethan and Jacobean Drama. Ed. David Scott Kastan and Peter Stallybrass. New York: Routledge, 1991.

The selections included in this book participated in the dramatic cultural reevaluation of Shakespeare undertaken in the 1980s and help to attest to the power of these "alternative shakespeares." Elaine Showalter's essay, reproduced here, first appeared in *The Woman's Part* and was reprinted in *Shakespeare and the Question of Theory.* Janet Adelman's early psychoanalytic feminist criticism was first published in *Representing Shakespeare* and in *Cannibals, Witches, and Divorce: Estranging the Renaissance* of which Marjorie Garber (author of another of the essays included in this volume) was the editor, and Bristol's political work is represented in *Shakespeare Reproduced.* As one might expect, however, critics with a psychoanalytic method or interest wrote more and earlier on *Hamlet* than have new historicist or Marxist writers. *Hamlet* has for nearly a century been a central text for psychoanalysis and perhaps thus has seemed to resist the historicizing and politicizing interests of much recent criticism. Karin S. Coddon's essay is one of the first important new historicist essays on the play.

This "strange eventful history" (a phrase used by Jaques in *As You Like It* to describe the story of each human life) cannot be concluded here, for like most good Renaissance histories it breaks off at the moment in which it reaches the present audience. The readers of this volume will be among the shapers of future understandings of *Hamlet,* which will serve, like those described here, to articulate the concerns of future ages as much as they do the moral lessons of the past. *Hamlet* will continue to puzzle and possess the minds of future generations, who can make the play their own only by in turn taking critical possession of it. "Remember me!" says the play, and we will not forget.

Susanne L. Wofford

WORKS CITED

Bowers, Fredson Thayer. *Hamlet as Scourge and Minister.* Charlottesville: U of Virginia P, 1989.

Bradley, A. C. *Shakespearean Tragedy.* 1904. Greenwich: Fawcett-Premier.

Cohen, Walter. "Political Criticism of Shakespeare." Howard and O'Connor 18–46.

Coleridge, Samuel Taylor. *Shakespearean Criticism.* 1930. 2 vols. Ed. Thomas Middleton Raysor. Everyman Library Edition. New York: Dutton, 1960. Based on reports of lectures Coleridge gave in 1811–19, supplemented by his notes.

Conklin, Paul. *A History of Hamlet Criticism: 1601–1821.* London: Routledge, 1947.

Donaldson, Peter S. *Shakespearean Films/Shakespearean Directors.* Boston: Unwin Hyman, 1990.

Edwards, Philip. Introduction. *Hamlet, Prince of Denmark.* New Cambridge Shakespeare. Cambridge, Eng.: Cambridge UP, 1985.

Eliot, T. S. "Hamlet." *Selected Essays.* Essay published 1919. New York: Harcourt, 1932.

Ferguson, Margaret. *"Hamlet:* Letters and Spirits." *Shakespeare and the Question of Theory.* Ed. Patricia Parker and Geoffrey Hartman. New York: Methuen, 1985.

Freud, Sigmund. *The Complete Letters of Sigmund Freud to Wilhelm Fliess, 1887–1904.* Ed. and trans. Jeffrey Moussaieff Masson. Cambridge: Harvard UP, 1985.

———. *The Interpretation of Dreams.* 1900. Standard Edition of the Complete Psychological Works, vols. 4, 5. Ed. and trans. James Strachey. New York: Avon, 1965.

———. "Mourning and Melancholia." 1915. Standard Edition 14: 237–58. See entry above for full publication information.

Frye, Roland. *The Renaissance Hamlet: Issues and Responses in 1600.* Princeton: Princeton UP, 1984.

Furness, Horace Howard, ed. *Hamlet.* New Variorum Edition of Shakespeare. 2 vols. 1877. N. p.: n. p., 1963.

Hawkes, Terence. "Telmah." *Shakespeare and the Question of Theory.* Ed. Patricia Parker and Geoffrey Hartman. London: Methuen, 1985. A study of Hamlet.

Howard, Jean, and Marion O'Connor, eds. *Shakespeare Reproduced: The Text in History and Ideology.* New York: Methuen, 1987.

Hunter, G. K. "Hamlet Criticism." *Critical Quarterly* 1 (1959): 27–32.

Jenkins, Harold. "*Hamlet* Then Till Now." *Shakespeare Survey* 18 (1965): 34–45.

Jones, Ernest. *Hamlet and Oedipus.* 1949. New York: Norton, 1976. Based on essays published between 1910 and 1923.

Jonson, Ben. *Ben Jonson's Literary Criticism.* Ed. James Redwine, Jr. Lincoln: U of Nebraska P, 1970.

Joyce, James. *Ulysses.* 1914. New York: Vintage-Random, 1961.

Kastan, David Scott, and Peter Stallybrass, eds. *Staging the Renaissance: Essays on Elizabethan and Jacobean Drama.* New York: Routledge, 1991.

Knight, G. Wilson. *The Wheel of Fire: Interpretations of Shakespearean Tragedy.* 1930. London: Methuen, 1949.

Knights, L. C. "How Many Children Had Lady Macbeth?" Rpt. in *Explorations* (1946).

Levin, Harry. *The Question of Hamlet.* New York: Oxford UP, 1959.

McGee, Arthur. *The Elizabethan Hamlet.* New Haven: Yale UP, 1987.

Mack, Maynard. "The World of Hamlet." *Yale Review* 41 (1952). Rpt. in the Signet Classic Edition of *Hamlet.* Ed. Edward Hubler. New rev. ed., 1987. 234–56.

Mills, John A. *Hamlet on Stage: The Great Tradition.* Westport: Greenwood, 1985.

Montrose, Louis. "'Shaping Fantasies': Figurations of Gender and Power in Elizabethan Culture." *Representations* 1.2 (Spring 1983): 61–94.

Rose, Jacqueline. "*Hamlet* — the *Mona Lisa* of Literature." *Critical Quarterly* 28 (1986): 35–49.

———. "Sexuality in the Reading of Shakespeare: *Hamlet* and *Measure for Measure*." *alternative shakespeares.* Ed. John Drakakis. London: Methuen, 1985. 95–118.

Spurgeon, Caroline. *Shakespeare's Imagery, and What It Tells Us.* 1935. Cambridge, Eng.: Cambridge UP, 1961.

Trewin, J. C. *Five and Eighty Hamlets.* London: Hutchison, 1987.

Van Doren, Mark. *Shakespeare.* 1939. Garden City: Doubleday, 1953.

Wayne, Don E. "Power, Politics, and the Shakespearean Text: Recent Criticism in England and the United States." Howard and O'Connor 47–67.

Wilson, J. Dover. *What Happens in "Hamlet."* New York: Macmillan, 1935.

Feminist Criticism
and
Hamlet

WHAT IS FEMINIST CRITICISM?

Feminist criticism comes in many forms, and feminist critics have a variety of goals. Some are interested in rediscovering the works of women writers overlooked by a masculine-dominated culture. Others have revisited books by male authors and reviewed them from a woman's point of view to understand how they both reflect and shape the attitudes that have held women back.

Since the early 1970s three strains of feminist criticism have emerged, strains that can be categorized as French, American, and British. These categories should not be allowed to obscure either the global implications of the women's movement or the fact that interests and ideas have been shared by feminists from France, Great Britain, and the United States. British and American feminists have examined similar problems while writing about many of the same writers and works, and American feminists have recently become more receptive to French theories about femininity and writing. Historically speaking, however, French, American, and British feminists have examined similar problems from somewhat different perspectives.

French feminists have tended to focus their attention on language, analyzing the ways in which meaning is produced. They have concluded that language as we commonly think of it is a decidedly male realm.

Drawing on the ideas of the psychoanalytic philosopher Jacques Lacan, French feminists remind us that language is a realm of public discourse. A child enters the linguistic realm just as it comes to grasp its separateness from its mother, just about the time that boys identify with their father, the family representative of culture. The language learned reflects a binary logic that opposes such terms as active/passive, masculine/feminine, sun/moon, father/mother, head/heart, son/daughter, intelligent/sensitive, brother/sister, form/matter, phallus/vagina, reason/emotion. Because this logic tends to group with masculinity such qualities as light, thought, and activity, French feminists have said that the structure of language is phallocentric: it privileges the phallus and, more generally, masculinity by associating them with things and values more appreciated by the (masculine-dominated) culture. Moreover, French feminists believe "masculine desire dominates speech and posits woman as an idealized fantasy-fulfillment for the incurable emotional lack caused by separation from the mother" (Jones 83).

In the view of French feminists, language is associated with separation from the mother. Its distinctions represent the world from the male point of view, and it systematically forces women to choose: either they can imagine and represent themselves as men imagine and represent them (in which case they may speak, but will speak as men) or they can choose "silence," becoming in the process "the invisible and unheard sex" (Jones 83).

But some influential French feminists have argued that language only *seems* to give women such a narrow range of choices. There is another possibility, namely that women can develop a *feminine* language. In various ways, early French feminists such as Annie Leclerc, Xavière Gauthier, and Marguerite Duras have suggested that there is something that may be called *l'écriture féminine:* women's writing. Recently, Julia Kristeva has said that feminine language is "semiotic," not "symbolic." Rather than rigidly opposing and ranking elements of reality, rather than symbolizing one thing but not another in terms of a third, feminine language is rhythmic and unifying. If from the male perspective it seems fluid to the point of being chaotic, that is a fault of the male perspective.

According to Kristeva, feminine language is derived from the preoedipal period of fusion between mother and child. Associated with the maternal, feminine language is not only threatening to culture, which is patriarchal, but also a medium through which women may be creative in new ways. But Kristeva has paired her central, liberating claim — that truly feminist innovation in all fields requires an understanding of the relation between maternity and feminine creation — with a warning. A feminist language that refuses to participate in "masculine" discourse, that places its future entirely in a feminine, semiotic discourse, risks being politically marginalized by men. That is to say, it risks being relegated to the outskirts (pun intended) of what is considered socially and politically significant.

Kristeva, who associates feminine writing with the female body, is joined in her views by other leading French feminists. Hélène Cixous, for instance, also posits an essential connection between the woman's body, whose sexual pleasure has been repressed and denied expression, and women's writing. "Write your self. Your body must be heard," Cixous urges; once they learn to write their bodies, women will not only realize their sexuality but enter history and move toward a future based on a "feminine" economy of giving rather than the "masculine" economy of hoarding (Cixous 250). For Luce Irigaray, women's sexual pleasure (*jouissance*) cannot be expressed by the dominant, ordered, "logical," masculine language. She explores the connection between women's sexuality and women's language through the following analogy: as women's *jouissance* is more multiple than men's unitary, phallic pleasure ("woman has sex organs just about everywhere"), so "feminine" language is more diffusive than its "masculine" counterpart. ("That is undoubtedly the reason . . . her language . . . goes off in all directions and . . . he is unable to discern the coherence," Irigaray writes [101–03].)

Cixous's and Irigaray's emphasis on feminine writing as an expression of the female body has drawn criticism from other French feminists. Many argue that an emphasis on the body either reduces "the feminine" to a biological essence or elevates it in a way that shifts the valuation of masculine and feminine but retains the binary categories. For Christine Fauré, Irigaray's celebration of women's difference fails to address the issue of masculine dominance, and a Marxist-feminist, Catherine Clément, has warned that "poetic" descriptions of what constitutes the feminine will not challenge that dominance in the realm of production. The boys will still make the toys and decide who gets to use them. In her effort to redefine women as political rather than as sexual beings, Monique Wittig has called for the abolition of sexual categories that Cixous and Irigaray retain and revalue as they celebrate women's writing.

American feminist critics have shared with French critics both an interest in and a cautious distrust of the concept of feminine writing.

Annette Kolodny, for instance, has worried that the "richness and variety of women's writing" will be missed if we see in it only its "feminine mode" or "style" ("Dancing" 78). And yet Kolodny herself proceeds, in the same essay, to point out that women *have* had their own style, which includes reflexive constructions ("she found herself crying") and particular, recurring themes (clothing and self-fashioning are two that Kolodny mentions; other American feminists have focused on madness, disease, and the demonic).

Interested as they have become in the "French" subject of feminine style, American feminist critics began by analyzing literary texts rather than philosophizing abstractly about language. Many reviewed the great works by male writers, embarking on a revisionist rereading of literary tradition. These critics examined the portrayals of women characters, exposing the patriarchal ideology implicit in such works and showing how clearly this tradition of systematic masculine dominance is inscribed in our literary tradition. Kate Millett, Carolyn Heilbrun, and Judith Fetterley, among many others, created this model for American feminist criticism, a model that Elaine Showalter came to call "the feminist critique" of "male-constructed literary history" ("Poetics" 25).

Meanwhile another group of critics including Sandra Gilbert, Susan Gubar, Patricia Meyer Spacks, and Showalter herself created a somewhat different model. Whereas feminists writing "feminist critique" have analyzed works by men, practitioners of what Showalter used to refer to as "gynocriticism" have studied the writings of those women who, against all odds, produced what she calls "a literature of their own." In *The Female Imagination* (1975), Spacks examines the female literary tradition to find out how great women writers across the ages have felt, perceived themselves, and imagined reality. Gilbert and Gubar, in *The Madwoman in the Attic* (1979), concern themselves with well-known women writers of the nineteenth century, but they too find that general concerns, images, and themes recur, because the authors that they treat wrote "in a culture whose fundamental definitions of literary authority are both overtly and covertly patriarchal" (45).

If one of the purposes of gynocriticism is to (re)study well-known women authors, another is to rediscover women's history and culture, particularly women's communities that have nurtured female creativity. Still another related purpose is to discover neglected or forgotten women writers and thus to forge an alternative literary tradition, a canon that better represents the female perspective by better representing the literary works that have been written by women. Showalter, in *A Literature of Their Own* (1977), admirably began to fulfill this purpose, providing a remarkably comprehensive overview of women's writing through three of its phases. She defines these as the "Feminine, Feminist, and Female" phases, phases during which women first imitated a masculine tradition (1840–80), then protested against its standards and values (1880–1920), and finally advocated their own autonomous, female perspective (1920 to the present).

With the recovery of a body of women's texts, attention has returned to a question raised a decade ago by Lillian Robinson: Doesn't American feminist criticism need to formulate a theory of its own practice? Won't reliance on theoretical assumptions, categories, and strategies developed by men and associated with nonfeminist schools of thought prevent feminism from being accepted as equivalent to these other critical discourses? Not all American feminists believe that a special or unifying theory of feminist practice is urgently needed; Showalter's historical approach to women's culture allows a feminist critic to use theories based on nonfeminist disciplines. Kolodny has advocated a "playful pluralism" that encompasses a variety of critical schools and methods. But Jane Marcus and others have responded that if feminists adopt too wide a range of approaches, they may relax the tensions between feminists and the educational establishment necessary for political activism.

The question of whether feminism weakens or fortifies itself by emphasizing its separateness — and by developing unity through separateness — is one of several areas of debate within American feminism. Another area of disagreement touched on earlier, between feminists who stress universal feminine attributes (the feminine imagination, feminine writing) and those who focus on the political conditions experienced by certain groups of women at certain times in history, parallels a larger distinction between American feminist critics and their British counterparts.

While it has been customary to refer to an Anglo-American tradition of feminist criticism, British feminists tend to distinguish themselves from what they see as an American overemphasis on texts linking women across boundaries and decades and an underemphasis on popular art and culture. They regard their own critical practice as more political than that of American feminists, whom they have often faulted for being uninterested in historical detail. They would join such American critics as Myra Jehlen to suggest that a continuing preoccupation with women writers might create the danger of placing women's texts outside the history that conditions them.

In the view of British feminists, the American opposition to male stereotypes that denigrate women has often led to counterstereotypes of feminine virtue that ignore real differences of race, class, and culture among women. In addition, they argue that American celebrations of individual heroines falsely suggest that powerful individuals may be immune to repressive conditions and may even imply that *any* individual can go through life unconditioned by the culture and ideology in which she or he lives.

Similarly, the American endeavor to recover women's history — for example, by emphasizing that women developed their own strategies to gain power within their sphere — is seen by British feminists like Judith Newton and Deborah Rosenfelt as an endeavor that "mystifies" male oppression, disguising it as something that has created for women a special world of opportunities. More important from the British standpoint, the universalizing and "essentializing" tendencies in both American practice and French theory disguise women's oppression by highlighting sexual difference, suggesting that a dominant system is impervious to political change. By contrast, British feminist theory emphasizes an engagement with historical process in order to promote social change.

In the essay that follows, Elaine Showalter focuses on the character of Ophelia, all but neglected by prefeminist criticism. Whereas those few earlier critics who did discuss Ophelia tended to see her as being "chiefly interesting . . . in what she says about Hamlet," Showalter proposes that Ophelia has a "story of her own," one that feminist criticism is now prepared to tell. In telling that story she sets out to combine French feminist thought about the "feminine" with a more American empirical and historical approach, thus "yok[ing]," in her own words, "French theory and Yankee know-how." In the process, she blends not only two versions of feminism but also feminism and cultural criticism — a contemporary critical approach that looks at, among other things, the way in which literature changes and is changed by popular culture over time.

Showalter argues that Ophelia's true story is the story of her representation, that is to say, the story of the changing way in which she has been interpreted by various kinds of artists (theatrical and nontheatrical), audiences, and critics. Showalter then begins to tell that story by disclosing what a contemporary Elizabethan would have thought of Ophelia. "Clinically speaking," Showalter writes, "Ophelia's behavior and appearance are characteristic of the malady the Elizabethans would have diagnosed as female love-melancholy, or erotomania." Throughout the seventeenth century, Ophelia's madness, in contrast to Hamlet's, was understood and, therefore, represented in productions and discussion, as a form of sexual — not intellectual — melancholy. Because of this fact, later ages played up or played down, emphasized or de-emphasized, Ophelia's part according to their own cultural attitudes toward or prohibitions against sexuality. Such varied interpretations, grounded in changing ideas about the relation of female sexuality and insanity, have in turn influenced the representations of Ophelia in the popular culture as well as on the stage. Given the fact that she is a minor character in comparison with Gertrude, who has gone virtually unrepresented on canvas and in fiction, the plethora of paintings and novels featuring Ophelia or "Ophelia-like" characters attests to the popular fascination with her. The Romantic Eugène Delacroix, Showalter tells us, puts Ophelia into the "erotic trance" of the "hypnotic"; the Pre-Raphaelite John Everett Millais managed to make the drowned Ophelia look simultaneously like a siren and a victim. To the Victorian mind, Ophelia typified the kind of mental breakdown women were believed to be prone to in adolescence, during the period of sexual awakening. Ophelia even embodied madness to such an extent that mad-women were expected to look and behave like her in order to be considered truly mad.

But it was during the Victorian period, too, that women began writing about Ophelia — women who saw in her character something different from what their male precursors had seen. On the stage as well, feminist interpretations began to represent Ophelia not as erotomaniac but as a "consistent psychological study in sexual intimidation, a girl terrified of her father, of her lover, and of life itself." In our own century, that feminist discourse has by and large persisted (though Freudian psychoanalytic critics have taken exception). As a result, Ophelia has come to be viewed perhaps as a madwoman but as a heroine as well, as a "sister" who "refuses to speak the language of the patriarchal order."

Recognizing that there is no *one* Ophelia — that interpretations of her have far exceeded Shakespeare's text — Showalter uses feminist criticism to describe, via the changing representations of Ophelia, the changing face not only of patriarchal ideology but also of the feminist response that exposes it. This is an important point, one that Showalter makes with particular terseness and cogency at the end of her essay:

in exposing the ideology of representation, feminist critics have also the responsibility to acknowledge and to examine the boundaries of our own ideological positions as products of our gender and our time.

The "humility" that this historical "self-consciousness" breeds is also a source of hope: hope that critics, in particular contemporary feminist critics, may now be in a position to afford Ophelia — and with her, woman — a fairer representation and reality.

Ross C Murfin

FEMINIST CRITICISM: A SELECTED BIBLIOGRAPHY

French Feminist Theories

Beauvoir, Simone de. *The Second Sex.* 1953. Trans. and ed. H. M. Parshley. New York: Bantam, 1961.

Cixous, Hélène. "The Laugh of the Medusa." Trans. Keith Cohen and Paula Cohen. *Signs* 1 (1976): 875–94.

Cixous, Hélène, and Catherine Clément. *The Newly Born Woman.* Trans. Betsy Wing. Minneapolis: U of Minnesota P, 1986.

French Feminist Theory. Special issue, *Signs* 7.1 (1981).

Irigaray, Luce. *This Sex Which Is Not One.* Trans. Catherine Porter. Ithaca: Cornell UP, 1985.

Jones, Ann Rosalind. "Writing the Body: Toward an Understanding of *L'Écriture féminine.*" Showalter, *New Feminist Criticism* 361–77.

Kristeva, Julia. *Desire in Language: A Semiotic Approach to Literature and Art.* Ed. Leon S. Roudiez. Trans. Thomas Gora, Alice Jardine, and Roudiez. New York: Columbia UP, 1980.

Marks, Elaine, and Isabelle de Courtivron, eds. *New French Feminisms: An Anthology.* Amherst: U of Massachusetts P, 1980.

Moi, Toril, ed. *French Feminist Thought: A Reader.* Oxford, Eng.: Basil Blackwell, 1987.

British and American Feminist Theories

Belsey, Catherine, and Jane Moore, eds. *The Feminist Reader: Essays in Gender and the Politics of Literary Criticism.* New York: Basil Blackwell, 1989.

Benhabib, Seyla, and Drucilla Cornell, eds. *Feminism as Critique: On the Politics of Gender.* Minneapolis: U of Minnesota P, 1987.

Butler, Judith. *Gender Trouble: Feminism and the Subversion of Identity.* New York: Routledge, 1990.

Collins, Patricia Hill. *Black Feminist Thought: Knowledge, Consciousness, and the Politics of Empowerment.* Boston: Unwin Hyman, 1990.

de Lauretis, Teresa, ed. *Feminist Studies/Critical Studies.* Bloomington: Indiana UP, 1986.

Feminist Readings: French Texts/American Contexts. Special issue, *Yale French Studies* 62 (1982). Essays by Jardine and Spivak.

Fuss, Diana. *Essentially Speaking: Feminism, Nature, and Difference.* New York: Routledge, 1989.

hooks, bell. *Ain't I a Woman? Black Women and Feminism.* Boston: South End, 1981.

Keohane, Nannerl O., Michelle Z. Rosaldo, and Barbara C. Gelpi, eds. *Feminist Theory: A Critique of Ideology.* Chicago: U of Chicago P, 1982.

Kolodny, Annette. "Dancing Through the Minefield: Some Observations on the Theory, Practice, and Politics of a Feminist Literary Criticism." Showalter, *New Feminist Criticism* 144–67.

The Lesbian Issue. Special issue, *Signs* 9 (Summer 1984).

Malson, Micheline, et al., eds. *Feminist Theory in Practice and Process.* Chicago: U of Chicago P, 1986.

Rich, Adrienne. *On Lies, Secrets, and Silence: Selected Prose, 1966–1979.* New York: Norton, 1979.

Showalter, Elaine. "Toward a Feminist Poetics." Showalter, *New Feminist Criticism* 125–43.

———, ed. *The New Feminist Criticism: Essays on Women, Literature, and Theory.* New York: Pantheon, 1985.

Warhol, Robyn, and Diane Price Herndl, eds. *Feminisms: An Anthology of Literary Theory and Criticism.* New Brunswick: Rutgers UP, 1991. Already a classic anthology.

The Feminist Critique

Fetterley, Judith. *The Resisting Reader: A Feminist Approach to American Fiction.* Bloomington: Indiana UP, 1978.

Greer, Germaine. *The Female Eunuch.* New York: McGraw, 1971.

Millett, Kate. *Sexual Politics.* Garden City: Doubleday, 1970.

Robinson, Lillian S. *Sex, Class, and Culture.* 1978. New York: Methuen, 1986.

Wittig, Monique. *Les Guérillères.* 1969. Trans. David Le Vay. New York: Avon, 1973.

Woolf, Virginia. *A Room of One's Own*. New York: Harcourt, 1929.

Women's Writing and Creativity

Abel, Elizabeth, ed. *Writing and Sexual Difference*. Chicago: U of Chicago P, 1982.

Abel, Elizabeth, Marianne Hirsch, and Elizabeth Langland, eds. *The Voyage In: Fictions of Female Development*. Hanover: UP of New England, 1983.

Auerbach, Nina. *Communities of Women: An Idea in Fiction*. Cambridge: Harvard UP, 1978.

Christian, Barbara. *Black Feminist Criticism: Perspectives on Black Women Writers*. New York: Pergamon, 1985.

Gilbert, Sandra M., and Susan Gubar. *The Madwoman in the Attic: The Woman Writer and the Nineteenth-Century Literary Imagination*. New Haven: Yale UP, 1979.

Jacobus, Mary, ed. *Women Writing and Writing about Women*. New York: Barnes, 1979.

Miller, Nancy K., ed. *The Poetics of Gender*. New York: Columbia UP, 1986.

Newton, Judith Lowder. *Women, Power and Subversion: Social Strategies in British Fiction, 1778–1860*. Athens: U of Georgia P, 1981.

Poovey, Mary. *The Proper Lady and the Woman Writer: Ideology as Style in the Works of Mary Wollstonecraft, Mary Shelley, and Jane Austen*. Chicago: U of Chicago P, 1984.

Showalter, Elaine. *A Literature of Their Own: British Women Novelists from Brontë to Lessing*. Princeton: Princeton UP, 1977.

Marxist and Class Analysis

Barrett, Michèle. *Women's Oppression Today: Problems in Marxist Feminist Analysis*. London: Verso, 1980.

Delphy, Christine. *Close to Home: A Materialist Analysis of Women's Oppression*. Trans. and ed. Diana Leonard. Amherst: U of Massachusetts P, 1984.

Hartsock, Nancy C. M. *Money, Sex, and Power: Toward a Feminist Historical Materialism*. Boston: Northeastern UP, 1985.

Kaplan, Cora. *Sea Changes: Culture and Feminism*. London: Verso, 1986.

Mitchell, Juliet. *Woman's Estate*. New York: Pantheon, 1971.

Newton, Judith, and Deborah Rosenfelt, eds. *Feminist Criticism and Social Change: Sex, Class and Race in Literature and Culture*. New York: Methuen, 1985.

Sargent, Lydia, ed. *Women and Revolution: A Discussion of the Unhappy Marriage of Marxism and Feminism.* Montreal: Black Rose, 1981.

Women's History/Women's Studies

Bridenthal, Renate, and Claudia Koonz, eds. *Becoming Visible: Women in European History.* Boston: Houghton, 1977.

Farnham, Christie, ed. *The Impact of Feminist Research in the Academy.* Bloomington: Indiana UP, 1987.

Kelly, Joan. *Women, History and Theory.* Chicago: U of Chicago P, 1984.

McConnell-Ginet, Sally, et al., eds. *Woman and Language in Literature and Society.* New York: Praeger, 1980.

Mitchell, Juliet, and Ann Oakley, eds. *The Rights and Wrongs of Women.* London: Penguin, 1976.

Newton, Judith L., et al., eds. *Sex and Class in Women's History.* London: Routledge, 1983.

Riley, Denise. *"Am I That Name?": Feminism and the Category of "Women" in History.* Minneapolis: U of Minnesota P, 1988.

Rowbotham, Sheila. *Woman's Consciousness, Man's World.* Harmondsworth, Eng.: Penguin, 1973.

Schipper, Mineke, ed. *Unheard Words: Women and Literature in Africa, the Arab World, Asia, the Caribbean, and Latin America.* London: Allison, 1985.

Scott, Joan Wallach. *Gender and the Politics of History.* New York: Columbia UP, 1988.

Smith-Rosenberg, Carroll. *Disorderly Conduct: Visions of Gender in Victorian America.* New York: Knopf, 1985.

Feminism and Other Critical Approaches

Armstrong, Nancy, ed. *Literature as Women's History I.* A special issue of *Genre* 19–20 (1986–87).

Diamond, Irene, and Lee Quinby, eds. *Feminism and Foucault: Reflections on Resistance.* Boston: Northeastern UP, 1988.

Feminist Studies 14 (1988). Special issue on feminism and deconstruction.

Gallop, Jane. *The Daughter's Seduction: Feminism and Psychoanalysis.* Ithaca: Cornell UP, 1982.

Keller, Evelyn Fox. *Reflections on Gender and Science.* New Haven: Yale UP, 1985.

Meese, Elizabeth, and Alice Parker, eds. *The Difference Within: Femi-*

nism and Critical Theory. Amsterdam/Philadelphia: John Benjamins, 1989.

Penley, Constance, ed. *Feminism and Film Theory.* New York: Routledge, 1988.

Feminist Studies of Shakespeare and *Hamlet*

Adelman, Janet. *Suffocating Mothers: Fantasies of Maternal Origin in Shakespeare, from "Hamlet" to "The Tempest."* New York: Routledge, 1992.

Bamber, Linda. *Comic Women, Tragic Men: A Study of Gender and Genre in Shakespeare.* Stanford: Stanford UP, 1982.

Belsey, Catherine. *The Subject of Tragedy: Identity and Difference in Renaissance Drama.* London: Methuen, 1985.

Erickson, Peter. *Patriarchal Structures in Shakespeare's Drama.* Berkeley: U of California P, 1985.

Ferguson, Margaret, Maureen Quilligan, and Nancy Vickers, eds. *Rewriting the Renaissance: The Discourses of Sexual Difference in Early Modern Europe.* Chicago: U of Chicago P, 1986.

Gohlke, Madelon Sprengnether. " 'I wooed thee with my sword': Shakespeare's Tragic Paradigms." *Representing Shakespeare.* Ed. Murray M. Schwartz and Coppélia Kahn. Baltimore: Johns Hopkins UP, 1980. 170–87.

Jardine, Lisa. *Still Harping on Daughters: Women and Drama in the Age of Shakespeare.* Brighton, Eng.: Harvester, 1983.

Kahn, Coppélia. *Man's Estate: Masculine Identity in Shakespeare.* Berkeley: U of California P, 1981.

Lenz, Carolyn Ruth Swift, Gayle Greene, and Carol Thomas Neely, eds. *The Woman's Part: Feminist Criticism of Shakespeare.* Urbana: U of Illinois P, 1980. The Showalter essay included here originally appeared in this important collection.

McLuskie, Kathleen. "The Patriarchal Bard: Feminist Criticism and Shakespeare — *King Lear* and *Measure for Measure.*" *Political Shakespeare.* Ed. Jonathan Dollimore and Alan Sinfield. Ithaca: Cornell UP, 1985. 88–108.

Neely, Carol Thomas. *Broken Nuptials in Shakespeare's Plays.* New Haven: Yale UP, 1985.

Newman, Karen. *Fashioning Femininity and English Renaissance Drama.* Chicago: U of Chicago P, 1991.

Novy, Marianne. *Love's Argument: Gender Relations in Shakespeare.* Chapel Hill: U of North Carolina P, 1984.

Rose, Jacqueline. "*Hamlet* — the *Mona Lisa* of Literature." *Critical Quarterly* 28 (1986): 35–49.

———. "Sexuality in *Hamlet* and *Measure for Measure.*" *alternative shakespeares.* Ed. John Drakakis. London: Methuen, 1985.

Women's Studies 9, nos. 1, 2 (1981–82). *Feminist Criticism of Shakespeare.*

A FEMINIST PERSPECTIVE

ELAINE SHOWALTER

Representing Ophelia: Women, Madness, and the Responsibilities of Feminist Criticism

"As a sort of a come-on, I announced that I would speak today about that piece of bait named Ophelia, and I'll be as good as my word" (11). These are the words which begin the psychoanalytic seminar on *Hamlet* presented in Paris in 1959 by Jacques Lacan. But despite his promising come-on, Lacan was *not* as good as his word. He goes on for some forty-one pages to speak about Hamlet, and when he does mention Ophelia, she is merely what Lacan calls "the object Ophelia" — that is, the object of Hamlet's male desire. The etymology of Ophelia, Lacan asserts, is "O-phallus," and her role in the drama can only be to function as the exteriorized figuration of what Lacan predictably and, in view of his own early work with psychotic women, disappointingly suggests is the phallus as transcendental signifier (20). To play such a part obviously makes Ophelia "essential," as Lacan admits; but only because, in his words, "she is linked forever, for centuries, to the figure of Hamlet" (23).[1]

The bait-and-switch game that Lacan plays with Ophelia is a cynical but not unusual instance of her deployment in psychiatric and critical texts. For most critics of Shakespeare, Ophelia has been an insignificant minor character in the play, touching in her weakness and madness but chiefly interesting, of course, in what she tells us about Hamlet. And

---

[1] Lacan is wrong about the etymology of Ophelia, which probably derives from the Greek for "help" or "succor." Charlotte M. Younge suggested a derivation from *ophis*, "serpent." See her *History of Christian Names* (1884, rpt. Chicago 1966), 346–47. I am indebted to Walter Jackson Bate for this reference.

while female readers of Shakespeare have often attempted to champion Ophelia, even feminist critics have done so with a certain embarrassment. As Annette Kolodny ruefully admits: "it is after all, an imposition of high order to ask the viewer to attend to Ophelia's sufferings in a scene where, before, he's always so comfortably kept his eye fixed on Hamlet" (7).

Yet when feminist criticism allows Ophelia to upstage Hamlet, it also brings to the foreground the issues in an ongoing theoretical debate about the cultural links between femininity, female sexuality, insanity, and representation. Though she is neglected in criticism, Ophelia is probably the most frequently illustrated and cited of Shakespeare's heroines. Her visibility as a subject in literature, popular culture, and painting, from Redon, who paints her drowning, to Bob Dylan, who places her on Desolation Row, to Cannon Mills, which has named a flowery sheet pattern after her, is in inverse relation to her invisibility in Shakespearean critical texts. Why has she been such a potent and obsessive figure in our cultural mythology? Insofar as Hamlet names Ophelia as "woman" and "frailty," substituting an ideological view of femininity for a personal one, is she indeed representative of Woman, and does her madness stand for the oppression of women in society as well as in tragedy? [Hamlet first uses these words for his mother, but from 3.1 they begin to include Ophelia as well.] Furthermore, since Laertes calls Ophelia a "document in madness," does she represent the textual archetype of woman *as* madness or madness *as* woman? And finally, how should feminist criticism represent Ophelia in its own discourse? What is our responsibility toward her as character and as woman?

Feminist critics have offered a variety of responses to these questions. Some have maintained that we should represent Ophelia as a lawyer represents a client, that we should become her Horatia, in this harsh world reporting her and her cause aright to the unsatisfied. Carol Neely, for example, describes advocacy — speaking *for* Ophelia — as our proper role: "As a feminist critic," she writes, "I must 'tell' Ophelia's story" (11). But what can we mean by Ophelia's story? The story of her life? The story of her betrayal at the hands of her father, brother, lover, court, society? The story of her rejection and marginalization by male critics of Shakespeare? Shakespeare gives us very little information from which to imagine a past for Ophelia. She appears in only five of the play's twenty scenes; the pre-play course of her love story with Hamlet is known only by a few ambiguous flashbacks. Her tragedy is subordinated in the play; unlike Hamlet, she does not struggle with moral choices or alternatives. Thus another feminist critic, Lee Edwards, concludes that it is impossible to reconstruct Ophelia's biography from the text: "We can imagine Hamlet's story without Ophelia, but Ophelia literally has no story without Hamlet" (36).

If we turn from American to French feminist theory, Ophelia might confirm the impossibility of representing the feminine in patriarchal discourse as other than madness, incoherence, fluidity, or silence. In French theoretical criticism, the feminine or "Woman" is that which escapes representation in patriarchal language and symbolism; it remains on the side of negativity, absence, and lack. In comparison to Hamlet, Ophelia is certainly a creature of lack. "I think nothing, my lord," she tells him in the Mouse-trap scene, and he cruelly twists her words:

HAMLET: That's a fair thought to lie between maids' legs.
OPHELIA: What is, my lord?
HAMLET: Nothing.

(3.2.111–13)

In Elizabethan slang, "nothing" was a term for the female genitalia, as in *Much Ado about Nothing*. To Hamlet, then, "nothing" is what lies between maids' legs, for, in the male visual system of representation and desire, women's sexual organs, in the words of the French psychoanalyst Luce Irigaray, "represent the horror of having nothing to see" (101). When Ophelia is mad, Gertrude says that "Her speech is nothing," mere "unshaped use." Ophelia's speech thus represents the horror of having nothing to say in the public terms defined by the court. Deprived of thought, sexuality, language, Ophelia's story becomes the Story of O — the zero, the empty circle or mystery of feminine difference, the cipher of female sexuality to be deciphered by feminist interpretation.[2]

A third approach would be to read Ophelia's story as the female subtext of the tragedy, the repressed story of Hamlet. In this reading, Ophelia represents the strong emotions that the Elizabethans as well as the Freudians thought womanish and unmanly. When Laertes weeps for his dead sister, he says of his tears that "when these are gone, / The woman will be out" [4.7.188–89] — that is to say, that the feminine and shameful part of his nature will be purged. According to David Leverenz, in an important essay called "The Woman in *Hamlet*," Hamlet's disgust at the feminine passivity in himself is translated into violent revulsion against women and into his brutal behavior toward Ophelia. Ophelia's suicide, Leverenz argues, then becomes "a micro-

---

[2]On images of negation and feminine enclosure, see Wilbern.

cosm of the male world's banishment of the female, because 'woman' represents everything denied by reasonable men" (303).

It is perhaps because Hamlet's emotional vulnerability can so readily be conceptualized as feminine that this is the only heroic male role in Shakespeare which has been regularly acted by women, in a tradition from Sarah Bernhardt to, most recently, Diane Venora, in a production directed by Joseph Papp. Leopold Bloom speculates on this tradition in *Ulysses,* musing on the Hamlet of the actress Mrs. Bandman Palmer: "Male impersonator. Perhaps he was a woman? Why Ophelia committed suicide?" (76).

While all of these approaches have much to recommend them, each also presents critical problems. To liberate Ophelia from the text, or to make her its tragic center, is to reappropriate her for our own ends; to dissolve her into a female symbolism of absence is to endorse our own marginality; to make her Hamlet's anima is to reduce her to a metaphor of male experience. I would like to propose instead that Ophelia *does* have a story of her own that feminist criticism can tell; it is neither her life story, nor her love story, nor Lacan's story, but rather the *history* of her representation. This essay tries to bring together some of the categories of French feminist thought about the "feminine" with the empirical energies of American historical and critical research: to yoke French theory and Yankee know-how.

Tracing the iconography of Ophelia in English and French painting, photography, psychiatry, and literature, as well as in theatrical production, I will be showing first of all the representational bonds between female insanity and female sexuality. Second, I want to demonstrate the two-way transaction between psychiatric theory and cultural representation. As one medical historian has observed, we could provide a manual of female insanity by chronicling the illustrations of Ophelia; this is so because the illustrations of Ophelia have played a major role in the theoretical construction of female insanity (126). Finally, I want to suggest that the feminist revision of Ophelia comes as much from the actress's freedom as from the critic's interpretation.[3] When Shakespeare's heroines began to be played by women instead of boys, the presence of the female body and female voice, quite apart from details of interpretation, created new meanings and subversive tensions in these roles, and perhaps most importantly with Ophelia. Looking at Ophelia's history on and off the stage, I will point out the contest between male and female

---

[3]See Goldman, for a stimulating discussion of the interpretative interaction between actor and audience.

representations of Ophelia, cycles of critical repression and feminist reclamation of which contemporary feminist criticism is only the most recent phase. By beginning with these data from cultural history, instead
of moving from the grid of literary theory, I hope to conclude with a
fuller sense of the responsibilities of feminist criticism, as well as a new
perspective on Ophelia.

"Of all the characters in *Hamlet,*" Bridget Lyons has pointed out,
"Ophelia is most persistently presented in terms of symbolic meanings"
(61). Her behavior, her appearance, her gestures, her costume, her
props, are freighted with emblematic significance, and for many generations of Shakespearean critics her part in the play has seemed to be
primarily iconographic. Ophelia's symbolic meanings, moreover, are
specifically feminine. Whereas for Hamlet madness is metaphysical,
linked with culture, for Ophelia it is a product of the female body and
female nature, perhaps that nature's purest form. On the Elizabethan
stage, the conventions of female insanity were sharply defined. Ophelia
dresses in white, decks herself with "fantastical garlands" of wildflowers,
and enters, according to the stage directions of the "Bad" Quarto, "distracted" playing on a lute with her "hair down singing." Her speeches
are marked by extravagant metaphors, lyrical free associations, and "ex-
plosive sexual imagery" (Charney and Charney 451, 457; see also Camden). She sings wistful and bawdy ballads and ends her life by drowning.
    All of these conventions carry specific messages about femininity
and sexuality. Ophelia's virginal and vacant white is contrasted with
Hamlet's scholar's garb, his "suits of solemn black." Her flowers suggest the discordant double images of female sexuality as both innocent
blossoming and whorish contamination; she is the "green girl" of pastoral, the virginal "Rose of May," and the sexually explicit madwoman
who, in giving away her wildflowers and herbs, is symbolically deflower-
ing herself. The "weedy trophies" and phallic "long purples" which she
wears to her death intimate an improper and discordant sexuality that
Gertrude's lovely elegy cannot quite obscure (Garber 155–57). In Elizabethan and Jacobean drama, the stage direction that a woman enters
with disheveled hair indicates that she might either be mad or the victim
of a rape; the disordered hair, her offense against decorum, suggests
sensuality in each case.[4] The mad Ophelia's bawdy songs and verbal license, while they give her access to "an entirely different range of expe-

---

[4]On disheveled hair as a signifier of madness or rape, see Charney and Charney 452–
53, 457, and Dessen 36–38.

rience" from what she is allowed as the dutiful daughter, seem to be her one sanctioned form of self-assertion as a woman, quickly followed, as if in retribution, by her death (Charney and Charney 456). Drowning too was associated with the feminine, with female fluidity as opposed to masculine aridity. In his discussion of the "Ophelia complex," the phenomenologist Gaston Bachelard traces the symbolic connections between women, water, and death. Drowning, he suggests, becomes the truly feminine death in the dramas of literature and life, one which is a beautiful immersion and submersion in the female element. Water is the profound and organic symbol of the liquid woman whose eyes are so easily drowned in tears, as her body is the repository of blood, amniotic fluid, and milk. A man contemplating this feminine suicide understands it by reaching for what is feminine in himself, like Laertes, by a temporary surrender to his own fluidity — that is, his tears; and he becomes a man again in becoming once more dry — when his tears are stopped (109–25).

Clinically speaking, Ophelia's behavior and appearance are characteristic of the malady the Elizabethans would have diagnosed as female love-melancholy, or erotomania. From about 1580, melancholy had become a fashionable disease among young men, especially in London, and Hamlet himself is a prototype of the melancholy hero. Yet the epidemic of melancholy associated with intellectual and imaginative genius "curiously bypassed women." Women's melancholy was seen instead as biological and emotional in origins[5] (Skultans 79–81).

On the stage, Ophelia's madness was presented as the predictable outcome of erotomania. From 1660, when women first appeared on the public stage, to the beginnings of the eighteenth century, the most celebrated of the actresses who played Ophelia were those whom rumor credited with disappointments in love. The greatest triumph was reserved for Susan Mountfort, a former actress at Lincoln's Inn Fields who had gone mad after her lover's betrayal. One night in 1720 she escaped from her keeper, rushed to the theater, and just as the Ophelia of the evening was to enter for her mad scene, "sprang forward in her place . . . with wild eyes and wavering motion" (Wingate 289). As a contemporary reported, "she was in truth *Ophelia herself,* to the amazement of the performers as well as of the audience — nature having made this last effort, her vital powers failed her and she died soon after" (Hiatt 11). These theatrical legends reinforced the belief of the age that female madness was a part of female nature, less to be imitated by an actress

---

[5]On historical cases of love-melancholy, see MacDonald.

than demonstrated by a deranged woman in a performance of her emotions.

The subversive or violent possibilities of the mad scene were nearly eliminated, however, on the eighteenth-century stage. Late Augustan stereotypes of female love-melancholy were sentimentalized versions which minimized the force of female sexuality and made female insanity a pretty stimulant to male sensibility. Actresses such as Mrs. Lessingham in 1772, and Mary Bolton in 1811, played Ophelia in this decorous style, relying on the familiar images of the white dress, loose hair, and wildflowers to convey a polite feminine distraction, highly suitable for pictorial reproduction, and appropriate for Samuel Johnson's description of Ophelia as young, beautiful, harmless, and pious. Even Mrs. Siddons in 1785 played the mad scene with stately and classical dignity. (See Figure 1.) For much of the period, in fact, Augustan objections to the levity and indecency of Ophelia's language and behavior led to censorship of the part. Her lines were frequently cut, and the role was often assigned to a singer instead of an actress, making the mode of representation musical rather than visual or verbal.

But whereas the Augustan response to madness was a denial, the Romantic response was an embrace.[6] The figure of the madwoman permeates Romantic literature, from the Gothic novelists to Wordsworth and Scott in such texts as "The Thorn" and *The Heart of Midlothian*, where she stands for sexual victimization, bereavement, and thrilling emotional extremity. Romantic artists such as Thomas Barker and George Shepheard painted pathetically abandoned Crazy Kates and Crazy Anns, while Henry Fuseli's "Mad Kate" is almost demonically possessed, an orphan of the Romantic storm.

In the Shakespearean theater, Ophelia's Romantic revival began in France rather than England. When Charles Kemble made his Paris debut as Hamlet with an English troupe in 1827, his Ophelia was a young Irish ingénue named Harriet Smithson. Smithson used "her extensive command of mime to depict in precise gesture the state of Ophelia's confused mind" (Raby 63). In the mad scene, she entered in a long black veil, suggesting the standard imagery of female sexual mystery in the Gothic novel, with scattered bedlamish wisps of straw in her hair. (See Figure 2.) Spreading the veil on the ground as she sang, she spread flowers upon it in the shape of a cross, as if to make her father's grave, and mimed a burial, a piece of stage business which remained in vogue for the rest of the century.

[6]See Byrd xiv and passim.

Figure 1. Sarah Siddons as Ophelia

The French audiences were stunned. Dumas recalled that "it was the first time I saw in the theatre real passions, giving life to men and women of flesh and blood" (Raby 68). The twenty-three-year-old Hector Berlioz, who was in the audience on the first night, fell madly in love and eventually married Harriet Smithson despite his family's frantic opposition. Her image as the mad Ophelia was represented in popular lithographs and exhibited in bookshop and printshop windows. Her costume was imitated by the fashionable, and a coiffure "à la folle," consisting of a "black veil with wisps of straw tastefully interwoven" in the hair, was widely copied by the Parisian beau monde, always on the lookout for something new (Raby 72, 75).

Although Smithson never acted Ophelia on the English stage, her intensely visual performance quickly influenced English productions as

Figure 2. Harriet Smithson as Ophelia

well; and indeed the Romantic Ophelia — a young girl passionately and visibly driven to picturesque madness — became the dominant international acting style for the next 150 years, from Helena Modjeska in Poland in 1871, to the eighteen-year-old Jean Simmons in the Laurence Olivier film of 1948.

Whereas the Romantic Hamlet, in Coleridge's famous dictum, thinks too much, has an "overbalance of the contempiative faculty" and an overactive intellect, the Romantic Ophelia is a girl who *feels* too much, who drowns in feeling. The Romantic critics seem to have felt that the less said about Ophelia the better; the point was to *look* at her. Hazlitt, for one, is speechless before her, calling her "a character almost too exquisitely touching to be dwelt upon" (Camden 247). While the

Augustans represent Ophelia as music, the Romantics transform her into an objet d'art, as if to take literally Claudius's lament, "poor Ophelia / Divided from herself and her fair judgment, / Without the which we are pictures" [4.5.83–85].

Smithson's performance is best recaptured in a series of pictures done by Delacroix from 1830 to 1850, which show a strong Romantic interest in the relation of female sexuality and insanity.[7] The most innovative and influential of Delacroix's lithographs is *La Mort d'Ophélie* of 1843, the first of three studies. Its sensual languor, with Ophelia half-suspended in the stream as her dress slips from her body, anticipated the fascination with the erotic trance of the hysteric as it would be studied by Jean-Martin Charcot and his students, including Janet and Freud. Delacroix's interest in the drowning Ophelia is also reproduced to the point of obsession in later nineteenth-century painting. The English Pre-Raphaelites painted her again and again, choosing the drowning, which is only described in the play, and where no actress's image had preceded them or interfered with their imaginative supremacy.

In the Royal Academy show of 1852, Arthur Hughes's entry shows a tiny waiflike creature — a sort of Tinker Bell Ophelia — in a filmy white gown, perched on a tree trunk by the stream. The overall effect is softened, sexless, and hazy, although the straw in her hair resembles a crown of thorns. Hughes's juxtaposition of childlike femininity and Christian martyrdom was overpowered, however, by John Everett Millais's great painting of Ophelia in the same show. (See Figure 3.) While Millais's Ophelia is sensuous siren as well as victim, the artist rather than the subject dominates the scene. The division of space between Ophelia and the natural details Millais had so painstakingly pursued reduces her to one more visual object; and the painting has such a hard surface, strangely flattened perspective, and brilliant light that it seems cruelly indifferent to the woman's death.

These Pre-Raphaelite images were part of a new and intricate traffic between images of women and madness in late nineteenth-century literature, psychiatry, drama, and art. First of all, superintendents of Victorian lunatic asylums were also enthusiasts of Shakespeare, who turned to his dramas for models of mental aberration that could be applied to their clinical practice. The case study of Ophelia was one that seemed particularly useful as an account of hysteria or mental breakdown in adolescence, a period of sexual instability which the Victorians regarded as

[7]See Raby 182.

Figure 3. John Everett Millais's *Ophelia*

risky for women's mental health. As Dr. John Charles Bucknill, president of the Medico-Psychological Association, remarked in 1859,
"Ophelia is the very type of a class of cases by no means uncommon.
Every mental physician of moderately extensive experience must have
seen many Ophelias. It is a copy from nature, after the fashion of the
Pre-Raphaelite school"[8] (110). Dr. John Conolly, the celebrated super-
intendent of the Hanwell Asylum and founder of the committee to
make Stratford a national trust, concurred. In his *Study of Hamlet* in
1863 he noted that even casual visitors to mental institutions could recognize an Ophelia in the wards: "the same young years, the same faded
beauty, the same fantastic dress and interrupted song" (177). Medical
textbooks illustrated their discussions of female patients with sketches of
Ophelia-like maidens.

But Conolly also pointed out that the graceful Ophelias who dominated the Victorian stage were quite unlike the women who had become the majority of the inmate population in Victorian public asylums.
"It seems to be supposed," he protested, "that it is an easy task to play
the part of a crazy girl, and that it is chiefly composed of singing and
prettiness. The habitual courtesy, the partial rudeness of mental disorder, are things to be witnessed. . . . An actress, ambitious of something

[8]For more extensive discussions of Victorian psychiatry and Ophelia figures, see
Showalter.

beyond cold imitation, might find the contemplation of such cases a not unprofitable study" (177–78, 180). Yet when Ellen Terry took up Conolly's challenge and went to an asylum to observe real madwomen, she found them "too *theatrical* " to teach her anything (Terry 154). This was because the iconography of the Romantic Ophelia had begun to infiltrate reality, to define a style for mad young women seeking to express and communicate their distress. And where the women themselves did not willingly throw themselves into Ophelia-like postures, asylum superintendents, armed with the new technology of photography, imposed the costume, gesture, props, and expression of Ophelia upon them. In England, the camera was introduced to asylum work in the 1850s by Dr. Hugh Welch Diamond, who photographed his female patients at the Surrey Asylum and at Bethlem. Diamond was heavily influenced by literary and visual models in his posing of the female subjects. His pictures of madwomen, posed in prayer, or decked with Ophelia-like garlands, were copied for Victorian consumption as touched-up lithographs in professional journals.[9] (See Figure 4.)

Reality, psychiatry, and representational convention were even more confused in the photographic records of hysteria produced in the 1870s by Jean-Martin Charcot. Charcot was the first clinician to install a fully equipped photographic atelier in his Paris hospital, La Salpêtrière, to record the performances of his hysterical stars. Charcot's clinic became, as he said, a "living theater" of female pathology; his women patients were coached in their performances for the camera, and, under hypnosis, were sometimes instructed to play heroines from Shakespeare. Among them, a fifteen-year-old girl named Augustine was featured in the published volumes called *Iconographies* in every posture of *la grande hystérie*. With her white hospital gown and flowing locks, Augustine frequently resembles the reproductions of Ophelia as icon and actress which had been in wide circulation.[10] (See Figure 5.)

But if the Victorian madwoman looks mutely out from men's pictures and acts a part men had staged and directed, she is very differently represented in the feminist revision of Ophelia initiated by newly powerful and respectable Victorian actresses and by women critics of Shakespeare. In their efforts to defend Ophelia, they invent a story for her drawn from their own experiences, grievances, and desires.

[9] Diamond's photographs are reproduced in Gilman, *The Face of Madness.*
[10] See Didi-Huberman, and Heath 36.

Figure 4. Hugh W. Diamond's photograph of a Victorian mad-woman at Surrey Asylum, by permission of the Royal Society of Medicine, London

Probably the most famous of the Victorian feminist revisions of the Ophelia story was Mary Cowden Clarke's *The Girlhood of Shakespeare's Heroines,* published in 1852. Unlike other Victorian moralizing and di-dactic studies of the female characters of Shakespeare's plays, Clarke's was specifically addressed to the wrongs of women and especially to the sexual double standard. In a chapter on Ophelia called "The rose of Elsinore," Clarke tells how the child Ophelia was left behind in the care of a peasant couple when Polonius was called to the court at Paris, and raised in a cottage with a foster-sister and brother, Jutha and Ulf. Jutha is seduced and betrayed by a deceitful knight, and Ophelia discovers the bodies of Jutha and her still-born child, lying "white, rigid, and still" in

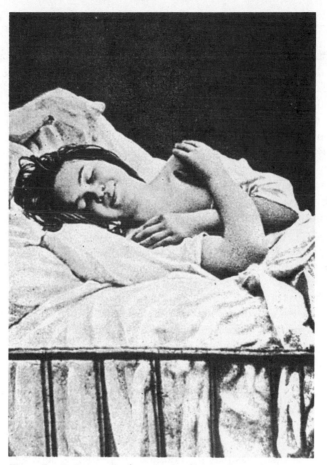

Figure 5. R. Regnard's photograph of "Augustine," *Iconographie photographique de la Salpêtrière,* 1878

the deserted parlor of the cottage in the middle of the night. Ulf, a "hairy loutish boy," likes to torture flies, to eat songbirds, and to rip the petals off roses, and he is also very eager to give little Ophelia what he calls a bear-hug. Both repelled and masochistically attracted by Ulf, Ophelia is repeatedly cornered by him as she grows up; once she escapes the hug by hitting him with a branch of wild roses; another time, he sneaks into her bedroom "in his brutish pertinacity to obtain the hug he had promised himself," but just as he bends over her trembling body, Ophelia is saved by the reappearance of her real mother.

A few years later, back at the court, she discovers the hanged body of another friend, who has killed herself after being "victimized and deserted by the same evil seducer." Not surprisingly, Ophelia breaks down

with brain fever — a staple mental illness of Victorian fiction — and has
prophetic hallucinations of a brook beneath willow trees where something bad will happen to her. The warnings of Polonius and Laertes
have little to add to this history of female sexual trauma.[11]

On the Victorian stage, it was Ellen Terry, daring and unconventional in her own life, who led the way in acting Ophelia in feminist
terms as a consistent psychological study in sexual intimidation, a girl
terrified of her father, of her lover, and of life itself. Terry's debut as
Ophelia in Henry Irving's production in 1878 was a landmark. According to one reviewer, her Ophelia was "the terrible spectacle of a normal
girl becoming hopelessly imbecile as the result of overwhelming mental
agony. Hers was an insanity without wrath or rage, without exaltation
or paroxysms" (Hiatt 114). Her "poetic and intellectual performance"
also inspired other actresses to rebel against the conventions of invisibility and negation associated with the part.

Terry was the first to challenge the tradition of Ophelia's dressing in
emblematic white. For the French poets, such as Rimbaud, Hugo, Mus-
set, Mallarmé, and Laforgue, whiteness was part of Ophelia's essential
feminine symbolism; they call her "blanche Ophélia" and compare her
to a lily, a cloud, or snow. Yet whiteness also made her a transparency,
an absence that took on the colors of Hamlet's moods, and that, for the
symbolists like Mallarmé, made her a blank page to be written over or
on by the male imagination. Although Irving was able to prevent Terry
from wearing black in the mad scene, exclaiming "My God, Madam,
there must be only *one* black figure in this play, and that's Hamlet!"
(Irving, of course, was playing Hamlet), nonetheless actresses such as
Gertrude Eliot, Helen Maude, Nora de Silva, and in Russia Vera
Komisarjevskaya, gradually won the right to intensify Ophelia's presence by clothing her in Hamlet's black (Terry 155–56).

By the turn of the century, there was both a male and a female discourse on Ophelia. A. C. Bradley spoke for the Victorian male tradition
when he noted in *Shakespearean Tragedy* (1906) that "a large number
of readers feel a kind of personal irritation against Ophelia; they seem
unable to forgive her for not having been a heroine" (160). The feminist counterview was represented by actresses in such works as Helena
Faucit [Martin]'s study of Shakespeare's female characters, and *The
True Ophelia*, written by an anonymous actress in 1914, which protested against the "insipid little creature" of criticism and advocated a
strong and intelligent woman destroyed by the heartlessness of men

[11]See Clarke, Gross 37–58, and Auerbach 210–15.

(Martin 4, 18; *The True Ophelia* 15). In women's paintings of the fin de siècle as well, Ophelia is depicted as an inspiring, even sanctified emblem of righteousness.[12]

While the widely read and influential essays of Mary Cowden Clarke are now mocked as the epitome of naive criticism, these Victorian studies of the girlhood of Shakespeare's heroines are of course alive and well as psychoanalytic criticism, which has imagined its own prehistories of oedipal conflict and neurotic fixation; and I say this not to mock psychoanalytic criticism, but to suggest that Clarke's musings on Ophelia are a pre-Freudian speculation on the traumatic sources of a female sexual identity. The Freudian interpretation of *Hamlet* concentrated on the hero but also had much to do with the resexualization of Ophelia. As early as 1900, Freud had traced Hamlet's irresolution to an Oedipus complex, and Ernest Jones, his leading British disciple, developed this view, influencing the performances of John Gielgud and Alec Guinness in the 1930s. In his final version of the study, *Hamlet and Oedipus*, published in 1949, Jones argued that "Ophelia should be unmistakably sensual, as she seldom is on stage. She may be 'innocent' and docile, but she is very aware of her body" (139).

In the theater and in criticism, this Freudian edict has produced such extreme readings as that Shakespeare intends us to see Ophelia as a loose woman and that she has been sleeping with Hamlet. Rebecca West has argued that Ophelia was not "a correct and timid virgin of exquisite sensibilities," a view she attributes to the popularity of the Millais painting; but rather "a disreputable young woman" (18). In his delightful autobiography, Laurence Olivier, who made a special pilgrimage to Ernest Jones when he was preparing his *Hamlet* in the 1930s, recalls that one of his predecessors as actor-manager had said in response to the earnest question, "Did Hamlet sleep with Ophelia?" — "In my company, always" (102, 152).

The most extreme Freudian interpretation reads *Hamlet* as two parallel male and female psychodramas, the counterpointed stories of the incestuous attachments of Hamlet and Ophelia. As Theodor Lidz presents this view, while Hamlet is neurotically attached to his mother, Ophelia has an unresolved oedipal attachment to her father. She has fantasies of a lover who will abduct her from or even kill her father, and when this actually happens, her reason is destroyed by guilt as well as by

---

[12]Among these paintings are the Ophelias of Henrietta Rae and Mrs. F. Littler. Sarah Bernhardt sculpted a bas-relief of Ophelia for the Women's Pavilion at the Chicago World's Fair in 1893.

lingering incestuous feelings. According to Lidz, Ophelia breaks down because she fails in the female developmental task of shifting her sexual attachment from her father "to a man who can bring her fulfillment as a woman" (88, 113). We see the effects of this Freudian Ophelia on stage productions since the 1950s, where directors have hinted at an incestuous link between Ophelia and her father, or more recently, because this staging conflicts with the usual ironic treatment of Polonius, between Ophelia and Laertes. Trevor Nunn's production with Helen Mirren in 1970, for example, made Ophelia and Laertes flirtatious doubles, almost twins in their matching fur-trimmed doublets, playing duets on the lute with Polonius looking on, like Peter, Paul, and Mary. In other productions of the same period, Marianne Faithfull was a haggard Ophelia equally attracted to Hamlet and Laertes, and, in one of the few performances directed by a woman, Yvonne Nicholson sat on Laertes' lap in the advice scene and played the part with "rough sexual bravado" (David 75).[13]

Since the 1960s, the Freudian representation of Ophelia has been supplemented by an antipsychiatry that represents Ophelia's madness in more contemporary terms. In contrast to the psychoanalytic representation of Ophelia's sexual unconscious that connected her essential femininity to Freud's essays on female sexuality and hysteria, her madness is now seen in medical and biochemical terms, as schizophrenia. This is so in part because the schizophrenic woman has become the cultural icon of dualistic femininity in the mid-twentieth century as the erotomaniac was in the seventeenth and the hysteric in the nineteenth. It might also be traced to the work of R. D. Laing on female schizophrenia in the 1960s. Laing argued that schizophrenia was an intelligible response to the experience of invalidation within the family network, especially to the conflicting emotional messages and mystifying double binds experienced by daughters. Ophelia, he noted in *The Divided Self,* is an empty space. "In her madness there is no one there. . . . There is no integral selfhood expressed through her actions or utterances. Incomprehensible statements are said by nothing. She has already died. There is now only a vacuum where there was once a person" (195n).

Despite his sympathy for Ophelia, Laing's readings silence her, equate her with "nothing," more completely than any since the Augustans; and they have been translated into performances which only make Ophelia a graphic study of mental pathology. The sickest Ophelias

---

[13]This was the production directed by Buzz Goodbody, a brilliant young feminist radical who killed herself that year. See Chambers, esp. 63–67.

on the contemporary stage have been those in the productions of the pathologist-director Jonathan Miller. In 1974 at the Greenwich Theatre his Ophelia sucked her thumb; by 1981, at the Warehouse in London, she was played by an actress much taller and heavier than the Hamlet (perhaps punningly cast as the young actor Anton Lesser). She began the play with a set of nervous tics and tuggings of hair which by the mad scene had become a full set of schizophrenic routines — head banging, twitching, wincing, grimacing, and drooling.[14] (David 75).

But since the 1970s too we have had a feminist discourse which has offered a new perspective on Ophelia's madness as protest and rebellion. For many feminist theorists, the madwoman is a heroine, a powerful figure who rebels against the family and the social order; and the hysteric who refuses to speak the language of the patriarchal order, who speaks otherwise, is a sister.[15] In terms of effect on the theater, the most radical application of these ideas was probably realized in Melissa Murray's agitprop play *Ophelia*, written in 1979 for the English women's theater group "Hormone Imbalance." In this blank-verse retelling of the Hamlet story, Ophelia becomes a lesbian and runs off with a woman servant to join a guerrilla commune.[16]

While I've always regretted that I missed this production, I can't proclaim that this defiant ideological gesture, however effective politically or theatrically, is all that feminist criticism desires or all to which it should aspire. When feminist criticism chooses to deal with representation, rather than with women's writing, it must aim for a maximum interdisciplinary contextualism, in which the complexity of attitudes toward the feminine can be analyzed in their fullest cultural and historical frame. The alternation of strong and weak Ophelias on the stage, virginal and seductive Ophelias in art, inadequate or oppressed Ophelias in criticism, tells us how these representations have overflowed the text and how they have reflected the ideological character of their times, erupting as debates between dominant and feminist views in periods of gender crisis and redefinition. The representation of Ophelia changes independently of theories of the meaning of the play or the Prince, for it depends on attitudes toward women and madness. The decorous and pious Ophelia of the Augustan age and the postmodern schizophrenic heroine who might have stepped from the pages of Laing can be derived

---

[14]Thanks to Marianne DeKoven, Rutgers University, for the description of the 1981 Warehouse production.
[15]See, for example, Cixous and Clément.
[16]For an account of this production, see Wandor 47.

from the same figure; they are both contradictory and complementary images of female sexuality in which madness seems to act as the "switching-point, the concept which allows the coexistence of both sides of the representation."[17] There is no "true" Ophelia for whom feminist criticism must unambiguously speak, but perhaps only a Cubist Ophelia of multiple perspectives, more than the sum of all her parts.

But in exposing the ideology of representation, feminist critics have also the responsibility to acknowledge and to examine the boundaries of our own ideological positions as products of our gender and our time. A degree of humility in an age of critical hubris can be our greatest strength, for it is by occupying this position of historical self-consciousness in both feminism and criticism that we maintain our credibility in representing Ophelia, and that, unlike Lacan, when we promise to speak about her, we make good our word.

WORKS CITED

Auerbach, Nina. *Woman and the Demon*. Cambridge, Eng.: Cambridge UP, 1983.

Bachelard, Gaston. *L'Eau et les rêves: Essai sur l'Imagination*. Paris, 1942.

Bradley, A. C. *Shakespearean Tragedy*. London: Macmillan, 1906.

Bucknill, J. C. *The Psychology of Shakespeare*. London, 1859. New York: Longman, 1970.

Byrd, Max. *Visits to Bedlam: Madness and Literature in the Eighteenth Century*. Columbia: U of South Carolina P, 1974.

Camden, Carroll. "On Ophelia's Madness." *Shakespeare Quarterly* 15 (1964): 247–55.

Chambers, Colin. *Other Spaces: New Theatre and the RSC*. London: Methuen, 1980.

Charney, Maurice, and Hanna Charney. "The Language of Madwomen in Shakespeare and His Fellow Dramatists." *Signs* 3.2 (1977): 451–60.

Cixous, Hélène, and Catherine Clément. *La Jeune Née*. Paris: Union Général, 1975.

Clarke, Mary Cowden. *The Girlhood of Shakespeare's Heroines*. London, 1852.

---

[17] I am indebted for this formulation to a critique of a draft of this paper by Carl Freedman, at the Wesleyan Center for the Humanities, April 1984.

Conolly, John. *Study of Hamlet.* London: Moxen, 1908.

David, Richard. *Shakespeare in the Theatre.* Cambridge, Eng.: Cambridge UP, 1978.

Dessen, Allan. *Elizabethan Stage Conventions and Modern Interpreters.* Cambridge, Eng.: Cambridge UP, 1984.

Didi-Huberman, Georges. *L'Invention de l'hystérie.* Paris, 1982.

Edwards, Lee. "The Labors of Psyche." *Critical Inquiry* 6 (1979): 33–98.

Garber, Marjorie. *Coming of Age in Shakespeare.* London: Methuen, 1987.

Gilman, Sander L. *The Face of Madness: Hugh W. Diamond and the Origin of Psychiatric Photography.* New York: Brunner/Mazel, 1976.

———. *Seeing the Insane: a Cultural History of Madness and Art in the Western World, Showing How the Portrayal of Stereotypes Has Reflected and Shaped the Perception and Treatment of the Disturbed.* New York: Wiley–Brunner/Mazel, 1982.

Goldman, Michael. *The Actor's Freedom: Toward a Theory of Drama.* New York: Viking, 1975.

Gross, George C. "Mary Cowden Clarke, *The Girlhood of Shakespeare's Heroines,* and the Sex Education of Victorian Women." *Victorian Studies* 16 (1972): 37–58.

Heath, Stephen. *The Sexual Fix.* London: n.p., 1983.

Hiatt, Charles. *Ellen Terry.* London: Bell, 1898.

Irigaray, Luce. Excerpts from *Ce sexe qui n'est pas un.* Rpt. in *New French Feminisms.* Ed. Elaine Marks and Isabelle de Courtivron. New York: Schocken, 1987. 99–106.

Jones, Ernest. *Hamlet and Oedipus.* New York: Doubleday, 1949.

Joyce, James. *Ulysses.* New York: Vintage, 1961.

Kolodny, Annette. "Dancing through the Minefield: Some Observations on the Theory, Practice, and Politics of Feminist Literary Criticism." *Feminist Studies* 6 (1980): 1–25.

Lacan, Jacques. "Desire and the Interpretation of Desire in *Hamlet.*" *Literature and Psychoanalysis: The Question of Reading: Otherwise.* Ed. Shoshana Felman. Baltimore: Johns Hopkins UP, 1982.

Laing, R. D. *The Divided Self.* Harmondsworth, Eng.: Penguin, 1965.

Leverenz, David. "The Woman in *Hamlet:* An Interpersonal View." *Signs* 4 (1978): 291–308.

Lidz, Theodor. *Hamlet's Enemy: Madness and Myth in "Hamlet."* New York: Basic, 1975.

Lyons, Bridget. "The Iconography of Ophelia." *English Literary History* 44 (1977): 60–74.

MacDonald, Michael. *Mystical Bedlam: Madness, Anxiety, and Healing in Seventeenth-Century England.* Cambridge, Eng.: Cambridge UP, 1982.

Martin, Helena Faucit. *On Some of Shakespeare's Female Characters.* Edinburgh: Blackwood, 1891.

Neely, Carol. "Feminist Modes of Shakespearean Criticism." *Women's Studies* 9 (1981): 3–15.

Olivier, Laurence. *Confessions of an Actor: An Autobiography.* New York: Simon, 1982.

Raby, Peter. *Fair Ophelia: Harriet Smithson Berlioz.* Cambridge, Eng.: Cambridge UP, 1982.

Showalter, Elaine. *The Female Malady: Women, Madness, and Culture in England, 1830–1980.* New York: Pantheon, 1985.

Skultans, Vieda. *English Madness: Ideas on Insanity 1580–1890.* London: Routledge, 1979.

Terry, Ellen. *The Story of My Life.* London: Hutchinson, 1908.

The True Ophelia; and other studies of Shakespeare's women, by an actress. London: Sidgwick, 1913. New York: n.p., 1914.

Wandor, Micheline. *Understudies: Theatre and Sexual Politics.* London: Methuen, 1981.

West, Rebecca. *The Court and the Castle.* New Haven: Yale UP, 1958.

Wilbern, David. "Shakespeare's 'Nothing'." *Representing Shakespeare: New Psychoanalytic Essays.* Ed. Murray M. Schwartz and Coppélia Kahn. Baltimore: Johns Hopkins UP, 1981. 244–63.

Wingate, C. E. L. *Shakespeare's Heroines on the Stage.* New York: Crowell, 1895.

Psychoanalytic Criticism
and
Hamlet

WHAT IS PSYCHOANALYTIC CRITICISM?

It seems natural to think about literature in terms of dreams. Works of literature, as well as dreams, tend to be inventions of the mind. Like a novel or a play, a dream may have some truth to tell, but it may need to be interpreted before that truth can be grasped. We can live vicariously through literary works, much as we can through daydreams. Terrifying tales and nightmares affect us in much the same way, plunging us into an atmosphere that continues to cling, even after the last chapter has been read or the alarm clock has sounded.

The notion that dreams allow such psychic explorations, of course, like the analogy between literary works and dreams, owes a great deal to the thinking of Sigmund Freud, the famous Austrian psychoanalyst who in 1900 published a seminal work, *The Interpretation of Dreams*. But is the reader who feels that the world of *Hamlet* is dreamlike a Freudian literary critic? And is it even *valid* to apply concepts advanced in 1900 to a play written at the turn of the seventeenth century?

To some extent the answer to the first question has to be yes. Freud is one of the reasons it *seems* "natural" to think of literary works in terms of dreams. We are all Freudians, really, whether or not we have read anything by Freud. At one time or another, most of us have referred to ego, libido, complexes, unconscious desires, and sexual repression. The premises of Freud's thought have changed the way the Western world thinks about itself. To a lesser extent, we are all psychoanalytic interpreters as well. Psychoanalytic criticism has influenced the teachers our teachers learned from, the works of scholarship and criticism they read, and the critical and creative writers *we* read as well.

What Freud did was develop a language that described, a model that explained, a theory that encompassed human psychology. Many of the elements of psychology he sought to describe and explain are present in the literary works of various ages and cultures, from Sophocles' *Oedipus Rex* to Shakespeare's *Hamlet* to Brontë's *Wuthering Heights*. When the great novel of the twenty-first century is written, many of these same elements of psychology will probably inform its discourse as well. If, by understanding human psychology according to Freud, we can appreciate literature on a new level, then we should acquaint ourselves with his insights.

Freud's theories are either directly or indirectly concerned with the nature of the unconscious mind. Freud didn't invent the notion of the unconscious; others before him had suggested that even the supposedly "sane" human mind was conscious and rational only at times, and even then at possibly only one level. But Freud went further, suggesting that the powers motivating men and women are *mainly* and *normally* unconscious.

Freud, then, powerfully developed an old idea: that the human mind is essentially dual in nature. He called the predominantly passionate, irrational, unknown, and unconscious part of the psyche the *id*, or "it." The *ego*, or "I," was his term for the predominantly rational, logical, orderly, conscious part. Another aspect of the psyche, which he called the *superego*, is really a projection of the ego. The superego almost seems to be outside of the self, making moral judgments, telling us to make sacrifices for the good causes even though self-sacrifice may not be quite logical or rational. And, in a sense, the superego *is* "outside," since much of what it tells us to do or think we have learned from our parents, our schools, or our religious institutions.

What the ego and superego tell us *not* to do or think is repressed, forced into the unconscious mind. One of Freud's most important contributions to the study of the psyche, the theory of repression, goes something like this: much of what lies in the unconscious mind has been put there by consciousness, which acts as a censor, driving underground unconscious or conscious thoughts or instincts that it deems unacceptable. Censored materials often involve infantile sexual desires, Freud postulated. Repressed to an unconscious state, they emerge only in disguised forms: in dreams, in language (so-called Freudian slips), in creative activity that may produce art (including literature), and in neurotic behavior.

According to Freud, all of us have repressed wishes and fears; we all have dreams in which repressed feelings and memories emerge disguised, and thus we are all potential candidates for dream analysis. One of the unconscious desires most commonly repressed is the childhood wish to displace the parent of our own sex and take his or her place in the affections of the parent of the opposite sex. This desire really involves a number of different but related wishes and fears. (A boy — and it should be remarked in passing that Freud here concerns himself mainly with the male — may fear that his father will castrate him, and he may wish that his mother would return to nursing him.) Freud referred to the whole complex of feelings by the word *oedipal*, naming the complex after the Greek tragic hero Oedipus; who unwittingly killed his father and married his mother.

Why are oedipal wishes and fears repressed by the conscious side of the mind? And what happens to them after they have been censored? As Roy P. Basler puts it in *Sex, Symbolism, and Psychology in Literature* (1975), "from the beginning of recorded history such wishes have been restrained by the most powerful religious and social taboos, and as a result have come to be regarded as 'unnatural,'" even though "Freud found that such wishes are more or less characteristic of normal human development":

> In dreams, particularly, Freud found ample evidence that such wishes persisted. . . . Hence he conceived that natural urges when identified as "wrong," may be repressed but not obliterated. . . .
> In the unconscious, these urges take on symbolic garb, regarded as nonsense by the waking mind that does not recognize their significance. (14)

Freud's belief in the significance of dreams, of course, was no more original than his belief that there is an unconscious side to the psyche. Again, it was the extent to which he developed a theory of how dreams work — and the extent to which that theory helped him, by analogy, to understand far more than just dreams — that made him unusual, important, and influential beyond the perimeters of medical schools and psychiatrists' offices.

The psychoanalytic approach to literature not only rests on the theories of Freud; it may even be said to have *begun* with Freud, who was interested in writers, especially those who relied heavily on symbols. Such writers regularly cloak or mystify ideas in figures that make sense only when interpreted, much as the unconscious mind of a neurotic disguises secret thoughts in dream stories or bizarre actions that need to be interpreted by an analyst. Freud's interest in literary artists led him to make some unfortunate generalizations about creativity; for example, in the twenty-third lecture in *Introductory Lectures on Psycho-Analysis* (1922), he defined the artist as "one urged on by instinctive needs that are too clamorous" (314). But it also led him to write creative literary criticism of his own, including an influential essay on "The Relation of a Poet to Daydreaming" (1908) and "The Uncanny" (1919), a provocative psychoanalytic reading of E. T. A. Hoffmann's supernatural tale "The Sandman."

Freud's application of psychoanalytic theory to literature quickly caught on. In 1909, only a year after Freud had published "The Relation of a Poet to Daydreaming," the psychoanalyst Otto Rank published *The Myth of the Birth of the Hero*. In that work, Rank subscribes to the notion that the artist turns a powerful, secret wish into a literary fantasy, and he uses Freud's notion about the "oedipal" complex to explain why the popular stories of so many heroes in literature are so similar. A year after Rank had published his psychoanalytic account of heroic texts, Ernest Jones, Freud's student and eventual biographer, turned his attention to a tragic text: Shakespeare's *Hamlet*. In an essay first published in the *American Journal of Psychology*, Jones, like Rank, makes use of the oedipal concept: he suggests that Hamlet is a victim of strong feelings toward his mother, the queen.

Between 1909 and 1949 numerous other critics decided that psychological and psychoanalytic theory could assist in the understanding of literature. I. A. Richards, Kenneth Burke, and Edmund Wilson were among the most influential to become interested in the new approach. Not all of the early critics were committed to the approach; neither were all of them Freudians. Some followed Alfred Adler, who believed that writers wrote out of inferiority complexes, and others applied the ideas of Carl Gustav Jung, who had broken with Freud over Freud's emphasis on sex and who had developed a theory of the *collective* unconscious. According to Jungian theory, a great work of literature is not a disguised expression of its author's personal, repressed wishes; rather, it is a manifestation of desires once held by the whole human race but now repressed because of the advent of civilization.

It is important to point out that among those who relied on Freud's models were a number of critics who were poets and novelists as well. Conrad Aiken wrote a Freudian study of American literature, and poets such as Robert Graves and W. H. Auden applied Freudian insights when writing critical prose. William Faulkner, Henry James, James Joyce, D. H. Lawrence, Marcel Proust, and Toni Morrison are only a few of the novelists who have either written criticism influenced by Freud or who have written novels that conceive of character, conflict, and creative writing itself in Freudian terms. The poet H. D. (Hilda Doolittle) was actually a patient of Freud's and provided an account of her analysis in her book *Tribute to Freud*. By giving Freudian theory credibility among students of literature that only they could bestow, such writers helped to endow earlier psychoanalytic criticism with a Freudian orientation that has only begun to be challenged in the last two decades.

The willingness, even eagerness, of writers to use Freudian models in producing literature and criticism of their own consummated a relationship that, to Freud and other pioneering psychoanalytic theorists, had seemed fated from the beginning; after all, therapy involves the close analysis of language. René Wellek and Austin Warren included "psychological" criticism as one of the five "extrinsic" approaches to literature described in their influential book, *Theory of Literature* (1942). Psychological criticism, they suggest, typically attempts to do at least one of the following: provide a psychological study of an individual writer; explore the nature of the creative process; generalize about "types and laws present within works of literature"; or theorize about the psychological "effects of literature upon its readers" (81). Entire books on psychoanalytic criticism even began to appear, such as Frederick J. Hoffman's *Freudianism and the Literary Mind* (1945).

Probably because of Freud's characterization of the creative mind as "clamorous" if not ill, psychoanalytic criticism written before 1950 tended to psychoanalyze the individual author. Poems were read as fantasies that allowed authors to indulge repressed wishes, to protect themselves from deep-seated anxieties, or both. A perfect example of author analysis would be Marie Bonaparte's 1933 study of Edgar Allan Poe. Bonaparte found Poe to be so fixated on his mother that his repressed longing emerges in his stories in images such as the white spot on a black cat's breast, said to represent mother's milk.

A later generation of psychoanalytic critics often paused to analyze the characters in novels and plays before proceeding to their authors.

But not for long, since characters, both evil and good, tended to be seen by these critics as the author's potential selves, or projections of various repressed aspects of his or her psyche. For instance, in *A Psychoanalytic Study of the Double in Literature* (1970), Robert Rogers begins with the view that human beings are double or multiple in nature. Using this assumption, along with the psychoanalytic concept of "dissociation" (best known by its result, the dual or multiple personality), Rogers concludes that writers reveal instinctual or repressed selves in their books, often without realizing that they have done so.

In the view of critics attempting to arrive at more psychological insights into an author than biographical materials can provide, a work of literature is a fantasy or a dream — or at least so analogous to daydream or dream that Freudian analysis can help explain the nature of the mind that produced it. The author's purpose in writing is to gratify secretly some forbidden wish, in particular an infantile wish or desire that has been repressed into the unconscious mind. To discover what the wish is, the psychoanalytic critic employs many of the terms and procedures developed by Freud to analyze dreams.

The literal surface of a work is sometimes spoken of as its "manifest content" and treated as a "manifest dream" or "dream story" would be treated by a Freudian analyst. Just as the analyst tries to figure out the "dream thought" behind the dream story — that is, the latent or hidden content of the manifest dream — so the psychoanalytic literary critic tries to expose the latent, underlying content of a work. Freud used the words *condensation* and *displacement* to explain two of the mental processes whereby the mind disguises its wishes and fears in dream stories. In condensation several thoughts or persons may be condensed into a single manifestation or image in a dream story; in displacement, an anxiety, a wish, or a person may be displaced onto the image of another, with which or whom it is loosely connected through a string of associations that only an analyst can untangle. Psychoanalytic critics treat metaphors as if they were dream condensations; they treat metonyms — figures of speech based on extremely loose, arbitrary associations — as if they were dream displacements. Thus figurative literary language in general is treated as something that evolves as the writer's conscious mind resists what the unconscious tells it to picture or describe. A symbol is, in Daniel Weiss's words, "a meaningful concealment of truth as the truth promises to emerge as some frightening or forbidden idea" (20).

In a 1970 article entitled "The 'Unconscious' of Literature," Norman Holland, a literary critic trained in psychoanalysis, succinctly sums up the attitudes held by critics who would psychoanalyze authors, but without quite saying that it is the *author* who is being analyzed by the psychoanalytic critic. "When one looks at a poem psychoanalytically," he writes, "one considers it as though it were a dream or as though some ideal patient [were speaking] from the couch in iambic pentameter." One "looks for the general level or levels of fantasy associated with the language. By level I mean the familiar stages of childhood development — oral [when desires for nourishment and infantile sexual desires overlap], anal [when infants receive their primary pleasure from defecation], urethral [when urinary functions are the locus of sexual pleasure], phallic [when the penis or, in girls, some penis substitute is of primary interest], oedipal," Holland continues by analyzing not Robert Frost but Frost's poem "Mending Wall" in terms of a specifically oral fantasy that is not unique to its author. "Mending Wall" is "about breaking down the wall which marks the separated or individuated self so as to return to a state of closeness to some Other" — including and perhaps essentially the nursing mother ("Unconscious" 136, 139).

While not denying the idea that the unconscious plays a role in creativity, psychoanalytic critics such as Holland began to focus more on the ways in which authors create works that appeal to *our* repressed wishes and fantasies. Consequently, they shifted their focus away from the psyche of the author and toward the psychology of the reader and the text. Holland's theories, which have concerned themselves more with the reader than with the text, have helped to establish another school of critical theory: reader-response criticism. Elizabeth Wright explains Holland's brand of modern psychoanalytic criticism in this way: "What draws us as readers to a text is the secret expression of what we desire to hear, much as we protest we do not. The disguise must be good enough to fool the censor into thinking that the text is respectable, but bad enough to allow the unconscious to glimpse the unrespectable" (117).

Whereas Holland came increasingly to focus on the reader rather than on the work being read, others who turned away from character and author diagnosis preferred to concentrate on texts; they remained skeptical that readers regularly fulfill wishes by reading. In determining the nature of the text, such critics may regard the text in terms of a dream. But no longer do they assume that dreams are meaningful in the way that works of literature are. Rather, they assume something more complex. "If we move outward" from one "scene to others in the

[same] novel," Meredith Skura writes, "as Freud moves from the dream to its associations, we find that the paths of movement are really quite similar" (181). Dreams are viewed more as a language than as symptoms of repression.

In fact, the French structuralist psychoanalyst Jacques Lacan treats the unconscious *as* a language, a form of discourse. Thus we may study dreams psychoanalytically in order to learn about literature, even as we may study literature in order to learn more about the unconscious. In Lacan's seminar on Poe's "The Purloined Letter," a pattern of repetition like that used by psychoanalysts in their analyses is used to arrive at a reading of the story. According to Wright, "the new psychoanalytic structural approach to literature" employs "analogies from psychoanalysis . . . to explain the workings of the text as distinct from the workings of a particular author's, character's, or even reader's mind" (125).

But Lacan, who is only one of a number of psychoanalytic theorists indebted to but attempting to improve on Freud, does far more than extend Freud's theory of dreams, literature, and the interpretation of both. More significantly, he takes Freud's whole theory of psyche and gender and adds to it a crucial third term — that of language. In the process, he uses but adapts Freud's ideas about the oedipal complex and oedipal stage, both of which Freud saw as crucial to the development of the child, and especially of male children. Lacan argues that girls do not enter language (and what Lacan calls the Symbolic order or the Law of the Father) in the way that boys do. Boys, according to Lacan, in their oedipal phase have to learn to desire substitutions for their mother. Therefore they move more easily into the linguistic realm, in which signs stand in or substitute for the things they represent.

Another thinker who has revised Freud significantly is D. W. Winnicott, an object-relations psychoanalyst who has had a significant impact on literary criticism. Critics influenced by Winnicott and his school have questioned the tendency to see reader/text as an either/or construct; instead, they have seen reader and text — or audience and play — in terms of a *relationship* taking place in what Winnicott calls a "transitional" or "potential space," a space in which binary terms like real and illusory, objective and subjective, have little or no meaning.

Psychoanalytic theorists of the Winnicottian school see the transitional, or potential, reader/text (or audience/play) space as being *like* the space entered into by psychoanalyst and patient. More important, they also see it as being similar to the space between mother and infant:

a space characterized by trust, in which categorizing terms (*knowing* and *feeling*, for instance) mix and merge and have little meaning apart from one another.

Whereas Freud saw the mother-son relationship in terms of the son and his repressed oedipal complex (and saw the analyst-patient relationship in terms of the patient and the repressed truth that the analyst could scientifically extract), object-relations analysts see both relationships as *dyadic* — that is, as being dynamic in both directions. Consequently, they don't depersonalize analysis or their analyses. It is hardly surprising, therefore, that contemporary literary critics who apply object-relations theory to the texts they discuss don't depersonalize critics or categorize their interpretations as "truthful," at least not in any objective or scientific sense. In the view of such critics, interpretations are made of language, itself a transitional object, and are themselves the mediating terms or transitional objects of a relationship.

Perhaps most characteristic of the theories of object relations is the turn to an earlier period in life as the basis of psychic life. Whereas Freud emphasized the period of early childhood in which the child works through the oedipal complex, object-relations theorists have stressed the primacy of a still earlier relationship to the mother, one dating as far back as the first days of infancy, according to Melanie Klein, who, like Winnicott, is an object-relations theorist. In the essay that follows, Janet Adelman stresses the overriding importance of Gertrude and the centrality of fantasies and anxieties about the sexualized body of the mother. In doing so, she combines gender studies and psychoanalytic criticism, the result being a feminist psychoanalytic reading of *Hamlet* that draws on the object-relations theory.

Adelman begins by discussing *Hamlet* in terms of the return of the mother and the mother's body to Shakespeare's plays. In the comedies and histories that precede *Hamlet,* mothers are surprisingly absent. Shakespeare focuses instead on the son-father relationship in works in which "the son attempts to become fully himself by identifying with the true father." Like *Julius Caesar* and the *Henry IV* plays, *Hamlet* presents a son who must choose between *two* father figures, but it makes things much more complicated by also presenting him with a mother who "threatens to annihilate the distinction between the fathers" by making, in Hamlet's view, no apparent distinction between her husband and her husband's evil and opposite brother.

Gertrude's passion for, and quick remarriage to, Claudius unleashes what Adelman calls "fantasies of maternal malevolence," causing Hamlet to see the whole world as an "unweeded garden," a phrase that reflects his view that his mother's body has been contaminated by an incestuous if not adulterous relationship. Adelman even suggests that, in Hamlet's view, the "psychic blame" for Old Hamlet's murder comes to rest with Gertrude. This shift of guilt from Claudius to Gertrude results from Hamlet's revulsion toward, and condemnation of, his mother's overt sexuality. Thus begins Hamlet's efforts to "save" and purify his mother, as evidenced by both "The Murther of Gonzago" (see *Hamlet* 3.2) and the closet scene (3.4).

Rather than seeing *Hamlet* in classic Freudian, oedipal terms as a play about a young man consumed by repressed passion for the mother (and/or repressed hatred of his true father), Adelman sees the play's psychological drama as being about Hamlet's complex relationships to several characters. These relationships ultimately involve fear of the mother (specifically of her sexuality), idealization of the father (and of the masculinity he represents), and a consequent "struggle . . . to free the masculine identity of both father and son from its origin in the contaminated maternal body."

The play is also, according to Adelman, about the madness that results as the distinction Hamlet wants to make between his dead father on one hand and Claudius on the other begins to break down. And it *does* break down: the ghost of Old Hamlet speaks of "foul crimes" done in his "days of nature"; Gertrude does not satisfy her son's need to hear her (re)assert the difference between the two men; and Hamlet himself, at one point, linguistically conflates Claudius's murder of the king with his father's crimes.

Adelman, like most contemporary psychoanalytic critics, does not attempt to analyze William Shakespeare; rather, she analyzes Hamlet and, more significantly, *Hamlet,* finding in the deep structures of the text's language a psychology complete with repressed infantile fantasies and fears (of being ruined at the point of origin; of the subjection of male to female; and of the annihilation that could result from "promiscuous mixture" and "boundary contamination" — in other words, the blurring of the line between the sexes). Furthermore, Adelman does not view the text in the way an old-fashioned Freudian might view it: as an object in need of surgical probing and cool, intellectual diagnosis. The play is viewed, rather, as being a vehicle in which we explore — at some cost to us and to the kind of community whose breakdown the play seems to lament — essentially destructive prejudices and passions. If, in Winnicottian terms, *Hamlet* is a transitional or potential space that remakes us even as we remake it through interpretive interplay, it is also space that, in Adelman's ominously Shakespearean words, "boils and bubbles like a witch's cauldron."

Ross C Murfin

PSYCHOANALYTIC CRITICISM: A SELECTED BIBLIOGRAPHY

Some Short Introductions to Psychological and Psychoanalytic Criticism

Holland, Norman. "The 'Unconscious' of Literature." *Contemporary Criticism*. Ed. Norman Bradbury and David Palmer, Stratford-upon-Avon Series, Vol. 12. New York: St. Martin's, 1970. 131–54.

Natoli, Joseph, and Frederik L. Rusch, comps. *Psychocriticism: An Annotated Bibliography*. Westport: Greenwood, 1984.

Scott, Wilbur. *Five Approaches to Literary Criticism*. London: Collier-Macmillan, 1962. See the essays by Burke and Gorer, as well as Scott's introduction to the section "The Psychological Approach: Literature in the Light of Psychological Theory."

Wellek, René, and Austin Warren. *Theory of Literature*. New York: Harcourt, 1942. See the chapter "Literature and Psychology" in pt. 3, "The Extrinsic Approach to the Study of Literature."

Wright, Elizabeth. "Modern Psychoanalytic Criticism." *Modern Literary Theory: A Comparative Introduction*. Ed. Ann Jefferson and David Robey. Totowa: Barnes, 1982. 113–33.

Freud, Lacan, and Their Influence

Basler, Roy P. *Sex, Symbolism, and Psychology in Literature*. New York: Octagon, 1975. See especially 13–19.

Clément, Catherine. *The Lives and Legends of Jacques Lacan*. Trans. Arthur Goldhammer. New York: Columbia UP, 1983.

Freud, Sigmund. *Introductory Lectures on Psycho-Analysis*. Trans. Joan Rivière. London: Allen, 1922.

Gallop, Jane. *Reading Lacan*. Ithaca: Cornell UP, 1985.

Hoffman, Frederick J. *Freudianism and the Literary Mind*. Baton Rouge: Louisiana State UP, 1945.

Kazin, Alfred. "Freud and His Consequences." *Contemporaries*. Boston: Little, 1962. 351–93.

Lacan, Jacques. *Écrits: A Selection*. Trans. Alan Sheridan. New York: Norton, 1977.

———. *Feminine Sexuality: Lacan and the école freudienne*. Ed. Juliet Mitchell and Jacqueline Rose. Trans. Jacqueline Rose. New York: Norton, 1982.

———. *The Four Fundamental Concepts of Psychoanalysis*. Trans. Alan Sheridan. London: Penguin, 1980.

Meisel, Perry, ed. *Freud: A Collection of Critical Essays*. Englewood Cliffs: Prentice, 1981.

Muller, John P. and William J. Richardson. *Lacan and Language: A Reader's Guide to "Écrits."* New York: International UP, 1982.

Porter, Laurence M. *The Interpretation of Dreams: Freud's Theories Revisited*. Twayne's Masterwork Studies Series. Boston: Hall, 1986.

Reppen, Joseph, and Maurice Charney. *The Psychoanalytic Study of Literature*. Hillsdale: Analytic, 1985.

Schneiderman, Stuart. *Jacques Lacan: The Death of an Intellectual Hero*. Cambridge: Harvard UP, 1983.

Selden, Raman. *A Reader's Guide to Contemporary Literary Theory*. Lexington: U of Kentucky P, 1985. See "Jacques Lacan: Language and the Unconscious."

Trilling, Lionel. "Art and Neurosis." *The Liberal Imagination*. New York: Scribner's, 1950. 160–80.

Wilden, Anthony. "Lacan and the Discourse of the Other." In Lacan, *Speech and Language in Psychoanalysis*. Trans. Wilden. Baltimore: Johns Hopkins UP, 1981. Published as *The Language of the Self* in 1968. 159–311.

Psychoanalysis, Feminism, and Literature

Chodorow, Nancy. *The Reproduction of Mothering: Psychoanalysis and the Sociology of Gender*. Berkeley: U of California P, 1978.

Gallop, Jane. *The Daughter's Seduction: Feminism and Psychoanalysis*. Ithaca: Cornell UP, 1982.

Garner, Shirley Nelson, Claire Kahane, and Madelon Sprengnether. *The (M)other Tongue: Essays in Feminist Psychoanalytic Interpretation*. Ithaca: Cornell UP, 1985.

Irigaray, Luce. *This Sex Which Is Not One*. Trans. Catherine Porter. Ithaca: Cornell UP, 1985.

———. *The Speculum of the Other Woman*. Trans. Gillian C. Gill. Ithaca: Cornell UP, 1985.

Jacobus, Mary. "Is There a Woman in This Text?" *New Literary History* 14 (1982): 117–41.

Kristeva, Julia. *The Kristeva Reader*. Ed. Toril Moi. New York: Columbia UP, 1986. See especially the selection from "Revolution in Poetic Language," 89–136.

Mitchell, Juliet. *Psychoanalysis and Feminism*. New York: Random House, 1974.

Mitchell, Juliet, and Jacqueline Rose. Introduction I and Introduction II. Lacan, *Feminine Sexuality: Jacques Lacan and the école freudienne* 1–26, 27–57.

Sprengnether, Madelon. *The Spectral Mother: Freud, Feminism, and Psychoanalysis*. Ithaca: Cornell UP, 1990.

Psychological and Psychoanalytic Studies of Literature

Bettelheim, Bruno. *The Uses of Enchantment: The Meaning and Importance of Fairy Tales*. New York: Knopf, 1976. Although this book is about fairy tales instead of literary works written for publication, it offers model Freudian readings of well-known stories.

Crews, Frederick C. *Out of My System: Psychoanalysis, Ideology, and Critical Method*. New York: Oxford UP, 1975.

———. *Relations of Literary Study*. New York: MLA, 1967. See the chapter "Literature and Psychology."

Hallman, Ralph. *Psychology of Literature: A Study of Alienation and Tragedy*. New York: Philosophical Library, 1961.

Hartman, Geoffrey, ed. *Psychoanalysis and the Question of the Text*. Baltimore: Johns Hopkins UP, 1978. See especially the essays by Hartman, Johnson, Nelson, and Schwartz.

Hertz, Neil. *The End of the Line: Essays on Psychoanalysis and the Sublime*. New York: Columbia UP, 1985.

Holland, Norman N. *Dynamics of Literary Response*. New York: Oxford UP, 1968.

———. *Poems in Persons: An Introduction to the Psychoanalysis of Literature*. New York: Norton, 1973.

Kris, Ernest. *Psychoanalytic Explorations in Art*. New York: International UP, 1952.

Lucas, F. L. *Literature and Psychology*. London: Cassell, 1951.

Natoli, Joseph, ed. *Psychological Perspectives on Literature: Freudian Dissidents and Non-Freudians: A Casebook*. Hamden: Archon Books–Shoe String, 1984.

Phillips, William, ed. *Art and Psychoanalysis.* New York: Columbia UP, 1977.

Rogers, Robert. *A Psychoanalytic Study of the Double in Literature.* Detroit: Wayne State UP, 1970.

Skura, Meredith. *The Literary Use of the Psychoanalytic Process.* New Haven: Yale UP, 1981.

Strelka, Joseph P. *Literary Criticism and Psychology.* University Park: Pennsylvania State UP, 1976. See especially the essays by Lerner and Peckham.

Weiss, Daniel. *The Critic Agonistes: Psychology, Myth, and the Art of Fiction.* Ed. Eric Solomon and Stephen Arkin. Seattle: U of Washington P, 1985.

Lacanian Psychoanalytic Studies of Literature

Davis, Robert Con, ed. *The Fictional Father: Lacanian Readings of the Text.* Amherst: U of Massachusetts P, 1981.

————, ed. "Lacan and Narration." *Modern Language Notes* 5 (1983): 843–1063.

Felman, Shoshana, ed. *Literature and Psychoanalysis: The Question of Reading: Otherwise.* Baltimore: Johns Hopkins UP, 1982. Includes Lacan's essay on *Hamlet.*

Froula, Christine. "When Eve Reads Milton: Undoing the Canonical Economy." *Canons.* Ed. Robert von Hallberg. Chicago: U of Chicago P, 1984. 149–75.

Homans, Margaret. *Bearing the Word: Language and Female Experience in Nineteenth-Century Women's Writing.* Chicago: U of Chicago P, 1986.

Muller, John P., and William J. Richardson, eds. *The Purloined Poe: Lacan, Derrida, and Psychoanalytic Reading.* Baltimore: Johns Hopkins UP, 1988. Includes Lacan's seminar on Poe's "The Purloined Letter."

Works by D. W. Winnicott

The Maturational Processes and the Facilitating Environment. London: Hogarth–Inst. of Psycho-Analysis, 1972.

Through Pediatrics to Psycho-Analysis. London: Hogarth–Inst. of Psycho-Analysis, 1975.

Psychoanalytic Criticism
of Shakespeare and *Hamlet*

Adelman, Janet. *Suffocating Mothers: Fantasies of Maternal Origin in Shakespeare's Plays, "Hamlet" to "The Tempest."* New York: Routledge, 1992. Includes this essay on *Hamlet* in full and two essays (on *Macbeth* and on *Coriolanus*) that have greatly influenced the direction of current psychoanalytic criticism.

Barber, C. L., and Richard Wheeler. *The Whole Journey: Shakespeare's Power of Development.* Berkeley: U of California P, 1986.

Erlich, Avi. *Hamlet's Absent Father.* Princeton: Princeton UP, 1977.

Fineman, Joel. "Fratricide and Cuckoldry: Shakespeare's Doubles." Schwartz and Kahn 86–91.

Gohlke, Madelon Sprengnether. "'I wooed thee with my sword': Shakespeare's Tragic Paradigms." Schwartz and Kahn 170–87.

Holland, Norman. *Psychoanalysis and Shakespeare.* New York: Octagon, 1989.

Jones, Ernest. *Hamlet and Oedipus.* 1949. New York: Norton, 1976. Influential early book by a disciple of Freud. Parts appeared in essay form in 1910 and 1923. Influenced the Olivier film version of *Hamlet.*

Leverenz, David. "The Woman in *Hamlet:* An Interpersonal View." Schwartz and Kahn 110–28.

Schwartz, Murray, and Coppélia Kahn, eds. *Representing Shakespeare: New Psychoanalytic Essays.* Baltimore: Johns Hopkins UP, 1980.

Wheeler, Richard. *Shakespeare's Development and the Problem Comedies.* Berkeley: U of California P, 1981.

Wilbern, David. "A Bibliography of Psychoanalytic and Psychological Writings on Shakespeare: 1964–1978." Schwartz and Kahn 264–86.

A PSYCHOANALYTIC PERSPECTIVE

JANET ADELMAN

"Man and Wife Is One Flesh": *Hamlet* and the Confrontation with the Maternal Body

In *Hamlet,* the figure of the mother returns to Shakespeare's dramatic world, and her presence causes the collapse of the fragile compact that had allowed Shakespeare to explore familial and sexual relationships in the histories and romantic comedies without devastating conflict; this collapse is the point of origin of the great tragic period. The son's acting out of the role of the father, his need to make his own identity in relationship to his conception of his father — the stuff of *1 and 2 Henry IV* and *Julius Caesar* — becomes deeply problematic in the presence of the wife/mother: for her presence makes the father's sexual role a disabling crux in the son's relationship with his father. At the same time, the relations between the sexes that had been imagined in the comedies without any serious confrontation with the power of female sexuality suddenly are located in the context of the mother's power to contaminate, with the result that they can never again be imagined in purely holiday terms. Here again, *Hamlet* stands as a kind of watershed, subjecting to maternal presence the relationships previously exempted from that presence.

The triangulated choice between two fathers that is characteristic of these plays is at the center of *Hamlet;* here, as in the earlier plays, assuming masculine identity means taking on the qualities of the father's name — becoming a Henry, a Brutus, or a Hamlet — by killing off a false father. Moreover, the whole weight of the play now manifestly creates one father true and the other false. Nonetheless, the choice is immeasurably more difficult for Hamlet than for his predecessors; for despite their manifest differences, the fathers in *Hamlet* keep threatening to collapse into one another, annihilating in their collapse the son's easy assumption of his father's identity. The initiating cause of this collapse is Hamlet's mother: her failure to serve her son as the repository of his

Adelman quotes from the Arden edition of Hamlet, *edited by Harold Jenkins (London: Methuen, 1982), which differs from the Riverside edition. Readers will therefore notice that the quotations in this essay occasionally differ slightly in form or in line number from the text printed in this volume. [Editor's note]*

father's ideal image by mourning him appropriately is the symptom of her deeper failure to distinguish properly between his father and his father's brother. Even at the start of the play, before the ghost's crucial revelation, Gertrude's failure to differentiate has put an intolerable strain on Hamlet by making him the only repository of his father's image, the only agent of differentiation in a court that seems all too willing to accept the new king in place of the old. Her failure of memory — registered in her undiscriminating sexuality — in effect defines Hamlet's task in relation to his father as a task of memory: as she forgets, he inherits the burden of differentiating, of idealizing and making static the past; hence the ghost's insistence on remembering (1.5.33,91) and the degree to which Hamlet registers his failure to avenge his father as a failure of memory (4.4.40). Hamlet had promised the ghost to remember him in effect by becoming him, letting his father's commandment live all alone within his brain; but the intensity of Hamlet's need to idealize in the face of his mother's failure makes his father inaccessible to him as a model, hence disrupts the identification from which he could accomplish his vengeance. As his memory of his father pushes increasingly in the direction of idealization, Hamlet becomes more acutely aware of his own distance from that idealization and hence of his likeness to Claudius,[1] who is defined chiefly by his difference from his father. Difference from the heroic ideal represented in Old Hamlet becomes the defining term common to Claudius and Hamlet: the very act of distinguishing Claudius from his father — "no more like my father/Than I to Hercules" (1.2.152–53) — forces Hamlet into imaginative identification with Claudius. The intensity of Hamlet's need to differentiate between true father and false thus confounds itself, disabling his identification with his father and hence his secure identity as son.

The female sexuality largely absent from the comedies invades *Hamlet* in the person of Gertrude, and, once there, it utterly contaminates sexual relationship, disabling holiday. In her presence, Hamlet sees his task as the disruption of marriage itself: "I say we will have no mo marriage" (3.1.149), he says to Ophelia as she becomes contaminated in his eyes, subject to the same "frailty" that names his mother. As he comes to identify himself with his cuckolded father — his "imaginations are as foul/As vulcan's stithy" (3.2.83–84) — he can think of Ophelia only as a cuckold-maker, like his mother: "if thou wilt needs marry, marry a fool, for wise men know well enough what monsters you make of them" (3.1.139–41). Moreover, Ophelia fuses with Gertrude not only as potential cuckold-maker but also as potential mother:

Get thee to a nunnery. Why, wouldst thou be a breeder of sinners? I am myself indifferent honest, but yet I could accuse me of
such things that it were better my mother had not borne me.
(3.1.121–24)

The implicit logic is: Why would you be a breeder of sinners like me? In
the gap between "breeder of sinners" and "I," Gertrude and Ophelia
momentarily collapse into one figure. It is no wonder that there can be
no more marriage: Ophelia becomes dangerous to Hamlet insofar as she
becomes identified in his mind with the contaminating maternal body,
the mother who has borne him.

Hamlet thus redefines the son's position between two fathers by
relocating it in relation to an indiscriminately sexual maternal body that
threatens to annihilate the distinction between the fathers and hence
problematizes the son's paternal identification; at the same time, the
play conflates the beloved with this betraying mother, undoing the
strategies that had enabled marriage in the comedies. The intrusion of
the adulterous mother thus disables the solutions of history and comedy
as Shakespeare has imagined them; in that sense, her presence initiates
tragedy. But how can we understand the mother whose presence has
the capacity to undermine the accommodations to which Shakespeare
had come? Why should the first mother powerfully present in Shakespeare since the period of his earliest works be portrayed as adulterous?
Why should her adulterous presence coincide with the start of
Shakespeare's great tragic period?

Given her centrality in the play, it is striking how little we know
about Gertrude; even the extent of her involvement in the murder of
her first husband is left unclear. We may want to hear her shock at
Hamlet's accusation of murder — "Almost as bad, good mother, / As
kill a king and marry with his brother" (3.4.28–29) — as evidence of
her innocence; but the text permits us to hear it alternatively as shock
either at being found out or at Hamlet's rudeness. The ghost accuses
her at least indirectly of adultery and incest — Claudius is "that incestuous, that adulterate beast" (1.5.42) — but he neither accuses her of nor
exonerates her from the murder. For the ghost, as for Hamlet, her chief
crime is her uncontrolled sexuality; that is the object of their moral revulsion, a revulsion as intense as anything directed toward the murderer
Claudius. But the Gertrude we see is not quite the Gertrude they see.
And when we see her in herself, apart from their characterizations of

her, we tend to see a woman more muddled than actively wicked; even her famous sensuality is less apparent than her conflicted solicitude both for her new husband and for her son. She is capable from the beginning of a certain guilty insight into Hamlet's suffering ("I doubt it is no other but the main, / His father's death and our o'er-hasty marriage" [2.2.56–57). Insofar as she follows Hamlet's instructions in reporting his madness to Claudius (3.4.189–90; 4.1.7), she seems to enact every son's scenario for the good mother, choosing his interests over her husband's. But she may of course believe that he is mad and think that she is reporting accurately to her husband; certainly her courageous defense of her husband in their next appearance together — where she bodily restrains Laertes, as 4.5.122 specifies — suggests that she has not wholly adopted Hamlet's view of Claudius. Here, as elsewhere, the text leaves crucial aspects of her action and motivation open. Even her death is not quite her own to define. Is it a suicide designed to keep Hamlet from danger by dying in his place? (Gertrude drinks the cup knowingly in Olivier's film of *Hamlet*.) She knows that Claudius has prepared the cup for Hamlet, and she shows unusual determination in disobeying Claudius's command not to drink it ("Gertrude, do not drink. / I will, my lord" [5.2.294–95]). In her last moment, her thoughts seem to be all for Hamlet; she cannot spare Claudius even the attention it would take to blame him ("O my dear Hamlet! / The drink, the drink! I am poison'd" [5.2.315–16].) Muddled, fallible, fully human, she seems ultimately to make the choice that Hamlet would have her make. But even here she does not speak clearly; her character remains relatively closed to us.

The lack of clarity in our impressions of Gertrude contributes, I think, to the sense that the play lacks, in Eliot's famous phrase, an "objective correlative."[2] For the character of Gertrude as we see it becomes for Hamlet — and for *Hamlet* — the ground for fantasies quite incongruent with it; although she is much less purely innocent than Richard III's mother, like that mother she becomes the carrier of a nightmare that is disjunct from her characterization as a specific figure. This disjunction is, I think, the key to her role in the play and hence to her psychic power: her frailty unleashes for Hamlet, and for Shakespeare, fantasies of maternal malevolence, of maternal spoiling, that are compelling exactly as they are out of proportion to the character we know, exactly as they seem therefore to reiterate infantile fears and desires rather than an adult apprehension of the mother as a separate person.

These fantasies begin to emerge as soon as Hamlet is left alone onstage:

O that this too too sullied flesh would melt,
Thaw and resolve itself into a dew,
Or that the Everlasting had not fix'd
His canon 'gainst self-slaughter. O God! God!
How weary, stale, flat, and unprofitable
Seem to me all the uses of this world!
Fie on't, ah fie, 'tis an unweeded garden
That grows to seed; things rank and gross in nature
Possess it merely. That it should come to this!
But two months dead. . .

                                              (1.2.129–38)

This soliloquy establishes the initial premises of the play, the psychic
conditions that are present even before Hamlet has met with the ghost
and has been assigned the insupportable task of vengeance. And what
Hamlet tells us in his first words to us is that he feels his own flesh as
sullied and wishes to free himself from its contamination by death, that
the world has become as stale and unusable to him as his own body, and
that he figures all this deadness and staleness and contamination in the
image of an unweeded garden gone to seed — figures it, that is, in the
familiar language of the fall. And he further tells us that this fall has been
caused not by his father's death, as both Claudius and Gertrude seem to
assume in their conventional consolations, but by his mother's remarriage, the "this" he cannot specify for fourteen lines, the "this" that
looms over the soliloquy, not quite nameable and yet radically present,
making his own flesh — "this . . . flesh" — dirty, disrupting his sense of
the ongoing possibility of life even as it disrupts his syntax.

   Hamlet's soliloquy is in effect his attempt to locate a point of origin
for the staleness of the world and his own pull toward death, and he
discovers this point of origin in his mother's body. He tells us that the
world has been transformed into an unweeded garden, possessed by
things rank and gross, because his mother has remarried. And if the
enclosed garden — the garden unpossessed — traditionally figures the
Virgin Mother, this garden, full of seed, figures his mother's newly contaminated body: its rank weeds localize what Hamlet will later call the
"rank corruption" of her sexuality (3.4.150–51), the "weeds" that will
grow "ranker" if that sexuality is not curbed (3.4.153–54). In this
highly compacted and psychologized version of the fall, death is the
sexualized mother's legacy to her son: maternal sexuality turns the enclosed garden into the fallen world and brings death into that world by
making flesh loathsome. If Hamlet's father's death is the first sign of

mortality, his mother's remarriage records the desire for death in his own sullied flesh. For in the world seen under the aegis of the unweeded garden, the very corporality of flesh marks its contamination: Hamlet persistently associates Claudius's fleshiness with his bloated sexuality — transforming the generalized "fatness of these pursy times" (3.4.155) into the image of the "bloat king" tempting his mother to bed (3.4.184) — as though in its grossness flesh was always rank, its solidness always sullied.[3]

The opening lines of the soliloquy point, I think, toward a radical confrontation with the sexualized maternal body as the initial premise of tragedy, the fall that brings death into the world: Hamlet in effect rewrites Richard III's sense that he has been spoiled in his mother's womb as the condition of mortality itself. The structure of *Hamlet* — and, I will argue, of the plays that follow from *Hamlet* — is marked by the struggle to escape from this condition, to free the masculine identity of both father and son from its origin in the contaminated maternal body. Hamlet's father's death is devastating to Hamlet — and to Shakespeare — partly, I think, because it returns Hamlet to this body, simultaneously unmaking the basis for the son's differentiation from the mother and the heroic foundation for masculine identity that Shakespeare had achieved in the histories.[4] As in a dream, the plot-conjunction of father's funeral and mother's remarriage expresses this return: it tells us that the idealized father's absence releases the threat of maternal sexuality, in effect subjecting the son to her annihilating power. But the dream-logic of this plot-conjunction is also reversible; if the father's death leads to the mother's sexualized body, the mother's sexualized body, I will argue, leads to the father's death. For the conjunction of funeral and marriage simultaneously expresses two sentences for the son: both "My idealized father's absence leaves me subject to my mother's overwhelming power," and "The discovery of my mother's sexuality kills my idealized father for me, making him unavailable as the basis for my identity." This fantasy-conjunction thus defines the double task of Hamlet and of Shakespeare in the plays to come: if Hamlet attempts both to remake his mother as an enclosed garden in 3.4 and to separate the father he idealizes from the rank place of corruption, Shakespearean tragedy and romance will persistently work toward the desexualization of the maternal body and the re-creation of a bodiless father, untouched by her contamination.

A small psychological allegory at the beginning of the play — the exchange between Horatio and Marcellus about the ghost's disappearance — suggests what is at stake in this double task. The first danger in *Hamlet* is the father's "extravagant and erring spirit" (1.1.159) wandering in the night, the father who is — Horatio tells us — "like a guilty thing" (1.1.153). As though in a kind of ghostly aubade, this father vanishes at the sound of the cock, who "with his lofty and shrill-sounding throat / Awake[s] the god of day" (1.1.156–57). At the approach of the sun-god, the guilty father is banished; and Marcellus's christianizing expansion of this conjunction explicates his banishment:

> It faded on the crowing of the cock.
> Some say that ever 'gainst that season comes
> Wherein our Saviour's birth is celebrated,
> This bird of dawning singeth all night long;
> And then, they say, no spirit dare stir abroad,
> The nights are wholesome, then no planets strike,
> No fairy takes, nor witch hath power to charm,
> So hallow'd and so gracious is that time.
> (1.1.162–69)

Through an incipient pun, Marcellus transforms the god of day into the Son who makes the night wholesome because he is born from the mother's desexualized body; and the dangers he protects against are increasingly identified not only with the father's guilty spirit but with the dark female powers of the night. The sequence here — from guilty thing, to sun-god, to the Son whose birth banishes the witch — follows the logic of a purifying fantasy: the female body of the night can be cleansed only as the guilty father gives way to the sun-god, allowing for the emergence of the purified Son.

The exchange between Horatio and Marcellus predicts both Hamlet's confrontation with the night-dangers of the female body and the fantasy-solution to that confrontation: it establishes the Son born of a bodiless father and a purified mother as the only antidote to her power. And it specifically predicts Hamlet's need to remake his father as Hyperion, his attempt to find a safe basis for his own identity as son in the father he would remake pure. As though in response to this initial encounter with the impure father, the initial strategy of both Hamlet (in the soliloquy) and *Hamlet* is to split the father in two,[5] deflecting his guilt onto Claudius and reconstituting him in the form of the bodiless sun-god:

That it should come to this!
But two months dead — nay, not so much, not two —
So excellent a king, that was to this
Hyperion to a satyr.

(1.2.137–40)

The identification of Old Hamlet with Hyperion makes him benignly
and divinely distant, separate from ordinary genital sexuality and yet im-
mensely potent, his sexual power analogous to God's power to impreg-
nate the Virgin Mother (often imaged as Spirit descending on the sun's
rays) and to such Renaissance mythologizings of this theme as the operation of the sun on Chrysogonee's moist body (*The Faerie Queene*
3.6.7). Ordinary genital sexuality then becomes the province of Claudius the satyr: below the human, immersed in the body, he becomes
everything Hyperion/Old Hamlet is not, and the agent of all ill.

This work of splitting is already implicit in Hamlet's initial image of
his mother's body as fallen garden, for that image itself makes a physio-
logically impossible claim: if Claudius's rank and gross possession now
transforms the garden that is the mother's body, then it must not before
have been possessed. Insofar as the soliloquy expresses Hamlet's sense
of his mother's body as an enclosed garden newly breached, it implies
the presence of a formerly unbreached garden; the alternatives that
govern Hamlet's imagination of his mother's body are the familiar ones
of virgin and whore, closed or open, wholly pure or wholly corrupt.
And the insistence that the garden has just been transformed functions to exonerate his father, separating him from his mother's sexualized body: it is the satyr Claudius, not the sun-god father, who has
violated the maternal space. Literalized in the plot, the splitting of the
father thus evokes the ordinary psychological crisis in which the son
discovers the sexuality of his parents, but with the blame handily shifted
from father onto another man as unlike father as possible — and yet as
like, hence his brother; in effect, the plot itself serves as a cover-up,
legitimizing disgust at paternal sexuality without implicating the idealized father. But thus arbitrarily separated, these fathers are always
prone to collapse back into one another. The failure to differentiate between Old Hamlet and Claudius is not only Gertrude's: the play frequently insists on their likeness even while positing their absolute difference; for the sexual guilt of the father — his implication in the mother's
body — is its premise, its unacknowledged danger. Even Hamlet's attempt to imagine a protective father in the soliloquy returns him to this
danger:

So excellent a king, that was to this
Hyperion to a satyr, so loving to my mother
That he might not beteem the winds of heaven
Visit her face too roughly. Heaven and earth,
Must I remember? Why, she would hang on him
As if increase of appetite had grown
By what it fed on; and yet within a month —
Let me not think on't . . .

$$(1.2.139–46)$$

This image of parental love is so satisfying to Hamlet in part because it
seems to enfold his mother safely within his father's protective embrace:
by protecting her against the winds of heaven, he simultaneously protects against her, limiting and controlling her dangerous appetite. But as
soon as that appetite has been invoked, it destabilizes the image of paternal control, returning Hamlet to the fact of his father's loss: for
Gertrude's appetite is always inherently frightening, always potentially
out of control; as the image of the unweeded garden itself implied, it has
always required a weeder to manage its overluxuriant growth. The existence of Gertrude's appetite itself threatens the image of the father's
godlike control; and in his absence, Gertrude's appetite rages, revealing
what had been its potential for voraciousness all along. Having sated
herself in a celestial bed, she now preys on garbage (1.5.55–57); and her
indifferent voraciousness threatens to undo the gap between then and
now, virgin and whore, Hyperion and satyr, on which Hamlet's defensive system depends. Despite the ghost's insistence on the difference,
sating oneself in bed and preying on garbage sound suspiciously like the
same activity: the imagery of devouring common to both tends to flat-
ten out the distinction. "Could you on this fair mountain leave to
feed / And batten on this moor?" Hamlet asks his mother (3.4.66–67),
insisting again on a difference that seems largely without substance, inadvertently collapsing the distance between the idealized and the debased versions of Gertrude's appetite and hence between the brothers
she feeds on. But in fact the strenuousness of the opposition between
them has indicated their resemblance all along: what they have in common is an appetite for Gertrude's appetite; and her appetite can't tell the
difference between them.

The ghost's revelation of Gertrude's adultery is horrifying not only
because it reveals that she has not been faithful to him — her rapid remarriage has already done that — but also because it threatens to undo
the structure of difference that Hamlet has had to maintain in order to
keep his father and Claudius apart. For if Gertrude's appetite for the

two men is the same, then Old Hamlet is as fully implicated in her sexuality as Claudius. Hence in part Hamlet's shock when he meets the
father he has idealized so heavily: when Old Hamlet appears to his son,
not in his mind's idealizing eye (1.2.185) but in the dubious form of
the ghost, he reveals not only Claudius's but also his own "foul crimes
done in [his] days of nature" (1.5.12). The fathers Hamlet tries so
strenuously to keep separated keep threatening to collapse into one another; even when he wants to kill one to avenge the other, he cannot
quite tell them apart. In 3.3, on his way to his mother's closet, he comes
across Claudius praying, a ready-made opportunity for revenge. But
knowing that his father has committed foul crimes, and seeing Claudius
praying, Hamlet becomes so unsure that there is an essential difference
between them that he worries that God might send the wrong man to
heaven. Even as he describes Claudius's murder of his father to himself,
he conflates it imagistically with his father's crimes: "A took my father
grossly, full of bread, / With all his crimes broad blown, as flush as
May" (3.3.80–81). Claudius's and Old Hamlet's crimes become
equally broad-blown, as the two sinful fathers merge linguistically: the
imagery of the rank garden, of overluxuriant and swollen growth, has
passed from Claudius to Old Hamlet, the "blossoms" of whose sin
(1.5.76) are now broad-blown and flush. The highly charged word
grossly registers this failure of differentiation: it hovers indeterminately
between the two men, attaching itself first to Claudius (Claudius killed
Old Hamlet grossly) and then to Old Hamlet (who died in a gross and
unsanctified state); and in its indeterminacy, it associates both Claudius
and Old Hamlet with the gross possession of Gertrude's unweeded garden.

Ultimately Hyperion and the satyr refuse to stay separated, so that
Hamlet — and *Hamlet* — have to do and redo the distinction over and
over again. Whatever Hamlet's original intentions in approaching his
mother in 3.4, his most immediate need after the crisis of differentiation
in 3.3 is to force her to acknowledge the difference between the two
fathers ("Hamlet, thou hast thy father much offended. / Mother, you
have my father much offended" [3.4.8–9]). But even as he attempts to
force this acknowledgment, he repeats the crisis of differentiation in yet
another form. He presents her (and us) with two pictures initially indistinguishable and linguistically collapsed into one another: "Look here
upon this picture, and on this, / The counterfeit presentment of two
brothers" (3.4.53–54). As he begins the work of distinguishing between them all over again, the sense of counterfeit presentment becomes descriptive not only of the portraits as works of art but of his own

portraiture, his own need both to present and to counterfeit these potentially similar false coins. Once again his father becomes a god, with "Hyperion's curls, the front of Jove himself, / An eye like Mars" (3.4.56–57); and Claudius becomes a "mildew'd ear / Blasting his wholesome brother" (3.4.64–65). But his words undermine the distinction he would reinstate: the most significantly contaminated ear in the play belongs to Old Hamlet.

Finally, the myth of his father as Hyperion cannot be sustained; and its collapse returns both father and son to the contaminated maternal body. No longer divinely inseminating, the sun-god becomes deeply implicated in matter in Hamlet's brutal parody of incarnation:

> HAMLET: If the sun breed maggots in a dead dog, being a good kissing carrion — Have you a daughter?
> POLONIUS: I have, my lord.
> HAMLET: Let her not walk i' th' sun. Conception is a blessing, but as your daughter may conceive — friend, look to't.
>
> (2.2.181–86)

Here is male spirit wholly enmeshed in female matter, kissing it, animating it with a vengeance; and — unlike the Son's — this conception is no blessing. If Marcellus's fantasy condenses father and son in a protective dyad, father and son here collapse into one another in their contamination: "Let her not walk i' th' sun," Hamlet warns Polonius; and his bitter pun locates the father-god's contamination in his own flesh. For this conception relocates the son in the dead matter of the unweeded garden: the horrific image of conception as the stirring of maggots in a corpse makes the son himself no more than one of the maggots, simultaneously born from and feeding on death in the maternal body.

In the myth of origins bitterly acknowledged here, the son is wedded to death by his conception, spoiled by his origin in the rank flesh of the maternal body; and there is no idealized father to rescue him from this body. This fantasy of spoiling at the site of origin is, I think, the undertext of the play; it emerges first in muted form as Hamlet waits for the appearance of his ghostly father and meditates on the dram of evil that ruins the noble substance of man. When Hamlet hears the drunken revel of Claudius's court, he first fixes blame on Claudius for the sense of contamination he feels: "They clepe us drunkards, and with swinish phrase / Soil our addition" (1.4.19–20). But as he continues, his bodily language rewrites the source of contamination, increasingly relocating it in the female body. "Indeed it takes / From our achievements, though perform'd at height, / The pith and marrow of our attribute" (1.4.20–22): through the imagery, the soiling of the male body — its pith and marrow emptied out at the height of performance — is grotesquely equated with intercourse and its aftermath. And this shadowy image of the male body spoiled by the female in intercourse predicts the rest of the speech, where the role of spoiler is taken not by Claudius and his habits but by an unnamed and unspecified female body that corrupts man against his will:

> So, oft it chances in particular men
> That for some vicious mole of nature in them,
> As in their birth, wherein they are not guilty
> (Since nature cannot choose his origin),
>   . . . these men,
> Carrying, I say, the stamp of one defect,
> Being Nature's livery or Fortune's star,
> His virtues else, be they as pure as grace,
> As infinite as man may undergo,
> Shall in the general censure take corruption
> From that particular fault.
>   (1.4.23–36, passim)

As Hamlet imagines man struggling against his one defect — the mark of his bondage to a feminized Nature or Fortune — the origin he cannot choose increasingly becomes not only the site but the agent of corruption. Even as Hamlet unorthodoxly proclaims man not guilty in his birth, that is, he articulates his own version of original sin: here, as in Richard III's fantasy of himself deformed by Nature in his mother's womb (*3 Henry VI* 3.2.153–64), man is spoiled in his birth by birth defects not of his own making, and he takes corruption from that particular fault.

Fall/fault/foutre: the complex bilingual pun registers the fantasy that moves under the surface of Hamlet's meditation. For *fault* allusively collapses the female genitals with the act of intercourse that engendered the baby there, and then collapses both with the fall and original sin[6] through its punning formulations, original sin becomes literally the sin of origin. "Virtue cannot so inoculate our old stock but we shall relish of it" (3.1.117–18): formed and deformed in his mother's womb, man takes his corruption from that particular fault. Hamlet is indeed "to the manner born" (1.4.15), as he says at the start of his meditation: "It were better my mother had not borne me," he tells Ophelia (3.1.123–24); but he is "subject to his birth" (1.3.18).

This subjection of male to female is, I think, the buried fantasy of *Hamlet*, the submerged story that it partly conceals and partly reveals; in its shift of contaminating agency from Claudius to the female body as the site of origin, Hamlet's meditation seems to me to be diagnostic of this fantasy. The poisoning of Old Hamlet is ostentatiously modeled on Cain's killing of Abel; Claudius cannot allude to his offense without recalling "the primal eldest curse upon't" (3.3.37). But this version of Cain and Abel turns out in part to be a cover for the even more primal story implicit in the unweeded garden, the prior explanation for the entrance of death into the world: the murder here turns not on the winning of a father's favor but on the body of a woman; and Old Hamlet is poisoned in his orchard-garden (1.5.35; 3.2.255) by the "serpent" who wears his crown (1.5.39). On the surface of the text, that is, the story of Adam and Eve has been displaced, the horrific female body at its center occluded: Eve is conspicuously absent from the Cain-and-Abel version of the fall. But if the plot rewrites the fall as a story of fratricidal rivalry, locating literal agency for the murder in Claudius, a whole network of images and associations replaces his literal agency with Gertrude's, replicating Eve in her by making her both the agent and the locus of death. Beneath the story of fratricidal rivalry is the story of the woman who conduces to death, of the father fallen not through his brother's treachery but through his subjection to this woman; and despite Gertrude's conspicuous absence from the scene in the garden, in this psychologized version of the fall, the vulnerability of the father — and hence of the son — to her poison turns out to be the whole story.

In an astonishing transfer of agency from male to female, malevolent power and blame for the murder tend to pass from Claudius to Gertrude in the deep fantasy of the play. We can see the beginnings of this shift of blame even in the Ghost's initial account of the murder, in which the emotional weight shifts rapidly from his excoriation of Claudius to his much more powerful condemnation of Gertrude's sexuality. And in "The Murder of Gonzago," Hamlet's version of his father's tale, the murderer's role is clearly given less emphasis than the Queen's: Lucianus gets a scant six lines, while her protestations of undying love motivate all the preceding dialogue of the playlet. Moreover, while the actual murderer remains a pasteboard villain, the Queen's protestations locate psychic blame for the murder squarely in her. "None wed the second but who kill'd the first," she tells us (3.2.175). In her formulation, remarriage itself is a form of murder: "A second time I kill my husband dead, / When second husband kisses me in bed" (3.2.179–80). We know that Hamlet has added some dozen or sixteen lines to the play (2.2.535), and though we cannot specify them, these protestations seem written suspiciously from the point of view of the child, whose mother's remarriage often seems like her murder of the image of his father. When Hamlet confronts his mother in her closet immediately after his playlet, he confirms that he at least has shifted agency from Claudius to her: his own killing of Polonius is, he says, "A bloody deed. Almost as bad, good Mother, / As kill a king and marry with his brother" (3.4.28–29). Given the parallel with his killing of Polonius, "as kill a king" first seems to describe Claudius's act; but when the line ends with "brother" rather than "queen" or "wife," the killing attaches itself irrevocably to Gertrude, playing out in miniature the shift of agency from him to her. For Claudius's crime is nearly absent here: in Hamlet's accusation, Claudius becomes the passive victim of Gertrude's sexual will; she becomes the active murderer.

And the play itself is complicit with Hamlet's shift of agency: though the degree of her literal guilt is never specified, in the deep fantasy of the play her sexuality itself becomes akin to murder. The second of the Player Queen's protestations — "A second time I kill my husband dead / When second husband kisses me in bed" — implicitly collapses the two husbands into one and thus makes the equation neatly: when her husband kisses her, she kills him. But this is in fact what one strain in the imagery has been telling us all along. As Lucianus carries the poison onstage in "The Murder of Gonzago," he addresses it in terms that associate it unmistakably with the weeds of that first unweeded garden:

> Thou mixture rank, of midnight weeds collected,
> With Hecate's ban thrice blasted, thrice infected,
> Thy natural magic and dire property
> On wholesome life usurps immediately.
>
> (3.2.251–54)

Even as we see him poison the Player King, the language insists that the poison is not his but hers, its usurpation on wholesome life derivative not from Claudius's political ambitions but from the rank weeds (3.4.153–54) of Gertrude's body. Its "mixture rank" merely condenses and localizes the rank mixture that is sexuality itself:[7] hence the subterranean logic by which the effects of Claudius's poison on Old Hamlet's body replicate the effects of venereal disease, covering his smooth body with the lazarlike tetter, the "vile and loathsome crust" (1.5.71–72) that was one of the diagnostic signs of syphilis.[8]

In Lucianus's words, the poison that kills Old Hamlet becomes less the distillation of a usurping fratricidal rivalry than the distillation of the horrific female body, the night-witch against whom Marcellus had invoked the protection of the Saviour born from a virgin birth; cursed by Hecate, it is in effect the distillation of midnight itself, the "witching time" when "hell itself breathes out / Contagion to this world" (3.2.379–81). The play here invokes the presence of an unbounded nightmare night-body, breathing out the contagion of her poison; and it gives shape to this horrific night-body through a curious and punning repetition. Horatio tells Hamlet that the ghost first appeared "in the dead waste and middle of the night" (1.2.198); and Hamlet repeats his phrase when he questions Rosencranz and Guildenstern about their relations with the lady Fortune:

> HAMLET: Then thou live about her waist, or in the middle of her favours?
> GUILDENSTERN: Faith, her privates we.
> HAMLET: In the secret parts of Fortune? O, most true! She is a strumpet.
>
> (2.2.232–36)

"Waste" and "waist" coalesce in the dangerous middle of this strumpet; and the idealized father turns out to be horribly vulnerable to the poison of her rank midnight weeds. For however mild-mannered Gertrude may be as a literal character, in fantasy she takes on the aspect of this night-body, herself becoming the embodiment of hell and death: the fires in which Hamlet's father is confined, the fires that burn and purge the foul crimes done in his days of nature (1.5.11–13), merely repro duce the fire of the "rebellious hell" that burns in her bones (3.4.82–88). In anticipation of Lear's anatomy — "there's hell, there's darkness, / There is the sulphurous pit" (King Lear 4.6.129–30) — punishment and crime coalesce: death is not only the consequence of sexuality but also its very condition.

This anatomy is in its own way perfectly orthodox; it condenses the story of the fall by making female sexuality itself the locus of death:

> Surely her house tendeth to death, & her paths unto the dead. All thei that go unto her, returne not againe, nether take they holde of the waies of life.

For she hathe caused manie to fall downe wounded, and the
strong men are all slayne by her. Her house is the waie unto the
grave, which goeth downe to the chambers of death. (*The Geneva
Bible*, Proverbs 2:18–19, 7:26–27)

Every encounter with the "strange woman" of Proverbs — and all
women are sexually strangers — is thus a virtual reliving of the fall into
mortality. But female sexuality in *Hamlet* is always maternal sexuality:
Gertrude's is the only fully sexualized female body in the play, and we
experience her sexuality largely through the imagination of her son.
In *Hamlet,* that is, Shakespeare re-understands the orthodox associations of woman with death by fusing the sexual with the maternal body,
reimagining the legacy of death consequent upon the fall as the legacy
specifically of the sexualized maternal body. And except in the saving
case of the Virgin Mother, the maternal body is always already sexual, corrupted by definition. The mother's body brings death into the
world because her body itself is death: in the traditional alignment of
spirit and matter, the mother gives us the stuff — the female matter —
of our bodies and thus our mortality. Birth itself thus immerses the
body in death: hence the power of Hamlet's grotesque version of
conception as the stirring of maggots in dead matter. Through this fusion of the sexual with the maternal body and the association of both
with death, Shakespeare in effect defamiliarizes the trope of the "womb
of earth" (1.1.140): death and sexuality are interchangeable in this
psychologized version of the fall because both lead back to this maternal
body. Hence also Shakespeare's punning equation of death and the
maternal body in his reformulation of the biblical source of danger: in
the deep fantasy of the play, the deadly woman of *Proverbs* — "thei that
go unto her, returne not againe" — is one with Hamlet's "undiscover'd
country, from whose bourn / No traveller returns" (3.1.79–80).

Both death and sexuality return the traveler to the undiscovered
country, familiar and yet utterly foreign, of the maternal body itself; and
in *Hamlet,* this body is always threatening to swallow up her children,
to absorb them back within her bourn, undoing their own boundaries.
Death itself is a hell-mouth, swallowing Old Hamlet up between its
"ponderous and marble jaws" (1.4.50), bringing him and Polonius
"not where he eats, but where a is eaten" (4.3.19), where all are subject
to "my Lady Worm" (5.1.87); and Gertrude is death's mouth, indiscriminately devouring her husbands "as if increase of appetite had
grown / By what it fed on" (1.2.144–45). In this grotesquely oral
world, everything is ultimately meat for a single table. Hence I think the

slight *frisson* of horror beneath Hamlet's wit as he describes "the funeral bak'd meats" that "Did coldly furnish forth the marriage tables" (1.2.180–84) we are never sure just what it is that is being consumed in the ceremonies of death and sexual union imagined here. And this momentary confusion is diagnostic of the play's fusion of eating and death and sex: in *Hamlet*, the turn toward the woman's body is always felt as the return to the devouring maternal womb, with all the potential not only for incestuous nightmare but for total annihilation implied by that return.

Hence, I think, the logic of the play's alternative name for poison: "union" (5.2.269, 331). For "union" is just another version of Hecate's "mixture rank," the poison that kills Old Hamlet: each is the poisonous epitome of sexual mixture itself and hence of boundary danger, the terrifying adulteration of male by female that does away with the boundaries between them.

> HAMLET: Farewell, dear mother.
> KING: Thy loving father, Hamlet.
> HAMLET: My mother. Father and mother is man and wife, man and wife is one flesh; so my mother.
>
> (4.3.52–55)

In this fantasy, it does not matter whether Hamlet is thinking of his father or of his incestuous stand-in; all sexuality — licit or illicit — is imagined as an adulterating mixture. And in this rank mixture, the female will always succeed in transforming the male, remaking him in her image, "for the power of beauty will sooner transform honesty from what it is to a bawd than the force of honesty can translate beauty into his likeness" (3.1.111–14). The imagined concourse of male honesty and female beauty ends in the contamination of the male by the female, his translation into a version of her. No wonder Marcellus associates the danger of invasion with the sweaty activity that makes "the night joint-labourer with the day" (1.1.81), obliterating the distinction between the realm of the witch-mother and that of the sun-god father; no wonder Hamlet is so intent upon keeping his father's commandment — or perhaps his father himself — all alone within his brain, "unmix'd with baser matter" (1.5.104).

For Hamlet is ultimately subject to the same adulterating mixture; the sexual anxiety registered through the play's two names for poison, like the incestuous marriage at its center, both covers and expresses a more primitive anxiety about the stability and security of individuating boundaries that finds its focus in Hamlet himself. Promiscuous mixture and boundary contamination everywhere infect this play, from its initial worry about invasion to its final heap of poisoned bodies: in a psychic world where boundaries cannot hold, where the self is invaded, its pales and forts broken down, its pith and marrow extracted, where mother-aunts and uncle-fathers (2.2.372) become indistinguishably one flesh, where even camels become weasels become whales (3.2.367–73), identity itself seems on the point of dissolving or being swallowed up. And the overwhelming use of images of oral contamination and oral annihilation to register these threats to the self suggests their origin in the earliest stages of emergent selfhood, when the nascent self is most fully subject to the mother's fantasied power to annihilate or contaminate. Hence, I think, the centrality of Gertrude: for the play localizes its pervasive boundary panic in Hamlet's relationship with his mother, whose contaminated body initially serves him as the metaphor for the fallen world that has sullied him. And the selfhood that Hamlet constructs in response to this threat becomes the crux of the play: withdrawing himself from the sullying maternal body of the world, Hamlet retreats into what he imagines as an inviolable core of selfhood that cannot be known or played upon (1.2.85; 3.2.355–63), constructing an absolute barrier between inner and outer as though there were no possibility of uncontaminating communication between them; unable to risk crossing this boundary in any creative way, through any significant action in the world, he fantasizes crossing it through magical thinking — imagining the revenge that could come "with wings as swift / As meditation" (1.5.29–30) or through the power of his horrid speech (2.2.557) — or he mimes crossing it from within the extraordinary distance of his withdrawal, taking up a variety of roles not to engage the world but to keep it at bay.[9] Hence in part his intense admiration for Horatio, who plays no roles and seems impervious to outer influence, who is "not a pipe for Fortune's finger / To sound what stop she please" (3.2.70–71); here as elsewhere, Hamlet figures the threat to (masculine) inner integrity as the sexualized female, aligning it with the strumpet Fortune in whose secret parts corrupt men live (2.2.232–36), as though all such threats were derivative from his unreliable mother's body. But there is no exemption from this body for Hamlet, no pure and unmixed identity for him; like honesty transformed into a bawd, he must eventually see the signs of her rank mixture in himself:

Why, what an ass am I! This is most brave,
That I, the son of a dear father murder'd,
Prompted to my revenge by heaven and hell,
Must like a whore unpack my heart with words
And fall a-cursing like a very drab,
A scullion!

(2.2.578–83)

He himself is subject to his birth: he would imagine himself the unmixed son of an unmixed father, but the whore-mother in him betrays
him, returning him to his own mixed origin, his contamination by the
sexual female within.[10]

The first mother to reappear in Shakespeare's plays is adulterous, I
think, because maternal origin is in itself felt as equivalent to adulterating betrayal of the male, both father and son; *Hamlet* initiates the period of Shakespeare's greatest tragedies because it in effect rewrites the
story of Cain and Abel as the story of Adam and Eve, relocating masculine identity in the presence of the adulterating female. This rewriting
accounts, I think, for Gertrude's odd position in the play, especially for
its failure to specify the degree to which she is complicit in the murder.
Less powerful as an independent character than as the site for fantasies
larger than she is, she is preeminently mother as other, the intimate unknown figure around whom these fantasies swirl. She is kept ambigu-
ously innocent as a character, but in the deep fantasy that structures the
play's imagery, she plays out the role of the missing Eve: her body is the
garden in which her husband dies, her sexuality the poisonous weeds
that kill him, and poison the world — and the self — for her son. This
is the psychological fantasy registered by the simultaneity of funeral and
marriage: the reappearance of the mother in *Hamlet* is tantamount to
the death of the idealized father because her presence signals his absence, and hence the absence of the son's defense against her rank mixture, her capacity to annihilate or contaminate; as in Marcellus's purifying fantasy, what the idealized father ultimately protects against is the
dangerous female powers of the night. The boy-child masters his fear of
these powers partly through identification with his father, the paternal
presence who has initially helped him to achieve separation from his
mother; but if his father fails him — if the father himself seems subject
to her — then that protective identification fails. This is exactly the psychological situation at the beginning of *Hamlet,* where Hamlet's father

has become unavailable to him, not only through the fact of his death but through the complex vulnerability that his death demonstrates. This father cannot protect his son; and his disappearance in effect throws Hamlet into the domain of the engulfing mother, awakening all the fears incident to the primary mother-child bond. Here as in Shakespeare's later plays, the loss of the father turns out in fact to mean the psychic domination of the mother: in the end, it is the specter of his mother, not his uncle-father, who paralyzes his will. The Queen, the Queen's to blame.

This shift of agency and of danger from male to female seems to me characteristic of the fantasy-structure of *Hamlet* and of Shakespeare's imagination in the plays that follow. The ghost's initial injunction sets as the prime business of the play the killing of Claudius; he specifically asks Hamlet to leave his mother alone, beset only by the thorns of conscience (1.5.85–87). But if Gertrude rather than Claudius is to blame, then Hamlet's fundamental task shifts; simple revenge is no longer the issue. Despite his ostensible agenda of revenge, the main psychological task that Hamlet seems to set himself is not to avenge his father's death but to remake his mother: to remake her in the image of the Virgin Mother who could guarantee his father's purity, and his own, repairing the boundaries of his selfhood. Throughout the play, the covert drama of reformation vies for priority with the overt drama of revenge, in fact displacing it both from what we see of Hamlet's consciousness and from center stage of the play: when Hamlet accuses himself of lack of purpose (3.4.107–10), of failing to remember his father's business of revenge (4.4.40), he may in part be right. Even as an avenger, Hamlet seems motivated more by his mother than by his father: when he describes Claudius to Horatio as "he that hath kill'd my king and whor'd my mother" (5.2.64), the second phrase clearly carries more intimate emotional weight than the first. And he manages to achieve his revenge only when he can avenge his mother's death, not his father's: just where we might expect some version of "rest, perturbed spirit" to link his killing of Claudius with his father's initial injunction, we get "Is thy union here? / Follow my mother" (5.2.331–32).

This shift — from avenging the father to saving the mother — accounts in part for certain peculiarities about this play as a revenge play: why, for example, the murderer is given so little attention in the device ostensibly designed to catch his conscience, why the confrontation of Hamlet with Gertrude in the closet scene seems much more central, much more vivid, than any confrontation between Hamlet and Claudius. Once we look at "The Murder of Gonzago" for what it is, rather than for what Hamlet tells us it is, it becomes clear that the playlet is in fact designed to catch the conscience of the queen: its challenge is always to her loving posture, its accusation "A second time I kill my husband dead / When second husband kisses me in bed." The confrontation with Gertrude (3.4) follows so naturally from this attempt to catch her conscience that Hamlet's unexpected meeting with Claudius (3.3) feels to us like an interruption of a more fundamental purpose. Indeed, Shakespeare stages 3.3 very much as an interruption: Hamlet comes upon Claudius praying as he is on his way to his mother's closet, worrying about the extent to which he can repudiate the Nero in himself; and we come upon Claudius unexpectedly in the same way. That is: the moment that should be the apex of the revenge plot — the potential confrontation alone of the avenger and his prey — becomes for the audience and for the avenger himself a lapse, an interlude that must be gotten over before the real business can be attended to. It is no wonder that Hamlet cannot kill Claudius here: to do so would be to make of the interlude a permanent interruption of his more fundamental purpose. Not even Hamlet could reasonably expect to manage his mother's moral reclamation immediately after he has killed her husband.

Nor would that avenging death regain the mother whom Hamlet needs: once his mother has been revealed as the fallen and possessed garden, she can be purified only by being separated from her sexuality. This separation is in fact Hamlet's effort throughout 3.4. In that confrontation, Hamlet first insists that Gertrude acknowledge the difference between Claudius and Old Hamlet, the difference her adultery and remarriage had undermined. But after the initial display of portraits, Hamlet attempts to induce in her revulsion not at her choice of the wrong man but at her sexuality itself, the rebellious hell that mutines in her matron's bones (3.4.82–83), the "rank corruption, mining all within" (3.4.150). Here, as in the play-within-the-play, Hamlet recreates obsessively, voyeuristically, the acts that have corrupted the royal bed, even when he has to subject his logic and syntax to considerable strain to do so:

QUEEN: What shall I do?
HAMLET: Not this, by no means, that I bid you do:
    Let the bloat King tempt you again to bed,
    Pinch wanton on your cheek, call you his mouse,
    And let him, for a pair of reechy kisses,
    Or paddling in your neck with his damn'd fingers,

Make you to ravel all this matter out
That I essentially am not in madness,
But mad in craft.
                                        (3.4.182–90)

There has to be an easier way of asking your mother not to reveal that your madness is an act. "Not this, by no means, that I bid you do": Hamlet cannot stop imagining, even commanding, the sexual act that he wants to undo. Moreover, the bloated body of this particular king is not particular to him: it is the sexualized male body, its act any sexual act. The royal bed of Denmark is always already corrupted, already a couch for luxury, as Hamlet's own presence testifies. "Go not to my uncle's bed" (3.4.161), Hamlet tells his mother; but his disgust at the incestuous liaison rationalizes a prior disgust at all sexual concourse, as his attempt to end the specifically incestuous union rationalizes an attempt to remake his mother pure by divorcing her from her sexuality.

Act 3 scene 4 records Hamlet's attempt to achieve this divorce, to recover the fantasied presence of the asexual mother of childhood, the mother who can restore the sense of sanctity to the world her sexuality has spoiled: his first and last word in the scene is "mother" (3.4.7, 219). And in his own mind at least, Hamlet does seem to achieve this recovery. He begins the scene by wishing that Gertrude were not his mother ("would it were not so, you are my mother" [3.4.15]); but toward the end, he is able to imagine her as the mother from whom he would beg — and receive — blessing:

Once more, good night,
And when you are desirous to be blest,
I'll blessing beg of you.
                                        (3.4.172–74)

This mother can bless Hamlet only insofar as she herself asks to be blessed by him, signaling her conversion from husband to son and inverting the relation of parent and child; Hamlet is very much in charge even as he imagines asking for maternal blessing. Nonetheless, coming near the end of Hamlet's long scene of rage and disgust, these lines seem to me extraordinarily moving in their evocation of desire for the maternal presence that can restore the sense of the world and the self as blessed.[11] And the blessedness they image is specifically in the relation of world and self: as mother and son mirror each other, each blessing each,

Shakespeare images the reopening of the zone of trust that had been foreclosed by the annihilating mother. For the first time, Hamlet imagines something coming to him from outside himself that will neither invade nor contaminate him: the recovery of benign maternal presence for a moment repairs the damage of the fall in him, making safe the boundary-permeability that had been a source of terror. Toward the end of the scene, all those night-terrors are gone: Hamlet's repeated variations on the conventional phrase "good night" mark his progression from rage at his mother's sexuality to repossession of the good mother he had lost. He begins with "Good night. But go not to my uncle's bed. . . . Refrain tonight" (3.4.161, 167), attempting to separate her from her horrific night-body; but by the end — through his own version of Marcellus's purifying fantasy — he has succeeded in imagining both her and the night wholesome. If he begins by wishing Gertrude were not his mother, he ends with the poignant repeated leave-taking of a child who does not want to let go of the mother who now keeps him safe: "Once more, good night . . . So again, good night. . . . Mother, good night indeed. . . . Good night, mother" (3.4.172, 179, 215, 219).

In the end, we do not know whether or not Gertrude herself has been morally reclaimed; it is the mark of the play's investment in Hamlet's fantasies that, even here, we are not allowed to see her as a separate person. To the extent that she looks into the heart that Hamlet has "cleft in twain" (3.4.158) and finds the "black and grained spots" (3.4.90) that he sees there, she seems to accept his version of her soiled inner body; in any case, her response allows him to think of his initial Nero-like aggression — speaking daggers though using none (3.2.387) — as moral reclamation. But as usual in this play, she remains relatively opaque, more a screen for Hamlet's fantasies about her than a fully developed character in her own right: whatever individuality she might have had is sacrificed to her status as mother. Nonetheless, though we might wonder just what his evidence is, Hamlet at least believes that she has returned to him as the mother he can call "good lady" (3.4.182). And after 3.4, her remaining actions are ambiguous enough to nourish his fantasy: though there are no obvious signs of separation from Claudius in her exchanges with him, in her last moments she seems to become a wonderfully homey presence for her son, newly available to him as the loving and protective mother of childhood, worrying about his condition, wiping his face as he fights, even perhaps intentionally drinking the poison intended for him.

In the end, whatever her motivation, he seems securely possessed of her as an internal good mother; and this possession gives him a new calm about his place in the world and especially about death, that domain of maternal dread. Trusting her, he can begin to trust in himself and in his own capacity for action; and he can begin to rebuild the masculine identity spoiled by her contamination. For his secure internal possession of her idealized image permits the return of his father to him, and in the form that he had always wanted: turning his mother away from Claudius, Hamlet wins her not only for himself but also for his father — for his father conceived as Hyperion, the bodiless godlike figure he had invoked at the beginning of the play. If her sexuality had spoiled this father, her purification brings him back; after 3.4, the guilty father and his ghost disappear, replaced by the distant heavenly father into whom he has been transformed, the one now acting through the sign of the other: "Why, even in that was heaven ordinant. / I had my father's signet in my purse" (5.2.48–49). Unexpectedly finding this sign of the father on his own person, Hamlet in effect registers his repossession of the idealized father within; and, like a good son, Hamlet can finally merge himself with this father, making His will his own. But though we may feel that Hamlet has achieved a new calm and self-possession, the price is high: for the parents lost to him at the beginning of the play can be restored only insofar as they are entirely separated from their sexual bodies. This is a pyrrhic solution to the problems of embodiedness and familial identity; it does not bode well for Shakespeare's representation of sexual union, or of the children born of that union.

In creating for Hamlet a plot in which his mother's sexuality is literally the sign of her betrayal and of her husband's death, Shakespeare recapitulates the material of infantile fantasy, playing it out with a compelling plot logic that allows its expression in a perfectly rationalized, hence justified, way. Given Hamlet's world, anyone would feel as Hamlet does — but Shakespeare has given him this world.[12] And the world Shakespeare gives him sets the stage for the plays that follow: from *Hamlet* on, all sexual relationships will be tinged by the threat of the mother, all masculine identity problematically formed in relationship to her. For despite Hamlet's tenuous recovery of his father's signet ring through the workings of Providence, the stabilizing father lost at the beginning of *Hamlet* — the father who can control female appetite, who can secure pure masculine identity for his son — cannot be brought back from the dead.

Notes

In its original form in Adelman's Suffocating Mothers: Fantasies of Maternal Origin in Shakespeare's Plays, *"Hamlet" to "The Tempest" (New York: Routledge, 1992), this essay is extensively footnoted. Readers interested in following up on any of the specific points mentioned here should consult that version of the essay. [Editors' note]*

¹This is the likeness registered stunningly, for example, in Hamlet's "How stand I then, / That have a father kill'd, a mother stain'd" (4.4.56–57), where *have* can indicate either possession or action. This likeness is the staple of most oedipal readings of the play, in which — in Ernest Jones's formulation — Claudius "incorporates the deepest and most buried part of [Hamlet's] own personality" (*Hamlet and Oedipus* [Garden City: Doubleday, 1954], 100); see Norman Holland's useful discussion of this and other oedipal readings in *Psychoanalysis and Shakespeare* (New York: Octagon, 1979), 163–206. These readings have been extended and challenged by Avi Erlich (*Hamlet's Absent Father* [Princeton: Princeton UP, 1977]), who sees the basic motive of the play not in Hamlet's covert identification with Claudius but in his desperate need for a strong father who can protect him from his own incestuous impulses and from the castrating mother they would lead to: "Much more than he wants to have killed his father, Hamlet wants his father back" (260). Although most oedipal accounts begin by acknowledging that Hamlet is initially more obsessed with his mother's remarriage than with his father's death, they usually go on to focus on the father-son relationship, discussing the mother merely as the condition that occasions the son's struggle with — or need for — his father. Without entirely discounting oedipal motives in the play, I want to restore what seems to me the mother's clear primacy in her son's imagination; I consequently emphasize pre-oedipal motives, in which fantasies of merger with and annihilation by the mother are prior to genital desire for her, and in which the strong father is needed more as an aid to differentiation and the establishment of masculine identity than as a superego protecting against incestuous desire. The extraordinary oral valence of both sex and killing in *Hamlet* — the extent to which both are registered in the language of eating and boundary diffusion — seems to me evidence of the extent to which even the more purely oedipal issues are strongly colored by pre-oedipal anxiety. My emphasis on Gertrude has to some extent been anticipated by those who stress matricidal impulses in the play, implicitly or explicitly making Orestes — rather than Oedipus — the model for *Hamlet*. See also Richard Wheeler's account of Hamlet's attempt to build a self both by incorporating the image of an ideal father and by recovering the trust shattered by disillusionment with his mother (*Shakespeare's Development and the Problem Comedies* [Berkeley: U of California P, 1981], 161, 190–200).

²T. S. Eliot, "Hamlet," *Selected Essays* (New York: Harcourt, 1932), 124. In Eliot's view, the discrepancy between Gertrude and the disgust she arouses in Hamlet is the mark of "some stuff that the writer could not drag to light, contemplate, or manipulate into art" (123) and hence of artistic failure; but, in concluding that Gertrude needs to be insignificant to arouse in Hamlet "the feeling which she is incapable of representing" (125), he inadvertently suggests the aesthetic power of fantasy disengaged from its adequate representation in a single character. For a brilliant analysis of the way in which the feminine stands for the failure of all kinds of representational stability in Eliot's aesthetic, in various psychoanalytic attempts to master the play, in *Hamlet* itself as the representative of Western tradition, see Jacqueline Rose, "*Hamlet* — the *Mona Lisa* of Literature," *Critical Quarterly* 28 (1986): 35–49.

³After giving the reasons for preferring Quarto 1 and 2's "sallied" (= sullied) to Folio's "solid," Jenkins concedes that Shakespeare may have intended a pun (see Arden *Hamlet* 436–37).

⁴In Linda Bamber's formulation, "What we see in Hamlet is not the Oedipal drama

itself but the unraveling of the resolution to the Oedipus complex" (*Comic Women*, *Tragic Men* [Stanford: Stanford UP, 1982], 156); Rose understands femininity as the scapegoated sign of this unraveling ("Hamlet — the *Mona Lisa* of Literature," esp. 40– 41, 46–47). Traditional Freudian theory locates the father's protective function at the point of this resolution (see, for example, Erlich's account of Hamlet's fantasy-search for the father who can protect him from his own incestuous impulses [*Hamlet's Absent Father*, esp. 23–37, 185–94]). But in object-relations theory, the father's protective role comes much earlier, when he helps the son in the process of differentiation from the potentially overwhelming mother of infancy (see, e.g., Nancy Chodorow, *The Reproduction of Mothering* [Berkeley: U of California P, 1978], 71, 79–82.

⁵The place of this dream-technique in the creation of Old Hamlet and Claudius was identified by Jones (*Hamlet and Oedipus* 138) and Maud Bodkin (*Archetypal Patterns in Poetry* [London: Oxford UP, 1934], 13–14) and has since been widely accepted by psychoanalytic critics; see especially, C. L. Barber and Richard Wheeler's account of its devastating effects on the son who thus loses the capacity to move toward independent selfhood by coming to terms with his father's imperfections in *The Whole Journey: Shakespeare's Power of Development* (Berkeley: U of California P, 1986), 249, 254–55. The overidealized father must be destructive to Hamlet's own selfhood (see Wheeler, *Shakespeare's Development* 143, 193–94); in discussing Hamlet's need to escape "from the shade of the dead hero," Levin strikingly anticipates more recent formulations of the problem in *The Question of Hamlet* (New York: Oxford UP, 1959), 57–58.

⁶See John H. Astington, "'Fault' in Shakespeare," *Shakespeare Quarterly* 36 (1985): 330–34, for *fault* as a slang term for the female genitals; he does not note its use in this passage. But *fault* could apparently carry the more general suggestion of sexual intercourse as well.

⁷*Oxford English Dictionary* 1 (e) gives "sexual intercourse" as one of the meanings for *mixture*. Holland cites several psychoanalytic critics who see the poisoning "as a childishly confused account of the sexual act" (*Psychoanalysis and Shakespeare* 194); see also Erlich (*Hamlet's Absent Father* 93), and especially Stanley Cavell, who reads the dumbshow poisoning as Hamlet's dream version of a primal scene fantasy. See Cavell's *Disowning Knowledge in Six Plays of Shakespeare* (Cambridge, Eng.: Cambridge UP, 1987), 185.

⁸Skin eruptions of the sort the ghost describes were one of the symptoms of syphilis (see James Cleugh, *Secret Enemy: The Story of a Disease* [London: Thames, 1954], 46–50. Both the ghost's "crust" and his odd "bark'd about" are anticipated in early descriptions of the disease: Francisco Lopez de Villalobos notes the "very ugly eruption of crusts upon the face and body," Josef Grunbeck the wrinkled black scabs, "harder than bark" (qtd. in English translation in Cleugh 48, 49).

⁹In this paragraph, as elsewhere, I am drawing on ideas expressed by D. W. Winnicott in a series of essays on the interface between inner and outer in earliest infantile development, especially on the ways in which a developing core of selfhood can meet with a reliable world in a transitional zone that makes creative interaction between inner and outer possible, and on the ways in which this zone can be destroyed (see especially "Transitional Objects and Transitional Phenomena," *Through Paediatrics to Psycho-Analysis* [London: Hogarth–Inst. of Psycho-Analysis, 1975], 229–42; "Ego Distortion in Terms of True and False Self," *The Maturational Processes and the Facilitating Environment* [London: Hogarth–Inst. of Psycho-Analysis, 1972], 140–52; and "Communicating and Not Communicating Leading to a Study of Certain Opposites," *The Maturational Processes* 179–92; and see ch. 8, nn. 83, 84, and 90, in my *Suffocating Mothers* for further discussion of Winnicott). See also Wheeler on Hamlet's "excruciating efforts to establish a self while hiding it from others" for a similarly Winnicottian account (*Shakespeare's Development* 198).

¹⁰Critics who use the model of Freud's "Mourning and Melancholia" generally assume that the lost object is Hamlet's father; but Hamlet's discovery of the whore inside

himself suggests that the lost, introjected, and then berated object is his mother (see, e.g., Paul A. Jorgensen, "Hamlet's Therapy," *The Huntington Library Quarterly* 27 [1964]: 254–55, and Stephen A. Reid, "Hamlet's Melancholia," *American Imago* 31 [1974]: 389–92). Psychoanalytic critics sometimes note Hamlet's difficulty in reconciling what they see as the masculine and feminine elements within him; see, for example, Murray M. Schwartz ("Shakespeare through Contemporary Psychoanalysis," *Representing Shakespeare: New Psychoanalytic Essays*, ed. Murray M. Schwartz and Coppélia Kahn [Baltimore: Johns Hopkins UP, 1980], 27) and especially Winnicott, in his not wholly successful attempt to gender the development of the objective subject ("Creativity and Its Origins," *Playing and Reality* [London: Tavistock, 1971], esp. 79–84; see also Rose's critique of Winnicott, "*Hamlet* — the *Mona Lisa* of Literature" 45). The fullest account of Hamlet's relation to his own "femaleness" is David Leverenz's "The Woman in Hamlet: An Interpersonal View" (*Representing Shakespeare* 110–28). For the basis of this construction of the masculine self in the theories of object-relations psychoanalysis, see my own *Suffocating Mothers*, ch. 1, p. 7; for *Hamlet* specifically, see Madelon Gohlke, " 'I wooed thee with my sword': Shakespeare's Tragic Paradigms," *Representing Shakespeare* 172–73.

    [11]Although C. L. Barber does not specifically discuss this moment in *Hamlet*, my sense of the importance of the sacred as a psychic category in Shakespeare is greatly indebted to him. His work locates the tragic need to find the sacred in familial relationships in the context of the Protestant dismantling of the Holy Family, especially of the Holy Mother, "whose worship could help meet the profound need for relationship to an ideal feminine figure, unsullied either by her own sexuality or by the sexual insecurities of men and unlimited in maternal solace and generosity" (Barber and Wheeler, *The Whole Journey* 32; see also "On Christianity and the Family: Tragedy of the Sacred," *Twentieth-Century Interpretations of "King Lear,"* ed. Janet Adelman [Englewood Cliffs: Prentice, 1978], 117–19, and "The Family in Shakespeare's Development: Tragedy and Sacredness," *Representing Shakespeare* 188–202, for earlier formulations of these ideas).

    [12]See Meredith Skura's account of the ways in which Hamlet's world embodies (and hence justifies) what he feels in *The Literary Use of the Psychoanalytic Process* (New Haven: Yale UP, 1981), 47.

Deconstruction
and
Hamlet

WHAT IS DECONSTRUCTION?

Deconstruction has a reputation for being the most complex and forbidding of contemporary critical approaches to literature, but in fact almost all of us have, at one time, either deconstructed a text or badly wanted to deconstruct one. Sometimes when we hear a lecturer effectively marshal evidence to show that a book means primarily one thing, we long to interrupt and ask what he or she would make of other, conveniently overlooked passages, passages that seem to contradict the lecturer's thesis. Sometimes, after reading a provocative critical article that *almost* convinces us that a familiar work means the opposite of what we assumed it meant, we may wish to make an equally convincing case for our former reading of the text. We may not think that the poem or novel in question better supports our interpretation, but we may recognize that the text can be used to support *both* readings. And sometimes we simply want to make that point: texts can be used to support seemingly irreconcilable positions.

To reach this conclusion is to feel the deconstructive itch. J. Hillis Miller, the preeminent American deconstructor, puts it this way: "Deconstruction is not a dismantling of the structure of a text, but a demonstration that it has already dismantled itself. Its apparently solid ground is no rock but thin air" ("Stevens' Rock" 341). To deconstruct a text isn't to show that all the high old themes aren't there to be found in it. Rather, it is to show that a text — not unlike DNA with its double helix — can have intertwined, opposite "discourses" — strands of narrative, threads of meaning.

Ultimately, of course, deconstruction refers to a larger and more complex enterprise than the practice of demonstrating that a text means contradictory things. The term refers to a way of reading texts practiced by critics who have been influenced by the writings of the French philosopher Jacques Derrida. It is important to gain some understanding of Derrida's project and of the historical backgrounds of his work before reading the deconstruction of *Hamlet* that follows, let alone attempting to deconstruct a text. But it is important, too, to approach deconstruction with anything but a scholar's sober and almost worshipful respect for knowledge and truth. Deconstruction offers a playful alternative to traditional scholarship, a confidently adversarial alternative, and deserves to be approached in the spirit that animates it.

Derrida, a philosopher of language who coined the term "deconstruction," argues that we tend to think and express our thoughts in terms of opposites. Something is black but not white, masculine and therefore not feminine, a cause rather than an effect, and so forth. These mutually exclusive pairs or dichotomies are too numerous to list, but would include beginning/end, conscious/unconscious, presence/absence, speech/writing, and construction/destruction (the last being the opposition that Derrida's word *deconstruction* tries to contain and subvert). If we think hard about these dichotomies, Derrida suggests, we will realize that they are not simply oppositions; they are also hierarchies in miniature. In other words, they contain one term that our culture views as being superior and one term viewed as negative or inferior. Sometimes the superior term seems only subtly superior (*speech, masculine, cause*), whereas sometimes we know immediately which term is culturally preferable (*presence* and *beginning* and *consciousness* are easy choices). But the hierarchy always exists.

Of particular interest to Derrida, perhaps because it involves the language in which all the other dichotomies are expressed, is the hierarchical opposition speech/writing. Derrida argues that the "privileging" of speech, that is, the tendency to regard speech in positive terms and writing in negative terms, cannot be disentangled from the privileging of presence. (Postcards are written by absent friends; we read Plato because he cannot speak from beyond the grave.) Furthermore, according to Derrida, the tendency to privilege both speech and presence is part of the Western tradition of *logocentrism,* the belief that in some ideal beginning were creative *spoken* words, words such as "Let there be light," spoken by an ideal, *present* God. According to logocentric tradition, these words can now only be represented in unoriginal speech or writing (such as the written phrase in quotation marks above). Derrida doesn't seek to reverse the hierarchized opposition between speech and writing, or presence and absence, or early and late, for to do so would be to fall into a trap of perpetuating the same forms of thought and expression that he seeks to deconstruct. Rather, his goal is to erase the boundary between oppositions such as speech and writing, and to do so in such a way as to throw the order and values implied by the opposition into question.

Returning to the theories of Ferdinand de Saussure, who invented the modern science of linguistics, Derrida reminds us that the association of speech with present, obvious, and ideal meaning and writing with absent, merely pictured, and therefore less reliable meaning is suspect, to say the least. As Saussure demonstrated, words are *not* the things they name and, indeed, they are only arbitrarily associated with those things. Neither spoken nor written words have present, positive, identifiable attributes themselves; they have meaning only by virtue of their difference from other words (*red, read, reed*). In a sense, meanings emerge from the gaps or spaces between them. Take "read" as an example. To know whether it is the present or past tense of the verb — whether it rhymes with *red* or *reed* — we need to see it in relation to some other word (for example, *yesterday*).

Because the meanings of words lie in the differences between them and in the differences between them and the things they name, Derrida suggests that all language is constituted by *différance*, a word he has coined that puns on two French words meaning "to differ" and "to defer": words are the deferred presences of the things they "mean," and their meaning is grounded in difference. Derrida, by the way, changes the *e* in the French word *différence* to an *a* in his neologism *différance;* the change, which can be seen in writing but cannot be heard in spoken French, is itself a playful, witty challenge to the notion that writing is inferior or "fallen" speech.

In *De la grammatologie* [*Of Grammatology*] (1967) and *Dissemination* (1972), Derrida begins to redefine writing by deconstructing some old definitions. In *Dissemination*, he traces logocentrism back to Plato, who in the *Phaedrus* has Socrates condemn writing and who, in all the great dialogues, powerfully postulates that metaphysical longing for origins and ideals that permeates Western thought. "What Derrida does in his reading of Plato," Barbara Johnson points out, "is to unfold dimen-

sions of Plato's *text* that work against the grain of (Plato's own) Plato-
nism" (xxiv). Remember: that is what deconstruction does according to
Miller; it shows a text dismantling itself.

In *Of Grammatology*, Derrida turns to the *Confessions* of Jean-
Jacques Rousseau and exposes a grain running against the grain. Rousseau, another great Western idealist and believer in innocent, noble origins, on one hand condemned writing as mere representation, a
corruption of the more natural, childlike, direct, and therefore undev-
ious speech. On the other hand, Rousseau admitted his own tendency
to lose self-presence and blurt out exactly the wrong thing in public. He
confesses that, by writing at a distance from his audience, he often expressed himself better: "If I were present, one would never know what
I was worth," Rousseau admitted (Derrida, *Of Grammatology* 142).
Thus, writing is a *supplement* to speech that is at the same time *necessary*.
Barbara Johnson, sounding like Derrida, puts it this way: "Recourse to
writing . . . is necessary to recapture a presence whose lack has not been
preceded by any fullness" (Derrida, *Dissemination* xii). Thus, Derrida
shows that one strand of Rousseau's discourse made writing seem a secondary, even treacherous supplement, while another made it seem necessary to communication.

Have Derrida's deconstructions of *Confessions* and the *Phaedrus* explained these texts, interpreted them, opened them up, and shown us
what they mean? Not in any traditional sense. Derrida would say that
anyone attempting to find a single, correct meaning in a text is simply
imprisoned by that structure of thought that would oppose two readings and declare one to be right and not wrong, correct rather than
incorrect. In fact, any work of literature that we interpret defies the laws
of Western logic, the laws of opposition and noncontradiction. In the
views of poststructuralist critics, texts don't say "A and not B." They say
"A and not-A," as do texts written by literary critics, who are also involved in producing creative writing.

Miller has written that the purpose of deconstruction is to show
"the existence in literature of structures of language which contradict
the law of non-contradiction." Why find the grain that runs against the
grain? To restore what Miller has called "the strangeness of literature,"
to reveal the "capacity of each work to surprise the reader," to demonstrate that "literature continually exceeds any formula or theory with
which the critic is prepared to encompass it" (Miller, *Fiction* 5).

Although its ultimate aim may be to critique Western idealism and
logic, deconstruction as it is practiced in literary criticism began as a

response to structuralism and to formalism, another structure-oriented theory of reading. (Deconstruction, which is really only one kind of a poststructuralist criticism, is sometimes referred to as poststructuralist criticism, or even as poststructuralism.)

Structuralism, Robert Scholes tells us, may now be seen as a reaction to modernist alienation and despair (3). Using Saussure's theory as Derrida was to do later, European structuralists attempted to create a *semiology,* or science of signs, that would give humankind at once a scientific and a holistic way of studying the world and its human inhabitants. Roland Barthes, a structuralist who later shifted toward poststructuralism, hoped to recover literary language from the isolation in which it had been studied and to show that the laws that govern it govern all signs, from road signs to articles of clothing. Claude Lévi-Strauss, a structural anthropologist who studied everything from village structure to the structure of myths, found in myths what he called *mythemes,* or building blocks, such as basic plot elements. Recognizing that the same mythemes occur in similar myths from different cultures, he suggested that all myths may be elements of one great myth being written by the collective human mind.

Derrida could not accept the notion that structuralist thought might someday explain the laws governing human signification and thus provide the key to understanding the form and meaning of everything from an African village to a Greek myth to Rousseau's *Confessions.* In his view, the scientific search by structural anthropologists for what unifies humankind amounts to a new version of the old search for the lost ideal, whether that ideal be Plato's bright realm of the Idea or the Paradise of Genesis or Rousseau's unspoiled Nature. As for the structuralist belief that texts have "centers" of meaning, in Derrida's view that derives from the logocentric belief that there is a reading of the text that accords with "the book as seen by God." Jonathan Culler, who thus translates a difficult phrase from Derrida's *L'Écriture et la différence* [*Writing and Difference*] (1967) in his book *Structuralist Poetics* (1975), goes on to explain what Derrida objects to in structuralist literary criticism:

> [When] one speaks of the structure of a literary work, one does so
> from a certain vantage point: one starts with notions of the mean-
> ing or effects of a poem and tries to identify the structures respon-
> sible for those effects. Possible configurations or patterns that
> make no contribution are rejected as irrelevant. That is to say,
> an intuitive understanding of the poem functions as the "centre"
> . . . : it is both a starting point and a limiting principle. (244)

For these reasons, Derrida and his poststructuralist followers reject the very notion of "linguistic competence" introduced by Noam Chomsky, a structural linguist. The idea that there is a competent reading "gives a privileged status to a particular set of rules of reading, . . . granting pre-eminence to certain conventions and excluding from the realm of language all the truly creative and productive violations of those rules" (Culler, *Structuralist Poetics* 241).

Deconstruction calls into question assumptions made about literature by formalist, as well as by structuralist, critics. Formalism, or the New Criticism as it was once commonly called, assumes a work of literature to be a freestanding, self-contained object, its meanings found in the complex network of relations that constitute its parts (images, sounds, rhythms, allusions, and so on). To be sure, deconstruction is somewhat like formalism in several ways. Both the formalist and the deconstructor focus on the literary text; neither is likely to interpret a poem or a novel by relating it to events in the author's life, letters, historical period, or even culture. And formalists, long before deconstructors, discovered counterpatterns of meaning in the same text. Formalists find ambiguity and irony; deconstructors find contradiction and undecidability.

Undecidability, as Paul de Man came to define it, is a complex notion easily misunderstood. There is a tendency to assume it has something to do with readers who, when forced to decide between two or more equally plausible and conflicting readings motivated by the same text, throw up their hands and decide that the choice can't be made. But undecidability in fact debunks this whole notion of reading as a decision-making process carried out on texts by readers. To say we are forced to choose or decide — or that we are unable to do so — is to locate the problem of undecidability falsely outside ourselves, and to make it reside within a text to which we come as an Other. The poststructuralist concept of undecidability, we might say, deconstructs the either/or–type distinction or opposition that structuralists and formalists have made between reader and text. It entails what de Man, in another context, calls the "mutual obliteration" not only of propositions apparently opposed but also of the subject/object relation.

Undecidability is thus rather different from ambiguity, as understood by formalists. Formalists believe a complete understanding of a literary work is possible, an understanding in which even the ambiguities will fulfill a definite, meaningful function. Deconstructors confront the apparently limitless possibilities for the production of meaning that develop when the language of the critic enters the language of the text.

They cannot accept the formalist view that a work of literary art has organic unity (therefore, structuralists would say, a "center"), if only we could find it. The formalist critic ultimately makes sense of ambiguity; undecidability, by contrast, is never reduced, let alone resolved, by deconstructive reading.

In recent years, deconstructive and poststructuralist critics have shown an increasing interest in the writings of Jacques Lacan, a psychoanalytic theorist who has extended Sigmund Freud's theory of dreams, literature, and the interpretation of both. Lacan took Freud's theory of psyche and gender and showed how there existed within Freud's own theory a crucial third term — that of language. In the process, he both used and significantly developed Freud's ideas about the oedipal stage and complex.

Lacan points out that the pre-oedipal stage, in which the child at first does not even recognize its independence from its mother, is also a preverbal stage, one in which the child communicates without the medium of language, or — if we insist on calling the child's communications a language — in a language that is perhaps best described as material. ("Coos," certainly, cannot be said to be figurative or symbolic.) In this pre-oedipal relation to its parents, the child enters the mirror stage.

During the mirror period, the child comes to view itself and its mother, later other people as well, as independent selves. This is the stage in which the child is first able to fear the aggressions of another, to desire what is recognizably beyond the self (initially the mother), and, finally, to want to compete with another for the same, desired object. This is also the stage at which the child first becomes able to feel sympathy with another person who is being hurt by a third, to cry when another cries. All of these developments involve projecting beyond the self and, by extension, constructing one's own self (or "ego" or "I") as others view one — that is, as another. Such constructions, according to Lacan, are just that: constructs, products, artifacts'— fictions of coherence that in fact hide what Lacan calls the "want-to-be" or the "lack in being" (manque à être).

The mirror stage, which Lacan also refers to as the Imaginary stage, is succeeded by the oedipal stage, although in Lacan's view, it should be pointed out, a new stage doesn't mark the end of an old one: a person never really or fully leaves any of the developmental stages behind. In Freud, of course, the oedipal stage begins when the child perceives gender and, more important, gender differences between itself and one of its parents; this is a time when male children, in particular, come to realize that the object of their desire (the mother) belongs to an older and more powerful rival (the father). In Lacan the oedipal stage begins when children — males but females as well — learn, through language, the social rules that restrain or prohibit individual desire, beginning (but not ending) with desire for the mother. Once introduced to this realm of rule or law, which Lacan refers to as the "Law of the Father" or the "Name-of-the-Father," boys and girls come to understand that what once seemed wholly their own and even indistinguishable from themselves is properly desired from a distance and in the form of socially and psychically acceptable *substitutes.*

The fact that the oedipal stage coincides with the entry of the child into language is extremely important for Lacan. The linguistic order, after all, is essentially a figurative or "Symbolic order"; words are not the things they stand for but are, rather, signifiers that stand in or substitute for the concepts of those things. For Lacan, the father need not be present in person, either as a signifier or as a signified concept, to trigger the oedipal stage or to catalyze the transition into the Symbolic order. Rather, Lacan argues, the oedipal stage involves a crisis over and subsequent adaptation to the system of names and naming, part of the larger system of substitutions we call language. A child has little doubt about who its mother is, but who is its father, and how would one know? The father's claim rests on the mother's *word* that he is in fact the father; the father's relationship to the child is thus established through language and a system of kinship — names — that in turn is basic to rules of everything from property to law. The name of the father (*nom du père*, which in French sounds like *non du père*, the "no of the father") involves, in a sense, nothing of the father: nothing, that is, except his word or name.

Lacan's psychoanalytic theory has proved of interest to deconstructors and other poststructuralists for a number of reasons. One of these involves Lacan's understanding of the "father" as a system of associated names and words, symbols, and laws. For Lacan, the father (who is only a name) is the "veiled phallus," a signified with the signifier missing. The notion of the missing signifier is of interest to deconstructive critics. For to say the signifier is missing is to suggest what deconstructors have also suggested, namely, that there is no possibility for absolute unmediated meaning — that meaning is always broken, made up of fragments that can never add up to an accessible totality. The absent signifier comes to stand for absent wholeness in language and, for Lacan, in the psyche. It is this link between the lack of completeness or closure or totality in language — the impossibility that language can express absolute presence — and Lacan's emphasis on a parallel absence or incompleteness in human psychic structure that makes deconstruction and Lacanian psychoanalysis such strong companion disciplines.

Deconstructive critics have thus been drawn to Lacanian theory insofar as it holds that the "subject," or self, is a product or construct, an artifact hiding a lack, a fiction covering an absence of being. Produced during the mirror stage, in which the child first sees itself as a self, the subject *seems* at once unified, consistent, and organized around a determinate center. In fact, however, the yoking together of fragments, of destructively dissimilar elements, takes its psychic toll, and Lacanian psychoanalysis (Lacan was an analyst with real patients, and not a literary critic) believes that there is therapeutic value in showing the integrated self to be an illusion; the job of a Lacanian analyst would thus be to "deconstruct," as it were, the patient's self, to show its continuities to be contradictions as well.

Marjorie Garber begins the essay that follows by discussing uncanny experiences, which involve the feeling that events are repeating themselves in an eerily unlikely way. She invokes Freud's theory that such experiences occur when something has happened that revives repressed, infantile feelings. According to a Freudian reading, there is something decidedly uncanny about the appearance of Hamlet's father's ghost, because the unlikely reappearance of Old Hamlet would be associated, in young Hamlet's mind, with the feeling that the murder of his father by Claudius only repeated in reality an act that he himself has committed in fantasy, as a result of infantile desire for his mother Gertrude.

In a move characteristic of much deconstruction today, Garber turns from a discussion of Freud to the theories of Lacan, who in an essay on *Hamlet* that has influenced most contemporary criticism of the play, associated Old Hamlet's ghost with what he calls the "veiled phallus" or "missing signifier." (See the beginning of Elaine Showalter's feminist contribution to this volume for an attack on this very essay by Lacan.) Lacan suggests that Hamlet's father's refusal to die (or refusal, in Hamlet's mind, to die), leaves Hamlet dominated by a phallic presence the reality of which is, at the same time, uncertain. Unable to affirm or deny the father, Hamlet becomes unable to affirm or deny the father's word and, more broadly, the "Law of the Father," which is to say, the whole patriarchal, symbolic order of things.

Lacan, Garber proceeds by pointing out, was fascinated by the figure of Hamlet's ghost, finding an "anamorphism" of him in the "ghostly skull" just visible in a famous Holbein painting. (An almost formless form, the skull is invisible from all angles but one.) Calling the

Holbein picture "a trap for the gaze," Lacan compares it to The Mouse-trap, *Hamlet's* play-within-the-play. In seeming to reveal something about the world outside its edges that, a moment later, it seems not to reveal, it too is a "trap for the gaze," a figure of the (veiled) phallus, another paralyzing version of the absent father and signifier. For what the play creates and represents is that unresolvable doubt and uncertainty about meaning that is suggested by the deconstructive term "undecidability," undecidability that in Lacan's view is signified by the ghost and characteristic of the modern subject or self.

In the second half of the essay, Garber makes more use of the thinking of Derrida and de Man. She quotes "On Shakespeare," a sonnet by Milton that, de Man has argued, articulates "the latent threat that inhabits prosopopoeia" (a poetical figure or "trope" involving the projection of voice and/or face on inanimate things). De Man, deconstructing this trope usually thought to prove the power of living poets to give voice to the inanimate world, reminds us that prosopopoeia involves invoking the dead. He goes on to suggest that, if the dead *were* to speak, "the living" would be "struck dumb," frozen like stone or marble, made dead themselves. *Hamlet,* Garber concludes, enacts dramatically the threat de Man finds latent in prosopopoeia. "I am dead," Hamlet continually says at the end of the play in which the dead King Hamlet speaks. And we are left frozen, too, in a certain uncertainty. For "what," finally, "does the Ghost say?" "What kind of commandment," Garber asks, "does the ghostly father in *Hamlet* hand down?" It tells Hamlet to "remember," but what Hamlet mainly has to remember is the loss that explains the present absence. As for the past that the ghost would have Hamlet speak about, the remembrance Hamlet promises to write "Within the book and volume of [his] brain," Garber uses Derrida to point out that "it" is "necessarily fictive, since it is only experienced," by Hamlet and by us, "*as* past, as tale, as narrative." And because it is fictive it inhibits the very revenge it would prompt.

Perhaps the most interesting aspect of this essay, which combines Lacanian psychoanalytic criticism, deconstruction, and even cultural criticism, is the way in which the notion of *repetition* is absorbed from Freud and Lacan and made applicable to literary memory, literary history. According to Freud and Lacan, the psychic system will deflect the representation of an initially traumatic (because desired, because problematic) event by repressing it, altering it, absorbing it into or displacing it onto something else. Similarly, a text gives rise to a literary history, and in the history of criticism a set of predictable repressions or displacements develop that are akin to those experienced pathologically in the "repetition" of a trauma. *Hamlet* thus acquires the status of an original trauma (but what was it? was it a fantasy? if so, whose?), and what we make of it through our readings of it becomes the culture's attempt to locate that trauma in a single originary presence, a ghost we call Shakespeare. Thus the past haunts the present uncannily, and we continually "speak of it" — an "it" we will not know.

Ross C Murfin

DECONSTRUCTION:
A SELECTED BIBLIOGRAPHY

Deconstruction, Poststructuralism, and Structuralism: Introductions, Guides, and Surveys

Arac, Jonathan, Wlad Godzich, and Wallace Martin, eds. *The Yale Critics: Deconstruction in America*. Minneapolis: U of Minnesota P, 1983. See especially the essays by Bové, Godzich, Pease, and Corngold.

Culler, Jonathan. *On Deconstruction: Theory and Criticism After Structuralism*. Ithaca: Cornell UP, 1982.

———. *Structuralist Poetics: Structuralism, Linguistics and the Study of Literature*. Ithaca: Cornell UP, 1975. See especially ch. 10.

Gasché, Rodolphe. "Deconstruction as Criticism." *Glyph* 6 (1979): 177–215.

Jefferson, Ann. "Structuralism and Post Structuralism." *Modern Literary Theory: A Comparative Introduction*. Totowa: Barnes, 1982. 84–112.

Leitch, Vincent B. *Deconstructive Criticism: An Advanced Introduction and Survey*. New York: Columbia UP, 1983.

Lentricchia, Frank. *After the New Criticism*. Chicago: U of Chicago P, 1981.

Melville, Stephen W. *Philosophy Beside Itself: On Deconstruction and Modernism*. Theory and History of Literature 27. Minneapolis: U of Minnesota P, 1986.

Norris, Christopher. *Deconstruction and the Interests of Theory*. Oklahoma Project for Discourse and Theory 4. Norman: U of Oklahoma P, 1989.

———. *Deconstruction: Theory and Practice*. London: Methuen, 1982.

Raval, Suresh. *Metacriticism*. Athens: U of Georgia P, 1981.

Scholes, Robert. *Structuralism in Literature: An Introduction.* New Haven: Yale UP, 1974.

Sturrock, John. *Structuralism and Since.* Oxford, Eng.: Oxford UP, 1975.

Selected Works by Jacques Derrida and Paul de Man

de Man, Paul. *Allegories of Reading.* New Haven: Yale UP, 1979. See especially ch. 1 ("Semiology and Rhetoric").

———. *Blindness and Insight.* New York: Oxford UP, 1971. Minneapolis: U of Minnesota P, 1983. The 1983 edition contains important essays not included in the original edition.

———. *The Resistance to Theory.* Minneapolis: U of Minnesota P, 1986.

Derrida, Jacques. *Dissemination.* 1972. Trans. Barbara Johnson. Chicago: U of Chicago P, 1981. See especially the concise, incisive "Translator's Introduction," which provides a useful point of entry into this work and others by Derrida.

———. *Of Grammatology.* Trans. Gayatri C. Spivak. Baltimore: Johns Hopkins UP, 1976. Trans. of *De la Grammatologie.* 1967.

———. *The Postcard: From Socrates to Freud and Beyond.* Trans. and introd. Alan Bass. Chicago: U of Chicago P, 1987.

———. *Speech and Phenomena, and Other Essays on Husserl's Theory of Signs.* 1973. Trans. David B. Allison. Evanston: Northwestern UP, 1978.

———. *Writing and Difference.* 1967. Trans. Alan Bass. Chicago: U of Chicago P, 1978.

Lacanian Psychoanalytic Studies of Literature

Davis, Robert Con, ed. *The Fictional Father: Lacanian Readings of the Text.* Amherst: U of Massachusetts P, 1981.

———, ed. "Lacan and Narration." *Modern Language Notes* 5 (1983): 843–1063.

Felman, Shoshana. *Jacques Lacan and the Adventure of Insight: Psychoanalysis in Contemporary Culture.* Cambridge: Harvard UP, 1987.

———, ed. *Literature and Psychoanalysis: The Question of Reading: Otherwise.* Baltimore: Johns Hopkins UP, 1982.

Froula, Christine. "When Eve Reads Milton: Undoing the Canonical

Economy." *Canons.* Ed. Robert von Hallberg. Chicago: U of Chicago P, 1984.

Homans, Margaret. *Bearing the Word.* Chicago: U of Chicago P, 1986.

Muller, John P., and William J. Richardson, eds. *The Purloined Poe: Lacan, Derrida, and Psychoanalytic Reading.* Baltimore: Johns Hopkins UP, 1988. Includes Lacan's seminar on Poe's "The Purloined Letter."

Essays in Deconstruction and Poststructuralism

Barthes, Roland. *S/Z.* Trans. Richard Miller. New York: Hill, 1974. In this influential work, Barthes turns from a structuralist to a poststructuralist approach.

Bloom, Harold, et al., eds. *Deconstruction and Criticism.* New York: Seabury, 1979. Includes essays by Bloom, de Man, Derrida, Miller, and Hartman.

Chase, Cynthia. *Decomposing Figures.* Baltimore: Johns Hopkins UP, 1986.

Harari, Josué, ed. *Textual Strategies: Perspectives in Post-Structuralist Criticism.* Ithaca: Cornell UP, 1979.

Johnson, Barbara. *The Critical Difference: Essays in the Contemporary Rhetoric of Reading.* Baltimore: Johns Hopkins UP, 1980.

———. *A World of Difference.* Baltimore: Johns Hopkins UP, 1987.

Miller, J. Hillis. "Ariadne's Thread: Repetition and the Narrative Line." *Critical Inquiry* 3 (1976): 57–77.

———. Introduction. *Bleak House.* By Charles Dickens. Ed. Norman Page. Harmondsworth, Eng.: Penguin, 1971. 11–34.

———. *The Ethics of Reading: Kant, de Man, Eliot, Trollope, James, and Benjamin.* New York: Columbia UP, 1987.

———. *Fiction and Repetition: Seven English Novels.* Cambridge: Harvard UP, 1982.

———. "Stevens' Rock and Criticism as Cure." *The Georgia Review* 30 (1976): 5–31, 330–48.

Poststructuralist or Deconstructionist Studies of Shakespeare and of *Hamlet*

Felperin, Howard. "'Tongue-tied our Queen?': The Deconstruction of Presence in *The Winter's Tale.*" *Shakespeare and the Question of Theory.* Ed. Patricia Parker and Geoffrey Hartman. New York: Methuen, 1985. 3–18.

Ferguson, Margaret. *"Hamlet:* Letters and Spirits." *Shakespeare and the Question of Theory.* Ed. Patricia Parker and Geoffrey Hartman. New York: Methuen, 1985. 292–309.

Garber, Marjorie. *Shakespeare's Ghost Writers: Literature as Uncanny Causality.* New York: Methuen, 1987.

Goldberg, Jonathan. *Voice Terminal Echo: Postmodernism and English Renaissance Texts.* London: Methuen, 1986.

———. *Writing Matter: From the Hands of the English Renaissance.* Stanford: Stanford UP, 1990. See especially chapter entitled "Hamlet's Hand."

Lezra, Jacques. "Pirating Reading: The Appearance of History in *Measure for Measure.*" *English Literary History* 56.2 (1989): 255–92.

Pye, Christopher. *The Regal Phantasm: Shakespeare and the Politics of Spectacle.* London: Routledge, 1990.

Waller, Marguerite. "Usurpation, Seduction, and the Problematics of the Proper: A 'Deconstructive,' 'Feminist' Rereading of the Seduction of Richard and Anne in Shakespeare's *Richard III.*" *Rewriting the Renaissance: The Discourses of Sexual Difference in Early Modern Europe.* Ed. Margaret Ferguson, Maureen Quilligan, and Nancy Vickers. Chicago: U of Chicago P, 1986. 159–74.

Other Work Referred to in "What Is Deconstruction?"

Abrams, M. H. "Rationality and the Imagination in Cultural History." *Critical Inquiry* 2 (1976): 447–64.

A DECONSTRUCTIONIST PERSPECTIVE

MARJORIE GARBER

Hamlet: Giving Up the Ghost

But the calling back of the dead, or the desirability of calling them back, was a ticklish matter, after all. At bottom, and boldly confessed, the desire does not exist; it is a misapprehension precisely as impossible as the thing itself, as we should soon see if nature once let it happen. What we call mourning for our dead is perhaps not so much grief at not being able to call them back as it is grief at not being able to want to do so.

— THOMAS MANN, *The Magic Mountain*

Everyone in the audience was once a budding Oedipus in fantasy, and each recoils in horror from the dream fulfillment here transplanted into reality, with the full quantity of repression which separates his infantile state from his present one.

Fleetingly the thought passed through my head that the same thing might be at the bottom of *Hamlet* as well. I am not thinking of Shakespeare's conscious intentions, but believe, rather, that a real event stimulated the poet to his representation, in that his unconscious understood the unconscious of his hero. How does Hamlet the hysteric justify his words, "Thus conscience does make cowards of us all?" How does he explain his irresolution in avenging his father by the murder of his uncle — the same man who sends his courtiers to their death without a scruple and who is positively precipitate in murdering Laertes? How better than through the torment roused in him by the obscure memory that he himself had contemplated the same deed against his father out of passion for his mother, and — "use every man after his desert, and who should 'scape whipping?" His conscience is his unconscious sense of guilt. And is not his sexual alienation in his conversation with Ophelia typically hysterical? And his rejection of the instinct that seeks to beget children? And, finally, his transferral of the deed from his own father to Ophelia's? And does he not in the end, in the same marvellous way as my hysterical patients do, bring down punishment on himself by suffering the same fate as his father of being poisoned by the same rival?

— SIGMUND FREUD, October, 1897, Letter to Wilhelm Fliess

The prince in the play, who had to disguise himself as a madman, was behaving just as dreams do in reality; so that we can
say of dreams what Hamlet says of himself, concealing the true
circumstances under a cloak of wit and unintelligibility: "I am
but mad north-north-west."

> — SIGMUND FREUD, *The Interpretation of Dreams*

Hamlet is a play not only informed *with* the uncanny but also informed *about* it. In *Hamlet*, Shakespeare instates the uncanny as sharply
as he does the Oedipus complex — or, to put the matter more precisely,
Freud's concept of uncanniness finds as explicit an expression in the play
as does his concept of the complicated sexual rivalry between father and
son. The Ghost is only the most explicit marker of uncanniness, the
ultimate articulation of "uncertainty whether something is dead or
alive" (Freud, "The Uncanny" 30). A similar uncanniness might be said
to inform the works of Shakespeare as they are received and used today.
Are they alive or dead? Why do we still maintain the centrality of
Shakespeare? Why in a time of canon expansion and critique of canonical literature does Shakespeare not only remain unchallenged, but in
fact emerge newly canonized, as the proliferation of new critical anthologies — *alternative shakespeares, Political Shakespeare, Shakespeare and
the Question of Theory* — attests? Why with the current renaissance in
Renaissance studies, is Shakespeare still the touchstone for new historicists, feminists, deconstructors? Why, in other words, do those who criticize canonical authority so often turn to Shakespeare to ratify the authority of their critique?

At the center of the question of uncanniness — both as it applies to
Hamlet and as it applies to the relation between *Hamlet* and its readers — lies not only the castration complex but also the compulsion to
repeat. "Whatever reminds us of this inner *repetition-compulsion* is perceived as uncanny" (Freud, "The Uncanny" 44). Repetition and the
repetition compulsion are figured throughout *Hamlet:* in the double
play, dumb show, and dialogue, their double existence never satisfactorily explained despite the ingenuity of critics; in the Queen's two marriages, the twin husbands ("Look here upon this picture, and on this, /
The counterfeit presentment of two brothers" [3.4.53–54]); in the
double murder of fathers, Hamlet's father killed by Claudius, Laertes'
father killed by Hamlet.

Every critical observation on doubling in the play, from the psycho-

analytic ("the decomposing of the original villain into at least three father figures, the ghost, Polonius, and Claudius"; "The splitting of the
hero into a number of brother figures: Fortinbras, Horatio, Laertes, and
Rosencrantz-and-Guildenstern" [Holland 165]) to the rhetorical ("the
most pregnant and interesting of [the play's] linguistic doublings is undoubtedly hendiadys" [Kermode 49]) is an implicit commentary on the
compulsion to repeat.

Moreover, *Hamlet* is a play that enacts the repetition compulsion
even as it describes it. (1) The ghost of old Hamlet appears to young
Hamlet and urges him to revenge; (2) the ghost of young Hamlet,
"pale as his shirt," "with a look so piteous in purport / As if he had been
loosed out of hell / To speak of horrors" (2.1.78–91) appears to
Ophelia in her closet and, in dumb show, raising a sigh both "piteous
and profound," returns from whence he has come; (3) the ghost of
Ophelia, mad, appears before her brother Laertes and incites him to
revenge for the death of their father Polonius.

What, indeed, is revenge but the dramatization and acculturation of
the repetition compulsion?

The Anamorphic Ghost

The agent of repetition here, clearly, is the ghost. And what is a
ghost? It is a memory trace. It is the sign of something missing, something omitted, something undone. It is itself at once a question, and the
sign of putting things in question. Thus Barnardo, one of the officers
on guard duty, suggests that "this portentous figure / Comes armed
through our watch so like the King / That was and is *the question* of
these wars" (1.1.109–11). Onstage, as in the plot of a tale or story, a
ghost is the concretization of a missing presence, the sign of what is
there by not being there. "'Tis here!" "'Tis here!" "'Tis gone!" cry the
sentries (1.1.141–42).

Horatio's learned disquisition, reminding his onstage hearers and
his offstage audience simultaneously of events in classical Rome and in
Shakespeare's recent play *Julius Caesar*, offers an historical (and stage-
historical) context for the ghost:

In the most high and palmy state of Rome
A little ere the mightiest Julius fell,
The graves stood [tenantless] and the sheeted dead
Did squeak and gibber in the Roman streets.
(1.1.113–16)

Horatio associates the appearance of a ghost with the death of Julius Caesar. Jacques Lacan associates it with the castration complex, the "veiled phallus."

> The hole in the real that results from loss, sets the signifier in motion. This hole provides the place for the projection of the missing signifier, which is essential to the structure of the Other. This is the signifier whose absence leaves the Other incapable of responding to your question, the signifier that can be purchased only with your own flesh and blood, the signifier that is essentially the veiled phallus. . . . swarms of images, from which the phenomena of mourning rise, assume the place of the phallus: not only the phenomena in which each individual instance of madness manifests itself, but also those which attest to one or another of the most remarkable collective madnesses of the community of men, one example of which is brought to the fore in *Hamlet*, i.e., the ghost, that image which can catch the soul of one and all unawares when someone's departure from this life has not been accompanied by the rites that it calls for. (Lacan, *Four Concepts* 38)

What does it mean to say that the ghost takes the place of the missing signifier, the veiled phallus? The ghost — itself traditionally often veiled, sheeted, or shadowy in form — is a cultural marker of absence, a reminder of loss. Thus the very plot of *Hamlet* replicates the impossibility of the protagonist's quest: "the very source of what makes Hamlet's arm waver at every moment, is the narcissistic connection that Freud tells us about in his text on the decline of the Oedipus complex: one cannot strike the phallus, because the phallus, even the real phallus, is a *ghost*" (Lacan, "Desire" 50).

Thus, not only is the ghost the veiled phallus, but the phallus is also a ghost. Lacan takes as his point of departure Freud's essay on "The Passing of the Oedipus Complex" (1925), which explores the dilemma of the child caught between his desires and his fear of castration. When the inevitable conflict arises between the child's narcissistic investment in his own body and the "libidinal cathexis of the parent-objects," writes Freud,

> the object-cathexes are given up and replaced by identification. The authority of the father or of the parents is introjected into the ego and there forms the kernel of the super-ego, which takes its severity from the father, perpetuates his prohibition against incest, and so insures the ego against a recurrence of the libinal object-cathexis. (Freud, "The Passing" 179)

We might think that Freud's "super-ego" and Lacan's "Name-of-the-Father" would both be names for the Ghost in *Hamlet*. Yet this Lacan seems explicitly to deny when, writing on the subject of certainty in "The Unconscious and Repetition," he remarks on "the weight of the sins of the father, borne by the ghost in the myth of Hamlet, which Freud couples with the myth of Oedipus."

> The father, the Name-of-the-Father, sustains the structure of desire with the structure of the law — but the inheritance of the father is that which Kierkegaard designates for us, namely, his sin.
> Where does Hamlet's ghost come from, if not from the place from which he denounces his brother for surprising him and cutting him off in the full flower of his sins? And far from providing Hamlet with the prohibitions of the Law that would allow his desire to survive, this too ideal father is constantly being doubted. (*Four Concepts* 34–35)

The Ghost is incompletely a representative of the Law, because both he and the tale he tells allow the son to doubt. He puts in question his own being as well as his message. Is he a spirit of health or goblin damn'd? Is this the real Law? Is this the truth? As long as the Law of the father is doubted or put in question, it cannot be (or is not) internalized, not assimilated into the symbolic, and therefore blocks rather than facilitates Hamlet's own passage into the symbolic, where he will find his desire. The finding of desire is the recognition of lack, the acceptance of castration. But the doubt Hamlet experiences gives him the idea that there is something left. "It is here," says Lacan, "that Freud lays all his stress — doubt is the support of his certainty."

He goes on to explain why: "This is precisely the sign," he says, "that there is something to preserve. Doubt, then, is a sign of resistance" (*Four Concepts* 35).

To put the matter in a slightly different way: the Name-of-the-Father is the dead father. *This* father — the Ghost — isn't dead enough. The injunction to "Remember me" suggests that he is not quite dead. Hamlet must renounce him, must internalize the Law by forgetting, not by remembering. This is the only way he can be put in touch with his own desires, and with the symbolic.

But Hamlet is the poet of doubt. Polonius reads aloud to the King and Queen Hamlet's love poem to Ophelia, a paean to negation:

Doubt thou the stars are fire,
Doubt that the sun doth move,

> Doubt truth to be a liar,
> But never doubt I love.
> (2.2.116–19)

The meaning of "doubt" is itself in doubt as the phrase is repeated, shifting from something like "dispute" or "challenge" to "suspect" or "fear." The litany of doubt here is an invitation to put things in question, at the same time that it puts in question the whole procedure of putting something in question. When we consider, additionally, the very dubious "truth" value of the statement that "the stars are fire" and "the sun doth move" — both presumptions put in question by Renaissance science — we find that a verse that purports to assert certainty and closure in fact undermines that certainty in every gesture.

In his essay on *Hamlet,* Lacan thus concerns himself with Shakespeare's play as a remarkable example of the topology of human desire, "the drama of Hamlet as the man who has lost the way of his desire" (12). This is not the only case in which Lacan finds the way of his own theoretical desire by turning to a Renaissance artifact. On another occasion he examines one of the most striking of Renaissance paintings, a painting which has lately excited a good deal of commentary among literary theorists, Holbein's portrait of 1533 called *The Ambassadors.* The famous work, which contains a preeminent example of the optical device known as the anamorphosis, discloses another ghost.

> Begin by walking out of the room, in which no doubt it has long held your attention. It is then that, turning around as you leave — as the author of the *Anamorphoses* describes it — you apprehend in this form . . . What? A skull. (Lacan, *Four Concepts* 88)

The object half obscured beneath the feet of the ambassadors in the depiction of *vanitas,* the skull, cannot fail to remind us of the skull in *Hamlet* — which is itself, in act 5, followed by what Lacan in fact identifies in the *Hamlet* essay as a *vanitas:* the objects wagered in the final duel scene, he writes, are "staked against death. This is what gives their presentation the character of what is called a *vanitas* in the religious tradition" (30). Holbein's skull, which is not seen as a skull except from an exceptional or eccentric angle, is called "the phallic symbol, the anamorphic ghost." Yet, Lacan insists, what we see here is "not the phallic symbol, the anamorphic ghost, but the gaze as such, in its pulsatile, dazzling and spread out function, as it is in this picture" (*Four Concepts* 84). "Look here upon this picture, and on this" (3.4.53). "The King is a thing . . . Of nothing" (4.2.27–29). The anamorphic ghost, the embedded, embodied, and distorted figure of a ghostly skull beneath the apparently solid feet of the ambassadors — what is this but an anamorphism of the ghost and the Ghost, the Ghost (once again, uncannily, inevitably) of Hamlet's father?

Lacan goes on:

> This picture is simply what any picture is, a trap for the gaze. In any picture, it is precisely in seeking the gaze in each of its points that you will see it disappear. (89)

"This picture is simply what any picture is, a trap for the gaze." What is *this* but the play within, the "Mouse-trap," "the image of a murther done in Vienna" (3.2.225). Long treated as a dramatic presentation that encodes misdirection, putting the real play in the audience, setting up Claudius and Gertrude as the real Player King and Player Queen, the "Mouse-trap," also known as "The Murther of Gonzago," appropriates the gaze and makes it the function of the play. Again Lacan's description (in *Four Concepts*) of *The Ambassadors* is apposite:

> In Holbein's picture I showed you at once — without hiding any more than usual — the singular object floating in the foreground, which is there to be looked at, in order to catch, I would almost say, *to catch in its trap*, the observer, that is to say us. . . . The secret of this picture is given at the moment when, moving slightly away, little by little, to the left, then turning around, we see what the magical floating object signifies. It reflects our own nothingness, in the figure of the death's head. (92)

> That is not how it is presented at first. . . . At the very heart of the period in which the subject emerged and geometral optics was an object of research, Holbein makes visible for us here something that is simply the subject as annihilated — annihilated in the form that is, strictly speaking, the imaged embodiment . . . of castration, which for us, centres the whole organization of the desires through the framework of the fundamental drives. (88–89)

Holbein's portrait shows "the subject as annihilated" — which is the subject of *Hamlet*, a play situated on the cusp of the emergence of what has come to be known as the modern subject.[1] For there is a way in

[1] See Francis Barker, *The Tremulous Private Body: Essays on Subjection* (London: Methuen, 1984), 25–40, for a compelling treatment of this question. The "modern subject" constituted here, of course, is male. Indeed, the centrality of *Hamlet* to the emergence of the "modern subject" seems connected to its *lack* of a powerful (or rather, an empowered) female presence.

which *Hamlet* performs the same operation as Holbein's painting upon the gaze and the trope of *vanitas*. Its final tableau of the death's head in the graveyard scene is another critique of the subject. What then is being caught in the trap Hamlet sets for the King, the King who is a thing of nothing? Is it Claudius who is caught in the "Mouse-trap," or Hamlet as the signifier of the modern subject, already marked by negation, already dressed in black?

Lacan's own theoretical fantasy of the distortion produced by an anamorphism is determinedly phallic:

> How is it that nobody has ever thought of connecting this with . . . the effect of an erection? Imagine a tattoo traced on the sexual organ *ad hoc* in the state of repose and assuming its, if I may say so, developed form in another state.
>
> How can we not see here . . . something symbolic of the function of the lack, of the appearance of the phallic ghost? (*Four Concepts* 87–88)

"My father, in his habit as he lived!" (3.4.135) "My father's spirit — in arms!" (1.2.254) "Thou, dead corse, again in complete steel" (1.4.52). The anamorphic ghost of Old Hamlet, erected to full form by the gaze, contrasts sharply with the same figure in the "state of repose," recumbent, passive, "Sleeping within my orchard" (1.5.35), who receives the poison in the ear, the incestuous rape of a brother. The Ghost recounts the fantasy-nightmare of his own castration: "Thus was I, sleeping, by a brother's hand / Of life, of crown, of queen, at once dispatch'd, / Cut off even in the blossoms of my sin" (1.5.74–76).

This is what Hamlet has already fantasized, what he recalls in his ejaculation, "O my prophetic soul!" (1.5.40) And as in the case of Julius Caesar, the dead man turned ghost is more powerful than he was when living, precisely because he crosses boundaries, is not only transgressive but *in* transgression, a sign simultaneously of limit and of the violation of that limit, the nutshell and the bad dreams. Thus the murder empowers the Ghost and his ghostly rhetoric, the language spoken in, by, and through the Name-of-the-Father. The Hyperion-father who obsesses Hamlet in his soliloquies and in his conversations with his mother is erected from this moment, from the moment of the father's absence and death, half-guiltily acknowledged as the son's desire. The castration fantasy of the sleeping father in the orchard enacts both Hamlet's desire and its repression, which are in this moment identical. Here again Lacan is suggestive, when he writes of the impossibility of not wanting to desire:

what does *not wanting to desire* mean? The whole of analytic experience — which merely gives form to what is for each individual at the very root of his experience — shows us that not to want to desire and to desire are the same thing.

To desire involves a defensive phase that makes it identical with not wanting to desire. Not wanting to desire is wanting not to desire. (235)

This is the condition in which we encounter Hamlet for much of the play, the condition of desiring not to desire. Look where his desires have gotten him — or not gotten him. He walks out of Ophelia's closet and into Gertrude's. Here again we have closet drama, and of a high order — plays not meant to be acted. Hamlet's accusation of his mother catches her in the trap set for the gaze: "O Hamlet, speak no more! / Thou turn'st my [eyes into my very] soul, / And there I see such black and [grained] spots / As will [not] leave their tinct" (3.4.88–91). The black spot she sees is Hamlet, Hamlet as marker, Hamlet as floating signifier, as his blackness becomes metonymically a sign of mourning, of negation, of absence, of the impossible desire to tell the difference between desire and the repression of desire.

What Would Your Gracious Figure?

The ghostly phallus as anamorphosis — that is, as *form* — assumes a certain visibility, however veiled. The Name-of-the-Father, on the other hand, is a function of the signifier, of language as a system of signs rather than shapes. As we shall see, the ghost — in *Hamlet,* as well as in a number of other literary guises — presents itself not only as a trap for the gaze but also a trope for the voice.

In an influential essay on prosopopoeia as the "fiction of the voice-from-beyond-the-grave," Paul de Man writes:

It is the figure of prosopopoeia, the fiction of an apostrophe to an absent, deceased, or voiceless entity, which posits the possibility of the latter's reply, and confers upon it the power of speech. Voice assumes mouth, eye, and finally face, a chain that is manifest in the etymology of the trope's name, *prosopon poiein,* to confer a mask or a face (*prosopon*). Prosopopoeia is the trope of autobiography, by which one's name, as in the Milton poem, is made as intelligible and memorable as a face. Our topic deals with the giving and taking away of faces, with face and deface, *figure,* figuration and disfiguration. ("Autobiography" 75–76)

The quotation from Milton with which de Man is here concerned is, perhaps inevitably, the sonnet "On Shakespeare" as cited and discussed in Wordsworth's *Essays upon Epitaphs*. De Man singles out the thirteenth and fourteenth lines of this sixteen-line sonnet for special commentary.

> Then thou our fancy of itself bereaving
> Dost make us marble with too much conceiving.

Here de Man observes that the phrase "dost make us marble," in the *Essays upon Epitaphs*, "cannot fail to evoke the latent threat that inhabits prosopopoeia, namely that by making the dead speak, the symmetrical structure of the trope implies, by the same token, that the living are struck dumb, frozen in their own death" (78).

Milton's sonnet "On Shakespeare" is dated 1630 and was published in the Second Folio of Shakespeare's Plays in 1632. Merritt Y. Hughes speculates that "Milton's questionable date, 1630, suggests that the poem was written some time before its publication, possibly with the expectation that the Stratford monument instead of the Droeshout portrait would be represented as the frontispiece of the Folio" (63). Thus the reference to "Marble," as well as the "piled Stones" of line 2, the "Monument" of line 8, and the "Tomb" of line 16 would be pertinent to the memorial occasion, and to the illustration accompanying the memorial verses. "Dost make us Marble," as Hughes also points out in a note, closely resembles the apostrophe to Melancholy in *Il Penseroso*, who is urged to "Forget thyself to Marble" (1.42). In the sonnet, however — and this is part of de Man's point — it is the spectator, the reader, the mourner who becomes marble. As Michel Riffaterre comments, paraphrasing de Man's argument:

> Chiasmus, the symmetrical structure of prosopopoeia, entails that, by making the dead speak, the living are struck dumb — they too become the monument. Prosopopoeia thus stakes out a figural space for the chiasmic interpretation: either the subject will take over the object, or it will be penetrated by the object. (112)

But in the case of the Stratford monument (or indeed, though less neatly, the Droeshout portrait), this exchange of properties has already taken place. The voice of the dead Shakespeare pictured on the tomb (and in the sonnet) speaks through the plays that succeed them in the Folio.

The question of whether the Ghost will speak is a central preoccupation of the whole first act of *Hamlet* and has a great deal to do with the way it is described and addressed. "It would be spoke to," says

Barnardo. Horatio, as a "scholar," is asked to do the job. Popular belief had it that "A ghost has not the power to speak till it has been first spoken to; so that, notwithstanding the urgency of the business on which it may come, everything must stand still till the person visited can find sufficient courage to speak to it" (Grose, qtd. in Jenkins 424). Horatio valiantly tries to interview it on two occasions in scene 1, urged on by Marcellus's apt invitation, "Question it, Horatio":

> HORATIO: What art thou that usurp'st this time of night,
>   Together with that fair and warlike form
>   In which the majesty of buried Denmark
>   Did sometimes march? By heaven I charge thee speak!
> MARCELLUS: It is offended.
> BARNARDO: See, it stalks away!
> HORATIO: Stay! Speak, speak, I charge thee speak!
>   *Exit Ghost*
>   (1.1.46–51)
> HORATIO: Stay, illusion!
>   If thou hast any sound or use of voice,
>   Speak to me.
>   If there be any good thing to be done
>   That may to thee do ease, and grace to me,
>   Speak to me.
>   If thou art privy to thy country's fate,
>   Which happily foreknowing may avoid,
>   O speak!
>   Or if thou hast uphoarded in thy life
>   Extorted treasure in the womb of earth,
>   For which, they say, your spirits oft walk in death,
>   Speak of it, stay and speak!
>   (1.1.127–39)

The cock crows, and though Barnardo thinks "it was about to speak," it starts away. We may notice that the constant pronoun here is *it*, not *he*, and that the "apparition" is carefully described as "*like* the King," as one who "usurp'st" the time of the night (a loaded word in the circumstances) and the "fair and warlike form" of the dead King, "buried Denmark," was wont to appear. "It" = King Hamlet. "It" is a space of conjecture, to be questioned. But the proof is to come, with the imparting of this tale to "young Hamlet." "For, upon my life," says Horatio, "This spirit, dumb to us, will speak to him" (170–71).

Cautiously, we may return to de Man's definition of prosopopoeia, the master trope, the trope of tropes: "the fiction of the voice-from-beyond-the-grave" (77), "the fiction of an apostrophe to an absent, deceased, or voiceless entity, which posits the possibility of the latter's reply and confers upon it the power of speech" (75–76). This description not only coincides with the dramatic circumstances of the first scene of *Hamlet,* it exemplifies it. "Our topic deals with the giving and taking away of faces, with face and deface, *figure,* figuration and disfiguration" (76).

When Hamlet is informed by Horatio of the appearance of "a figure like your father" (1.2.199), he asks, inevitably, "Did you not speak to it?" But the other question, on which he is curiously insistent, is whether the sentries saw the apparition's *face:* "saw you not his face?" "look'd he frowningly?" "Pale, or red?" "And fix'd his eyes upon you?" (229–33). We know that the Elizabethans often used *its* and *his* interchangeably but still there is something striking about Hamlet's recurrent use of *he* and *his* after all the *its* of scene 1. Hamlet himself will return to the neuter pronoun after this exchange ("Perchance 'twill walk again" [242]; "If it assume my noble father's person / I'll speak to it" [243–44]) so that the brief gendering of the figure comes as a moment of achieved personating or animation, to be followed by a return to the objectification of *it,* which, as the *Oxford English Dictionary* tells us, is used "now only of things without life." Is the Ghost animate or inanimate? Certainly it is animated — but the he/it distinction marks an act of naming that is an act of choice, confirmed when Hamlet sees the Ghost face to face:

> HORATIO: Look, my lord, it comes!
> HAMLET: Angels and ministers of grace defend us!
>   Be thou a spirit of health, or goblin damn'd,
>   Bring with thee airs from heaven, or blasts from hell,
>   Be thy intents wicked, or charitable,
>   Thou com'st in such a questionable shape
>   That I will speak to thee. I'll call thee Hamlet,
>   King, father, royal Dane. O, answer me!
>   (1.4.38–45)

Critical attention has usually been focused on the spirit/goblin, heaven/hell problem here — is this a false ghost or a true ghost, a delusion or a sign? But what seems equally central is the structure of address. Hamlet *chooses* to name the Ghost with those names which are for him most problematical: King, father, royal Dane.

Hamlet addresses the "questionable shape" and brings it to speech, and therefore to a kind of life. Does he, in doing so, fulfill de Man's dire prophecy: "the latent threat that inhabits prosopopoeia, namely that by making the dead speak, the symmetrical structure of the trope implies, by the same token, that the living are struck dumb, frozen in their own death?" (78).

In the fiction of address, what Jonathan Culler suggestively terms "this sinister reciprocity" (148) is always present *as* a threat. But if it is latent in lyric, it may become manifest in drama, and in *Hamlet* it does. *This* is the nature of revenge in *Hamlet*, the unremitting demand of the Ghost, leading to Hamlet's final paradoxical declaration, "I am dead." De Man elsewhere points out that "the object of the apostrophe is only addressed in terms of the activity that it provokes in the addressing subject" (de Man, *Allegories* 29; see also Chase 82–112). Our attention is focused on the *speaker*. Culler interestingly comments on this argument that "apostrophe involves a drama of 'the one mind's modifications'" (148), and I would like to take his metaphor here seriously — for it is precisely a *dramatic* situation that is produced by this structure of address, which is why it is plausible to say that Hamlet constructs his own Ghost, makes use of the "gracious figure" of his father by utilizing the equally gracious figure of prosopopoeia. Since apostrophe and prosopopoeia so often involve a sensation of loss (not only in the post-Enlightenment lyric as observed by commentators like de Man, Culler, and Hartman, but in the elegiac tradition and the epitaphic texts of the Renaissance), the fiction of address itself performs a paradoxical function, not unlike that performed by Hamlet's "I am dead": it instates that which it mourns, makes present that which it declares absent and lost. "The poem," says Culler, "denies temporality in the very phrases — recollections — that acknowledge its claims," the narrator can "find, in his poetic ability to invoke [the mourned object] as a transcendent presence, a sense of his own transcendent continuity" (152). This is the transaction that takes place in *Hamlet*. "I am dead" and "I am alive to contemplate and mourn — and avenge — the dead" coexist in the same sensibility, in the same moment of naming. And this capacity, on the part of apostrophe and prosopopoeia, is, exactly, *dramatic:* "Apostrophe is not the representation of an event; if it works, it produces a fictive, discursive event" (153). In *Hamlet* (as in *The Winter's Tale*) the effect of the dramatic mode is to dis-figure the trope of address to a dead or inanimate object, and ventriloquize its response as part of the ongoing dramatic action. "Marry, how? tropically?" (*Hamlet* 3.2.224)

The Ghost is not — or not only — an instance of the unmetaphoring[2] of prosopopoeia. It is also the *manifestation* of that "latent threat" implicit in the trope itself. The rhetorical figure ("a figure like your father," 1.2.199), under the operation of the uncanny, comes to life, is dis- or un-figured ("then saw you not his face" [1.2.229]), and exacts its sinister reciprocity: "that the living are . . . frozen in their own death" (de Man, "Autobiography" 78).

Begging the Question

Uncanny reciprocity is thus created by the transference of death to the living and voice to the dead. But what does the dead voice say? What kind of commandment does the ghostly father in *Hamlet* hand down?

The Ghost's commandment comes in the form of a double imperative: "Remember me!" and "revenge!" What I will attempt to demonstrate here is that this double imperative is in fact a double bind. But first, a look at the first part of the commandment, the imperative to remember.

Hamlet is indeed a play obsessively concerned with remembering and forgetting. Not only does the Ghost in his first appearance call upon Hamlet to "Remember me," and provoke his son to take that "commandement" as his "word" (1.5.95–110); when he appears again in the Queen's closet he makes the same demand, this time in the negative: "Do not forget!" (3.4.110). Claudius, the new King, acknowledges that "Though yet of Hamlet our dear brother's death / The memory be green" (1.2.1–2) and a fit circumstance for grief, yet insists that "we with wisest sorrow think on him / Together with remembrance of ourselves" (6–7). Hamlet, in soliloquy, is pained by the memory of his mother's passionate attachment to his father: "Heaven and earth, / Must I remember? Why, she should hang on him / As if increase of appetite had grown / By what it fed on" (1.2.142–45). And "O God, a beast that wants discourse of reason / Would have mourn'd longer" (150–51). In a sardonic mood he laments the frailty of memory two months after his father's death (and his mother's remarriage):

> O heavens, die two months ago, and not forgotten yet? Then there's hope a great man's memory may outlive his life half a year, but, by'r lady, 'a must build churches then, or else shall 'a suffer

[2]For "unmetaphoring," see Rosalie Colie 11.

not thinking on, with the hobby-horse, whose epitaph is, "For O,
for O, the hobby-horse is forgot."

$(3.2.122-27)^3$

When he comes to her closet, Gertrude, chiding him for his flippancy,
asks "Have you forgot me?" and receives a stinging reply: "No, by the
rood, not so; / You are the Queen, your husband's brother's wife, /
And would it were not so, you are my mother" (3.4.14–16). When in
the same scene, after the Ghost's injunction: "Do not forget!" Hamlet
reminds her that he must go to England, she answers, "Alack, / I had
forgot" (200–01).

Ophelia herself is constantly associated with the need to remember.
Laertes urges her to "remember well" (1.3.84) his cautions about
Hamlet's untrustworthiness as a suitor, and she answers that " 'Tis in my
memory lock'd" (85). In the scene where she is "loosed" to Hamlet in
the lobby he says to her, "Nymph, in thy orisons / Be all my sins
rememb'red" (3.1.88–89) and she offers him "remembrances of yours
/ That I have longed long to redeliver" (92–93). Her next offerings of
remembrance will be the flower-giving, when she gives her brother
"rosemary, that's for remembrance; pray you, love, remember. And
there is pansies, that for thoughts" (4.5.174–75). "A document in madness, thoughts and remembrance fitted," he concludes (4.5.176–77).

Forgetting, and especially forgetting oneself, is closely connected to
manners, but also to something more. Hamlet greets Horatio, whom
he has not seen since Wittenberg, with "Horatio — or I do forget myself" (1.2.161). Much later in the play he apologizes for grappling with
Laertes: "I am very sorry, good Horatio, / That to Laertes I forgot
myself, / For by the image of my cause I see / The portraiture of his"
(5.2.75–78). At the beginning of act 5 scene 2 he takes up his tale of the
voyage to England, checking to see if Horatio "remember[s] all the circumstance" (2). "Remember it, my lord!" Horatio exclaims (3).
Hamlet describes the moment on shipboard when he opened Claudius's death-warrant, "making so bold, / My fears forgetting manners,
to [unseal] / Their grand commission" (5.2.16–18), and comments on
his pretense of aristocratic carelessness: "I once did hold it, as our
statists do, / A baseness to write fair, and labor'd much / How to

---

^{3} "For O, for O, the hobby-horse is forgot' was the refrain of a popular song. . . .
From its frequent use we seem to have an instance of a catch-phrase continuing in popularity after the original point of it had been lost. What is certain is that the hobby-horse,
while very much remembered, became a byword for being forgotten and as such the occasion for numerous jokes in Elizabethan plays" (Jenkins 500–01).

forget that learning, but, sir, now / It did me yeman's service" (5.2.33–36). "Antiquity forgot, custom not known" (4.5.104), the rabble call for Laertes to be king. Hamlet presses Osric to forgo courtesy and to put his hat back on his head: "I beseech you remember" (5.2.101). Hamlet's dying request is for Horatio to tell his story, and in the final moments Fortinbras asserts that he has "some rights of memory in this kingdom" (371) which, with the support of Hamlet's "dying voice," he is now prepared to claim.

Recent critical discussions of the two Hegelian terms for memory, *Erinnerung* and *Gedächtnis*, can shed light on the problem we are considering, the relationship between memory and revenge. Initiated by Paul de Man in an essay on "Sign and Symbol in Hegel's *Aesthetics*," the discourse on memory has since developed in a number of provocative directions (see Chase 113–26).

Erinnerung, ("recollection") as de Man defines it, after Hegel, is "the inner gathering and preserving of experience" ("Sign and Symbol" 771), while *Gedächtnis* ("memory") is "the learning by rote of *names*, or of words considered as names, and it can therefore not be separated from the notation, the inscription, or the writing down of these names. In order to remember, one is forced to write down what one is likely to forget" (772).

How can this distinction help us to understand the complexity of Hamlet's mandate to turn his mourning into revenge?

When Hamlet first appears on stage, he is beset by *Erinnerung*, interiorizing recollection, the consciousness of loss. Loss is what he thinks he *has* — not just "the trappings and the suits of woe," but "that within which passes show" (1.2.86, 85). He will not relinquish this memory, which he hugs to himself. Claudius has a number of motives for calling his "obstinate condolement" "a course / Of impious stubbornness" (1.2.93–94), but he is not altogether wrong. Loss is what Hamlet has instead of both mother and father — and loss is what he must lose, or learn to live with.

Freud describes such immersion, when it reaches the state of melancholia, as a kind of fetishization, a privatizing and husbanding of grief, a refusal to let go (Freud, "Mourning"). In Hamlet this condition is exemplified by the first soliloquy, "O that this too too sallied flesh would melt" (1.2.129), with its longing for dissolution, its flirtation with self-slaughter, and its fragmented and particularized memory of both his father and his mother.

The encounter with the Ghost disrupts his absorption in the past as recollection. Abruptly Hamlet is wrenched from *Erinnerung* to

Gedächtnis, from symbol to sign, or, to use de Man's terms, from symbol to allegory. From this point forward he is compelled to constitute the past by memorization, by inscription, by writing down.

> Remember thee!
> Ay, thou poor ghost, whiles memory holds a seat
> In this distracted globe. Remember thee!
> Yea, from the table of my memory
> I'll wipe away all trivial fond records,
> All saws of books, all forms, all pressures past
> That youth and observation copied there,
> And thy commandement all alone shall live
> Within the book and volume of my brain,
> Unmix'd with baser matter. Yes, by heaven!
> O most pernicious woman!
> O villain, villain, smiling, damned villain!
> My tables — meet it is I set it down
> That one may smile, and smile, and be a villain!
> At least I am sure it may be so in Denmark! [*He writes.*]
> So, uncle, there you are. Now to my word:
> It is, 'Adieu, adieu! remember me.'
> I have sworn't.
>   (1.5.95–112)

The "tables" of act 1 scene 5 are writing tables, somewhat like Freud's "Mystic Writing-Pad,"[4] which is, in turn, somewhat like the operations of memory as inscription of memory, *Gedächtnis.* Polonius alludes to a similar kind of table when he repudiates the role of "desk or table-book" (2.2.136) in his conversation with the Queen, announcing that he could not, like such inanimate objects, merely remain "mute and dumb" (137) when he learned of Hamlet's overmastering love for Ophelia. Polonius's choice of mute and dumb objects is suggestive, since both desk and table-book are surfaces for writing. His refusal to "play" the desk or table-book denies the possibility of prosopopoeia, of a speaking record. Thus while Polonius declines to be such a table, Hamlet takes dictation from the Ghost so as to carry about with him the transcribed and inscribed "word," whether his "tables" are tables of wax, of paper, or of memory.

The writing tables, then, must take the place of another kind of

[4]See Freud, "A Note upon the 'Mystic Writing-Pad,'" *General Psychological Theory* 207–12; Derrida, "Freud and the Scene of Writing," *Writing and Difference* 196–231.

"table" in *Hamlet,* the table at which one eats and drinks, the kind of table associated not with *Gedächtnis* but with *Erinnerung.* For the language of *Erinnerung,* of interiorization, in this play is the language of digestion, of eating: "the funeral bak'd-meats / Did coldly furnish forth the marriage tables" (1.2.180–81); "Heaven and earth, / Must I remember? Why, she should hang on him / As if increase of appetite had grown / By what it fed on" (143–45). Even the famous soliloquy on the sullied-sallied-solid flesh, the wish that the flesh would "melt / Thaw, and resolve itself into a dew!" (1.2.129–30) reflects this burden of interiorization. Hamlet, unable either to escape or to complete the desired *Erinnerung,* is caught between cannibalism and anorexia, spewing forth in language what he cannot swallow, taunting Claudius with a reminder of "how a king may go a progress through the guts of a beggar" (4.3.29–30). Caught, that is, until he is catapulted into an even more difficult trap by the double pull of the paternal imperative, an imperative so indigestible that it must be written down.

Jacques Derrida, writing on memory and mourning, writing in memory of and in mourning for Paul de Man, suggests that *Gedächtnis* and *Erinnerung* are central to "the possibility of mourning," and that "the inscription of memory" is "an effacement of interiorizing recollection" (Derrida, *Memoires* 56). In the "tables" speech, Hamlet limns precisely the effacement of *Erinnerung* by *Gedächtnis.* By writing down the Ghost's "commandment" he both inscribes and constitutes the paternal story of a past which, in its pastness, is necessarily fictive, since it is only experienced *as* past, as tale, as narrative.

But what, exactly, does Hamlet write? (Or does he write at all? Critics and editors divide on this question, as to whether he whips out a table or mimes the taking of dictation.) What he claims to record is "thy commandment," and the conjunction of "table" and "commandment" is suggestive. Implicit in the scene, but not always explicitly noted, is its relationship to the moment in Exodus when God gives to Moses "two tables of testimony, tables of stone, written with the finger of God" (Exod. 31:18). In the Mosaic case, *God* writes, and Moses, angry with the idolatrous Israelites dancing about the golden calf, casts the tables out of his hands and breaks them. Moses then returns to God and pleads with Him to show him His glory. And God says to him, "Thou canst not see my face: for there shall no man see me, and live" (Exod. 33:20). Contrary to the case of prosopopoeia, there must here be voice without face, speech without face. And God commands Moses to hew "two tables of stone like unto the first: and I will write upon *these* tables the words that were in the first tables, which thou brakest" (34:1). The tables that Moses brings to the Israelites, the foundations of the Law, are thus themselves copies, the second version written by God in substitution for the first, the originals, which were broken, which were lost. Moses breaks the tablets because the people were breaking the commandments they did not yet have. Even this law, the great original, is a copy and a substitution.

When we turn our attention once again to Hamlet's tables, we can see the operation of substitution here through erasure, the inscription on the tables of "thy commandment," which is — to revenge? to remember? to do the one through the agency of the other? We may notice that the same word, "commandment," is used to denote Hamlet's other act of inscription as substitution, the "new commission" that sends Rosencrantz and Guildenstern, instead of Hamlet, to be executed in England. The Ambassador from England arrives upon the bloody scene at the close of the play and comments — in a figure that recalls the murder of King Hamlet — "The ears are senseless that should give us hearing, / To tell him his commandment is fulfill'd, / That Rosencrantz and Guildenstern are dead" (5.2.351–53), and Horatio, taking "his commandment" to refer to Claudius's original intent, replies, "He never gave commandement for their death" (356).

Hamlet's writing is thus already a copy, a substitution, a revision of an original that does not show its face in the text. Whether it be the revisionary "tables," the interpolated "dozen or sixteen lines," or the redirected "new commission" signed with a usurped signature, Hamlet's writing is always, in fact, ghost writing.

Forgetting the Hobbyhorse

What, then, are we to make of the reminders of remembering, the cautions against forgetting, of which the Ghost's two visitations are the benchmarks? It might seem natural to assume that remembering would facilitate reparation, restitution, and recuperation — that the way to rectify an error, or expiate a crime, is through a memory of the act, and even of the historical circumstances that produced, provoked, or surrounded the act. Yet this is precisely what the play of *Hamlet* does *not* tell us. Rather than facilitating action, remembering seems to block it, by becoming itself an obsessive concern, in effect fetishizing the remembered persons, events, or commands so that they become virtually impossible to renounce or relinquish. Our contemporary sense of "hobbyhorse" as a constant preoccupation sums up this fetishizing instinct fairly well: the hobbyhorse must *be* forgot in order for action to follow.

Consider the Ghost's two visitations and his reiterated command. The Ghost asks Hamlet to do two things: to remember and to revenge. Repeatedly on the first occasion he urges revenge. "If thou didst ever thy dear father love . . . Revenge his foul and most unnatural murther" (1.5.23–25). "Bear it not" (81). "Let not the royal bed of Denmark be / A couch for luxury and damned incest" (82–83). Hamlet is to "[pursue] this act" (84) to revenge his father's murder, while sparing his mother any punishment: "Taint not thy mind, nor let thy soul contrive / Against thy mother aught" (85–86). But he is *to act*, he is *to revenge*. "Adieu, adieu, adieu! remember me" (111). Remember and revenge. But these two injunctions are not only different from one another, they are functionally at odds. For the more Hamlet remembers, the more he meditates the "word" that he takes as the Ghost's "commandment" and inscribes on his tables, the more he is trapped in a round of obsessive speculation. Far from goading him to action, the Ghost's twice iterated instruction, "Remember me," "do not forget," impedes that action, impedes revenge. What Hamlet needs to do is not to remember, but to *forget*.

> Imagine the extremest possible case of a man who did not possess the power of forgetting at all and who was thus condemned to see everywhere a state of becoming: such a man would no longer believe in his own being, would no longer believe in himself, would see everything flowing asunder in moving points and would lose himself in this stream of becoming. . . . Forgetting is essential to action of any kind . . . it is altogether impossible to love at all without forgetting. Or, to express my theme even more simply: there is a degree of sleeplessness, or of rumination, of the historical sense, which is harmful and ultimately fatal to the living thing, whether this living thing be a man or a people or a culture.
>
> To determine . . . the boundary at which *the past has to be forgotten if it is not to become the gravedigger of the present,* one would have to know exactly how great the *plastic* power of a man, a people, or a culture is: I mean by plastic power the capacity to develop out of oneself in one's own way, to transform and incorporate into oneself what is past and foreign, to heal wounds, to replace what has been lost, to recreate broken moulds. (62; emphasis added)

The "boundary at which the past has to be forgotten if it is not to become the gravedigger of the present." This is Nietzsche in "The Use and Abuse of History." Nietzsche's grave-digger is also Hamlet's, a talismanic figure who digs up the pate of a politician, the skull of a lawyer, the bones of a great buyer of land, and jowls them indifferently to the ground (5.1.72–105). It is Hamlet, on this occasion, who "consider[s] too curiously" (192), who speculates about the noble dust of Alexander stopping a bunghole, and "Imperious Caesar, dead and turn'd to clay" who "Might stop a hole to keep the wind away" (199–200). Hamlet, who is still prey to the "rumination, of the historical sense, which is harmful and ultimately fatal to the living thing, whether this living thing be a man or a people or a culture" ("Use and Abuse" 62). The grave-digger himself marks Hamlet's boundaries. He came to his trade "that day that our last king Hamlet overcame Fortinbras" (134–35), "that very day that young Hamlet was born" (138). Harold Jenkins in the Arden edition of *Hamlet* remarks,

> What matters is that when Hamlet came into the world a man began to dig graves and has now been at it for a lifetime. . . . As Hamlet's talk with the grave-digger thus links the grave-digger's occupation with the terms of Hamlet's life, will it not seem to us that the hero has come face to face with his own destiny? (554)

Yet the grave-digger has the same uncanny valence as the Mower in Marlowe's *Edward II;* he is the figuration of Hamlet's mortality, as the skull of Yorick is the fragmented emblem of that mortality. Re-membering is here reconstituted through a process of dis-membering, of disarticulation of parts, of dislocation of bones and members.

But there is more that is uncanny in this passage of Nietzsche, for it seems throughout to be haunted by the ghost of *Hamlet.* "I have striven," he writes in the foreword to "The Use and Abuse of History," "to depict a feeling by which I am constantly tormented; I *revenge myself upon it* by handing it over to the public" (Nietzsche 59; emphasis added). "It" is the abuse of history, the preoccupation with the past that can inhibit life, making it "stunted and degenerate" (ibid.). Nietzsche's *revenge* is to be a "meditation" he describes as "untimely" — but then it must *be* untimely in order to be effective: "for I do not know what meaning classical studies could have for our time if they were not un-timely — that is to say, acting counter to our time and thereby acting on our time and, let us hope, for the benefit of a time to come" (100). It is not, I think, entirely fanciful to wish to juxtapose these remarks to Hamlet's famous *cri de coeur,* "The time is out of joint — O cursed spite, / That ever I was born to set it right!" (1.5.188–89). And we may perhaps go further and suggest that Nietzsche in this exclamation, this profession of revenge — like Hamlet in his own professions of belated-ness and determination — is himself a revenant, a ghost, a figure dislo-

cated in and from history ("classical studies"; "earlier times") and constituted (or self-constituted) as not only critic but critique.

This is Hamlet's use of the classical past as well as Nietzsche's; the
Pyrrhus play ("Aeneas's Tale to Dido"); the constant reminders that his
father was Hyperion to Claudius's satyr, that he himself is confronted
with a choice of Hercules — these too are uses of history that verge
upon the abusive because they place Hamlet rhetorically on the margins
of history rather than in the midst of historical process. It is only when
he writes himself back into that process, with the agency of his father's
signet ring, later claiming his place in history ("This is I, / Hamlet the
Dane!" [5.1.243–44]) by an act of self-naming, that he moves beyond
untimely meditation, the belatedness of soliloquy, toward action. For
action is inextricably bound with forgetting.

> Consider the cattle, grazing as they pass you by: they do not know
> what is meant by yesterday or today, they leap about, eat, rest, di-
> gest, leap about again, and so from morn till night and from day
> to day, fettered to the moment and its pleasure or displeasure, and
> thus neither melancholy nor bored. This is a hard sight for a man
> to see. . . . A human being may well ask an animal: "Why do you
> not speak to me of your happiness but only stand and gaze at
> me?" The animal would like to answer, and say: "The reason is I
> always forget what I was going to say" — but then he forgot this
> answer, too, and stayed silent: so that the human being was left
> wondering.
> But he also wonders at himself, that he cannot learn to forget
> but clings relentlessly to the past: however far and fast he may run,
> this chain runs with him. And it is a matter for wonder: a mo-
> ment, *now here and then gone*, nothing before it came, again noth-
> ing after it has gone, nonetheless *returns as a ghost* and disturbs
> the peace of a later moment. (Nietzsche 61; emphasis added)

"'Tis here." "'Tis here." "'Tis gone." Nietzsche's meditation, Nietzsche's revenge, incorporates (or "incorpses")[5] *Hamlet* as a manifestation of the haunting presentness of the past. Hamlet remembers;
Polonius forgets. "What was I about to say? / By the mass, I was about
to say something. / Where did I leave?" Reynaldo: "At 'closes in the
consequence'" (2.1.49–51). What Polonius forgets is precisely what
closes in the consequence: causality, history. "'The reason is I always
forget what I was going to say' — but then he forgot this answer, too."

---

[5]See Margaret W. Ferguson, "*Hamlet:* Letters and Spirits," Parker and Hartman
302.

Polonius forgets: Hamlet remembers. Hamlet's own meditation on revenge and bestial oblivion is so close to Nietzsche's that we may wonder
whether Nietzsche's complex of ideas, from revenge to the ghost to the
beast to the grave-digger, does not derive in some way from Shakespeare's great untimely meditation, and in particular, from the soliloquy
in act 4 scene 4:

> How all occasions do inform against me,
> And spur my dull revenge! What is a man,
> If his chief good and market of his time
> Be but to sleep and feed? a beast, no more.
> Sure He that made us with such large discourse,
> Looking before and after, gave us not
> That capability and godlike reason
> To fust in us unus'd. Now whether it be
> Bestial oblivion, or some craven scruple
> Of thinking too precisely on th' event —
> A thought which quarter'd hath but one part wisdom
> And ever three parts coward — I do not know
> Why yet I live to say, "This thing's to do,"
> Sith I have cause, and will, and strength, and means
> To do't.
>   (4.4.32–46)

Now, what does it mean to say that Nietzsche's meditation on revenge and forgetting situates itself as a rewriting of *Hamlet*? Is this
merely a way of repositioning Shakespeare as the great authority, the
great original, in whose work all ideas, all controversies, all contestations
are already present? Is Shakespeare the *locus classicus* (or the *locus
renascens*) of the move to place subversion within containment? And/or
is *Hamlet* — as I have suggested above — the play that articulates, or
represents, the construction of the modern subject?

I think that the last of these questions can be answered, tentatively,
in the affirmative, and that this accounts at least in part for the befuddle-
ment and irritation some contemporary critics demonstrate when they
are asked to come face to face with this play. It is too close to us. What
look like critiques, analyses, implementations of *Hamlet* to make some
other point (philosophical, political, psychoanalytic) dissolve to bring us
back to the play itself, not as referent, but as origin — or marker of the
unknowability of origins. That critics write their own Hamlets, as, for
example, Coleridge, Goethe, and T. S. Eliot, have done, is something of
a commonplace for us. That they are *compelled* to do so — that this is
their compulsion to repeat — because the play limns a preconscious

moment that can only be retrieved *through* repetition and not through
memory, reinscribes the paradox of the play as itself a *mise en abyme*
without (exactly, precisely, without) the primal scene at which it is constantly hinting, and which we are constantly on the brink of remembering, falsely, fictively. The ghost of *Hamlet* — the ghost *in Hamlet* — is
this illusion of the articulation of our own perception of desire and its
denial, our own conviction that what Freud, in speaking of dreams,
called "the spot where it reaches down to the unknown" *can* be
plumbed, even if it is found to be a hollow void. *Hamlet* is the play of
undecidability. But/and it is the play of the uncanny, the play in which
the *Heimlich* and the *Unheimlich* are opposite and identical, the play
that demonstrates that you can't go home again. Why? Because you *are*
home — and home is not what you have always and belatedly (from
*un*home) fantasized it to be. Hence, once again, forgetting and remembering. And revenge. In other words, *transference*.

Indeed, it is not surprising to think of *Hamlet* as the story of an
analysis, for what is analysis but a contemporary restaging of the pattern
of deferral and substitution that we recognize in *Hamlet*? If our question, or one of our questions, concerns the relationship of memory and
revenge, it is here answered, at least in part, by the compulsion to repeat. "As long as he is under treatment he never escapes from this compulsion to repeat; at last one understands that it is his way of remembering." This compulsion to repeat, "which is now replacing the impulse to
remember," encompasses the killing (and not killing) of fathers, the accusation of women, the plays within the play, dumb show, and talking
cure. The transference-neurosis is induced as a kind of therapeutic substitution, which *can* be cured or worked on because it is present rather
than lost, and because it is, in some sense, play. "We admit it into the
transference as to a playground" (Freud, "Further Recommendations"
160–61).

> The transference thus forms a kind of intermediary realm between
> illness and real life, through which the journey from the one to
> the other must be made. The new state of mind has absorbed all
> the features of the illness; it represents, however, an artificial ill-
> ness which is at every point accessible to our interventions. It is at
> the same time a piece of real life, but adapted to our purposes by
> specially favourable conditions, and it is of a provisional character.
> From the repetition-reactions which are exhibited in the transfer-
> ence the familiar paths lead back to the awakening of the memo-
> ries, which yield themselves without difficulty after the resistances
> have been overcome. (165)

This is a reasonably appropriate description of the role played by the play-within-the-play in *Hamlet,* and also by Hamlet's role as chorus (analyst) of the "Mouse-trap" (or even of the first Player's Pyrrhus speech). Real and provisional, "adapted to our purposes" with or without the addition of a dozen or sixteen lines, close enough to the original or originary situation (at least as it is fantasized or retold) yet safely "artificial" and thus able to be discounted or bounded, the play-within-the-play does exhibit many of the symptoms of transference-neurosis, as in fact do the soliloquies that problematize the *activity* of others (Fortinbras, the First Player, Pyrrhus, even Laertes) as contrasted with the ruminative passivity of Hamlet.

The connection between repressed thoughts and memories and the compulsion to repeat is also strongly argued in *Beyond the Pleasure Principle* (1920), and it is not surprising that both of these Freudian texts have been used by narratologists to develop strategies of narrative displacement, substitution, and delay. In *Beyond the Pleasure Principle* Freud again states that "the compulsion to repeat must be ascribed to the unconscious repressed" (41) and comments on the odd but undeniable fact that people often compulsively repeat things that are not, and seem never to have been, pleasurable. How then is the compulsion to repeat related to the pleasure principle?

> The artistic play and artistic imitation carried out by adults, which, unlike children's, are aimed at an audience, do not spare the spectators (for instance, in tragedy) the most painful experiences and yet can be felt by them as highly enjoyable. This is convincing proof that, even under the dominance of the pleasure principle, there are ways and means enough of making what is in itself unpleasurable into a subject to be recollected and worked over in the mind. (37)

Tragedy — whether exemplified by *Hamlet* or by "The Murther of Gonzago" — thus can produce pleasure when it is received as a repetition. But if the illusion represented by the players conduces to pleasure when categorized as play, what of the kind of compulsion to repeat that results in a different sort of illusion — the terrifying spectacle of the ghost? "Stay, illusion!" (1.1.127). Three times in *Beyond the Pleasure Principle* Freud evokes the image of some "daemonic" power produced by the repetition-compulsion.

> What psycho-analysis reveals in the transference phenomena of neurotics can also be observed in the lives of some normal people. The impression they give is of being pursued by a malignant fate

or possessed by some "daemonic" power; but psycho-analysis has always taken the view that their fate is for the most part arranged by themselves and determined by early infantile influences. (44)

The manifestations of a compulsion to repeat (which we have described as occurring in the early activities of infantile mental life as well as among the events of psycho-analytic treatment) exhibit to a high degree an instinctual character and, when they act in opposition to the pleasure principle, give the appearance of some "daemonic" force at work. (65)

It may be presumed, too, that when people unfamiliar with analysis feel an obscure fear — a dread of rousing something that, so they feel, is better left sleeping — what they are afraid of at bottom is the emergence of this compulsion with its hint of possession by some "daemonic" power. (67)

In the terms of *Hamlet,* this "daemonic" force or power, if it is to be ascribed to or even personified by the Ghost, is the compulsion to repeat which repression substitutes for remembering. Confronted with the Ghost's command, "Remember me!" Hamlet remembers that he is commanded to remember, but displaces that which he is unable to remember into compulsive behavior of a kind that translates *him* into a daemon, into a ghost. Thus he appears as a silent spectacle in Ophelia's closet, pale, sighing, as if "loosed out of hell" (2.1.80). The passivity of Hamlet, his apparent position of being acted on rather than acting, is also commensurate with the impression of being possessed, while in fact giving the name of "possession" to the repetition compulsion.

Turning the Tables

For Hamlet himself, who or what is the Ghost? We could say that for Hamlet the Ghost is — or at least, is supposed to be — what Lacan calls the *sujet supposé savoir,* the subject who is supposed to know. "As soon as the subject who is supposed to know exists somewhere," says Lacan, "there is transference" (*Four Concepts* 232). Who is, who *can* be, invested with such authority, such being-in-knowledge? For Lacan, "If there is someone to whom one can apply there can be only one such person. This *one* was Freud, while he was alive" (*Four Concepts* 232). What a muted accolade is this — "This *one was* Freud, while he was alive." And now that he is dead? Lacan does not say, or does not say directly, who is the new *one,* the new *sujet supposé savoir.* But does he need to? The King is dead, long live . . . And so in *Hamlet,* also, the investment of authority is not without a sense of question and cost. Can the Ghost be the subject who is supposed to know only *because* he is dead? "O my prophetic soul," cries Hamlet (1.5.40). The Ghost is supposed to know — that is, to confirm — what Hamlet did not know he knew.

"The analyst," says Lacan, "occupies this place in as much as he is the object of the transference. Experience shows us that when the subject enters analysis, he is far from giving the analyst this place" (*Four Concepts* 232). Then when does Hamlet enter into a transferential relationship with the Ghost? When, precisely, he is given to think that his own authority is confirmed. Notice how much like an analytic situation is Hamlet's own response to this uncanny consultant.

> Given that analysis may, on the part of certain subjects, be put in question at its very outset, and suspected of being a lure — how is it that around this *being mistaken* something stops? Even the psycho-analyst put in question is credited at some point with a certain infallibility, which means that certain intentions, betrayed, perhaps, by some chance gesture, will sometimes be attributed even to the analyst put in question, *"You did that to test me!"* (234)

For Hamlet's testing of the Ghost ("The spirit that I have seen / May be a [dev'l] and the [dev'l] hath power / T' assume a pleasing shape . . . yea, and perhaps, / Out of my weakness and my melancholy, / As he is very potent with such spirits, / Abuses me to damn me. I'll have grounds / More relative than this" [2.2.578–84]) is really in many ways the provision of a test for himself. Does he believe the Ghost, or not? Does the Ghost have authority?

The Ghost that comes "in such a questionable shape" (1.4.43) is immediately put in question, is in fact, as we have begun to see, the shape or sign of putting things in question. We could almost designate him as is done in Spanish with an inverted question mark before each appearance, before each utterance, and with another question mark following each. Plain as the Ghost's utterances may seem, Hamlet *wants* them to be a riddle, a problem, a question.

> Be thy intents wicked, or charitable,
> Thou com'st in such a questionable shape
> That I will speak to thee. I'll call thee Hamlet,
> King, father, royal Dane.
> (1.4.42–45)

"Certain intentions, betrayed, perhaps, by some chance gesture" seem to provoke in Hamlet a wish to name, to pin upon his *sujet supposé savoir* the signifier Lacan has called *"le nom-du-père"* [the Name-of-the-Father]. Lacan's term derives in part from a critique of the traditional Christian invocation all too appropriate to *Hamlet:* "In the name of the Father, the Son, and the Holy Ghost." Coupling this formula with the biological indeterminacy of paternity, Lacan notes that

> the attribution of procreation to the father can only be the effect of a pure signifier, of a recognition, not of a real father, but of what religion has taught us to refer to as the Name-of-the-Father.
> Of course, there is no need of a signifier to be a father, any more than to be dead, but without a signifier, no one would ever know anything about either state of being.
> . . . insistently Freud stresses the affinity of the two signifying relations that I have just referred to, whenever the neurotic subject (especially the obsessional) manifests this affinity through the conjunction of the themes of the father and death.
> How, indeed, could Freud fail to recognize such an affinity, when the necessity of his reflexion led him to link the appearance of the signifier of the Father, as author of the Law, with death, even to the murder of the Father — thus showing that if this murder is the fruitful moment of debt through which the subject binds himself for life to the Law, the symbolic Father is, in so far as he signifies this Law, the dead Father. (*Écrits* 199)

Lacan extends this view further by underscoring the homonymic double meaning of *"nom-du-père,"* which in French sounds identical to the expression *"non-du-père"* — "no" of the father. The father — the dead father, the symbolic father — is the Law. For Freud, of course, this symbolic father is not the Christian father but the father of Jewish law. And the law commands, "thou shalt *not*": "If thou hast nature in thee, bear it *not*, / Let *not* the royal bed of Denmark be / A couch for luxury and damned incest. / But howsomever thou pursues this act, / Taint *not* thy mind, *nor* let thy soul contrive / Against thy mother aught" (Ghost to Hamlet, 1.5.81–86); "Do *not* forget" (Ghost to Hamlet, 3.4.110, in Gertrude's closet).

Freud, it will be recalled, made much of the connection between the writing of *Hamlet* and the death of Shakespeare's father. In *The Interpretation of Dreams,* he cites the Shakespearean scholar Georg Brandes to demonstrate that

> *Hamlet* was written immediately after the death of Shakespeare's father (in 1601), that is, under the immediate impact of the bereavement and, as we may well assume, while his childhood feel-

ings about his father had been freshly revived. It is known, too, that Shakespeare's own son who died at an early age bore the name of "Hamnet," which is identical with "Hamlet." (299)

Yet there is another father involved here, as Freud's preface to the second edition of *The Interpretation of Dreams* (1908) makes clear. For that masterpiece of analytic invention was itself written right after the death of Freud's *own* father. In his preface, Freud writes:

this book has a further subjective significance for me personally — a significance which I only grasped after I had completed it. It was, I found, a portion of my own self-analysis, my reaction to my father's death — that is to say, to the most important event, the most poignant loss, of a man's life. (xxvi)

There may therefore be a connection between Freud's interpretation of Hamlet and the death not only of *Shakespeare's* father but also of *Freud's* father.

Similarities between Freud's story and Hamlet's have been noticed by recent revisionist biographers, often in connection with his recantation of (or "suppression of") the seduction theory, which held that neuroses originated in actual sexual encounters — with adults, often parents, servants, or older children — experienced in childhood. Marianne Krüll, for example, argues that Hamlet's situation — "a son dwelling with impotent rage on the ruthlessness of his mother and his uncle — had parallels with Freud's own family" (63). The "uncle" in the Freud story was his half-brother Philip, called "Uncle" by Freud's niece and nephew, and represented in Freud's own dream associations in such a way as to suggest some real or imagined sexual relationship between Philip and his (Freud's) mother (Krüll 124–25). Krüll's book argues that Freud received from his father, Jacob, an ambivalent mandate: he was commanded to show filial piety, to honor his father as instructed by the Fifth Commandment, and above all not to inquire into his father's secrets, or his past; at the same time, he was commanded to seek success in the secular world, to become a great man. The son's resentment at this impossible double task was identical, says Krüll, to that felt by Jacob Freud toward *his* father, Schlomo (Sigmund's Hebrew name). "Neither of them rebelled against his father, and both shouldered the contradictory mandate of making his own way, even while remaining dutiful sons" (180). "To complete its hold over him" writes John Gross, "the mandate forbade him to acknowledge the feelings of resentment that it inspired, his rage against Jacob for saddling him with an insoluble problem" (C25). This "mandate," we may notice, is very like the "word" Hamlet receives from the Ghost in the "tables" scene, together with the troublesomely ambivalent command, "Remember me!"

A dream mentioned by Freud in slightly different versions in the letters to Fliess and *The Interpretation of Dreams*[6] concerns the arrangements he made for his father's funeral, and the criticism he incurred from relatives for choosing "the simplest possible ritual" (*Interpretation of Dreams* 353) though he did so in accordance with his understanding of his father's wishes. It is this dream that Krüll has in mind when she writes that like Hamlet,

> Freud too has been given orders by his late father in a dream which, though the subject was not revenge, as in Hamlet's case, nevertheless caused the son comparable qualms of conscience. Another reason for Freud, in my view, to feel so drawn to the Hamlet theme. (63)

Not only the funeral of old Hamlet, swiftly followed by Gertrude's remarriage, but even more particularly the "hugger-mugger" interment (4.5.83) of Polonius and the "maimed rites" accompanying Ophelia's obsequies (5.1.205) — so disturbingly punctuated by Laertes's twice iterated demand, "What ceremony else?" (5.1.209, 211) — correspond to Freud's own anxieties about performing his duty to the dead.

In the dream — which he tells Fliess took place *after* his father's funeral, and which in *The Interpretation of Dreams* he describes as taking place *before* — he sees a notice-board inscribed with the phrase, "You are requested to close the eyes," which he interprets as an ambivalent statement; in *The Interpretation of Dreams* the ambivalence has made its way onto the notice-board itself, so that the sign reads "*either*

"You are requested to close the eyes"
or, "You are requested to close an eye."

I usually write this [says Freud] in the form:

"You are requested to close $\frac{\text{the}}{\text{an}}$ eye(s)." (352; emphasis added)

Closing the eyes is a funerary rite, a service performed on the eyes of the dead; closing *an* eye is winking at (overlooking) an offense or slight. As Freud writes to Fliess, "The sentence on the sign has a double meaning:

[6]Masson, ed., November 2, 1896, 202; Freud, *Interpretation of Dreams* 352–53.

One should do one's duty toward the dead (an apology, as though I had not done it and were in need of leniency) and the actual duty itself. The dream thus stems from the inclination to self-reproach that regularly sets in among the survivors" (202).

The generalization at the end denies any *particular* ambivalence occasioned by this specific bereavement, but the whole letter, like the ones preceding it during his father's illness, speaks openly of Freud's own feeling. Jacob Freud died on November 23, 1896. A little less than a year later, with affirmations of relief and release rather than "disgrace," Freud abandoned the seduction theory. Whatever else his motivations were for making this crucial change, the seduction theory came dangerously close to an accusation of the father, as is pointed out in the famous letter to Fliess of September 1897. Jeffrey Masson, whose controversial book, *The Assault on Truth: Freud's Suppression of the Seduction Theory,* has occasioned much disputation among psychoanalysts, notes that the original English edition of the letters (itself provocatively entitled *The Origins of Psychoanalysis*) omitted the reference to Freud's own father, by using an ellipsis: "in every case . . . blame was laid on perverse acts by the father." The three dots appear in the letter in place of the phrase Masson translates as "the father, not excluding my own." The editors, Marie Bonaparte, Ernst Kris, and Freud's daughter Anna, comment that their editorial principle was one of "omitting or abbreviating everything publication of which would be inconsistent with professional or personal confidence. . . . Omissions have been indicated by dots" (xi–xii). Even translation, here, acts out the story of suppression. Thus the discarding of the seduction theory, and the substitution of the Oedipus complex, not only opened the way for the discovery of the inner life of the child and the foundations of modern psychoanalysis, but also paid a kind of filial duty, honoring the memory of the father, and of fathers. The child's (Freud's own) fantasies, not the parent's actions, were to blame. Or if no blame was to be attached, at least there was no accusation against the parent. Are we — and were Freud's fellow analysts — being requested to close an/the eye(s)?

The story by means of which Freud substitutes infantile fantasy for child abuse is the story of Oedipus, who, by killing his father and marrying his mother, acts out in reality what every man is said to live in fantasy. Oedipus, then, becomes a paradigm for every man. Or does he? In the course of a discussion of the differences between *Oedipus* and *Hamlet,* Freud indicates that the later play represents a cultural advance: "The changed treatment of the same material reveals the whole difference in the mental life of these two widely separated epochs of civilization: the secular advance of repression in the emotional life of mankind" (*Interpretation of Dreams* 298). What Oedipus *does* (kills his father, marries his mother), Hamlet *fantasizes* but *represses*, so that "we only learn of [this fantasy's] existence from its inhibiting consequences" (298). And yet this, to Freud, is very much more interesting than the straightforward enactment of the desire. Oedipus gives his name to the complex Freud discovered in every child's fantasy life, but it is Hamlet rather than Oedipus who engages Freud's own fascination, and his most extended discussion on the subject.

It is therefore not entirely clear which of the two dramas is "closer to home." *Hamlet* looks like a repressed version of the Oedipus story but in being a story *of* repression, it may in fact be closer to the story of "modern" man. There may, in other words, be *two* originary stories in Freud's mind, *both* of which are too close for comfort, and between which the story of Oedipus emerges as a compromise formation: the story of the father's sins, to which Freud dutifully closes his eyes by abandoning the seduction theory; and the story of repressed filial ambivalence, hesitation, and resentment toward an impossible paternal mandate, which Freud relegates to the status of secondary revision. The story of killing the father, which would seem to express Freud's filial ambivalence, in fact represses it: the murdered father can forever remain innocent while the son shoulders the guilt. The Oedipus story does not account for filial love.

If anything is clear, it is that the Ghost is not — or not merely — Shakespeare *père* or Shakespeare *fils,* the son of John Shakespeare or the father of Hamnet — but rather "Shakespeare" itself. The ambiguous and ambivalent pronoun of act 1 is appropriately used here, because Shakespeare is a concept — and a construct — rather than an author. We thus hear of the Shakespeare establishment, and of "Shakespeare" as a corpus of plays — a corpus "incorpsed" in innumerable authoritative editions, yet one that breaks the bounds — the margins — set to contain it, stalking the battlements of theory:

> tell
> Why thy canoniz'd bones, hearsed in death,
> Have burst their cerements; why the sepulchre,
> Wherein we saw thee quietly [inurn'd,]
> Hath op'd his ponderous and marble jaws
> To cast thee up again.
>   (1.4.46–51)

The Ghost is Shakespeare. He is the one who comes as a revenant, belatedly instated, regarded as originally authoritative, rather than retrospectively and retroactively canonized, and deriving increased authority from this very instatement of authority backward, over time. "The ghost, *le re-venant*, the survivor, appears only as a means of figure or fiction, but its appearance is not nothing, nor is it a mere semblance." This "presence without present of a present which, coming back, only *haunts*" haunts Freud, haunts Nietzsche, haunts Lacan, haunts postmodern England and postmodern America. The Ghost's command, his word, is "Remember me!" and we have done so, to the letter, *avant la lettre*, moving our remembrance further and further back until it becomes an originary remembrance, a remembrance of remembrance itself. "Remember me!" cries the Ghost, and Shakespeare is for us the superego of literature, that which calls us back to ourselves, to an imposed, undecidable, but self-chosen attribution of paternity. "Remember me!" The canon has been fixed against self-slaughter.

"A little more than kin and less than kind." Hamlet's bitter phrase inflects not only the problem of a ghostly genre, the unwriting and rewriting of revenge tragedy, but also the continuous attempt to render Shakespeare both kind and kin, of our time, our contemporary, always already postmodern, decentered. "Yet his modernity too like Nietzsche's, is a forgetting or a suppression of anteriority" (de Man, "Literary History" 157). This is de Man on Baudelaire. But it could be said of Hamlet — and of Shakespeare. This Baudelairization is not Bowdlerization, but transference, con-texting. We know that Shakespeare played the part of the Ghost in *Hamlet*. What could not be foreseen, except through anamorphic reading, was that he would *become* that Ghost. "Remember me!" the Ghost cries. "Do not forget." And, indeed, we do not yet seem quite able to give up that ghost.

WORKS CITED

Barker, Francis. *The Tremulous Private Body: Essays on Subjection*. London: Methuen, 1984.

Brandes, Georg. *William Shakespeare: A Critical Study*. New York: Macmillan, 1909.

Chase, Cynthia. *Decomposing Figures*. Baltimore: Johns Hopkins UP, 1986.

Colie, Rosalie. *Shakespeare's Living Art*. Princeton: Princeton UP, 1974.

Culler, Jonathan. "Apostrophe." *The Pursuit of Signs*. Ithaca: Cornell UP, 1981.

de Man, Paul. *Allegories of Reading*. New Haven: Yale UP, 1979.

———. "Autobiography as Defacement." *The Rhetoric of Romanticism*. New York: Columbia UP, 1984. 67–81.

———. "Literary History and Literary Modernity." *Blindness and Insight*. Minneapolis: U of Minnesota P, 1983. 142–65.

———. "Sign and Symbol in Hegel's *Aesthetics*." *Critical Inquiry* 8 (1982): 761–75.

Derrida, Jacques. "Freud and the Scene of Writing." *Writing and Difference*. Trans. Alan Bass. Chicago: U of Chicago P, 1978. 196–231.

———. *Mémoires: for Paul de Man*. Trans. Cecile Lindsay, Jonathan Culler, and Eduardo Cadava. New York: Columbia UP, 1986.

Dollimore, Jonathan, and Alan Sinfield, eds. *Political Shakespeare*. Ithaca: Cornell UP, 1985.

Drakakis, John, ed. *alternative shakespeares*. London: Methuen, 1985.

Ferguson, Margaret. "*Hamlet:* Letters and Spirits." Parker and Hartman 292–309.

Freud, Sigmund. *Beyond the Pleasure Principle*. Trans. James Strachey. New York: Bantam, 1959.

———. *The Complete Letters of Sigmund Freud to Wilhelm Fliess, 1887–1904*. Ed. and trans. Jeffrey Moussaieff Masson. Cambridge: Harvard UP, 1985.

———. "Further Recommendations in the Technique of Psychoanalysis: Recollection, Repetition, and Working Through" (1914). *Therapy and Technique*. Ed. Philip Rieff. New York: Macmillan, 1963.

———. *General Psychological Theory*. Ed. Philip Rieff. New York: Macmillan, 1963.

———. *The Interpretation of Dreams*. Ed. and trans. James Strachey. New York: Avon, 1965.

———. "Mourning and Melancholia" (1917). *General Psychological Theory*.

———. "A Note upon the 'Mystic Writing-Pad'" (1925). *General Psychological Theory*.

———. *The Origins of Psychoanalysis. Letters to Wilhelm Fliess*. Ed. Marie Bonaparte, Anna Freud, and Ernst Kris. Trans. Eric Mosbacher and James Strachey. New York: Basic, 1954.

———. "The Passing of the Oedipus Complex." *Sexuality and the Psychology of Love*. Ed. Philip Rieff. New York: Macmillan, 1963.

———. "The Uncanny." *Studies in Parapsychology*. Ed. Philip Rieff. New York: Collier, 1963.

Gross, John. Rev. of *Freud and His Father*, by Marianne Krüll. *New York Times* 15 Aug. 1986.

Holland, Norman. *Psychoanalysis and Shakespeare*. New York: Octagon, rpt. 1976.

Jenkins, Harold, ed. *Hamlet*. By William Shakespeare. The Arden Shakespeare. London: Methuen, 1982.

Kermode, Frank. *Forms of Attention*. Chicago: U of Chicago P, 1985.

Krüll, Marianne. *Freud and His Father*. Trans. Arnold J. Pomerans. New York: Norton, 1986.

Lacan, Jacques. "Desire and the Interpretation of Desire in *Hamlet*." Ed. Jacques-Alain Miller. Trans. James Hulbert. In *Literature and Psychoanalysis*. Ed. Shoshana Felman. Baltimore: Johns Hopkins UP, 1982.

———. *Écrits: A Selection*. Trans. Alan Sheridan. New York: Norton, 1977.

———. *The Four Fundamental Concepts of Psychoanalysis*. Ed. Jacques-Alain Miller. Trans. Alan Sheridan. New York: Norton, 1981.

Masson, Jeffrey Moussaieff. *The Assault on Truth: Freud's Suppression of the Seduction Theory*. New York: Penguin, 1985.

Milton, John. *John Milton: Complete Poems and Major Prose*. Ed. Merritt Y. Hughes. New York: Odyssey, 1957.

Nietzsche, Friedrich. "The Use and Abuse of History." *Untimely Meditations*. Trans. R. J. Hollingdale. Cambridge, Eng.: Cambridge UP, 1983.

Parker, Patricia, and Geoffrey Hartman, eds. *Shakespeare and the Question of Theory*. New York: Methuen, 1985.

Riffaterre, Michel. "Prosopopoeia." *The Lesson of Paul de Man. Yale French Studies* 69 (1985): 107–23.

Marxist Criticism
and
Hamlet

WHAT IS MARXIST CRITICISM?

To the question "What is Marxist criticism?" it may be tempting to respond with another question: "What does it matter?" In light of the rapid and largely unanticipated demise of Soviet-style communism in the former USSR and throughout Eastern Europe, it is understandable to suppose that Marxist literary analysis would disappear too, quickly becoming an anachronism in a world enamored with full market capitalism.

In fact, however, there is no reason why Marxist criticism should weaken, let alone disappear. It is, after all, a distinct phenomenon from Soviet and Eastern European communism, having had its beginnings nearly eighty years before the Bolshevik revolution and having thrived, since the 1940s, mainly in the West — not as a form of communist propaganda but rather as a form of critique, a discourse for interrogating *all* societies and their texts in terms of certain specific issues. Those issues — including race, class, and the attitudes shared within a given culture — are as much with us as ever, not only in contemporary Russia but also in the United States.

The argument could even be made that Marxist criticism has been strengthened by the collapse of Soviet-style communism. There was a time, after all, when few self-respecting Anglo-American journals would use Marxist terms or models, however illuminating, to analyze Western issues or problems. It smacked of sleeping with the enemy. With the collapse of the Kremlin, however, old taboos began to give way. Even the staid *Wall Street Journal* now seems comfortable using phrases like "worker alienation" to discuss the problems plaguing the American business world.

The assumption that Marxist criticism will die on the vine of a moribund political system rests in part on another mistaken assumption, namely, that Marxist literary analysis is practiced only by people who would like to see society transformed into a Marxist-communist state, one created through land reform, the redistribution of wealth, a tightly and centrally managed economy, the abolition of institutionalized religion, and so on. In fact, it has never been necessary to be a communist political revolutionary to be classified as a Marxist literary critic. (Many of the critics discussed in this introduction actually *fled* communist societies to live in the West.) Nor is it necessary to like only those literary works with a radical social vision or to dislike books that represent or even reinforce a middle-class, capitalist world-view. It is necessary, however, to adopt what most students of literature would consider a radical definition of the purpose and function of literary criticism.

More traditional forms of criticism, according to the Marxist critic Pierre Macherey, "set . . . out to deliver the text from its own silences by coaxing it into giving up its true, latent, or hidden meaning." Inevitably, however, non-Marxist criticism "intrude[s] its own discourse between the reader and the text" (qtd. in Bennett 107). Marxist critics, by contrast, do not attempt to discover hidden meanings in texts. Or, if they do, they do so only after seeing the text, first and foremost, as a material product to be understood in broadly historical terms. That is to say, a literary work is first viewed as a product *of* work (and hence of the realm of production and consumption we call economics). Second, it may be looked upon as a work that *does* identifiable work of its own. At one level, that work is usually to enforce and reinforce the prevailing ideology, that is, the network of conventions, values, and opinions to which the majority of people uncritically subscribe.

This does not mean that Marxist critics merely describe the obvious. Quite the contrary: the relationship that the Marxist critic Terry Eagleton outlines in *Criticism and Ideology* (1978) between the soaring cost of books in the nineteenth century, the growth of lending libraries, the practice of publishing "three-decker" novels (so that three borrowers could be reading the same book at the same time), and the changing *content* of those novels is highly complex in its own way. But the complexity Eagleton finds is not that of the deeply buried meaning of the

text. Rather, it is that of the complex web of social and economic relationships that were prerequisite to the work's production. Marxist criticism does not seek to be, in Eagleton's words, "a passage from text to
reader." Instead, "its task is to show the text as it cannot know itself, to
manifest those conditions of its making (inscribed in its very letter)
about which it is necessarily silent" (43).

As everyone knows, Marxism began with Karl Marx, the nineteenth-
century German philosopher best known for writing *Das Kapital,* the
seminal work of the communist movement. What everyone doesn't
know is that Marx was also the first Marxist literary critic (much as Sigmund Freud, who psychoanalyzed E. T. A. Hoffmann's supernatural tale
"The Sandman," was the first Freudian literary critic). During the
1830s Marx wrote critical essays on writers such as Goethe and Shakespeare (whose tragic vision of Elizabethan disintegration he praised).
The fact that Marxist literary criticism began with Marx himself is
hardly surprising, given Marx's education and early interests. Trained in
the classics at the University of Bonn, Marx wrote literary imitations, his
own poetry, a failed novel, and a fragment of a tragic drama *(Oulanem)*
before turning to contemplative and political philosophy. Even after he
met Friedrich Engels in 1843 and began collaborating on works such as
The German Ideology and *The Communist Manifesto,* Marx maintained a
keen interest in literary writers and their works. He and Engels argued
about the poetry of Heinrich Heine, admired Hermann Freiligrath (a
poet critical of the German aristocracy), and faulted the playwright Ferdinand Lassalle for writing about a reactionary knight in the Peasants'
War rather than about more progressive aspects of German history.
As these examples suggest, Marx and Engels would not — indeed,
could not — think of aesthetic matters as being distinct and independent from such things as politics, economics, and history. Not surprisingly, they viewed the alienation of the worker in industrialized, capitalist societies as having grave consequences for the arts. How can people
mechanically stamping out things that bear no mark of their producer's
individuality (people thereby "reified," turned into things themselves)
be expected to recognize, produce, or even consume things of beauty?
And if there is no one to consume something, there will soon be no one
to produce it, especially in an age in which production (even of something like literature) has come to mean *mass* (and therefore profitable)
production.
In *The German Ideology* (1846), Marx and Engels expressed their

sense of the relationship between the arts, politics, and basic economic reality in terms of a general social theory. Economics, they argued, provides the "base" or "infrastructure" of society, but from that base emerges a "superstructure" consisting of law, politics, philosophy, religion, and art.

Marx later admitted that the relationship between base and superstructure may be indirect and fluid: every change in economics may not be reflected by an immediate change in ethics or literature. In *The Eighteenth Brumaire of Louis Bonaparte* (1852), he came up with the word *homology* to describe the sometimes unbalanced, often delayed, and almost always loose correspondence between base and superstructure. And later in that same decade, while working on an introduction to his *Political Economy*, Marx further relaxed the base-superstructure relationship. Writing on the excellence of ancient Greek art (versus the primitive nature of ancient Greek economics), he conceded that a gap sometimes opens up between base and superstructure — between economic forms and those produced by the creative mind.

Nonetheless, *at* base the old formula was maintained. Economics remained basic and the connection between economics and superstructural elements of society was reaffirmed. Central to Marxism and Marxist literary criticism was and is the following "materialist" insight: consciousness, without which such things as art cannot be produced, is not the source of social forms and economic conditions. It is, rather, their most important product.

Marx and Engels, drawing upon the philosopher G. W. F. Hegel's theories about the dialectical synthesis of ideas out of theses and antitheses, believed that a revolutionary class war (pitting the capitalist class against a proletarian, antithetical class) would lead eventually to the synthesis of a new social and economic order. Placing their faith not in the idealist Hegelian dialectic but, rather, in what they called "dialectical materialism," they looked for a secular and material salvation of humanity — one in, not beyond, history — via revolution and not via divine intervention. And they believed that the communist society eventually established would be one capable of producing new forms of consciousness and belief and therefore, ultimately, great art.

The revolution anticipated by Marx and Engels did not occur in their century, let alone lifetime. When it finally did take place, it didn't happen in places where Marx and Engels had thought it might be successful: the United States, Great Britain, and Germany. It happened, rather, in 1917 Russia, a country long ruled by despotic czars but also enlightened by the works of powerful novelists and playwrights, including Chekhov, Pushkin, Tolstoy, and Dostoyevsky.

Perhaps because of its significant literary tradition, Russia produced revolutionaries like Nikolai Lenin, who shared not only Marx's interest in literature but also his belief in literature's ultimate importance. But it was not without some hesitation that Lenin endorsed the significance of texts written during the reign of the czars. Well before 1917 he had questioned what the relationship should be between a society undergoing a revolution and the great old literature of its bourgeois past.

Lenin attempted to answer that question in a series of essays on Tolstoy that he wrote between 1908 and 1911. Tolstoy — the author of *War and Peace* and *Anna Karenina* — was an important nineteenth-century Russian writer whose views did not accord with all of those of young Marxist revolutionaries. Continuing interest in a writer like Tolstoy may be justified, Lenin reasoned, given the primitive and unenlightened economic order of the society that produced him. Since superstructure usually lags behind base (and is therefore usually *more* primitive), the attitudes of a Tolstoy were relatively progressive when viewed in light of the monarchical and precapitalist society out of which they arose.

Moreover, Lenin also reasoned, the writings of the great Russian realists would *have* to suffice, at least in the short run. Lenin looked forward, in essays like "Party Organization and Party Literature," to the day in which new artistic forms would be produced by progressive writers with revolutionary political views and agendas. But he also knew that a great proletarian literature was unlikely to evolve until a thoroughly literate proletariat had been produced by the educational system.

Lenin was hardly the only revolutionary leader involved in setting up the new Soviet state who took a strong interest in literary matters. In 1924 Leon Trotsky published a book called *Literature and Revolution,* which is still acknowledged as a classic of Marxist literary criticism.

Trotsky worried about the direction in which Marxist aesthetic theory seemed to be going. He responded skeptically to groups like Proletkult, which opposed tolerance toward pre- and nonrevolutionary writers, and which called for the establishment of a new, proletarian culture. Trotsky warned of the danger of cultural sterility and risked unpopularity by pointing out that there is no necessary connection between the quality of a literary work and the quality of its author's politics.

In 1927 Trotsky lost a power struggle with Josef Stalin, a man who believed, among other things, that writers should be "engineers" of "human souls." After Trotsky's expulsion from the Soviet Union, views held by groups like Proletkult and the Left Front of Art (LEF), and by theorists such as Nikolai Bukharin and A. A. Zhdanov, became more prevalent. Speaking at the First Congress of the Union of Soviet Writers in 1934, the Soviet author Maxim Gorky called for writing that would "make labor the principal hero of our books." It was at the same writer's congress that "socialist realism," an art form glorifying workers and the revolutionary State, was made Communist party policy and the official literary form of the USSR.

Of those critics active in the USSR after the expulsion of Trotsky and the unfortunate triumph of Stalin, two critics stand out. One, Mikhail Bakhtin, was a Russian, later a Soviet, critic who spent much of his life in a kind of internal exile. Many of his essays were written in the 1930s and not published in the West or translated until the late 1960s. His work comes out of an engagement with the Marxist intellectual tradition as well as out of an indirect, even hidden, resistance to the Soviet government. It has been important to Marxist critics writing in the West because his theories provide a means to decode submerged social critique, especially in early modern texts. He viewed language — especially literary texts — in terms of discourses and dialogues. Within a novel written in a society in flux, for instance, the narrative may include an official, legitimate discourse, plus another infiltrated by challenging comments and even retorts. In a 1929 book on Dostoyevsky and a 1940 study titled *Rabelais and His World*, Bakhtin examined what he calls "polyphonic" novels, each characterized by a multiplicity of voices or discourses. In Dostoyevsky the independent status of a given character is marked by the difference of his or her language from that of the narrator. (The narrator's voice, too, can in fact be a dialogue.) In works by Rabelais, Bakhtin finds that the (profane) language of the carnival and of other popular festivals play against and parody the more official discourses, that is, of the king, church, or even socially powerful intellectuals. Bakhtin influenced modern cultural criticism by showing, in a sense, that the conflict between "high" and "low" culture takes place not only between classic and popular texts but also between the "dialogic" voices that exist within many books — whether "high" or "low."

The other subtle Marxist critic who managed to survive Stalin's dictatorship and his repressive policies was Georg Lukács. A Hungarian who had begun his career as an "idealist" critic, Lukács had converted to Marxism in 1919; renounced his earlier, Hegelian work shortly thereafter; visited Moscow in 1930–31; and finally emigrated to the

USSR in 1933, just one year before the First Congress of the Union of Soviet Writers met. Lukács was far less narrow in his views than the most strident Stalinist Soviet critics of the 1930s and 1940s. He disliked much socialist realism and appreciated prerevolutionary, realistic novels that broadly reflected cultural "totalities" — and were populated with characters representing human "types" of the author's place and time. (Lukács was particularly fond of the historical canvasses painted by the early nineteenth-century novelist Sir Walter Scott.) But like his more rigid and censorious contemporaries, he drew the line at accepting non-revolutionary, modernist works like James Joyce's *Ulysses*. He condemned movements like Expressionism and Symbolism, preferring works with "content" over more decadent, experimental works characterized mainly by "form."

With Lukács its most liberal and tolerant critic from the early 1930s until well into the 1960s, the Soviet literary scene degenerated to the point that the works of great writers like Franz Kafka were no longer read, either because they were viewed as decadent, formal experiments or because they "engineered souls" in "nonprogressive" directions. Officially sanctioned works were generally ones in which artistry lagged far behind the politics (no matter how bad the politics were).

Fortunately for the Marxist critical movement, politically radical critics *outside* the Soviet Union were free of its narrow, constricting policies and, consequently, able fruitfully to develop the thinking of Marx, Engels, and Trotsky. It was these non-Soviet Marxists who kept Marxist critical theory alive and useful in discussing all *kinds* of literature, written across the entire historical spectrum.

Perhaps because Lukács was the best of the Soviet communists writing Marxist criticism in the 1930s and 1940s, non-Soviet Marxists tended to develop their ideas by publicly opposing those of Lukács. German dramatist and critic Bertolt Brecht countered Lukács by arguing that art ought to be viewed as a field of production, not as a container of "content." Brecht also criticized Lukács for his attempt to enshrine realism at the expense not only of other "isms" but also of poetry and drama, both of which had been largely ignored by Lukács.

Even more outspoken was Brecht's critical champion Walter Benjamin, a German Marxist who, in the 1930s, attacked those conventional and traditional literary forms conveying a stultifying "aura" of culture. Benjamin praised Dadaism and, more important, new forms of art ushered in by the age of mechanical reproduction. Those forms — including radio and film — offered hope, he felt, for liberation from capitalist culture, for they were too new to be part of its stultifyingly ritualistic traditions.

But of all the anti-Lukácsians outside the USSR who made a contribution to the development of Marxist literary criticism, the most important was probably Théodor Adorno. Leader since the early 1950s of the Frankfurt school of Marxist criticism, Adorno attacked Lukács for his dogmatic rejection of nonrealist modern literature and for his belief in the primacy of content over form. Art does not equal science, Adorno insisted. He went on to argue for art's autonomy from empirical forms of knowledge, and to suggest that the interior monologues of modernist works (by Beckett and Proust) reflect the fact of modern alienation in a way that Marxist criticism ought to find compelling.

In addition to turning against Lukács and his overly constrictive canon, Marxists outside the Soviet Union were able to take advantage of insights generated by non-Marxist critical theories being developed in post–World War II Europe. One of the movements that came to be of interest to non-Soviet Marxists was structuralism, a scientific approach to the study of humankind whose proponents believed that all elements of culture, including literature, could be understood as parts of a system of signs. Using modern linguistics as a model, structuralists like Claude Lévi-Strauss broke the myths of various cultures down into "mythemes" in an attempt to show that there are structural correspondences or homologies between the mythical elements produced by various human communities across time.

Of the European structuralist Marxists, one of the most influential was Lucien Goldmann, a Rumanian critic living in Paris. Goldmann combined structuralist principles with Marx's base-superstructure model in order to show how economics determines the mental structures of social groups, which are reflected in literary texts. Goldmann rejected the idea of individual human genius, choosing to see works, instead, as the "collective" products of "trans-individual" mental structures. In early studies, such as *The Hidden God* (1955), he related seventeenth-century French texts (such as Racine's *Phèdre*) to the ideology of Jansenism. In later works, he applied Marx's base-superstructure model even more strictly, describing a relationship between economic conditions and texts unmediated by an intervening, collective consciousness.

In spite of his rigidity and perhaps because of his affinities with structuralism, Goldmann came to be seen in the 1960s as the proponent of a kind of watered-down, "humanist" Marxism. He was certainly viewed that way by the French Marxist Louis Althusser, a disciple not of

Lévi-Strauss and structuralism but rather of the psychoanalytic theorist
Jacques Lacan and of the Italian communist Antonio Gramsci, famous
for his writings about ideology and "hegemony." (Gramsci used the
latter word to refer to the pervasive, weblike system of assumptions and
values that shapes the way things look, what they mean, and therefore
what reality *is* for the majority of people within a culture.)

Like Gramsci, Althusser viewed literary works primarily in terms of
their relationship to ideology, the function of which, he argued, is to
(re)produce the existing relations of production in a given society. Dave
Laing, in his book on *The Marxist Theory of Art* (1978), has attempted
to explain this particular insight of Althusser's by saying that ideologies,
through the "ensemble of habits, moralities, and opinions" that can be
found in any literary text, "ensure that the work-force (and those responsible for re-producing them in the family, school, etc.) are maintained in their position of subordination to the dominant class" (91).
This is not to say that Althusser thought of the masses as a brainless
multitude following only the dictates of the prevailing ideology: Althusser followed Gramsci in suggesting that even working-class people
have some freedom to struggle against ideology and change history.
Nor is it to say that Althusser saw ideology as being a coherent, consistent force. In fact, he saw it as being riven with contradictions that
works of literature sometimes expose and even widen. Thus Althusser
followed Marx and Gramsci in believing that although literature must
be seen in *relation* to ideology, it — like all social forms — has some
degree of autonomy.

Althusser's followers included Pierre Macherey, who in *A Theory of
Literary Production* (1966) developed Althusser's concept of the relationship between literature and ideology. A realistic novelist, he argued,
attempts to produce a unified, coherent text, but instead ends up producing a work containing lapses, omissions, gaps. This happens because
within ideology there are subjects that cannot be covered, things that
cannot be said, contradictory views that aren't recognized as contradictory. (The critic's challenge, in this case, is to supply what the text cannot say, thereby making sense of gaps and contradictions.)

But there is another reason why gaps open up and contradictions
become evident in texts. Works don't just reflect ideology (which Goldmann had referred to as "myth" and which Macherey refers to as a system of "illusory social beliefs"); they are also "fictions," works of art,
products of ideology that have what Goldmann would call a "world-
view" to offer. What kind of product, Macherey implicitly asks, is identical to the thing that produced it? It is hardly surprising, then, that

Balzac's fiction shows French peasants in two different lights, only one of which is critical and judgmental, only one of which is baldly ideological. Writing approvingly on Macherey and Macherey's mentor Althusser in *Marxism and Literary Criticism* (1976), Terry Eagleton says: "It is by giving ideology a determinate form, fixing it within certain fictional limits, that art is able to distance itself from [ideology], thus revealing . . . [its] limits" (19).

A follower of Althusser, Macherey is sometimes referred to as a "post-Althusserian Marxist." Eagleton, too, is often described that way, as is his American contemporary, Fredric Jameson. Jameson and Eagleton, as well as being post-Althusserians, are also among the few Anglo-American critics who have closely followed and significantly developed Marxist thought.

Before them, Marxist interpretation in English was limited to the work of a handful of critics: Christopher Caudwell, Christopher Hill, Arnold Kettle, E. P. Thompson, and Raymond Williams. Of these, Williams was perhaps least Marxist in orientation: he felt that Marxist critics, ironically, tended too much to isolate economics from culture; that they overlooked the individualism of people, opting instead to see them as "masses"; and that even more ironically, they had become an elitist group. But if the least Marxist of the British Marxists, Williams was also by far the most influential. Preferring to talk about "culture" instead of ideology, Williams argued in works such as *Culture and Society 1780–1950* (1958) that culture is "lived experience" and, as such, an interconnected set of social properties, each and all grounded in and influencing history.

Terry Eagleton's *Criticism and Ideology* (1978) is in many ways a response to the work of Williams. Responding to Williams's statement, in *Culture and Society*, that "there are in fact no masses; there are only ways of seeing people as masses" (289), Eagleton writes: "That men and women really are now unique individuals was Williams's (unexceptionable) insistence; but it was a proposition bought at the expense of perceiving the fact that they must mass and fight to achieve their full individual humanity. One has only to adapt Williams's statement to 'There are in fact no classes; there are only ways of seeing people as classes' to expose its theoretical paucity" (*Criticism* 29).

Eagleton goes on, in *Criticism and Ideology*, to propose an elaborate theory about how history — in the form of "general," "authorial," and "aesthetic" ideology — enters texts, which in turn may revivify, open up, or critique those same ideologies, thereby setting in motion a process that may alter history. He shows how texts by Jane Austen, Matthew Arnold, Charles Dickens, George Eliot, Joseph Conrad, and T. S. Eliot deal with and transmute conflicts at the heart of the general and authorial ideologies behind them: conflicts between morality and individualism, individualism and social organicism and utilitarianism.

As all this emphasis on ideology and conflict suggests, a modern British Marxist like Eagleton, even while acknowledging the work of a British Marxist predecessor like Williams, is more nearly developing the ideas of continental Marxists like Althusser and Macherey. That holds, as well, for modern American Marxists like Fredric Jameson. For although he makes occasional, sympathetic references to the works of Williams, Thompson, and Hill, Jameson makes far more *use* of Lukács, Adorno, and Althusser as well as non-Marxist structuralist, psychoanalytic, and poststructuralist critics.

In the first of several influential works, *Marxism and Form* (1971), Jameson takes up the question of form and content, arguing that the former is "but the working out" of the latter "in the realm of superstructure" (329). (In making such a statement Jameson opposes not only the tenets of Russian Formalists, for whom content had merely been the fleshing out of form, but also those of so-called vulgar Marxists, who tended to define form as mere ornamentation or windowdressing.) In his later work *The Political Unconscious* (1981), Jameson uses what in *Marxism and Form* he had called "dialectical criticism" to synthesize out of structuralism and poststructuralism, Freud and Lacan, Althusser and Adorno, a set of complex arguments that can only be summarized reductively.

The fractured state of societies and the isolated condition of individuals, he argued, may be seen as indications that there originally existed an unfallen state of something that may be called "primitive communism." History — which records the subsequent divisions and alienations — limits awareness of its own contradictions and of that lost, Better State, via ideologies and their manifestation in texts, whose strategies essentially contain and repress desire, especially revolutionary desire, into the collective unconscious. (In Conrad's *Lord Jim*, Jameson shows, the knowledge that governing classes don't *deserve* their power is contained and repressed by an ending that metaphysically blames Nature for the tragedy and that melodramatically blames wicked Gentleman Brown.)

As demonstrated by Jameson in analyses like the one mentioned above, textual strategies of containment and concealment may be discovered by the critic, but only by the critic practicing dialectical criticism, that is to say, a criticism aware, among other things, of its *own* status as ideology. All thought, Jameson concludes, is ideological; only through ideological thought that knows itself as such can ideologies be seen through and eventually transcended.

In the essay that follows, Michael D. Bristol acknowledges his debt to Mikhail Bakhtin's notion that texts often contain double discourses: one reflecting the political ideology of the "official" culture; the other reflecting popular or traditional culture. Bakhtin associated the latter discourse with Carnival, not just with the excessive celebrations held before Lent, but also, and more generally, with "a class of social occasions held together by broad family resemblance — fairs, theatrical performances, public executions, and even spontaneous 'social dramas.'" For Bristol, *Hamlet* is "a play that typifies Shakespeare's use of Carnival as the basis of his dramatic art."

The discourse of Carnival, as Bakhtin understood it, is infused by the down-to-earth priorities and values held by the underprivileged or plebeian "second world" of commoners, or "folk." Because that world was necessarily concerned with basic issues of survival, with the sustenance and reproduction of life, the language of Carnival is substantially concerned with the body, with eating, with sex, and with death. In carnivalesque discourse, as well as actual practice, matters of the body are treated with a kind of profound humor — neither simply "funny" as we might say about a situation comedy, nor "serious" as we expect a high drama like *Hamlet* to be, but something in between. This doubleness produces an "ambivalent" or "grotesque" quality to Carnival imagery that allows it to contrast starkly with the language of power and propriety.

Bakhtinian criticism is meant to help us understand Renaissance popular culture, where popular means something traditional shared by all people but especially preserved and respected by the nonelite segments of society. In England this divergence was complicated by the strength of puritanism, for Puritans from any part of the social order might criticize these traditional festive and communal practices, which were seen (from the point of view of the radical Protestants) as tainted by their association with the Catholic Church. Bristol uses a Bakhtinian approach to show how the text of *Hamlet* is traversed by a kind of popular discourse with its own political meaning, a discourse of which we have little direct textual evidence other than the language and imagery of Carnival.

According to Bristol's reading of *Hamlet*, Claudius is something like Carnival's Lord of Misrule. For one thing, he has deposed the legitimate ruler. For another, the celebration he declares in honor of the dead king and his own marriage to the widowed queen is grotesque in the way that Carnival can be grotesque, mingling sex and death, comedy and tragedy, festivity and mourning in a way that is improper from the vantage point of the official discourse. Finally, though, Claudius only *seems* like an interloper from the world of Carnival. The realm he governs is a dark parody of Carnival society; he is not so much the Lord of Misrule as he is the Lord of Misrule's evil twin. True, he has upset the social order, but he has done so through a cowardly murder that would in no way be countenanced by the folk and their values. Furthermore, he has uncrowned a king only to wear the crown himself; he has not so much mocked authority as he has coveted it.

What Bristol calls the "carnivalesque pattern of uncrowning" in *Hamlet* is thus not reflected so much in Claudius and his grotesque doings as it is in the grave-diggers' scene, in which the poor and their laughter rule the day. On one hand the grave-digging clowns, "who typify underprivileged labor in their work, their language, and the[ir] social attitudes," understand all too well how privilege and money influence the treatment of people — even when they are dead. ("If this had not been a gentlewoman," one says to the other as they dig the grave of the suicide Ophelia, "she should have been buried out a' Christian burial" [5.1.22–24].) On the other hand, the grave-diggers know that, at the site on which they perform their work, all claims of political, economic, or class superiority are ultimately laughable. As their jokes make all too clear, the only real rules of the world are death and change.

Although Bakhtin's ideas have been mentioned in the foregoing discussion of Marxist criticism, Bakhtin would not have called himself a Marxist, and many who have recently applied his literary theories do not consider themselves Marxists either. Then again, as Bristol points out in the opening paragraph of his essay, Marx *himself* was "famous for the paradoxical claim that he was not a Marxist." What, then, makes a critic a Marxist? Calling himself a Marxist critic, Bristol suggests that it is the tendency to see literature in light of "class consciousness and class struggle." Few critics before Bristol have illuminated so powerfully the way in which *Hamlet* represents a struggle between the proletarian consciousness and that of the prevailing patriarchy. The theories of Bakhtin about the carnivalesque countercurrent within texts allow Bristol to show how that struggle informs the play in image, structure, and genre.

Ross C Murfin

MARXIST CRITICISM:
A SELECTED BIBLIOGRAPHY

Marx, Engels, Lenin, and Trotsky

Engels, Friedrich. *The Condition of the Working Class in England.* Ed. and trans. W. O. Henderson and W. H. Chaloner. Stanford: Stanford UP, 1968.

Lenin, V. I. *On Literature and Art.* Moscow: Progress, 1967.

Marx, Karl. *Selected Writings.* Ed. David McLellan. Oxford, Eng.: Oxford UP, 1977.

Trotsky, Leon. *Literature and Revolution.* New York: Russell, 1967.

General Introductions to and
Reflections on Marxist Criticism

Bennett, Tony. *Formalism and Marxism.* London: Methuen, 1979.

Demetz, Peter. *Marx, Engels, and the Poets.* Chicago: U of Chicago P, 1967.

Eagleton, Terry. *Literary Theory: An Introduction.* Minneapolis: U of Minnesota P, 1983. See chapter on Marxism.

——. *Marxism and Literary Criticism.* Berkeley: U of California P, 1976.

Elster, Jon. *An Introduction to Karl Marx.* Cambridge, Eng.: Cambridge UP, 1985.

——. *Nuts and Bolts for the Social Sciences.* Cambridge, Eng.: Cambridge UP, 1989.

Fokkema, D. W., and Elrud Kunne-Ibsch. *Theories of Literature in the Twentieth Century: Structuralism, Marxism, Aesthetics of Reception, Semiotics.* New York: St. Martin's, 1977. See ch. 4, "Marxist Theories of Literature."

Frow, John. *Marxism and Literary History.* Cambridge: Harvard UP, 1986.

Jefferson, Ann, and David Robey. *Modern Literary Theory: A Critical Introduction.* Totowa: Barnes, 1982. See the essay "Marxist Literary Theories," by David Forgacs.

Laing, Dave. *The Marxist Theory of Art.* Brighton, Eng.: Harvester, 1978.

Selden, Raman. *A Reader's Guide to Contemporary Literary Theory.* Lexington: U of Kentucky P, 1985. See ch. 2, "Marxist Theories."

Slaughter, Cliff. *Marxism, Ideology and Literature.* Atlantic Highlands: Humanities, 1980.

Some Classic Marxist Studies and Statements

Adorno, Théodor. *Prisms: Cultural Criticism and Society.* Trans. Samuel Weber and Sherry Weber. Cambridge: MIT P, 1982.

Althusser, Louis. *For Marx.* Trans. Ben Brewster. New York: Pantheon, 1969.

Althusser, Louis, and Etienne Balibar. *Reading Capital.* Trans. Ben Brewster. New York: Pantheon, 1971.

Benjamin, Walter. *Illuminations.* Ed. with introd. by Hannah Arendt. Trans. H. Zohn. New York: Harcourt, 1968.

Caudwell, Christopher. *Illusion and Reality.* 1935. New York: Russell, 1955.

———. *Studies in a Dying Culture.* London: Lawrence, 1938.

Goldmann, Lucien. *The Hidden God.* New York: Humanities, 1964.

———. *Towards a Sociology of the Novel.* London: Tavistock, 1975.

Gramsci, Antonio. *Selections from the Prison Notebooks.* Ed. Quintin Hoare and Geoffrey Nowell Smith. New York: International UP, 1971.

Kettle, Arnold. *An Introduction to the English Novel.* New York: Harper, 1960.

Lukács, Georg. *The Historical Novel.* Trans. H. Mitchell and S. Mitchell. Boston: Beacon, 1963.

———. *Studies in European Realism.* New York: Grosset, 1964.

———. *The Theory of the Novel.* Cambridge: MIT P, 1971.

Marcuse, Herbert. *One-Dimensional Man.* Boston: Beacon, 1964.

Thompson, E. P. *The Making of the English Working Class.* New York: Pantheon, 1964.

———. *William Morris: Romantic to Revolutionary.* New York: Pantheon, 1977.

Williams, Raymond. *Culture and Society 1780–1950.* New York: Harper, 1958.

———. *The Long Revolution.* New York: Columbia UP, 1961.

———. *Marxism and Literature.* Oxford, Eng.: Oxford UP, 1977.

Wilson, Edmund. *To the Finland Station.* Garden City: Doubleday, 1953.

Studies by and of
Post-Althusserian Marxists

Dowling, William C. *Jameson, Althusser, Marx: An Introduction to "The Political Unconscious."* Ithaca: Cornell UP, 1984.

Eagleton, Terry. *Criticism and Ideology: A Study in Marxist Literary Theory.* London: Verso, 1978.

———. *Exiles and Émigrés.* New York: Schocken, 1970.

Jameson, Fredric. *Marxism and Form: Twentieth-Century Dialectical Theories of Literature.* Princeton: Princeton UP, 1971.

———. *The Political Unconscious: Narrative as a Socially Symbolic Act.* Ithaca: Cornell UP, 1981.

Macherey, Pierre. *A Theory of Literary Production.* Trans. G. Wall. London: Routledge, 1978.

Works by Bakhtin and Studies
of the Carnivalesque and the Grotesque Body

Bakhtin, Mikhail. *The Dialogic Imagination: Four Essays.* Ed. Michael Holquist. Trans. Caryl Emerson. Austin: U of Texas P, 1981.

———. *Rabelais and His World.* Trans. Hélène Iswolsky. Cambridge: MIT P, 1968.

Bristol, Michael. *Carnival and Theatre: Plebeian Culture and the Structure of Authority in Renaissance England.* London: Methuen, 1985.

Stallybrass, Peter. "Patriarchal Territories: The Body Enclosed." *Rewriting the Renaissance: The Discourses of Sexual Difference in Early Modern Europe.* Ed. Margaret Ferguson, Maureen Quilligan, and Nancy Vickers. Chicago: U of Chicago P, 1986. 123–42. On Bakhtin and on *Othello.*

Stallybrass, Peter, and Allon White. *The Politics and Poetics of Transgression.* Ithaca: Cornell UP, 1986.

Other Cultural Materialist Studies of Shakespeare

Belsey, Catherine. *The Subject of Tragedy: Identity and Difference in Renaissance Drama.* London: Methuen, 1985.

Dollimore, Jonathan. *Radical Tragedy: Religion, Ideology and Power in the Drama of Shakespeare and His Contemporaries.* Chicago: U of Chicago P, 1984.

———. "Introduction: Shakespeare, Cultural Materialism, and the New Historicism." Dollimore and Sinfield 2–17.

Dollimore, Jonathan, and Alan Sinfield, eds. *Political Shakespeare: New Essays in Cultural Materialism.* Ithaca: Cornell UP, 1985. An influential collection of essays.

Drakakis, John, ed. *alternative shakespeares.* London: Methuen, 1985.

Howard, Jean, and Marion O'Connor, eds. *Shakespeare Reproduced: The Text in History and in Ideology.* New York: Methuen, 1987.

Jardine, Lisa. *Still Harping on Daughters: Women and Drama in the Age of Shakespeare.* 2nd ed. New York: Columbia UP, 1989.

Kavanagh, James. "Shakespeare in Ideology." Drakakis 144–65.

Marxist Studies of Shakespeare or of *Hamlet*

Cohen, Walter. *The Drama of a Nation: Public Theater in Renaissance England and Spain.* Ithaca: Cornell UP, 1985.

———. "Political Criticism of Shakespeare." Howard and O'Connor 18–46. Includes extensive, useful bibliography.

Eagleton, Terry. *William Shakespeare.* Oxford, Eng.: Basil Blackwell, 1986.

Weimann, Robert. *Shakespeare and the Popular Tradition in the Theater: Studies in the Social Dimension of Dramatic Form and Function.* Ed. Robert Schwartz. Baltimore: Johns Hopkins UP, 1978.

———. "Mimesis and *Hamlet.*" *Shakespeare and the Question of Theory.* Ed. Patricia Parker and Geoffrey Hartman. New York: Methuen, 1985. 275–91.

———. "History and the Issue of Authority in Representation: The Elizabethan Theater and Its Reformation." *New Literary History* 17 (1986): 449–76.

A MARXIST PERSPECTIVE

MICHAEL D. BRISTOL

"Funeral Bak'd-Meats": Carnival and the Carnivalesque in *Hamlet*

Marx is famous for the paradoxical claim that he was not a Marxist, and in a sense this is a perfectly accurate description. What Marx meant by this was that he did not regard his own research as a substantive theory, and did not expect his writings to become a kind of secular scripture. The orientation known as "Marxist criticism" should not require loyalty to any of the substantive doctrines found in Marx, and indeed the very notion of criticism demands open-endedness, doubt, and genuine curiosity as fundamental to any real knowledge. Following Jon Elster, in his admirable *Introduction to Karl Marx,* I would characterize myself as a Marxist in the sense that many of my basic orientations to research and critical thinking have their ancestry in the writings of Marx.

Marx was an ambitious and prolific thinker, who had important and influential things to say on a wide variety of topics. Working with the best evidence he could gather at the time he proposed a broad theory of human practice, touching in particular on the domains of history, economic theory, and social structure. Many of Marx's arguments were based on what we now know to be faulty or incomplete evidence, and this is compounded by the fact that he was often distracted by wishful thinking, faulty logic, or by the rigorous imperatives of short-term political struggle. In order to do good Marxist criticism, it is crucial to recognize that many of the substantive doctrines of classical Marxism have to be substantially modified in the light of more recent research. Nevertheless, Marxism retains its value as a type of social and cultural criticism that focuses on social conflict, social creativity, and the struggle for positive social change. More specifically, Marx's notions of distributive justice, and his discussion of topics such as alienation and exploitation still retain considerable value. The most fundamental idea in Marxism, the theory of class consciousness and class struggle still has enormous importance in providing a basic orientation for research. Marxist research demands a commitment to the belief that real social and historical explanation is possible, and that this explanation is most likely to be found in the analysis of social struggle and conflict. It is these principles that I have tried to adhere to in the critical work that I have done on Shakespeare.

The action of *Hamlet* takes place against two contrasting backdrops. One of these is a world of international politics, characterized by diplomatic missions, intellectual and cultural exchange, and geopolitical struggle (see Metscher). All of the young men in this story are engaged in this dynamic and cosmopolitan world that echoes the intellectual and political dynamism of Shakespeare's actual society. Claudius belongs to this world as well, but, as the representative of an older generation, he takes care to place himself and the activities of his court in a quite different social and cultural milieu when he proclaims a period of festive celebration that will honor simultaneously his dead predecessor and his own marriage to the widowed queen. The funeral for Hamlet's father is combined with a wedding feast, and this odd mingling of grief and of festive laughter is typical of the play as a whole.

The personal struggle of Hamlet, his profound doubts about what to do and his agonized, sometimes hilarious reflections about his own uncertainty are the aspect of the play that modern audiences find most accessible and sympathetic. But this very private and personal tension is both clearer and more meaningful when it can be understood in the context of larger movements of social and cultural change. Hamlet has internalized strong oppositions in basic social values; he has a passionately felt loyalty to the traditional ethos of his murdered father and yet in some ways he more closely resembles his archenemy Claudius in his understanding of a more typically modern political reality. These fundamentally historical differences are experienced by Hamlet as psychological conflicts. Hamlet's question, "What must I do?" can be usefully reinterpreted as the question of "Where do I belong?" or even "How can my life make sense within a social landscape of irreconcilable social difference?" The most effective critical strategy to adopt in this context, therefore, is to concentrate on the way Shakespeare has deployed the resources of Carnival to represent and at the same time to criticize important beliefs and practices in the official culture of his own time. Carnival is a vivid, intense, and highly dramatic way to make the complex social dialogue that is *Hamlet* much more audible.

Hamlet is a play that typifies Shakespeare's use of Carnival as the basis of his dramatic art. It is a text in which the language of popular festive form is deeply embedded in the structure of action and where the meanings privileged in the culture of Carnival are fully actualized. Although the play is filled with tragedy and horror, many of the scenes are extremely funny, and indeed for much of the action Hamlet and Claudius stalk each other like two murderous clowns attempting to achieve strategic advantage over the other. Claudius adopts certain popular, carnivalesque attitudes as a way to conceal his aggressive, rational calculation of self-interest behind a mask of traditional pieties, folk wisdom, and festive distractions. Hamlet's "antic disposition" is also a kind of carnivalesque disguise or camouflage, although Hamlet is much more genuinely in touch with the popular festive sources of Carnival than Claudius, especially in his understanding of the corrosive and clarifying power of laughter. For Hamlet and for the audience as well, however, the larger meaning of Carnival emerges only gradually and is fully revealed in the grave-diggers' scene as a powerful transformation downward, or "uncrowning," of the world of official culture, geopolitical conflict, and royal intrigue.

Carnival was observed throughout Europe during the early modern period, reaching its climax on Shrove Tuesday or Mardi Gras, just before the beginning of Lent. Traditionally this is a time of hedonistic excess and transgression. Carnival permits and actually encourages the unlimited consumption of special foods, drunkenness, and a high degree of sexual license, which often leads to street violence and civil commotion. The custom of masking and disguise makes it easier for the participants to get away with these violations of social order, and indeed it is typical of Carnival that social order is literally turned upside down. Despite its notoriety as a time of excess, license, and derangement, the word *Carnival* actually refers to and marks the beginning of a period of lenten renunciation; the word is derived from the Latin expression *carnem levare*, the taking away of meat or "farewell to the flesh." It is precisely this ambivalent, paradoxical, and unstable character that gives Carnival its social importance.

Misrule, inversion, and travesty are the typical strategies of the carnivalesque. A Carnival masquerade embodies an alternative set of rules for interpreting social reality. In these participatory celebrations traditional religious and political symbols are combined with humble objects from the kitchen and the workshop, and with images of bodily functions, especially those relating to food and eating. In Brueghel's painting *The Battle of Carnival and Lent,* the personification of Carnival rides on a wine barrel instead of a horse, and the combatants brandish cooking utensils instead of weapons. Various figures in Carnival's entourage wear articles of food or kitchenware on their heads — a kettle, a hat made of waffles — and Carnival himself is crowned with a meat pie that someone has bitten into (see Gaignebet, "Le Combat," and Davis).

The comprehensive rethinking of the social world in terms of common everyday material and physical experience is central to the practice of "uncrowning" — the fundamental transformation downward of popular festive imagery. Here the kettle or meat pie takes the place of the crown or helmet as the "topmost" principle. In this way Carnival brings our knowledge of social reality down to earth and substitutes the body, its needs, and its capabilities, for more abstract and restrictive "laws" of society and its organization. Carnival draws attention to the relative and arbitrary character of official versions of political order. In this way the experience of Carnival opens up alternative possibilities for action and helps to facilitate creativity in the social sphere.

Although Carnival specifically refers only to festivities that immediately precede Lent, the typical Carnival experience of excess and social derangement is not limited to a single annual blowout. In fact, during the early modern period there were many regularly occurring feasts with typical carnivalesque features of material abundance, license, and social effervescence (see Gaignebet, *Le Carnaval*). In a further extension of the term, Carnival may also take in a class of social occasions held together by broad family resemblance — fairs, theatrical performances, public executions, and even spontaneous "social dramas." Carnival in this broader sense is characterized by its negativity and in-betweenness. It is the liminal occasion par excellence, something that happens betwixt and between the regularly scheduled events of ordinary life.

The combined sense of ambiguity and exteriority (or marginality) points to a further meaning for Carnival, not as a specific feast, a general type of celebration, or even a class of social occasions, but rather as a mode-of-being-in-the-world or mode-of-being-together-with-others. This is what Mikhail Bakhtin refers to when he speaks of Carnival as a "second life of the people," with its own liturgy and its own system for the production and distribution of the good things of this life (Bakhtin 1968).

Bakhtin's theories of Carnival are central to a more comprehensive and ambitious set of theories of human action, social initiative, and collective authority, all based on Bakhtin's highly original and distinctive theories of human language. For Bakhtin, language is not limited to verbal behavior but encompasses gestures, physical actions, and even the organization of space and time. Furthermore, language is characterized by a social diversity of "speech types," the distinctive idiom, slang, or "shop talk" of groups and communities. The visual, verbal, and gestural repertoires of Carnival are of particular importance as a kind of expressive resistance to the authorized and permitted languages of official culture. It is this possibility of purposeful opposition to injustice and oppression that gives the carnivalesque a particular importance for the many variants of Marxist critique or for any type of criticism that puts social struggle or conflict in the foreground of its concerns.

In Bakhtin's account, Carnival is very much more than just a particularly boisterous and extended holiday. For Bakhtin, Carnival expresses a fundamental truth about the world; its down-to-earth vocabularies, its affirmation of the body, its grotesque exaggeration and aggressive annihilation of all reified modes of legitimation in fact interpret the world in a more comprehensive, universal, and practical way than the official world-views and serious philosophies of elite culture. Furthermore, the knowledge of the social world sedimented in carnivalesque symbolic and participatory practice is available to the people as a resource to be used in defense of their own values, practices, and their own version of the "good life" against the expropriations of a colonizing social structure, whether feudal or capitalist. Carnival may inform actual strategic deliberations aimed at correcting specific injustices, but there is an even more fundamental tendency in the carnivalesque to abolish class difference and social inequality. Carnival both interprets the world and acts upon it, even when the participants cannot fully articulate what they are doing.

According to Bakhtin, then, Carnival constitutes a second world, or second culture, outside the world of official culture and political authority, where ordinary, unprivileged people act out a distinctive pattern of values. These values are generated out of the practical details of everyday life, and in particular from the various activities such as agricultural labor or the preparation of food by means of which human life is produced and reproduced. A central feature of this symbolic regime is a way of interpreting the human form in terms of what Bakhtin calls the grotesque body. Classical aesthetics represents the body in terms of closure, integrity, and rational proportion. In contrast to this, the grotesque body is open, unfinished, and unrestrained. The intact surfaces and well-defined contours of the classical body give way to a celebration of growth and bodily expansion. Instead, exaggerated shapes and openings — fat bellies, swollen breasts, open mouths, enlarged genitals — are affirmed and celebrated, but also ridiculed. The body as represented in its grotesque aspect is involved in continual exchange of materials with its environment; the enjoyment of food and sexuality, as well as the satisfactions of copious excretion, are represented as ambivalent. The grotesque interpretation acknowledges the body as both desirable *and* disgusting. The openness, vulnerability, and transience of the body are typically occasions for laughter. The ability of life to reproduce itself through eating and through sexuality are privileged metaphors that overturn formal ideologies based on rigid categories of status and privilege. In this pattern, death and physical dissolution are part of a system of symbols that represent a social and biological process of continuous rebirth and renewal. In this context, death may even be treated as an occasion for both laughter and grief.

The first scenes of *Hamlet* take place during a period of mourning for a dead king, Old Hamlet. His brother and successor Claudius proclaims a period of ambiguous festivity that serves as both funeral and wedding celebration. Dramatically, this gesture appears to be very sim-

ilar to Duke Theseus's in *A Midsummer Night's Dream*. For Theseus
the celebration of his wedding called for the banishment and exclusion
of melancholy — a unison and concord of emotions that parallels the
social unity of the various ranks and functions in the community.
Claudius's call to the wedding feast reveals a deep ambivalence, however. The marriage is in many ways scandalous, tainted by intimations of
incest, adultery, and indecorous haste. And, as the play very quickly reveals, there is no real and enduring social unity in Denmark that
Claudius can appeal to. Nevertheless, Claudius tries to establish the
legitimacy of his situation by a careful balancing of two evidently contradictory forms of celebration.

> KING: Though yet of Hamlet our dear brother's death
> The memory be green, and that it us befitted
> To bear our hearts in grief, and our whole kingdom
> To be contracted in one brow of woe,
> Yet so far hath discretion fought with nature
> That we with wisest sorrow think on him
> Together with remembrance of ourselves.
> Therefore our sometime sister, now our queen,
> Th' imperial jointress to this warlike state,
> Have we, as 'twere with a defeated joy,
> With an auspicious and a dropping eye,
> With mirth in funeral, and with dirge in marriage,
> In equal scale weighing delight and dole,
> Taken to wife.
>   (1.2.1–14)

Where Theseus wished to banish melancholy, Claudius must embrace
it; his revels require a mixed decorum, the unification of contrary impulses. Claudius compares the mortality of a king as a specific human
being with the immortality of his office, and affirms that the continuing
vitality of society is independent of the transience of contingent individuals. The death of the old gives scope to the new and emergent. The
marriage to Gertrude expresses this idea of succession and renewal at a
sexual and bodily level; the disturbing candor with which that sexuality
is expressed on stage is essential to the situation, since it "brings down"
the projects and ambitions of kingship to the material and earthly level
of appetite and desire.

Taken out of context, Claudius's speech expresses a truthful intu-
ition about death, change, and human individuality that is in many ways
typical of the folk wisdom embedded in the carnivalesque. Individuals

are never static entities but instead experience manifold changes and transformations. Communal life and its institutions create a background of relative permanency against which the multifarious transformations, substitutions, and surprises of each individual life must be played out. The transgressive character of Claudius's marriage to Gertrude expresses this carnivalesque understanding of death both in its affirmation of sexual appetite and in its endorsement of shifting social identity. In a sense, Claudius functions here as a complex variant of the Lord of Misrule. He violates decorum and makes a mockery of kingship by appearing in the usurped finery of the "real" king. As a Lord of Misrule Claudius is no doubt intended to prompt our derision by virtue of the falseness of his claims, but he is also likely to encourage our mockery both for the office he usurps and for its rightful holder. He has killed his predecessor and replaced him in the queen's bed. His coronation and marriage, a kind of joke at his victim's expense, can be an occasion of Carnival mirth — an affirmation of continuing sexual, as well as political, life.

In the specific context of *Hamlet,* however, Claudius cannot really embody or represent the values of Carnival and plebeian culture in any simple or straightforward way. The link of death with marriage and sexuality as well as the affirmation of misrule are carnivalesque themes that Claudius appropriates in order to make legitimate his own questionable authority. Although he appears to understand popular culture, he is in fact both the agent and the beneficiary of a social order that excludes the popular element and expropriates its resources. Furthermore, his use of the carnivalesque is intended only as a mask for the strategic advancement of private goals and ambitions. Such a "privatizing" of carnivalesque transgression and sensuality is a fundamental distortion of the collective and communal orientations typical of plebeian culture. There is no sense in which Claudius acts in the interests of the excluded plebeian culture and although he is associated with misrule he is neither a popular king nor a champion of the popular element.

Claudius does not rely exclusively on a vocabulary of carnivalesque celebration of change as the source of his legitimacy. He also employs more conventional philosophical rhetoric to disguise the aspect of misrule in his claim to kingship.

> KING: 'Tis sweet and commendable in your nature, Hamlet,
>   To give these mourning duties to your father.
>   But you must know your father lost a father,
>   That father lost, lost his, and the survivor bound

In filial obligation for some term
To do obsequious sorrow. But to persever
In obstinate condolement is a course
Of impious stubbornness, 'tis unmanly grief.
                                            (1.2.87–94)

This is a traditional language of Christian patience and resignation that
is linked to the language of Carnival in seeing death as "a part of life as
a whole — its indispensable component, the condition of its constant
renewal and rejuvenation. . . . Death is included in life, and together
with Birth determines its eternal movement" (Bakhtin 50). Of course
Claudius's appropriation of Christian doctrine is no more "truly legitimate" than his appropriation of the spirit of Carnival. And there is a
further irony in all of this. Claudius evidently wants to use Carnival as a
means for reinforcing and making legitimate his otherwise dubious political authority. But Carnival typically mocks and uncrowns all authority. And, as the action will make clear, Carnival cannot be controlled
"from above"; Claudius's scheme to consolidate his power by means of
a carnivalized variant of kingly authority will be fatally compromised by
other versions of a downward carnivalesque movement articulated by
Hamlet, the players, and the grave-diggers.
    Although the Danish court participates in the traditional festive ob-
servance of political succession and regal hospitality, Hamlet sees himself as excluded from the conviviality of this society. The custom of excessive drinking, evidently a traditional practice in the Danish court, is
viewed by Hamlet as corruption and decadence. His initial rejection of
all forms of carnivalesque derangement, whether traditional or not, is
symbolized by his black suit and his mournful attitude. The motivation
of that exclusion is his revulsion toward the ambivalent and contradictory decorum of the festive practices of the Danish court. His perception of the feasting and revelry is expressed in his first greeting to
Horatio, where he complains of his mother's haste in remarrying.

    HAMLET: Thrift, thrift, Horatio, the funeral bak'd-meats
        Did coldly furnish forth the marriage tables.
                                            (1.2.180–81)

It is a bitter jest about the unseemliness, the indecorousness of the situation, that is at once a moral judgment on the behavior of Claudius and
Gertrude as well as a philosophically principled objection to what he
takes to be a scandalous adherence to certain carnivalesque customs

within the court. He has already explained how the outward presentation of self ought to correspond to the inner state. His own suit of woe, he insists, bears a constant and natural resemblance to the grief that excludes all other feeling in Hamlet. But conventional signs of grief are not enough in themselves to "[denote][him] truly" (1.2.83); since others dissemble and falsify outward symbols, strong action — but of a kind he may not yet recognize — will be required to reinvest signs with their true meanings.

In the strained and deceptively festive atmosphere of Claudius's court, Hamlet stands firmly for the values of seriousness; as the action begins, he does not perform nor play nor dissimulate. His laughter is satiric and judgmental, the laughter of rational evaluations. He feels particular revulsion about eating and drinking; the funeral meats that grace the wedding banquet are offensive to Hamlet in the way they actualize a process of continuity oblivious to the distinctions he wishes to make. Meat is the link between the living and the dead; in the wedding feast/funeral banquet, the continuity of social life is affirmed over the finite individual.

Claudius then can be interpreted as an individual representation of the grotesque body — incomplete, unfinished, deeply implicated in the lower functions of sexuality — and of its appetites, yet the full implications of carnivalesque uncrowning never enter his self-understanding. Carnival laughter, acknowledgment of the body in its open and festive manifestations, ambivalence of emotion, and mixed decorum have all been co-opted by power and authority, without the recognition that these strategies necessarily entail a critique of authority that is inimical to the interests of power. Hamlet's deliberate self-exclusion from the festive rests upon hunches and suspicions about the real meaning of the feasting in the Danish court that are more fully developed later in the play. He cannot return to Wittenberg and to the life of rational clarity it evidently represents for him; he must instead become part of and in a sense accept the complex and ambivalent world of courtly and popular festivity in order to understand it.

The environment of Denmark's court is dominated by dissimulation and intrigue; Hamlet defines his problem as the penetration of this intrigue, the unmasking and exposure of all dissimulation (see Mack, Colie). And yet neither his own rhetoric nor the interrogation of others is sufficient to consolidate his knowledge, let alone persuade others. Even his counterfestivity — the antic disposition, the dumb show, and the reenactment of the murder — falls short of producing knowledge. A more decisive act is required and this comes finally with the killing of

Polonius. This murder is a mistake, but Polonius's identity is fixed at last, and, for Hamlet, words begin to have more solid meanings, as he laughs the guts offstage.

The killing reveals to Hamlet the clarifying possibilities of violence, the way in which the identity of a thing may be known by killing it and removing it from the changes of living experience. It also forces Hamlet back to the issues of the body and to a new understanding of "funeral bak'd-meats."

> KING: Now, Hamlet, where's Polonius?
> HAMLET: At supper.
> KING: At supper? where?
> HAMLET: Not where he eats, but where 'a is eaten; a certain con-
> vocation of politic worms are e'en at him. Your worm is your
> only emperor for diet: we fat all creatures else to fat us, and we
> fat ourselves for maggots; your fat king and your lean beggar
> is but variable service, two dishes, but to one table — that's
> the end.
>
> (4.3.16–24)

Here the rhetoric Hamlet uses is carnivalized; emperors are uncrowned so as to be used as food while worms have become "politic" and impe-rial.

By opening Polonius's body with the sword, Hamlet has fixed his identity in the endless circular process in which life devours life and in-dividual pretension is brought down to earth by the constant struggles for existence of "worms" human and natural.

> HAMLET: A man may fish with the worm that hath eat of a king,
> and eat of the fish that hath fed of that worm.
> KING: What dost thou mean by this?
> HAMLET: Nothing but to show you how a king may go a progress
> through the guts of a beggar.
>
> (4.3.26–30)

According to the principles of rationality by which he tried to operate at first, Hamlet was required to make distinctions between father and uncle, between Hyperion and satyr, king and beggar, human and worm. Using the logic of grotesque Carnival equivocation, he can now see an equivalence between Old Hamlet and Claudius. The royal "progress," which affirms hierarchy, social superiority, and political power, is brought down to the lower functions of the body — a king's pretensions are devoured by the unprivileged.

Hamlet has learned the language of grotesque equivocation and its critique of power as an outsider in the intrigues of the court, but he is not yet acquainted with the popular sources of that language within the everyday life and practical conscious of the common people. The fullest elaboration of the carnivalesque pattern of uncrowning is presented in the grave-diggers' scene. Here actual representatives of the unprivileged appear as clowns who give direct articulation to the perspective of a culture in which the meanings of Carnival are most fully and accurately understood. The opening dialogue of the clowns anchors the graveyard scene in a concrete social milieu; the clowns typify unprivileged labor in their work, their language, and the social attitudes they express.

> FIRST CLOWN: Will you ha' the truth an't? If this had not been a gentlewoman, she should have been buried out a' Christian burial.
> SECOND CLOWN: Why, there thou say'st, and the more pity that great folk should have count'nance in this world to drown or hang themselves more than their even-Christen.
>
> (5.1.22–27)

Christian burial is, of course, given in accordance with the spiritual condition of the deceased at the presumed moment of death. The clowns perceive very clearly, however, how wealth and privilege influence such determination, so that social distinction seems to persist into the afterlife. But the joking about suicide as a privilege reserved for "great folk" is extremely complicated. There is the direct implication of resentment over privilege of any kind, resentment grounded in the principle of "even-Christen," the belief that all men are equal in God's sight. At the same time the grave-digger expresses a certain grim satisfaction with the particular privilege in question — let them all drown themselves if that's the privilege they insist on.

The preoccupation with privilege and social class is given even more direct expression in the grave-diggers' discussion of the ancient origins of "gentlemen."

> FIRST CLOWN: There is no ancient gentlemen but gard'ners, ditchers, and grave-makers. They hold up Adam's profession.

SECOND CLOWN: Was he a gentleman?
FIRST CLOWN: 'A was the first that ever bore arms.
SECOND CLOWN: Why, he had none.
FIRST CLOWN: What, art a heathen? How dost thou understand the
   Scripture? The Scripture says Adam digg'd. Could he dig with-
   out arms?

(5.1.28–36)

This is a clear and explicit critique of the basis for social hierarchy in
gentility and the privilege of "bearing arms." The grave-digger's reference to Adam digging restores a subordinated meaning for "arms" not
as the signifier of social difference, but rather as the sign of social equality. All men and women have real arms, as opposed to a symbolic "coat
of arms," and all men and women thus share the capacity to work so as
to create subsistence. The grave-digger's speech clearly echoes the nascent egalitarian ideology expressed in the following anonymous verse
that was popular in various early modern protest movements such as the
diggers or the levelers.

   When Adam delved
   And Eve span
   Who was then
   The Gentleman?

Gardeners and grave-makers, and by extension everyone who does productive labor, are the true descendants of Adam and thus the only real
"gentlefolk."

   Against the perspective of death and burial all claims to hierarchical
superiority are nullified, all the "serious" claims of economic, political,
or moral systems become the objects of laughter. The doomsday image
of the grave is from this perspective not something grim and gloomy
but, on the contrary, the occasion for "drink" and merriment. The
grave-diggers' jokes reflect an alternative hierarchy of ontological categories in which death and change are sovereign and permanent, while
such symbolic edifices as church, state, and society are killed, buried,
dissolved back into the earth by the patient and persistent labor of the
grave-digger.

   In the grave-diggers' world-view, doomsday is a horizon that corresponds to the overthrow of social inequality. The grave-digger enacts
this philosophy by staging the grotesque exchange between life and
death as he tosses various skulls and bones out of the grave. Hamlet and

Horatio enter as he works; after some extended raillery, the clown shows Hamlet a particularly interesting skull.

> CLOWN: Here's a skull that hath lien you i' th' earth three and
> twenty years. . . . A pestilence on him for a mad rogue! 'a
> poured a flagon of Rhenish on my head once. This same skull,
> sir, was, sir, Yorick's skull, the King's jester.
>
> (5.1.161–69)

There is no reason to doubt the grave-digger's assertion about the skull's identity — but there is nothing to confirm it either. A skull presents no identifying features, no countenance, that allows us to recognize individuality. As far as the audience can tell, Yorick's skull looks just like the other skulls that have by now been tossed about onstage. But this absence of individual features does not make the grave-digger's identification of the skull less cogent. The entity known as "Yorick" consists of a relationship between social integument (guise, false-face, persona) and a "viewer" or "spectator" (social Other) to acknowledge it.

Using the prop to focus his imagination Hamlet reconstitutes the social meaning sedimented in a grinning skull.

> HAMLET: Alas, poor Yorick! I knew him, Horatio, a fellow of infi-
> nite jest, of most excellent fancy. He hath bore me on his back
> a thousand times, and now how abhorr'd in my imagination it
> is! my gorge rises at it. Here hung those lips that I have kiss'd
> I know not how oft. Where be your gibes now, your gambols,
> your songs, your flashes of merriment, that were wont to set
> the table on a roar?
>
> (5.1.172–78)

The genuine "community" the prince remembers is dead and buried, but this is the moment of its resurrection as an object of nostalgia. The old jester is dead, but the power of laughter is indestructible. Even a dead jester can make us laugh; here the "dead" mock the "living," by reminding us that there is a kind of equality between "a pestilent rogue" and "my lady." The contemplation of mortality becomes funny.

> HAMLET: Imperious Caesar, dead and turn'd to clay,
> Might stop a hole to keep the wind away.
> O that that earth which kept the world in awe
> Should patch a wall t' expel the [winter's] flaw!
>
> (5.1.199–202)

All the categories of social existence, gender, rank, metier, and so on, are relative and impermanent; the skull is the negation of identity, an ominous parody of the human face. The imperial image of glory and majesty — Caesar, Alexander — is uncrowned by plebeian consciousness that views power as a bloody and farcical masquerade. In addition, the scene fundamentally disrupts the genre to which the play nominally belongs.

Hamlet is a tragedy, and the story the play tells happens long after the jester has died. In a sense this might be taken as an exemplary definition of tragedy, that is, as a story in which the skull as a memento mori replaces the actual jester. But in this play the jester's absence is more than offset by the appearance of a number of other clowns, including most notably Hamlet himself. The image of a man in a graveyard contemplating a skull is the typical representation of *memento mori*, but here this dark, forbidding symbol of the values of seriousness and penitential self-renunciation has itself been carnivalized. The sense of the tragic is not, however, diminished or "subverted" by this; instead the laughter typical of the carnivalesque takes on greater philosophical depth and complexity.

The complex "knowledge" Hamlet achieves at the edge of the grave does not stop with Caesar's return to dust, for at this moment the funeral procession for Ophelia comes onstage. The scene is a counterstatement to the grave-diggers' laughter. Ceremony is preserved, social convention is affirmed because even in these unhappy circumstances the value of the person remains. Imperious Caesar, whose function now is to stop a bunghole, is a suitable object for laughter and derision, but Ophelia's death is no joking matter. The ceremonies at the grave link death and marriage again, but in a more obviously disturbing way than before, for here death does not give birth to new possibility — death proscribes marriage and forestalls possibility of renewed life. A moment earlier the prince reflected on the impermanence of individuality; now he "goes down" into the grave, to give himself a definite name and title, to struggle with an enemy, and in spite of the lessons in equivocation he learned from the grave-digger, to proclaim his love in heightened and theatrical rhetoric.

> HAMLET: 'Swounds, show me what thou't do.
>   Woo't weep? woo't fight? woo't fast? woo't tear thyself?
>   Woo't drink up eisel, eat a crocadile?
>   I'll do't. Dost thou come here to whine?

To outface me with leaping in her grave?
Be buried quick with her, and so will I.
And if thou prate of mountains, let them throw
Millions of acres on us, till our ground,
Singeing his pate against the burning zone,
Make Ossa like a wart! Nay, and thou'lt mouth,
I'll rant as well as thou.

(5.1.260–70)

To experience the grave is to pass beyond all histrionics; having seen this, Hamlet now indulges in a moment of exaggerated theatricality, reaching for the grand gesture, challenging Laertes to "outface" him. Even standing in the grave Hamlet cannot stop acting, he cannot refrain from "making a scene." The laughing or grinning skull may objectify or represent an existence that is beyond dissimulation, it may instruct us in the impermanence of social categories, it may even humble us by dissolving our claims to status in a grim and frightening laugh — but the knowledge offered by the skull is never actualized on this side of the grave. This knowledge applies to everyone, whether aristocratic or plebeian. What typifies plebeian consciousness in this respect is the blunt and fearless acknowledgment of death as a process of social leveling.

At this point it is useful to raise a question about staging. What happens to the grave-digger when the coffin of Ophelia is brought onstage? The text provides no answer to this question, since the stage directions indicate only that all exit after the king's speech to Laertes. The director is faced with a number of choices — the grave-digger can retire discreetly, or he can remain onstage in a visible position without joining the mourners — in effect upstaging the entire proceeding. The director, in making this decision, must commit herself on the question of social distinction, dramatic tone — that is, on the entire complex of issues related to social degree and social hierarchy.

If the grave-digger discreetly exits during the burial sequence, his function as a popular chorus interpreting the values and the conflicts of the dominant culture is weakened. Plebeian values and popular critique would be given only limited expression in order to return with great assurance to the "real" or official problematics of the court. But if he remains onstage throughout the burial, the grave-digger can gather up the skulls and prepare for the next scene. The grave-digger's resulting presence through Ophelia's burial would then amplify his function as a Plebeian chorus. He is the man whose houses last till doomsday. His presence would alter the audience's perception of Ophelia (who has the privilege to kill herself), of Laertes, of Hamlet, of the whole court. He can watch the grief, the ambition, the anxiety over privilege, decorum, and ceremony with an attitude of amused indifference.

The pattern of festivity is completed in the final scene, where Claudius again presides over a scene of revelry. The main festive sequence is from ritual to dramatic entertainment to game and sport: Claudius celebrates a marriage and a funeral, Claudius views a play, Claudius welcomes home a nobleman and enjoys a bout of fencing. In each of these scenes the king acts as host at a feast. We see him display the gestures and attitudes of merriment, or holiday, turning away from serious business, to indulge his appetites. Hamlet refuses participation in the festive process at the stage of ritual; he commits himself to partial but conditional involvement through dramatic artifice; when festivity opens into game, when genuine hazard and exercise of skill create a series of dynamic possibilities, his participation in the festive scene is complete.

But what does it mean to be fully engaged in a "festive process" in the world of this play? The logic of everything that has come before is by now transparent; the stage must be piled high with slaughtered "meat." The two most powerful families have been completely exterminated; old kinship relationships are eliminated, traditional claims to the throne are canceled and the situation is open for whatever is new and emergent. The redundancy of Claudius's assassination (execution) by Hamlet is of course entirely appropriate here; both aspects of Claudius's kingship — the active and the festive, the sword and cup of wine, are turned against him.

An important tendency in Carnival is fulfilled in this final scene. While it would be unusual for an actual Carnival to result in an organized insurrection of the common people, violent social protest was not uncommon and sometimes this violence could take the form of large-scale class warfare (see LeRoy Ladurie). In *Hamlet* the violence and bloodshed latent in a Carnival arises from factional antagonism rather than class conflict, but it really does bring about a change in the political order. However, the regime of Fortinbras hardly represents the overthrow of aristocratic authority in favor of a popular and egalitarian redistribution of power. To the contrary, it seems likely that a stringent administrative and social discipline amounting to martial law will be imposed.

The party's over. The festive process we witness here does not move from rigidity through release to clarification, at least not in the basically reassuring sense of a controlled and exceptional "holiday" turning us back to an unquestioned harmony. The real logic of festivity is the dissolution, and finally the extinction of identity, the annihilation of the individual in the historical continuum. The process, on the other hand, does not come to an end, and so witnesses must be implicated in what has been acted out.

> HAMLET: You that look pale and tremble at this chance,
> That are but mutes or audience to this act,
> Had I but time — as this fell sergeant, Death,
> Is strict in his arrest — O, I could tell you —
> But let it be.
>
> (5.2.316–20)

Hamlet is about to leave the stage and his concern with how his story will be told to the "mutes and audience" suggest that there is no real end to the histrionics. Horatio will "stand in" for him, so that Hamlet must compel his friend to "refuse festivity" just as he has done before.

"Mutes and audience" may be passive, they may be excluded from privileged knowledge, and yet somehow the record of one's deed vis-à-vis this witnessing body remains crucial.

> O God, Horatio, what a wounded name,
> Things standing thus unknown, shall I leave behind me!
>
> (5.2.326–27)

Fortinbras enters to the sound of drums and trumpets; melancholy joins with mirth again as Hamlet becomes a prop in someone else's political pageantry — pageantry offered to an audience of ordinary men and women in the "yet unknowing world." The play opens toward a future that is not all that different in certain respects from the events so far acted out, at least as far as the tension between "high" political drama and a "low" audience of nonparticipating witnesses is concerned. The grave-digger represents that "low audience" on the stage and serves as a chorus expressing their way of seeing the events of high political struggle.

Carnival, with its ambivalent and contradictory language, uncrowns the shifting rationales used to explicate political intrigue and supplies an alternative reading of history based on the arbitrariness and transience of political authority.

And so they said that these matters bee Kynges games, as it were
stage playes, and for the more part plaied upon scafoldes. In
which pore men be but lookers on. . . . (More 81)

These "pore men" know and understand the action through the Carnival linking of life and death, their rhythmic alternation, and the mixed
emotions this rhythm brings forth.

WORKS CITED

Bakhtin, Mikhail. *The World of Rabelais.* Trans. Hélène Iswolsky.
Cambridge: MIT P, 1968.

Barber, C. L. *Shakespeare's Festive Comedy.* New York: Meridian
Books, 1963.

Burke, Peter. *Popular Culture in Early Modern Europe.* New York:
New York UP, 1978.

Capp, Bernard. "English Youth Groups and *The Pinder of Wakefield.*"
Past and Present 76 (1977): 127–133.

Colie, Rosalie. *Shakespeare's Living Art.* Princeton: Princeton UP,
1974.

Davis, Natalie Z. "The Reasons of Misrule." *Society and Culture in
Early Modern France.* Stanford: Stanford UP, 1975. 97–123.

Elster, Jon. *An Introduction to Karl Marx.* Cambridge, Eng.: Cambridge UP, 1985.

Gaignebet, Claude. *Le Carnaval: Essais de mythologie populaire.* Paris:
Payot, 1974.

———. "Le Combat de Carnaval et de Carême de P. Breughel
(1559)." *Annales: Économies, Sociétés, Civilizations* 27 (1972):
313–43.

———. "Le Cycle annuel des fêtes à Rouen au milieu du XVIe
siècle." *Les Fêtes de la Renaissance, III.* Paris: Éditions du Centre
National de la Recherche Scientifique, 1975. 569–78.

LeRoy Ladurie, Emmanuel. *Carnival in Romans.* Trans. Mary
Feeney. New York: Braziller, 1979.

Mack, Maynard. "The World of Hamlet." *Yale Review* 41 (1959):
502–23.

Margolin, Jean Claude. "Charivari et marriage ridicule au temps de la
Renaissance." *Les Fêtes de la Renaissance, III.* Paris: Éditions du
Centre National de la Recherche Scientifique, 1975. 579–601.

Metscher, Thomas. "Shakespeare in the Context of Renaissance Europe." *Science and Society* 41 (1976): 17–24.

More, Thomas. *The History of King Richard III*. Ed. Richard S. Sylvester. *Yale Edition of the Complete Works of St. Thomas More.* New Haven: Yale UP, 1963.

Mullaney, Steven. *The Place of the Stage: License, Play, and Power in Renaissance England.* Chicago: U of Chicago P, 1988.

Thompson, E. P. "Rough Music: Le Charivari Anglais." *Annales: Économies, Sociétés, Civilizations* 27 (1972): 285–312.

The New Historicism
and
Hamlet

WHAT IS THE NEW HISTORICISM?

The new historicism is, first of all, *new:* one of the most recent developments in contemporary theory, it is still evolving. Enough of its contours have come into focus for us to realize that it exists and deserves a name, but any definition of the new historicism is bound to be somewhat fuzzy, like a partially developed photographic image. Some individual critics that we may label new historicist may also be deconstructors, or feminists, or Marxists. Some would deny that the others are even writing the new kind of historical criticism.

All of them, though, share the conviction that, somewhere along the way, something important was lost from literary studies: historical consciousness. Poems and novels came to be seen in isolation, as urnlike objects of precious beauty. The new historicists, whatever their differences and however defined, want us to see that even the most urnlike poems are caught in a web of historical conditions, relationships, and influences. In an essay titled "The Historical Necessity for — and Difficulties with — New Historical Analysis in Introductory Literature Courses" (1987), Brook Thomas suggests that discussions of Keats's "Ode on a Grecian Urn" might begin with questions such as the following: Where would Keats have seen such an urn? How did a Grecian urn end up in a museum in England? Some very important historical and political realities, Thomas suggests, lie behind and inform Keats's definitions of art, truth, beauty, the past, and timelessness. They are realities that psychoanalytic and reader-response critics, formalists and feminists and deconstructors, might conceivably overlook.

Although a number of influential critics working between 1920 and 1950 wrote about literature from a psychoanalytic perspective, the majority of critics took what might generally be referred to as the historical approach. With the advent of the New Criticism, or formalism, however, historically oriented critics almost seemed to disappear from the face of the earth. Jerome McGann writes: "A text-only approach has been so vigorously promoted during the last thirty-five years that most historical critics have been driven from the field, and have raised the flag of their surrender by yielding the title 'critic' to the victor, and accepting the title 'scholar' for themselves" (*Inflections* 17). Of course, the title "victor" has been vied for by a new kind of psychoanalytic critic, by reader-response critics, by so-called deconstructors, and by feminists since the New Critics of the 1950s lost it during the following decade. But historical scholars have not been in the field, seriously competing to become a dominant critical influence.

At least they haven't until now. In the late 1970s and early 1980s the new historicism first began to be practiced and articulated in the ground-breaking work of Louis Montrose and Stephen Greenblatt. Through their work and that of others, the new historicism transformed the field of Renaissance studies and later began to influence other fields as well. By 1984, Herbert Lindenberger could write: "It comes as something of a surprise to find that history is making a powerful comeback" (16). E. D. Hirsch, Jr., has also suggested that it is time to turn back to history and to historical criticism: "Far from being naive, historically based criticism is the newest and most valuable kind . . . for our students (and our culture) at the present time" (Hirsch 197). McGann obviously agrees. In *Historical Studies and Literary Criticism* (1985), he speaks approvingly of recent attempts to make sociohistorical subjects and methods central to literary studies once again.

As the word *sociohistorical* suggests, the new historicism is not the same as the historical criticism practiced forty years ago. For one thing, it is informed by recent critical theory: by psychoanalytic criticism, reader-response criticism, feminist criticism, and perhaps especially by deconstruction. The new historicist critics are less fact- and event-oriented than historical critics used to be, perhaps because they have come to wonder whether the truth about what really happened can ever be purely and objectively known. They are less likely to see history as linear and progressive, as something developing toward the present.

As the word "sociohistorical" also suggests, the new historicists view history as a social science and the social sciences as being properly historical. McGann most often alludes to sociology when discussing the future of literary studies. "A sociological poetics must be recognized not only as relevant to the analysis of poetry, but in fact as central to the analysis" (*Inflections* 62). Lindenberger cites anthropology as particularly useful in the new historical analysis of literature, especially anthropology as practiced by Victor Turner and Clifford Geertz. Geertz, who has related theatrical traditions in nineteenth-century Bali to forms of political organization that developed during the same period, has influenced some of the most important critics writing the new kind of historical criticism. Due in large part to Geertz's influence, new historicists such as Stephen Greenblatt have asserted that literature is not a sphere apart or distinct from the history that is relevant to it. That is what old historical criticism tended to do, to present history as information you needed to know before you could fully appreciate the separate world of art. Thus the new historicists have discarded old distinctions between literature, history, and the social sciences, while blurring other boundaries. They have erased the line dividing historical and literary materials, showing that the production of one of Shakespeare's plays was a political act and that the coronation of Elizabeth I was carried out with the same care for staging and symbol lavished on a work of dramatic art.

In addition to breaking down barriers that separate literature and history, history and the social sciences, new historicists have reminded us that it is treacherously difficult to reconstruct the past as it really was — rather than as we have been conditioned by our own place and time to believe that it was. And they know that the job is utterly impossible for anyone who is unaware of the difficulty and of the nature of his or her own historical vantage point. "Historical criticism can no longer make any part of [its] sweeping picture unselfconsciously, or treat any of its details in an untheorized way," McGann wrote in 1985 (*Historical Studies* 11). "Unselfconsciously" and "untheorized" are key words here; when the new historicist critics of literature describe a historical change, they are highly conscious of, and even likely to discuss, the *theory* of historical change that informs their account. They know that the changes they happen to see and describe are the ones that their theory of change allows or helps them to see and describe. And they know, too, that their theory of change is historically determined. They seek to minimize the distortion inherent in their perceptions and representations by admitting that they see through preconceived notions; in other words, they learn and reveal the color of the lenses in the glasses that they wear.

All three of the critics whose recent writings on the so-called back-to-history movement have been quoted thus far — Hirsch, Lindenberger, and McGann — mention the name of the late Michel Foucault. As much an archaeologist as a historian and as much a philosopher as either, Foucault in his writings brought together incidents and phenomena from areas of inquiry and orders of life that we normally regard as unconnected. As much as anyone, he encouraged the new historicist critic of literature outwardly to redefine the boundaries of historical inquiry.

Foucault's views of history were influenced by Friedrich Nietzsche's concept of a *wirkliche* ("real" or "true") history that is neither melioristic nor metaphysical. Foucault, like Nietzsche, didn't understand history as development, as a forward movement toward the present. Neither did he view history as an abstraction, idea, or ideal, as something that began "In the beginning" and that will come to THE END, a moment of definite closure, a Day of Judgment. In his own words, Foucault "abandoned [the old history's] attempts to understand events in terms of . . . some great evolutionary process" (*Discipline and Punish* 129). He warned new historians to be aware of the fact that investigators are themselves "situated." It is difficult, he reminded them, to see present cultural practices critically from within them, and on account of the same cultural practices, it is almost impossible to enter bygone ages. In *Discipline and Punish: The Birth of the Prison* (1975), Foucault admitted that his own interest in the past was fueled by a passion to write the history of the present.

Like Marx, Foucault saw history in terms of power, but his view of power owed more perhaps to Nietzsche than to Marx. Foucault seldom viewed power as a repressive force. Certainly, he did not view it as a tool of conspiracy used by one specific individual or institution against another. Rather, power represents a whole complex of forces; it is that which produces what happens. Thus, even a tyrannical aristocrat does not simply wield power, because he is formed and empowered by discourses and practices that constitute power. Viewed by Foucault, power is "positive and productive," not "repressive" and "prohibitive" (Smart

63). Furthermore, no historical event, according to Foucault, has a single cause; rather, it is intricately connected with a vast web of economic, social, and political factors.

A brief sketch of one of Foucault's major works may help clarify some of his ideas. *Discipline and Punish* begins with a shocking but accurate description of the public drawing and quartering of a Frenchman who had botched his attempt to assassinate King Louis XV. Foucault proceeds, then, by describing rules governing the daily life of modern Parisian felons. What happened to torture, to punishment as public spectacle? he asks. What complex network of forces made it disappear? In working toward a picture of this "power," Foucault turns up many interesting puzzle pieces, such as that in the early revolutionary years of the nineteenth century, crowds would sometimes identify with the prisoner and treat the executioner as if *he* were the guilty party. But Foucault sets forth a related reason for keeping prisoners alive, moving punishment indoors, and changing discipline from physical torture into mental rehabilitation: colonization. In this historical period, people were needed to establish colonies and trade, and prisoners could be used for that purpose. Also, because these were politically unsettled times, governments needed infiltrators and informers. Who better to fill those roles than prisoners pardoned or released early for showing a willingness to be rehabilitated? As for rehabilitation itself, Foucault compares it to the old form of punishment, which began with a torturer extracting a confession. In more modern, "reasonable" times, psychologists probe the minds of prisoners with a scientific rigor that Foucault sees as a different kind of torture, a kind that our modern perspective does not allow us to see as such.

Thus, a change took place, but perhaps not so great a change as we generally assume. It may have been for the better or for the worse; the point is that agents of power didn't make the change because mankind is evolving and, therefore, more prone to perform good-hearted deeds. Rather, different objectives arose, including those of a new class of doctors and scientists bent on studying aberrant examples of the human mind.

Foucault's type of analysis has recently been practiced by a number of literary critics at the vanguard of the back-to-history movement. One of these critics, Stephen Greenblatt, has written on Renaissance changes in the development of both literary characters and real people. Like Foucault, he is careful to point out that any one change is connected with a host of others, no one of which may simply be identified as the cause or the effect. Greenblatt, like Foucault, insists on interpreting literary devices as if they were continuous with other representational devices in a culture; he turns, therefore, to scholars in other fields in order to better understand the workings of literature. "We wall off literary symbolism from the symbolic structures operative elsewhere," he writes, "as if art alone were a human creation, as if humans themselves were not, in Clifford Geertz's phrase, cultural artifacts." Following Geertz, Greenblatt sets out to practice what he calls "anthropological or cultural criticism." Anthropological literary criticism, he continues, addresses itself "to the interpretive constructions the members of a society apply to their experience," since a work of literature is itself an interpretive construction, "part of the system of signs that constitutes a given culture." He suggests that criticism must never interpret the past without at least being "conscious of its own status as interpretation" (Greenblatt, *Renaissance Self-Fashioning* 4).

Not all of the critics trying to lead students of literature back to history are as "Foucauldian" as Greenblatt. Some of these new historicists owe more to Marx than to Foucault. Others, like Jerome McGann, have followed the lead of Soviet critic M. M. Bakhtin, who was less likely than Marx to emphasize social class as a determining factor. (Bakhtin was more interested in the way that one language or style is the parody of an older one.) Still other new historicists, like Brook Thomas, have clearly been more influenced by Walter Benjamin, best known for essays such as "Theses on the Philosophy of History" and "The Work of Art in the Age of Mechanical Reproduction."

Moreover, there are other reasons not to declare that Foucault has been the central influence on the new historicism. Some new historicist critics would argue that Foucault critiqued old-style historicism to such an extent that he ended up being antihistorical or, at least, nonhistorical. As for his commitment to a radical remapping of relations of power and influence, cause and effect, in the view of some critics, Foucault consequently adopted too cavalier an attitude toward chronology and facts. In the minds of other critics, identifying and labeling a single master or central influence goes against the very gain of the new historicism. Practitioners of the new historicism have sought to decenter the study of literature and move toward the point where literary studies overlap with anthropological and sociological studies. They have also struggled to see history from a decentered perspective, both by recognizing that their own cultural and historical position may not afford the best understanding of other cultures and times and by realizing that events seldom have any single or central cause. At this point, then, it is appropriate to pause and suggest that Foucault shouldn't be seen as *the* cause of the new historicism, but as one of several powerful, interactive influences.

It is equally useful to suggest that the debate over the sources of the movement, the differences of opinion about Foucault, and even my own need to assert his importance may be historically contingent; that is to say, they may all result from the very *newness* of the new historicism itself. New intellectual movements often cannot be summed up or represented by a key figure, any more than they can easily be summed up or represented by an introduction or a single essay. They respond to disparate influences and almost inevitably include thinkers who represent a wide range of backgrounds. Like movements that are disintegrating, new movements embrace a broad spectrum of opinions and positions.

But just as differences within a new school of criticism cannot be overlooked, neither should they be exaggerated, since it is the similarity among a number of different approaches that makes us aware of a new movement under way. Greenblatt, Hirsch, McGann, and Thomas all started with the assumption that works of literature are simultaneously influenced by and influencing reality, broadly defined. Thus, whatever their disagreements, they share a belief in referentiality — a belief that literature refers to and is referred to by things outside itself — that is fainter in the works of formalist, poststructuralist, and even reader-response critics. They believe with Greenblatt that the "central concerns" of criticism "should prevent it from permanently sealing off one type of discourse from another or decisively separating works of art from the minds and lives of their creators and their audiences" (*Renaissance Self-Fashioning* 5).

McGann, in his introduction to *Historical Studies and Literary Criticism,* turns referentiality into a rallying cry:

> What will not be found in these essays . . . is the assumption, so common in text-centered studies of every type, that literary works are self-enclosed verbal constructs, or looped intertextual fields of autonomous signifiers and signifieds. In these essays, the question of referentiality is once again brought to the fore. (3)

Elsewhere in "Keats and the Historical Method in Literary Criticism," he outlines a program for those who have rallied to the cry. These procedures, which he claims are "practical derivatives of the Bakhtin school," assume that historicist critics, who must be interested in a work's point of origin and in its point of reception, will understand the former by studying biography and bibliography. After mastering these details, the critic must then consider the expressed intentions of the author, because, if printed, these intentions have also modified the developing history of the work. Next, the new historicist must learn the history of the work's reception, as that body of opinion has become part of the platform on which we are situated when we study the book. Finally, McGann urges the new historicist critic to point toward the future, toward his or her *own* audience, defining for its members the aims and limits of the critical project and injecting the analysis with a degree of self-consciousness that alone can give it credibility (*Inflections* 62).

In the essay that follows, Karin S. Coddon discusses Robert Devereux, second earl of Essex, reportedly a model for Hamlet — and reputedly mad. Essex, who for a while courted Queen Elizabeth, ended up being executed for his leadership role in an unsuccessful insurrection against the queen. Without trying to determine whether Essex *was* mad or not, or what madness *is* in modern terms, Coddon defines madness as it was understood in the context of late sixteenth- and early seventeenth-century English culture. Using a contemporary Elizabethan diary in which Essex is discussed, she shows that in Elizabethan culture madness and ambition (especially treasonous ambition) were closely associated, tightly linked.

Coddon then connects Essex's mad treason with the emergence of the modern concept of subjectivity from the medieval concept of the (more orderly) soul. It was surely subjectivity — which involves seeing the world in an individual, even idiosyncratic way — that allowed Essex to confer knighthood without the queen's permission, return to London against Her Majesty's wishes, and "burst in upon a half-dressed Elizabeth in her private chamber." (Little wonder it is that King Claudius remarks in *Hamlet,* "Madness in great ones must not unwatched go"! [3.1.187])

For the Elizabethans, explains Coddon, madness resulted from the "internalization of disobedience" and its consequent overthrow of what Shakespeare calls the "pales and forts of reason" — reason that normally contains subjectivity. Such abolition of the usual constraints led to *dis*ordered subjectivity, which, in the Elizabethan view became synonymous with madness. Hence subjectivity became the object of control by authority, leading Coddon to pose a central question: Is madness ever *not* political?

Marked by the strong influence of Michel Foucault, Coddon's essay depicts the struggle between Essex and the queen not in terms of a struggle between two individuals but, rather, as a contest between "subjectivity and power." Historically, that struggle was usually brought to a "sane" conclusion, she argues, with punishment being visited upon the body of the unwilling subject. In Essex's case, insane ambition was banished when Essex confessed his transgressions before the executioner, prayed for forgiveness, and "affirmed" the "justice" of the "authority" that had condemned him. These kinds of speeches, Coddon argues, were part of the theater of punishment; they reinforced power and predominant cultural values by proving the triumph and reaffirming the validity of both.

Coddon takes the new historicist position that, just as politics is a form of theater, so is theater a form that politics takes; art and society cannot be understood apart from each other since they are but different forms through which the ideologies of a culture achieve representation and are thus empowered. Certainly, *Hamlet* ends up showing the tragic results of mad ambition; furthermore, subjectivity is contained and a conservative ideology, if not order, reasserts itself in the play's final scene, where death, as the single absolute authority, has the power to renounce madness and restore identity. Just as the confessional, repentant scaffold speech delivered by Essex just before his execution reestablished his (legitimate) identity (and with it, existing power relationships), so does Hamlet's last-minute apology to Laertes.

But does *Hamlet*, finally, amount to a typical Elizabethan scaffold speech, a rather predictable apologia for the prevailing ideological currents? Coddon suggests that it does and yet does not. Like many other new historicists, Foucault included, Coddon is interested in the Renaissance, its politics, and its art, because the historical dramas of that period (literary and otherwise) seem, from the vantage point of our own period, to have been liminal or transitional. That is to say, they seem to have represented, reproduced, and reasserted the values of the previous ages while also resisting those values — in ways we call modern. *Hamlet* performs this cultural role but only while also utterly exceeding it. For the play is, after all, among the forces that encouraged subjectivity, inwardness, independence, and alienation. Permeated by Renaissance cultural discourse, *Hamlet*, like so many of Shakespeare's plays, also changed that discourse unalterably.

Ross C Murfin

THE NEW HISTORICISM: A SELECTED BIBLIOGRAPHY

New Historicism is a method of criticism that was defined in large part by a number of critics working in the area of English Renaissance literature. For further reading, see "Other Cultural Materialist Studies of Shakespeare" in the selected bibliography of Marxist criticism.

The New Historicism: Further Reading

Graff, Gerald, and Gerald Gibbons, eds. *Criticism in the University*. Evanston: Northwestern UP, 1985. This volume, which contains Hirsch's essay, "Back to History," in the section entitled "Pedagogy and Polemics," also includes sections devoted to the historical backgrounds of academic criticism; the influence of Marxism, feminism, and critical theory in general on the new historicism; and varieties of "cultural criticism."

Greenblatt, Stephen. "The Circulation of Social Energy." *Shakespearean Negotiations: The Circulation of Social Energy in Renaissance England*. Berkeley: U of California P, 1985. 1–20.

Hirsch, E. D., Jr. "Back to History." Graff and Gibbons 189–97.

Howard, Jean. "The New Historicism in Renaissance Studies." *English Literary Renaissance* 16 (1986): 13–43.

Howard, Jean, and Marion O'Connor, eds. *Shakespeare Reproduced: The Text in History and Ideology*. New York: Methuen, 1987.

Lindenberger, Herbert. "Toward a New History in Literary Study." *Profession: Selected Articles from the Bulletins of the Association of Departments of English and the Association of Departments of Foreign Languages*. New York: MLA, 1984. 16–23.

Liu, Alan. "The Power of Formalism: The New Historicism." *English Literary History* 56 (1989): 721–71.

McGann, Jerome. *The Beauty of Inflections: Literary Investigations in Historical Method and Theory*. Oxford: Clarendon–Oxford UP, 1985. See especially the introduction and ch. 1, "Keats and the Historical Method in Literary Criticism."

———. *Historical Studies and Literary Criticism*. Madison: U of Wisconsin P, 1985. See especially the introduction and the essays in the following sections: "Historical Methods and Literary Interpretations" and "Biographical Contexts and the Critical Object."

Montrose, Louis Adrian. "Renaissance Literary Studies and the Subject of History." *English Literary Renaissance* 16 (1986): 5–12.

Morris, Wesley. *Toward a New Historicism*. Princeton: Princeton UP, 1972.

Thomas, Brook. "The Historical Necessity for — and Difficulties with — New Historical Analysis in Introductory Literature Courses." *College English* 49 (1987): 509–22.

Wayne, Don E. "Power, Politics, and the Shakespearean Text: Recent Criticism in England and the United States." Howard and O'Connor 47–67.

New Historicist Studies of Shakespeare and of *Hamlet*

Dollimore, Jonathan. *Radical Tragedy: Religion, Ideology, and Power in the Drama of Shakespeare and His Contemporaries*. Brighton, Eng.: Harvester, 1984.

Dollimore, Jonathan, and Alan Sinfield, eds. *Political Shakespeare: New Essays in Cultural Materialism*. Manchester, Eng.: Manchester UP, 1985. See esp. the essays by Dollimore, Greenblatt, and Tennenhouse.

Goldberg, Jonathan. *James I and the Politics of Literature*. Baltimore: Johns Hopkins UP, 1983.

Greenblatt, Stephen. "Invisible Bullets: Renaissance Authority and Its Subversion, *Henry IV* and *Henry V*." Dollimore and Sinfield 18–47. Revised and expanded in Greenblatt, *Shakespearean Negotiations*. One of the most influential early new historicist essays.

———. *Renaissance Self-Fashioning: From More to Shakespeare*. Chicago: U of Chicago P, 1980. See ch. 1 and the chapter on *Othello* entitled "The Improvisation of Power."

———. *Shakespearean Negotiations: The Circulation of Social Energy in Renaissance England*. Berkeley: U of California P, 1985.

Marcus, Leah. *Puzzling Shakespeare: Local Reading and Its Discontents*. Berkeley: U of California P, 1988.

Montrose, Louis Adrian. "The Purpose of Playing: Reflections on a Shakespearean Anthropology." *Helios* n.s. 7.2 (1980): 51–74.

———. "'Shaping Fantasies': Figurations of Gender and Power in Elizabethan Culture." *Representations* 2 (1983): 61–94. One of the most influential early new historicist essays.

Moretti, Franco. "'A Huge Eclipse': Tragic Form and the Deconsecration of Sovereignty." *The Power of Forms in the Renaissance*. Ed. Stephen Greenblatt. Norman: Pilgrim, 1982. 7–40.

Mullaney, Steven. *The Place of the Stage: License, Play, and Power in Renaissance England*. Chicago: U of Chicago P, 1987.

Newman, Karen. "'And wash the Ethiop White': Femininity and the Monstrous in Othello." Howard and O'Connor 143–62.

Tennenhouse, Leonard. *Power on Display: The Politics of Shakespeare's Genres.* New York: Methuen, 1986.

Foucault and His Influence

As I point out in the introduction to the new historicism, some new historicists would question the "privileging" of Foucault implicit in this section heading ("Foucault and His Influence") and the following one ("Other Writers and Works"). They might cite the greater importance of one of these other writers or point out that to cite a central influence or a definitive cause runs against the very spirit of the movement. See also "Works by Bakhtin" and "Other Cultural Materialist Studies of Shakespeare" in the selected bibliography of Marxist criticism.

Dreyfus, Hubert L., and Paul Rabinow. *Michel Foucault: Beyond Structuralism and Hermeneutics.* Chicago: U of Chicago P, 1983.

Foucault, Michel. *Discipline and Punish: The Birth of the Prison.* 1975. Trans. Alan Sheridan. New York: Pantheon, 1978.

———. *The History of Sexuality.* Vol. 1. Trans. Robert Hurley. New York: Pantheon, 1978.

———. *Language, Counter-Memory, Practice.* Ed. Donald F. Bouchard. Trans. Bouchard and Sherry Simon. Ithaca: Cornell UP, 1977. Selected essays and interviews.

———. *The Order of Things: An Archaeology of the Human Sciences.* New York: Vintage, 1973.

Sheridan, Alan. *Michel Foucault: The Will to Truth.* New York: Tavistock, 1980.

Smart, Barry. *Michel Foucault.* New York: Ellis Horwood–Tavistock, 1985.

Other Writers and Works of Interest to New Historicist Critics

Benjamin, Walter. *Illuminations.* Trans. Harry Zohn. New York: Schocken, 1969. Includes "The Work of Art in the Age of Mechanical Reproduction" (1936) and "Theses on the Philosophy of History" (1950).

Geertz, Clifford. *The Interpretation of Cultures.* New York: Basic, 1973.

———. *Negara: The Theatre State in Nineteenth-Century Bali.* Princeton: Princeton UP, 1980.

Goffman, Erving. *Frame Analysis.* New York: Harper, 1974.

Jameson, Fredric. *The Political Unconscious.* Ithaca: Cornell UP, 1981.
Koselleck, Reinhart. *Futures Past.* Trans. Keith Tribe. Cambridge:
    MIT P, 1985.
Representations. This quarterly journal, printed by the University of
    California Press, regularly publishes new historical studies and cul-
    tural criticism.
Said, Edward. *Orientalism.* New York: Columbia UP, 1978.

A NEW HISTORICIST PERSPECTIVE

KARIN S. CODDON

"Suche Strange Desygns":
Madness, Subjectivity, and Treason
in *Hamlet* and Elizabethan Culture

"For, to define true madness/What is't but to be nothing else but
mad?" reasons Polonius (2.2.93–94). Whether Robert Devereux, second earl of Essex, was actually mad in any clinical sense of the word is
not an issue for historicism.[1] But that his "madness" was poor Robert's
— and ultimately, the Tudor state's — enemy may be as illuminating
for discussions of madness in Shakespearean tragedy as humoral psychology and the vogue of melancholy. Essex seems to have suffered
from what Timothie Bright would have called a "melancholie
madnesse," replete with bouts of near-stuporous despair and religious
mania (2). The possibility that the earl was punished with a "sore distraction" is frequently viewed as a kind of colorful biographical sidelight
to the rebellion of 1601: Essex, "brilliant, melancholy and ill-fated,"
becomes the embodiment of the Elizabethan *mal du siècle,* his Icarian
fall mirroring the fate of a generation of aspiring minds (Wilson 228;
Esler 97–99). "The flowre of chivalrie" who fell heir in his own lifetime
to the heroic legacy of Sir Philip Sidney, Essex has been identified as the
historical inspiration for Henry Bolingbroke, Hamlet, and Antony. But
the affinities between Essex and the heroes of Shakespearean drama

---

[1]Lacey Baldwin Smith has recently argued that the apparent madness of Essex, as well
as of a number of other Tudor traitors, was a manifestation of a more insidious "cultural
paranoia." That is, the cause of irrationality need not lie exclusively in the tortured chambers of the mind; it can be external, and the self-destructive traitor can be a symptom of
his society as well as a victim of his private insanity" (*Treason in Tudor England* 12). For
an acute commentary and critique, see Christopher Hill's review.

evoked in contemporary accounts of the earl's madness suggest a reciprocity more complex than a mere one-to-one correspondence between history and fictions. Essex's madness, whatever its precise pathological nature, was profoundly engaged in his transgressions as subject, according to John Harington's diary entry of a few months prior to the insurrection:

> It resteslhe wythe me in opynion, that ambition thwarted in its career, dothe speedilie leade on to madnesse; herein I am strengthened by what I learne in my Lord of Essex, who shyftethe from sorrowe and repentaunce to rage and rebellion so suddenlie, as well provethe him devoide of good reason or righte mynde; in my last discourse, he uttered suche strange desygns that made me hastene forthe, and leave his absence; thank heaven I am safe at home, and if I go in suche troubles againe, I deserve the gallowes for a meddlynge foole: His speeches of the Queene becomethe no man who hathe *mens sana in corpore sano* ["sound mind in sound body"]. He hathe ill advysors, and much evyll hathe sprunge from thys source. The Queene well knowethe how to humble the haughtie spirit, the haughtie spirit knowethe not how to yield, and the mans soule seemeth tossede to and fro, like the waves of a troubled sea. (225–26)

Harington attributes Essex's madness to "ambition thwarted in its career," articulating a Tudor and Stuart commonplace: "Ambition, madam, is a great man's madness" (Webster, *The Duchess of Malfi* 1.2.125). But in Harington's discourse the causal relation between overreaching and insanity is ambiguous; ambition may "speedilie leade on to madnesse," but madness spurs the subjective overthrow of the pales and forts of reason that should constrain the "haughtie spirit." The discourse of madness becomes virtually indistinguishable from the discourse of treason: "he uttered . . . strange desygns"; "His speeches of the Queene becomethe no man who hathe *mens sana in corpore sano*"; "the haughtie spirit knowethe not how to yield." Harington finds Essex's madness so alarming not because it is irrational but because it speaks "strange desygns": reason, or treason, in madness. And yet he represents Essex nonetheless as a victim as well as violator subjected by his own disordered subjectivity: "the mans soule seemeth tossede to and fro, like the waves of a troubled sea." The man Robert Devereux is, then, as radically self-divided a subject as Hamlet, though not because the fictive prince was "inspired" by the historical earl. Madness is the mighty opposite of the ideology of self-government, or what Mervyn James has called the "internalization of obedience" (44). As such, madness disintegrates the identity so precariously fashioned by notions of inward control and self-vigilance, notions whose contradictions become increasingly critical toward the end of Elizabeth's rule. Madness renders the subject not more but less himself; it becomes the internalization of *dis*obedience, prerequisite and portent of the external violation of order.

Not all of Essex's transgressions against Elizabethan authority, of course, were merely internal. Yet even at the height of his political/erotic courtship of the queen, his potentially unruly disposition is a topic of courtly conversation. William Camden recalls of Essex, "Nor was he excusable in his deportment to the Queen herself, whom he treated with a sort of insolence, that seemed to proceed rather *from a mind that wanted ballast, than any real pride in him* . . ." (qtd. in Matter 5; emphasis mine). That Camden casts the earl's "insolence" as a psychological rather than spiritual defect is a telling qualification. Essex's subjectivity becomes the site of the displacement of sin by disorder; the Luciferean sin of pride has metamorphosed into a dangerous inward unfixity. This apparent displacement does not mitigate the earl's "insolence" so much as it inscribes the inextricable — but here, disturbingly precarious — relation between subject and subjectivity; the instability of the latter is reciprocally engaged in the performance of the former, as in Harington's description of the "haughtie spirit." This shift from soul to subjectivity is bound up in the cultural shift from medieval ecclesiastical authority to Renaissance secular authority; as the sinner was to the church, now the disordered subjectivity is to the secular state. Subjectivity, "a mind that want[s] ballast," is identified as the site of potential transgression and the object of authority and control.

The period between 1597 and 1601 saw the deterioration of Essex's favored position with Elizabeth, a change that would culminate in the queen's fateful refusal to renew the lucrative sweet wines monopoly. But Essex's fall from grace was only partly due to the parsimony and caprice of the aging queen. In 1598 occurred the notorious ear-boxing incident, in which Essex responded to Elizabeth's sharp cuff on the ear by reaching for his sword. The apparent if swiftly checked impulse toward regicide was compounded by Essex's self-justification questioning the infallibility of the sovereign will. "What, cannot Princes err? cannot subjects receive wrong? Is an earthly power or authority infinite?" he wrote in a letter to Sir Thomas Egerton. "Pardon me, pardon me, my good lord, I can never subscribe to such principles" (qtd. in Lacey 213). But "such principles" were precisely those to which Tudor propaganda demanded subscription:

al subjectes are bounden to obey [Magistrates] as god's ministers: yea although they be evil, not only for feare, but also for conscience's sake . . . let al marke diligently, that it is not lawful for inferiours and subjectes, in any case to resist or stand against the superior powers: for s. Paule's words be plain, that whosoever withstandeth the ordinaunce of god. (*An Exhortation concerning good order and obedience, to rulers and Magistrates*)[2]

Moreover, the writer of the *Exhortation* deems it "an intolerable ignoraunce, *madnes*, and wickednes, for subjectes to make any murmuring, rebellyon, resistance or withstanding, commocion, or insurrection against there most dere and most dred soveraygne Lord and king . . ." (66; emphasis mine). Essex's outrage may have been as temperamental as political, the effect of what Egerton diplomatically referred to as his need "to conquer [him]self," but the surly defiance of his letter accords with the "strange desygns" that perturbed Harington and the sometimes flagrant insubordination that characterized the earl's misadventures in Ireland in 1599. Openly disregarding the queen's orders, Essex conferred knighthood upon over eighty members of his company "without even the justification of a military victory" (Stone 401). But when he chose to return to England against the queen's wishes, and burst in upon a half-dressed Elizabeth in her private chamber, his violation of the boundaries of subject took on yet more dangerous implications. If his making for his sword symbolically threatened the queen's body politic, his intrusion into her private room also threatened the sacred, gendered body of the royal virgin. Just as the subject's identity was enabled by his inward and outward adherence to the prescriptions of authority, the monarch's identity depended upon the uniformity of obedience, as Elizabeth well understood: "I am no Queen. That man is above me," she raged to her godson Harington (*Nugae Antiquae* 134). Like Diana surprised by Actaeon, Elizabeth exacted physical punishment upon the intruder, though confinement, not dismemberment, was Essex's sentence. Essex spent nearly six months in the custody of the Lord Keeper Egerton. A letter from John Donne, then secretary to the Lord Keeper, to Henry Wotton provides a window into the perception of the prisoner's condition:

He withers still in his sicknes & plods on to his end in the same pace where you left us. the worst accidents of his sicknes are that

---

[2]Reprinted in Kinney 63. For a valuable discussion of the inadequacy of "the orthodox Elizabethan framework . . . to absorb effectively the facts of heterodoxy and social flux" (59), see Montrose, "The Purpose of Playing."

he conspires with it & that it is not here beleeved. that which was sayd of Cato that his age understood him not I feare may be averted of your lord that he understood not his age: for it is a naturall weaknes of innocency. that such men want lockes for themselves and keyse for others. (Qtd. in Bald 108)[3]

While Essex was hardly suspected of putting on an antic disposition, Donne's comments reveal the degree to which the physical and mental anguish of the insubordinate earl was subjected to political scrutiny. "Madness in great ones must not [unwatch'd] go" (3.1.187), Claudius observes in *Hamlet*. With Essex's most erratic behavior explicitly bound up in gestures of disobedience, his inward distress ("he conspires with it") becomes as suspect as his public comportment. Donne's conclusion "that such men want lockes for themselves and keyse for others" is of a piece with Harington's comment that "the Queene well knowethe how to humble the haughtie spirit, the haughtie spirit knowethe not how to yield," and with Camden's reference to Essex's "mind that wanted ballast." All three observations imply an antagonism not only between the subject and power, but between *subjectivity* and power, anticipating both the confrontation and the outcome. It is an agon in which the subject necessarily turns upon the "self" as well as upon authority. For if, as Foucault has suggested, power is realized and resisted in its effects, i.e., in its "government of individualization," contestation disrupts the "form of power which makes individuals subjects" — subjects in both senses of the word.[4] The problem of containment becomes one of confinement. The disruption of the internalized relation between authority and inwardness transforms the dialogue of "subjectification" into a problem of material subjugation: as authority gives way to coercion, the body, not subjectivity, becomes its object. Ultimately, "a mind that want[s] ballast" can be disciplined only by the exaction of punishment upon the body. In *Hamlet,* the restoration of the "mad" hero's wits is necessarily punctuated by the death that swiftly follows his recovery of sanity. If the deployment of physical punishment

---

[3] R. C. Bald holds that "the writer shows the kind of knowledge of Essex's condition that one would expect from an inmate of York house, and more perhaps than the current gossip would furnish him with" (108, n. 2).

[4] Foucault writes, "This form of power applies itself to immediate everyday life which categorizes the individual, marks him by his own individuality, attaches him to his own identity, imposes a law of truth on him which he must recognize and which others must recognize in him. . . . There are two meanings of the word 'subject': subject to someone else by control and dependence; and tied to his own identity by a conscience or self knowledge, both meanings suggest a form of power which subjugates and makes subject to" ("The Subject and Power" 781).

transforms as much as fulfills power relations ("The Subject and Power" 794–95), the literal silencing of madness by confinement, constraint, or extinction of the body is itself an unstable strategy of containment. For the division of inwardness and the body that enables post-Reformation subjectivity situates madness nonetheless in the equivocal space between interiority and exteriority. Neither wholly confined to nor estranged from inwardness, madness in its semiotic excess problematizes the closure that is the object of rites of punishment, on both the stage and the scaffold.

Historian Lacey Baldwin Smith remarks that "by the time Essex turned to treason, the deterioration in his character had passed beyond the point of hysteria: it was bordering on insanity which led him to confuse the fantasies of his own sick brain with reality" (*Elizabethan World* 266). Smith's reference to the rebellion as "an act of political madness" seems particularly resonant precisely because it may be tacitly redundant: Was Essex's madness — or the madness of great ones, both onstage and at court — ever *not* "political," that is, charged with implications *against* the inscription of order, obedience, and authority that fashioned and controlled identity in late Tudor and early Stuart England? When Essex's "strange desygns" finally bodied forth action on February 8, 1601, the equivocal boundaries between representation and rebellion almost wholly collapse, though not quite in the way the earl had planned. If the playing of Shakespeare's *Richard II* "40 times in open streets and houses" failed to rouse the support of the citizens for the rebels, the consequences of the failed insurrection produced a spectacle of trial, repentance, and noble death that seemed to duplicate the form and effect of the tragic denouement. Although Essex repeatedly declared his innocence during the trial, once his fate was decided paranoiac self-justifications gave way to compliance with the art of dying. Entailing confession, repentance, and "the return of the traitor to society and to himself," as Steven Mullaney puts it (33), such performances were commonly described and perhaps, implicitly *prescribed* in *ars moriendi* handbooks, published accounts of executions, and penultimate moments in contemporary tragedy.

On February 25 Essex faced the executioner with a noble set speech in which he confessed his spiritual and political transgressions, forgave and prayed for forgiveness, and affirmed throughout the absolute justice of the authority that condemned him:

Lord Jesus, forgive it us, and forgive it me, the most wretched of all; and I beseech her Majesty, the State, and Ministers thereof, to forgive it us. The Lord grant her Majesty a prosperous reign and a long one, if it be His will. O Lord, bless her and the nobles and ministers of the Church and State. And I beseech you and the world to have a charitable opinion of me for my intention toward her Majesty, whose death, upon my salvation and before God, I protest I never meant, nor violence to her person; yet I confess I have received an honourable trial, and am justly condemned. And I desire all the world to forgive me, even as I do freely and from my heart forgive the world. (Qtd. in Harrison 323)

As J. A. Sharpe has discussed in a suggestive essay, the theatricality of "last dying speeches" on the scaffold in sixteenth- and seventeenth-century England served a specific ideological function: noble traitors and common criminals alike became "willing central participants in a theatre of punishment, which offered not merely a spectacle, but a reinforcement of certain values. . . . they were helping to assert the legitimacy of the power which had brought them to their sad end" (156). And following James's analysis of Tudor and Stuart "ideological controls" in the face of limited coercive power, Sharpe has suggested that this "theatre of the gallows" demonstrated the condemned man's "internalization of obedience," the willing representation of inward acquiescence to good order (158–61; cf. James 43–54). The case of Essex, then, seems particularly stirring: not only the avowed traitor, but the disordered, self-divided subjectivity is restored, identity — as noble, Christian subject to her majesty and her ministers — recovered in the assertion of the righteousness and coherence of authority.[5] "I am no Queen," Elizabeth had complained upon Essex's violation of her royal imperatives; in dying, Essex effectively reaffirmed the monarch's identity as well as his own.

Yet there was enough uncertainty about semiotic containment in such spectacles of death that Essex's execution, like Mary Queen of Scots's beheading, was kept a semiprivate affair, printed transcriptions of the event rather than the event itself entrusted with the dissemination of its ideological significance. Hence the ideological efficiency of "the theatre of the gallows" may be no less equivocal than the "strange desygns" that prefaced the performance. As Foucault has remarked,

[5]Mullaney has written suggestively on the condemned traitor's recovery of decorum in the ritual of execution: "Confession, execution, and dismemberment, unsettling as they may seem, were not so much punishment as they were the demonstration that what had been a traitor was no longer, and that which had set him off from man and nature had been . . . lifted from him. When the body bleeds, reason has been effaced; execution is treason's epilogue, spoken by the law" (33–34).

"there was . . . on the part of the state power, a political fear of the effects of these ambiguous rituals" (*Discipline and Punish* 65). The willingness to spare Essex the humiliation of public execution may have stemmed in part from fear that the propaganda value of such a spectacle could backfire, especially given the popularity of the earl with the citizens (59–69). Nor was the proliferation of official propaganda any insurance that the populace would be duly awed by the terrible enactment of power and punishment:

> The condemned man found himself transformed into a hero by the sheer extent of his widely advertised crimes, and sometimes the affirmation of his belated repentance. Against the law, against the rich, the powerful, the magistrates, the constabulary or the watch, against taxes and their collectors, he appeared to have waged a struggle with which one all too easily identified. . . . If the condemned man was shown to be repentant, accepting the verdict, asking both God and man for forgiveness for his crimes, it was as if he had come through some process of purification: he died, in his own way, like a saint. (*Discipline and Punish* 67)

Indeed, three years after Essex's death one Robert Pricket published a tributory poem about the earl, "Honor's Fame in Triumph Riding," in which the earl's downfall is attributed chiefly to the machinations of his enemies, just as he had claimed during his trial. The verses sent Pricket to prison (Matter 78). For while the poem is not explicitly subversive, such lines as "He died for treason; Yet no Traitor. Why?" stand in sharp contradiction with the official exegeses of the earl's demise (78).

The ways in which that other great Elizabethan spectacle of death — tragedy — duplicates, appropriates, and, sometimes, questions the strategies of power informing productions of authority and punishment on the scaffold are thus ideologically as well as aesthetically significant. As Leonard Tennenhouse has commented, "The strategies of theater resembled those of the scaffold, as well as court performance . . . in observing a common logic of figuration that both sustained and testified to the monarch's power . . ." (15). But the apparent exclusion of madness, of unreason, of disorder, from the final transcriptions of the actual traitor's death is consistently called into question, even subverted, in the punishment meted out by an ostensible tragic order. In the middle tragedies of Shakespeare, discrepancies between the spectacle and its discursive record bequeathed to the survivors undermine the closure apparently evoked in the hero's "restoration to himself" in death; the words of Horatio, Edgar, and Macduff seem glaringly inadequate even as plot summaries. "In Shakespeare . . . madness still occupies an extreme place, in that it is beyond appeal. Nothing ever restores it either to truth or reason. It leads only to laceration and thence to death" (Foucault, *Madness and Civilization* 31–32); the highly stylized return to self before death is unsettled by the madness that outlives the individual subject in the gulf between tragic experience and its final retelling.[6] Madness does not deny authority so much as testify to a fissure in the structure of authority — and subjectivity, an excess that is not recuperated by the "government of individualization," to disrupt both subjection *and* subjectivity. As such, its discourse of "wild and whirling words," of a "soule . . . tossede to and fro, like the waves of a troubled sea," is peculiarly resistant to strategies of containment.

Accordingly, among the most important mandates of Foucault's landmark if controversial work is that madness and its representations be investigated in terms of their functions within—and against — structures of power.[7] If the political drama of Essex's madness, rebellion, and noble death shares marked affinities with the tragedies contemporary to it, so does the theater itself duplicate and reflect upon a more insidious crisis of authority swelling in late Elizabethan England. What will distinguish madness in such plays as *Hamlet* (1601) and *King Lear* (1605) from its depictions in the equally pathologically fixated tragedy of the late 1580s and early 1590s is the subordination to which it will subject other plot elements: madness does not serve narrative so much as narrative serves madness. This narrative *non serviam* constructs a split not so much between "plot" and "character" as between agency and inwardness, a division clearly manifest in the so-called problem of Hamlet but also informing tragedies as early as Marlowe's *Edward II* (1593) and as late as Webster's *Duchess of Malfi* (1613). The antagonism between subjectivity and the drama's "syntygmatic axis" (Moretti 55–64), between disorder and a linear mimesis, duplicates the position of power's subject in relation to the authority that, like the narrative, both constricts and constrains him. But the notion of tragic madness as overtly or even covertly "subversive" is problematic. In fact, madness displaces action, metaphorizing it but also taking its place. If madness seems to privilege and enlarge the tragic hero's subjectivity, so does it also fragment, check, and defer it. As an inversion of internalized "ideological

---

[6]Cf. Franco Moretti's commentary on Jacobean tragedy: "Fully realized tragedy is the parable of the degeneration of the sovereign inserted in a context that *can no longer understand it*" (55).
[7]For critiques of *Madness and Civilization* and of Foucault's methodology, see Midelfort and see Feder 29–34. Shoshana Felman offers a comparative critique of Foucault and Derrida on madness in her *Writing and Madness* (35–55).

controls" madness by definition precludes the realization of a stable, coherent subjectivity in opposition to the disorder from without. Foucault has discussed the historical liminality of the Renaissance madman positioned between the wandering lunatic of the Middle Ages and the construction of bourgeois individualist subjectivity, the rise of the modern "anatomo-politics of the body" that banishes unreason (*Madness and Civilization* 35–64; *History of Sexuality* 139–45). Recent critical works by Francis Barker, Catherine Belsey, and Terry Eagleton have applied the Foucauldian notion of liminality to the Shakespearean subject, particularly in the paradigmatic case of Hamlet.[8] The absolute impenetrability of Hamlet's mystery, the absence of the full interiority apparently promised in the prince's claim that "I have that within which passes show" (1.2.85), leads Belsey to conclude that "Hamlet is . . . the most discontinuous of Shakespeare's heroes," riddled almost to the point of unintelligibility by the "repressed discontinuities of the allegorical tradition" (41–42). Barker and Eagleton go a step further; because humanist subjectivity has yet to fully emerge in the late sixteenth century, "in the interior of [Hamlet's] mystery, there is, in short, nothing."[9] But this nothing's more than matter; because the privatized subjectivity is incomplete, "wild and whirling words" are never wholly opaque, much less transcendent. The discourse of madness, feigned, real, or a combination of both, remains in Shakespeare's plays as in Harington's diary a language of "strange desygns," of matter and impertinency mixed. The break between subject and society is equivocal rather than absolute, and the idiom of unreason in Shakespeare retains resolutely social resonances. The idealization of madness as a transcendent world metaphysically autonomous of its material conditions is a Romantic and post-Romantic construct: " 'Garde tes songes: / Les sages n'en ont pas d'aussi beaux que les fous!' " (Guard your dreams: the wise do not have dreams as beautiful as those of madmen) concludes Baudelaire's poem "La Voix" (the Voice) in *Fleurs du Mal*. But in Elizabethan and Jacobean theater the mad hero is never an absolute exile; even when banished, like Lear, he is accompanied, if only by a parodic progress. His threat transgressive more than nihilistic, the mad tragic hero, unlike the fully demonized savage or "ungovernable man," violates and recognizes social boundaries simultaneously.[10] In his tragedy

---

[8]See Barker 25–41; Belsey 41–42; Eagleton 70–75.
[9]Barker 37. Eagleton concurs: Hamlet is a "kind of nothing . . . because he is never identical with himself" (73).
[10]On the "ungovernable man," see Greenblatt 147–48.

he lingers in the dangerous, equivocal space of "reason in madness," but he is never completely marginalized. For he remains bound up in the social situation from which he is (subjectively) divided, linked to the specter of a former self whose public form he reassumes in dying.[11]

Therefore, to consider the problem of madness in Hamlet — and in *Hamlet* — is to examine its manifestly political implications in the play. Political not in the sense of topical allusions to historical persons such as Essex, but rather in the sense that Hamlet's madness articulates and represents a historically specific division by which inwardness, breaking down the pales and forts of reason, enacts the faltering of ideological prescriptions designed to define, order, and constrain subjectivity. The similarities between the madness of fictive Hamlet and that of historical Robert Devereux, the unreason that violates the sanctity of a virgin's private chamber or defies a monarch's command, derive from the transgression of ideological boundaries governing both treason and madness. That Shakespeare problematizes Hamlet's "antic disposition" at every turn is significant; the fact that Hamlet's madness cannot be pinned down, clarified, or debunked allows its consistent perception as a conduct of "strange desygns" and a threat to the sovereign. The various attempts at diagnosing Hamlet's malaise ventured by Claudius, Polonius, and Gertrude are informed by a recognition that in the ambiguous space in which reason and madness intersect lies treason. As with Essex, it is not madness itself but the insidious presence of method in it that constitutes "strange desygns." This particular danger characterizes no less the madness of Ophelia:

> Her speech is nothing,
> Yet the unshaped use of it doth move
> The hearers to collection; they yawn at it,
> And botch the words up to fit their own thoughts,
> Which as her winks and nods and gestures yield them,
> Indeed would make one think there might be thought,
> Though nothing sure, yet much unhappily.
>   (4.5.7–13)

As Laertes quite rightly observes, "This nothing's more than matter" (173); Ophelia's "unshaped" speech no less than Hamlet's "wild and

---

[11]On the death of the tragic hero Barker comments, "Tragic heroes have to die because in the spectacular kingdom death is in the body. There is no 'merely' or metaphorically ethical death which does not at the same time entail the extinction of the body, and even its complete and austere destruction" (40).

whirling words" threatens to inscribe its disorder on the "ill-breeding minds" of the body politic. In *Hamlet* it is not transcendent truth that unreason speaks, but "dangerous conjectures" rooted in the subject's problematic relation to the authority against which his — or her — inwardness is constructed.

Madness in *Hamlet*, then, while engaging and even subjecting subjectivity, is not contained within it. As a particular mode of discourse it continually threatens to be construed — or misconstrued — into an incitement of social and political disorder. The metonymic markers for order — moderation, stoicism, obedience — are undermined throughout the play by the dangerous if impenetrable subjectivity of the hero. When Claudius urges Hamlet to give over his obdurate mourning, he invokes a series of maxims on authority and obedience to natural and divine order:

> But to persever
> In obstinate condolement is a course
> Of impious stubbornness, 'tis unmanly grief,
> It shows a will most incorrect to heaven,
> A heart unfortified, a mind impatient,
> An understanding simple and unschool'd:
> For what we know must be, and is as common
> As any the most vulgar thing to sense,
> Why should we in our peevish opposition
> Take it to heart? Fie, 'tis a fault to heaven,
> A fault against the dead, a fault to nature,
> To reason most absurd, whose common theme
> Is death of fathers.
> (1.2.92–104)

Claudius may be "a little more than kin, and less than kind," but his reasoning articulates views about mourning and self-government that were commonplaces of Elizabethan religious as well as psychological thought (see MacDonald 72–85). The Protestant emphasis on an all-encompassing providence identified the will of God in all human experience regardless of how apparently arbitrary or unpleasant, while the government of passions was particularly imperative in a culture with more than its share of life-threatening hazards (see Thomas 1–21). Similarly, Claudius's insinuation that such mourning is effeminate tacitly genders melancholy; it is worth noting that Ophelia's madness, with its "unshaped" content of sexual and political allusions, doubles and even parodies Hamlet's distraction (cf. Showalter 80–83 [pp. 224–28 in this volume]). That Claudius is so eager to attribute Ophelia's madness to "the poison of deep grief" (4.5.74), indeed, the filial grief for which he upbraids Hamlet in 1.2, suggests that the feminization of madness in later periods has its seeds in the cultural construction of the rational, obedient male subject (see Foucault, *History of Sexuality* 104, 121).

But the claims of obedience upon inwardness are deflected by "that within which passes show," by the implication that the wisdom of authority — divine, royal, filial — can neither order nor account for the subject's perception of his own experience. The moralization of the inward space ("'tis a fault to heaven"), designed to encourage the subject's self-surveillance against the possible disruption of "unmanly" passion and madness, fails to dissuade Hamlet from his melancholy. But with the failure of inward constraints, authority seeks to impose its will on the subject's body: Hamlet must stay in Denmark while Laertes is allowed to return to France. The inward refusal of covert ideological controls moves power to expose and flex its coercive underpinnings. As the play develops and Hamlet's melancholy intensifies into the more dangerous "antic disposition," the question of his physical constraint becomes all the more literal and imperative. Denmark does become a prison: Rosencrantz warns Hamlet, "You do surely bar the door upon your own liberty if you deny your griefs to your friend" (3.2.318–19), while Claudius plots the ultimate physical curtailment: "For we will put fetters about this fear,/Which now goes too free-footed" (3.3.25–26).

But while madness addresses and reproduces the problematics of authority, the internalization of disobedience precludes taking arms against a sea of troubles. The radical inutility of unreason divides subjectivity and agency, and hence the question of Hamlet's "delay" should be considered in light of the more pervasive antagonism between inwardness and authority. The appearance of the ghost does not counter the vacuity of the preceding exercises in patriarchal authority but rather duplicates and even literalizes it in the equivocal space of the supernatural.[12] Hamlet's initial address to the ghost identifies its ambivalence:

> Be thou a spirit of health, or goblin damn'd,
> Bring with thee airs from heaven, or blasts from hell,
> Be thy intents wicked, or charitable,
> Thou com'st in such a questionable shape
> That I will speak to thee.
>
> (1.4.40–44)

[12]On the interplay of the equivocal, the irrational, and the supernatural (with particular reference to *Macbeth*), see Mullaney; Coddon.

As a figure of boundless semiotic ambiguity the ghost is aligned with madness and "breaking down the pales and forts of reason" (1.4.28). Horatio, the paradigmatic reasonable man, is even more ineffectual than Claudius against unreason:

> What if it tempt you toward the flood, my lord,
> Or to the dread summit of the cliff
> That beetles o'er his base into the sea,
> And there assume some other horrible form,
> Which might deprive your sovereignty of reason,
> And draw you into madness?
>
> (1.4.69–74)

The threat of madness or demonic possession, like Claudius's admonishment of unnatural grief bound up in the ideology of self-vigilance, holds no sway over the prince, who "waxes desperate with [imagination]" (1.4.87).

The uncertain origins of King Hamlet's ghost have been well documented. But its eschatological ambiguities may be less significant than the rhetoric of filial duty and natural bonds, the very idiom that Claudius employs in 1.2, in which the ghost couches its exhortations to revenge: "If thou didst ever thy dear father love"; "If thou hast nature in thee, bear it not" (1.5.23, 81). But unlike the apparitions of *The Spanish Tragedy* and *Antonio's Revenge,* the specter of King Hamlet is a figure of contamination as much as one of justice. "Taint not thy mind" (1.5.85), it urges Hamlet, yet it is not revenge but its own sickly idiom that the ghost inscribes within the "distracted globe" of Hamlet. The ghost claims in what is actually a mode of *occupatio:*

> But that I am forbid
> To tell the secrets of my prison-house,
> I could a tale unfold whose lightest word
> Would harrow up thy soul, freeze thy young blood,
> Make thy two eyes like stars start from their spheres,
> Thy knotted and combined locks to part,
> And each particular hair to stand an end,
> Like quills upon the fearful porpentine.
>
> (1.5.13–20)

But in reappearing to Hamlet in Gertrude's closet the ghost seemingly effects its own prophecy on Hamlet, whom Gertrude describes almost exactly as the ghost has hypothetically in 1.5:

Forth at your eyes your spirits wildly peep,
And as the sleeping soldiers in th' alarm,
Your bedded hair, like life in excrements
Start up and stand an end.
                                        (3.4.119–22)

Although speaking from the conventional position of justice, the ghost shapes its claims on the government and direction of the subject through fragmentation, contamination, madness. It is worth noting that the so-called problems of Hamlet's character — the obscurely motivated "antic disposition," the delay, the swift transitions from brooding soliloquy to "a kind of joy" — do not arise until the end of 1.5, after the encounter with King Hamlet's ghost. The radically ambivalent nature of the ghost serves as an almost emblematic contradiction that subsumes the play's manifest attempts at narrative coherence. Intention and consequences will diverge wildly and overtly; wills and fates will so contrary run. Hamlet's subjectivity is riven by an exhortation to obedience undermined by its own ontological and discursive equivocation.

That the dead king's exhortation to revenge and remembrance is neglected by the play as well as the prince demonstrates *Hamlet*'s consistent reluctance to privilege wholeheartedly any generic or hierarchic discourse of authority, with the possible exception of playing itself.[13] "The time is out of joint," Hamlet says at the end of 1.5, words that are all but literalized in the act that follows. The elapse of fictive time between the first and second acts, during which Hamlet has apparently done nothing save "put on" the ambiguous "antic disposition," and the centering of the plot almost exclusively on his "transformation" serve to turn the play away from the revenge plot commanded and authorized by the ghost. The discontinuities between 1.5 and 2.1 are as provocative as those informing Hamlet's "too much changed" character, the only striking "remembrance" of the precedent scene Ophelia's description of Hamlet surprising her in her closet. Because the strange encounter takes place offstage, the authenticity of Hamlet's demeanor remains, as is true of almost all of his "mad" conduct, uncertain. But if Ophelia gives a typical enough picture of the conventional melancholy lover for Polonius to make an immediate, confident diagnosis, her reference to his "look so piteous in purport / As if he had been loosed out of hell / To speak of horrors" (2.1.79–81) contradicts the relative benignity of

---

[13]On the theater's construction of — and reflections on — its own authority see Montrose, " 'Shaping Fantasies': Figurations of Gender and Power in Elizabethan Culture."

love-madness with an evocation of the supernatural, irrational incident of the prior scene. Again, it is significant to note that Ophelia speaks of Hamlet in terms markedly similar to those in which the ghost describes "the secrets of my prison-house."

It is not until well over four hundred lines into 2.2 that madness gives way to the subject of revenge, and even here it is a player's speech, "a dream of passion," that recalls to Hamlet — and to *Hamlet* — the purpose exhorted by the ghost. But while playing is aligned neither with the specious aphorisms of the ideology of self-moderation nor with the radically disintegrating forces of unreason, *Hamlet's* play-within-the-play, unlike Hieronymo's in *The Spanish Tragedy*, speaks daggers but uses none. Its purpose falls upon the inventor's head, alerting Claudius not only to Hamlet's knowledge of the fratricide but also to an apparent threat to the king's own life. Far from a vehicle of revenge, the play-within-the-play comprises but another obstacle. Significantly, closure for "The Mouse-trap" is literally disrupted when the king, "frighted with false fire," hastily departs. In "The Mouse-trap," as in *Hamlet,* in the place of closure there is madness; the ostensible revenger sings snatches of ballads, calls for music, and boasts to Horatio, "Would not this, sir, and a forest of feathers — if the rest of my fortunes turn Turk with me — with [two] Provincial roses on my raz'd shoes, get me a fellowship in a cry of players?" (3.2.260–63). Hamlet's antic foolery and incongruous festivity counter and parody the sober purpose and implication of the preceding performance. Thus the authority of playing is problematized by the play's contradictory and ambiguous effects.

Hamlet's crisis of subjectivity, then, is *Hamlet's* crisis of authority; the ideological constructs that shape power and subjection as mutually constitutive, specifically, the ideology of inward obedience designed to bolster the pales and forts of reason, are scrutinized and exposed as ineffectual. The disintegration of subjective identity — madness — corresponds to the airy nothing of ghostly authority, to the "king of shreds and patches," to the "dream of passion" of the players. If his "mouse-trap" incites Hamlet to act, he nonetheless inverts the ghost's express command, bypassing the opportunity to kill Claudius and instead focusing on Gertrude, against whom he was told not to "contrive." First confronting the queen with words so "wild and whirling" she fears for her life, then inadvertently stabbing the eavesdropping Polonius, Hamlet proceeds to deliver, ironically enough, a high-minded lecture on the queen's failure to govern her passions. But his argument for self-restraint swiftly gives way to a morbid explication of the particularly sexual nature of Gertrude's betrayal, the source of Hamlet's melancholy even before he learns of his father's murder. As madness impedes narrativity, purpose degenerates into repetition, a motif Shakespeare manifestly explores in *King Lear*. In *Hamlet*, a play still marked by the absent linear form of revenge narrative, hollow gestures toward purpose are approached only to be reversed. The sudden appearance of the ghost functions not only to remind Hamlet of his "almost blunted purpose," but also to rehearse the earlier encounter. Yet when it departs, Hamlet promptly reverts to another argument for sexual self-restraint ("Assume a virtue if you have it not"). As for Polonius, whose corpse has been almost comically forgotten for over a hundred lines, Hamlet asserts rather decorously that

> For this same lord,
> I do repent; but heaven hath pleas'd it so,
> To punish me with this, and this with me,
> That I must be their scourge and minister.
> I will bestow him, and will answer well
> The death I gave him.
>   (3.4.172–77)

But identity — as noble revenger — is no sooner restored than overthrown by madness, which resists closure and subverts purpose. Hamlet requests "One word more, good lady," then launches into an "antic" tirade upon Gertrude's sexual relations with "the bloat king." And in overt contradiction of his lofty repentance of lines 172–77, Hamlet announces that "I'll lug the guts into the neighbor room" (212) and far from "answering well" for Polonius's slaying, stashes the body in a cupboard.

The fragmentation displaced in the grotesque mutilations of earlier revenge tragedies has become in *Hamlet* the condition of the hero's subjectivity, the principle governing dramatic structure, the violence inscribed on the body of the play instead of on the body of the villain. Indeed, Hamlet's strange business with the body of Polonius replaces what is in the source stories the actual dismemberment of the spying minister. In the very brief scene 4.2, often cut from stage productions, and in the ensuing interrogation by the king ("Now, Hamlet, where's Polonius?" / "At supper." [4.3.16–17]), Hamlet's mysterious inwardness intersects with the contradiction of the body, the body that is at once absent and material, a thing and a thing of nothing. Madness, a discourse that collapses the ostensible distinction between the body and the "self," speaking an idiom that conflates and confuses the political and the "private," here posits as its referent the great leveler of differences, death. As Michael Bristol has commented, "Hamlet's 'extreame show of doltishness' reinterprets the basic distinctions of life: between food and corrupt, decaying flesh, between human and animal, between king and beggar. Temporal authority and indeed all political structures of difference are turned inside out" (187).

> Your worm is your only emperor for diet: we fat all creatures else
> to fat us, and we fat ourselves for maggots; your fat king and your
> lean beggar is but variable service, two dishes, but to one table —
> that's the end.
>
> (4.3.20–24)

Madness, then, is not so much metaphor as metonymy for death, a moment in which the materiality of the body overturns the authority of distinctions out of which coherent, unified subjectivity is constructed. For in *Hamlet* subjectivity is still engaged in materiality even as the autonomy of the "self" ("is") from the body ("seems") is being asserted. By the graveyard scene the death-madness of 4.2 and 4.3 has become externalized, literalized in the representation of a grave-digger who "sings in grave-making" (5.1.63–64), in Hamlet's hypothetical histories of the skulls of courtiers, politicians, as "Imperious Caesar" (5.1.199) whose dust may stop a bunghole. There is Yorick, too, the "mad rogue" whose literal antic disposition was "wont to set the table on a roar" (178). The prince and the grave-digger discuss "Young Hamlet, he that is mad and sent to England," in the third person, as though the radically fragmented hero of acts 2 through 4 has been banished across the imaginary sea. Madness, death, fragmentation, heretofore located in Hamlet's "wild and whirling words," are in 5.1 presented as conditions of the play's world. Hamlet is again "good as a chorus," pointing out, commenting upon, and interpreting the old bones in the graveyard, the "maimed rites" of Ophelia's funeral. At once justification and near-parodic literalization of the stuff of Hamlet's privileged subjectivity, the gross materiality of the grave seems to claim an authority that subsumes inwardness and difference. If the scene owes a debt to the *memento mori* tradition, the skulls emblematize not so much the vanity of the world as the material necessity that implicates subject and authority alike.[14] Hamlet recognizes the authority of death as absolute and inviolable, yet even as recognition of authority confers, accordingly, the unified identity ("This is I, Hamlet the Dane!" [5.1.243–44]) disrupted by the more problematic relations to power, Hamlet's "towering passion" returns to destabilize the seemingly restored noble self. The scuffle with Laertes has an almost black comic aspect in contrast to the sober meditations on mortality that precede it, given the "bravery" of Laertes' speech, reasonable Horatio's typically ineffectual "Good my lord, be quiet" (251), and Hamlet's somewhat incongruous question to the man whose father he has killed, "What is the reason that you use me thus? / I lov'd you ever" (275–76). The containment apparently evoked in the dialogue with the grave-diggers is contradicted as soundly as Hamlet's promise to "answer well" for Polonius's death, madness once again violently usurping narrative order.

Yet Hamlet's outburst at Ophelia's grave exhausts his "wild and whirling words." In the final scene the hero at last becomes the "courtier, soldier, scholar" of Ophelia's tribute, recounting to Horatio the rash but providentially sanctioned actions on the ship, bantering wittily with Osric the waterfly, graciously agreeing to the king's request for the conciliatory game with Laertes. Hamlet's placid fatalism despite his premonition of death and his acquiescence to providential design transform "distracted" subjectivity into noble subjection to the "divinity that shapes our ends." Hence Hamlet's apology to Laertes renounces madness, the unruly and disruptive force in the play as well as in his own "distracted globe": "His madness is poor Hamlet's enemy" (5.2.221). In the past, critics have debated over the sincerity or lack thereof of Hamlet's apology, a consequence of overemphasis on Hamlet as a naturalistic character rather than as central feature of a play in which the ambiguities, the "strange desygns," of madness are so foregrounded. Even when considered in a theatrical rather than purely textual context, wherein an actor is personating Hamlet, the tragic hero's last formal set speech, like that of Othello or even the premature "Let's away to prison" speech of Lear, engages the public dimension informing rites of symbolic closure in Elizabethan England. In *Hamlet* as in the scaffold speech of Essex, an eloquent if stylized confession redeems the transgressing subject and affirms the order he has violated, disclaims "a purposed evil" and restores the speaker to himself. Because the audience

[14]Ferguson's essay considers the complex function of the *memento mori* in *Hamlet* (302–05). For a reading of *Hamlet* as a "*memento mori* poem," see Morris 311–41.

knows what Hamlet only presciently suspects, his death seems inevitable, in accord with the narrative logic so consistently violated before by the now-renounced madness.

But Shakespeare's decorous ritual of death, for all that it *seems* to observe a form of ideological closure, does not contain madness even by the hero's death and the extinction of his problematic subjectivity. "Madness dissipated can be only the same thing as the imminence of the end. . . . But death itself does not bring peace; madness will still triumph — a truth mockingly eternal, beyond the end of a life which yet had been delivered from madness by this very end" (Foucault, *Madness and Civilization* 32). For Hamlet "the rest is silence"; he bequeaths his "story" to reasonable Horatio. But Horatio's recapitulation of the tragic events contradicts Hamlet's own providential interpretation of his tragedy:

> So shall you hear
> Of carnal, bloody, and unnatural acts,
> Of accidental judgments, casual slaughters,
> Of deaths put on by cunning and [forc'd] cause,
> And in this upshot, purposes mistook
> Fall'n on th' inventors' heads.
> (5.2.362–67)

Moreover, Horatio urges that the rather skeletal tale be recounted to ward off the semiotic slippage aligned with disruptive madness; his task must be performed "Even while men's minds are wild, lest more mischance / On plots and errors happen" (376–77). If Hamlet has retracted his madness, *Hamlet* stops short of following suit. The division that breeds "dangerous conjectures" rests unreconciled; the condemned man's words enact a rite of obedience but affirm an order that is still estranged from the disorderly social reality of "wild minds." Shakespeare's tragedy, performed on the public stage, makes no attempt to contain the potentially dangerous play of signification that moved Tudor authority to make the executions of Mary and Essex semiprivate affairs whose printed reports are as safely decontextualized as Horatio's account of what happens in *Hamlet*. Indeed, Shakespeare's investigation of the interplay of unreason's "strange desygns" and the "wild minds" of the body politic stands in reciprocal rather than imitative relation to the offstage drama of disobedience and melancholy, treason and madness, that led Robert Devereux to the scaffold. Whether Shakespeare's reflections were actually prompted by the ill-fated career of the queen's last favorite is ultimately less important than the pervasive crisis of inwardness and authority, enacted in *Hamlet,* acted upon by the earl of Essex. The ambiguous boundaries between treason and madness in Elizabethan England testify to the politicization of subjectivity, the traces of which essentialist readings of Hamlet — and of the history of "the self" — have repressed but not effaced.[15]

WORKS CITED

Bald, R. C. *John Donne: A Life.* New York: Oxford UP, 1970.

Barker, Francis. *The Tremulous Private Body: Essays on Subjection.* London: Methuen, 1984.

Belsey, Catherine. *The Subject of Tragedy: Identity and Difference in Renaissance Drama.* London: Methuen, 1985.

Bright, Timothie. *A Treatise of Melancholie.* 1586. New York: Columbia UP, 1940.

Bristol, Michael D. *Carnival and Theater: Plebeian Culture and the Structure of Authority in Renaissance England.* New York: Methuen, 1985.

Coddon, Karin S. "Unreal Mockery: Unreason and the Problem of Spectacle in *Macbeth.*" *English Literary History* 56 (1989): 485–501.

Dollimore, Jonathan. *Radical Tragedy: Religion, Ideology, and Power in the Drama of Shakespeare and His Contemporaries.* Chicago: U of Chicago P, 1984.

Dollimore, Jonathan, and Alan Sinfield, eds. *Political Shakespeare: New Essays in Cultural Materialism.* Ithaca: Cornell UP, 1985.

Eagleton, Terry. *William Shakespeare.* Oxford: Blackwell, 1986.

Esler, Anthony. *The Aspiring Mind of the Elizabethan Younger Generation.* Durham: Duke UP, 1966.

Feder, Lillian. *Madness in Literature.* Princeton: Princeton UP, 1980.

Felman, Shoshana. *Writing and Madness: (Literary/Philosophy/Psychoanalysis).* Trans. Martha Noel Evans and Shoshana Felman. Ithaca: Cornell UP, 1985.

Ferguson, Margaret W. "*Hamlet:* Letters and Spirits." Parker and Hartman 292–309.

---

[15]In each of its many metamorphoses, this essay has benefited from the criticism, guidance, and encouragement I have received from Louis A. Montrose; to him I extend my gratitude.

Foucault, Michel. *Discipline and Punish: The Birth of the Prison*. 1975. Trans. Alan Sheridan. New York: Vintage, 1977.

——. *History of Sexuality*. Vol. 1. Trans. Robert Hurley. New York: Pantheon, 1978.

——. *Madness and Civilization: A History of Insanity in the Age of Reason*. Trans. Richard Howard. London: Tavistock, 1967.

——. "The Subject and Power." *Critical Inquiry* 8 (1982): 777–81.

Greenblatt, Stephen. *Renaissance Self-fashioning: From More to Shakespeare*. Chicago: U of Chicago P, 1980.

Harington, John. *Nugae Antiquae*. Vol. 2. 1779. Hildesheim, Ger.: Olms, 1968.

Harrison, G. B. *The Life and Death of Robert Devereux, Earl of Essex*. New York: Holt, 1937.

Hill, Christopher. Rev. of *Treason in Tudor England: Politics and Paranoia* by Lacy Baldwin Smith. *New York Review of Books* 7 May 1987: 36–38.

James, Mervyn. *English Politics and the Concept of Honour, 1485–1642*. Past and Present Supplement 3. London: Past and Present Society, 1975.

Kinney, Arthur F., ed. *Elizabethan Backgrounds: Historical Documents of the Age of Elizabeth I*. Hamden: Archon, 1975.

Lacey, Robert. *Robert, Earl of Essex*. New York: Atheneum, 1970.

MacDonald, Michael. *Mystical Bedlam: Madness, Anxiety, and Healing in Seventeenth-Century England*. Cambridge: Cambridge UP, 1981.

Matter, Joseph Allen. *My Lords and Lady of Essex: Their State Trials*. Chicago: Regency, 1969.

Midelfort, H. C. Erik. "Madness and Civilization in Early Modern Europe: A Reappraisal of Michel Foucault." *After the Reformation: Essays in Honor of J. H. Hexter*. Ed. Barbara C. Malament. Philadelphia: U of Pennsylvania P, 1980. 247–65.

Montrose, Louis Adrian. "The Purpose of Playing: Reflections on a Shakespearean Anthropology." *Helios* n.s. 7.2 (1980): 53–76.

——. " 'Shaping Fantasies': Figurations of Gender and Power in Elizabethan Culture." *Representations* 44.2 (1983): 61–94.

Moretti, Franco. *Signs Taken for Wonders: Essays in the Sociology of Literary Forms*. Trans. Susan Fisher, David Forgacs, and David Miller. London: Verso, 1983.

Morris, Harry. *Last Things in Shakespeare*. Tallahassee: Florida State UP, 1985.

Mullaney, Steven. "Lying Like Truth: Riddle, Representation, and

Treason in Renaissance England." *English Literary History* 47 (1980): 32–47.

Neill, Michael. "'Exeunt with a Dead March': Funeral Pageantry on the Shakespearean Stage." *Pageantry in the Shakespearean Theater.* Ed. David M. Bergeron. Athens: U of Georgia P, 1985. 153–93.

Parker, Patricia, and Geoffrey Hartman, eds. *Shakespeare and the Question of Theory.* New York: Methuen, 1985.

Sharpe, J. A. "Last Dying Speeches: Religion, Ideology, and Public Execution in Seventeenth-Century England." *Past and Present* 107 (1985): 144–67.

Showalter, Elaine. "Representing Ophelia: Women, Madness, and the Responsibilities of Feminist Criticism." Parker and Hartman 77–94. Also reprinted in this volume on pp. 220–40.

Smith, Lacey Baldwin. *The Elizabethan World.* Boston: Houghton, 1967.

———. *Treason in Tudor England: Politics and Paranoia.* Princeton: Princeton UP, 1986.

Stone, Lawrence. *The Crisis of the Aristocracy, 1558–1641.* Abridged ed. New York: Methuen, 1986.

Tennenhouse, Leonard. *Power on Display: The Politics of Shakespeare's Genres.* New York: Methuen, 1986.

Thomas, Keith. *Religion and the Decline of Magic.* New York: Scribner, 1971.

Weimann, Robert. "Mimesis in *Hamlet.*" Parker and Hartman 275–91.

Wilson, J. Dover. *What Happens in "Hamlet."* 1935. Cambridge, Eng.: Cambridge UP, 1982.

Glossary of Critical
and Theoretical Terms

Most terms have been glossed parenthetically where they first appear in the text. Mainly, the glossary lists terms that are too complex to define in a phrase or a sentence or two. A few of the terms listed are discussed at greater length elsewhere (feminist criticism, for instance); these terms are defined succinctly and a page reference to the longer discussion is provided.

AFFECTIVE FALLACY First used by William K. Wimsatt and Monroe C. Beardsley to refer to what they regarded as the erroneous practice of interpreting texts according to the psychological responses of readers. "The Affective Fallacy," they wrote in a 1946 essay later republished in the *Verbal Icon* (1954), "is a confusion between the poem and its *results* (what it *is* and what it *does*). . . . It begins by trying to derive the standards of criticism from the psychological effects of a poem and ends in impressionism and relativism." The affective fallacy, like the intentional fallacy (confusing the meaning of a work with the author's expressly intended meaning), was one of the main tenets of the New Criticism, or formalism. The affective fallacy has recently been contested by reader-response critics, who have deliberately dedicated their efforts to describing the way individual readers and "interpretive communities" go about "making sense" of texts.

See also: Authorial Intention, Formalism, Reader-Response Criticism.

AUTHORIAL INTENTION Defined narrowly, an author's intention in writing a work, as expressed in letters, diaries, interviews, and conversations. Defined more broadly, "intentionality" involves unexpressed motivations, designs, and purposes, some of which may have remained unconscious.

The debate over whether critics should try to discern an author's intentions (conscious or otherwise) is an old one. William K. Wimsatt and Monroe C. Beardsley, in an essay first published in the 1940s, coined the term "intentional fallacy" to refer to the practice of basing interpretations on the expressed or implied intentions of authors, a practice they judged to be erroneous. As proponents of the New Criticism, or formalism, they argued that a work of literature is an object in itself and should be studied as such. They believed that it is sometimes helpful to learn what an author intended, but the critic's real purpose is to show what is actually in the text, not what an author intended to put there.

See also: Affective Fallacy, Formalism.

BASE *See* Marxist Criticism.

BINARY OPPOSITIONS *See* Oppositions.

BLANKS *See* Gaps.

CANON Since the fourth century, used to refer to those books of the Bible that the Christian church accepts as being Holy Scripture. The term has come to be applied more generally to those literary works given special status, or "privileged," by a culture. Works we tend to think of as "classics" or the "Great Books" produced by Western culture — texts that are found in every anthology of American, British, and world literature — would be among those that constitute the canon.

Recently, Marxist, feminist, minority, and Third World critics have argued that, for political reasons, many excellent works never enter the canon. Canonized works, they claim, are those that reflect — and respect — the culture's dominant ideology and/or perform some socially acceptable or even necessary form of "cultural work." Attempts have been made to broaden or redefine the canon by discovering valuable texts, or versions of texts, that were repressed or ignored for political reasons. These have been published both in traditional and in nontraditional anthologies. The more outspoken critics of the canon, especially radical critics practicing cultural criticism, have called into question the whole concept of canon or "canonicity." Privileging no form of artistic expression that reflects and revises the culture, these critics treat cartoons, comics, and soap operas with the same cogency and respect they accord novels, poems, and plays.

See also: Cultural Criticism, Feminist Criticism, Ideology, Marxist Criticism.

CONFLICTS, CONTRADICTIONS *See* Gaps.

CULTURAL CRITICISM A critical approach that is sometimes referred to as "cultural studies" or "cultural critique." Practitioners of cultural criticism oppose "high" definitions of culture and take seriously popular cultural forms. Grounded in a variety of continental European influences, cultural criticism nonetheless gained institutional force in England, in 1964, with the founding of the Centre for Contemporary Cultural Studies at Birmingham University. Broadly interdisciplinary in its scope and approach, cultural criticism views the text as the locus and catalyst of a complex network of political and economic discourses. Cultural critics share with Marxist critics an interest in the ideological contexts of cultural forms.

DECONSTRUCTION A poststructuralist approach to literature that is strongly influenced by the writings of the French philosopher Jacques Derrida. Deconstruction, partly in response to structuralism and formalism, posits the undecidability of meaning for all texts. In fact, as the deconstructionist critic J. Hillis Miller points out, "deconstruction is not a dismantling of the structure of a text but a demonstration that it has already dismantled itself." See "What Is Deconstruction?" pp. 283–93.

DIALECTIC Originally developed by Greek philosophers, mainly Socrates and Plato, as a form and method of logical argumentation; the term later came to denote a philosophical notion of evolution. The German philosopher G. W. F. Hegel described dialectic as a process whereby a thesis, when countered by an antithesis, leads to the synthesis of a new idea. Karl Marx and Friedrich Engels, adapting Hegel's idealist theory, used the phrase "dialectical materialism" to discuss the way in which a revolutionary class war might lead to the synthesis of a new social economic order. The American Marxist critic Fredric Jameson has coined the phrase "dialectical criticism" to refer to a Marxist critical approach that synthesizes structuralist and poststructuralist methodologies.
See also: Marxist Criticism, Structuralism, Poststructuralism.

DIALOGIC *See* Discourse.

DISCOURSE Used specifically, can refer to (1) spoken or written discussion of a subject or area of knowledge; (2) the words in, or text of, a narrative as opposed to its story line; or (3) a "strand" within a given narrative that argues a certain point or defends a given value system.

More generally, "discourse" refers to the language in which a subject or area of knowledge is discussed or a certain kind of business is transacted. Human knowledge is collected and structured in discourses. Theology and medicine are defined by their discourses, as are politics, sexuality, and literary criticism.

A society is generally made up of a number of different discourses or "discourse communities," one or more of which may be dominant or serve the dominant ideology. Each discourse has its own vocabulary, concepts, and rules, knowledge of which constitutes power. The psychoanalyst and psychoanalytic critic Jacques Lacan has treated the unconscious as a form of discourse, the patterns of which are repeated in literature. Cultural critics, following Mikhail Bakhtin, use the word "dialogic" to discuss the dialogue *between* discourses that takes place within language or, more specifically, a literary text.
See also: Cultural Criticism, Ideology, Narrative, Psychoanalytic Criticism.

FEMINIST CRITICISM An aspect of the feminist movement whose primary goals include critiquing masculine-dominated language and literature by showing how they reflect a masculine ideology; writing the history of unknown or undervalued women writers, thereby earning them their rightful place in the literary canon; and helping create a climate in which women's creativity may be fully realized and appreciated. See "What Is Feminist Criticism?" pp. 208–15.

FIGURE *See* Metaphor, Metonymy, Symbol.

FORMALISM Also referred to as the New Criticism, formalism reached its height during the 1940s and 1950s but it is still practiced today. Formalists treat a work of literary art as if it were a self-contained, self-referential object. Rather than basing their interpretations of a text on the reader's response, the author's stated intentions, or parallels between the text and historical contexts (such as the author's life), formalists concentrate on the relationships *within* the text that give it its own distinctive character or form. Special attention is paid to repetition, particularly of images or symbols, but also of sound effects and rhythms in poetry.

Because of the importance placed on close analysis and the stress on the text as a carefully crafted, orderly object containing observable formal patterns, formalism has often been seen as an attack on Romanticism and impressionism, particularly impressionistic criticism. It has sometimes even been called an "objective" approach to literature. Formalists are more likely than certain other critics to believe and say that the meaning of text can be known objectively. For instance, reader-response critics see meaning as a function either of each reader's experience or of the norms that govern a particular "interpretive community," and deconstructors argue that texts mean opposite things at the same time.

Formalism was originally based on essays written during the 1920s and 1930s by T. S. Eliot, I. A. Richards, and William Empson. It was significantly developed later by a group of American poets and critics, including R. P. Blackmur, Cleanth Brooks, John Crowe Ransom, Allen Tate, Robert Penn Warren, and William K. Wimsatt. Although we associate formalism with certain principles and terms (such as the "Affective Fallacy" and the "Intentional Fallacy" as defined by Wimsatt and Monroe C. Beardsley), formalists were trying to make a cultural statement rather than establish a critical dogma. Generally Southern, religious, and culturally conservative, they advocated the inherent value of literary works (particularly of literary works regarded as beautiful art objects) because they were sick of the growing ugliness of modern life and contemporary events. Some recent theorists even suggest that the rising popularity of formalism after World War II was a feature of American isolationism, the formalist tendency to isolate literature from biography and history being a manifestation of the American fatigue with wider involvements.

See also: Affective Fallacy, Authorial Intention, Deconstruction, Reader-Response Criticism, Symbol.

GAPS When used by reader-response critics familiar with the theories of Wolfgang Iser, refers to "blanks" in texts that must be filled in by readers. A gap may be said to exist whenever and wherever a reader perceives something to be missing between words, sentences, paragraphs, stanzas, or chapters. Readers respond to gaps actively and creatively, explaining apparent inconsistencies in point of view, accounting for jumps in chronology, speculatively supplying information missing from plots, and resolving problems or issues left ambiguous or "indeterminate" in the text.

Reader-response critics sometimes speak as if a gap actually exists in a text; a gap is, of course, to some extent a product of readers' perceptions. Different readers may find gaps in different texts, and different gaps in the same text. Furthermore, they may fill these gaps in different ways, which is why, a reader-response critic might argue, works are interpreted in different ways.

Although the concept of the gap has been used mainly by reader-response critics, it has also been used by critics taking other theoretical approaches. Practitioners of deconstruction might use "gap" when speaking of the radical contradictoriness of a text. Marxists have used the term to speak of everything from the gap that opens up between economic base and cultural superstructure to the two kinds of conflicts or contradictions to be found in literary texts. The first of these, they would argue, results from the fact that texts reflect ideology, within which certain subjects cannot be covered, things cannot be said, contradictory views cannot be recognized as contradictory. The second kind of conflict, contradiction, or gap within a text results from the fact that works don't just reflect ideology: they are also fictions that, consciously or unconsciously, distance themselves from the same ideology.

See also: Deconstruction, Ideology, Marxist Criticism, Reader-Response Criticism.

GENRE A French word referring to a kind or type of literature. Individual works within a genre may exhibit a distinctive form, be governed by certain conventions, and/or represent characteristic subjects. Tragedy, epic, and romance are all genres.

Perhaps inevitably, the term "genre" is used loosely. Lyric poetry is a genre, but so are characteristic *types* of the lyric, such as the sonnet, the ode, and the elegy. Fiction is a genre, as are detective fiction and science fiction. The list of genres grows constantly as critics establish new lines of connection between individual works and discern new categories of works with common characteristics. Moreover, some writers form hybrid genres by combining the characteristics of several in a single work.

Knowledge of genres helps critics to understand and explain what is conventional and unconventional, borrowed and original, in a work.

HEGEMONY Given intellectual currency by the Italian communist Antonio Gramsci, the word (a translation of *egemonia*) refers to the pervasive system of assumptions, meanings, and values — the web of ideologies, in other words — that shapes the way things look, what they mean, and therefore what reality *is* for the majority of people within a given culture.

See also: Ideology, Marxist Criticism.

IDEOLOGY A set of beliefs underlying the customs, habits, and/or practices common to a given social group. To members of that group, the beliefs seem obviously true, natural, and even universally applicable. They may seem just as obviously arbitrary, idiosyncratic, and even false to outsiders or members of another group who adhere to another ideology. Within a society, several ideologies may coexist, or one or more may be dominant.

Ideologies may be forcefully imposed or willingly subscribed to. Their component beliefs may be held consciously or unconsciously. In either case, they come to form what Johanna M. Smith has called "the unexamined ground of our experience." Ideology governs our perceptions, judgments, and prejudices — our sense of what is acceptable, normal, and deviant. Ideology may cause a revolution; it may also allow discrimination and even exploitation.

Ideologies are of special interest to sociologically oriented critics of literature because of the way in which authors reflect or resist prevailing views in their texts. Some Marxist critics have argued that literary texts reflect and reproduce the ideologies that produced them; most, however, have shown how ideologies are riven with contradictions that works of literature manage to expose and widen. Still other Marxists have focused on the way in which texts themselves are characterized by gaps, conflicts, and contradictions between their ideological and anti-ideological functions. Feminist critics have addressed the question of ideology by seeking to expose (and thereby call into question) the patriarchal ideology mirrored or inscribed in works written by men — even men who have sought to counter sexism and break down sexual stereotypes. New historicists have been interested in demonstrating the ideological underpinnings not only of literary representations but also of our interpretations of them. Fredric Jameson, an American Marxist critic, argues that all thought is ideological, but that ideological thought that knows itself as such stands the chance of seeing through and transcending ideology.

See also: Cultural Criticism, Feminist Criticism, Marxist Criticism, New Historicism.

IMAGINARY ORDER One of the three essential orders of the psychoanalytic field (see Real and Symbolic Order), it is most closely associated with the senses (sight, sound, touch, taste, and smell). The infant, who by comparison to other animals is born premature and thus is wholly dependent on others for a prolonged period, enters the Imaginary order when it begins to experience a unity of body parts and motor control that is empowering. This usually occurs between six and eighteen months and is called by Lacan the "mirror stage" or "mirror phase," in which the child anticipates mastery of its body. It does so by identifying with the *image* of wholeness (i.e., seeing its own image in the mirror, experiencing its mother as a whole body, etc.). This sense of oneness, and also difference from others (especially the mother or primary caretaker), is established through an image or vision of harmony that is both a mirroring and a "mirage of maturation" or false sense of individuality and independence. The Imaginary is a metaphor for unity, is related to the visual order, and is always part of human subjectivity. Because the subject is fundamentally separate from others and also internally divided (conscious/unconscious), the apparent coherence of the Imaginary, its fullness and grandiosity, is always false, a *mis*recognition that the ego (or "me") tries to deny by imagining itself as coherent and empowered. The Imaginary operates in conjunction with the Real and Symbolic and is not a "stage" of development equivalent to Freud's "pre-oedipal stage," nor is it prelinguistic.

See also: Psychoanalytic Criticism, Real, Symbolic Order

IMPLIED READER A phrase used by some reader-response critics in place of the phrase "the reader." Whereas "the reader" could refer to any idiosyncratic individual who happens to have read or to be reading the text, "the implied reader" is *the* reader intended, even created, by the text. Other reader-response critics seeking to describe this more generally conceived reader have spoken of the "informed reader" or the "narratee," who is "the necessary counterpart of a given narrator."

See Reader-Response Criticism.

INTENTIONAL FALLACY *See* Authorial Intention.

INTENTIONALITY *See* Authorial Intention.

INTERTEXTUALITY The condition of interconnectedness among texts. Every author has been influenced by others, and every work contains explicit and implicit references to other works. Writers may consciously or unconsciously echo a predecessor or precursor; they may also consciously or unconsciously disguise their indebtedness, making intertextual relationships difficult for the critic to trace.

Reacting against the formalist tendency to view each work as a free-standing object, some poststructuralist critics suggested that the meaning of a work only emerges intertextually, that is, within the context provided by other works. But there has been a reaction, too, against this type of intertextual criticism. Some new historicist critics suggest that literary history is itself too narrow a context and that works should be interpreted in light of a larger set of cultural contexts.

There is, however, a broader definition of intertextuality, one that refers to the relationship between works of literature and a wide range of narratives and discourses that we don't usually consider literary. Thus defined, intertextuality could be used by a new historicist to refer to the significant interconnectedness between a literary text and nonliterary discussions of or discourses about contemporary culture. Or it could be used by a poststructuralist to suggest that a work can only be recognized and read within a vast field of signs and tropes that is *like* a text and that makes any single text self-contradictory and "undecidable."

See also: Discourse, Formalism, Narrative, New Historicism, Poststructuralism, Trope.

MARXIST CRITICISM An approach that treats literary texts as material products, describing them in broadly historical terms. In Marxist criticism, the text is viewed in terms of its production and consumption, as a product *of* work that does identifiable cultural work of its own. Following Karl Marx, the founder of communism, Marxist critics have used the terms "base" to refer to economic reality and "superstructure" to refer to the corresponding or "homologous" infrastructure consisting of politics, law, philosophy, religion, and the arts. Also following Marx, they have used the word "ideology" to refer to that set of cultural beliefs that literary works at once reproduce, resist, and revise. See "What Is Marxist Criticism?" pp. 331–43.

METAPHOR The representation of one thing by another related or similar thing. The image (or activity or concept) used to represent or "figure" something else is known as the "vehicle" of the metaphor; the thing represented is called the "tenor." In other words, the vehicle is what we substitute for the tenor. The relationship between vehicle and tenor can provide much additional meaning. Thus, instead of saying, "Last night I read a book," we might say, "Last night I plowed through a book." "Plowed through" (or the activity of plowing) is the vehicle of our metaphor; "read" (or the act of reading) is the tenor, the thing being figured. The increment in meaning through metaphor is fairly obvious. Our audience knows not only *that* we read but also *how* we read, because to read a book in the way that a plow rips through earth is surely to read in a relentless, unreflective way. Note that in the sentence above, a new metaphor — "rips through" — has been used to explain an old one. This serves (which is a metaphor) as an example of just how thick (another metaphor) language is with metaphors!

Metaphor is a kind of "trope" (literally, a "turning," i.e., a figure that alters or "turns" the meaning of a word or phrase). Other tropes include allegory, conceit, metonymy, personification, simile, symbol, and synecdoche. Traditionally, metaphor and symbol have been viewed as the principal tropes; minor tropes have been categorized as *types* of these two major ones. Similes, for instance, are usually defined as simple metaphors that usually employ "like" or "as" and state the tenor outright, as in "My love is like a red, red rose." Synecdoche involves a vehicle that is a *part* of the tenor, as in "I see a sail" meaning "I see a boat." Metonymy is viewed as a metaphor involving two terms commonly if arbitrarily associated with (but not fundamentally or intrinsically related to) each other. Recently, however, deconstructors such as Paul de Man and J. Hillis Miller have questioned the "privilege" granted to metaphor and the metaphor/metonymy distinction or "opposition." They have suggested that all metaphors are really metonyms and that all figuration is arbitrary.

See also: Deconstruction, Metonymy, Oppositions, Symbol.

METONYMY The representation of one thing by another that is commonly and often physically associated with it. To refer to a writer's handwriting as his or her "hand" is to use a metonymic "figure" or "trope." The image or thing used to represent something else is known as the "vehicle" of the metonym; the thing represented is called the "tenor."

Like other tropes (such as metaphor), metonymy involves the replacement of one word or phrase by another. Liquor may be referred to as "the bottle," a monarch as "the crown." Narrowly defined, the vehicle of a metonym is arbitrarily, not intrinsically, associated with the tenor. In other words, the bottle just happens to be what liquor is stored in and poured from in our culture. The hand may be involved in the production of handwriting, but so are the brain and the pen. There is no special, intrinsic likeness between a crown and a monarch; it's just that crowns traditionally sit on monarchs' heads and not on the heads of university professors. More broadly, "metonym" and "metonymy" have been used by recent critics to refer to a wide range of figures and tropes. Deconstructors have questioned the distinction between metaphor and metonymy.

See also: Deconstruction, Metaphor, Trope.

NARRATIVE A story or a telling of a story, or an account of a situation or of events. A novel and a biography of a novelist are both narratives, as are Freud's case histories.

Some critics use the word "narrative" even more generally; Brook Thomas, a new historicist, has critiqued "narratives of human history that neglect the role human labor has played."

NEW CRITICISM *See* Formalism.

NEW HISTORICISM One of the most recent developments in contemporary critical theory, its practitioners share certain convictions, the major ones being that literary critics need to develop a high degree of historical consciousness and that literature should not be viewed apart from other human creations, artistic or otherwise. See "What Is the New Historicism?" pp. 368–76.

See also: Authorial Intention, Deconstruction, Formalism, Ideology, Poststructuralism, Psychoanalytic Criticism.

OPPOSITIONS A concept highly relevant to linguistics, since linguists maintain that words (such as "black" and "death") have meaning not in themselves but in relation to other words ("white" and "life"). Jacques Derrida, a poststructuralist philosopher of language, has suggested that in the West we think in terms of these "binary oppositions" or dichotomies, which on examination turn out to be evaluative hierarchies. In other words, each opposition — beginning/end, presence/absence, or consciousness/unconsciousness — contains one term that our culture views as superior and one term that we view as negative or inferior.

Derrida has "deconstructed" a number of these binary oppositions, including two — speech/writing and signifier/signified — that he believes to be central to linguistics in particular and Western culture in general. He has concurrently critiqued the "law" of noncontradiction, which is fundamental to Western logic. He and other deconstructors have argued that a text can contain opposed strands of discourse and, therefore, mean opposite things: reason *and* passion, life *and* death, hope *and* despair, black *and* white. Traditionally, criticism has involved choosing between opposed or contradictory meanings and arguing that one is present in the text and the other absent.

French feminists have adopted the ideas of Derrida and other deconstructors, showing not only that we think in terms of such binary oppositions as male/female, reason/emotion, and active/passive, but that we also associate reason and activity with masculinity and emotion and passivity with femininity. Because of this, they have concluded that language is "phallocentric" or masculine-dominated.

See also: Deconstruction, Discourse, Feminist Criticism, Poststructuralism.

PHALLUS The symbolic value of the penis that organizes libidinal development and which Freud saw as a stage in the process of human subjectivity. Lacan viewed the Phallus as the representative of a fraudulent power (male over female) whose "law" is a principle of psychic division (conscious/unconscious) and sexual difference (masculine/feminine). The Symbolic order (see Symbolic Order) is ruled by the Phallus, which of itself has no inherent meaning *apart from* the power and meaning given it by individual cultures and societies and represented by the Name of the Father as lawgiver and namer.

POSTSTRUCTURALISM The general attempt to contest and subvert structuralism initiated by deconstructors and certain other critics associated with psychoanalytic, Marxist, and feminist theory. Structuralists, using linguistics as a model employing semiotic (sign) theory, posit the possibility of knowing a text systematically and revealing the "grammar" behind its form and meaning. Poststructuralists argue against the possibility of such knowledge and description. They counter that texts can be shown to contradict not only structuralist accounts of them but also themselves. In making their adversarial claims, they rely on close readings of texts and on the work of theorists such as Jacques Derrida and Jacques Lacan.

Poststructuralists have suggested that structuralism rests on distinctions between "signifier" and "signified" (signs and the things they point toward), "self" and "language" (or "text"), texts and other texts, and text and world that are overly simplistic, if not patently inaccurate. Poststructuralists have shown how all signifieds are also signifiers, and they have treated texts as "intertexts." They have viewed the world as if it *were* a text (we desire a certain car because it *symbolizes* achievement) and the self as the subject, as well as the user, of language; for example, we may shape and speak through language, but it also shapes and speaks through us.

See also: Deconstruction, Feminist Criticism, Intertextuality, Psychoanalytic Criticism, Semiotics, Structuralism.

PSYCHOANALYTIC CRITICISM   Grounded in the psychoanalytic theories of Sigmund Freud, it is one of the oldest critical methodologies still in use. Freud's view that works of literature, like dreams, express secret, unconscious desires led to criticism that interpreted literary works as manifestations of the authors' neuroses. More recently, psychoanalytic critics have come to see literary works as skillfully crafted artifacts that may appeal to *our* neuroses by tapping into our repressed wishes and fantasies. Other forms of psychological criticism that diverge from Freud, although they ultimately derive from his insights, include those based on the theories of Carl Jung and Jacques Lacan. See "What Is Psychoanalytic Criticism?" pp. 241–51.

READER-RESPONSE CRITICISM   An approach to literature that, as its name implies, considers the way readers respond to texts, as they read. Stanley Fish describes the method by saying that it substitutes for one question, "What does this sentence mean?" a more operational question, "What does this sentence do?" Reader-response criticism shares with deconstruction a strong textual orientation and a reluctance to define a single meaning for a work. Along with psychoanalytic criticism, it shares an interest in the dynamics of mental response to textual cues.

REAL   In Lacanian psychoanalysis, one of the three orders of subjectivity (see Imaginary Order and Symbolic Order), the Real is the intractable and substantial world that resists and exceeds interpretation. The Real cannot be imagined, symbolized, or known directly. It constantly eludes our efforts to name it (death, gravity, the physicality of objects are examples of the Real) and thus challenges both the Imaginary and the Symbolic orders. The Real is fundamentally "Other," the mark of the divide between conscious and unconscious, and is signaled in language by gaps, slips, speechlessness, and the sense of the uncanny. The Real is not what we call "reality." It is the stumbling block of the Imaginary (which thinks it can "imagine" anything, including the Real) and of the Symbolic, which tries to bring the Real under its laws (the Real exposes the "phallacy" of the Law of the Phallus). The Real is frightening; we try to tame it with laws and language and call it "reality."

See also: Imaginary Order, Psychoanalytic Criticism, Symbolic Order.

SEMIOLOGY, SEMIOTIC   *See* Semiotics.

SEMIOTICS   The study of signs and sign systems and the way meaning is derived from them. Structuralist anthropologists, psychoanalysts, and literary critics developed semiotics during the decades following 1950, but much of the pioneering work had been done at the turn of the century by the founder of modern linguistics, Ferdinand de Saussure, and the American philosopher Charles Sanders Peirce.

Semiotics is based on several important distinctions, including the distinction between "signifier" and "signified" (the sign and what it points toward) and the distinction between "langue" and "parole." *Langue* (French for "tongue," as in "native tongue," meaning language) refers to the entire system within which individual utterances or usages of language have meaning; *parole*

(French for "word") refers to the particular utterances or usages. A principal tenet of semiotics is that signs, like words, are not significant in themselves, but instead have meaning only in relation to other signs and the entire system of signs, or langue.

The affinity between semiotics and structuralist literary criticism derives from this emphasis placed on langue, or system. Structuralist critics, after all, were reacting against formalists and their procedure of focusing on individual words as if meanings didn't depend on anything external to the text.

Poststructuralists have used semiotics but questioned some of its underlying assumptions, including the opposition between signifier and signified. The feminist poststructuralist Julia Kristeva, for instance, has used the word "semiotic" to describe feminine language, a highly figurative, fluid form of discourse that she sets in opposition to rigid, symbolic masculine language.

See also: Deconstruction, Feminist Criticism, Formalism, Poststructuralism, Oppositions, Structuralism, Symbol.

SIMILE *See* Metaphor.

SOCIOHISTORICAL CRITICISM *See* New Historicism.

STRUCTURALISM A science of humankind whose proponents attempted to show that all elements of human culture, including literature, may be understood as parts of a system of signs. Structuralism, according to Robert Scholes, was a reaction to "'modernist' alienation and despair."

Using Ferdinand de Saussure's linguistic theory, European structuralists such as Roman Jakobson, Claude Lévi-Strauss, and Roland Barthes (before his shift toward poststructuralism) attempted to develop a "semiology" or "semiotics" (science of signs). Barthes, among others, sought to recover literature and even language from the isolation in which they had been studied and to show that the laws that govern them govern all signs, from road signs to articles of clothing.

Particularly useful to structuralists were two of Saussure's concepts: the idea of "phoneme" in language and the idea that phonemes exist in two kinds of relationships: "synchronic" and "dichronic." A phoneme is the smallest consistently significant unit in language; thus, both "a" and "an" are phonemes, but "n" is not. A diachronic relationship is that which a phoneme has with those that have preceded it in time and those that will follow it. These "horizontal" relationships produce what we might call discourse or narrative and what Saussure called "parole." The synchronic relationship is the "vertical" one that a word has in a given instant with the entire system of language ("langue") in which it may generate meaning. "An" means what it means in English because those of us who speak the language are using it in the same way at a given time.

Following Saussure, Lévi-Strauss studied hundreds of myths, breaking them into their smallest meaningful units, which he called "mythemes." Removing each from its diachronic relations with other mythemes in a single myth (such as the myth of Oedipus and his mother), he vertically aligned those mythemes that he found to be homologous (structurally correspondent). He then studied the relationships within as well as between vertically aligned columns, in an attempt to understand scientifically, through ratios and proportions, those thoughts and processes that humankind has shared, both at one particular time and across time. One could say, then, that structuralists followed Saussure in preferring to think about the overriding langue or language of myth, in which each mytheme and mytheme-constituted myth fits meaningfully, rather than about isolated individual paroles or narratives. Structuralists followed Saussure's lead in believing what the poststructuralist Jacques Derrida later decided he could not subscribe to — that sign systems must be understood in terms of binary oppositions. In analyzing myths and texts to find basic structures, structuralists tended to find that opposite terms modulate until they are finally resolved or reconciled by some intermediary third term. Thus, a structuralist reading of *Paradise Lost* would show that the war between God and the bad angels becomes a rift between God and sinful, fallen man, the rift then being healed by the Son of God, the mediating third term.

See also: Deconstruction, Discourse, Narrative, Poststructuralism, Semiotics.

SUPERSTRUCTURE *See* Marxist Criticism.

SYMBOL A thing, image, or action that, although it is of interest in its own right, stands for or suggests something larger and more complex — often an idea or a range of interrelated ideas, attitudes, and practices.

Within a given culture, some things are understood to be symbols: the flag of the United States is an obvious example. More subtle cultural symbols might be the river as a symbol of time and the journey as a symbol of life and its manifold experiences.

Instead of appropriating symbols generally used and understood within their culture, writers often create symbols by setting up, in their works, a complex but identifiable web of associations. As a result, one object, image, or action suggests others, and often, ultimately, a range of ideas.

A symbol may thus be defined as a metaphor in which the "vehicle," the thing, image, or action used to represent something else, represents many related things (or "tenors") or is broadly suggestive. The urn in Keats's "Ode on a Grecian Urn" suggests many interrelated concepts, including art, truth, beauty, and timelessness.

Symbols have been of particular interest to formalists, who study how meanings emerge from the complex, patterned relationships between images in a work, and psychoanalytic critics, who are interested in how individual authors and the larger culture both disguise and reveal unconscious fears and desires through symbols. Recently, French feminists have also focused on the symbolic. They have suggested that, as wide-ranging as it seems, symbolic language is ultimately rigid and restrictive. They favor semiotic language and writing, which, they contend, is at once more rhythmic, unifying, and feminine.

See also: Feminist Criticism, Metaphor, Psychoanalytic Criticism, Trope.

SYMBOLIC ORDER In Lacanian psychoanalysis, one of the three orders of subjectivity (see Imaginary Order and Real), it is the realm of law, language, and society; it is the repository of generally held cultural beliefs. Its symbolic system is language, whose agent is the father or lawgiver, the one who has the power of naming. The human subject is commanded into this pre-established order by language (a process that begins long before a child can speak) and must submit to its orders of communication (grammar, syntax, etc.). Entrance into the symbolic order determines subjectivity according to a primary law of referentiality that takes the male sign (see Phallus) as its ordering principle. Lacan states that both sexes submit to the Law of the Phallus (the law of order, language, and differentiation) but their individual relation to the Law determines whether they see themselves as — and are seen by others to be — either "masculine" or "feminine." The Symbolic institutes repression (of the Imaginary), thus creating the unconscious, which itself is structured like the language of the Symbolic. The unconscious, a timeless realm, cannot be known directly, but it can be understood by a kind of translation that takes place in language — psychoanalysis is the "talking cure." The Symbolic is not a "stage" of development (as is Freud's "oedipal stage") nor is it set in place once and for all in human life. We constantly negotiate its threshold (in sleep, in drunkenness) and can "fall out" of it altogether in psychosis.

See also: Imaginary Order, Psychoanalytic Criticism, Real.

SYNECDOCHE See Metaphor, Metonymy.

TENOR See Metaphor, Metonymy, Symbol.

TROPE A figure, as in "figure of speech." Literally a "turning," i.e., a turning or twisting of a word or phrase to make it mean something else. Principal tropes include metaphor, metonymy, simile, personification, and synecdoche.

See also: Metaphor, Metonymy.

VEHICLE See Metaphor, Metonymy, Symbol.

About the Contributors

THE VOLUME EDITOR

Susanne L. Wofford is associate professor of English at the University of Wisconsin–Madison. In addition to articles on Spenser and Shakespeare, she has written *The Choice of Achilles: The Ideology of Figure in the Epic* (1992). She is currently completing a book on Shakespeare entitled *Theatrical Power: The Politics of Representation on the Shakespearean Stage.*

THE CRITICS

Janet Adelman is professor of English at the University of California at Berkeley. In addition to articles on Shakespeare, she is the author of *Suffocating Mothers: Fantasies of Maternal Origin in Shakespeare's Plays, "Hamlet" to "The Tempest"* (1992), and *The Common Liar: An Essay on "Antony and Cleopatra"*, (1973).

Michael D. Bristol is professor of English at McGill University in Montreal. In addition to essays on Shakespeare, theater, and cultural history and theory, he is author of *Shakespeare's America/America's Shakespeare* (1990) and *Carnival and Theater: Plebeian Culture and the Structure of Authority in Renaissance England* (1985).

Karin S. Coddon is assistant professor of English at Brown University. She has published numerous essays on Shakespeare, Renaissance drama, and postmodern popular culture.

Marjorie Garber is professor of English at Harvard University and director of Harvard's Center for Literary and Cultural Studies. In addition to essays on Shakespeare, Renaissance drama, and cultural studies, she has written four books: *Vested Interests: Cross-Dressing and Cultural Anxiety* (1991), *Shakespeare's Ghost Writers: Literature as Uncanny Causality* (1987), *Coming of Age in Shakespeare* (1981), and *Dream in Shakespeare: From Metaphor to Metamorphosis* (1974). She was also the editor of *Cannibals, Witches, and Divorce: Estranging the Renaissance* (1987).

Elaine Showalter is professor of English at Princeton University and the author of numerous influential works on feminist theory, literature by women, and nineteenth-century culture, including *Sister's Choice: Tradition and Change in American Women's Writing* (1991), *Sexual Anarchy: Gender and Culture at the Fin de Siècle* (1990), *The Female Malady: Women, Madness, and Culture in England, 1830–1980* (1985), *A Literature of Their Own: British Women Novelists from Brontë to Lessing* (1976), and *Women's Liberation and Literature* (1971). She has also edited several anthologies of works about feminism, including *Speaking of Gender* (1989) and *The New Feminist Criticism: Essays on Women, Literature, and Theory* (1985).

THE SERIES EDITOR

Ross C Murfin, general editor of Case Studies in Contemporary Criticism and volume editor of Conrad's *Heart of Darkness* and Hawthorne's *Scarlet Letter* in the series, is provost and vice president for academic affairs at Southern Methodist University. He has taught at the University of Miami, Yale University, and the University of Virginia, and has published scholarly studies on Joseph Conrad, Thomas Hardy, and D. H. Lawrence.

(continued from page iv)

"'Man and Wife Is One Flesh': *Hamlet* and the Confrontation with the Maternal Body" by Janet Adelman. From *Suffocating Mothers: Fantasies of Maternal Origin in Shakespeare's Plays*. New York: Routledge, 1992. Copyright © Routledge, Chapman, and Hall, Inc.

"'Suche Strange Desygns': Madness, Subjectivity, and Treason in *Hamlet* and Elizabethan Culture" by Karin S. Coddon. From *Renaissance Drama: New Series 1989*. Vol. XX. Ed. Mary Beth Rose. Evanston, IL: Northwestern University Press and The Newberry Center for Renaissance Studies, 1989. Copyright © 1990 by Northwestern University Press. All rights reserved.

"*Hamlet:* Giving Up the Ghost" by Marjorie Garber. From *Shakespeare's Ghost Writers*. London: Methuen & Co., 1987. Copyright © Methuen & Co., a Division of Routledge, Chapman, and Hall, Inc.

"Representing Ophelia: Women, Madness, and the Responsibilities of Feminist Criticism" by Elaine Showalter. From *Shakespeare and the Question of Theory*, eds. Patricia Parker and Geoffrey Hartman. London: Routledge, 1985. Copyright © Routledge, Chapman, and Hall, Inc.

"Sarah Siddons as Ophelia," "Harriet Smithson as Ophelia," and John Everett Millais's "Ophelia." From the Art Collection of the Folger Shakespeare Library.

Hugh W. Diamond's photograph of a Victorian madwoman at Surrey Asylum. By permission of the Royal Society of Medicine, London.